The Mammoth Book of

Jokes

The Mammoth Book of

Jokes

Edited by

Geoff Tibballs

RUNNING PRESS
PHILADELPHIA · LONDON

Collection copyright © Geoff Tibballs 2000, 2006
First published in the United States in 2006 by
Carroll & Graf Publishers
This edition published in 2007 by Running Press Book Publishers
All rights reserved under the Pan-American and International Copyright Conventions
Printed and bound in the EU

9 8 7 6 5 4 3
Digit on the right indicates the number of this printing

Library of Congress Cataloging-in-Publication Data is available on file

978-0-7867-1839-9

Running Press Book Publishers
2300 Chestnut Street
Philadelphia, PA 19103-4371

Visit us on the web!
www.runningpress.com

CONTENTS

INTRODUCTION

Have you ever wondered who told the first joke? And did anyone think it was funny? And if so, did they know they had to laugh? It's a reasonably safe bet to assume that it wouldn't have been Adam cracking a mother-in-law joke, but it would be comforting to think that it might have been a riddle that has stood the test of time, like "Why did the chicken cross the Roman road?" That one would surely have had them rolling around in the Colosseum . . . although it might have lost a little of its appeal if you were next in the queue to be thrown to the lions.

That's one of the things about humour – it's so subjective. For example, the sort of joke or story that goes down well at a stag night is unlikely to be quite so well received at a ladies' flower-arranging convention. And that is where this book can prove invaluable. Within the pages of this revised and expanded edition of *The Mammoth Book of Jokes*, there are some 7,400 jokes, quips and quotations for every occasion. There are clean jokes, dirty jokes and shaggy dog stories; excruciating puns, merciless put-downs and philosophical one-liners; humorous quotations and thoughtful epigrams from the likes of Oscar Wilde, Dorothy Parker and Mark Twain; wisecracks by the world's favourite comedians, ranging from Groucho Marx and Bob Hope to modern-day performers such as Jerry Seinfeld and Steven Wright; graveyard humour in the form of notable epitaphs; limericks fair and foul; an alternative dictionary; misprints and bloomers, including the world's strangest signs and most baffling headlines; exam-paper blunders; optimistic pick-up lines and razor-sharp rejections; and a collection of toasts to suit any circumstance.

So that you can find a joke, quote or quip to fit your requirements, every item in the book is numbered. Simply look up your chosen topic – from aardvark to zoo – in the comprehensive index and consult the appropriate numbers.

Let's face it, you can never know too many jokes. Who knows what's just around the corner? You could be at an interview for a high-powered job tomorrow and your prospective employer says: "Tell me a good aardvark joke and the job's yours!"

In particular, I am delighted to give due prominence to that most maligned of humorous devices: the pun. Having spent much of my formative years promoting the cause of the pun with Joan-of-Arc-like zeal – and being frequently threatened with the same fate – it is a pleasure to be able to include a number of outstanding examples in this field. As someone once said: "A good pun is its own reword." Although a few golden oldies have crept in, the vast majority of the jokes are right up to date, much of it culled from that essential new humour source: the Internet. And all the favourite targets are there – lawyers, bankers, blondes, estate agents, politicians, the police and, of course, elephants. Until researching this book, I had assumed that elephant jokes went out with beehive hairdos and Tiny Tim in the 1960s when they were an essential part of every playground conversation. But judging from the number of elephant joke sites on the Internet, they are still thriving. I suppose that's the thing about elephant jokes – you never forget them. And maybe elephants carry a clue as to the world's oldest joke. "My mastodon's got no nose . . ."

Geoff Tibballs
April 2006

Part 1
STORIES, JOKES AND ONE-LINERS

Absent-mindedness

1 After stopping off for lunch on a day trip, an elderly couple had driven ten miles down the road when the woman remembered that she had left her glasses at the restaurant. Her husband was irritated at having to go back for them. "How could you forget your glasses?" he moaned. "This is going to add an hour to the journey. The whole day is wasted!"

He was still complaining when they pulled up again outside the restaurant. As his wife got out of the car, he grumbled: "While you're in there, you may as well get my hat too."

2 Three elderly women were discussing the problems of growing old. One said: "Sometimes I find myself in front of the refrigerator with a jar of mayonnaise and I can't remember if I am putting it away or making a sandwich."

Another said: "And I can trip on the stairs and not remember if I was walking up or down."

"Oh well, I don't have those sort of problems, touch wood," said the third, tapping her knuckles on the table, before adding: "That must be the door – I'll get it."

3 A couple had become forgetful in their old age and sought a remedy by attending special memory classes where they were taught to remember things by word association. The husband was telling his neighbour how beneficial the classes had been.

"Who was the instructor?" asked the neighbour.

"Oh, um, what was the name now?" said the husband. "What's that flower that smells nice and has thorns?"

"A rose?"

"That's it," said the husband triumphantly. He turned towards the house and called: "Hey, Rose, what's the name of the guy in charge of the memory class?"

4 An old man asked his wife to make him a hot fudge sundae. She went to the kitchen and twenty minutes later came back with a plate of scrambled eggs instead. Seeing this, he flew into a rage and yelled: "Where's the bacon? I asked for bacon!"

5 First you forget names, then you forget faces. Next you forget to pull your zipper up and finally, you forget to pull it down. (GEORGE BURNS)

6 The young girl student was puzzled why the ageing college professor needed three pairs of glasses.

He explained: "I have one pair for long sight, one pair for short sight, and the third pair to look for the other two."

7 Another college professor called on a pharmacist. "Give me some prepared tablets of acetylsalicylic acid."

"Do you mean aspirin?" asked the pharmacist.

"That's it. I can never remember that name!"

8 An elderly widow and a widower had been dating for five years. He finally asked her to marry him and she immediately said "yes". But the next morning he couldn't remember what her answer had been. In desperation, he decided to call her.

"This is really embarrassing," he began, "but when I asked you to marry me yesterday, well, this morning I just couldn't remember what your answer was."

"Oh, I'm so glad you called," she said. "I remembered saying 'yes' to someone, but I couldn't remember who it was!"

9 My grandfather's a little forgetful, but he likes to give me advice. One day, he took me aside and left me there. (RON RICHARDS)

10 An absent-minded professor was moving to a new house further along the same street. His wife knew that he was prone to forgetting things and so she wrote down the new address on a piece of paper before he went off to college. She handed him the paper and the key to the new house and reminded him not to go back to the old address.

That morning, one of his students asked him a complex question and the professor wrote the answer down on the back of the slip of paper. The student asked whether he could keep the paper. Forgetting what was on the other side, the professor said, "Certainly."

In the evening, he returned out of habit to the old house, tried the key and couldn't get in. Realizing his mistake, he searched in his pockets for the slip of paper with the new address, but of course there was no sign of it. So he wandered along the street and stopped the first personable-looking lad whom he saw.

"Excuse me, I'm Professor Galbraith. You wouldn't happen to know where I live, would you?"

"Sure, Dad," said the boy.

11 A 90-year-old man was sitting on a park bench sobbing. A young man asked him what was wrong.

"I'm in love with a 20-year-old girl," wailed the old man. "She's gorgeous looking, kind, considerate, she's a great cook and we have the most fantastic sex three times a day, every day."

"So why are you crying?"

"I've forgotten where we live!"

12 Three old men were at the doctor's for a memory test. The doctor asked the first old man: "What is two times two?"

"194," came the reply.

The doctor turned to the second old man. "What is two times two?"

"Thursday," replied the second old man.

Finally the doctor addressed the third old man. "What is two times two?"

"Four," came the answer.

"That's great," said the doctor. "How did you get that?"

"Simple," said the third old man. "I subtracted 194 from Thursday!"

Accidents

13 A stranger rushed into a bar and ordered a double whisky. "Tell me," he asked the bartender agitatedly, "how high does a penguin grow?"

"Oh, about so high," replied the bartender, placing his hand some two feet from the floor.

"Are you sure?" said the stranger.

"Positive," said the bartender.

"Damn. I guess I just ran over a nun!"

14 A young man was shipwrecked on a desert island and didn't see another human being for 20 years. Then out of the blue, a beautiful woman was washed ashore.

"How have you survived all these years?" she asked, water dripping from her velvety skin.

"I existed by digging for clams and eating berries," he replied.

"What did you do for love?" she purred.

"What's love?"

With that, she showed him, not once, not twice, but three times.

"So, how do you like love?" she said afterwards.

"It's great," he said. "But look what you did to my clam digger!"

15 It's been a rough day. I got up this morning, put on a shirt and a button fell off. I picked up my briefcase and the handle came off. I'm afraid to go to the bathroom. (RODNEY DANGERFIELD)

16 A huge fire broke out near a farm. The county fire department were called out but the blaze was too big for them to tackle, so a call for additional assistance was made to a part-time volunteer force. The volunteer brigade turned up in a dilapidated old truck which spluttered along the track leading to the fire. The county fire chief was about to apologize to the farmer for the embarrassment the volunteer force were causing when, to his amazement, the volunteer truck fearlessly drove into the very heart of the fire. Within minutes, the centre of the fire was extinguished, breaking the blaze into two controllable sections. An hour later the entire fire was out.

The farmer was so impressed that he immediately presented the captain of the volunteer force with a cheque for 1,000 dollars.

A local newspaperman asked the captain what he was going to spend it on. "I'm gonna get the brakes on that damn truck fixed!"

17 A woman phoned her husband at work for a chat. "Sorry, darling," he said, "I'm really busy at the moment. I haven't got time to talk."

"Oh, this won't take long. It's just that I've got good news and bad news."

"Look," he repeated, "I really am busy. Just give me the good news."

"Well," she said, "the air bag works."

18 I told my wife she looks sexy with black fingernails. Now she thinks I slammed the car door on her hand on purpose. (EMO PHILIPS)

19 Wife: "The big clock fell off the wall this afternoon. A moment sooner, and it would have landed on Mother's head."

Husband: "That's it! I'm getting rid of that clock. It's always been slow."

20 A man was out walking when he fell over the edge of a cliff. As he hurtled towards the ground, he just managed to hang on to a protruding tree branch. Staring down at a 200-foot drop to almost certain death, he cried out: "Help me, please! Is anybody up there?"

A deep voice came back: "Yes, my son, I am up here."

"Who is it?" called the man.

"It is The Lord."

"Can you help me?"

"Certainly, my son. Just let go of the branch and I will catch you."

The man thought for a moment, then shouted: "Is anybody else up there?"

21 I spilt some stain remover on my sleeve. How do you get that out? (BOB MONKHOUSE)

22 Two small boys were listening while a woman told her friend about a recent accident in which a man had driven into the back of her car. "He blamed me," she said, "and called me every rude, dirty name in the book!"

One of the boys turned to the other and said wide-eyed: "There's a book?"

23 A car broke down on the expressway. The driver pulled over to the shoulder and jumped out of the vehicle. Then he opened the trunk and pulled out two men in trenchcoats. The men stood behind the car, opened up their coats and began exposing themselves to oncoming traffic. The result was a terrible pile-up.

A police officer arrived on the scene and surveyed the carnage. He raged at the driver: "Why on earth did you put these two perverts at the side of the road?"

The driver explained: "I broke down, and I was just using my emergency flashers."

24 A parachutist jumped from a plane, only to discover that his chute was broken. As he plunged towards the ground, frantically trying to fix the parachute, he passed another man on the way up.

"Do you know anything about parachutes?" he cried.

"No," replied the other man. "Do you know anything about gas cookers?"

25 What has four legs, is big, green, fuzzy and if it fell out of a tree would kill you? – A pool table.

26 I saw a sign by the side of the road that said, "Tiredness can kill." I never knew that. Last Saturday I stayed up watching films! I could have died! (ARDAL O'HANLON)

You can tell it's going to be a bad day when:

27 You wake up face down on the pavement.

28 Your boss tells you not to bother taking off your coat.

29 You wake up to discover your waterbed has broken, then you remember you don't have a waterbed.

30 You put both contact lenses in the same eye.

31 The dog chews the presentation you've been working on all weekend.

32 You put your bra on backwards and it fits better.

33 You call suicide prevention and they put you on hold.

34 Your twin sister forgets your birthday.

35 Your birthday cake collapses from the weight of candles.

36 You find a TV news team waiting in your office.

37 Your wife wakes up feeling amorous and you have a headache.

38 You find Yellow Pages open at "hitmen".

39 Your car horn goes off accidentally and remains stuck as you follow a group of Hell's Angels down the motorway.

40 You wake up in the office naked in front of your workmates.

41 Your blind date turns out to be your ex-wife.

42 You turn on the news and they're showing emergency routes out of the city.

43 Your birthday cake has so many candles that the fire service have to be called out to extinguish the flames.

44 Two drivers climbed out of their cars after colliding at a road junction. One produced a hip flask from his pocket and said to the other: "Here, have a nip of whisky to calm your nerves."

"Thanks," said the other driver, taking a swig from the flask. "Here, you have one too," he added, handing back the whisky.

"No, I'd rather not – the police will be here soon."

The following are genuine comments on accident insurance claims forms:

45 The car in front hit the pedestrian but he got up so I hit him again.

46 An invisible car came from nowhere, struck my car and vanished.

47 There was no damage to the car as the gate post will testify.

48 The guy was all over the road. I had to swerve a number of times before I hit him.

49 I had one eye on a parked car, another on approaching lorries, and another on the woman behind.

50 The telephone pole was approaching. I was attempting to swerve out of its way when it struck my front end.

51 I knocked over a man. He admitted it was his fault and that he had been knocked over before.

52 I collided with a stationary truck coming the other way.

53 I pulled away from the side of the road, glanced at my mother-in-law and headed over the embankment.

54 I believe if I had lost my head the accident could have been worse.

55 I started to slow down but the traffic was more stationary than I thought.

56 I pulled into a lay-by with smoke coming from under the bonnet. I realized the car was on fire so took my dog and smothered it with a blanket.

57 The pedestrian had no idea which way to run, so I ran over him.

58 To avoid a collision I ran into the other car.

59 In an attempt to kill a fly, I drove into a telegraph pole.

60 A lamp-post bumped into my car, damaging it in two places.

61 Coming home I drove into the wrong house and collided with a tree I don't have.

62 Leaving home for work I drove out of my drive straight into a bus. The bus was five minutes early.

63 I consider neither vehicle to blame, but if either was to blame it was the other one.

64 I saw a slow-moving, sad-faced old gentleman as he bounced off the roof of my car.

65 I collided with a stationary tree.

66 As I approached the intersection, a sign suddenly appeared in a place where no stop sign had ever appeared before. I was unable to stop in time to avoid the accident.

67 To avoid hitting the bumper in front, I struck the pedestrian.

68 I had been driving for 40 years when I fell asleep at the wheel and had an accident.

69 The other car collided with mine without giving warning of its intentions.

70 I blew my horn but it would not work as it was stolen.

71 A truck backed through my windshield into my wife's face.

72 I was on my way to the doctor's with rear end trouble when my universal joint gave way, causing me to have an accident.

73 A pedestrian hit me and went under my car.

74 I was sure the old fellow would never make it to the other side of the road when I struck him.

75 Q: Could either driver have done anything to avoid the accident?
A: I could have travelled by bus.

76 (Following a collision between a motorist and a cow]
Q: What warning did you give the other party before the collision?
A: Horn.
Q: What warning was given by the other party?
A: Moo.

Accountants

77 A woman went to the doctor who told her she had only six months to live.
"Oh my God," said the woman. "What shall I do?"
"Marry an accountant," suggested the doctor.
"Why," asked the woman. "Will that make me live longer?"
"No," replied the doctor. "But it will seem longer."

78 What's an actuary? – An accountant with a sense of humour.

79 Why do some accountants become actuaries? – They find bookkeeping too exciting.

80 What do accountants do to liven up their office party? – Invite a funeral director.

81 What's an accountant's idea of trashing his hotel room? – Refusing to fill out the guest comment card.

82 What's the wildest thing a group of young accountants can do? – Go into town and gang-audit someone.

83 Three engineers and three accountants were on board a train. "I can't believe how expensive my ticket was," said one of the accountants, "50 dollars for such a relatively short journey."

"You should do what we do," said the chief engineer. "We three always travel together but only buy one ticket. That way, we pay a third of the price each."

The accountant was puzzled. "But how do you get away with only buying one ticket? The ticket collector always comes round."

"It's easy," said the engineer. "Watch this."

At the first sign of the ticket collector, the three engineers huddled into a restroom and shut the door. When the collector knocked on the restroom door and called "Ticket please", a single arm held out one ticket. The collector stamped the ticket and went on his way.

The accountant was impressed and, knowing a thing or two about money, decided that he and his two colleagues would try the same trick the next time they travelled together. So the accountants bought just one ticket between them. The engineers happened to be on the same train and, to the accountants' surprise, hadn't even bought one ticket.

"You'll never get away with that," said the accountants.

"You wait and see," replied the engineers.

When the ticket collector approached, both groups squeezed together in separate restrooms and shut the doors. Then one of the engineers knocked on the door of where the accountants were hiding and said: "Ticket, please."

84 The company accountant is shy and retiring. He's shy a quarter of a million dollars. That's why he's retiring. (MILTON BERLE)

85 How do you know when you've met a good tax accountant? — He has a loophole named after him.

86 An accountant was having difficulty sleeping at night. He went to the doctor.

"Have you tried counting sheep?" inquired the doctor.

"That's the problem," said the accountant. "I make a mistake and spend the next six hours trying to find it."

87 What's the definition of an extrovert accountant? — One who looks at your shoes while he's talking to you instead of his own.

88 How do you drive an accountant insane? — Tie him to a chair, stand in front of him and fold up a road map the wrong way.

89 Out of the blue, an accountant decided to leave his wife. He left her a note saying: "Dear Diane, I am 54 years old and have never done anything wild in my life. But now I'm leaving you for a stunning 18-year-old model. We'll be staying at the Savoy."

When he arrived at the hotel, there was a message waiting from his wife. It read: "Dear Clive, I too am 54 years old. I have followed your example and am staying at the Royal with an 18-year-old Italian hunk. And I'm sure that you, as an accountant, will appreciate that 18 goes into 54 many more times than 54 goes into 18 . . ."

90 An accountant was accosted in the street by a tramp begging for money.

"Spare some change, sir?" asked the tramp.

"Why should I?" asked the accountant.

"Because I haven't a penny to my name and I haven't had a hot meal in three months."

"Hmm," said the accountant. "And how does this compare to your previous quarter?"

Acting

91 Acting is all about honesty. If you can fake that, you've got it made. (GEORGE BURNS)

92 A Jewish actor was excited to land a major part in a new play and rushed home to tell his mother the good news.

"Momma, Momma," he cried. "I got the part. I play the husband."

His mother looked at him disdainfully. "You couldn't get a speaking part?"

93 The leading lady in a stage musical was in a filthy mood before curtain-up. Two members of the chorus line were discussing it.

"What's the matter with her?" asked one.

"She only received nine bouquets tonight."

"Only nine! Isn't that enough for her?"

"Not when she'd paid for ten!"

94 They asked Jack Benny if he would do something for the Actors' Orphanage, so he shot both his parents and moved in. (BOB HOPE)

95 An agent found out that an actress he represented was selling her body at night for 100 dollars a time. Seeing her in a new light, he asked whether he too could have sex with her, but she told him that he'd have to pay like the others. She wouldn't even allow him his 10 per cent agent's fee as a discount. He wasn't happy about the arrangement, but the following night, he went to her apartment, turned out the lights and had sex with her. She fell asleep afterwards but an hour later, she was woken and made love to again. Then half an hour after that she was made love to once more, and every 30 minutes for the next three hours.

Impressed with his virility, she purred: "I'm so lucky to have you as my agent."

"I'm not your agent, lady," a strange voice answered. "He's at the door selling tickets."

96 An actor was recalling the latest performance of his one-man show. "It took the audience nearly an hour to leave the theatre."

"My!" said his agent. "It must have been a packed house."

"Actually no," sighed the actor. "He was on crutches."

97 I went to an audition the other day, they were casting 13 people to be clouds. But 14 people showed up — it was overcast. (JAY LONDON)

98 Two actors got married, but fell out almost immediately. The day after the wedding, the bride went to see a lawyer about obtaining a divorce.

"What's gone wrong?" asked the lawyer. "You've been married less than a day."

The actress said grandly: "I could tell at the church that things wouldn't work between us, when he signed his name in the register in bigger letters than mine."

99 Why don't actors stare out of the window in the morning? – Because if they did, they'd have nothing to do in the afternoon.

Adultery

100 One evening, a guy was sent out by his wife to buy cigarettes from a store. But the store was closed so he went instead to a nearby bar to use the vending machine there. Having got the cigarettes, he decided to have a quick drink before leaving for home. As he sat down at the bar, he noticed this stunning brunette perched on the next stool. He couldn't believe how gorgeous she looked and so he started chatting to her. He bought her a drink – and another and another – and when the bar closed, she invited him back to her apartment.

When they reached her apartment, they went straight to bed. The sex was fantastic. When it was all over, he looked at his watch and saw that it was one o'clock in the morning.

"Jesus Christ!" he exclaimed, leaping out of bed. "I hadn't realized it was so late. My wife's gonna kill me. Have you got any talcum powder?"

The girl looked puzzled but handed him a container of talcum powder which he rubbed into his hands. Then without saying a word, he quickly left.

Back home, his wife was waiting for him. "Where have you been?" she demanded angrily. "Do you know what time it is? I only sent you out for a packet of cigarettes and you've been gone nearly four hours!"

"Look, I'm really sorry," he said. "I went to the store for your cigarettes but the store was shut. So I tried the vending machine at the bar round the corner and while I was there I met this great looking chick and we ended up in bed together."

"Let me see your hands!" said the wife, and he showed her his hands covered in talcum powder. "You goddamn liar!" she boomed "You went bowling again!"

101 What do you call a woman who knows where her husband is every night? – A widow.

102 A couple were celebrating their golden wedding anniversary, but the husband had something on his mind.

"There's something that's always bugged me about the children," he said. "I can't help noticing that out of our eight kids, Ben looks different from all the others. I know it's a terrible thing to ask, but does he have a different father?"

The wife couldn't bear to look him in the eye. "Yes, it's true," she admitted. "Ben does have a different father from the other seven."

The husband's heart sank. Fighting back the tears, he said: "You have to tell me. Who is Ben's father?"

She looked at him sorrowfully and said: "You."

103 An old man went into confession and told the priest: "Father, I'm 81, married with six children and 13 grandchildren. Last night I had an affair and made love to two 18-year-old girls. Twice."

"I see," said the priest. "When was the last time you were in confession?"

"Never, Father," replied the old man. "I'm Jewish."

"So why are you telling me?"

"I'm telling everybody!"

104 A husband arrived home early from work to find his wife on the bed having a heart attack. He was just about to call the doctor when his little boy said: "Dad, there's a naked man in the wardrobe."

"What!" said the husband. He opened the wardrobe and there was his best friend Tom.

"I don't believe this!" screamed the husband. "There's Julie having a heart attack, and you're playing games with the kids!"

105 A married man took a solo trip to Bermuda that was part work, part vacation. He fell so in love with the place that he wired his friend: "Catch next plane out. Bring my wife and your mistress."

The friend wired back: "Your wife and I arriving tomorrow 4.30 p.m. How long have you known about us?"

106 My wife gives me no respect. I took her to a drive-in movie. I spent the whole night trying to find out what car she was in. (RODNEY DANGERFIELD)

107 A married couple were celebrating their fiftieth wedding anniversary. The husband asked the wife: "Darling, have you ever cheated on me?"

"What a strange question to ask after all these years," she said. "But, if you must know, yes, I have cheated on you. Three times."

The husband was saddened by this admission but wanted to know when.

She said: "The first time was when you were 31. Remember you wanted to start a business but no bank would give you a loan? And remember how the bank president came to our house in person and signed the papers? Well . . ."

The husband was touched. "You mean, you slept with the president of the bank so that I could start up my business? That's the kindest thing anyone's ever done for me. When was the second occasion?"

"Remember when you were 48 you had a heart attack and no surgeon would operate on you? And then Dr Forrest came all the way up here to carry out the surgery himself, and after that you were in good shape again? Well . . ."

The husband was genuinely moved. "So you slept with Dr Forrest to save my life? What a wonderful woman you are! And when was the third time?"

"Remember how a few years ago when you really wanted to be president of the golf club? But you were 52 votes short?"

108 Two middle-aged businessmen, Mark and Miles, went to the gym for a workout. As they undressed beforehand, Mark was stunned to find Miles wearing a corset beneath his shirt.

"Since when have you been wearing a corset?" asked Mark.

"Since my wife found it in the glove compartment."

109 Packing for a business trip, a husband noticed that his wife had packed a condom in his briefcase. "Why do you do that whenever I go away?" he asked. "You know I'd never cheat on you."

"I know you wouldn't," she said, "and I really trust you, but with AIDS and everything, I'd just feel safer in the knowledge that if anything did happen, you'd be protected. So please, darling, take the condom with you. For my sake."

"OK," he agreed, "if you put it like that, I will. But for God's sake, give me more than one!"

110 An errant husband kept a wife and a mistress who had never met. He wanted to find out whether both women were faithful to him, so he packed them off on the same cruise with the intention of questioning each on the other's behaviour. When his wife returned, he asked her a few general questions about the people on the cruise before focusing on the behaviour of the passenger who was his secret mistress.

"She was a total slut," reported the wife. "She must have slept with almost every man on the ship."

The husband was crestfallen and later asked his cheating mistress how his wife had behaved on the cruise.

"She was a real lady," said the mistress.

The husband brightened. "Really?"

"Yes, she came on board with her husband and never left his side."

111 A man came home with some hot gossip. "Do you know what they're saying?" he told his wife. "They're saying our janitor has slept with every woman in this apartment block except for one!"

The wife said: "That must be that girl from number 36 – nobody likes her."

112 A guy on a date parked his car in a quiet street late at night and climbed in the back seat for sex. His partner was more than willing and asked him to do it four times. After a couple of hours of this, he was exhausted, but she was still up for more.

"Excuse me," he said, "but I must go for a pee."

He climbed out of the car and noticed a man further down the street struggling to change a tyre. He went over to him and said: "Look, I've got this woman in my car and I've given it to her four times but she still wants more. I don't think I can manage it. So if I change your tyre, will you take over from me?"

So the second guy took his place in the back seat and was just getting down to business when a police officer knocked on the window and shone a light on them.

"What are you doing in there?" asked the cop.

"I'm making love to my wife," replied the man hesitantly.

"This is a public place. Can't you do that at home?"

"If you must know, officer, I didn't know it was my wife till you shined the light on her!"

113 Throughout her married life, a wife kept a padlocked chest at the foot of the bed. Her husband often asked her what was in the chest, but she always refused to divulge the contents. Then, on their twenty-fifth wedding anniversary, she finally agreed to open it.

Inside were two ears of corn and 30,000 dollars. The wife explained: "Every time I cheated on you, I put in an ear of corn."

The husband didn't mind too much that she had only been unfaithful to him twice in 25 years. "But what about the money?" he asked.

"Well," she replied, "every time I reached a bushel, I sold it."

114 Guns don't kill people — husbands who come home early kill people. (DON ROSE)

115 A married couple were dining out when a beautiful girl strolled over to their table and kissed the husband warmly.

"Who was that?" demanded the wife.

"That's my mistress," replied the husband.

"Your mistress! I want a divorce."

"Are you sure about that, honey? Do you really want to give up your big house, the swimming pool, the Mercedes, your jewellery, your furs, the vacation home in Mexico?"

For the next half-hour there was a frosty atmosphere between the two. Then the wife nudged the husband and said: "Isn't that Richard over there? Who's he with?"

"That's his mistress," said the husband.

"Huh," said the wife, taking a mouthful of dessert. "Ours is much cuter."

116 A man sleeps around, no questions asked, but if a woman makes 19 or 20 mistakes, she's a tramp. (JOAN RIVERS)

117 A business executive dialled his home phone number from work and was surprised when a strange woman answered.

"Who is this?" he asked.

"This is the maid," replied the voice on the other end.

"But we don't have a maid," he said.

"You do now. I was hired this morning by the lady of the house."

"I see. Well, this is her husband. Is she there?"

There was a moment's silence before the maid replied: "Er, well actually she's upstairs in the bedroom with someone I thought was her husband."

The man couldn't believe what he was hearing, but decided to act swiftly and decisively. "Would you like to make 50,000 dollars?" he asked the maid.

"Sure would," came the reply.

"Right. Now listen carefully. I want you to go into my study, look in the top drawer of my desk and take out my gun. Then I want you to go to the bedroom and shoot that bitch and the guy she's with. Do you understand?"

"Yes," answered the maid and she put down the phone. The man listened and heard two shots ring out. The maid returned to the phone.

"What should I do with the bodies?" she asked.

"Throw them in the swimming pool," said the man.

"What pool?"

"Er, this is 366-2940?"

118 Young Tommy came home from school early and found his father in bed with the maid. His mother arrived home half an hour later and Tommy rushed to tell her: "Mum, when I got home from school, I saw Dad in bed with the maid. They were . . ."

His mother interrupted him: "Wait till dinner tonight, Tommy, and when the maid serves the meal, I'll wink at you, and then you can tell the story."

That evening the maid served dinner as usual. She was in the middle of serving the vegetables when Tommy's mother winked at him. Tommy took the hint and said: "Mum, when I got home from school, I saw Dad in bed with the maid. They were doing the same thing I saw you and Uncle Dennis doing at the cottage last summer."

119 A wife slapped her husband around the face after discovering a piece of paper in his jacket pocket with the name Marylou written on it.

He protested: "It was the name of a horse I bet on yesterday."

The following day she slapped him again.

"What was that for?" he said.

"Your horse called last night."

120 "I have a confession to make," announced the husband. "I've been seeing a psychiatrist."

"Don't worry," said the wife. "I've been seeing a night club owner and a footballer."

121 Colin led a hectic life. When he wasn't working hard, he was bowling or playing tennis. One weekend his wife decided he needed a break so she took him to a strip club. He protested that it wasn't really his scene, but she insisted that it would do him good.

When they arrived, the club doorman said: "Hello, Colin. How are you tonight?"

The wife registered her surprise.

"He's just one of the guys I bowl with," explained Colin.

Once inside the club, they sat down and a waitress came over. "Nice to see you, Colin," she said. "Your usual Scotch on the rocks?"

The wife's eyes widened. "You must come here a lot!"

"No, no. She's a member of the tennis club."

Moments later, a stripper sauntered over to the table, threw her arms around Colin and purred: "Your favourite table dance, Colin?"

At this, the wife stormed out. Colin followed her and spotted her getting into a taxi cab. He jumped into the passenger seat and she started ranting and raving at him. After a few yards, the cabbie leaned over and said: "Looks like you picked up a bitch tonight, Colin!"

122 A man came home to find evidence that his wife had been unfaithful. "Was it my friend Ted?" he demanded.

"No, it wasn't."

"Was it my friend Pete?"

"No, it wasn't?"

"Was it my friend Larry?"

"No it wasn't," she screamed. "What is it — don't you think I have any friends of my own?"

123 A little boy was hiding in the closet listening to his mum entertaining her lover. Suddenly he heard a car pull up on the drive and his mum say: "Oh no, it's my husband. Quick, hide in the closet." With that, her lover joined the boy in the closet.

"Gee, it's real dark in here," said the boy. "I'm scared. I'm gonna scream."

"No, don't," pleaded the lover. "I'll give you five dollars if you don't scream."

"Gee, it's real dark in here," repeated the boy, "I'm real scared. I can feel a scream coming on."

"Look, I'll give you ten dollars," said the lover, "so long as you keep quiet."

"Gee, it's real dark in here," continued the boy. "So scary. I don't know if I can stop myself screaming."

"All right," said the lover. "Here's 50 dollars for you if you promise not to scream."

The boy stuffed the money into his pocket and kept quiet. Twenty minutes later, the car drove off and the lover left in a hurry shortly afterwards.

Later that afternoon, the boy went shopping with his mother. As they passed a cycle shop, the boy said: "I really like that red bike in the window. And I can afford it — I've got 50 dollars."

"Where did you get 50 dollars from?" asked the mother.

"I promised I wouldn't say," said the boy.

"What do you mean you promised you wouldn't say? You must have done something bad if you won't say."

"I haven't," insisted the boy.

"How am I expected to believe you," said the mother, "if you keep secrets from me? No, I'm taking you to church and you can tell the priest how you got that money in confession."

The little boy went into the confessional and when the door closed, it was pitch black inside. The boy said nervously: "Gee, it's real dark in here."

And the priest said: "Let's not start THAT again."

Advertising

124 When KFC sales hit a lean patch, Colonel Sanders came up with a brilliant advertising idea. He got in touch with the Pope and asked the pontiff whether he could change the words of the Lord's Prayer from "Give us this day our daily bread" to "Give us this day our daily chicken."

"I can't possibly do that," said the Pope.

"Not even for 100,000 dollars?" asked the Colonel.

"No, not for 100,000 dollars," replied the Pope.

Six months on and KFC sales were declining still further. The Colonel was getting desperate and made another call to the Pope. This time he offered 500,000 dollars for the words of the Lord's Prayer to be changed to "Give us this day our daily chicken."

Again the Pope refused. "I can't possibly change the wording of the Lord's Prayer from bread to chicken," he repeated.

Another six months and KFC sales had reached an all-time low. The company was in danger of going out of business. Colonel Sanders made one last attempt to persuade the Pope to change the wording of the Lord's Prayer.

"I'll donate 50 million dollars to the Vatican if you change the word 'bread' to 'chicken' in the Lord's Prayer."

"That's a lot of money," conceded the Pope.

"So you'll do it?"

"I'll have to discuss it with the cardinals."

So the Pope called a meeting of the cardinals. He began: "I have good news and bad news. The good news is, KFC are going to donate 50 million dollars to the Vatican. The bad news is, we lost the Wonder Bread account."

125 Now they show you how detergents take out blood stains – a pretty violent image there. I think if you've got a T-shirt with a bloodstain all over it, maybe laundry isn't your biggest problem. Maybe you should get rid of the body before you do the wash. (JERRY SEINFELD)

126 In the last couple of weeks I have seen the ads for the Wonder Bra. Is that really a problem in this country – men not paying enough attention to women's breasts? (JAY LENO)

127 Two advertising executives – one junior and one senior – had lunch together. Midway through the meal, the junior executive asked: "What's happened to Fred Zimmerman? I haven't seen him around lately."

"Haven't you heard?" said the senior. "Fred died last week – he's gone to that great ad. agency in the sky."

"My God!" exclaimed the younger man. "What did he have?"

"Nothing much – a small toothpaste account, a couple of discount stores, nothing worth going after."

128 Today I met with a subliminal advertising executive for just a second. (STEVEN WRIGHT)

The following are genuine examples of product slogans which did not translate well:

129 Pepsi's "Come alive with the Pepsi generation" was translated into Chinese as "Pepsi brings your ancestors back from the grave".

130 The Ford Pinto car met with a lukewarm response in Brazil where "pinto" is slang for "tiny male genitals'. So Ford renamed the car the Corcel, meaning "horse".

131 When Coors translated its slogan "Turn it loose" into Spanish, it came out as "Suffer from diarrhoea".

132 Clairol introduced the "Mist Stick", a curling iron, into Germany, only to discover that "mist" is German slang for manure.

133 Scandinavian vacuum-cleaner manufacturer Electrolux ran a US campaign: "Nothing sucks like an Electrolux". In America, "sucks" is less than complimentary.

134 General Motors' Chevrolet Nova flopped in Spain because "no va" means "won't go".

135 The KFC slogan "finger-lickin' good" came across in Chinese as "eat your fingers off".

136 When Parker Pens marketed a ball-point in Mexico, the advert should have read: "It won't leak in your pocket and embarrass you". However, because the company thought "embarazar" (to impregnate] meant "to embarrass", the ad. actually read: "It won't leak in your pocket and make you pregnant."

137 In Italy, a campaign for Schweppes Tonic Water was translated as Schweppes Toilet Water.

138 Bacardi concocted a fruit drink with the name Pavian to suggest French chic, only to learn that in Germany "Pavian" means baboon.

139 Chicken magnate Frank Perdue's slogan: "It takes a strong man to make a tender chicken" was translated into Spanish as "It takes an aroused man to make a chicken affectionate".

140 When Braniff translated a slogan touting its upholstery: "Fly in leather" — it came out in Spanish as "Fly naked".

141 The Coca-Cola name in China was first read as "Ke-kou-Ke-la", meaning "Bite the wax tadpole".

142 When translated into Arabic, Jolly Green Giant comes out as Intimidating Green Ogre.

Age

143 An elderly woman was driving her husband in the country when she was pulled over by the highway patrol.

The officer stepped out of his car and quizzed the old woman. "Ma'am, did you know you were speeding?"

"What did he say?" said the woman to her husband.

The husband shouted: "He says you were speeding."

"May I see your licence?" said the officer.

"What did he say?" said the old woman.

"He wants to see your licence," shouted the husband.

She handed the officer her licence. The officer studied it carefully.

"I see you're from South Carolina," he said. "I spent some time there once, had the worst sex with a woman I've ever had in my life."

"What did he say?" said the old woman.

The husband yelled: "He thinks he knows you."

144 An elderly couple went to the doctor for their annual physicals. The old man went in first, and after he was finished, the doctor sent him back out to the waiting room and called in the old woman.

The doctor said: "Before I examine you, I'd like to talk about your husband for a moment. I'm a bit concerned about him. I asked him how he was feeling and he said he had never felt better. He said that when he got up this morning, he went to the bathroom, opened the door and God turned the light on for him. And when he was done, he shut the door and God turned the light out for him."

"Oh, no," sighed the wife. "He's been peeing in the fridge again."

145 The best thing to do is to behave in a manner befitting one's age. If you are 16 or under, try not to go bald. (WOODY ALLEN)

146 An old lady went to the doctor and asked for birth control pills.
"Why do you want them at your age?" asked the doctor.
"They help me sleep better," replied the old lady.
"How come?"
"Well, doctor, I put them in my granddaughter's orange juice, and I sleep better at night."

147 What does a 75-year-old woman have between her breasts that a 25-year-old doesn't? – Her navel.

148 An old man went to the doctor for his annual physical. The doctor listened to his heart and pronounced: "I'm afraid you have a serious heart murmur. Do you smoke at all?"
"No."
"Do you drink to excess?"
"No."
"Do you still have a sex life?"
"Yes."
"Well, I'm sorry to have to tell you, that with this heart murmur, you'll have to give up half of your sex life."
"Which half – the looking or the thinking?"

149 Andy Williams went to pay a charity visit to an old people's home to cheer up the residents. But he was dismayed that none of the residents seemed to recognize him. Instead they all looked mystified. Finally he went up to one old lady and said: "Do you know who I am?"
The old lady whispered: "Don't worry, dear. Matron will tell you."

150 I'm at an age where my back goes out more than I do. (PHYLLIS DILLER)

151 An 83-year-old man went to the doctor's and said: "Doc, my sex drive is too high. I want it lowered."
The doctor couldn't believe what he was hearing. "You're 83 and you want your sex drive lowered?"
"That's right," said the man pointing to his head. "It's all up here. I want it lowered."

152 A group of old people in a nursing home were discussing their ailments. One said: "My arthritis is so bad I can hardly grip this cup."

Another said: "My cataracts are so bad I can't even see to pour my coffee."

Another said: "I can't turn my head because of the constant pains in my neck."

Another said: "I have regular dizzy spells because of my blood pressure."

Another said: "I guess that's what happens when you get old."

Another said: "But we should be grateful that we can all still drive."

153 What's the best way to get a youthful figure? – Ask a woman her age.

154 Eighty-eight-year-old Mabel walked into the recreational room of an old people's home. Holding her clenched fist in the air, she proclaimed: "Anyone who can guess what's in my hand can have sex with me tonight."

A disinterested old man called out: "An elephant."

Mabel thought for a minute and said: "Near enough."

155 I bought Victoria Principal's old car. No matter how far you drive it the clock keeps going back to 33,000 miles. (JOAN RIVERS)

156 An elderly couple were lying in bed one night. The husband was falling asleep but the wife was in a romantic mood and wanted to talk.

She said: "You used to hold my hand when we were courting."

Wearily he reached across, held her hand for a second and tried to get back to sleep.

A few moments later she said: "Then you used to kiss me."

Mildly irritated, he reached across, gave her a peck on the cheek and settled down to sleep.

Thirty seconds later she said: "Then you used to bite my neck."

Angrily, he threw back the bedclothes and got out of bed.

"Where are you going?" she asked.

"To get my teeth!"

157 I'm 63 now, but that's just 17 Celsius. (GEORGE CARLIN)

158 Two old ladies were sitting in their armchairs sipping tea and talking about their dead husbands. One turned to the other and said: "Did you have mutual orgasms?"

"No, I think we were with the Prudential."

159 A man decided to give his 88-year-old father a nice surprise by fixing a visit from a call-girl.

"Hi," said the call-girl, "I'm here to give you super sex."

"Thanks," said the old man. "I'll have the soup."

160 Middle age is when you choose your cereal for the fibre, not the toy.

161 A couple in their eighties decided to consult a fertility expert to discover whether it was possible for them to have another child. The doctor said recent scientific developments meant that there was a chance, and he gave them a jar and asked them to return with a semen sample.

The following day they went back to the doctor's with an empty jar. The husband was most apologetic. He told the doctor: "I tried my right hand, I tried my left hand. My wife tried her right hand, my wife tried her left hand. She took her teeth out and used her mouth. But still we couldn't get the lid off the jar."

Telltale signs that you're getting old:

162 Your wife gives up sex for Lent and you don't find out until Easter.

163 You stoop to tie your shoes and wonder what else you can do while you're down there.

164 Your ears are hairier than your head.

165 The gleam in your eyes is from the sun hitting your bifocals.

166 Everything hurts, and what doesn't hurt, doesn't work.

167 You can remember when everything was fields.

168 Your little black book contains only names that end in M.D.

169 You get out of breath playing chess.

170 You're still chasing women, but can't remember why.

171 You keep in touch with friends through the obituary column.

172 Your friends compliment you on your alligator shoes but you're not wearing any.

173 You sink your teeth into a steak and they stay there.

174 You feel like the morning after and you haven't been anywhere.

175 Whenever you fall asleep, people worry that you're dead.

176 You can remember cover versions of songs the first time around.

177 You no longer think of speed limits as a challenge.

178 You take a metal detector to the beach.

179 You can live without sex, but not without glasses.

180 You can remember when the Dead Sea was only sick.

181 Your knees buckle, but your belt won't.

182 Your children begin to look middle-aged.

183 You enjoy hearing about other people's operations.

184 You start doing jigsaw puzzles again.

185 You are proud of your lawnmower.

186 You sing along with the elevator music.

187 A fortune-teller offers to read your face.

188 The little grey-haired old lady you help across the street is your wife.

189 Your doctor doesn't give you x-rays anymore – he just holds you up to the light.

190 You get into a heated argument about pension plans.

191 You sit in a rocking chair and can't get it going.

192 After painting the town red, you have to take a long rest before applying the second coat.

193 You got cable TV for the weather channel.

194 You have a party and the neighbours don't even realize it.

195 Your blood type is discontinued.

American towns, cities and states

Alaska
You know you're in Alaska when:

196 You know which leaves make good toilet paper.

197 You find minus 60 degrees a mite chilly.

198 When it warms up to minus 35, you go out in your shirt sleeves to wash your car.

199 The trunk of your car doubles as a deep freeze.

200 You design your Hallowe'en costumes to fit over a snowsuit.

201 You have more miles on your snow blower than on your car.

202 You have over a dozen favourite recipes for moose meat.

203 You think sexy lingerie is fleece socks and a flannel nightie with only eight buttons.

204 You have ever worn a tie with waders.

205 You never say to your kids: "Be home by dark."

206 You can see the road through the floorboard of your pickup truck.

207 The mayor greets you on the street by your first name.

Boston

208 I have just returned from Boston. It is the only thing to do if you find yourself up there. (FRED ALLEN)

Chicago

209 I think that's how Chicago got started. A bunch of people in New York said, "Gee, I'm enjoying the crime and the poverty, but it just isn't cold enough. Let's go west." (RICH JENI)

Colorado

210 A Californian, a Texan and a guy from Colorado were attending a business convention near Las Vegas. On their first night, they went for a drink together in a local bar.

The Californian drank a wine spritzer which he downed in one before hurling his empty glass against the wall, smashing the glass to pieces. Explaining his actions to the bartender, he said: "The standard of living is so high in California that we never drink out of the same glass twice."

Next the Texan downed a Margarita and threw the empty glass against the wall, explaining: "In Texas, we're all so rich from the oil industry that we never drink out of the same glass twice."

Then it was the turn of the man from Colorado. He drank his beer before pulling a gun and shooting his two companions dead. He explained to the bartender: "In Colorado we have so many Californians and Texans that we never have to drink with the same ones twice."

Detroit

211 The Detroit Lions football team were in desperate need of a classy quarterback to help them in their quest for the Super Bowl. After scouring countless colleges without success, their coach was watching CNN when he saw footage of a war scene in Bosnia. At the heart of the action was a young Bosnian soldier who twice scored a direct hit with a hand grenade from a distance of 200 yards. The coach immediately thought that this guy had the perfect throwing arm and set out to sign him.

Following protracted negotiations, the young Bosnian signed and became an instant hero, helping the Lions to win the Super Bowl for the first time in their history. Immediately after the game, he called his mother.

"I've just won the Super Bowl for the Lions," he said excitedly.

"I don't want to talk to you," snapped his mother. "You're not my son any more. At this very moment, there are gunshots all around us. The neighbourhood is a pile of rubble. Your two brothers were beaten within an inch of their lives last week, and your sister was attacked in broad daylight. No, I'll never forgive you for what you've done — making us move to Detroit."

Louisiana

212 An Alabama man was looking for a place to live. Eventually he came to a remote farm but the farmer said the only room he had left was the outhouse. Undeterred, the guy moved in. The next day the farmer saw two TV antennae on top of the outhouse. "What's going on," he asked?

The guy explained: "I sublet the basement to a guy from Louisiana."

Michigan

213 What's the only sign of intelligent life in Ann Arbor? – Columbus: 187 miles.

214 Why do they throw out a sack of manure at University of Michigan weddings? – To keep the flies off the bride.

Minnesota

215 Two guys from Minnesota drove 50 miles to a gas station for a fill-up just because they had heard about a special offer to customers who bought a full tank of gas. The men asked the gas station attendant about the contest.

He explained: "If you win, you're entitled to free sex."

"Great!" they said. "How do we enter?"

The attendant continued: "I'm thinking of a number between one and ten. If you guess right, you win free sex."

They thought for a moment and then one of them said: "Seven."

"No, sorry," said the attendant, "the number I was thinking of was five. Bad luck."

Undeterred, the pair drove back to the station the following week and asked if the contest was still running. The attendant told them it was.

"Right," said one, "I reckon you're thinking of the number eight."

"That's real bad luck," said the attendant. "It was nine."

As they left, cursing their misfortune, one turned to the other and said: "I'm beginning to think this contest is rigged."

"No way," said his friend. "My wife won twice last week."

216 What do you call an intelligent person in Minnesota? – A tourist.

217 Ed from Minnesota went on his first parachute jump. The instructor told Ed exactly what to do and, on leaving the plane, he pulled the ripcord and floated downwards. The instructor followed him out of the plane, but his 'chute failed to open and he plummeted past Ed heading towards the ground. Seeing this, Ed immediately undid the straps to his 'chute and shouted: "So you wanna race, huh?"

218 A man from St Cloud was walking down the street, carrying a brown paper bag. He met a friend who asked him what he had got in the bag.

"Fish," he replied.

"Well," said the friend, "I'll make a bet with you. If I can guess how many fish you've got in that bag, you have to let me have one."

"I'll tell you what. If you tell me how many fish I have in this bag, I'll give you both of them."

219 Why wasn't Christ born in Minnesota? — They couldn't find three wise men and a virgin.

Oklahoma

220 The young man from Oklahoma and his new bride went to a smart hotel for their honeymoon. But that night, while she climbed into bed, he stood by the window, gazing at the moon and stars.

"Honey," she called, "why don't you come to bed?"

"Nope. Momma told me tonight would be the most wonderful night of my life, and I ain't gonna miss a minute of it."

221 The library at the University of Oklahoma burned down last week. The students were very upset — some of the books hadn't been coloured in yet.

222 What do tornadoes and graduates from the University of Oklahoma have in common? — They both end up in trailer parks.

223 Two guys from Oklahoma went to the pet shop to buy two budgerigars.

"What colour do you want?" asked the pet shop owner. "Blue, green or white?"

"We don't care," they said. "Any colour will do."

That afternoon they went to the top of a 100-foot cliff. The first guy grabbed one of the budgerigars in his hand, threw himself off the cliff and landed with a thud at the bottom. Then his friend picked up the other bird and hurled himself off the cliff, landing in a heap at the bottom. As they came round, battered and bruised, one said to the other: "If you ask me, this budgie jumping ain't all it's cracked up to be."

Pasadena

224 A cemetery with lights. (ANON)

Philadelphia

225 Last week I went to Philadelphia, but it was closed. (W.C. FIELDS)

South Carolina

226 How do you know when you're in a South Carolina hotel? – When you call the front desk to say "I've gotta leak in my sink" and the reply is "go ahead".

Utah

227 A guy walked into a Utah bar, ordered a drink and asked the bartender if he'd like to hear a good Brigham Young University joke.

"Listen, buddy," growled the bartender, "see those two big guys on your left? They were both linemen in the BYU football team. And that huge fellow on your right was a top wrestler there. That guy in the corner was the Y's all-time champion weightlifter. And I lettered in three sports at the Y. Now are you absolutely positive you want to tell your joke here?"

"Nah, guess not," said the guy. "I wouldn't want to have to explain it five times."

Vermont

228 After working in the computer business for 20 years, a man decided to take early retirement and escape from the stresses of modern life by buying 50 acres of land in Vermont. His home was totally isolated and, for the first six months, the only people he saw were the mailman and the grocery delivery man. Then one evening, he was surprised by a knock at the door. Standing there was this big Vermontan.

"I'm Caleb, your neighbour from four miles over the ridge. I'm having a party Saturday night and I thought you might like to come."

"That sounds good – I'd like to meet some local folks."

"Oh, but I gotta warn you – there's gonna be some heavy drinkin'."

"Don't worry about that. I used to be in computers and those guys could drink for America."

"Oh, and there's more than likely gonna be some fightin' too."

"That's no problem. I get on with most people."

"Oh, and I've seen some wild sex at these parties."

"Great, after six months' isolation, I'm up for that."

"Right, see you Saturday then," said Caleb.

"One thing. What should I wear?"

"Whatever you want – it's just gonna be the two of us."

Wyoming

229 A theology professor asked a student from Wyoming: "What's the opposite of joy?"

"Sadness," replied the student.

"What's the opposite of depression?"

"Elation."

"And what's the opposite of woe?"

"Giddy up."

Animals

230 A Canadian national park ranger was warning a group of tourists about the danger posed by grizzly bears. He said: "Problems can occur when people unexpectedly stumble across bears. To avoid this, we advise hikers to wear tiny bells on their clothing in order to warn the bears of their presence. And always be on your guard when you know bears are in the area, particularly if you see bear droppings."

One tourist asked: "How do you identify bear droppings?"

"Easy," replied the ranger. "They're the ones with the tiny bells in them."

231 Two lions were strolling down Broadway. One turned to the other and said: "Not many people around today, are there?"

232 At two o'clock in the morning, two bats were hanging upside down in their cave. The first bat turned to the other and said: "How about getting some nice tasty blood for a late-night snack?"

"Where are we gonna find blood at that this time of night?" asked the other.

"All right," said the first, "I'll go off by myself."

Half an hour later, the first bat returned with blood dripping from his mouth and covering his body.

"Wow!" said the second bat. "Where did you get all that blood?"

"See that tree over there?"

"Yeah."

"Well, I didn't!"

233 A man just back from an African safari was relating his adventures to a friend. "It was quite a trip, I can tell you. One day, I was out in the jungle and I heard a noise. I turned round to see this huge lion — bigger than anything I'd ever seen on TV — just a few yards away. I froze for a second, then ran for my life. The lion bounded after me. He was almost at my shoulder when he slipped and I managed to get ahead. But within a matter of seconds, I could feel his hot breath on the back of my neck again, but luckily just as he was about to pounce, he slipped once more. In the distance I saw a house and ran for it as fast as my legs would take me. As I got close to the house, the lion caught up again and was almost on top of me when he slipped for a third time. That enabled me to get in the house and slam the door in the lion's face."

"Wow! That's some story," said the friend. "If I'd been in that situation, I would have shit my pants."

"What do you think the lion kept slipping on?"

234   Apparently bears are attracted to women in their menstrual cycles. A 1,000lb grizzly against a 120lb woman with cramps. I say fair fight. (SIMON COTTER)

235   What's a zebra? – 26 sizes larger than an "A" bra.

236   A tiny turtle began to climb a tree very slowly. Three hours later, it reached the top, climbed on to an outside branch, jumped into the air waving its front legs and crashed to the ground. Saved by its shell, the tiny turtle started to climb the tree again. Four hours later, it reached the top, climbed on to a branch, jumped into the air waving its front legs and crashed to the ground. Undaunted, the tiny turtle tried again. This time it took five hours to climb to the top of the tree. Once there, it stumbled on to an outside branch, jumped into the air waving its front legs and crashed to the ground. As the tiny turtle dusted itself down for yet another laborious ascent of the tree, two birds were watching from above. The female bird turned to the male and said: "Darling, don't you think it's time we told him he's adopted?"

237   Why did the monkey fall out of the tree? – Because he was dead.

238   Why did the second monkey fall out of the tree? – Because he was tied to the first monkey.

239   Why did the third monkey fall out of the tree? – Peer pressure.

240   Why did the squirrel fall out of the tree? – He was doing a monkey impression.

241   What is it with chimpanzees and that middle parting? Stuck in the Twenties, aren't they? (HARRY HILL)

242 A circus owner advertised for a new lion tamer and two young people showed up for an audition. One was a good-looking lad; the other was a gorgeous blonde girl.

The circus owner told them: "I'm going to give it to you straight. This is one ferocious lion. He ate my last tamer, so you guys had better be good or you're history. Here's your equipment: a chair, a whip and a gun. Who wants to try out first?"

The girl said: "I'll go first." She walked past the chair, the whip and the gun and stepped right into the lion's cage. The lion started to snarl and pant and began to charge her. But about half way there, she threw open her coat to reveal her beautiful naked body. The lion stopped dead in his tracks, sheepishly crawled up to her and started licking her ankles. Then he started licking her calves and kissing them tenderly before resting his head at her feet.

The circus owner was stunned. "I've never seen a display like that in my life," he said, before turning to the young man and asking: "Can you top that?"

The young man replied: "No problem. First, get that lion out of the way."

243 What do you call a donkey with three legs? – A wonkey.

244 What do you call a cow with no legs? – Ground beef.

245 What do you call a cow with two legs? – Lean beef.

246 What do you call a deer with no eyes? – No eye idea.

247 What do you call a deer with no eyes and no legs? – Still no eye idea.

248 Animals may be our friends. But they won't pick you up at the airport. (BOBCAT GOLDTHWAITE)

249 A giant panda walked into a restaurant. He ordered some food, ate it, then pulled a gun and blew the brains out of the waiter. Alerted by the shots, the manager appeared just as the panda was making his way to the door.

"Hey, you!" yelled the manager. "You just shot my waiter. Where do you think you're going?"

The beast replied calmly: "I'm a panda. Look it up in the dictionary."

When the panda had gone, the manager thumbed through the dictionary. Sure enough, under panda it said : "Furry mammal, lives in China. Eats shoots and leaves."

250 Why do ducks have webbed feet? To stamp out fires. Why do elephants have flat feet? To stamp out burning ducks.

251 I had a linguistics professor who said that it's man's ability to use language that makes him the dominant species on the planet. That may be, but I think there's one other thing that separates us from animals — we aren't afraid of vacuum cleaners. (JEFF STILSON)

252 What did the doe say as she came running out of the trees? — That's the last time I do that for two bucks.

253 What do you get if you cross a Frisbee with a cow? — Skimmed milk.

254 A horse and a ram were sitting in a bar.

"Fancy another beer?" said the horse. "It's thirsty work pulling that cart all day."

"I know what you mean," replied the ram. "I've been stuck in a field all afternoon with no protection whatsoever from the sun. And the only water we get comes in a trough that is filled with grass, muck and wool. I've been gasping for a cold beer since about three o'clock."

"It's appalling the working conditions we have to endure," said the horse.

"Tell me about it," said the ram. "But if any of us dares to complain, we're threatened with the slaughterhouse. You wouldn't mind, but I can't imagine the farmer and his wife drinking dirty water from a trough."

"You're right there," said the horse. "It's a national disgrace." He reached over for the menu. "I wouldn't mind something to eat as well, as long as it doesn't contain oats. I don't think my boss has ever heard of a healthy balanced diet."

"No, none of them have got a clue about nutrition," said the ram. "You've only got to look at them though. They're all fat and ruddy-faced — heart attacks waiting to happen."

"I fancy a burger," said the horse, "with extra cheese."

"Good idea," replied the ram. "Will you order two? But before that, I must go to the lavatory. Any idea where it is?"

"No, I haven't," said the horse. "Like you, it's the first time I've been here."

Just then a pig sitting at a nearby table said: "The lavatory is through the door by the pool table."

The ram looked at the horse with a puzzled expression and said: "Fancy that, a talking pig!"

255 Why do gorillas have big nostrils? — Because they have big fingers.

256 What's black and white and goes round and round? – A zebra stuck in a revolving door.

257 Two rabbits and a hedgehog were sitting talking by the side of a busy road. The hedgehog was keen to see what was on the other side of the road but was frightened of attempting the journey for fear of being run over by a car. The rabbits gave him a piece of advice: "If there's a vehicle coming," they said, "look it right between the headlights, curl up in a tight ball, let it pass over the top and away you go. It's as simple as that."

A few minutes later, the first rabbit tried to cross the road. Half-way across, he saw a car approaching. Lining himself up directly between the car's headlights, he curled up in a ball and allowed the wheels to pass either side of him. Then he scampered to the safety of the grass verge on the other side. Shortly afterwards, the second rabbit crossed the road. He was almost at the other side when he saw the headlights of a huge lorry. Lining himself up directly between the headlights, he curled up in a ball and allowed the wheels to pass either side of him. Then he too scampered to the grass verge.

Five minutes later, the hedgehog finally plucked up the courage to try and cross the road. He had only gone a few yards when he saw headlights approaching. He lined himself up dircctly between the headlights, curled up in a ball and splat! He was run over.

One rabbit turned to the other and said. "That was bad luck. How many Reliant Robins do you get on this road?"

258 What's got horns and a beard and walks through walls? – Casper the friendly goat.

259 Zebra: "Let's switch roles for a while."
Lion: "OK, I'm game."

260 Two guys were out hiking one day when they came across a disused mine shaft. They were curious as to how deep it was and so they threw a pebble into the hole and waited for the sound of it hitting the foot of the shaft. Instead they heard nothing. So they fetched a larger rock and threw that down the shaft. Still nothing. Then they searched for something bigger and found a railroad tie. With great difficulty, they carried the tie to the mine and dropped it down the shaft. As they stood back to wait for the sound of it hitting the bottom, a goat suddenly darted between them and leaped into the open shaft. The men were still recovering from the shock when a stranger approached.

"Anyone seen a goat?" he asked.

"Yeah," they said, "one just jumped into the mine shaft."

"No, that couldn't have been my goat," said the stranger. "Mine was tethered to a railroad tie."

261 Why did the homeless turtle cross the road? – To get to the Shell station.

262 A guy walked into a bar and saw a horse behind the bar serving drinks. The guy couldn't help but stare, prompting the horse to ask: "What's the matter? Haven't you seen a horse serving drinks before?"

"It's not that," said the guy. "I just never thought the bear would sell this place."

263 Two silkworms had a race – it ended in a tie.

264 A lion woke up one morning with the urge to inflict his superiority on his fellow beasts. So he strode over to a monkey and roared: "Who is the mightiest animal in the jungle?"

"You are, Master," said the monkey, quivering.

Then the lion came across a warthog.

"Who is the mightiest animal in the jungle?" roared the lion.

"You are, Master," said the warthog, shaking with fear.

Next the lion met an elephant.

"Who is the mightiest animal in the jungle?" roared the lion.

The elephant grabbed the lion with his trunk, slammed him against a tree half a dozen times, dropped him like a stone and ambled off.

"All right," shouted the lion. "There's no need to turn nasty just because you don't know the answer."

265 Where do you get virgin wool from? – Ugly sheep.

266 A man arrived home from work to find his dog with his neighbour's pet rabbit in its mouth. The man grabbed the rabbit from the dog, but the pet was clearly already dead. Terrified by what his neighbour would think, he took the bedraggled corpse indoors, gave it a bath, blow-dried its fur and put it back into the cage in his neighbour's garden. That way, he hoped that his neighbour would think the rabbit had simply died of natural causes.

A few days later, the neighbour leaned over the garden fence and said: "Did you know that Fluffy had died?"

"Oh, no," said the man, feigning ignorance.

"It was really strange," continued the neighbour. "We found him dead in his cage, but the day after we buried him in the garden, someone dug him up, gave him a bath and put him back in his cage. How sick can some people get!"

267 I ask people why they have deer heads on their walls. They always say because it's such a beautiful animal. I think my mother is attractive, but I have photographs of her. (ELLEN DEGENERES)

268 Two slugs were slithering along the pavement. Rounding a corner, they found themselves stuck behind two snails. "Oh no!" groaned one of the slugs. "Caravans!"

269 A rabbit escaped from the research laboratory where he had been born and bred. On his first taste of freedom, he met a group of wild rabbits frolicking in a field.

"Hi," he said, introducing himself, "I've escaped from the laboratory and I've never been outside before. What do you rabbits do all day?"

"See that field over there?" they said. "It's full of plump, juicy carrots. Care to try some?"

So they all went off and ate some carrots. "That was great," said the escaped rabbit afterwards. "What else do you do?"

"See that field over there?" they said. "It's full of fat lettuces. Care to try some?"

So they all went off and devoured the lettuces. "This is brilliant," said the escaped rabbit. "I really love it out here in the wild."

"So are you going to stay with us?" they asked.

"I'd really like to, but I must get back to the laboratory. I'm dying for a cigarette."

270 A missionary was chased through the jungle for a week by a ferocious lion. Finally the missionary found himself cornered and, in despair, fell to his knees and prayed for salvation. To his amazement, the lion also began to pray.

"It's truly a miracle," said the missionary, "you, a killer lion, joining me in prayer just when I thought my life was about to end!"

"Shut up," said the lion, "I'm saying grace."

Army

271 The Swiss have an interesting army. Five hundred years without a war, pretty impressive. Also pretty lucky for them. Ever see that little Swiss army knife they have to fight with? Not much of a weapon there – corkscrews, bottle openers.

"Come on, buddy, let's go. You get past me, the guy behind me, he's got a spoon! Back off, I've got the toe clippers right here!" (JERRY SEINFELD)

272 On leaving the army, an old soldier got a white-collar job. One day he arrived at the office to find that he had been given a new young secretary. While taking dictation, she noticed that his fly was open. She wondered whether or not to mention it but in the end she thought she had better say something. So she said discreetly: "Did you know your barracks door is open?"

The old man looked mystified but later realized what she had meant when he himself discovered that his zipper was open. He caught up with her in the corridor. "By the way, Miss Perlman," he said with a grin, "when you saw my barracks door open this morning, did you see a soldier standing to attention?"

"No," she replied coolly, "all I saw was a disabled veteran sitting on two old duffel bags."

273 During camouflage training, a private was disguised as a tree. But he made a sudden noise which was spotted by a visiting general.

The general took him to task. "Don't you know that by yelling and jumping the way you did, you could have endangered the lives of the entire company!"

"I'm sorry, sir," replied the private. "But I can explain. You see, I stood still when a flock of pigeons used me for target practice. And I didn't move a muscle when a large dog peed on my lower branches. But when two squirrels ran up the leg of my pants and I heard the bigger one say: 'Let's eat one now and save the other till winter' . . . that did it."

274 We have women in the military, but they don't put us in the front lines. They don't know if we can fight, if we can kill. I think we can. All the general has to do is walk over to the women and say: "You see the enemy over there? They say you look fat in those uniforms." (ELAYNE BOOSLER)

275 The general received word that the mother of Lance Corporal Perkins had died. At parade, the sergeant major volunteered to break the sad news to Perkins. "I'll go and tell him, shall I, sir?"

"Steady on, sergeant major," said the general. "You can't just barge over and tell the poor man that his mother has died, in front of the rest of the regiment. This calls for tact and diplomacy. Subtlety."

"Very well, sir," said the sergeant major. "I shall be at my most diplomatic and subtle."

With that, he marched over to the line of soldiers and bellowed the command: "All those with mothers still alive, one pace forward . . . Not so fast, Perkins."

276 During an army war game a commanding officer's jeep got stuck in the mud. The CO saw some men lounging around nearby and asked them to help him get unstuck.

"Sorry, sir," said one of the loafers, "but we've been classified dead and the umpire said we couldn't contribute in any way."

The CO turned to his driver and said: "Go drag a couple of those dead bodies over here and throw them under the wheels to give us some traction."

277 Why are soldiers so tired on 1 April? – Because they just had a 31-day March.

278 I think I've worked out how medieval armies broke through the defences of castles. They chose the weakest spot – the gift shop. All a determined enemy had to do was overpower the two old ladies who work there and the whole castle was taken. (BILL BAILEY)

279 Two military cops were chasing a fleeing draftee from a military base. He fled into a nearby convent where he spotted a nun sitting in the courtyard.

"Quick, sister," he said. "Hide me. I don't want to be drafted and the military police are after me."

The nun lifted her skirt and told the young man to hide under it.

"You've got nice legs for a nun," he remarked from beneath the skirt.

"If you look up a little farther," said the nun, "you'll find a set of balls. I don't wanna be drafted either!"

280 Military intelligence is a contradiction in terms. (GROUCHO MARX)

281 A crusty old general was confined to military hospital with a minor ailment. During his stay, he made everyone's life a misery. He complained about the food, he complained about his bed, he complained about the lack of facilities in his room. The staff couldn't wait for him to leave.

One day, an orderly came to take his temperature. After grumbling about the inconvenience, the general finally opened his mouth. But the orderly explained that it was his rectal temperature that needed to be taken and requested that the general turn over. The general blustered some more, but eventually rolled over and lay on his stomach to have his temperature taken. After making the insertion, the orderly told him: "Stay like that for five minutes. Don't move. I'll be back to check up on you."

An hour later, the head nurse entered the room and said: "What's going on?"

The general barked: "What's the matter? Haven't you ever seen someone having their temperature taken?"

"Yes, I have, General, but never before with a daffodil!"

Art

282 Two statues, one male and one female, had religiously guarded the door of an old church for four centuries so one day God, in his mercy, decided to give them both a day off.

"Spend the day how you want," said God who then watched as the male and female statues disappeared behind a bush. Soon the bush began rattling and shaking in a frenzy of activity.

Twelve hours later, the pair emerged but God said: "You've still got half a day left. Go off and have some more fun."

The female statue turned to the male and said: "OK, this time you hold the pigeon and I'll crap on it."

283 If Michelangelo had been a heterosexual, the Sistine Chapel would have been painted basic white and with a roller. (RITA MAE BROWN)

284 Mrs Bloom decided to have her portrait painted. She told the artist: "I want you to paint me with diamond earrings, a diamond necklace, emerald bracelets and a ruby pendant."

The artist replied: "But you're not wearing any of those things."

"I know," she said. "It's in case I die before my husband. I'm certain he'll get married again right away, and I want his new wife to go crazy looking for the jewellery!"

285 I inherited a painting and a violin which turned out to be a Rembrandt and a Stradivarius. Unfortunately, Rembrandt made lousy violins and Stradivarius was a terrible painter. (TOMMY COOPER)

286 Two American ladies were in London admiring a well-endowed male statue. While discussing its artistic merits, one of the women shook her head and said: "I don't think so, dear. Big Ben's a clock."

287 A visitor to an art gallery was perplexed by what appeared to be nothing more than a blank canvas. As chance would have it, the artist responsible was standing next to him.

"I don't wish to appear offensive, but what exactly is it supposed to be?" asked the visitor.

"That, sir, is a cow grazing," replied the artist proudly.

"Where's the grass?"

"The cow has eaten it, sir."

"But where's the cow?"

"You don't think she'd be daft enough to stay after she'd eaten all the grass, do you?"

288 A woman visited an art gallery. One picture was bright blue with vivid orange swirls while the one next to it was black with lime green blobs. The artist was standing nearby so she said to him: "I'm sorry, but I don't understand your paintings."

He replied loftily: "I paint what I feel inside me."

The woman said: "Have you tried Alka-Seltzer?"

289 I went to the museum where they had all the heads and arms from the statues that are in all the other museums. (STEVEN WRIGHT)

290 An artist and his model were kissing passionately on the couch when he heard a car pull up. "Quick, it's my wife," he said. "Get your clothes off and pretend we're working!"

Automobiles

291 A young couple went out on a date in the guy's new car. A few miles down the road, he turned to her and said: "If I do 100 mph, will you take your clothes off?" She said it sounded like fun and so he stepped on the gas. When the speedo touched 100, she began to strip off. Distracted by her state of undress, he took his eyes off the road for a second and crashed into a hedge. The girl was thrown clear without a scratch but all her clothes were trapped in the car, along with her boyfriend.

"Go and get help," he screamed.

"I can't," she said. "I'm stark naked."

Seeing one of his shoes had also been thrown clear, he pointed to it and said: "Cover your crotch with that and go and get help. Please."

So she picked up the shoe, covered herself with it and ran half a mile to the nearest gas station. "Help! Help!" she yelled to the elderly attendant. "My boyfriend's stuck!"

The attendant glanced down at the shoe covering her crotch and said: "I'm sorry, miss. He's too far in."

292 What do you do if a bird craps on your car? – Don't ask her out again.

293 A traffic cop pulled over a nun for driving her little old car too slow on the highway. "This is a 65 mph highway, Sister," he said. "How come you were doing less than 25? You're a danger to other vehicles."

"I'm sorry, officer," she replied, "but I saw a lot of signs which said 22 not 65."

"That's not the speed limit," said the cop. "That's the name of the highway."

Just then he looked in the back of the car and saw two more nuns trembling with fear. "What's the matter with them?" he asked.

The Sister replied: "We've just come off Highway 119."

For the following jokes you can substitute Skoda or Lada:

294 How do you double the value of a Yugo? – Fill the tank with gasoline.

295 What is worse than owning a Yugo? – Owning two Yugos.

296 What do you call an open-topped Yugo? – A skip.

297 What information is contained in each new Yugo owner's manual? – The bus timetable.

298 What's the difference between a Yugo and a golf ball? – You can drive a golf ball more than 200 yards.

299 What's the difference between a Yugo and the flu? – You can get rid of the flu.

300 Why does a Yugo have a heated rear windscreen? – To keep your hands warm when you push it.

301 A guy was driving a Yugo on the interstate when it broke down. A short while later, a Porsche stopped and the driver offered to give the Yugo a tow. "If I go too fast," said the Porsche driver, "honk your horn."

So the Porsche set off with the Yugo on tow. A few miles down the road, a Corvette pulled alongside the Porsche.

The Corvette driver called out: "I bet I can outrace you with that thing on tow behind you."

The Porsche driver was up for the challenge and the two cars sped off side by side down the highway. Two State Troopers watched in disbelief as the cars flew by.

"Did you see that Porsche and Corvette racing neck and neck?" said one.

The other said: "Yeah. And what about that little Yugo flying along behind them, honking his horn, trying to pass?"

302 A small boy was walking along the road when a car pulled up alongside. The driver leaned out and said: "If you get in my car, I'll give you a bag of sweets." The boy ignored him.

"OK," said the driver, "if you get in my car, I'll give you two bags of sweets." Still the boy ignored him.

"Listen," persisted the driver, "if you get in my car, I'll give you all the sweets you want and ten dollars."

The boy turned to the driver and said: "Dad, for the last time, I'm not getting into that Yugo!"

303 My licence plate says PMS. Nobody cuts me off! (WENDY LIEBMAN)

304 Two friends were driving through London. When they came to a set of traffic lights, the driver went straight through on red.

"You just jumped that light," said his astonished passenger.

The driver responded: "Don't worry, my brother does it all the time."

A few minutes later, the driver shot through another red light.

"You jumped another one – you'll get us killed!" protested the friend.

But he was reassured once more: "Don't worry, my brother does it all the time."

However at the next set of lights, showing green, the driver came to a halt.

"Why are you stopping on green?" asked the passenger.

"My brother might be coming."

305 A man saw an advertisement in a paper which read, "Porsche for sale: 200 dollars." He went round to view it, expecting to find a battered heap of rust, but instead found himself face to face with a gleaming new model in mint condition. "Why are you selling it for 200 dollars?" he asked the lady vendor.

"Simple. Last week, my husband ran off with his secretary. He said: 'You can keep the house, but sell my Porsche and send the money on to me.'"

306 I saw a sign: "Rest Area 25 Miles." That's pretty big. Some people must be really tired. (STEVEN WRIGHT)

307 A State Trooper pulled a car over on a quiet country road and walked up to the driver. "Excuse me, ma'am," he said, "but is there any explanation for your erratic driving? You were weaving all over the road."

"Thank goodness you're here, officer," she gasped. "I almost had an accident. I looked up and there was a tree right in front of me. I swerved to the left and there was another tree. So I swerved to the right and there was another tree. It was the most terrifying experience."

Calmly the officer reached through the side window to the rear-view mirror and said: "Ma'am, there was no tree. It was your air freshener."

308 A driver was speeding down a country lane when he turned a corner and was horrified to see two farmhands standing talking in the middle of the road. As he swerved to avoid them, his car ran up an embankment, did a triple somersault and landed in an adjacent field.

One farmhand turned to the other and said: "That was lucky. I reckon we got out of that field just in time."

309 When I get real bored, I like to drive downtown and get a great parking spot, then sit in my car and count how many people ask me if I'm leaving. (STEVEN WRIGHT)

310 An irate motorist went back to the garage where he had bought an expensive battery for his car six months previously. He told the garage owner: "When you sold me that battery, you told me it would be the last battery my car would ever need. Now, six months later, it's dead."

"Yeah, I'm sorry," said the garage owner. "I just didn't think your car would last longer than that."

311 A man was driving his wife home after a night out when they were stopped by the police.

"Did you know you were speeding, sir?" asked the officer.

"No, I had no idea that I was speeding," replied the driver.

"Of course you were," interrupted the wife. "You're always speeding."

The officer looked at the rear of the vehicle. "And did you know your brake light is broken, sir?"

"No, I had no idea that it was broken," replied the driver.

Again the wife interrupted. "Of course you knew it was broken. You're always saying you'll get it repaired, but you never have."

The officer began to sympathize with the driver. "Does she always talk to you like this?"

"Only when he's drunk," said the wife.

312 Men drive too fast, we are told, because the car is an extension of the penis. But if it were, men would surely not drive too fast; they would just back in and out of the garage. Or maybe just polish it all the time. (JEREMY HARDY)

313 "The car won't start," said a wife to her husband. "I think there's water in the carburettor."

"How do you know?" said the husband scornfully. "You don't even know what the carburettor is."

"I'm telling you," repeated the wife, "I'm sure there's water in the carburettor."

"We'll see," mocked the husband. "Let me check it out. Where's the car?"

"In the swimming pool."

314 An old man was driving on the freeway when his car phone rang. It was his wife. "Herman," she cried, "I just heard on the news that there's a car going the wrong way on 280. Please be careful."

"Hell," exclaimed Herman. "It's not just one car. It's hundreds of them!"

Genuine answers given on written driving exams in California:

315 Q: Do you yield when a blind pedestrian is crossing the road?

A: What for? He can't see my licence plate.

316 Q: Who has the right of way when four cars approach a four-way stop at the same time?

A: The pick-up truck with the gun rack and the bumper sticker saying, "Guns don't kill people. I do."

317 Q: When driving through fog, what should you use?

A: Your car.

318 Q: What is the difference between a flashing red traffic light and a flashing yellow traffic light?

A: The colour.

319 Q: What are the important safety tips to remember when backing your car?

A: Always wear a condom.

320 Q: What are some points to remember when passing or being passed?

A: Make eye contact and wave "hello" if she's cute.

321 Three men – Eric, Ray and Steve – were killed in a car crash and made their way up to heaven. St Peter was waiting for them and outlined the facilities which heaven had to offer. He announced: "For the purposes of travelling around heaven, you will each be given a means of transportation appropriate to your past deeds."

First, St Peter turned to Eric. "Eric, you cheated on your wife on four separate occasions. You will drive around heaven in a battered old Dodge."

Next, St Peter turned to Ray. "Ray, you cheated on your wife twice. You will be given a Toyota station-wagon."

Finally, St Peter turned to Steve. "Steve, you led a blameless life. You never cheated on your wife and were totally faithful, a loyal loving husband. Your reward is a top-of-the-range Ferrari."

Steve was overjoyed and drove around heaven in his gleaming red Ferrari.

Eric and Ray were envious but, two months later, they spotted Steve crying at the wheel of his car. "What's the matter?" they asked. "You've got everything you could want – the best car in heaven."

"I know," sobbed Steve, "but I just saw my wife go by on a skateboard."

322 I love the way garages leave black buckets outside for your dead flowers. (JACK DEE)

323 A juggler was driving to a show when he was stopped by a traffic cop. The cop peered inside the car, looked at the back seat and demanded to know: "What are matches and lighter fuel doing in your car?"

"I'm a juggler," replied the driver.

"Oh yeah?" said the cop suspiciously. "Let's see you prove it."

So the driver collected his props and began juggling three blazing torches at the roadside. Just then an elderly couple drove by. The husband turned to his wife and said: "I'm glad I quit drinking. Look at the test they're giving now!"

324 While working on a car, a mechanic accidentally swallowed some brake fluid. To his surprise, he quite liked the taste. The next day he took another swig and enjoyed it so much that by the end of the week he was hooked on the stuff.

His friend said: "You must be mad drinking brake fluid! It's poisonous. You've got to give it up."

"Don't worry," said the mechanic. "I can stop any time."

Aviation

325 On boarding an aeroplane, a man was surprised to find that the occupant of the next seat was a parrot. The parrot didn't say anything until the stewardess came round with the drinks trolley shortly after take-off. The man ordered a coffee but the parrot squawked loudly: "Get me a brandy, you stupid cow."

The stewardess was so taken aback by the parrot's outburst that she forgot all about the man's coffee but did remember the parrot's brandy. A few minutes later when the stewardess was passing again, the man politely reminded her that he still hadn't had his coffee. No sooner had he finished speaking than the parrot squawked: "Get me another brandy, you lazy mare."

Moments later, the flustered stewardess returned with the parrot's second brandy, but again forgot the man's coffee.

By now, the man was getting irritated and so he decided to copy the parrot's approach. So the next time the stewardess appeared, the man barked: "Fetch me a coffee, whore."

The next thing he knew both he and the parrot had been hurled out of the plane by two burly stewards. As they plunged towards the ground, the parrot turned to the man and said: "For someone who can't fly, you're a lippy bastard."

Actual airline announcements:

326 Weather at our destination is fifty degrees with some broken clouds, but they'll try to have them fixed before we arrive.

327 Your seat cushions can be used for flotation and in the event of an emergency water landing, please take them with our compliments.

328 We ask you to please remain seated as Captain Kangaroo bounces us to the terminal.

329 Please remain in your seats with your seatbelts fastened while the Captain taxis what's left of our airplane to the gate!

330 Thank you for flying with us. We hope you enjoyed giving us the business as much as we enjoyed taking you for a ride.

331 There may be fifty ways to leave your lover, but there are only four ways out of this airplane . . .

332 Feel free to move about as you wish, but please stay inside the plane till we land.

333 In the event of a sudden loss of cabin pressure, oxygen masks will descend from the ceiling. Stop screaming, grab the mask, and pull it over your face.

334 We'd like to thank you folks for flying with us today. And the next time you get the insane urge to go blasting through the skies in a pressurized metal tube, we hope you'll think of us here at US Airways.

335 Last one off the plane must clean it.

336 A plane was delayed nearly an hour on take-off. When it eventually took to the air, the passengers asked the stewardess the reason for the late departure.

"Well," she explained, "the pilot was worried about a noise he heard coming from one of the engines and it took us a while to get a new pilot."

337 Bad weather forced a plane to keep circling over JFK airport for nearly two hours. Finally the pilot announced over the public address system: "Ladies and gentlemen, I have some bad news and some good news. The bad news is that we are running out of fuel. The good news is that I'm parachuting down to get help."

338 There are only two reasons to sit in the back row of an airplane: either you have diarrhoea, or you're anxious to meet people who do. (RICH JENI)

339 The flight attendant listened patiently to the man's complaints: "You bring me cold coffee, you give me lousy food, I can't see the movie – not that it matters anyway because you didn't bring me any headphones – and my window doesn't have a shade, so I can't close it and go to sleep."

When he had finally finished, she said: "Just shut up and land the plane!"

340 How do you know if there's a pilot at your party? – He'll tell you.

341 Before going on his first plane journey, a man was told that chewing gum would stop his ears popping during the flight. As they landed, the man turned to his friend and said: "The chewing gum works fine, but how do I get it out of my ears?"

342 A woman on her first plane trip found herself a nice window seat in a no smoking area. But no sooner had she settled down than a man appeared and insisted that it was his seat.

Despite a lengthy argument, she flatly refused to move and told him to go away.

"OK, madam," he said, "if that's the way you want it, you fly the plane!"

343 Did you ever notice that the first piece of luggage on the carousel never belongs to anyone? (ERMA BOMBECK)

344 When the Pope landed in Dublin on a ceremonial visit to Ireland, the first thing he did was kneel down and kiss the soil.

"I wonder why he did that?" remarked an onlooker.

The man next to him said: "You would too, if you'd flown Alitalia and landed safely!"

345 How do you know it's an Alitalia plane? – By the hairs under the wings.

346 An elderly man and a Baptist minister were sitting next to each other on a plane. Since the flight had been delayed, the pilot announced that once they were airborne, free drinks would be brought round to the passengers by way of an apology.

Ten minutes after take-off, the pretty young flight attendant came round with the drinks trolley. The old man requested a whisky and soda. "And what would you like?" the attendant asked the Baptist minister.

"No, no," he roared. "I would rather commit adultery than drink alcohol!"

The old man looked confused and, handing his drink back to the attendant, said: "Sorry, I didn't know there was a choice . . ."

347 In aeroplanes, why is there no window in the toilet? Who on earth is going to see in? (BILLY CONNOLLY)

348 A farmer and his wife went to an air fair. The farmer had always been fascinated by planes and asked the pilot of a light aircraft how much it would be for a ride.

"150 dollars," said the pilot.

"Can't afford that," said the farmer. "That's a real shame cos I've always wanted to go up in one of them things."

The pilot was touched by his enthusiasm. "I'll tell you what I'll do – I'll make a deal with you. You and your wife can ride for free provided you don't make a sound at any time during the flight. But if you make a sound, it'll cost you the full 150 dollars."

The couple agreed and climbed into the plane. The pilot really showed off, performing loops, dives and twists. Half an hour later, when he came in to land, he asked the farmer whether he'd enjoyed it.

"It was wild," said the farmer. "Unbelievable."

"Well, I want to congratulate you on your bravery," said the pilot. "You didn't make a sound."

"It was a close call though," said the farmer. "I nearly said something when my wife fell out!"

349 After a really bumpy landing, the ashen-faced passengers left the aircraft. Last one off was a little old lady who paused at the exit door and said shakily to the flight attendant: "Can I ask you a question?"

"Sure."

"Did we land or were we shot down?"

350 I love flying. I've been to almost as many places as my luggage. (BOB HOPE)

351 An old lady was terrified of flying to visit her family in Australia because she was always afraid that there would be a bomb on board. Her family tried to convince her that the risk of such an occurrence was remote and persuaded her to consult an actuary.

"What are the chances of someone having a bomb on a plane?" she asked.

"Very small," replied the actuary, "about one in 10,000."

"And what are the chances of two people having a bomb on the same plane?"

"Even smaller," said the actuary. "Something like one in a billion. Practically zero."

After that, the old lady was happy to fly . . . so long as she always took a bomb on board with her.

352 As Concorde landed in New York, the pilot announced: "Ladies and gentlemen, thank you for flying on Concorde and, on behalf of the crew, I hope that we shall have the pleasure of your company on future flights." Then, forgetting that his microphone was still switched on, he added: "Now all I need is a nice cup of coffee and a woman."

Hearing the gaffe, a pretty young flight attendant rushed up the gangway towards the cockpit. Halfway up the aisle, an old lady patted her on the arm and said: "Don't hurry, dear. Give him time to have his coffee."

353 Airline hostesses show you how to use a seat belt in case you haven't been in a car since 1965. (JERRY SEINFELD)

354 An aircraft with four engines was flying over the ocean when one of the engines failed. "Quick," said the pilot to his crew, "dump all the food."

Soon afterwards, a second engine failed. "Quick," said the pilot, "dump the empty seats."

A few minutes later, a third engine failed. "Quick," said the pilot, "dump all the luggage."

Then the fourth engine failed. "Can I have your attention please," announced the pilot over the tannoy. "All four engines have failed. There's no chance of us reaching Kennedy Airport so I'm going to attempt to make a water landing. All the passengers who can swim should move to the right side of the plane; all those who can't swim should move to the left side. Those of you who can swim, head for the island on your right. Those of you who can't swim, I'd just like to thank you for flying Delta Air . . ."

Rules of the air:
355 Every take-off is optional. Every landing is mandatory.
356 If you push the stick forward, the houses get bigger. If you pull the stick back, they get smaller. That is, unless you keep pulling the stick all the way back, then they get bigger again.
357 Flying isn't dangerous. Crashing is what's dangerous.
358 The only time you have too much fuel is when you're on fire.
359 When in doubt, hold on to your altitude. No one has ever collided with the sky.
360 A good landing is one from which you can walk away. A great landing is one after which they can use the plane again.

361 Always try to keep the number of landings you make equal to the number of take-offs you've made.

362 The propeller is just a big fan in front of the plane used to keep the pilot cool. When it stops, you can actually watch the pilot start sweating.

363 Never let an aircraft take you somewhere your brain didn't get to five minutes earlier.

364 Stay out of clouds. The silver lining everyone keeps talking about might be another aircraft going in the opposite direction.

365 It's always a good idea to keep the pointy end going forward as much as possible.

366 Remember, gravity is not just a good idea – it's the law, and it's not subject to repeal.

367 If all you can see out of the window is ground that's going round and round and all you can hear is screaming from the passenger compartment, things are not at all as they should be.

368 Good judgment comes from experience. Unfortunately the experience usually comes from bad judgment.

369 The three most useless things to a pilot are the altitude above you, the runway behind you, and a tenth of a second ago.

370 In the ongoing battle between objects made of aluminium going hundreds of miles per hour and the ground going zero miles per hour, the ground has yet to lose.

Babies

371 A man was pushing a pram containing a screaming baby along the street. All the while the man kept repeating quietly: "Keep calm, George." "Don't scream, George." "It'll be OK, George."

A woman heard this and said to the man: "You really are doing your best to soothe your son George."

The man looked at her and replied stonily: "I'm George."

372 Thanks to the miracle of fertility treatment, a woman was able to have a baby at 65. When she was discharged from hospital, her relatives came to visit. "Can we see the baby?" they asked.

"Not yet," said the 65-year-old mother.

Twenty minutes later, they asked again. "Can we see the baby?"

"Not yet," said the mother.

Another twenty minutes later, they asked again. "Can we see the baby?"

"Not yet," said the mother.

The relatives were growing impatient. "Well, when can we see the baby?"
"When it cries."
"Why do we have to wait until the baby cries?"
"Because I forgot where I put it."

373 I've been breastfeeding for two years. I could light the gas ring with my nipples. (JO BRAND)

374 When they brought their first baby home from hospital, the wife suggested to her husband that he should have a go at changing the baby's nappy.
"I'm busy," he said. "I'll change the next one."
So three hours later, she tried again: "Darling, will you change baby's nappy?"
"No," he said. "I meant the next baby."

Reasons why men can't change the baby in the middle of the night:
375 "I'm sure he called for Mummy."
376 "I'm having a really good dream, and I don't want to spoil it."
377 "I've got an important meeting the day after next."
378 "You're so much better with him than me."
379 "I've got cramp."
380 "You must admit, I need my beauty sleep much more than you do."
381 "I couldn't face a nappy after that late-night curry."
382 "I can't find my dressing-gown."
383 "You know how I get the baby cream and the oven cleaner mixed up."
384 "I got up last time . . . all right, the time before that."
385 "I'm asleep."

386 A boy went to visit his mother in hospital and to see his new baby brother. While there, he slipped into an adjoining ward and started talking to a woman with her leg in traction.
"How long have you been here?" he asked.
"Six weeks," she replied.
"Can I see your baby?"
"I haven't got a baby."
"Gee, you're slow. My mum's only been here two days but she's got one!"

387 A woman was walking along the street with her blouse open. A passer-by stopped her and said: "Excuse me, madam, your breast is hanging out."
She looked down and shrieked: "Oh my God, I left the baby on the bus!"

388 Three men were waiting anxiously outside the maternity ward at the city hospital. After a few minutes, a nurse came out to tell the first man: "Congratulations. You're the father of twins."

"Twins!" he exclaimed. "How about that? I work for the Doublemint Chewing Gum Company!"

Shortly afterwards, a nurse came out to tell the second man: "Congratulations. You're the father of triplets."

"Triplets" he said. "What a coincidence! I work for the 3M Organization!"

The third man stood up ashen-faced and muttered: "I need some air. I work for 7-Up!"

389 If I ever have twins, I'd use one for parts. (STEVEN WRIGHT)

390 In the backwoods of Canada in a shack with no electricity, a man's wife went into labour in the middle of the night. The local doctor was fetched to help with the delivery. The doctor gave the nervous father-to-be a lantern to hold, partly to keep him occupied and partly so that he could see what he was doing. After a few minutes, a baby boy was born and the husband put down the lantern to hold him.

"Don't put that lantern down just yet," said the doctor. "I think there's another one on the way."

Shortly afterwards, a baby daughter was born and the husband put down the lantern to hold her.

"Don't put that lantern down yet," said the doctor. "I think there may be another one still to come."

Sure enough, a few minutes later, another baby girl was born. The father scratched his head and said to the doctor: "D'you think it's the light that's attracting them?"

391 I love being a grandmother. It's great to finally be greeted by someone who's bald, drooling, and wearing a diaper who's not my date. (JOAN RIVERS)

392 Mr and Mrs Harris were desperate to start a family, but after trying for years, they became convinced that it was not meant to happen. So, as a last resort, they decided to employ the services of a proxy father whom they had never met. On the morning that the sperm donor was due to call, Mr Harris set off for work as usual and wished his wife good luck. She wasn't looking forward to it.

As chance would have it, that same morning a travelling baby photographer was also in the area and called at the Harrises' house. Mrs Harris answered the door. She was expecting the sperm donor.

"Good morning, madam," said the photographer. "You don't know me, but I've come to . . ."

"Yes, I know," she interrupted. "There's no need to explain. Come in. I've been expecting you."

"Really?" said the photographer, thinking that his advertising must have paid off. "I must say I have made a speciality of babies."

"That's what my husband and I were hoping," she said. "So where do we start?"

"Well, I usually try two in the bathtub, one on the couch and perhaps a couple on the bed. That seems to work for me."

"No wonder George and I haven't had much luck . . ."

"If we try several different positions and I shoot from six or seven angles, I'm sure you'll be pleased with the results."

"I do hope so," she said nervously. "Can we get this over with quickly?"

"In my line of work, I have to take my time," he replied. "It's no good rushing these things. I'd love to be in and out in five minutes, but I think you'd be disappointed with that."

"That's true," she sighed knowingly.

The photographer opened his briefcase and pulled out a portfolio of baby pictures. "This one was done on top of a bus," he explained.

"Oh my!" exclaimed Mrs Harris.

"And these twins turned out really well considering the fact that their mother was difficult to work with."

"In what way was she difficult?" asked Mrs Harris anxiously.

"She insisted we go out outdoors, so I had to take her over to Hyde Park to get the job done properly. People were crowding four deep to watch. It took over three hours in all. It was really exhausting."

By now Mrs Harris was looking decidedly worried.

"Right," he said. "I'll just get my tripod."

"Tripod?"

"Yes, I need a tripod on which to rest my Canon."

At that point Mrs Harris fainted.

Banking

393 A man walked into a bank and asked to borrow the sum of 2,000 dollars for three weeks. The loan officer asked what collateral the man had. He replied: "I've got a Rolls-Royce. Keep it until the loan is paid off. Here are the keys."

So the loan officer arranged for the car to be driven into the bank's underground parking for safe-keeping and gave the man the 2,000 dollars.

Three weeks later, the man walked back into the bank, paid back the 2,000 dollars loan plus 10 dollars interest and regained possession of his Rolls-Royce. The loan officer was mystified: "Tell me, sir," he said, "why would someone who drives a Rolls-Royce need to borrow 2,000 dollars?"

The man replied: "I had to go abroad for three weeks and where else could I store a Rolls-Royce for that length of time for 10 dollars?"

394 What's the difference between a dead skunk and a dead banker on the road? – There are skid marks near the skunk.

395 A man went into a bank and withdrew 1,000 dollars in cash. To keep the bills together, he bound them with a rubber band. Then he stuffed the wad of money in his pocket and headed for the door. However he had only gone a few yards down the street when he found to his horror that the money was missing. He was sure that he hadn't been targeted by a pickpocket and could only presume that the bundle of bills had fallen out of his pocket. He dashed back into the bank and collided with an elderly customer.

"Have you lost some money tied in a rubber band?" asked the old man.

"Yes, I have!"

"Well, I've found the rubber band."

396 They usually have two tellers in my local bank, except when it's very busy, when they have one. (RITA RUDNER)

397 A little old lady went into the Chase Manhattan Bank and announced that she wanted to open a savings account.

"Certainly," said the accounts manager. "How much would you like to put in?"

"Three million dollars," replied the old lady.

The accounts manager gasped. "That's a lot of money. In what form would you like to open your account?"

"Cash. I've got it here in this bag. See for yourself if you want."

The manager looked into a plastic bag and, sure enough, there were several bundles of crisp green bills. This was a most unusual scenario and the manager decided to notify the bank president who duly escorted the old lady into his office so that he could deal with the matter personally.

The president was charm itself. He arranged for tea and biscuits to be brought in for the bank's valued new client. "If you don't mind me asking," he said. "where did you get the money?"

"Gambling," replied the old lady.

The president found this hard to take in. "What sort of gambling?"

"Oh, I make bets with people on all sorts of things, and I usually win. For example, I've got 100,000 dollars right here which says that by noon tomorrow your balls will be square. And I'll give you odds of four to one. You got 25,000 dollars you'd be willing to wager on that?"

The president was almost lost for words. "It wouldn't be ethical for me to take your money because I'm afraid there is no way you can win that particular bet."

"Well, if you ain't willing to take a gamble, I have to wonder whether this is the right bank for me and my money."

The president was desperate not to lose her custom. "Let's not be hasty," he said. "OK, I'll go along with your bet if you're absolutely sure about it."

"Absolutely," said the little old lady. "And don't worry about me. I know what I'm doing. I'll see you at 11.45 tomorrow morning."

All that night, the president woke up at hourly intervals to check that his balls hadn't gone square. Everything in that department was fine. At 11.45 the following morning, the little old lady arrived at the bank with her lawyer.

"My lawyer's here to act as a witness," she explained as they entered the president's office.

As noon struck, the president claimed that he had won the bet, but the little old lady demanded that he drop his pants so that she could check. He obliged, she had a feel around and pronounced that his balls weren't square.

"I guess you've won the bet," she said, handing him the 100,000 dollars. As she did so, the lawyer began banging his head against the wall.

"What's up with him?" asked the president.

"He's just a sore loser," said the little old lady. "You see, I bet him 1 million dollars that I would have the president of the Chase Manhattan Bank by the balls by noon today!"

398 A young woman went to cash a cheque from her husband. The bank cashier asked her to endorse it. So she wrote on the back: "My husband is a wonderful man."

399 A student went into a bank to see the manager with regard to extending his overdraft. At first, the manager refused point blank but when the student pleaded, he reconsidered.

"I'll tell you what I'll do," said the manager. "I'm a sporting man and I like a bet. I've got a glass eye and if you can tell me which one it is, I'll extend your overdraft."

"It's your left eye," said the student without hesitation.

"Good God!" exclaimed the manager. "That's amazing. You're the first person ever to guess correctly. People always think my right eye is the glass one. How did you know?"

The student replied: "It's a damn sight more sympathetic than your right eye."

400 I don't have a bank account because I don't know my mother's maiden name. (PAULA POUNDSTONE)

401 A guy walked into a bank and said to the female teller at the window: "I want to open a bloody account."

"I beg your pardon," said the teller. "What did you say?"

"Listen, damn you," snarled the man. "I said I want to open a bloody account – right now."

"I'm terribly sorry, sir," said the teller, "but I am afraid we do not tolerate that kind of language in this bank." And with that, she left her window and reported the customer's behaviour to the manager. The manager returned to confront the man.

"Now what seems to be the problem?" asked the bank manager.

"There's no damn problem," said the man. "I just won 50 million in the lottery and I want to open a bloody account in this damn bank."

"I see," said the manager, "and this bitch is giving you a hard time?"

402 A man went into a bank and said to the cashier: "Will you check my balance?" So she pushed him.

Bartenders

403 A penguin walked into a bar and asked the bartender: "Have you seen my brother?"

The bartender said: "I don't know. What does he look like?"

404 A termite walked into a bar and said: "Is the bar tender here?"

405 A guy walked into a bar carrying a crocodile and a chicken. He put them down on a stool and said to the bartender: "I'll have a Scotch and soda."

And the crocodile added: "And I'll have a Whiskey Sour."

The bartender was amazed. "That's incredible," he gasped, "I've never seen a crocodile that could talk!"

"He can't," said the guy. "The chicken's a ventriloquist."

406 A man walked into a bar. Ow! It was an iron bar.

407 Celine Dion walked into a bar. "Why the long face?" said the bartender.

408 A customer walked into a bar and started dialling numbers on his hand as if it were a phone. The bartender looked at him warily. "Look," warned the bartender, "I don't know what you're up to, but this is a tough neighbourhood and I don't want any trouble."

The customer said: "I'm not out to cause trouble, I promise. Let me explain. I'm very hi-tech and I had a phone installed in my hand because I got tired of carrying around my mobile."

The bartender looked at him as if he were a crank. "I don't believe a word of it."

"OK," said the customer, "I'll prove it to you." And he pressed the digits on his hand, held his wrist up to his ear and began conducting a conversation. Then he gave his hand to the bartender and, to the bartender's amazement, he could hear a voice coming through the hand.

"That's incredible," said the bartender at the end of the call. "I was able to talk to someone through your hand."

"It's ingenious," said the customer. "It means I can keep in touch with my broker, my wife, anyone, without needing a conventional phone. By the way, where is the men's room?"

The bartender directed him down the corridor to the toilets but began to get a bit worried when the customer hadn't returned 20 minutes later. Knowing the reputation of the neighbourhood, he thought he'd better go and check that he was all right. On opening the door, he found the customer spreadeagled against the wall, with his pants down and a roll of toilet paper rammed up his butt.

"Oh God," exclaimed the bartender. "Did they rob you? Are you hurt?"

"No, I'm fine," answered the customer. "I'm just waiting for a fax."

409 Two hamburgers walked into a bar. The bartender said: "Sorry, we don't serve food."

410 A snail slid into a bar and ordered a beer. The bartender said: "Get out, you're a snail." And he picked up the snail, threw him out of the door and across the street.

Eleven months later, while collecting glasses, the bartender felt a tap at his ankle. The snail said: "What the hell did you do that for?"

411 A guy walked into a bar and said to the bartender: "I've got this great Polish joke."

The bartender glared at him and warned him: "Before you go telling that joke, I think you ought to know that I'm Polish, the two bouncers on the door are Polish and most of my customers are Polish."

"OK," said the guy. "I'll tell it slowly."

412 A skeleton walked into a bar and said: "I'll have a Budweiser and a mop, please."

413 A guy walked into a bar. The bartender said: "You've got a steering wheel down your pants."

"Yeah, I know," said the guy. "It's driving me nuts!"

414 Shakespeare walked into a bar and asked for a beer. The bartender said: "I can't serve you — you're bard."

415 A smartly dressed man entered a plush Manhattan bar and took a seat. The bartender came over and asked: "What can I get you to drink, sir?"

"Nothing, thank you," replied the man. "I tried alcohol once but I didn't like it, and I haven't drunk it since."

The bartender was a little perplexed but being a friendly, outgoing sort, he pulled out some cigarettes from his pocket, flipped the top of the pack and offered one to the man. But the man refused, saying: "I tried smoking once, didn't like it, and I have never smoked since. Look, actually, I wouldn't be in here at all, except that I'm waiting for my son."

To which the bartender said: "Your only child, I presume?"

416 Did you hear about the bailiff who moonlighted as a bartender? — He served subpoena coladas.

417 A man went into a bar and ordered a succession of Martinis. After each one, he removed the olive and put it into a jar.

After two hours, the bartender felt compelled to ask: "Why do you keep doing that?"

"Because," slurred the man, "my wife sent me out for a jar of olives."

418 A grasshopper walked into a bar. The bartender said: "Hey, we have a drink named after you."

The grasshopper said: "You have a drink named Marlon?"

419 A vagrant walked into a bar and was told by the bartender to get out.

"All right," said the vagrant, "If you give me a cocktail stick, I'll leave."

So the bartender handed him a cocktail stick and he left.

Two minutes later, another vagrant came in. Again, the bartender ordered him to leave.

"Very well," said the vagrant, "Give me a cocktail stick and I'll go."

So the bartender handed him a cocktail stick and he left.

Two minutes later, a third vagrant entered the bar. The bartender immediately offered him a cocktail stick to leave.

"I don't want a cocktail stick," said the vagrant. "I want a straw. Give me a straw and I'll go."

The bartender was puzzled. "How come you want a straw when the other two wanted cocktail sticks?"

"Well," said the vagrant, "someone's been sick outside and now all the lumpy bits have gone."

420 A little pig walked into a bar, ordered a drink and asked where the toilet was.

"Just along the corridor," said the bartender.

Then a second little pig walked into the bar, ordered a drink and asked where the toilet was.

"Just along the corridor," said the bartender.

Then a third little pig walked into the bar and ordered a drink. The bartender said: "I suppose you want to use the toilet too?"

"No, I'm the little pig that goes wee wee wee wee all the way home."

421 A sheriff walked into a bar and said: "Has anyone seen Brown Paper Jake? He wears a brown paper hat, a brown paper waistcoat, a brown paper shirt, brown paper boots, brown paper pants and a brown paper jacket."

The bartender said: "What's he wanted for?"

"Rustlin'."

422 A baby seal walked into a bar and sat down. "What can I get you?" asked the bartender.

The baby seal said: "Anything but a Canadian Club."

423 A guy walked into a bar and ordered a double scotch, bourbon on the rocks, and a triple vodka. He said to the bartender: "I shouldn't be drinking this with what I've got."

"Why, what have you got?"

"Thirty cents."

424 Two fonts walked into a bar. The bartender said: "Sorry, we don't want your type in here."

425 A businessman walked into a bar and ordered a hot dog and a Budweiser. He downed the beer, put the hot dog on his head, smashed it with his hand and walked out before the bartender could say a word.

The next day the businessman returned and once again ordered a hot dog and a Budweiser. The bartender watched in amazement as the businessman drank the beer, put the hot dog on his head, smashed it with his hand and walked out.

The businessman was back again the following day and placed his regular order of a hot dog and a Budweiser. But this time the bartender was waiting to catch him out. "I'm sorry, we're out of hot dogs," he said.

"Right," said the businessman. "I'll have a packet of chilli-flavoured potato chips and a Budweiser."

He downed the beer, put the packet of chilli flavoured potato chips on his head, smashed it with his hand and headed for the door.

"Wait!" called the bartender, overcome by curiosity. "Why did you smash that packet of chilli-flavoured potato chips on your head?"

The businessman replied: "Because you didn't have any hot dogs."

426 A guy walked into a bar with a giraffe. They both drank so much that the giraffe passed out on the floor. There was no way the guy could get the giraffe back on its feet so he decided to go home and collect it in the morning. But as he headed for the door, the bartender called out: "Hey, you can't leave that lyin' there."

The guy said: "That's not a lion – it's a giraffe."

427 A neutron walked into a bar and asked the bartender: "How much for a beer?"
The bartender said: "For you, no charge."

Baseball

428 A small boy got lost at a baseball game. He went up to a police officer and said: "I've lost my dad."

"What's he like?" asked the officer sympathetically.

"Beer and women," said the boy.

429 After spending so much time in Hollywood, Hugh Grant decided to get involved in the local community. Someone suggested he take up baseball, so he joined a local team.

During their first game, Grant came out to bat. On the very first pitch, he knocked the ball out of the park. The team members stood there, dumbfounded. Unfortunately, so did Grant.

"Run!" his team-mates yelled.

Grant turned and stared at them icily. "There's no need for me to run away," he replied. "I'm more than willing to reimburse you chaps for the cost of your ball."

430 A baseball team manager who had an ulcer visited his doctor.

"Remember," said the doctor, "don't get excited, don't get angry and forget all about baseball when you're off the field." Then he added: "By the way, how come you let the pitcher bat yesterday with the tying run on second and two men out in the ninth?"

431 Baseball is very big with my people. It figures. It's the only time we can get to shake a bat at a white man without starting a riot. (DICK GREGORY)

432 God and Satan arranged a baseball game between heaven and hell. God was supremely confident and told Satan he hadn't a chance. God reeled off the list of players on his team – Mickey Mantle, Joe DiMaggio, Lou Gherig, Babe Ruth and all the other legends of the game.

Satan said: "Yeah, but I have the umpires."

433 During a game of baseball between teams of eight year olds, the coach went over to one of his young players and began to read him the riot act.

"Do you understand what co-operation is?" barked the coach.

"Yes," replied the boy.

"And do you understand what a team is?"

"Yes."

"So when a strike is called, or you're out at first, you don't argue or curse, or attack the umpire. Do you understand all that?"

"Yes."

"Then go and explain it to your mother!"

434 A Scotsman on a visit to Chicago was attending his first baseball game. After a base hit, he heard the fans roaring "Run, run." So when the next batter made a good hit, the Scotsman joined in the shouts of "run, run". Keen to show how quickly he had picked up the rules of the game, the Scotsman rose to his feet when the third batter slammed a hit and led the chorus of "run, run". The next batter held his swing at three and two, and as the umpire called a walk, the

Scotsman stood up alone and yelled "Run, run." As everybody around him began to snigger, the Scotsman sat down in embarrassment, totally confused.

The person in the next seat leaned over and explained: "He doesn't have to run, he's got four balls."

The Scotsman immediately stood up and shouted: "Walk with pride, man."

Beauty

435 Sleeping Beauty, Tom Thumb and Quasimodo were talking one day. Sleeping Beauty said: "I believe myself to be the most beautiful girl in the world."

Tom Thumb said: "I must be the smallest person in the world."

Quasimodo said: "And I absolutely have to be the ugliest person in the world."

So they went to the Guinness Book of World Records to have their claims verified. Sleeping Beauty went first and came out looking deliriously happy. "It's official. I AM the most beautiful girl in the world."

Tom Thumb went next, and emerged triumphant. "I am officially the smallest person in the world."

Some time later Quasimodo came out looking bewildered and confused, asking: "Who is Camilla Parker Bowles?"

436 You know how you can tell whether a woman's had her face lifted? Every time she crosses her legs, her mouth snaps open. (JOAN RIVERS)

437 Plastic surgery fanatic Jocclyne Wildenstein was knocked down by a car. As she lay unconscious on the roadside, she felt herself drifting through a long, dark tunnel towards the light, where she met God.

"It's not your time to die yet," said God. "You have another 30 or 40 years to live." So she went back to Earth where she made a full recovery.

Jocelyne was so grateful for her lucky escape that, when she was discharged from hospital, she decided to embark on a new way of life. She went to doctors for a complete make-over to reverse all her plastic surgery and restore her body to its original state.

Facing the world with renewed confidence, she was leaving her home one morning and failed to notice a speeding car. Seriously injured again, she found herself before God once more — but this time it was for good.

Furious, she screamed at him: "You said I'd have another 30 or 40 years!"

Embarrassed, God said: "I'm sorry, I didn't recognize you."

438 Where lipstick is concerned, the important thing is not colour, but to accept God's final word on where your lips end. (JERRY SEINFELD)

439 I've got no bosoms. In Africa they want to name an underdeveloped nation after me. (JOAN RIVERS)

440 How does Michael Jackson pick his nose? — Through a catalogue.

441 A wife bought a whole range of cosmetics designed to knock years off her age. After five hours applying the various creams and potions, she asked her husband: "Tell me honestly, darling, what age do you think I look?"
He said: "From your skin — 21; from your hair — 18; from your figure — 23."
"Oh, you flatterer," she gushed.
"Wait a minute," he said, "I haven't added them up yet."

442 It's a good thing that beauty is only skin deep, or I'd be rotten to the core. (PHYLLIS DILLER)

443 A woman in her fifties went to see a plastic surgeon. "What can you do for me?" she asked.
"Well," said the surgeon, "it depends how much you are prepared to pay. You have bags under your eyes — I can remove those for you. And you have crow's feet around your eyes — I can tighten the skin up there."
"I want more than that."
"Well, you've got a few wrinkles on your forehead — I can pull that tight. Also, your jowls droop down — I can sort that out."
"I still want more — money is no object."
"In that case, I can give you the full treatment from the neck up. I can fix your double chin. Your neck and throat are a bit baggy — I can pull that tight. As an extra, I'll put a small screw in the back of your neck beneath your hair. When your wrinkles start to reappear, all you have to do is come in and I'll tighten the screw a little. That will tighten your skin right up."
The woman had the work done and looked great. But ten months later, she called on the surgeon in a state of high anxiety. "Doctor, see these huge bags under my eyes? They've never been this bad before. You must do something about them!"
"Madam," replied the surgeon, "those aren't bags — they're your breasts. And if you don't stop turning that screw, you're going to end up with a goatee!"

444 I look just like the girl next door . . . if you happen to live next door to an amusement park. (DOLLY PARTON)

Birds

445 A sailor went to an auction and bid for a parrot. The sailor bid 10 dollars, but someone else bid 20 dollars. The sailor bid 25 dollars, but someone else bid 30 dollars. The sailor bid 35 dollars, but someone else bid 40 dollars. The sailor was determined to buy the bird and put in a final bid of 45 dollars. This time there were no other bids and the parrot was sold to the sailor.

"That's a lot of money I've paid for this bird," said the sailor to the auctioneer. "I hope he can talk."

"Of course he can," replied the auctioneer. "Who do you think was bidding against you?"

446 Two parrots sitting on a perch. One said to the other: "Can you smell fish?"

447 What goes cluck, cluck, boom? – A chicken in a minefield.

448 Why did the chicken go halfway across the road? – Because it wanted to lay it on the line.

449 Why doesn't a chicken wear pants? – Because his pecker is on his head.

450 A boy wandered into a pet store and asked for a quarter's worth of bird seed. The store assistant smiled at this odd request and asked: "How many birds do you have?"

"None yet," said the boy, "but I'm hoping to grow some."

451 What do you get when you cross a parrot with a lion? – I don't know, but when it talks, you'd better listen.

452 How do you turn a duck into a soul singer? – Put it in a microwave until its bill withers.

453 A duck walked into a general store, waddled up to the counter and asked: "Got any peanuts?"

"No," said the assistant.

The following day the duck was back again. "Got any peanuts?"

"No," said the assistant firmly.

The next day the duck came in again. "Got any peanuts?"

"No," yelled the assistant. "I've told you we don't have any peanuts. If you come back in here again and ask for peanuts, I'll nail your webbed feet to the floor."

The next day the duck came in again. "Got any nails?"

"No," said the assistant.

"Good. Got any peanuts?"

454 I saw a robin redbreast in Central Park today, but it turned out to be a sparrow with an exit wound. (DAVID LETTERMAN)

455 What's the difference between a pigeon and a yuppie? – A pigeon can still lay a deposit on a Porsche.

456 "If your father could see you now," said the mother turkey to her wayward son, "he'd turn over in his gravy!"

457 Why do swallows fly south in the autumn? – Because walking would take too long.

458 What do you call a woodpecker with no beak? – A headbanger.

459 Why did the one-eyed chicken cross the road? – To get to the birds' eye shop.

460 A man bought a parrot but got annoyed because it wouldn't stop swearing. So as punishment, he put the bird in the freezer. An hour later, the shivering parrot begged to be let out of the freezer. "I promise never to swear again," it said. "I've learned my lesson. Just tell me one thing: what on earth did that turkey do?"

461 I can levitate birds. No one cares. (STEVEN WRIGHT)

462 A circus owner walked into a bar and found everyone gathered around a table. On the table was a duck tap dancing on an upturned flower pot. The circus owner was so impressed he immediately bought the duck and the flower pot for 1,500 dollars.

Hundreds flocked to see the duck's first performance in the Big Top but, to everyone's disappointment, the duck didn't dance a step. The angry circus owner went back to the bar to seek out the man who had sold it to him.

"That duck is a fraud," raged the circus owner. "He hasn't danced a step for me."

"That's odd. Did you remember to light the candle under the pot?"

463 Why did the chicken run on to the soccer pitch? – Because the referee blew for a fowl.

464 A burglar broke into a house and started to search for valuables. As he did so, he passed a budgie in a cage and the bird said: "I can see you and so can Jesus." The burglar paid no attention and continued ransacking the room. Again the budgie called out: "I can see you and so can Jesus." The burglar still ignored the budgie but the bird repeated: "I can see you and so can Jesus."

The burglar decided to show that he wasn't intimidated by the bird. "What are you going to do about it?" he snarled. "You're only a budgie."

"Maybe," replied the budgie, "but Jesus is a rottweiller."

465 Imagine if birds were tickled by feathers . . . (STEVEN WRIGHT)

466 Why did the parrot wear a raincoat? – So that it could be Polly unsaturated.

467 A woman was walking along the street when a parrot in a pet shop window squawked: "Hey, lady, you're ugly." The woman tried to ignore the insult and hurried on her way.

The next day when she passed the pet shop, she quickened her stride in the hope that the parrot wouldn't notice her, but he did and squawked loudly: "Hey, lady, you're ugly." The woman was hugely embarrassed.

When the same thing happened for a third and a fourth day, she'd had enough. She stormed into the shop and demanded to speak to the owner. She threatened to sue him and to have the parrot put down unless the abuse stopped. The owner promised faithfully that the bird wouldn't say it again.

The following day, she walked past the pet shop and the parrot called out: "Hey, lady."

The woman turned round and glared at the bird. "Yes?"

"You know . . ."

468 What's black, white, black, white, black, white, black, white, black, white, black? – A penguin rolling down the stairs.

Birth

469 A man took his pregnant wife to the hospital to give birth. There the doctor revealed that he had developed an experimental machine which could take some of the pain of childbirth from the mother and give it to the father instead. He asked the couple whether they were interested in giving it a try, and they agreed. Since the machine was largely untested, the doctor thought it wise to start at the lowest setting. He strapped the man down, switched on the machine and asked him whether he could feel any pain.

"No, I feel fine."

So the doctor turned the machine to a slightly higher setting. Again the man reported feeling no discomfort. And all the while the wife was going through pain free childbirth.

Greatly encouraged, the doctor turned the machine to its highest setting. Still the man felt no pain. "This is truly amazing," said the doctor excitedly. "A veritable breakthrough in childbirth."

After his wife had given birth, the husband climbed off the machine and calmly drove home. There he found the mailman dead on the doorstep.

470 Having a baby is like taking your lower lips and forcing them over your head. (CAROL BURNETT)

471 A woman was lying in hospital, giving birth. After half an hour of pushing, panting and sweating, the baby's head suddenly popped out. The baby took one look at the doctor and asked: "Are you my daddy?"

"No, I'm not," replied the doctor, startled. And the baby popped back into the womb.

The obstetrician was called to look into this unusual occurrence. No sooner had he arrived than the baby's head popped out again.

"Are you my daddy?" asked the baby.

"No, I'm not," answered the obstetrician.

The obstetrician decided to fetch the boy's father. "The baby seems reluctant to come out," said the worried medic. "He keeps asking for his father, so would you please come to the delivery room?"

The father entered the delivery room and the baby's head popped out again.

"Are you my daddy?" asked the baby.

The father knelt down and answered proudly: "Yes, son, I'm your father."

The baby immediately began tapping his index finger violently and repeatedly on his father's forehead and said: "This is pretty damned annoying, isn't it?"

472 I had a Jewish delivery. They knock you out with the first pain and wake you up when the hairdresser shows. (JOAN RIVERS)

473 A group of pregnant women and their partners were attending an ante-natal class. The instructor was emphasizing the importance of keeping healthy during pregnancy.

"Ladies, exercise is good for you. Walking is particularly beneficial. And, gentlemen, it wouldn't hurt you to take the time to go walking with your partner."

Hearing this, a male voice asked: "Is it all right if she carries a golf bag while we walk?"

474 A woman in labour with her first child yelled repeatedly: "Shouldn't, wouldn't, couldn't, mustn't, can't."

Her worried husband asked the doctor what the problem was.

"Don't worry," said the doctor. "Your wife is just having contractions."

475 I was born by Caesarean Section, but not so you'd notice. It's just that when I leave a house, I go out through the window. (STEVEN WRIGHT)

476 A keen soccer fan was about to be a father for the first time. His friend asked: "What if your wife is having the baby on the same day as the match?"

"No problem. I've just bought a video recorder. So I can watch the birth after the game."

477 Watching a baby being born is a little like watching a wet St Bernard coming in through the cat door. (JEFF FOXWORTHY)

478 A man phoned the hospital in a state of excitement. "My wife is pregnant. Her contractions are only two minutes apart."

The doctor said: "Is this her first child?"

"No, you idiot. This is her husband!"

Birthdays

479 Little Johnny was heard praying in a loud voice a week before his birthday. "Dear God, I pray that I will get a computer game for my birthday."

"Why are you shouting?" asked his mother. "God isn't deaf."

"I know," replied Johnny, "but Granny is."

480 A husband was at a loss what to get his wife as a birthday present. He was looking for something different, so a friend suggested: "For a laugh, why don't you have a special certificate made up which says that she can have two hours of great sex, any way she wants it? She'll love it . . . and so will you."

The husband thought it was a great idea and went to a printer's to have the certificate drawn up.

A week later, the friend bumped into the husband in the street. "Well, how did it go?"

"She loved it," said the husband. "She jumped up, kissed me passionately on the mouth and ran out the door yelling, 'I'll see you in two hours'."

481 For my sister's fortieth birthday, I sent her a singing mammogram. (STEVEN WRIGHT)

482 A husband asked his wife what she wanted for her birthday. "Oh, just give me something with diamonds," she replied.

So he bought her a pack of playing cards.

483 A young man went shopping for his girlfriend's birthday present in company with his girlfriend's sister. He chose an expensive pair of beige gloves and the sister bought a pair of white panties. Unfortunately in the process of wrapping, the gifts became mixed up with the result that the parcel from the boy contained the panties. Inside was a note which read:

"Dear Alison, I chose these because I noticed you're not in the habit of wearing any when we go out. If it hadn't been for your sister, I would have chosen long ones with buttons, but she wears short ones that are easier to remove.

"I hope you like the shade. I know they're pale but the lady in the store showed me a pair she had been wearing for the past month and they were hardly soiled. I had her try yours on for me and she looked really smart.

"I wish I was there to put them on you for the first time, as no doubt other hands will come in contact with them before I see you again. Just think how many times I will kiss them over the coming year. I do hope you wear them on Friday. Love, Adam.

PS. The latest style is to wear them folded down with a little fur showing."

484 When a man has a birthday he takes a day off. When a woman has a birthday she takes a year off.

485 A husband and his wife were out shopping. "Darling," said the wife, "it's my mother's birthday tomorrow. What can we buy her? She'd like something electric."

"How about a chair?" suggested the husband.

486 The wife said: "I'm looking forward to my fortieth birthday."

"Yes," replied the husband sourly, "but you're looking in the wrong direction."

487 A man was on his way home from work when he realized that he had forgotten his young daughter's birthday. Knowing she liked dolls, he stopped off at a toy store and asked the sales assistant whether they had any Barbie dolls in stock.

"Sure," replied the sales girl. "We have Barbie Goes to the Gym at 19.95 dollars; Barbie Goes to the Ball at 19.95 dollars; Barbie Goes Shopping at 19.95 dollars; Barbie Goes Nightclubbing at 19.95 dollars; and Divorced Barbie at 250 dollars."

The man was perplexed. "Why are the others all .19.95 dollars and yet Divorced Barbie costs 250 dollars?"

"Because," replied the sales girl, "divorced Barbie comes with Ken's house, Ken's car, Ken's boat and Ken's furniture."

Bosses

488 An office manager had too much drink at a party and embarrassed himself in front of his boss. His wife told him the awful truth the following morning.

"Your behaviour was appalling," she said. "At one point you went up to your boss and started jabbing him in the stomach and verbally abusing him. You were swearing like a trooper."

"Really?" said the husband, shocked.

"Yes," said the wife. "You really told him what you thought of him. He was furious."

"Well," said the husband, in a display of bravado, "it serves him right. He's an asshole. Piss on him!"

"You did," said the wife, "and he fired you."

"Well, screw him!"

"I did," said the wife. "You're back at work on Monday."

489 A man asked his boss for a raise. "A raise?" thundered the boss. "Why should you have a raise? You're never here. Listen. There are 365 days in the year – 366 this year because it's a Leap Year. The working day is eight hours. That's one third of the day, so in a year that comes to 122 days. The office is shut on Sundays so that's 52 off, leaving 70. Then you have two weeks' holiday – take off 14, which leaves 56. Then there are four Bank Holidays, so if you remove them, that leaves 52. The office is closed on Saturdays. There are 52 Saturdays in a year, so you see, you don't do anything at all!"

490 A young employee turned to his colleague and said: "I feel like punching the boss in the face again."

"Again? Did you say again?"

"Yeah, I felt like punching him in the face once before."

491 Kill my boss? Do I dare live out the American dream? (HOMER SIMPSON)

492 An employee went in to see his boss. "Boss," he said, "we're doing some heavy house-cleaning at home tomorrow, and my wife needs me to help with clearing stuff out of the attic, the shed and the garage and with scrubbing down all the kitchen cupboards."

"I'm sorry," said the boss, "but we're short-handed at the moment. There's no way I can give you a day off."

"Thanks, boss. I knew I could rely on you!"

493 A boss at a business convention in Las Vegas decided to visit a brothel. He was a stickler for the rules of the workplace and asked the madam: "Is this a union house?"

"No, it's not," she replied.

"So if I pay 100 dollars, what do the girls get?"

"The house takes 80 dollars and the girls get 20 dollars."

"Well I think that's grossly unfair," said the boss. "I shall take my custom elsewhere."

Further down the street, he found another brothel. "Is this a union house?" he asked.

"Yes," said the madam. "It is."

"So if I pay 100 dollars, how much do the girls get to keep?"

"The girls get 80 dollars, the house gets 20 dollars."

"That's more like it," he said. He looked around the room and pointed to a pretty girl. "I'd like her for the night."

"I'm sure you would, sir," said the madam, gesturing at a 70-year-old woman in the corner, "but Ethel here has seniority."

494 Happiness is seeing your boss's face on the side of a milk carton.

495 The boss ticked off one of his employees. "I know you were skiving yesterday. You were out playing golf!"

"That's a lie!" insisted the employee. "And I have the fish to prove it!"

496 The boss rebuked the young employee. "You're 25 minutes late again, boy. Don't you know what time we start work in this office?"

"No, sir, everyone's already hard at it when I get here."

497 A boss was confused about paying an invoice so he asked his secretary for help. "You graduated from the University of Georgia," he said. "If I were to give you $20,000, minus 14 per cent, how much would you take off?"

She thought for a moment and replied: "Everything but my earrings."

498 The boss asked a new employee his name.

"Stuart," replied the young man.

The boss scowled. "I don't know what kind of namby-pamby place you worked at before, but we don't use first names here. In my view, it breeds familiarity which ultimately leads to a breakdown in authority. So I always call my employees by their last names only – Smith, Jones, Brown etcetera. They in turn refer to me only as Mr Harvey. Understood? Right. Now that we've got that straight, what's your last name?"

"Darling," replied the young man. "My name is Stuart Darling."

"OK, Stuart, the next thing I want to tell you is . . ."

Things not to say to your prospective boss at a job interview:

499 I want your job.

500 Who's that old hag in the photo on your desk?

501 Do you want to hear about my police record?

502 I never work in the afternoon – I'm too drunk.

503 Have you just farted?

504 Where in God's name did you get that tie?

505 I'm only here because there's nothing good on TV.

506 I bet you and your secretary get it together after work.

507 I hear nobody does much work in this place.

508 Which route do your cashiers take to the bank?

509 The last six jobs I've had, I've walked out with 50,000 dollars in compensation for wrongful dismissal.

510 The voices in my head told me to come for this interview.

511 Want to buy some porno films?

512 Hey, dog breath, what sort of salary will I be on?

George W. Bush

513 George W. Bush was invited to address a major gathering of the American Indian nation. He spoke for almost an hour on his plans for increasing every Native American's standard of living. He referred to his career as Governor of Texas, how he had signed "yes" 1,533 times – for every Indian issue that came to his desk for approval. Although the President was vague on the details of his plan, he seemed most enthusiastic about his future ideas for helping his "red brothers". At the end of his speech, the tribes presented the President with a plaque inscribed with his new Indian name – Walking Eagle. The proud President then departed in his motorcade, waving to the crowds.

A news reporter later asked the group of chiefs how they came to select the new name given to the President. They explained: "Walking Eagle is the name given to a bird so full of shit it can no longer fly."

514 Donald Rumsfeld was giving Bush his daily war briefing. He concluded by saying, "Yesterday, three Brazilian soldiers were killed."

"Oh no!" exclaimed Bush. "That's terrible!"

His staff were stunned at this display of emotion and watched nervously as the President sat, head in hands. Finally Bush looked up and asked: "OK, so how many is a Brazillion?"

515 *The Weakest Link* is a fascinating programme. They ask a bunch of people questions and they keep getting rid of the dumbest person, so just the smartest person is left. It's kind of the opposite way we elect a President. (JAY LENO)

516 Bush was waiting to give a keynote speech when he was suddenly overcome with nerves. Dick Cheney told him to get a grip but Bush reached straight for the Bourbon. Ten minutes later Bush was desperate for a piss. Cheney told him to go piss in the corner and then come out and give his speech. When Bush reappeared, he had a big wet patch on the front of his pants.

Cheney said: "George, I thought I told you to take a piss in the corner of your room!"

"But Dick," replied Bush, "that's the Oval Office. It ain't got no corners!"

517 A traffic cop found George W. Bush on the highway in a distressed state. With no money to pay his lawyers and convinced that his family all hated him, he was threatening to douse his clothes in gasoline and set fire to himself.

A passer-by asked what was going on. The cop explained, adding that because he felt sorry for the President, he was going from car to car asking for donations.

"How much have you collected so far?" asked the passer-by.

"About 25 gallons . . ."

518 US soldiers in Iraq say that one of the things that's keeping them going and inspiring them is all the letters they're receiving from schoolchildren around the country. Then someone explained that those letters are actually from President George W. Bush. (CONAN O'BRIEN)

519 Keen to let the world know he was still alive, Osama bin Laden sent Bush a letter in his own handwriting. Opening the letter, Bush saw only a coded message: "370HSSV-0773H". Bush couldn't figure it out so he asked Dick Cheney what it meant. Cheney didn't know either but suggested sending it to Donald Rumsfeld.

After scratching his head for a few minutes, Rumsfeld said: "Why not try Condi? She has a doctorate, which means she's smart."

Dr Rice studied the letter but she was baffled too.

As Bush continued to ponder the mysterious message lying on the desk before him, a White House cleaner entered the Oval Office. Reading the message, the cleaner asked: "Sir, where did that come from?"

Bush said: "Supposedly it's a message from Osama bin Laden. But what the hell does '370HSSV-0773H' mean?"

The cleaner cleared her throat and said: "Mr President, I think you've been looking at the message upside down."

520 George W. Bush went into Burger King and asked for two whoppers. The guy serving said: "You're an intellectual giant and the best President we've ever had."

521 George W. Bush, the Pope and a hippie were on board a small private plane when the pilot announced that they were in trouble and should bale out. Unfortunately there were only two parachutes between the three passengers, meaning that someone would be left to face almost certain death. Before they could discuss it, Bush snatched a parachute, ran for the door and jumped, screaming: "I'm far too important a person to die!"

The Pope and the hippie looked at the one remaining parachute. The Pope said: "My son, I have lived a good, long life and I have faith that I will go to a better place. You take the last parachute."

"It's OK, you have it," said the hippie, reaching down. "I'll have this one. The President of the United States just jumped out holding my rucksack!"

522   Three sharks met in the ocean and talked about the people they'd recently eaten. The first said: "I swallowed bin Laden yesterday but the guy had eaten so much garlic I still feel sick."

The second shark said: "I swallowed Vladimir Putin last week but he had so much vodka in him that I'm still drunk."

The third shark said: "You're lucky. I swallowed George W. Bush three weeks ago and the guy has so much air in his head, I still can't dive!"

523   An aide to the Prime Minister of Canada called President Bush a moron. Well that's not fair. Here's a guy who never worked a day in his life, got rich off his dad's money, lost the popular vote and ended up President. That's not a moron, that's genius! (JAY LENO)

524   George W. Bush fell into a lake and was rescued from drowning by three small boys. He was so grateful that he told the boys: "I'll give you anything you want for saving my life."

The first boy said: "I'd like a Ferrari."

"No problem," said Bush. "You will have a sparkling new red Ferrari."

The second boy said: "I'd like a computer."

"Sure," said Bush. "You'll be sent a brand new, top-of-the range computer."

The third boy said: "I'd like a motorized wheelchair."

"Why?" said Bush. "You look pretty healthy to me."

"Because," said the boy, "I'll need a wheelchair when my dad finds out I saved George W. Bush from drowning."

525   What do golf and Florida elections have in common? – Low score wins.

526   The President finally explained why he sat in that classroom on 9/11 for seven minutes after he was told the country was under attack. He said he was "collecting his thoughts". What a time to start a new hobby! (BILL MAHER)

527   When President Bush went to Russia, they asked him if he wanted to see Lenin's tomb. He said he didn't – he wasn't really a Beatles fan. (JOAN RIVERS)

528   American soldiers were patrolling a desolate road near Baghdad when they came upon an armed Iraqi soldier, lying dead in a ditch. Just then, they heard a

groan from across the road and rushed over to find a badly wounded US soldier. As they lifted him into their jeep, they asked what happened.

He said: "I was face to face with that Iraqi, right here in the middle of the road, my gun on him, his pointed at me . . . neither one of us making the first move. Finally the tension was too much, so I shouted out: 'Saddam is an asshole!' Well, he stared right back at me and said: 'George Bush is a son of a bitch!' We were still shaking hands when the truck hit us."

529 *Newsweek* magazine says that President Bush is determined not to make the same mistakes his father did, you know, like letting his kids get involved in politics. (JAY LENO)

530 Donald Rumsfeld, Dick Cheney and George W. Bush went into a bar.
Rumsfeld: "I'll have a B and C."
Bartender: "What's a B and C?"
Rumsfeld: "Bourbon and Coke."
Cheney: "And I'll have a G and T."
Bartender: "What's a G and T?"
Cheney: "Gin and tonic."
Bush: "And I'll have a 15."
Bartender: "What's a 15?"
Bush: "Seven and seven."

531 St Peter was on extended leave and so a minor saint was left in charge of admissions to Heaven. He was told to get proof of identity before letting anyone in. First up was Beethoven.

"I need proof of identity," said the saint. So Beethoven played a few bars of his Fifth Symphony and was admitted.

Next up was Einstein.

"I need proof of identity," said the saint. So Einstein explained the theory of relativity and was admitted.

Next up was George W. Bush.

"I need proof of identity," said the saint.

"But I'm George W. Bush, President of the United States."

"Sorry. Everyone needs proof. Even Beethoven and Einstein needed proof."

"Who?"

"OK, through you go."

532 One day, George W. Bush found a bottle lying on the ground. He opened it and a genie popped out and granted him one wish.

"I'd like to wish for peace in the Middle East," said the President.

"Sorry," answered the genie, "there are some things even a genie can't arrange. You'll have to make another wish."

"OK," said Bush. "I wish people didn't think I was so dumb."

"Hmmm," said the genie. "Let me take a second look at that map of the Middle East."

533 Having George W. Bush giving a lecture on business ethics is like having a leper give you a facial. (ROBIN WILLIAMS)

534 Dubya and George Bush Sr were dragging the deer they'd just shot back to their truck. Another hunter saw them and said: "Sirs, I don't want to tell you how to do something, but I can tell you it's much easier if you drag the deer the other way. Then the antlers won't dig into the ground."

After the hunter left, Dubya said: "You know, that guy was right. This is a lot easier."

"Yeah," said George Sr, "but we're getting farther from the truck."

Business

535 On his first morning in new premises, a young businessman began sorting out his office. He was in the middle of arranging his desk when there was a knock at the door. Eager to imply that he had gone up in the world and that business was brisk, he quickly picked up the phone and called to the person at the door: "Come in." A tradesman entered the office, but the young businessman talked into the phone as if he were conducting a meaningful conversation with a client.

"I agree," he said. "Yes . . . I agree . . . Yes . . . sure. No problem . . . We can fix that . . ."

After a minute, he broke off from his imaginary conversation and said to the tradesman: "Can I help you with something?"

"Yes," he replied. "I'm here to hook up the phone."

536 A man went to his bank manager and said: "I'd like to start a small business. How do I go about it?"

"Simple," said the bank manager. "Buy a big one and wait."

537 When the middle manager was sacked, not only did he have to give back his company credit card and his company car, he even had to give back his ulcer.

538 As a gesture to welcome him into the family, a successful businessman gave his new son-in-law a half share of the firm. "From now on," said the businessman, "we're equal partners. All you have to do is go down to the factory each day and learn the ropes."

"I couldn't do that," said the son-in-law. "I hate factories. They're such noisy places."

"That's no problem," said the businessman. "We'll put you in the office. You can oversee the clerical side."

"No way!" said the son-in-law. "I'm not being stuck behind a desk all day."

Not surprisingly, the businessman was becoming irritated by this display of ingratitude.

"I've just made you half-owner of this thriving company. First, I offer you a management position in the factory, but you don't want it; then I offer you a management post in the office, but you don't want that either. What am I going to do with you?"

"You could always buy me out."

539 I'll keep it short and sweet. Family, Religion, Friendship. These are the three demons you must slay if you wish to succeed in business. (MONTGOMERY BURNS, *The Simpsons*)

540 Did you hear about the guy who trained in origami and opened a shop in New York? – The business folded.

541 A chicken and a pig were drinking in a bar one night when the chicken said: "Why don't we go into business together? We could open a ham and egg restaurant."

"Not so fast," said the pig. "For you, it's just a day's work. For me, it's a matter of life and death."

Cabs

542 A drunk stumbled out of the Metropole Hotel, fell into a cab and told the driver: "Take me to the Metropole."

"We're there," said the cabbie.

"OK," said the drunk, taking a 5 dollar bill from his wallet, "but next time don't drive so fast."

543 An Englishwoman and her young son took a taxi in New York. Driving through a run-down district of the city, the boy was fascinated by the women in short skirts and tight tops who were accosting men.

"What are those ladies doing?" he asked his mother.

The mother was embarrassed. "I expect they're lost and are asking for directions."

But the taxi driver interrupted: "Hey, lady, why not tell the kid the truth! They're prostitutes."

"What are prostitutes?" asked the boy.

"They're women who sell their bodies," replied the mother, still angry at the taxi driver's outburst.

"Do they have children like other ladies?" asked the boy.

"Yes," said the mother icily. "Their children become New York taxi drivers."

544 When a passenger tapped him on the shoulder to ask a question, the taxi driver screamed, lost control of the vehicle and nearly ran into a crowd of pedestrians. "Don't ever do that again!" he yelled.

"I'm sorry," said the passenger. "It was only a tap on the shoulder."

"Maybe, but this is my first day as a cab driver. I've been driving hearses for the last twenty years!"

545 A New York taxi driver and a priest went to heaven on the same day. St Peter was waiting to greet them.

"You must be Phil O'Donnell, the New York taxi driver," said St Peter. "Come through and try on your silk robe with your golden sceptre."

While the taxi driver was being fitted out, St Peter returned to attend to the priest. "And you must be Father Flynn, the priest of St Mark's. Come through and try on your cloth robe with your wooden sceptre."

"Excuse me," interrupted the priest, "but how come I, a man of the cloth, only get a cloth robe and a wooden sceptre while that New York taxi driver gets a silk robe and a golden sceptre?"

"Well," said St Peter, "we work on a performance scale. You see, while you preached, everyone slept; but when he drove a taxi, everyone prayed."

546 On a business trip to Las Vegas, a guy lost all his money in the casinos. There was plenty of cash back home in Boston, but first he needed to get to the airport. As he came out of the casino, a lone taxi cab was waiting.

"How much for a ride to the airport?" asked the businessman.

"Fifteen dollars."

"Look, I haven't got fifteen dollars. I've only got three dollars fifty. I've had a bad time in the casinos. I'm good for the money. And the moment I get home I'll send you a cheque. So will you please take me to the airport?"

"No way, buster. No money, no ride." And he slammed the door in the businessman's face.

A year later, the businessman was back in Las Vegas. This time he enjoyed a profitable night in the casinos and as he came out, a line of taxi cabs was waiting. Last in line was the driver who had been so rude to him the previous year. The businessman planned his revenge. He walked up to the first cab in line and said: "How much for a ride to the airport?"

"Fifteen dollars."

"And how much for you to give me a blow job on the way?"

"What! Don't be so disgusting! Get out of my cab!"

Then he went to the second cab in line. "How much for a ride to the airport?"

"Fifteen dollars."

"And how much for you to give me a blow job on the way?"

"How dare you! Get out of my cab!"

This went on all the way down the line until he reached the last cab – the one driven by his old adversary. The businessman peered in and said: "How much for a ride to the airport?"

"Fifteen dollars."

"OK. Fine."

And off they went. As they drove slowly past the long line of cabs, the businessman gave a big smile and a thumbs up sign to each driver . . .

California

547 A fine place to live, if you happen to be an orange. (FRED ALLEN)

548 The Los Angeles Police Department, the FBI and the CIA were each determined to prove that they were the best at apprehending criminals. So the President decided to set them a test. He released a rabbit into the forest and each organization had to catch it.

The CIA went in first. They placed animal informants throughout the forest and questioned all plant and mineral witnesses. After three months of extensive investigation, they concluded that rabbits don't exist.

Next it was the FBI's turn. After two weeks with no leads, they set fire to the forest, killing everything in it, including the rabbit. They remained unrepentant for their actions, maintaining that the rabbit had provoked them.

Finally the LAPD went in. They came out an hour and a half later with a badly beaten bear. The bear was yelling: "OK. OK. I'm a rabbit! I'm a rabbit!"

549 In California, they don't throw their garbage away – they make it into TV shows. (WOODY ALLEN)

550 Two die-hard Californians could only watch in embarrassment as a torrential downpour hit Los Angeles. Finally, after a long silence, one turned to the other and said: "Boy, some terrible weather certainly blows in from Nevada, doesn't it?"

551 California is wonderful. On a clear day when the fog lifts, you can see the smog.

552 In California, handicapped parking is for women who are frigid. (JOAN RIVERS)

553 Three California girls were strolling along the beach when they saw a man lying naked on the sand. He quickly grabbed at the only clothing within reach – a baseball cap – and covered his face with it.
The three girls stopped and looked at him.
"Well, it's not my husband," said the first.
"No, you're quite right," said the second. "It's definitely not your husband."
The third said: "In fact, he's a stranger – he doesn't live in Long Beach."

554 What's the difference between LA and yoghurt? – Yoghurt has real culture.

555 Oh to be in LA when the polyethyl-vinyl trees are in bloom. (HERB GOLD)

556 Three men – a Nebraskan, a Californian and a Washingtonian – were out walking when they came across a lantern. As they examined it, a genie popped out and declared: "I'll give you each one wish."
The Nebraskan said: "I am a farmer, my father was a farmer and my son will be a farmer. So I want the land in Nebraska to be fertile for ever." There was a puff of smoke, and the genie said the wish had been granted.
Next it was the Californian's turn. He told the genie: "I want a wall around California so that no foreigners can come into our precious state." There was a puff of smoke, and the genie said the wish had been granted.
Finally it was the Washingtonian's turn. He asked the genie: "Tell me more about this wall around California."

"Well," said the genie, "it's 150 feet high, 50 feet thick and completely surrounds the state. Nothing can get in or out."

"Interesting," mused the Washingtonian. "Fill it with water."

You know you're from California when:
557 You were actually born somewhere else.
558 Your pet has its own psychiatrist.
559 You don't exterminate your cockroaches, you smoke them.
560 You consult your horoscope before planning your day.
561 If you need a TV, you can go to the local riot and pick one up.
562 You'd kill your parents to be in movies.
563 You have killed your parents to be in movies.
564 You spend more on facelifts than on groceries.
565 You don't write letters, you write screenplays.
566 You go to a tanning salon before going to the beach.
567 You invite your analyst to Christmas dinner.

Cannibals

568 A cannibal is a guy who goes into a restaurant and orders the waiter. (JACK BENNY)

569 Three men lost in the jungle were captured by cannibals. The cannibal king told the men they could live if they successfully undertook a trial. The first step of the trial was for each to go into the forest and collect ten pieces of the same kind of fruit. So the three went their separate ways into the forest. Soon the first came back with ten apples. The king then explained the trial: "You have to shove the fruits up your ass without any expression on your face. If you make any expression or sound, you will be eaten."

The first man shoved the first apple up his ass, but on the second he winced and was eaten by the cannibals.

Then the second man returned with ten berries. He inserted the first nine without making a sound, but on the tenth he suddenly burst out laughing and was eaten by the cannibals.

The two dead men met up in heaven. The first said: "Why did you laugh on the tenth berry – you were almost home?"

"I know," he said, "but I saw the third guy coming with an armful of pineapples!"

570 Two cannibals were eating dinner. One said: "I really hate my sister."

The other said: "Well, just eat the noodles."

571 Did you hear about the cannibal student who was suspended from school for buttering up his teacher?

572 And have you heard about the cannibal restaurant where dinner costs an arm and a leg?

573 A man was captured by cannibals. "What," asked the cannibal chief, licking his lips, "was your job before you were captured?"

"I was a newspaper man," came the reply.

"An editor?"

"No, merely a sub-editor."

"Cheer up. Promotion awaits you. After dinner you will be editor-in-chief."

574 It had been a trying few months for two cannibals. Food had been scarce, so when they finally caught and killed a missionary, each was determined to have his fair share. Finally they agreed that they should start eating from opposite ends of the missionary's body and meet in the middle. That way they would both get equal portions.

After a while, the guy starting from the head asked the other one: "How are you doing down there?"

"I'm having a ball."

"No, no, you're eating too fast!"

575 A Frenchman, an Englishman and a New Yorker were captured by cannibals. The chief told them: "You will each be killed, cooked and eaten, and then we will use your skins to build a canoe. As a concession, I will allow you to choose how you want to die."

The Frenchman asked for a sword, yelled "Vive La France!" and ran himself through.

The Englishman asked for a gun, shouted "God Save The Queen!" and blew his brains out.

The New Yorker said, "Gimme a fork," and immediately started jabbing himself all over his body until blood was pouring out through hundreds of holes.

"What on earth are you doing?" demanded the chief.

The New Yorker snapped back: "There goes your goddam canoe!"

576 What is the title of the best-selling cannibal book? — How To Serve Your Fellow Man.

577 What did the cannibal get when he was late for dinner? – The cold shoulder.

578 What do cannibals do at a wedding? – They toast the bride and groom.

579 Two cannibals were sitting around a fire. One turned to the other and said: "I've never yet met a man I didn't like."

580 A saint was sent as a missionary to a tribe of cannibals, but the cannibals snatched him and ate him. Afterwards they were all violently sick. The witch doctor told them: "It's true what they say – you can't keep a good man down!"

581 Two cannibals were sitting beside the fire after a sumptuous meal. One turned to the other and said: "Your wife sure makes a good roast."
"Yeah, I'm really going to miss her."

582 Two cannibals were eating a clown. One said to the other: "Does this taste funny to you?"

Cats

583 A woman famous for her charitable work was granted three wishes by a fairy godmother.
"My," she said, "I have everything I could possibly want in life. What more can I wish for?" Then she thought for a moment and said, "Well, I suppose a new living-room chair would be nice. I've had that one for 33 years."
Within seconds, the fairy godmother had delivered a new chair. "Now what about your second wish?"
"Well, if you insist, I suppose a new car would be nice to get me to church."
No sooner were the words spoken than a brand new car appeared on the drive.
"And for your third wish?" asked the fairy godmother.
"Well, I suppose there's no point in having a new car without somebody to share it with. Could you possibly turn my loyal and loving cat into a handsome young man?"
Almost immediately, the cat was turned into a handsome hunk. The young man strolled over to the woman and said: "I bet you're sorry you had me neutered now."

584 I gave my cat a bath the other day. They love it. He just sat there and enjoyed it. It was fun for me. The fur kept sticking to my tongue, but other than that . . .
(STEVE MARTIN)

585 How did a cat take first prize at the bird show? – By reaching into the cage.

586 A ginger tom cat and a pretty tortoiseshell were courting in the back garden one night. The tom looked at her wistfully and purred: "I'd die for you?"
She gazed back into his eyes and said: "How many times?"

587 What's the difference between a cat and a comma? – One has the paws before the claws and the other has the clause before the pause.

588 The problem with cats is that they get the exact same look on their face whether they see a moth or an axe-murderer. (PAULA POUNDSTONE)

589 What happened when the cat swallowed a penny? – There was some money in the kitty.

590 An old lady's two cats – a ginger tom and a pretty tortoiseshell – died within a few weeks of each other. She couldn't bear the thought of being without them, so she decided to take the bodies to a taxidermist and have them put on display in her living room.
"These are my two cats," said the old lady. "They used to get on so well together."
"Ah, that's nice," said the taxidermist. "Tell me, do you want them mounted?"
"No," replied the old lady. "Just holding hands."

Signs that your cat is planning to kill you:
591 He suddenly seems really friendly with the dog.
592 You wake up to find a sparrow's head in your bed.
593 His ball of yarn is tied playfully into a hangman's noose.
594 He now sharpens his claws on your car's brake lines.
595 He has taken a sudden interest in the wood chipper.
596 He takes notes whenever Tom and Jerry are on.
597 There are cyanide pawprints all over the house.
598 The droppings in his litter tray spell out DEATH.
599 Instead of dead birds, he leaves packets of Marlboros on your doorstep.
600 He actually *does* have your tongue.

601 Cats have nine lives, which makes them ideal for experimentation. (JIMMY CARR)

602 A cat died and went to heaven. God said: "You've been a good cat all your life. Is there anything you desire?"

The cat replied: "I lived on a farm and always had to sleep on a hard floor, so a soft pillow would be great. Then I could sleep peacefully in heaven."

God provided a soft pillow for the cat.

The following day six mice died and went to heaven. God told them: "You have been good mice all your lives. Is there anything you desire?"

"Yes," they said. "We've always had to run everywhere, being chased by cats or people. We'd love a pair of roller skates each so that we can get around heaven without having to use our little legs so much."

And God provided each mouse with a pair of roller skates.

A week or so later, God thought he'd check up on the cat who was fast asleep on his new pillow.

"Is everything OK?" asked God.

The cat stretched out. "I've never been happier," he said. "The pillow is so comfortable and those meals on wheels you've been sending over are simply the best."

Children

603 The boss of a big multinational company urgently needed to speak to one of his management team at the weekend, so he phoned him at home.

A small boy's voice answered the phone in hushed tones.

"Hello," said the boss. "Is your daddy home?"

"Yes," whispered the child.

"May I talk with him?"

"No."

The boss was not used to hearing the word "no". "Well, is your mummy there?"

"Yes," whispered the child.

"May I talk with her?"

"No."

Knowing that it was unlikely that a small boy would have been left home alone, the boss tried again. "Is anyone else there?"

"Yes," said the boy. "A policeman."

The boss was startled to hear that the police were there. "Well, may I speak with him?"

"No, he's busy," whispered the boy.

"Busy doing what?" asked the boss, beginning to wonder what was going on at the house.

"Talking to Daddy, Mummy and the firemen."

Just then, the boss heard the sound of a helicopter down the phone. "What's that noise?" he asked.

"A helicopter," whispered the boy.

"Exactly what's going on there?"

"The search team just landed the helicopter," confided the boy.

"What are they doing there?"

"They're looking for me."

604 When I was a kid, I had two imaginary friends. They would only play with each other. (RITA RUDNER)

605 When I was a kid, I had a friend who worked in a radio station. Whenever we walked under a bridge, you couldn't understand what he said. (STEVEN WRIGHT)

606 What do you get when you cross LSD with a birth control pill? – A trip without the kids.

607 "I'm glad you named me John," said the small boy.

"Why?" asked his mother.

"Because that's what all the kids at school call me."

608 I've got two wonderful children – and two out of five isn't bad. (HENNY YOUNGMAN)

609 A little girl made a cup of tea for her mother.

"I didn't know you could make tea," said mum taking a sip.

"Yes, I boiled some water, added the tea leaves like you do, and then strained it into a cup. But I couldn't find the strainer, so I used the fly swatter."

"What!" exclaimed mum, choking on her tea.

"Oh, don't worry. I didn't use the new fly swatter. I used the old one."

610 A small boy confessed to his mother that he had accidentally smashed a vase while playing at his friend's house. "But, Mom," he added, "you don't have to worry about buying a new one because Michael's mother said it was irreplaceable."

611 When I was in the Boy Scouts, I slipped on the ice and hurt my ankle. A little old lady had to help me across the street. (STEVEN WRIGHT)

612 A drunk was staggering along the road when he saw a woman walking a young child. "Lady," said the drunk, "that is the ugliest kid I've ever seen in my life. God, that child is ugly!"

As the drunk wandered off, the woman burst into tears. A mailman went to her rescue.

"What's the matter, madam?" he asked.

"I've just been terribly insulted," sobbed the woman.

"There, there," said the mailman, reaching into his pocket. "Have this tissue to dry your eyes. And here's a banana for the chimp."

613 I figure if the children are alive when he gets home, I've done my job.
(ROSEANNE BARR)

614 Bored out of his mind, a small boy was playing up in church during the Sunday morning service. His constant chattering and whistling began to upset the other worshippers. Finally his father lost patience and dragged him out of the church. On the way out, the boy called loudly to the congregation: "Pray for me!"

Some truths about life which children have learned:
615 No matter how hard you try, you can't baptize cats.
616 When your mum is mad at your dad, don't let her brush your hair.
617 If your sister hits you, don't hit her back. They always catch the second person.
618 Wear a hat when feeding seagulls.
619 Don't ever be too full for dessert.
620 Don't flush the toilet when your dad's in the shower.
621 Never ask a two year old to hold a tomato.
622 You can't trust dogs to watch your food.
623 When your dad is mad and asks you, "Do I look stupid?" don't answer him.
624 Never spit when on a rollercoaster.
625 Never do pranks at a police station.
626 A piece of chewing gum stuck under the dining-room table will return to haunt you.
627 You can't hide a piece of broccoli in a glass of milk.
628 Don't wear polka-dot underwear beneath white shorts.
629 Forget the cake, go for the icing.
630 Don't sneeze when someone is cutting your hair.
631 Puppies still have bad breath even after eating a tic-tac.
632 Never dare your little brother to paint the family car.
633 Never hold a dustbuster and a cat at the same time.

634   School lunches stick to the wall.

635   Stay away from prunes.

636   A little girl was attending a church service with her mother when she started to complain that she was feeling unwell. "I think I need to throw up," said the girl.

"Well, go outside," said the mother, "and use the bushes by the front door of the church."

The little girl went off but was back less than a minute later.

"That was quick," said the mother. "Did you throw up?"

"Yes, but I didn't need to go outside," replied the little girl. "I used a box near the door that says 'For the sick' ".

637   When I was a kid, we had a quicksand box in the backyard. I was an only child . . . eventually. (STEVEN WRIGHT)

638   "Johnny," scolded the small boy's mother, "your face is clean but how did you manage to get your hands so dirty?"

"Washing my face," replied Johnny.

639   My husband and I are either going to buy a dog or have a child. We can't decide whether to ruin our carpet or ruin our lives. (RITA RUDNER)

640   A small boy went on a school trip to a local church. On the walls, he saw a gallery of photographs of men in uniform. He asked a nearby usher who they were.

"Those are our boys who died in service."

The youngster queried: "Was that the morning service or the evening service?"

641   When I was a kid I used to pray every night for a new bike. Then I realized that the Lord doesn't work that way, so I stole one and asked him to forgive me. (EMO PHILIPS)

642   A father spotted his four-year-old daughter out in the backyard brushing the family dog's teeth.

"What are you doing?" he asked.

"I'm brushing Bruno's teeth," she replied. "But don't worry, I'll put your toothbrush back, like I always have."

643 When you have a fat friend, there are no seesaws, only catapults. (DEMETRI MARTIN)

644 Noticing that his four-year-old daughter was tired, a father gave her a ride on his shoulders. But after a few minutes, she started tugging at his hair.

"Stop that, darling," he said. "It hurts."

"But daddy," she replied, "I'm only trying to get my gum back."

Christmas

645 It was Christmas Eve and the entire house was decorated with lights and tinsel. It was a magical sight. The little boy turned to his father and asked: "Dad, how did the fairy get on top of the Christmas tree?"

"You want to know how the fairy got on top of the Christmas tree? I'll tell you a story, son. Once upon a time, there was a fairy who was helping Santa Claus with the preparations for Christmas. She was helping to decorate Santa's grotto, but Santa couldn't be bothered. He was in a bad mood. He had been let down by two of the reindeer, Mrs Claus was giving him a hard time and he had been drinking heavily. So the last thing he was interested in was decorating his grotto. But the fairy was keen and wanted everything to look as pretty as possible.

"'What shall I do with this gold tinsel, Santa?' asked the fairy politely.

"'Oh, I don't know,' growled Santa. 'And I don't care either.'

"Two minutes later, the fairy appeared with a box of beautiful silver balls.

"'What shall I do with these beautiful silver balls?' asked the fairy.

"'How should I know!' snarled Santa. 'Do what you like with them.'

"Two minutes later, the fairy came back with a Christmas tree.

"'What shall I do with this Christmas tree?' asked the fairy.

"This was too much for Santa. 'As far as I'm concerned, you can stick it up your . . .'

"And that, son, is how the fairy got on top of the Christmas tree."

646 How is the Italian version of Christmas different? – One Mary, one Jesus and 33 Wise guys.

647 A New York mother took her young son to Gimbels department store to meet Santa Claus.

"What would you like for Christmas, young man?" asked the jolly Santa.

"A computer games console, a bicycle and an Action Man," replied the boy.

"I'll do my best to see that you're lucky," said Santa.

Later that day the mother took the boy to Macy's department store and once again they visited Santa's grotto.

"What would you like for Christmas, young man?" asked the Santa.

"A computer games console, a bicycle and an Action Man," replied the boy.

"And are you going to be a good boy and help your mother?" asked Santa.

The boy turned to his mother and said: "Let's go back to Gimbels. I didn't have to make any promises there."

648 I love Christmas. I receive a lot of wonderful presents I can't wait to exchange. (HENNY YOUNGMAN)

649 A father asked his young daughter what she would like for Christmas. She said that what she wanted more than anything else was a baby brother. And it so happened that on Christmas Eve her mother came from hospital clutching a baby boy.

The following year, the father again asked his daughter what she would like for Christmas.

"Well," she replied, "if it's not too uncomfortable for Mummy, I'd like a pony."

650 What weighs eight pounds and won't be plucked next Christmas? — John Denver's guitar.

651 Why is Christmas just like a day at the office? — Because you do all the work and the fat guy in the suit gets all the credit.

652 A mother had twin children Will and Jenny. The two had entirely different outlooks on life — Will was a born pessimist while Jenny was an eternal optimist. These attitudes caused the mother a great deal of concern, particularly when it came to buying presents for them. So she decided to consult a child psychiatrist with regard to what she should buy them for Christmas. The psychiatrist told her to spend as much as she could afford on Will the pessimist but said that Jenny would probably be happy with anything. "Why not get a pile of manure and wrap that up for Jenny?" he suggested. "I'm sure she'd be fine with that."

The mother took his advice and spent 300 dollars on presents for Will and wrapped up a heap of manure for Jenny.

Come Christmas morning and the kids were opening their presents. "What has Santa Claus bought you?" she asked Will.

He answered gloomily. "A bike, but I'll probably get run over while riding it; football boots, but I'll probably break my leg while playing; and an electric train set, but I'll probably electrocute myself."

Realizing this wasn't going as planned, she turned swiftly to Jenny. "And what has Santa Claus bought you?"

"I think I got a pony," said Jenny, up to her elbows in manure, "but I haven't been able to find him yet!"

Bill Clinton

653 Monica Lewinsky went to the dry cleaners and handed her suit to the attendant. "There's a stain on the lapel," she said. "Can you get it off?"

The attendant, a little hard of hearing, replied: "Come again?"

"No, no," said Monica. "It's coffee this time."

654 What's the difference between John F. Kennedy and Bill Clinton? – One had his head blown off, the other was assassinated.

655 A survey in Washington DC asked 1,000 women: "Would you sleep with Bill Clinton if you had the chance?" Seventy-seven per cent answered, "Never again."

656 Bill Clinton looked up from his desk in the Oval Office to see an aide approaching nervously. "What is it?" asked Clinton.

"It's this Abortion Bill, Mr President."

"Oh, just go ahead and pay it."

657 What's Bill Clinton's idea of safe sex? – When Hillary is out of town.

658 Why does Bill Clinton wear boxer shorts? – To keep his ankles warm.

659 Clinton stepped off from Air Force One carrying a small dog. One of his secret service men said: "Nice dog, sir."

"Thanks," said the President. "I got it for Hillary."

"Nice trade, sir!"

660 What ad did Monica Lewinsky answer? – Be a White House intern and get a taste of the Presidency.

661 The Pope and Bill Clinton were on a plane when it crashed. Both were killed. Owing to a mix-up, Clinton went to heaven while the Pope went to hell. Two

days later, St Peter realized his mistake and arranged for the Pope to be moved to heaven. When he arrived there, the Pope said that he had waited all his life to meet the Virgin Mary. Clinton grinned and said: "You're a day too late."

662 Hillary Clinton visited a new doctor in Washington for a thorough examination. To his alarm, he discovered that she'd got crabs. He thought to himself, "How can I tell the First Lady she's got crabs?"

He decided to break the news to her gently. "It appears that you're suffering from Nixon's Disease," he told her.

"Nixon's Disease? What's that?" she demanded. "Give it to me straight, doc."

"Well, in simple terms," he said, "you've got bugs in your oval office."

663 What was Bill Clinton's New Year's Resolution? – He said he wouldn't splash out on any more dresses.

664 Monica Lewinsky died and tried to get into heaven disguised as a nun. She lined up with the other nuns and waited to be interviewed at the Pearly Gates. St Peter asked the first nun in line: "Sister, have you ever touched a man in your life and, if so, with what part of your body?"

"I have only touched a man once," said the nun, "and that was with my fingertip."

"Very well," said St Peter, "dip your fingertip in the bowl of holy water and proceed through to heaven."

St Peter turned to the second nun in line and asked her: "Sister, have you ever touched a man in your life and, if so, with what part of your body?"

"I have only touched a man once," replied the nun, "and that was with my hand."

"Very well," said St Peter, "dip your hand in the holy water and proceed through to heaven."

Next it was Monica's turn, but before St Peter could speak she told him: "Look, you can forget the holy water routine. After one nun's put her dirty finger in it and another's put her dirty hand in it, there's no way I'm gonna gargle with it!"

665 Why was Monica Lewinsky different from all other Americans? – When other Americans want some dick in the White House, they just vote.

666 Al Gore and Bill Clinton were discussing premarital sex. Gore said to Clinton: "I never slept with my wife before we were married. Did you?"

"I dunno," said Clinton. "What was Tipper's maiden name?"

667 Everyone knows you can get Aids from sex. But Bill Clinton got sex from aides.

668 Hillary Clinton was shocked to find that she was pregnant. In a rage, she phoned her husband at the White House and screamed: "You bastard! You bastard! You got me pregnant!"
Bill Clinton replied: "Who is this?"

College and university

669 A college boy delivered a pizza to an old man's house. "I suppose you want a tip?" said the old man grumpily.
"That would be much appreciated," said the college boy, "but the other guy who does pizza deliveries told me not to expect much from you. He said if I got a quarter from you, I'd be lucky."
The old timer was hurt by the accusation. "Well, to prove him wrong, here's five dollars."
"Thank you," said the college boy, "I'll put this in my school fund."
"What are you studying?" asked the old man.
"Applied psychology."

670 A father visited his son's college. Watching students in a chemistry class, he was told they were conducting experiments to find a universal solvent.
"What's that?" he asked.
"A liquid which will dissolve anything," replied the students.
"It sounds good," said the father. "But when you find it, what kind of container will you keep it in?"

671 When I went to college, my parents threw a going away party for me, according to the letter. (EMO PHILIPS)

672 A graduate with a science degree asks: "Why does it work?"
A graduate with an engineering degree asks: "How does it work?"
A graduate with an accounting degree asks: "How much will it cost?"
A graduate with an arts degree asks: "Do you want fries with that?"

673 A freshman at Harvard was looking for the library, so he approached an upperclassman and asked: "Excuse me, but where's the library at?"
The upperclassman looked down his nose at the freshman and replied haughtily: "At Harvard, we never end a sentence with a preposition."
"Sorry," said the freshman. "Where's the library at, asshole?"

674 I was thrown out of college for cheating on the metaphysics exam; I looked into the soul of the boy next to me. (WOODY ALLEN)

675 Taking a new class, a college lecturer was intent on instilling discipline. So he said sarcastically: "If there are any idiots in the room, will they please stand up."

A few moments later, a freshman rose to his feet.

"So why do you consider yourself to be an idiot?" demanded the lecturer.

"I don't," he replied. "But I hate to see you standing up there all by yourself!"

676 What is half of infinity? – nity.

677 Two engineering students were walking to class when one said: "Where did you get such a great bike?"

The second engineer replied: "Well, yesterday I was on my way home when this beautiful girl rode in front of me, tossed her bike and the clothes to the ground and declared: 'Take what you want!'"

The first engineer nodded in approval: "Good choice – the clothes probably wouldn't have fitted."

678 A professor was removing parts of a dead man's body before a class full of medical students. "This is the heart, this is the liver, this is the kidney . . ."

"What's he doing?" asked a latecomer.

"Sssh. He's giving an organ recital."

679 A student was fed up. "What's the matter?" asked his flat mate.

"I wrote home asking my parents to send money so that I could buy a laptop, and they sent me the laptop!"

680 A college professor had a strict rule regarding mid-term exams – that anyone seen writing after the bell would automatically be given zero marks. On this occasion, the bell sounded for the end of the exam but while everybody else stopped writing, one student carried on regardless for another five minutes before calmly handing in his paper.

"That's a zero for you," said the professor.

"Don't you know who I am?" said the student.

"I don't care who you are!" snapped the professor. "You could be the president's nephew for all I care. You get zero."

"So you don't know who I am?" persisted the student.

"No."

"Good."

And with that the student slipped his exam paper into the middle of the stack of the other students' papers and walked out.

Computers

681 A salesman for a major West Coast computer company was demonstrating the latest model at a convention. He boasted that no matter what question the computer was asked, it would come up with the correct answer.

While everyone else asked the computer questions about mathematical problems and the circumference of the Earth, one smartass decided to show off by asking the computer: "Where is my father?"

A minute later came the printout: "Your father is working in a bar in Chicago."

"Ha!" crowed the smartass. "The supposedly infallible computer is wrong. My father is dead."

The salesman was anxious not to lose face over this so he came up with a suggestion. "Perhaps if you rephrased the question, the computer might understand it better?"

So the smartass amended the question to "Where is my mother's husband?" and waited for the reply.

A minute later came the printout: "Your mother's husband is dead. But your father is still working in a bar in Chicago."

682 The Web brings people together because no matter what kind of a twisted sexual mutant you happen to be, you've got millions of pals out there. Type in, "Find people who have sex with goats that are on fire" and the computer will say, "Specify type of goat." (RICH JENI)

683 A computer once beat me at chess, but it was no match for me at kick boxing. (EMO PHILIPPS)

Maxims for the Internet age:

684 Home is where you hang your @.

685 You can't teach an old mouse new clicks.

686 Great groups from little icons grow.

687 The geek shall inherit the earth.

688 Don't byte off more than you can view.

689 What boots up must come down.

690 Virtual reality is its own reward.

691 There's no place like http://www.home.com.

692 Windows will never cease.

693 Three women were comparing their love lives. The first woman said: "My husband is an architect. When we make love, it has power, form and function. It's wonderful."

The second woman said: "My husband is an artist. When we make love, it has passion, emotion and vision. It's wonderful."

The third woman said: "My husband works for Microsoft. When we make love, he just sits at the end of the bed and tells me how great it's going to be when it gets here."

694 What is the new O.J. Simpson website address? Slash slash backslash escape.

695 The Army installed a computer. As a demonstration, an officer fed in the question: "How far is it from these barracks to the coast?"

"Seven hundred," replied the computer.

The officer fed in another question. "Seven hundred what?"

The computer printed out its answer. "Seven hundred, sir!"

696 How do you stop your husband reading your e-mail? – Rename the folder "instruction manual".

697 A computer lets you make more mistakes faster than any invention in human history – with the possible exceptions of hand guns and tequila. (MITCH RATLIFFE)

698 A Canadian went on vacation to Florida. His wife was on a business trip and was planning to meet him in Miami the following day. When he reached his hotel room, he decided to send his wife a quick e-mail. Unable to find the scrap of paper on which he had written her e-mail address, he did his best to type it from memory. Unfortunately he missed one letter and his message was directed instead to an elderly vicar's wife whose husband had passed away only the day before.

When the grieving widow checked her e-mail, she took one look at the screen, let out a shriek of horror and fell to the floor in a dead faint. Hearing the commotion, her family rushed into the room and saw the message on the screen which read: "Dearest wife. Just checked in. Everything prepared for your arrival tomorrow. PS: Sure is hot down here."

699 What kills 99 per cent of all known computer germs? – MS Dos.

You might be a computer nerd if:

700 Your web page is more popular than you.

701 You think Bill Gates is a "cool guy".

702 You refer to going to the bathroom as "downloading".

703 You've ever considered getting a tattoo of the "intel inside" logo.

704 The closest you ever come to having sex is downloading nude pictures off the Internet.

705 You wake at 3 a.m. to go to the bathroom and, on your way back to bed, you stop to check your e-mail.

706 You've never actually met any of your friends.

707 Your favourite sport is Tetris.

708 You haven't played solitaire with real cards in years.

709 You have an identity crisis if someone is using a screen name close to your own.

710 The optician looks deep into your eyes and sees a screen saver.

711 You run back into your burning home to rescue your computer rather than your family.

712 You'd prefer to buy *Computer Weekly* than *Playboy*.

713 You try to enter your password on the microwave.

714 You e-mail your buddy who works at the desk next to you.

715 When someone yells out, "Where's Tommy?", you do a search for tommy.com.

716 You spend a plane trip with your laptop on your lap and your child in the overhead baggage compartment.

717 When someone asks "What did you say?", you reply "Scroll up."

718 You get in an elevator and double-click the button for the floor you want.

719 You decided to stay on at college for an extra year just for the free Internet access.

720 Tech support calls *you* for help.

721 You know exactly how much hard space drive you have free, but you don't know your spouse's birthday.

722 You turn off your modem and get an awful empty feeling, like you just pulled the plug on a loved one.

723 You have called out someone's screen name while making love to your significant other.

724 You've read more books over the Internet than in real life.

725 Your dog has its own home page.

726 You can't speak to your mother because she doesn't have a modem.

727 You name your daughter Dotcom.

728 When Microsoft boss Bill Gates died suddenly, St Peter offered him a choice of going to heaven or hell. Gates said he'd like to take a look at hell first. Gates could hardly believe his eyes. The place was full of beautiful, hard-working women, each hanging on his every word.

"This is all virtual, isn't it?" said Gates.

"Sure," replied St Peter. "And no bugs."

"So what's heaven like?"

"It's people wearing robes and playing harps while sitting on clouds."

"It's no contest," said Gates. "Hell is the place for me. It's amazing."

Three weeks later, St Peter dropped in to hell on a flying visit. An angry Gates was waiting for him. "What happened?" he raged. "This place is terrible. The temperature is over 200 degrees, the music is awful and there are vermin everywhere. Where are the beautiful women, the virtual wonders? Where is the splendid hell you promised me?"

"Oh, that," said St Peter. "That was just a demo."

Crime

729 A snail was mugged in an alley by two slugs. Later a detective asked him for a description of his assailants. "Gee," said the snail, "I'm not sure. It all happened so fast."

730 A defence attorney told his client: "I've got good news and bad news. The bad news is your blood test came back and your DNA is an exact match with the sample found on the victim's dress."

"Oh, no!" said the client. "I'm finished. What's the good news?"

"Your cholesterol is down to 140."

731 A man tried to hijack a busload of Japanese tourists. Luckily the police had 500 photos of the suspect.

732 An escaped convict broke into a house and bound and gagged a young married couple in their bedroom. While the intruder was ransacking the place downstairs, the husband managed to loosen his gag. "Honey," he gasped, "this guy hasn't seen a woman in years. Just do what he says. If he wants sex, go along with it. Our lives could depend on it."

Just then she managed to spit out her gag too. "I'm so relieved you feel that way, darling," she said, "because he just told me what a nice tight ass he thought you'd got."

733 Did you hear about the thief who stole a calendar? – He got 12 months.

734 A driver appeared in court on a charge of speeding. "I understand you were travelling at 65 mph in a 30 mph zone," said the judge.
"That's not true," protested the driver. "I wasn't even doing 30, in fact I wasn't even doing 15, I was barely . . ."
"That's enough," interrupted the judge. "I'm going to hurry and fine you 20 dollars before you back into something!"

735 We had gay burglars the other night. They broke in and rearranged the furniture. (ROBIN WILLIAMS)

736 Two burglars were robbing an apartment block when they heard the sound of police car sirens.
"Quick! Jump!" said one.
"But we're on the thirteenth floor," protested his accomplice.
The first burglar said: "This is no time to be superstitious!"

737 Two teenagers arrested for mugging an old lady were taken to the police station. The sergeant told them that they were entitled to one phone call.
Twenty minutes later a man entered the station. "I assume you're the kids' lawyer?" said the sergeant.
"No," said the man, "I'm here to deliver a pizza."

738 What did Jack the Ripper's mother say to him? – "How come you never go out with the same girl twice?"

739 A cross-eyed judge looked at the three defendants in the dock and asked the first: "How do you plead?"
"Not guilty," said the second defendant.
"I wasn't talking to you," snapped the judge.
"I never said a word," replied the third defendant.

740 Why did the escaped convict saw the legs off his bed? – He wanted to lie low.

741 A man was jumped in an alley by two muggers. He put up a heroic resistance, but was eventually overpowered and the attackers went through his pockets. They didn't find much.

"You mean you fought like that for 48 cents?" said one mugger incredulously.

"Is that all you wanted?" said the man, relieved. "I thought you were after the 500 dollars in my shoe."

742 A shoplifter was caught red-handed trying to steal a watch from an exclusive jewellery store. The shoplifter pleaded with the manager not to call the police and said he would happily buy the watch. After careful deliberation, the manager agreed.

"That's 500 dollars then."

"Hmmm," said the shoplifter, "that's more than I planned to spend. Could you show me something less expensive?"

743 A thief who steals ladies' underwear from washing lines evaded capture yesterday. He gave police the slip.

744 An 89-year-old woman arrived home from bingo to find her husband in bed with another woman. In a jealous rage, she pushed him off the balcony of their apartment and sent him plunging to his death. She was charged with murder and when her case was heard, the judge asked her whether there was anything she wished to say in her own defence.

"Well, your honour," she said calmly, "I figured that at 94, if he could make love to another woman, he could fly too!"

745 The defendant stood defiantly in the dock and told the judge: "I don't recognize this court."

"Why?" rapped the judge.

"Because it's been decorated since the last time I was here."

746 A lawyer was talking to a client who had just been found guilty of murder.

"There's good news and bad news," said the lawyer. "The bad news is you're getting the electric chair. The good news is I got the voltage lowered."

747 A gang of bank robbers ordered the staff to take off their clothes and lie face down on the floor. A nervous blonde pulled off her clothes but lay on her back.

"Turn over, Mandy," whispered the girl lying beside her. "This is a stick-up, not the office party."

Dating

748 The year was 1959 and college boy Mike went to pick up Cathy, his date for the evening. While Cathy was getting ready, her father was asking Mike about his plans for the evening.

"We'll probably go to a soda shop or a movie," said Mike.

Her father calmly replied: "Why don't the pair of you go out and screw?"

Mike was taken aback by the suggestion. "You think we should go out and screw?" he queried.

"Absolutely," said the father. "After all, you're only young once. And I know how Cathy loves to screw. She'd screw all night if we let her."

Mike was lost for words, but reckoned it was going to be a date to remember.

Shortly afterwards, Cathy appeared and off they went. Her father sat back to watch the TV but 20 minutes later, the door burst open and Cathy ran in, sobbing.

"Dammit, Daddy!" she screamed. "It's called the twist!"

749 My last girlfriend looked like Claudia Schiffer – only shorter and Korean. (MAX KAUFFMAN)

750 An old hillbilly had three pretty teenage daughters of whom he was very protective. He used to sit on the front porch, shotgun in hand, and run his eye over any potential suitors. If he didn't like the look of them, he'd send them on their way.

One night, all three girls were due to go out on dates. The first's boyfriend drove up and announced: "Hi, my name is Joe, I'm here to get Flo, we're going to the show, is she ready to go?" The old man decided that the boy sounded OK and he gave his blessing for the date.

Ten minutes later, another car pulled up. The driver called out: "Hi, my name is Freddy, I'm here to get Betty, we're going for spaghetti, is she ready?" The old man thought the boy was decent enough so he gave permission for the date.

Ten minutes later, a third car arrived. The driver called out: "Hi, my name is Chuck . . ." And the old man shot him.

751 I date this girl for two years, and then the nagging starts: "I wanna know your name . . ." (MIKE BINDER)

752 A guy contacted a computer dating agency in search of his ideal mate. He said: "I want a partner who is small and cute, who loves water sports and enjoys group activities." Ten seconds later, the computer printed out the identity of his dream companion: a penguin.

753 There's a fine line between cuddling and holding someone down so they can't get away. (DAVE ATTELL)

754 My girlfriend told me I should be more affectionate. So I got two girlfriends.

755 I was with this girl the other night and from the way she was responding to my skilful caresses, you would have sworn that she was conscious from the top of her head to the tag on her toes. (EMO PHILIPS)

756 A girl went over to her friend and said: "I hear you broke off your engagement to Rob? Why?"

"It's just that my feelings towards him aren't the same any more."

"Are you returning his ring?"

"No way! My feelings towards the ring haven't changed a bit!"

757 I just broke up with someone and the last thing she said to me was, "You'll never find anyone like me again."

I'm thinking: "I should hope not! If I don't want you, why would I want someone like you?" (LARRY MILLER)

758 A rich, handsome playboy took a girl on a first date to an amusement park. After going on half a dozen rides, he said: "What do you want to do next?"

"Get weighed," she said.

He thought that was a strange request, but he took her to the weighing booth. After going on a few more rides, he asked again: "What do you want to do next?"

"Get weighed," she replied.

"What, again?"

"Get weighed," she repeated.

By now, the guy was convinced she was seriously weird, so he made an excuse and took her home early. Her mother wasn't expecting her back so soon. "What is it, dear?" she said. "Didn't you have a nice time tonight?"

"Wousy," said the girl.

759 A girl phoned me the other day and said, "Come on over, there's nobody home." I went over. Nobody was home. (RODNEY DANGERFIELD)

760 Once upon a time there was a famous black knight on a black horse who desired the hand of a fair princess. So he rode to the castle where the princess lived to seek permission from her father, the king.

"Who goes there?" demanded the castle gatekeeper.

"It is the black knight on the black horse," replied the knight. "I wish to see the king."

"Not the black knight on the black horse?" replied the gatekeeper.

"Yes, the black knight on the black horse."

"Very well. You may come through."

The knight entered the royal chamber.

"Who is it?" boomed the king.

"It is the black knight on the black horse. I have come to ask for the hand of your daughter, the Princess Romana."

"Not the black knight on the black horse?" said the king.

"Yes, the black knight on the black horse."

"Well," said the king, "before you can marry my daughter, you must obtain a golden ring from the golden dragon."

"I shall do that," replied the knight, and he rode off to find the golden dragon.

The golden dragon was in its lair. "Who goes there?" it called at the sound of approaching hoofs.

"It is the black knight on the black horse. I have come to claim the golden ring with which I may marry the king's daughter, the Princess Romana."

"Not the black knight on the black horse?" said the golden dragon.

"Yes, the black knight on the black horse."

The golden dragon handed him the golden ring and he rode back to the castle.

"Who goes there?" demanded the gatekeeper.

"It is the black knight on the black horse."

"Not the black knight on the black horse?"

"Yes, the black knight on the black horse. I am here to see the king."

"Very well. Come through."

The black knight entered the royal chamber.

"Who is it?" boomed the king.

"It is the black knight on the black horse."

"Not the black knight on the black horse?"

"Yes, the black knight on the black horse. I have obtained the golden ring from the golden dragon. Now may I ask for the hand of your daughter, the Princess Romana?"

"Before you can marry my daughter," replied the king, "you must also obtain the emerald ring from the green dragon."

"I shall do that," said the knight and he rode off in search of the green dragon.

The green dragon was in its lair. "Who goes there?" it said, hearing the sound of approaching hoofs.

"It is the black knight on the black horse. I have come to claim the emerald ring with which I may marry the king's daughter, the Princess Romana."

"Not the black knight on the black horse?"

"Yes, the black knight on the black horse."

The green dragon handed the emerald ring to the black knight and he rode back to the castle.

"Who goes there?" demanded the gatekeeper.

"It is the black knight on the black horse. I am here to see the king."

"Not the black knight on the black horse?"

"Yes, the black knight on the black horse."

"Very well. Come through."

The knight entered the royal chamber.

"Who is it?" boomed the king.

"It is the black knight on the black horse."

"Not the black knight on the black horse?"

"Yes, the black knight on the black horse. I have obtained the emerald ring from the green dragon and now I have come to ask for the hand of your daughter, the Princess Romana."

"Before you can marry my daughter," replied the king, "you must also obtain the ruby ring from the red dragon."

"Then I shall do that," said the knight and he rode off in search of the red dragon.

The dragon was in its lair. "Who goes there?" called the dragon, hearing the sound of approaching hoofs.

"It is the black knight on the black horse."

"Not the black knight on the black horse?"

"Yes, the black knight on the black horse. I have come to claim the ruby ring so that I may marry the king's daughter, the Princess Romana."

The red dragon handed the black knight the ruby ring and the knight rode back to the castle.

"Who goes there?" demanded the gatekeeper.

"It is the black knight on the black horse."

"Not the black knight on the black horse?"

"Yes, the black knight on the black horse. I am here to see the king."

"Very well. Come through."

The knight entered the royal chamber.

"Who is it?" boomed the king.

"It is the black knight on the black horse."

"Not the black knight on the black horse?"

"Yes, the black knight on the black horse. I have obtained the ruby ring from the red dragon and now I wish to ask for the hand of your daughter, the Princess Romana."

"Very well," said the king, "you have obtained all three rings. You may ask for the hand of my daughter, the Princess Romana."

The knight was escorted to the princess's chamber.

"Who is it?" asked the princess.

"It is the black knight on the black horse."

"Not the black knight on the black horse?"

"Yes, the black knight on the black horse. Your father, the king, has given me permission to ask for your hand in marriage. So, fair princess, will you marry me?"

"No way."

761 "I stepped out for a walk. My girlfriend asked how long I would be out. I said, 'The whole time'." (STEVEN WRIGHT)

762 A boy promised his girlfriend: "We're going to have a great time Saturday. I got three tickets for the big game."

"Why do we need three?" she asked.

"One for your father, one for your mother and one for your kid sister . . ."

763 I've been on so many blind dates, I should get a free dog. (WENDY LIEBMAN)

764 A young couple parked in a lovers' lane. "It's lovely out here tonight," she sighed romantically. "It's so quiet and peaceful. Just listen to the crickets."

"They're not crickets," replied her boyfriend. "They're zippers."

765 Dating is pressure and tension. What is a date, really, but a job interview that lasts all night? The only difference between a date and a job interview is that in not many job interviews is there a chance you'll end up naked at the end of it. (JERRY SEINFELD)

Death

766 It's not that I'm afraid to die, I just don't want to be there when it happens. (WOODY ALLEN)

767 Three guys were standing on the roof of the Empire State Building. The first said: "You know, the wind currents here in New York are so strong that you could step off the edge of this building and literally float in mid-air due to the upward thrust of the thermal air current."

"You're crazy," said the second guy.

"You don't believe me?" said the first. "Watch this."

And with that, the first guy stepped off the edge of the Empire State Building, floated around in mid-air for 30 seconds and returned safely to the roof.

"That was amazing," said the second guy. "I've got to try that."

And so the second guy stepped off the roof. But instead of floating, he dropped like a stone to the street more than 1,000 feet below.

Seeing this, the third guy, who had remained silent until then, turned to the first guy and said: "You know something, there are times when you can be a real asshole, Superman."

768 For three days after death, hair and fingernails continue to grow but phone calls taper off. (JOHNNY CARSON)

769 After 40 years of misery together, a man didn't shed too many tears when his wife died. He begrudged spending anything on her funeral and, to save on burial costs, he arranged for her to be buried privately in their back garden. A week later, a friend of the deceased came round to pay her respects and was surprised to see the wife's bottom protruding from the soil.

"Did you bury her like that as a token of affection?" asked the friend. "So that you could always see her, be in touch with her?"

"No way," said the husband. "It's somewhere to park my bike!"

Famous last words:

770 Don't worry, it's fireproof.

771 Are you sure the power is off?

772 Pull the pin and count to what?

773 Don't be so superstitious.

774 I've seen this done on TV.

775 What does this button do?

776 I wonder where the mother bear is?

777 Which wire was I supposed to cut?

778 This tastes funny.

779 You wouldn't hit a guy with glasses, would you?

780 Good doggie, nice doggie . . .

781 An Englishman, a Scotsman and an Irishman were due to face a firing squad. The Englishman was first to be lined up against the wall. As the soldiers raised their rifles and took aim, he suddenly shouted "Avalanche!" The soldiers instinctively turned round to look and by the time they realized it was a hoax, the Englishman had escaped.

The Scotsman then prepared to meet his doom. Just as the soldiers raised their rifles and took aim, he shouted "Flood!" Again they turned round to see what the problem was, and by the time it dawned on them that it was a hoax, the Scotsman had escaped.

Finally it was the turn of the Irishman who had been greatly impressed by his colleagues' cunning ruses and was determined to come up with a similar diversion. So just as the soldiers raised their rifles and took aim, he shouted "Fire!"

782 A man had his wife cremated. As smoke came out, he said to his friend: "That's the first time I ever saw her hot."

783 My cousin just died. He was only 19. He got stung by a bee – the natural enemy of a tightrope walker. (EMO PHILIPS)

784 An old lady was proud of being a virgin. Before she passed away, she gave strict instructions to the funeral director regarding her headstone. She said: "I want it to read: 'Born as a virgin, lived as a virgin, died as a virgin.'"

When she died, the funeral director relayed the instructions to the men inscribing her headstone. But they were lazy, and instead of carving out the full inscription, they just wrote: "Returned unopened."

785 How many men do you need for a mafia funeral? Only one: to slam the car boot shut.

786 To me, funerals are like bad movies. They last too long, they're overacted, and the ending is predictable. (GEORGE BURNS)

787 The day after losing his wife in a boating accident, a man answered the door to two grim-faced police officers. They announced: "We have some bad news, some good news, and some great news. Which would you like to hear first?"

"Give me the bad news first," said the man.

"Sir, I'm afraid we found your wife's body in San Francisco Bay."

"Oh, no," sobbed the man. "My poor wife. My poor darling wife. What can be the good news?"

"When we pulled her up, she had two 5 lb lobsters and a dozen large edible crabs on her."

"That's awful," said the man. "So what's the great news?"

"We're going to pull her up again tomorrow."

788 I'll tell you what makes my blood boil – crematoriums. (TIM VINE)

789 A man was telling his friend: "My grandfather predicted in advance the very year in which he was going to die. What's more, he knew the exact month he was going to die, the precise day he was going to die and even the time of day he was going to die. And he was right on every count."

"That's uncanny," said the friend. "How did he know all that?"

"The judge told him."

790 When someone close to you dies, move seats. (JIMMY CARR)

791 A man went to the doctor's for his annual physical. The man was stunned when the doctor said: "I'm afraid you've only got six weeks to live."

"I can't believe it," said the man. "I feel great. Isn't there anything that can be done?"

"Well," said the doctor, "you could try taking a mud bath every day."

"Why, will that cure me?" said the man hopefully.

"No, but it'll get you used to the dirt."

792 My wife and I took out life insurance policies on each other. So now it's just a waiting game. (BILL DWYER)

793 First guy: "Why are you putting a wreath on that fuse box?"

Second guy: "A year ago today my brother got the electric chair."

794 "Mum," said the son to his ageing mother, "when you go, do you want to be buried or cremated?"

"I don't mind," replied the mother. "Surprise me."

795 "I don't want to achieve immortality through my work – I want to achieve it through not dying." (WOODY ALLEN)

796 Minutes before her husband's funeral, a widow took one last look at his body. To her horror, she saw that he was wearing a brown suit whereas she had issued strict instructions to the undertaker that she wanted him buried in a blue suit. She sought out the undertaker and demanded that the suit be changed. At first, he tried to tell her that it was too late but when he could see that she wasn't going to back down, he ordered the mortician to wheel the coffin away.

A few minutes later, just as the funeral was about to start, the coffin was wheeled back in and, incredibly, the corpse was now wearing a blue suit. The widow was delighted and, after the service, praised the undertaker for his swift work.

"Oh, it was nothing," he said. "It so happened there was another body in the back room and he was already dressed in a blue suit. All we had to do was switch heads."

797 The chief problem about death, incidentally, is the fear that there may be no afterlife – a depressing thought, particularly for those who have bothered to shave. Also, there is the fear that there is an afterlife but no one will know where it's being held. (WOODY ALLEN)

798 I don't believe in an afterlife, although I am bringing a change of underwear. (WOODY ALLEN)

Ways to be offensive at a funeral:

799 Tell the widow she looks horny in black.

800 Take bets on how long it takes a body to decompose.

801 Drive behind the hearse and keep honking your horn.

802 Tell the undertaker your dog died and ask if you can sneak him into the coffin.

803 Put a hard-boiled egg in the mouth of the deceased.

804 Punch the body and tell people he hit you first.

805 Goose the widow as she bends over to throw dirt on to the coffin.

806 Ask someone to take a Polaroid of you shaking hands with the deceased.

807 Go around telling people that you've seen the will and that they're not in it.

808 Listen to your Walkman at the graveside.

809 Ask the widow for the $50 the deceased owed you.

810 Tell the widow that you're the deceased's secret gay lover.

811 Put a whoopee cushion on the widow's chair.

812 Use the deceased's tongue to lick a postage stamp.

813 Climb on the headstone to get a better view.

814 Take a flower from the wreath as a buttonhole.

815 Attend the funeral wearing a clown's costume.

816 Whenever the widow cries, blow a raspberry every time she wipes her nose.

817 Toss a handful of cooked rice on to the deceased, scream "Maggots, Maggots!", then pretend to faint.

818 Tell the widow that the deceased's last wish was that she make love to you.

819 Slip plastic vampire teeth into the deceased's mouth.

820 Two old ladies met in the park. After inquiring about each other's health, the topic of conversation turned to their respective husbands.

"Oh," said one, "Harry died last week. He went out to the garden to dig up a cabbage for dinner, had a heart attack and dropped dead in the middle of the vegetable patch."

"Oh, my," said the other. "What did you do?"

"I opened a can of peas instead."

821 A prisoner in the electric chair got a sudden attack of the hiccups just as the warden was about to pull the switch.

"Any last requests?" asked the warden.

"Yeah, hic. Could you please, hic, do something to scare me?"

Dentists

822 A young woman had terrible toothache but was reluctant to go to the dentist because she was frightened of his drill. Eventually, however, she was in such discomfort that she decided to pluck up courage.

"I really am scared," she told the dentist as she entered the surgery. "I don't know which is worse – having a tooth filled or having a baby."

"Well," said the dentist, "make up your mind before I adjust the chair."

823 Patient: "I have yellow teeth. What should I do?"

Dentist: "Wear a brown tie."

824 A man walked into a dentist's and asked how much it cost to extract two wisdom teeth.

"80 dollars," replied the dentist.

"80 dollars!" groaned the man. "That's a bit steep. Isn't there any way you can do it cheaper?"

"Well, I suppose if you don't have anaesthetic, I can knock it down to 60."

"That's still too expensive."

The dentist scratched his head. "OK, if I save on the anaesthetic and simply rip out the teeth with a pair of pliers, I could get away with charging 20 dollars."

"That's still too much."

"Well, I suppose as a last resort, I could let one of my students do it for the experience. That way, I could charge you just 10 dollars."

"That's better," said the man. "Book my wife in for next Monday."

825 I'm always amazed to hear of air-crash victims so badly mutilated that they have to be identified by their dental records. What I can't understand is, if they don't know who you are, how do they know who your dentist is? (PAUL MERTON)

826 A dentist was filling a cavity when he turned to the patient and said: "Would you mind doing me a favour? Could you let out a loud, piercing scream?"

The patient said: "But it doesn't hurt so bad this time."

The dentist said: "I know. But I've got a waiting room full of people and I don't want to miss the four o'clock ball game."

827 What does the dentist of the year get? – A little plaque.

828 Patient: "How much to have a tooth pulled?"

Dentist: "80 dollars."

Patient: "80 dollars for a few minutes work?"

Dentist: "I can extract it very slowly if you like."

829 As a dentist prepared to extract a tooth from a lady patient, she suddenly grabbed him by the balls and said ominously: "Now we're not going to hurt each other, are we?"

830 I went to the dentist. He said, "Say aaah."

I said, "Why?".

He said, "My dog's died." (TIM VINE)

831 A speaker was about to address a public meeting when he realized that he had left his false teeth at home. He shuffled around anxiously for a few moments before informing the lady who was chairing the meeting that he would be unable to give his speech because he had forgotten his false teeth.

His predicament was overheard by a man in the front row of the audience who immediately produced a pair of false teeth from his pocket and said: "Why don't you try these?"

The speaker put the set of false teeth in his mouth but they were too tight. "By chance, I have another pair," said the man. "Try these."

The speaker put the second set of teeth in his mouth but they were too loose. "It's no good," he said. "I'll have to pull out."

"Wait," said the man. "It so happens that I have one more pair of false teeth in my pocket. Try these."

The speaker did, and they fitted perfectly. "Well, thank you," he said, "I've been looking for a good dentist."

"I'm not a dentist," said the man. "I'm an undertaker."

Diets

832 A woman had been advised by her doctor to go on a strict diet but she couldn't discipline herself and would spend most of the day raiding the fridge. As her weight ballooned, one day she got stuck on the lavatory seat. "Jim, Jim!" she called to her husband. "The lavatory seat's stuck to my butt. Fetch the doctor."

The husband asked the doctor to come round as soon as he could but didn't explain what the problem was. In the meantime, the husband managed to remove the seat from the lavatory bowl but it was still wedged fast to his wife's backside. He suggested she go and kneel on the bed until the doctor arrived.

When the doctor showed up, the husband showed him straight into the bedroom where the wife was kneeling with her back to the door.

"What do you think, doc?" asked the husband.

"I think it's very nice," replied the doctor, "but why such a cheap frame?"

833 I'm on a whisky diet. I've lost three days already. (TOMMY COOPER)

834 Patient: "How can I lose 12 lbs of ugly fat?"
Doctor: "Cut your head off."

835 It's easy to distract fat people. It's a piece of cake. (CHRIS ADDISON)

836 A husband was standing on the bathroom scales, desperately holding his stomach in. His wife, thinking he was trying to reduce his weight, remarked: "I don't think that helps."

"It does," he said. "It's the only way I can read the numbers!"

837 My wife is on a diet. Coconuts and bananas. She hasn't lost any weight, but she can sure climb a tree. (HENNY YOUNGMAN)

838 A woman was overweight so her doctor put her on a diet. "I want you to eat regularly for two days, then skip a day, and repeat the procedure for two weeks. Next time I see you, you'll have lost at least 5 lbs."

But when the woman returned two weeks later, she had lost 20 lbs. The doctor was amazed. "Did you follow my instructions?"

"Yes," she said, "but I thought I was going to drop dead that third day."

"From hunger, you mean?"

"No, from skipping."

839 I don't know what all this fuss is about weight. My wife lost two stone swimming last year. I don't know how. I tied them round her neck tight enough. (LES DAWSON)

840 An elderly couple died within days of each other and were shown round heaven by St Peter. It was a fabulous place – permanent sunshine, swimming pools, bars and tennis courts. "Heck, Ethel," hissed the husband, "we could have been here ten years ago if you hadn't heard about all them fancy low-fat diets."

Dinner parties

841 A wife was holding a lavish dinner party at the family apartment and had invited the cream of San Franciscan society to attend. To ensure that she was serving only the freshest food at the party, that afternoon she sent her husband down to the beach to fetch some snails. But while he was collecting snails on the beach, he met a beautiful woman. Well, one thing led to another and they ended up going back to her place, drinking several bottles of wine and making passionate love.

He was so smitten with her that he completely forgot about the time and it was the following morning before he woke up. "My God!" he thought. "My wife's dinner party!" He frantically got dressed and ran back to the apartment just as the sun was rising. But he was in such a hurry that as he reached the top of the stairs leading to the apartment, he dropped the bucket of snails and they fell to the floor. There were snails all the way down the stairs.

Just then his wife opened the door. She was furious. "Where have you been all night?" she screamed.

He looked at her and then at the trail of snails down the stairs. "Come on guys," he said, "we're almost there."

842 The small girl was allowed to stay up for the start of her parents' dinner party and as a treat was given the chance to say grace.

"But I don't know what to say," she whispered nervously in front of the guests.

Her mother helped her out. "Just say what Daddy said before breakfast this morning. You know, 'Oh God . . .' "

"Oh yes, I remember," said the little girl. "Oh God, why have we got to have these boring people to dinner tonight?"

843 As a special treat, little Johnny was allowed to stay up for a dinner party which his parents were giving for friends. As his mother collected the plates after the main course, Johnny piped up: "Is the dessert not good for me or is there enough to go round?"

844 A fraught housewife answered the phone and was relieved to hear a friendly voice on the other end. "Oh, Mother," she sobbed, "I've had a terrible day. I sprained my ankle this morning and so I haven't been able to go shopping. The washing machine's broken, the baby won't eat, the house is a mess and I'm supposed to be hosting a dinner party tonight."

"Now, don't you worry about a thing. I'll be over in half an hour. I'll do the shopping, clean up the house and cook your dinner. I'll feed the baby and I'll call a repairman to fix the washing machine. I'll do everything. And I'll call George at the office and tell him he ought to come home and help."

"George? Who's George?"

"George – your husband! This is 314 4628?"

"No, this is 314 4629."

"Oh."

"Does this mean you're not coming over?!"

Divorce

845 Mrs Czernak appeared before the judge in a divorce action.

"How old are you?" asked the judge.

"Thirty-five," said Mrs Czernak.

The judge noted her greying hair and wrinkled cheeks. "May I see your birth certificate?"

She handed the judge her birth certificate.

"Madam," he said severely, "according to this certificate you are not 35 but 50."

"Your honour," replied Mrs Czernak, "the last 15 years I spent with my husband I'm not counting. You call that a life?"

846 It was partially my fault that we got divorced. I tended to place my wife under a pedestal. (WOODY ALLEN)

847 A couple in their nineties appeared before a judge to ask for a divorce. The wife moaned: "He gambles, he stays out nights, he runs around with women. I can't take any more."

The husband countered: "She doesn't do any housework, her cooking is atrocious, she has no time for me, she sleeps around."

"How long has this been going on?" asked the judge.

"About 70 years," they chorused.

The judge was bemused. "So why did you wait till now to get a divorce?"

"Well, we were waiting for the kids to die."

848 Marriages don't last. When I meet a guy, the first question I ask myself is: "Is this the man I want my children to spend their weekends with?" (RITA RUDNER)

849 A travelling salesman was testifying in divorce proceedings against his wife. His attorney said: "Please describe the incident that first caused you to entertain suspicions regarding your wife's infidelity."

The salesman answered: "I'm on the road during the week so naturally when I am home at weekends, I'm particularly attentive to my wife. One Sunday morning we were in the middle of a heavy session of love-making when the old lady in the apartment next door pounded on the wall and yelled: 'Can't you at least stop all that racket at the weekend?' "

850 A woman with 12 children aged between one and 12 decided to sue her husband for divorce on the grounds of desertion.

"When did he desert you?" asked the judge.

"Eleven years ago."

"But if he left you 11 years ago, where did all the children come from?"

"He kept coming back to say he was sorry."

851 A man consulted his priest about getting a divorce. The priest was surprised. "Why on earth would you want to divorce such a lovely wife? She is soft and gentle and, if I may say so, she is also quite beautiful and nicely proportioned. I really can't see what you have to complain about."

The man took off his shoe. "See this shoe," he said, showing it to the priest, "the leather is soft and gentle. It is a beautiful piece of work and nicely proportioned."

"Ah," said the priest, "a parable."

"In a way, Father," replied the man. "I'm the only one who knows it pinches."

852   A divorce court judge said to the husband: "Mr Geraghty, I have reviewed this case very carefully and I've decided to give your wife 800 dollars a week."

"That's very fair, your honour," he replied. "And every now and then I'll try to send her a few bucks myself."

853   Julie-Ann and Joan were discussing problems in their respective marriages. "I'm going to get a divorce," said Julie-Ann. "Yesterday I saw my louse of a husband going into a movie with another woman."

"Oh, dear," said Joan. "I am sorry. But, you know, there could have been a perfectly innocent explanation. Why didn't you follow them into the cinema?"

"I couldn't," said Julie-Ann. "The guy I was with had already seen the film."

854   Two newlyweds quickly realized that the marriage wasn't working and filed for divorce. The judge wanted to know what the problem was.

The husband answered: "In the seven weeks that we've been together, we haven't been able to agree on a single thing."

The judge turned to the wife: "Have you anything to say?"

She replied: "It's been eight weeks, your honour."

855   Divorce is having your genitals torn off through your wallet. (ROBIN WILLIAMS)

856   After 35 years of marriage, a husband said he wanted a divorce. His wife was stunned. "But John," she pleaded, "how could you want to divorce me after all we've been through together? Remember how just after we met, you caught malaria and nearly died, but I looked after you? Then when your family were wiped out in a hurricane, I was there for you. Then when you were falsely accused of armed robbery, I stood by you. Then when you lost 40,000 dollars on the horses, I sympathized. And when that fire destroyed your office, I comforted you. How could you leave me? We've been through so much."

"That's the problem, Sue. Face it, you're just bad luck."

857 A woman went to an attorney to ask about a divorce.

"What grounds do you have, madam?"

"About six acres."

"No, I don't think you quite understand. Let me rephrase the question. Do you have a grudge?"

"No, just a parking space."

"I'll try again. Does your husband beat you up?"

"No, I always get up at least an hour before he does."

The attorney could see he was fighting a losing battle. "Madam, are you sure you want a divorce?"

"I'm not the one who wants a divorce," she said. "My husband does. He claims we don't communicate."

Doctors

858 A man with a heavy cold went to see his doctor. The doctor prescribed a course of tablets but they had no effect. On the man's next visit the doctor administered an injection but that didn't work either. On the third visit, the doctor told the man: "I want you to go home, take a hot bath, then open all the windows in your house and stand in the draught."

"But if I do that, doctor, I'll catch pneumonia."

"I know," said the doctor. "But I can cure pneumonia."

859 A woman went to the doctor's clutching the side of her face.

"What seems to be the problem?" asked the doctor.

"Well," said the woman, removing her hand, "it's this pimple on my cheek. There's a small tree growing from it, and a table and chairs, and a picnic basket. What on earth can it be?"

"It's nothing to worry about," said the doctor. "It's only a beauty spot."

860 A man went to the doctor's with a cucumber in his left ear, a carrot in his right ear and a banana up his nose. "What's wrong with me?" he asked.

"Simple," said the doctor. "You're not eating properly."

861 Doctor examining a woman: "You have acute angina."

Woman: "Why thank you, doctor!"

862 What has thick glasses and a wet nose? – A short-sighted gynaecologist.

863 What is the difference between God and an orthopaedic surgeon? – God doesn't think he's an orthopaedic surgeon.

864 I went to the doctor the other day. All this guy did was suck blood out of my neck. Never go to see Dr Acula. (MITCH HEDBERG)

865 A man went to the doctor's complaining of a pain in the stomach. The doctor gave him a thorough examination but could not find anything obviously wrong.

He doctor sighed: "I'm afraid I can't diagnose your complaint. I think it must be drink."

"All right then," said the patient, "I'll come back when you're sober."

866 My doctor gave me six months to live but when I couldn't pay the bill he gave me six months more. (WALTER MATTHAU)

867 I went to the doctor and said: "Doctor, every morning when I get up and I look in the mirror, I feel like throwing up. What's wrong with me?"

The doctor said: "I don't know, but your eyesight's perfect." (RODNEY DANGERFIELD)

868 I went to the doctor because I'd swallowed a bottle of sleeping pills. He told me to have a few drinks and get some rest. (RODNEY DANGERFIELD)

869 A woman went to the doctor's. The doctor said: "You've got tuberculosis."

"I don't believe you," said the shocked woman. "I want a second opinion."

"OK," said the doctor. "You're ugly as well."

870 A woman visited her doctor because she was worried that she had been wetting the bed at night. The doctor asked her the usual questions, then told her to go behind the screen and remove her clothes. The woman was surprised at this request, but agreed. When she was undressed, he asked her to stand on her hands in front of and facing a full-length mirror. She couldn't understand why he wanted her to do this, but was prepared to do anything to cure her problem. Then he asked her to open her legs and he put his head between them and rested his chin on her private parts.

"Yes, yes," he muttered. "Yes, I see. Right, would you get dressed again, please?"

After she had got dressed, he sat her down and informed her that the cause of her bed-wetting was that she was drinking too much liquid immediately before going to bed.

The woman was puzzled. "So what did the exercise in front of the mirror tell you?" she asked.

"Oh, that. I just wanted to find out whether a beard would suit me."

871 My kid is a born doctor. Nobody can read anything he writes. (HENNY YOUNGMAN)

872 A young medical student approached a patient in bed brandishing a syringe. "Nothing to worry about," said the student, "just a little prick with a needle."

"Yes, I know you are," said the patient. "But what are you going to do?"

873 Four nurses decided to play a trick on a doctor who they thought was arrogant. Later, each discussed what they had done.

The first nurse said: "I stuffed cotton wool in his stethoscope so that he couldn't hear."

The second nurse said: "I let the mercury out of his thermometers and painted them all to read 107 degrees."

The third nurse said: "I poked holes in all of the condoms he keeps in his desk drawer."

And the fourth nurse fainted.

874 A woman went to the doctor and told him: "Every time I sneeze, I have an orgasm."

"Hmmm. What are you taking for it?"

"Pepper."

875 A doctor prescribed suppositories for a man suffering from constipation but a week later the man returned to the doctor and complained that the treatment wasn't working.

"Have you been taking them regularly?" asked the doctor.

"What do you think I've been doing?" snapped the man. "Shoving them up my ass?"

876 A guy walked into the doctor's with a lettuce leaf sticking out of one ear. "That's unusual," said the doctor.

The man said: "That's just the tip of the iceberg."

877 An 86-year-old man was having his annual check-up. He boasted to the doctor: "I've got an 18-year-old bride who is pregnant with my child. How about that, eh, doc?"

The doctor thought for a moment and said: "Let me tell you a story. I knew a guy who was a keen hunter, but one day he left home in a hurry and accidentally picked up his umbrella instead of his gun. Later that day, he came face to face with a huge grizzly bear. The hunter raised his umbrella, pointed it at the bear and squeezed the handle. And guess what, the bear dropped dead."

"That's impossible," said the old man. "Someone else must have shot that bear."

"That's kind of what I'm getting at," said the doctor.

878 Doctor, doctor, I keep thinking I'm a pair of curtains.
     For heaven's sake, woman, pull yourself together.

879 Doctor, doctor, I feel like a pack of cards.
     I'll deal with you later.

880 Doctor, doctor, I've only got 59 seconds to live.
     Wait a minute, please.

881 Doctor, doctor, I think I've swallowed a pillow.
     How do you feel?
     A little down in the mouth.

882 Doctor, doctor, I can't control my aggression.
     How long have you had this problem?
     Who wants to know?

883 Doctor, doctor, I've swallowed the film from my camera.
     We'll just have to see what develops.

884 Doctor, doctor, I'm a manic depressive.
     Calm down, cheer up, calm down, cheer up, calm down . . .

885 Doctor, doctor, I can't pronounce my Fs, Ts or Hs.
     Well, you can't say fairer than that, then.

886 Doctor, doctor, I keep thinking I'm a piece of chalk.
     Get to the end of the cue.

887 Doctor, doctor, my leg hurts. What can I do?
     Limp.

888   Doctor, doctor, my son swallowed a razor blade.
Don't panic, I'm coming right away. Have you done anything yet?
Yeah, I shaved with an electric razor.

889   Doctor, doctor, I can't stop singing "The Green Green Grass of Home."
That's what we doctors call Tom Jones' Syndrome.
Oh, really? Is it common?
It's not unusual.

090   Doctor, doctor, I have a split personality.
Nurse, bring in another chair.

891   Doctor, doctor, I keep thinking I'm a clock.
OK, relax. There's no need to get yourself wound up.

892   Doctor, doctor, I think I'm a bridge.
What's come over you?
Two cars, a truck and a coach.

893   Doctor, doctor, my hair keeps falling out. What can you give me to keep it in?
A shoebox. Next.

894   Doctor, doctor, I think I'm a chicken.
How long has this been going on?
Ever since I was an egg.

895   Doctor, doctor, last night I dreamed I was a tepee. The night before, I dreamed
I was a wigwam.
Just relax — you're two tents.

896   Doctor, doctor, I've got a cricket ball stuck in my ear.
How's that?
Oh, don't start . . .

897   Doctor, doctor, I keep thinking I'm a bell.
If the feeling persists, give me a ring.

898   Doctor, doctor, I have a serious memory problem. I can't remember a thing.
How long have you had this problem?
What problem?

899 Doctor, doctor, I think I'm a moth.
Get out of the way, you're in my light.

900 Doctor, doctor, I get so nervous and frightened during driving tests.
Don't worry, you'll pass eventually.
But I'm the examiner!

901 Doctor, doctor, people keep ignoring me.
Next!

902 Doctor, doctor, what's good for excessive wind?
A kite.

903 Doctor, doctor, people tell me I'm a wheelbarrow.
Don't let them push you around.

904 Doctor, doctor, I think I'm shrinking.
Well, you'll just have to be a little patient.

905 Doctor, doctor, my wife thinks she's a lift.
Tell her to come in.
I can't. She doesn't stop at this floor!

906 Doctor, doctor, I can't stop stealing things.
Take these pills for a week and if they don't work, I'll have a colour TV.

907 Nurse: "Doctor, there's an invisible man in the waiting room."
Doctor: "Tell him I can't see him."

908 Doctor: "We need to get these people to a hospital."
Nurse: "What is it?"
Doctor: "It's a big building with lots of doctors, but that's not important now!"

909 A woman went to the doctor's office with a strawberry in her ear.
The doctor said: "I've got some cream for that."

910 A man wasn't feeling well so he went to the doctor. The doctor asked him what he ate.
"Well, doctor," said the man, "for breakfast I have two pool balls – one

yellow, one purple. For lunch I have two more pool balls – a blue and a white. And for dinner I have two reds and two blacks."

"I'm not surprised you're not well," said the doctor. "You're not having enough greens."

911 At an out-of-town medical convention which both were attending, a male medic got chatting to a pretty woman. He asked her to dinner and they went to a smart restaurant. Before and after dinner, she made a point of washing her hands. The dinner was a great success and she invited him back to her hotel room. She slipped into the bathroom to wash her hands and then they made love. After sex, she washed her hands again.

When she returned, he said: "I bet you're a surgeon."

"Yes, I am. How did you know?" she asked.

"Because you're always washing your hands."

She said: "And I bet you're an anaesthetist."

"That's right. How did you guess?"

"Because I didn't feel a thing."

912 The doctor said to the patient: "I want you take your clothes off and stick your tongue out of the window."

"What will that do?"

"Not much. But I hate my neighbour!"

913 A doctor was woken at four o'clock in the morning to make a house call. With great reluctance, he got dressed and stepped out into a terrible snowstorm. After examining the patient, the doctor told him to send immediately for his lawyer, friends and relatives and to make a will.

When the doctor got home, he told his wife what he had done.

"Why, was the man that bad?" asked the wife.

"No," said the doctor, "I just didn't want to be the only one called out on such a filthy night."

914 The doctor put a stethoscope to the patient's chest. The patient said: "Doc, how do I stand?"

The doctor replied: "That's what puzzles me."

915 A man went to the doctor because he thought he watched too much TV. The doctor asked: "What are the symptoms?"

The man replied: "A yellow cartoon family."

916 A patient told the doctor: "That medicine you prescribed makes me walk like a crab."

"Ah," said the doctor. "Those will be the side effects."

917 An elderly patient went to the doctor. "I need help, doctor. Do you remember those voices in my head which I've been complaining about for years?"

"Yes."

"Well, they've suddenly stopped."

"That's good. So what's the problem?"

"I think I'm going deaf."

918 A woman went to the doctor and complained that she felt constantly exhausted.

"How often do you have sex?" asked the doctor.

"Every Monday, Wednesday and Friday," replied the woman.

"Well, perhaps you should cut out Wednesdays."

"I can't – that's the only night I'm home with my husband."

919 When a pipe burst in a doctor's house, he was forced to call the plumber. The plumber came over, fiddled around for half an hour and presented the doctor with a bill for 600 dollars.

"600 dollars for half an hour's work! This is ridiculous! I don't even make that much as a doctor!"

The plumber replied: "Neither did I when I was a doctor."

920 Doctor to patient: "I've got some bad news and I've got some very bad news."

Patient: "You'd better let me have the bad news first."

Doctor: "The results of your tests have come back and they say you've only got 24 hours to live."

Patient: "Only 24 hours. Gee. That's terrible. It's no time at all. What's the very bad news?"

Doctor: "I've been trying to reach you since yesterday."

921 Doctor to patient: "I'm afraid you're dying."

Patient: "How long have I got?"

Doctor: "Ten . . ."

Patient: "Ten what? Ten months, Ten weeks, Ten days . . . ?"

Doctor: "Ten, nine, eight, seven . . ."

Dogs

922 A blind man was walking along the street with his guide dog when it suddenly stopped and cocked its leg against the blind man's leg. Immediately, the blind man felt in his pocket, produced a biscuit and fed it to the dog.

A passer-by was amazed at what she had just witnessed. "In view of what the dog just did to you," she told the blind man, "that was an incredible act of kindness."

"Nonsense," said the blind man. "I only did it to find out which end of the dog to kick!"

923 Outside of a dog, books are a man's best friend; inside of a dog, it's too dark to read. (GROUCHO MARX)

924 A meek little man walked into a bar and said: "Does anyone own that rottweiler outside?"

"Yeah, I do," said a big, burly biker, rising to his feet. "What about it?"

"Well, I think my chihuahua just killed him."

"What are you talking about?" snarled the biker. "How could your puny little chihuahua kill my mighty rottweiler?"

"It seems she got stuck in your dog's throat."

925 John saw Bill studying a chess board. Opposite him sat a dog.

"What's going on?" asked John.

"Just playing chess with my dog," answered Bill.

"You're kidding!" exclaimed John. "Whoever heard of a dog that could play chess? That's the smartest dog I've ever seen."

"Oh, I don't know about that," said Bill, "I've beaten him three games out of four."

926 A woman went into an exclusive pet store and asked for a tartan sweater for her dog. The sales assistant suggested it would be better to bring the dog in for a proper fitting.

"I can't do that!" said the customer. "The sweater is a surprise!"

927 Where do you find a dog with no legs? – The same place you left him.

928 What do you call a dog with no legs? – It doesn't matter, he won't come anyway.

929 What has four legs and one arm? – A pit bull leaving a playground.

930 What's the difference between a poodle humping your leg and a pit bull humping your leg? – You let the pit bull finish.

931 What do you do when a pit bull is humping your leg? – Fake an orgasm.

932 There's a new breed of dog – a pit bull crossed with a collie. It bites your leg off, then goes for help.

933 A boy called on his girlfriend at her tenth-storey apartment in readiness for their date. While she was getting dressed, he played ball in the lounge with her small dog. Unfortunately the door to the balcony was open and when the ball bounced out the door and over the ledge of the balcony, the little dog followed it.

A few moments later, the girl appeared. The boy said: "Have you noticed your dog has been acting depressed lately?"

934 Did you ever walk in a room and forget why you walked in? I think that's how dogs spend their lives. (SUE MURPHY)

935 A corgi went to the job centre to look for work and the man behind the desk was delighted. "A talking dog!" he enthused. "I'll fix you up with a job in no time."

After a few minutes on the phone, he declared: "There you are, you start at the circus on Monday."

"That's no good to me," protested the corgi. "I'm a plumber."

936 A Christian fundamentalist couple went shopping for a pet which adhered to Christian fundamentalist principles. They heard about a kennels which specialized in devoutly religious dogs and were shown one particular dog that could perform religious tricks. When asked to fetch the bible, it did so immediately. And when ordered to look for Psalm 23, it pawed its way through the pages until it found the relevant passage. The couple were most impressed and bought the dog.

That evening, a friend came to visit. "Does your dog do ordinary tricks?" she asked.

The couple were unsure but decided on a test. So they issued the standard command of "Heel". Instantly the dog jumped up, put one paw on the man's forehead, closed its eyes in concentration and bowed its head.

937 A little man walked into a bar with a dachshund under his arm. "Look at that silly dog," sneered a burly guy with a rottweiler. "Look at that long nose and those stumpy little legs. That's the ugliest dog I've ever seen."

"Yeah?" said the little man bravely. "But he's real mean."

"Don't make me laugh! I'll bet you 50 dollars my rottweiler can finish him off in two minutes."

"OK. You're on."

The dachshund and the rottweiler lined up nose to nose, and the dachshund suddenly lunged forward and bit the rottweiler in half. The rottweiler owner couldn't believe it. "What kind of a dog is that?" he growled.

"Well, before I cut off his tail, he was an alligator."

938 Why do dogs always race to the door when the doorbell rings? – Because it's hardly ever for them. (HARRY HILL)

939 A talent scout walking down the street noticed an accordionist with a singing puppy. The scout immediately saw the potential of such an act and took them to his office to sign them up. "I'll have you playing in Vegas within a month," he promised. But just as they were about to put pen to paper, a big dog marched into the office, picked the puppy up by the scruff of its neck and ran off with it.

"My act! You've stolen my act!" screamed the talent scout. "What can we do?"

"Nothing," said the accordionist. "That was his mother. She doesn't want him to be an entertainer. She wants him to be a doctor."

940 What do you get if you cross a malamute with a pointer? – A moot point.

941 A man went to the vet to collect his sick dog. The vet came in carrying the dog and said: "I'm really sorry, but I'm going to have to put your dog down."

The man burst into tears. "Why?"

"Because he's too heavy."

942 Two dogs were walking down the street when one suddenly crossed the road, sniffed a lamp post for a minute, then crossed back again.

"What was that all about?" asked the other dog.

"Just checking my messages."

943 A young girl loved to walk her dog after school but when the dog came on heat, the girl's father advised her that it would be best to keep the pet indoors for a few days. However, the girl was so distraught that the father felt he had to come up with a solution. So he sprayed some gasoline on the dog's rear end to deter any male dogs.

The girl took her pet out as usual but came home half an hour later without the dog.

"Where's Trudy?" asked the father.

"Oh," replied the girl, "she ran out of gas a few blocks back and is being pushed home by another dog."

944 A dog is not intelligent. Never trust an animal that's surprised by its own farts. (FRANK SKINNER)

945 Did you ever notice when you blow in a dog's face he gets mad at you? But when you take him in a car he sticks his head out the window. (STEVE BLUESTONE)

946 First woman: "My dog is so smart that every morning he waits for the paper boy to come round and then he takes the newspaper and brings it to me."
Second woman: "I know."
First woman: "How?"
Second woman: "My dog told me."

947 Entering a small country store, a stranger saw a sign saying "Beware of the dog". He looked round but all he could see was a harmless old dog lying fast asleep on the floor next to the counter. The stranger said to the store manager: "Is that the dog folks are supposed to beware of?"
"Yep."
"Well, he doesn't look dangerous to me. Why did you put the sign up?"
"Cos people kept tripping over him."

You know you're a dog person when:
948 Poop has become a source of conversation for you and your partner.
949 You can't see out the passenger side of the car windscreen because there are nose-prints all over the inside.
950 You think being told you have "dog breath" is a compliment.
951 You have 29 different names for your dog.
952 You carry dog biscuits in your pocket at all times.
953 You keep eating even after finding a dog hair in your pasta.
954 You put an extra blanket on your bed so your dog can be comfortable.
955 You have a paddling pool in the garden, but no children.

956 Your licence plate is FID O.

957 You match your clothes to the colour of your dog.

958 The only picture on your office desk is one of your dog.

959 Your friend's dog acts as Best Dog at your wedding.

960 Your freezer mainly contains bones.

961 You've changed your name by deed poll to Jack Russell.

962 You use your dog's brush on your own hair.

963 Your house isn't carpeted – the fuzzy furballs under your feet are soft enough.

964 You own at least six squeaky hedgehogs.

965 A German shepherd dog went to a Western Union office, took out a blank form and wrote "Woof, woof, woof, woof, woof, woof, woof, woof, woof."

The clerk studied the form and said: "There are only nine words here. You could send another 'woof' for the same price."

The dog said: "But that would be silly."

966 I wonder if other dogs think poodles are members of a weird religious cult. (RITA RUDNER)

967 A dog applied for a job as a high-powered secretary. The advertisement stated that the successful applicant must have good keyboard skills, a command of shorthand, and be able to speak a second language. The interviewer sat the dog at the computer and watched in Amazement as the animal performed the most complex functions, including spreadsheets and e-mail. Then he gave the dog dictation and was impressed by the hound's ability to write 120 words a minute in immaculate shorthand.

"Well," he said at the end of the interview, "it looks as if the job's yours. There's just one thing though. What about the second language?"

To which the dog replied, "Miaow!"

968 I poured spot remover on my dog. Now he's gone. (STEVEN WRIGHT)

969 Two men – one with a doberman pinscher, the other with a chihuahua – were hoping to gain admission to a restaurant despite the "No dogs" sign on the door.

"There's no way we'll get in," said the man with the chihuahua.

"You watch me," said the doberman owner. "I bet I can get in if I pretend to be blind." With that, he put on a pair of dark glasses and went up to the doorman.

"No pets allowed," said the doorman.

"But this is my guide dog," protested the man.

"A doberman?" queried the doorman.

"Yes, they're using them now."

"Well, OK, come on in."

With his friend safely inside, the chihuahua owner tried the same trick. He put on a pair of dark glasses and went up to the doorman.

"No pets allowed," said the doorman.

"But this is my guide dog."

"A chihuahua?" said the doorman in disbelief.

"A chihuahua?" repeated the man. "They gave me a chihuahua?"

970 Did you hear about the cowboy who got himself a dachshund . . . because everyone kept telling him to get a long, little doggie.

971 Three kids saw a dog riding on the front seat of a fire truck which was racing along the road with its siren going. Each wondered what the dog was doing there.

"I think he's there to keep onlookers away from the fire," said the first.

"I think he's there to bring the firemen good luck," said the second.

The third said: "I reckon he's there to find the hydrant!"

972 Dogs are the leaders of the planet. If you see two life forms, one of them's making a poop, the other's carrying it for him, who would you assume is in charge? (JERRY SEINFELD)

973 Why aren't dogs good dancers? – Because they've got two left feet.

974 A guy walked into a bar with a dog under his arm and bet anyone present 100 dollars that his dog could talk. The bartender took up the challenge. The owner looked at the dog and asked: "What is on the top of this building to prevent the rain coming in?"

The dog answered: "Roof."

"Are you kidding?" said the bartender. "I'm not falling for that."

"OK," said the dog owner. "How about double or quits? I'll ask him another question: who was the greatest baseball player of all time?"

The dog answered: "Roof."

"Right, that's it," said the bartender, and he threw them both out into the street.

As they bounced on the sidewalk, the dog looked at the owner and said: "DiMaggio?"

975 Two dogs walked over to a parking meter. One said to the other: "How do you like that? Pay toilets!"

976 No animal should ever jump up on the dining-room furniture unless absolutely certain that he can hold his own in the conversation. (FRAN LEBOWITZ)

977 Three men and a dachshund were sitting at a table playing poker. The stakes were high and an onlooker was amazed to see the dachshund win two hands in a row.

"That's incredible," said the onlooker, "I've never seen such a smart dog."

"He ain't that smart," whispered one of the players. "Whenever he gets a good hand, he wags his tail."

978 A boy was riding along the street in a home-made cart pulled by a dog with a rope attached to the dog's genitals. On the side of the cart the boy had written "POLICE".

A passer-by watched with interest. When the cart stopped, he told the boy: "You know, your police car would go faster if you tied the rope around your dog's neck."

"I know," said the boy, "but I wouldn't get the cool siren."

979 What's the difference between a businessman and a warm dog? – The businessman wears a suit, the dog just pants.

980 A woman watched a dog go into a butcher's shop.

"What is it today?" asked the butcher. "Pork?"

The dog shook its head.

"Beef?"

The dog shook its head.

"Lamb chops?"

The dog wagged its tail furiously.

The butcher wrapped up two lamb chops, gave them to the dog and the dog trotted out. The same thing happened the following day and the woman was so intrigued she decided to follow the dog out of the shop. She saw the dog walk up the steps to a house, stand on his hind legs and ring the doorbell with his nose. A man answered the door and immediately started shouting angrily at the dog.

The woman was incensed. "You should be ashamed of yourself," she told the man. "That is the cleverest dog I've ever seen. He goes to the butcher's, fetches your dinner, brings it home and rings the doorbell. And you treat him like that!"

"Maybe," said the man, "but it's the third time this week he's forgotten his key."

Drunks

981 A man spent six hours in a bar before rolling home to his wife blind drunk. "Where have you been?" she demanded.

"I've been to this amazing bar," he slurred, rocking on his feet. "It's called the Golden Saloon and everything there is golden. At the front there are two huge golden doors, the floors are golden and even the urinals are golden."

"What rubbish," snapped the wife. "I don't believe a word of it."

"Here," said the husband, rummaging in his pocket for a piece of paper. "Ring this number if you don't believe me."

So the following day she phoned the number on the slip of paper. "Is this the Golden Saloon?" she asked.

"It is," replied the bartender.

"Tell me," said the wife, "do you have two huge golden doors at the front of the building?"

"Sure do," said the bartender.

"And do you have golden floors?"

"Yup."

"What about golden urinals?"

There was a long pause and then the wife heard the bartender yell: "Hey, Duke, I think I got a lead on the guy that pissed in your saxophone last night!"

982 When I read about the evils of drinking, I gave up reading. (HENNY YOUNGMAN)

983 A cop stopped a drunk wandering along the street at five o'clock in the morning. The officer said: "Can you explain why you're out at this hour?"

The drunk replied: "If I could, I'd be home by now!"

984 A guy was swaying down the street when he saw two nuns approaching. As they reached him, they split, one walking to his left, the other to his right. The drunk then turned round, scratched his head and said: "How did she do that?"

985 One more drink and I'd be under the host. (DOROTHY PARKER)

986 Late at night, a drunk was on his knees beneath a street-light, evidently looking for something. A passer-by, being a good Samaritan, offered to help. "What is it you have lost?" he asked.

"My watch," replied the drunk. "It fell off when I tripped over the pavement."

The passer-by joined in the search but after a quarter of an hour, there was still no sign of the watch.

"Where exactly did you trip?" asked the passer-by.

"About half a block up the street," replied the drunk.

"Then why are you looking for your watch here if you lost it half a block up the street?"

The drunk said: "Because the light's a lot better here."

987 Alcohol is good for you. My grandfather proved it. He drank two quarts of booze every mature day of his life and lived to the age of 103. I was at the cremation – that fire would *not* go out! (DAVE ASTOR)

988 A man was sitting outside a bar enjoying a quiet drink when a nun started lecturing him on the evils of alcohol.

"How do you know alcohol is evil?" said the man. "Have you ever tasted it?"

"Of course not," answered the nun.

"Then let me buy you a drink and, afterwards, if you still believe that it's evil, I promise I'll never touch another drop."

"But I can't possibly be seen to be drinking," said the nun.

"Right. Well, I'll get the bartender to put it in a teacup for you."

The man went inside and asked for a beer and a vodka. "And would you mind putting the vodka in a teacup?"

"Oh no," said the bartender. "It's not that bloody nun again, is it?"

989 Two drunks were staggering home along the railway tracks.

The first said: "There's a hell of a lot of steps here."

The second nodded: "And this handrail is bloody low down!"

990 A little man walked into a bar and slipped on a pile of dog poo by the door. Moments later, a burly biker came in and slipped on it as well.

The little man said: "I just did that."

And the biker hit him.

991 My favourite drink is a cocktail of carrot juice and whiskey. I'm always drunk but I can see for miles. (ROY "CHUBBY" BROWN)

992 A drunk rolled into a bar, but the bartender refused to serve him. "You've had too much to drink," he said. "I'm not serving you."

Five minutes later, the drunk came in again. The bartender stood firm. "There's no way I'm serving you more alcohol. You've had more than enough already."

Five minutes later, the doors opened and the drunk lurched in once more. "Look," said the bartender, "I'm not serving you. You're too drunk."

The drunk nodded. "I guess I must be, " he said. "The last two places said the same thing."

993 I saw a wino; he was eating grapes. I said, "Man, you have to wait!" (MITCH HEDBERG)

994 A wife was in bed with her lover when she heard her husband's key in the door. "Stay where you are," she said. "He's so drunk he won't even notice you're in bed with me."

Sure enough, the husband lurched into bed none the wiser, but a few minutes later, through a drunken haze, he saw six feet sticking out at the end of the bed. He turned to his wife: "Hey, there are six feet in this bed. There should only be four. What's going on?"

"Nonsense," said the wife. "You're so drunk you miscounted. Get out of bed and try again. You can see better from over there."

The husband climbed out of bed and counted. "One, two, three, four. You're right, you know."

995 I can't think of anything worse after a night of drinking than waking up next to someone and not being able to remember their name, or how you met, or why they're dead. (LAURA KIGHTLINGER)

996 A drunk staggered into a Catholic church and ended up in the confession booth. After a few moments, the priest said: "What do you need my son?"

The drunk asked: "Is there any paper on your side?"

997 A woman drove me to drink and I never even had the courtesy to thank her. (W.C. FIELDS)

998 A young stockbroker was unwinding in a bar after a hard week's work. He was in the mood for a bit of fun and so he announced: "If anyone can drink 20 pints of Guinness, I'll give them 150 dollars."

The bartender lined up the 20 pints on the bar, but there were no immediate takers. Without saying a word, one man got off his stool, popped out, came back a few minutes later and declared that he could drink all 20. And to everyone's amazement he did.

The stockbroker handed over the money and asked the man where he had nipped out to.

"Well," he said, "first I had to go to the bar next door to make sure I could do it!"

999 They're trying to put warning labels on liquor saying, "Caution, alcohol can be dangerous to pregnant women." That's ironic. If it weren't for alcohol, most women wouldn't even be that way. (RITA RUDNER)

1000 A man rolled home drunk to find his wife waiting for him. "What do you think you're doing coming home half drunk?" she bellowed.

"Sorry, honey," he replied. "I ran out of money."

1001 A pair of London businessmen staggered out of a company party in New York. Colin crossed the street while Neville stumbled into a subway entrance. When Colin reached the other side, he saw Neville emerging from the subway stairs.

"Where have you been?" slurred Colin.

"Dunno," said Maurice. "But you should see the train set that guy has got in his basement!"

1002 You're not drunk if you can lie on the floor without holding on. (DEAN MARTIN)

1003 A drunk guy walked up to a parking meter and put in a quarter. He stared at the needle that had stopped at 60 and exclaimed: "Jesus, I can't believe I lost 100 pounds!"

1004 A guy went out drinking every night of the week before coming home drunk at midnight to a frosty welcome from his long-suffering wife. She was telling a friend about how unbearable the atmosphere was becoming between herself and her husband, and the friend suggested she try a different tack. She advised that instead of haranguing him when he got in, she should treat him with compassion.

That night, the husband staggered in late as usual but this time he was greeted with a friendly kiss. She sat him in his favourite chair, brought him his slippers and made him a nice cup of tea. He could hardly believe it. Where were the insults and accusations? After a while she said: "It's getting late now, dear. I think we'd better go upstairs to bed."

"We might as well," slurred the husband. "I'll be in trouble when I get home anyway."

1005 I was in a bar the other night, moving from stool to stool, trying to get lucky – but there wasn't gum under any of them. (EMO PHILIPS)

1006 Two guys were sitting in a bar in Dublin when one turned to the other and said: "You see that chap over there? Don't you think he looks just like me?"

The man went over to his doppelganger and said: "Excuse me, but I couldn't help noticing that you're a dead ringer for me."

"You're right, I do look like you."

"Where are you from?"

"Dublin."

"Me too."

"Which street?"

"Kilfoyle Road."

"Kilfoyle Road? That's incredible. That's my road too. What number?"

"76."

"76. I don't believe it. Me too. What are your parents' names?"

"Joe and Kitty."

"Joe and Kitty. Unbelievable. So are mine."

Just then, the bartenders changed shifts. "Anything happened?" said the new bartender.

"Nothing much," said the old one. "Oh, except the Murphy twins are drunk again."

1007 What do American beer and a rowing-boat have in common? – They're both close to water.

1008 Without question, the greatest invention in the history of mankind is beer. Oh, I grant you that the wheel was also a fine invention, but the wheel does not go nearly as well with pizza. (DAVE BARRY)

1009 A drunk guy was driving the wrong way down a one-way street. A cop pulled him over and said: "Didn't you see the arrows?"

"Arrows? I didn't even see the Indians!"

1010 A guy in a bar ordered two shots of vodka. He drank the first and poured the second over his right hand. Then he ordered another two shots of vodka, drank one and tipped the other over his right hand. After watching the guy do the same thing for a third time, the bartender asked: "Why do you keep wasting good drink?"

The guy slurred: "I have to get my date drunk."

1011 I drink to make other people interesting. (DAVE BARRY)

1012 A drunk was carrying a box with holes in the side when he bumped into an old friend. "What have you got there?" asked the friend, pointing to the box.

"A mongoose," replied the drunk.

"Why have you got a mongoose?"

"Well, you know I sometimes get a bit drunk. And when I do, I see snakes. And I'm scared to death of snakes. So I've got this mongoose for protection."

"But those snakes are imaginary."

"That's OK," said the drunk. "So is this mongoose."

Elephants

1013 What do you call two elephants on a bicycle? – Optimistic.

1014 How do you know if there's an elephant in your fridge? – Footprints in the butter.

1015 Why did the elephant paint his toenails different colours? – So he could hide in a dish of M & Ms/Smarties.

1016 Why didn't the elephant cross the road? – Because he didn't want to be mistaken for a chicken.

1017 How do you get down from an elephant? – You don't, you get down from a duck.

1018 What did Tarzan say when he saw 500 elephants coming over the hill? – "Look, there's 500 elephants coming over the hill."

1019 What did Tarzan say when he saw 500 elephants in sunglasses coming over the hill? – Nothing, he didn't recognize them.

1020 How do you know if there's an elephant under your bed? – Your nose is touching the ceiling.

1021 How do you know if there's an elephant in your bed? – By the "E" on his pyjamas.

1022 What do you call someone who treats elephants' skin complaints? – A pachydermatologist.

1023 What has two grey legs and two brown legs? – An elephant with diarrhoea.

1024 What do you give an elephant with diarrhoea? – Plenty of room.

1025 A man bought an old circus elephant but couldn't afford its upkeep. So he decided to raise money by organizing a contest with a first prize of 30,000 dollars. Entry was 10 dollars a head and the prize was for anyone who could make the elephant jump four feet in the air. People came from far and wide to try and win the 30,000 dollars, but nobody was able to persuade the elephant to jump until a Texan pulled up in a stretch limo. Taking a baseball bat from the vehicle, he proceeded to whack the elephant hard in the nuts. The poor elephant jumped four feet in the air and the Texan claimed the 30,000 dollars.

Sadly, the event had failed to attract sufficient entrants to cover the prize money and so the elephant's owner arranged another contest. This time he offered 30,000 dollars to anyone who could get the elephant to swing its head back and forth as if it were saying "no". Once again, nobody proved successful until the Texan in the stretch limo appeared on the scene.

"Remember me?" said the Texan, stepping from the car.

The elephant nodded a worried-looking "yes".

The Texan held up the baseball bat. "Want me to use this again?"

The elephant took one look at the bat and swung its head from side to side . . .

1026 What would you get if you crossed an elephant with a fish? – Swimming trunks.

1027 How does an elephant hide in the jungle? – He paints his privates red and climbs up a cherry tree.

1028 What is the loudest noise in the jungle? – A giraffe eating cherries.

1029 How do you know if you pass an elephant? – You can't get the lavatory seat down.

1030 Why are elephants wrinkled? – Have you ever tried to iron one?

1031 What is more difficult than getting an elephant in the back seat of your car? – Getting a pregnant elephant in the back seat of your car.

1032 What is more difficult than getting a pregnant elephant in the back seat of your car? – Getting an elephant pregnant in the back seat of your car.

1033 What do you get when you cross an elephant with a hooker? – A two-ton pick-up.

1034 An elephant was drinking from a river one day when he spotted a turtle asleep on a log. Without any warning, he went over and kicked the turtle right across to the other side of the river.
"Why did you do that?" asked a passing zebra.
"Because," said the elephant, "I recognized it as the same turtle that nipped me on the trunk 44 years ago."
"Wow!" exclaimed the zebra. "What a memory."
"Yes," said the elephant. "Turtle recall."

1035 What is grey and white on the inside and red on the outside? – An insideout elephant.

1036 What is grey and white on the inside and red and white on the outside? – Campbell's Cream of Elephant soup.

1037 What is grey, has large ears, a trunk, and squeaks? – An elephant wearing new shoes.

1038 What has two tails, two trunks and five legs? – An elephant with spare parts.

1039 Why do elephants drink so much? – To try to forget.

1040 What do you get when you cross an elephant with a kangaroo? – Great big holes all over Australia.

1041 What do elephants have for lunch? – An hour, like everyone else.

1042 What do you get if an elephant sits on your best friend? – A flat mate.

1043 The elephants were playing the ants at soccer. It was a close match but when the ants' star player dribbled towards goal, an elephant defender lumbered over towards him, trod on him and killed him.

"What did you that for?" demanded the referee.

"I didn't mean to kill him," said the elephant. "I was just trying to trip him up."

1044 What was the elephant doing on the motorway? – About 5 mph.

1045 Why can't two elephants go into the swimming pool at the same time? – Because they've only got one pair of trunks.

1046 How can you tell if an elephant is sitting behind you in the bathtub? – You can smell the peanuts on his breath.

1047 What is the red stuff between elephants' toes? – Slow pygmies.

1048 An ant and an elephant shared a night of passion but in the morning the ant awoke to find that the elephant had died. "Damn," sighed the ant. "One night of passion and I spend the rest of my life digging a grave!"

England

1049 A foreign visitor to England was completely baffled by the language and struggled with the pronunciation of words such as "enough", "bough" and "though". He finally gave up altogether when he read a local newspaper headline: "FETE PRONOUNCED SUCCESS."

1050 If an Englishman gets run down by a truck, he apologizes to the truck. (JACKIE MASON)

1051 Julia Roberts, an Englishman and a Frenchman were all sitting in the same train compartment. Nothing much happened until the train went into a tunnel. Through the darkness could be heard the sound of a loud slap and a cry of pain. When the train emerged from the tunnel, Julia Roberts and the Englishman were sitting perfectly normally, but the Frenchman was rubbing his cheek and nursing a swollen eye.

Julia immediately thought: "The Frenchman must have tried to kiss me when we went in the tunnel, but kissed the Englishman by mistake and got a slap for his pains."

The Frenchman thought: "The Englishman must have tried to kiss Julia and she slapped me by mistake."

And the Englishman thought: "This is great. Every time we go into a tunnel, I can smack that French prat!"

1052 We know Jesus wasn't English because he wore sandals – but never with socks. (LINDA SMITH)

1053 An Italian, a Frenchman and an Englishman were sitting in a hotel lounge.

Suddenly the Italian announced: "I made love to my wife four times last night. This morning she told me how much she loved me."

"Pah!" scoffed the Frenchman "That is nothing. Last night I made love to my wife six times. This morning she told me I was the world's greatest lover and that she could never go with another man."

The Englishman was quietly reading his paper. The Frenchman turned to him and said smugly: "And how many times did you make love to your wife last night?"

"Once," said the Englishman.

"Only once?" snorted the Frenchman. "And what did she say to you this morning?"

"Don't stop."

1054 Erith isn't twinned with anywhere, but it does have a suicide pact with Dagenham. (LINDA SMITH)

Sure signs that you're English:

1055 You treat anybody foreign with suspicion.

1056 You never leave home without an umbrella.

1057 You haven't been to the Millennium Dome.

1058 On holiday in Spain, you search for a bar that serves roast beef.

1059 You think Marty Wilde was every bit as good as Elvis.

1060 You have little sense of rhythm.

1061 You understand the rules of cricket.

1062 You care about the rules of cricket.

1063 You think dried pig's blood is a delicacy.

1064 You're still mentally at war with Germany, France, Scotland, the American colonies, the Danes, the Celts, the Vikings, the Romans.

1065 You think the weather is a more exciting topic of conversation than baseball.

1066 You don't expect any form of public transport to run on time.

1067 You think sarcasm is the highest form of wit.

1068 You think France begins and ends at the Calais hypermarket.

1069 You have a proverb to cover any eventuality.

Excuses

1070 A woman saw an electrician walking up her drive. She rushed to the door. "Why have you come today?" she barked. "You were supposed to repair the doorbell yesterday."

"Yes, I know," said the electrician. "I rang three times but there was no answer, so I thought you must be out."

1071 A traffic cop pulled over a guy who was driving erratically. "Blow into this breathalyzer tube, please," he ordered.

"Sorry, officer, I can't," replied the driver. "I'm asthmatic. If I do that, I'll have a bad asthma attack."

"OK, come to the station and give a blood sample."

"Sorry, officer, I can't. I'm haemophilic. If I do that, I'll bleed to death."

"Well then we'll need a urine sample."

"Sorry, officer, I can't. I'm diabetic. If I do that, I'll get really low blood sugar."

"All right. Then I need you to step out of your car and walk along this white line."

"Sorry, officer, I can't."

"Why not?"

"Because I'm drunk."

1072 "Do you believe in life after death?" the company boss asked one of his young employees.

"Yes, sir."

"That's good, because after you left early yesterday to go to your grandmother's funeral, she called in to see you."

1073 Did you hear about the office worker who ran out of sick days, so he called in dead?

1074 A woman was in bed with her husband's best friend when the phone rang. After hanging up, she turned to her lover and said: "That was Jim, but don't worry, he won't be home for a while. He's playing cards with you."

1075 A driver was speeding down the highway late in the afternoon when he saw a police car behind. For a while he tried to out-race his pursuer, but, after touching 120 and still not managing to shake him off, he realized it was a lost cause and pulled over.

The cop stepped out of his car. "Listen, buddy," he said. "I've had a really lousy day and all I want to do is get home to my wife and kids. So if you can come up with a good excuse as to why you were doing 120 back there, I'll let you off."

The driver thought for a moment and said: "Three weeks ago, my wife ran off with a cop. When I saw you in my rear-view mirror, I thought you were that officer and that you were trying to hand her back."

Excuses to offer for being asleep at the office:

1076 They told me at the blood bank that this might happen.

1077 Damn. Why did you interrupt me? I'd almost figured out a solution to our problem.

1078 My entire family was wiped out last night by machine-gun wielding burglars, and I didn't get much sleep afterwards.

1079 I must have left the top off the correction fluid.

1080 I was testing the keyboard for drool-resistance.

1081 I was trying to pick up my contact lens without using my hands.

1082 This is in return for the six hours last night when I dreamed about work.

1083 I was psyching myself up for the rest of the day.

1084 I was doing a highly specific yoga exercise to relieve work-related stress.

1085 The mailman flipped out and pulled a gun, so I was playing dead to avoid getting shot.

Families

1086 An 18-year-old boy came home excitedly one night and announced: "Janie and me are getting married."

His father's face fell. He took the boy to one side and said: "I'm sorry, son, you can't marry Janie. When I was first married to your mother, I'm afraid I fooled around a lot. You see, Janie is your half-sister."

The boy was devastated and it took him six months to start dating again. But a year on, he came home with more good news. "Kirsty and me are getting married."

His father's face dropped. Once again he took the boy to one side and explained: "I'm sorry, son, you can't marry Kirsty. She's your half-sister too."

The boy ran to his room in tears. Later his mother came up to comfort him.

"Dad's done a lot of bad things," sobbed the boy. "He keeps saying I can't marry the girl I love."

"Oh, don't pay any attention to him," she said. "He's not your real father."

1087 Why are families like a box of chocolates? – They're mostly sweet, with a few nuts.

1088 "That wife of mine is a liar," confided a husband to his best friend.

"How do you know?"

"Because she didn't come home last night, and when I asked her where she'd been, she said she'd spent the night with her sister Emma."

"So?"

"So she's a liar. I spent the night with her sister Emma!"

1089 My dad is Irish and my mum is Iranian, which basically means we spent most of our family holidays in customs. (PATRICK MONAHAN)

1090 A French husband and wife were travelling through Eastern Europe with the wife's aged aunt. The old woman had been a pain in the butt from the word go, complaining about everything – the food, the hotels, the weather, the people. Finally she went too far and insulted a small nation's queen. As a result, all three members of the family were sentenced to corporal punishment in the form of 50 lashes. However, because the nation did not wish to be viewed as hostile to foreign visitors, the queen agreed that each be granted a wish before receiving the punishment.

The wife said: "I would like a pillow to be bound to my rear end." The pillow was tied in place and the wife received her 50 lashes.

Next it was the aunt's turn. Seeing her niece's pain, she said: "I would like two pillows – one to be bound to my rear end and one to be bound to my back." The pillows were tied in place and the aunt received her 50 lashes.

Finally it was the husband's turn. "I have two wishes, if that is possible," he said.

"That is acceptable," said the chief of police. "I am empowered by her royal highness to grant you two wishes. What are your wishes?"

"Firstly, I would like to be given 100 lashes instead of 50."

"Are you sure? That is a most unusual request."

"I am certain. I definitely want 100 lashes."

"And what is your second wish?"

"I want my mother's aunt to be bound to my back."

Farming

1091 An American and an Irishman met at a farming convention in Kilkenny. The American owned a huge farm back in Texas while the Irishman had no more than a couple of acres outside Wexford.

"Tell me about your farm," said the Irishman.

"It's enormous," began the American, "the biggest farm you ever did see in your life. It stretches halfway across the county. Do you know I can get in my truck first thing in the morning, drive around my land and still not cover it all by sundown?"

"To be sure," said the Irishman, "I used to have a truck like that."

1092 Why do they bury farmers only three feet deep? – So they can still get a hand out.

1093 A farmer was sitting in a bar one afternoon, getting slowly drunk. A man came over to talk to him.

"You look down," said the man. "It's a beautiful day. How can you be miserable on a day like this?"

The farmer mumbled: "Some things you just can't explain."

"Come on, tell me about it," said the man. "It might help to talk to someone."

"If you really want to know," said the farmer, "I was sitting in the barn this morning milking my cow and I'd just got the bucket full when she kicked it over with her left leg."

"Is that all? It's not exactly the end of the world."

"Some things you just can't explain," mumbled the farmer.

"So what did you do?"

"I took her left leg and tied it to a post on the left with some rope. Then I carried on milking. And just as I'd got the bucket full again, she kicked it over with her right leg."

"I can see that would be annoying."

The farmer mumbled: "Some things you just can't explain."

"So what did you do next?"

"I tied her right leg to the post on the right and carried on milking. And just as the bucket was filling up, she knocked it over with her tail."

"You must have been angry by now?"

"Some things you just can't explain," mumbled the farmer.

"What did you do?"

"I didn't have any more rope, so I took off my belt and tied her tail to the rafter. At that moment, my pants fell down and my wife walked in. Some things you just can't explain."

1094 A young farmhand was sent out in a truck to do some repair work on a fence. It should only have taken him an hour and the farmer became concerned when, after two hours, he still hadn't returned. Just then, the farmer's mobile phone rang.

"I'm on the way back but I've hit a pig," said the farmhand.

"Don't worry," said the farmer. "These things happen. But drag the carcass off the road so that nobody else hits it."

"But he's not dead," said the farmhand. "He's kicking and squealing. I'm afraid he's gonna hurt me."

"OK then," said the farmer. "There's a shotgun in the back of the truck. Fetch that, shoot the pig and drag the carcass off the road. Understand?"

"Yeah, I understand."

Half an hour later, the farmer's mobile rang again.

"I'm still stuck," said the farmhand.

"Why?" asked the farmer. "Did you shoot the pig and drag the carcass off the road like I said?"

"Yeah, I did, but his motorcycle is still jammed under the truck?"

1095 Two snowmen in a field. One looked at the other and said: "Can you smell carrots?"

1096 Why was the farmer hopping mad? — Because someone stepped on his corn.

1097 A visitor to a farm spotted a pig with only three legs. He said to the farmer: "Why don't you put it out of its misery and have it put down?"

The farmer drew a deep breath, shook his head and said: "Let me tell you about that pig. One night last year, the house caught fire and the pig ran through the house and woke everyone up. Thanks to the pig, we all got out safely. Then last month my tractor overturned and that pig went to get help. He saved my life."

"I understand," said the visitor, "but look at him — he can hardly walk. Wouldn't it be kinder to take him to a vet and have him put to sleep?"

"Listen, buddy," snapped the farmer. "If you had a pig that was that smart, would you eat him all at once?"

1098 A man walked apprehensively into a field containing a bull. Spotting the farmer on the other side of the fence, he asked: "Is this bull safe?"

"He's as safe as can be," replied the farmer, "but I can't say the same for you."

1099 An old rooster had ruled the farm for years but just lately he hadn't been performing to standard. Fewer chicks were being born than ever before. So the farmer decided that the bird was past his best and bought a strutting young rooster to replace him. "This should keep the hens happy," announced the farmer as he introduced the handsome newcomer.

The old rooster was furious and was determined not to give up without a fight. So he challenged the youngster to a race of three laps of the yard.

"OK, you're on," said the young rooster. "I can outrun you any day of the week."

"If you're so confident," replied the old rooster, "you won't mind giving me a head start. After all, your legs are much younger than mine."

"No problem," crowed the young rooster. "You can have half a lap start and I'll still beat you."

The race began with the old rooster hotly pursued round the yard by his younger rival. Hearing the commotion, the farmer ran to investigate. Seeing the two roosters, he immediately picked up his rifle and shot the younger bird dead.

"Damn," groaned the farmer. "That's the third gay rooster I've bought this month."

Fashion

1100 "If you really loved me, you'd buy me a nice mink," said the wife sulkily.

"All right," groaned the husband, "I'll buy you a mink if it's that important to you, but only on one condition."

"Condition? What kind of condition?"

"You have to keep its cage clean!"

1101 Some women hold up dresses that are really ugly and they always say the same thing: "This looks much better on." On what? On fire? (RITA RUDNER)

1102 A woman in church one Sunday morning suddenly had a terrible coughing fit. Afterwards a friend said to the woman's husband: "I felt really sorry for Jean having that bout of coughing, and the way everyone turned to look at her."

"Don't worry," said the husband. "She was wearing a new hat."

1103 My dad's pants kept creeping up on him. By 65 he was just a pair of pants and a head. (JEFF ALTMAN)

1104 How can you get four suits for a dollar? – Buy a pack of cards.

1105 A man bought his wife a fur coat made from hamsters. He took her to Blackpool for the day and she spent six hours on the big wheel.

1106 The judge glared at the accused: "So you admit breaking into the dress shop?"

"Yes, your honour."

"And why was that?"

"Because my wife wanted a dress."

The judge consulted his notes. "But it says here that you broke into the same shop four nights in a row."

"Yes, sir. She made me exchange it three times."

1107 Did you hear about the secondhand Indian clothing store called Whose Sari Now?

Clothes not to wear at an interview for an office job:

1108 A suit of armour.

1109 Camouflage combat jacket and trousers.

1110 A Hannibal Lecter T-shirt.

1111 The national costume of Holland.

1112 Prison uniform.

1113 A Richard Nixon mask.

1114 A pink satin jump suit (if you're a man).

1115 Scuba diving gear.

1116 A Big Bird costume.

1117 Anything dripping in blood.

1118 A guy was walking along the street wearing only one shoe. A woman went up to him and asked: "Have you just lost a shoe?"

"No, I've just found one."

1119 I saw a woman wearing a sweatshirt with "Guess" on it. I said, "Thyroid problem?" (EMO PHILIPS)

1120 A teenage boy with spiked hair, a nose ring and baggy combat trousers told his friend: "I don't really like dressing like this, but it stops my parents dragging me everywhere with them."

1121 A wife said to her husband: "Darling, I really need a new dress."
"Why? What's wrong with the one you've got?"
"Well, it's too long and, besides, the veil keeps getting in my eyes."

1122 A wife was throwing out some old clothes for a charity jumble sale when she reached into the pocket of one of her husband's old suits and discovered a shoe repairer's ticket. She showed the ticket to her husband.
"This ticket must be 20 years old," he said. "I must have forgotten to collect those shoes. That shop is still there so I'll take the ticket in and see whether they've still got my shoes."
So he went back to the shoe shop with the ticket. The sales assistant said: "They'll be ready Thursday."

1123 My daughter wanted some trainers. I said, "You're eleven. Go to Taiwan and make some." (JEREMY HARDY)

1124 A young man went to a lake for a swim but when he got there, he realized he had forgotten his swimming trunks. Since there was nobody about, he decided to jump in naked. An hour later, he climbed out and was just about to get dressed when he saw two old ladies approaching. He hastily grabbed a small bucket, held it over his privates and breathed a huge sigh of relief. But when the old ladies started to stare at him, he felt decidedly awkward.
One said to him: "You know, I have a special gift. I can read minds. And I bet I can read yours."
The young man scoffed: "So you reckon you know what I'm thinking, do you?"
"Yes," she said. "Right now, I bet you think that the bucket you're holding has a bottom."

Ways to tell someone their fly is unzipped:
1125 The gate is open but the beast is asleep.
1126 The cucumber has left the salad.
1127 Your soldier ain't so unknown now.
1128 Quasimodo needs to go back in the tower and tend to his bells.
1129 Elvis Junior has left the building.
1130 You've got a security breach at Los Pantalones.
1131 You've got your fly set for "Monica" instead of "Hillary".

1132 Don't spend two dollars to dryclean a shirt. Donate it to the Salvation Army instead. They'll clean it and put it on a hanger. Next morning buy it back for 75 cents.

1133 If high heels were so wonderful, men would still be wearing them. (SUE GRAFTON)

1134 A woman tried to board a bus but her skirt was so tight that she couldn't make the step up. So she reached behind her, lowered her zip and tried again. Still the skirt was too tight. So again she reached behind her, lowered her zip a little more and tried to negotiate the step. But still the skirt was too tight. Determined to catch this bus, she once more reached behind her, lowered the zip a little and attempted to climb aboard. Then suddenly she felt two hands on her butt which helped her on to the bus. She turned around angrily and told the man behind her: "Sir, I don't know you well enough for you to behave in such a manner."

The man replied: "Lady, I don't know you well enough for you to unzip my fly three times either!"

1135 I was with my wife and she was reading a magazine and she showed me a photograph of a fur coat. She said: "I'd like that." So I cut it out and gave it to her. (TOMMY COOPER)

1136 A man walked into an army surplus store and asked if they had any camouflage trousers.

"Yes, we have," said the sales assistant, "but we can't find them!"

Fish and fishing

1137 Two fish are in a tank. One says to the other: "Can you drive this thing?"

1138 It was a bitterly cold winter day. A man went fishing and cut a hole in the ice, but didn't catch a thing. Then a young boy came along, cut a hole in the ice nearby and proceeded to catch fish after fish. Eventually the man went over to the boy and said: "I've been here six hours and haven't caught one fish. Yet you've been here 45 minutes and you've caught at least ten. What's your secret?"

The boy replied: "Roo raf roo reep ra rurms rarm."

"Sorry," said the man. "I didn't catch that."

"Roo raf roo reep ra rurms rarm."

"I'm sorry. I can't understand a word you're saying."

The boy spat a wad of ugly brown slime into his hand and said: "You have to keep the worms warm!"

1139 A man was skulking around in his back garden digging a hole. His neighbour decided to investigate.

"What are you doing?" he asked.

The man replied: "My goldfish died and I'm burying him."

"That's an awfully big hole just for a goldfish, isn't it?" said the neighbour.

The man shouted back: "That's because he's inside your cat."

1140 What do you call a fish without an eye? — A fsh.

1141 How did they know the man eaten by a shark had dandruff? — They found his head and shoulders on the beach.

1142 Young Kenny burst into the house crying after a day out fishing with his dad. His mother asked him what was wrong.

The boy explained: "Dad and I were fishing and he hooked this giant fish, the biggest he'd ever seen. But while he was reeling it in, the line broke and the fish got away."

"Come on, Kenny," she said, "a big boy like you shouldn't be crying about an accident. You should have just laughed it off."

"But that's just what I did, Mum."

1143 A man went into a fish shop carrying a trout under his arm. "Do you make fishcakes?" he asked.

"Yes, we do," replied the fishmonger.

"Great," said the man. "It's his birthday."

1144 Why don't oysters give to charity? — They're shellfish.

1145 What did the fish say when he ran into a wall? — "Dam!"

1146 On fishing shows they always throw the fish back. They don't want to eat them — they just want to make them late for something. (MITCH HEDBERG)

1147 A woman walked into a bait and tackle shop to find a blind man serving behind the cash desk. She asked for a fishing line for her husband but, taking advantage of the blind man's disability, craftily slipped a 70-dollar reel into her bag. The blind man was just starting to ring up her purchase when the phone rang. It was the store manager who had positioned himself behind a one-way mirror at the back counter.

The manager whispered into the phone: "The lady whose purchase you are ringing up just put a 70-dollar reel into her bag. Don't make a big deal about it, but just make sure you charge her for it."

The blind man put down the phone and told the woman: "That'll be 4 dollars 50 for the line and 70 dollars for the reel."

The woman was so embarrassed at being caught out that she passed wind loudly.

The blind man continued: "And that'll be 2 dollars 50 more for the Duck Call and a dollar for the Musk Scent!"

Florida

1148 Sophie and Daphne – two elderly widows in Florida – were curious about the latest arrival in their apartment block. He was a quiet, distinguished gentleman who seemed to believe in keeping himself to himself.

One day, Daphne said: "Sophie, you know I'm shy. Why don't you catch him at the pool and find out a little more about him? He looks so lonely."

So Sophie went over to talk to the man as he was sitting beside the pool. "My friend and I were wondering why you look so lonely," she said.

"Of course I'm lonely," he answered. "I've spent the past 20 years in prison."

"Oh, why?"

"I strangled my third wife."

"Oh. What happened to your second wife?"

"I shot her."

"And what about your first wife?"

"We had a fight and she fell off a building."

"Oh, my." Then Sophie turned to her friend on the other side of the pool and called out: "Yoo hoo, Daphne! It's OK. He's single!"

1149 Florida: God's waiting room. (GLENN LE GRICE)

1150 A little old lady was sitting directly behind the bus driver on a journey from Miami. After 15 minutes, she tapped the driver on the shoulder and said: "Are we at Orlando yet?"

He said: "No, lady. I'll tell you when we are."

Fifteen minutes later, she tapped him on the shoulder again. "Are we at Orlando yet?"

"No, lady," he snapped. "I'll tell you when we are."

This went on every 15 minutes so that by the time they eventually arrived in

Orlando, he was close to throttling her. And so it was with great delight that he announced: "This is Orlando. Out you get, lady."

"Oh, no," she said, "I'm going all the way to Jacksonville. It's just that before we set off, my daughter told me that when we got to Orlando, I should take my blood pressure pill."

1151 My parents didn't want to move to Florida, but they turned 60, and that's the law. (JERRY SEINFELD)

Food and drink

1152 Scientists have discovered a food that diminishes a woman's sex drive by 90 per cent — wedding cake.

1153 A family were given some venison by a friend. The wife cooked the deer steaks and served them up for dinner.

"What is this?" asked their young daughter. "Is it beef?"

"No," said the father.

"Is it pork?" said their young son.

"No," said the father. "I'll give you a clue. It's what Mum sometimes calls me."

"Spit it out, sis," yelled the boy. "We're eating asshole!"

1154 Why did the raisin go out with the prune? — Because he couldn't find a date.

1155 An American woman travelling in south-east Asia was horrified to be served bird's nest soup.

"Do you mean to say this actually is a bird's nest?" she protested.

The chef assured her that it was, explaining that the bird built the nest using its own saliva as glue.

"Are you saying I'm supposed to eat saliva from a bird?" she demanded. "I can't imagine anyone eating bird's saliva."

Realizing that there was no hope of converting her, the chef asked what she would prefer instead. She answered: "Oh, just fix me an omelette."

1156 What's 50 metres high and made of dough? — The Leaning Tower of Pizza

1157 What's smelly, round and laughs? — A tickled onion.

1158 Did you hear about the man who died in a bowl of muesli? He was pulled under by a strong currant.

1159   A man went into a butcher's and asked: "Do you keep dripping?"
"Yes," said the butcher, "and it's very embarrassing."

1160   Two students were talking about cooking. "I got a cookbook a couple of years back," said one, "but I could never do anything with it."
"Was it too demanding?" asked his friend.
"Absolutely. Every one of the recipes began the same way – 'Take a clean dish.' "

1161   Rice is great when you're hungry and want 2,000 of something. (MITCH HEDBERG)

1162   Did you hear about the guy who was half-French, half-pygmy? He was a great cook, but he could never reach the grill.

1163   Two tomatoes were walking across the street, one in front of the other. The first tomato was getting impatient because the second one was so slow. Then halfway across, the second tomato was run over by a car. The first tomato shouted: "Hey, ketchup."

1164   How does Good King Wenceslas like his pizzas? – Deep pan, crisp and even.

1165   I put instant coffee in a microwave and almost went back in time. (STEVEN WRIGHT)

Signs that you're drinking too much coffee:
1166   You get a speeding ticket even when you're parked.
1167   You haven't blinked since the last lunar eclipse.
1168   You grind your coffee beans in your mouth.
1169   Your eyes stay open when you sneeze.
1170   The nurse needs a scientific calculator to take your pulse.
1171   You can jump-start your car without cables.
1172   You have a picture of your coffee mug on your coffee mug.
1173   Cocaine is a downer.
1174   You go to AA meetings just for the free coffee.
1175   Your nervous twitch registers on the Richter scale.
1176   You don't tan, you roast.
1177   You walk 20 miles on your treadmill before you realize it's not plugged in.
1178   Your birthday is a national holiday in Brazil.

1179 A millionaire was driving along in his stretch limo when he saw a humble man eating grass by the roadside. Ordering his driver to stop, he wound down the window and called to the man: "Why are you eating grass?"

"Because, sir, we don't have the money for real food."

"Come with me then," said the millionaire.

"But, sir, I have a wife, two sisters and six children."

"That's fine – bring them all along."

The man and his family climbed into the limo. "Sir, you are too kind. How can I ever thank you for taking all of us with you, offering us a new home?"

"No, you don't understand," said the millionaire, "the grass at my home is 4 feet high. No lawn mower will cut it."

1180 Why did the baby strawberry cry? – Because his mother was in a jam.

1181 Wife: "The two things I cook best are meatloaf and apple pie."
Husband: "Which is this?"

1182 I never eat on an empty stomach. (TALLULAH BANKHEAD)

1183 When he and his mother returned home from the supermarket, the small boy pulled out the box of animal crackers he'd begged for and emptied them on the counter.

"What are you doing?" asked his mother.

The boy replied: "The box says you can't eat them if the seal is broken. I'm looking for the seal."

1184 Why did the tomato blush? – Because it saw the salad dressing.

1185 What's the difference between roast beef and pea soup? – Anyone can roast beef.

1186 Ever wonder about those people who spend 2 dollars a time on little bottles of Evian water? Try spelling Evian backwards.

1187 I drank some boiling water because I wanted to whistle. (MITCH HEDBERG)

1188 Boy: "Are caterpillars good to eat?"
Father: "I've told you before: don't talk about such things at the dinner table."

Mother: "Anyway, why do you ask?"
Boy: "Cos I saw one on Daddy's lettuce, and now it's gone."

1189 What do you call cheese that isn't yours? – Nacho Cheese.

1190 What is Snow White's favourite drink? – 7 Up.

1191 I'm not saying my wife is a terrible cook, but our garbage disposal has developed an ulcer. (HENNY YOUNGMAN)

1192 Three tortoises went on a picnic. It took them ages to crawl to a suitable spot and when they eventually got there, they realized that they had forgotten the chocolate biscuits. The two older tortoises turned to the youngest and said: "Will you pop home and fetch the biscuits?"
"Why me?" he asked.
"Because you've got younger legs."
After much persuasion, he relented, but only on condition that they didn't start drinking the Coca-Cola until he returned.
"We promise not to touch a drop," they said.
So the young tortoise set off on the long crawl back home. After two hours, the others were gasping for a drink and so they took out the bottle of Coke. As they did so, a little head peered round a nearby rock and said: "If you do, I won't go."

1193 The most remarkable thing about my mother is that for 30 years she served nothing but leftovers. The original meal was never found. (TRACEY ULLMAN)

1194 Two carrots were walking down the road when one was hit by a truck. It was taken to hospital and rushed in for an emergency operation. After an anxious six hours, the surgeon came out and told the other carrot: "Your friend will live, but I'm afraid he's going to be a vegetable for the rest of his life."

Football (American)

1195 A college football coach addressed a newcomer to the team and said: "Look, I know I'm not supposed to let you play since you failed maths, but we really need you on the team. I'm gonna do a deal with you: if you can answer one simple maths question, you can play. OK?"
The newcomer nodded.
"Right," said the coach. "What's two plus two?"

The new boy thought for a moment and answered "Four."

Before the coach could say anything, the rest of the team started screaming: "Oh come on, coach, give him another chance."

1196 After spending all day watching football on TV, a man fell asleep and spent the night in the chair. His wife woke him in the morning.

"It's twenty to seven," she called.

"In whose favour?"

1197 A football fan had a lousy seat at the stadium, offering a really bad view. But through his binoculars he spotted an empty seat on the 50-yard line and so he made his way there. When he got there, he asked the man in the next seat whether the empty seat was taken.

"This is my wife's seat," he replied solemnly. "She passed away. She was a big Packers fan."

"I'm terribly sorry to hear of your sad loss. May I ask why you didn't give the ticket to a friend or a relative?"

"They're all at the funeral."

1198 A huge college freshman decided to try for the football team.

"Can you tackle?" asked the coach.

"Watch this," said the freshman who proceeded to run smack into a telegraph pole, shattering it into splinters.

"Wow!" exclaimed the coach. "Can you run?"

"Of course I can run," said the freshman. He was off like a shot and did 100 metres in just over ten seconds.

"Great!" enthused the coach. "But can you pass a ball?"

The freshman rolled his eyes and hesitated for a moment. "Well, sir," he replied, "if I can swallow it, I can probably pass it."

1199 Bowing to political correctness and pressure from Native Americans, the Washington Redskins have changed their name. They will now be known as the Washington Tampons — a name chosen because the team is good for only one period and doesn't have a second string.

1200 Three men died and went to heaven where St Peter quizzed each one.

"What's your IQ?" St Peter asked the first man.

"210."

"Maybe we can discuss the theory of relativity some time." St Peter turned to the second man. "What's your IQ?"

"170."

"Maybe we can discuss quantum mechanics some time." St Peter turned to the third man. "What's your IQ?"

"40."

"Hey, how about those San Francisco 49ers?"

1201 A wife was watching the television news and said to her husband: "Did you hear that? A man in Baltimore swapped his wife for a season ticket to Colts' games. Would you do a thing like that?"

"Heck, no. The season's half over!"

1202 A wife was having an affair with the TV repair man. She complained: "My husband never pays any attention to me – all he's ever bothered about is watching the football game on TV. That's why we've got the biggest set in the neighbourhood – so he can watch the game."

Just then, she heard a key in the front door. Her husband had arrived home unexpectedly. She said to her lover: "Quick, hide in the back of the TV."

So the lover hid in the TV while the husband sat down to watch the football game. After ten minutes, it became so hot and uncomfortable in the back of the TV set that the lover climbed out, walked straight past the husband and out of the front door.

The husband turned to his long-suffering wife and said: "Hey, honey, I didn't see the referee send that guy off, did you?"

1203 Why did the hopeless football team change their name to the Opossums? – Because they play dead at home and get killed on the road.

1204 A sportswriter was interviewing a college football coach about his star player. "He's great on the field," said the writer, "but how's his scholastic work?"

"He makes straight As," said the coach.

"That's terrific!"

"Yes, but his Bs are a little crooked."

Golf

1205 A young man went for a round of golf with a girl he liked from work. Beforehand, he slipped into the professional's shop and bought a couple of golf balls which he put in his pocket. When he met the girl on the first tee, she couldn't help noticing the bulge in his pocket.

"It's only golf balls," he explained.

"Oh, I'm sorry," she replied. "Is it something like tennis elbow?"

1206 A golf nut met the Pope on a trip to Rome. "Your Holiness," he said, "I'm crazy about golf. I play every day of the year. But, tell me, is there a golf course in heaven?"

"I'm not sure," said the Pope. "I'll have to ask God."

A few days later, the man bumped into the Pope again. "Any news from God about the golf course in heaven?" he asked.

"Oh, yes," replied the Pope. "Apparently there is a beautiful course in heaven with velvet-smooth greens and lush fairways. The bad news is you have a tee time for tomorrow morning."

1207 Give me my golf clubs, fresh air and a beautiful partner, and you can keep my golf clubs and the fresh air. (JACK BENNY)

1208 A guy from out of town visited a golf club and was paired up with Joe, one of the members. Playing left-handed, the visitor shot a round of two under par. Joe thought this was a remarkable score for a strange course and saw the potential for making money from bets. So he asked the visitor whether he was available to play at ten o'clock the following morning.

"Yes," he said, "but I may be two minutes late."

Next day the visitor turned up on the dot of ten and, this time playing right-handed, helped Joe to victory over another pair and the 200 dollars which was riding on the result. Joe was amazed at the visitor's ambidextrous play and asked him whether he was available for another money match, at eleven the next day.

"Certainly," he replied, "but I may be two minutes late."

The next day the visitor arrived on the stroke of eleven and, reverting to playing left-handed, helped Joe to another win and another 200 dollars. As they celebrated in the bar afterwards, Joe said: "I notice you are equally good playing left- and right-handed. How do you decide which to play?"

"It's simple. If my wife is sleeping on her left side when I wake up in the morning, I play left-handed. If she's sleeping on her right side, I play right-handed."

"What if she's sleeping on her back?"

"That's when I'm two minutes late."

1209 "I'd move heaven and earth to break 100," puffed the rookie golfer as he thrashed away at the ball in deep rough.

"Try heaven," advised his playing partner. "I think you've already moved enough earth."

1210 The other day I broke 70. That's a lot of clubs. (HENNY YOUNGMAN)

1211 Phil and Dave went for a game of golf one Saturday afternoon, but Phil was under strict instructions from his wife to be back by four o'clock because she wanted him to take her shopping. Four o'clock passed, so did five o'clock and six o'clock. Eventually Phil arrived home at seven.

"Where on earth have you been?" she screamed.

"Honey," said Phil, "a terrible thing happened. We made it to the first green when Dave dropped dead of a heart attack."

The wife felt guilty. "That's awful," she said.

"You're telling me," said Phil. "The rest of the round it was hit the ball, drag Dave, hit the ball, drag Dave . . ."

1212 Two golfers went to see the professional at their club. "Can you give me any tips?" asked one of the men as he stood on the practice ground.

The professional said: "You're standing too close to the ball."

The man's partner added: ". . . After you've hit it."

1213 Four married guys went away on a golfing weekend. On the second fairway, they began discussing the problems they'd had getting permission from their wives.

The first said: "I had no end of trouble getting away. I had to promise my wife I'll paint the whole house next weekend."

The second said: "It was no easier for me. I've had to promise my wife I'll go shopping with her next weekend."

The third said: "I know what you mean. I've promised my wife she can have a new fitted kitchen."

The fourth guy said: "It was no problem for me. I just set my alarm for 5.30 this morning. When it went off, I gave my wife a nudge and said: 'Golf course or intercourse?' And she said: 'Don't forget your sweater.'"

1214 After a long day on the course, an exasperated golfer turned to his caddie and said: "You must be the worst caddie in the world."

"I don't think so," replied the caddie. "That would be too much of a coincidence."

1215 A keen golfer stood trial for killing his wife. After initially denying the offence, he finally broke down in court and admitted his guilt.

"How did you kill her?" asked the judge.

"With three strokes of a five-iron."

"Three strokes?" queried the judge.

"Yes. On the first two, I lifted my head."

1216 Finding his ball in deep rough, a golfer took an almighty swing, but struck nothing more than a divot. He swung again, missed the ball again and got another big chunk of turf. Just then, two ants climbed on to the ball, saying: "Let's get up here before we get killed!"

1217 A golfer was poised over his tee shot for ages. "For goodness sake, hurry up!" said his partner.

"But my wife is watching from the clubhouse. I want to make this a perfect shot."

"Forget it – you'll never hit her from here!"

1218 A preacher was an avid golfer and couldn't help sneaking off to play a round one Sunday. An angel watching him from above was furious and told God: "Look at that preacher down there, abandoning his duties to play golf on a Sunday. He should be punished."

God agreed and promised to act. A few minutes later, the preacher hit a superb hole-in-one on a 350-yard hole. The angel rounded on God: "I thought you were going to punish him! Instead he's just hit a perfect hole-in-one."

God smiled: "Think about it – who can he tell?"

Why golf is better than sex:

1219 A below par performance is considered good.

1220 You can stop in the middle for a cheeseburger and a couple of beers.

1221 It's much easier to find the sweet spot.

1222 Foursomes are encouraged.

1223 You can have a golf calendar on your office wall without being accused of harassment.

1224 You can still make money doing it as a senior.

1225 You don't have to sneak golf magazines into the house.

1226 Three times a day is possible.

1227 There's no such thing as a golf-transmitted disease.

1228 If you want to watch golf on TV, you don't have to subscribe to a premium cable channel.

1229 If your equipment gets old and rusty, you can replace it.

1230 If you are having trouble with golf, it is perfectly acceptable to pay a professional to show you how to improve your technique.

1231 Nobody ever tells you that you'll go blind if you play golf by yourself.

1232 When dealing with a golf pro, you never have to worry if he/she is really an undercover cop.

1233 A man had been stranded on a desert island for ten years and in that time hadn't seen another living person. Then one day, to his amazement, a gorgeous blonde stepped out of the sea wearing a wet suit and scuba diving gear. She walked over to him and started caressing his beard. "How long is it since you last had a cigarette?" she asked.

"Ten years," he gasped.

She slowly unzipped a waterproof pocket on her left sleeve and produced a packet of cigarettes and a box of matches. He lit the cigarette and sighed: "I've been desperate for a cigarette. This is fantastic."

When he had finished the first cigarette, she said: "And how long is it since you last tasted whisky?"

"Ten years," he replied.

And she slowly unzipped the waterproof pocket on her right sleeve and brought out a bottle of whisky.

"Gee, this is great," he said, drinking half of the bottle. "I'd forgotten how good whisky tasted."

Then she began to unzip the long fastening at the front of her wet suit and purred seductively: "How long is it since you had some real fun?"

The man could hardly believe his luck. "Don't tell me you've got a set of golf clubs in there!"

1234 Golfer: "This is the worst golf course I've ever played on."

Caddie: "This isn't the golf course, sir. We left that half an hour ago!"

How golf is like urinating in a public restroom:

1235 Keep your back straight, knees bent, feet shoulder width apart.

1236 Form a loose grip.

1237 Keep your head down.

1238 Avoid a quick backswing.

1239 Stay out of the water.

1240 Try not to hit anybody.

1241 If you are taking too long, you should let others go ahead of you.

1242 You shouldn't stand directly in front of others.

1243 Be quiet while others are about to go.

1244 Keep strokes to a minimum.

1245 A London street market trader went for his first game of golf. His partner hit a wayward drive on the first tee and shouted "Fore".

"Three ninety-five," yelled the market trader instinctively.

1246 A couple were out playing golf when the husband hit a wayward tee shot into a greenhouse. His wife dutifully held the greenhouse door open for him so that he could play back on to the fairway, but the husband sliced his shot, the ball hit his wife on the temple and killed her instantly.

Fifteen years later, the widower was playing with a friend when his wayward tee shot landed in the same place in the same greenhouse. The friend held the greenhouse door open for him and dared him to play the shot.

"No way," said the widower. "I tried that shot 15 years ago and I ended up taking a triple bogey."

1247 St Peter and God were playing golf. St Peter teed off first and hit a beautiful drive straight down the centre of the fairway. Then it was God's turn, but he hit a terrible drive which was heading towards the deep rough until, from nowhere, a squirrel caught his ball and dropped it in the middle of the fairway. Then amazingly a bird swooped down, picked up God's ball, flew towards the green and dropped it in the hole for a hole in one.

St Peter turned to God and said: "Are we gonna play golf or are we gonna piss about?"

1248 I never kick my ball in the rough or improve my lie in a sand trap. For that I have a caddie. (BOB HOPE)

1249 "Why don't you play golf with Jim any more?" the wife asked her husband.

"Would you play with someone who moves his ball to a better lie when no one is looking, who deliberately coughs halfway through his opponent's backswing and who lies about his handicap?"

"Well, no," said the wife.

"Neither will Jim."

1250 During a frustrating round, a golfer said to his caddie: "Will you stop checking your watch all the time – it's distracting me."

The caddie replied: "It's not a watch – it's a compass."

1251 Asked what his handicap was, Sammy Davis Jr. replied: "I'm a coloured, one-eyed Jew. Do I need anything else?"

1252 A husband and wife were both keen golfers. The wife was feeling neglected and wanted to know how much he loved her.

"If I were to die tomorrow," she said, "and you remarried, would you give your new wife my jewellery?"

"What an awful thing to ask!" exclaimed the husband. "But no, of course not."

"And would you give her any of my clothes?"

"No, honey, of course not."

"What about my golf clubs?"

"No. She's left-handed."

1253 A man came home from a game of golf to be greeted by his young son.

"Daddy, Daddy," he cried, "did you win?"

"Well," explained the father, "in golf it doesn't matter so much if you win. But I tell you one thing – I got to hit the ball more times than anybody else."

1254 After a whirlwind romance, a couple were on their honeymoon when the guy announced: "Honey, I have a confession to make. I'm a golf nut. I play every weekend in the summer. You'll hardly see me."

The wife took a deep breath and said: "And I have a confession to make too. I'm a hooker."

"That's no big deal," said the husband. "Just keep your head down and your left arm straight."

1255 Standing on the first tee, a golfer said to his playing partner: "Why don't you try this ball – you can't lose it?"

"How do you mean, you can't lose it?"

"It's a special ball. If you hit into the woods, it beeps. If you hit it in water, it sends up bubbles, if it lands in deep rough, it emits a plume of smoke."

"Wow! That's fantastic. Where did you get it?"

"I found it."

1256 An employee went for a game of golf with his boss who owned a small white poodle. The dog always used to accompany its master on the course and every time the boss hit a good drive or sank a long putt, the poodle stood on its hind legs and applauded with its two front paws.

The employee was amazed. "What happens," he asked, "if you land in a bunker or miss a short putt?"

"Oh," said the boss, "the dog turns somersaults."

"How many?"

The boss replied: "Depends on how hard I kick him up the butt."

Grandparents

1257 A boy visited his grandmother with his friend. While the boy was talking to his granny in the kitchen, his friend was eating peanuts from a bowl on the living room table. When it was time to go, the friend called out: "Thanks for the peanuts."

"That's OK," said Granny. "Since I lost my dentures I can only suck the chocolate off 'em."

1258 A little boy said to his grandfather. "Make a frog noise for me, Grandad."

"No, son, I don't feel like making a frog noise right now."

"Oh, please, Grandad, make a frog noise."

"No, I don't want to."

"Oh, please, Grandad, make a frog noise."

"Why is it so important to you that I make a frog noise?"

"Cos Mum says when you croak we can go to Disneyworld."

1259 A little boy and his grandad were raking leaves in the garden. The boy saw an earthworm trying to get back into its hole.

"Grandad, I bet I can put that worm back in that hole."

"I'll bet you 5 dollars you can't. It's too wriggly and limp to put back in that little hole. You'll never get it in."

The boy went into the house, came back with a can of hairspray and sprayed the worm until it was straight and stiff. Then he stuffed the worm back into the hole.

His grandad gave him the 5 dollars and trotted indoors with a smile on his face. Thirty minutes later, he reappeared and gave his grandson another 5 dollars.

"But, Grandad, you already gave me 5 dollars."

"I know. That's from your Grandma."

1260 A man came home from work and noticed that his father seemed to be avoiding the grandchildren. "What's the problem?" he asked. "Normally you love playing with them."

The old man whisked a medicine prescription from his pocket and said: "Read that label. That's why!"

The son took the bottle and read the label: "Take two pills a day. KEEP AWAY FROM CHILDREN."

1261 Timmy was sitting at the tea table with his granny. They were chatting about television and comics when suddenly he asked: "How old are you, Grandma?"

"That's private, Timmy," she replied. "I'm not saying."

A few moments later, Timmy asked: "How much do you weigh, Grandma?"

"My, you are inquisitive!" said Grandma. "But I'm afraid I'm not going to tell you how much I weigh either. You see, it's personal."

The next day at school, Timmy recounted the conversation to his friends. They said if he wanted to find out how old his granny was and how much she weighed, he should look in her drivers' licence. So on his next visit to his grandmother's, Timmy sneaked a look at her drivers' licence. When they sat down for tea, he told her excitedly: "I know all about you now. You're 65 and you weigh 125 lb." Then he hesitated for a moment before whispering to her: "I also know you got an 'F' in Sex."

1262 A ten-year-old boy was stuck with his maths homework. "Grandpa," he pleaded, "could you help me with this?"

"I could," replied his grandfather, "but it wouldn't be right, would it?"

"I don't suppose it would, Grandpa," said the boy, "but have a shot at it anyway."

Hair

1263 A man went to the same hairdresser every month. The hairdresser had the annoying habit of belittling whatever the customer said. One month the customer said he had bought a new car.

"What sort?" asked the hairdresser.

"A BMW," replied the customer.

"Oh, you shouldn't have got a BMW," said the hairdresser. "You'd be much better off with a Ferrari. Much classier, more comfortable, better road-holding."

The following month the customer revealed that he had bought an executive house on a new development on the outskirts of town. "Oh, you don't want to move there," sneered the hairdresser. "It's miles from the shops. And there's no decent pubs. You see, they'll be giving those houses away soon."

At his next appointment, the customer said that he was going on holiday to Rome.

"What do you want to go to Rome for?" asked the hairdresser. "There's nothing much there. It's all ruins."

"Well," replied the customer patiently, "it's always been my ambition to meet the Pope and, if possible, to speak to him."

"No chance," laughed the hairdresser. "You won't get anywhere near him. I bet you £100 the Pope doesn't talk to you."

The customer was so fed up with the hairdresser's attitude that he accepted the bet. A month later he returned for his next haircut and was asked how he had got on in Rome.

"Don't forget our £100 bet," crowed the hairdresser. "You can pay by cheque."

"No, actually you owe me £100," said the customer. "The Pope did speak to me."

"How?" spluttered the hairdresser.

"Well," said the customer, "I was wandering around St Peter's Square one morning hoping to catch a glimpse of the Pope when, to my surprise, I saw him walking towards me. And to my amazement, he stopped beside me and started talking to me."

"What did he say?" asked the hairdresser.

"He said: 'Where on earth did you get that terrible haircut?' "

1264 There's one thing about baldness; it's neat. (DON HEROLD)

1265 Celebrating their silver wedding anniversary, the wife turned to her husband and said: "Will you still love me when my hair has gone grey?"

"Why not?" he replied. "Haven't I loved you through six other shades?"

1266 A guy went into a barber shop and said: "I want my hair cut so that it's all different lengths round the front and back, there's a strange spiky bit on top and bald patches here, here and here."

"I don't think I can do that," said the barber.

"Why not? You did last time I was here!"

1267 I recorded my hair this morning; tonight I'm watching the highlights. (JAY LONDON)

1268 A teenager had just passed his driving test and asked his father, who was a church minister, whether he could borrow his car.

"Yes, you may borrow my car, if you study the Bible, work hard at college and get your hair cut."

A month later, the lad asked again whether he could borrow the car.

His father said: "I'm very proud of you, son. You've been studying your Bible and your college results are excellent. But the only thing is, you haven't had your hair cut."

The lad replied: "I've been thinking about that. You know, Samson had long hair, so did Moses, Noah and even Jesus."

"That's very true," said his father. "And they walked everywhere."

1269 After being nicked twice by the barber's razor, the customer asked for a glass of water.

"Sorry, sir," said the barber. "Is there a hair in your mouth?"

"No, I want to see if my neck leaks!"

1270 A man and a boy entered a barber's shop together. After the man had received a shave and a haircut, he sat the boy in the chair and said: "I'm just popping to buy a packet of Corn Flakes from the supermarket. I'll be back in a few minutes."

When the boy's hair was cut and the man still hadn't returned, the barber said: "It looks like your dad's forgotten you."

"That wasn't my dad," said the boy. "He just walked up, took me by the hand and said, 'Come on, we're going to get a free haircut.'"

1271 My pubic hair is going grey. In a certain light you'd swear it was Stewart Granger down there. (BILLY CONNOLLY)

1272 A bald man sat down in the barber shop and said to the barber: "I went for a hair transplant, but I couldn't stand the pain. If you can make my hair look like yours without causing me any discomfort, I'll pay you 5,000 dollars."

So the barber quickly shaved his own head.

1273 A man on his first visit to a new barber shop remarked: "Your dog takes great interest in watching you cut hair."

"Yep," said the barber, "that's because sometimes I snip off a bit of a customer's ear."

Hallowe'en

1274 A married couple were invited to a masked Hallowe'en party. They were eagerly looking forward to it but at the last minute the wife cried off with a headache. However she didn't want to spoil her husband's fun and insisted that he went on his own. So he set off for the party in full costume.

After lying on the bed for an hour, the wife began to feel better and decided that she was well enough to go to the party after all. When she arrived, the party was in full swing. She quickly spotted her husband but chose to keep her presence a secret from him, something she was able to do since he had no idea what her costume was. Instead she preferred to observe him, to see how he behaved when he thought she wasn't around. She watched from afar as he flirted, kissed and danced with other women and then figured it was time to make a move on him herself, still without revealing her identity.

Disguising her voice, she sidled up to him and said: "Fancy a breath of fresh air?"

"Sure," he replied. "I know the very place."

And with that, he led her to his car where they had sex on the back seat.

Both returned to the party but shortly before the unmasking at midnight, she slipped home alone, removed her costume and went to bed. Waiting for her husband to come home, she wondered how he would manage to explain his behaviour at the party.

"How was it?" she asked when he finally arrived.

"Oh, you know I never have a good time when you're not there, darling."

"Did you dance?"

"No, not one dance. In fact, when I got there, I met a few mates and we went to the den and played poker all evening."

"Oh, yeah?" said the wife.

"But I tell you," he continued. "The guy I loaned my costume to sure had a good time!"

Health

1275 Health is what my friends are always drinking to before they fall down. (PHYLLIS DILLER)

1276 A woman went with her husband for his routine medical check-up. But afterwards the doctor took her to one side and said: "I'm afraid I have some bad news. Unless you adhere to a strict routine, your husband will die. Every morning, you must give him a good healthy breakfast and you must cook him a nutritional meal at night. Furthermore, you must not burden him with household chores and you must keep the house spotless and germ-free. I know it places a great deal of work on your shoulders, but it really is the only way to keep him alive."

On their way home, the husband asked his wife what the doctor had said to her.

"Oh," she replied, "he said you're going to die."

1277 I bought all those Jane Fonda videos. I love to sit and eat cookies and watch them. (DOLLY PARTON)

1278 What is the difference between herpes and true love? – Herpes lasts for ever.

1279 An overweight man went to the doctor who advised him to lose three stone. The doctor recommended that the man should run five miles every day for the next 100 days. The patient phoned the doctor exactly 100 days later.
"Have you lost the weight?" asked the doctor.
"I have," said the patient, "but I'm not at all happy with the situation."
"Why not?"
"Because I'm 500 miles from home!"

1280 I had Anthrax this week – diarrhoea, blood in the urine, the liver was disintegrating, and I found the only thing that really helped was Lemsip. Just took the edge off. (HARRY HILL)

1281 A man went to his local gym to ask about yoga classes for beginners.
The instructor asked: "How flexible are you?"
"Well," replied the man, "I can't do Wednesdays."

1282 I'm Jewish and I don't work out. If God had wanted us to bend over he'd put diamonds on the floor. (JOAN RIVERS)

1283 A man went to the optician's. "I keep seeing spots in front of my eyes."
Receptionist: "Have you seen a doctor?"
Man:"No, just spots."

1284 The left side of the brain is responsible for speech, but then it *would* say that, wouldn't it? (HARRY HILL)

1285 Have you heard about the disease found in soft butter? – Doctors say it spreads very easily.

1286 I hate people who think it's clever to take drugs . . . like customs officers. (JACK DEE)

1287 A puny bus driver pulled up at the stop and a giant of a man climbed on board. "Big John doesn't pay," said the man and marched straight to a seat. Given the difference in build between the two men, the driver was not about to argue.

The next day, the same thing happened. The man mountain got on the bus, glared at the driver and said: "Big John doesn't pay." And then he went to a seat.

This went on for several days, by the end of which the driver was starting to resent Big John's attitude. Why should he not pay when everyone else had to? So the driver went to the gym and began an intensive course of body-building so that he could stand up and face Big John like a man.

Two weeks later and with rippling muscles where there was once skin and bone, the driver looked forward to his daily encounter. At his usual stop, the colossal passenger got on and announced: "Big John doesn't pay."

But this time, the driver wasn't going to take it lying down. He rose to his feet and said: "Oh, yeah. And why doesn't Big John pay?"

The man reached into his inside pocket. The driver momentarily feared the worst. And the man said: "Because Big John got bus pass."

1288 A lady with a clipboard stopped me in the street and said, "Can you spare a few minutes for cancer research?" I said, "All right, but we're not going to get much done." (JIMMY CARR)

Ways of relieving stress:

1289 Jam miniature marshmallows up your nose and sneeze them out.

1290 Leaf through *National Geographic* and draw underwear on the natives.

1291 When someone tells you "have a nice day", tell them you have other plans.

1292 Dance naked in front of your pets.

1293 Write a short story using alphabet soup.

1294 Stare at people through the prongs of a fork and pretend they're in jail.

1295 Put your toddler's clothes on backwards and send him to pre-school as if nothing is wrong.

1296 Fill out your tax form using Roman numerals.

1297 Braid the hairs in each nostril.

1298 Tape pictures of your boss on watermelons and launch them from high places.

1299 Tattoo "Out to Lunch" on your forehead.

1300 Polish your car with earwax.

1301 Read the dictionary upside down and look for secret messages.

1302 Start a nasty rumour and see if you recognize it when it comes back to you.

1303 Invent a language and ask people for directions in it.

1304 Did you hear about the constipated accountant? – He couldn't budget.

1305 Did you hear about the constipated composer? – He couldn't finish his last movement.

1306 Did you hear about the constipated mathematician? – He worked it out with a pencil.

1307 My whole family is lactose intolerant; when we take pictures we can't say "cheese". (JAY LONDON)

1308 A bear, a lion and a chicken were discussing which of them was the scariest.
"When I snarl," said the bear, "the forest rumbles."
"When I roar," countered the lion, "the jungle trembles."
The chicken smiled: "And when I cough, the whole world shits itself!"

1309 Two gas company servicemen – one old, one young – were calling on houses in a neighbourhood, checking the meters. At the final house on their round, a lady watched through the window as they checked the meter. Their truck was parked at the end of the street and, to prove his fitness, the older man challenged the youngster to a race. As they ran to the truck, they were surprised to find the woman from the last house huffing and puffing right behind them.
"What's wrong?" they said.
She gasped: "When I saw two gas men running as hard as you, I figured I'd better run too!"

1310 The price of Prozac went up 50 per cent last year. When Prozac users were asked about it, they said, "Whatever." (CONAN O'BRIEN)

1311 Reason to be cheerful: statistics say that every seven minutes of every day, someone in an aerobics class pulls a hamstring.

1312 A man went into a drug store and asked the pharmacist if he could give him something for hiccups. Without warning, the pharmacist suddenly reached out and slapped the man hard across the face.
"What did you do that for?" asked the man indignantly.
"Well, you haven't got hiccups any more, have you?"
"I haven't got hiccups – my wife has!"

1313 The worst time to have a heart attack is during a game of charades. (DEMETRI MARTIN)

1314 What do aerobics instructors and people who process bacon have in common?
– They both tear hams into shreds.

1315 Why did the aerobics instructor cross the road? – Someone on the other side
could still walk.

1316 Is it fair to say there'd be less litter if blind people were given pointed sticks?
(ADAM BLOOM)

1317 First man: "I tried to kill myself yesterday by taking 1,000 aspirin."
Second man:"What happened?"
First man: "Oh, after the first two I felt better."

1318 You have to stay in shape. My grandmother, she started walking five miles a
day when she was 60. She's 97 today and we don't know where the hell she
is. (ELLEN DEGENERES)

1319 After receiving his medication from the pharmacist, the customer inquired:
"Are these time-release pills?"
"Yes," said the pharmacist. "They begin to work after your cheque clears."

1320 A sure cure for seasickness is to sit under a tree. (SPIKE MILLIGAN)

Heaven and hell

1321 A man died and went up to heaven where he was greeted by St Peter.
"And who are you?" asked St Peter.
"My name is Steven Richards."
"And what did you do for a living?" asked St Peter.
"I was unemployed."
"Unemployed, hmmm?" mused St Peter. "And have you ever done anything
good in your life?"
"As a matter of fact I have. I was walking along the street once and I saw a
group of bikers who were threatening to beat up a defenceless girl. So I rushed
to her rescue, pulled the ringleader off by his hair, kicked him hard where it
hurts and told him and his gang to clear off."
"That's highly commendable," said St Peter flicking through the man's file,
"but I can't see any report of this incident. When did it happen?"
"About five minutes ago."

1322 God was talking to one of his angels. He said: "I've just created a 24-hour period of alternating light and darkness on Earth."
  The angel said: "What are you going to do now?"
  And God replied: "I think I'll call it a day."

1323 St Peter became aware of a man pacing up and down outside the pearly gates. "Can I help you?" asked St Peter.
  The man looked at his watch impatiently. "No, it's OK. I won't be long."
  Five minutes later, St Peter looked out again and saw that the man still seemed agitated about something. "What is it?" asked St Peter.
  The man stopped his pacing. "Look," he said, "you know I'm dead; I know I'm dead. So will someone please tell the cardiac arrest team?"

1324 Maybe there is no actual place called hell. Maybe hell is just having to listen to our grandparents breathe through their noses when they're eating sandwiches. (JIM CARREY)

1325 To the horror of the locals, Satan suddenly appeared in the main street of a small town one Sunday morning. Everyone rushed indoors except for one old timer who calmly stayed on his porch reading a book. Satan was furious that this one person should not be afraid of him and went over to challenge him.
  "Are you scared of me?" screamed Satan at his most menacing.
  "Nope," said the old timer.
  "Aren't you terrified that I'm going to wreak havoc in your nice little community?"
  "Nope."
  By now steam was coming out of Satan's ears. He raged: "You do know who I am, don't you?"
  "Should do. Been married to your sister for 46 years."

1326 Two lovers who were interested in spiritualism and reincarnation promised that if either died, the survivor would try to contact the partner in the other world exactly 30 days after death. A few weeks after making this pact, the young man was killed in a car crash. Thirty days later, his sweetheart tried to contact him via a seance.
  "Can you hear me, Joel?" she wailed.
  A voice came back: "Yes, Lauren, this is Joel. I hear you."
  "Oh, Joel, it's so good to hear your voice. What is it like where you are?"
  "It's beautiful, Lauren. There are clear blue skies, a soft breeze and warm sunshine."

"What do you do all day, Joel?"

"Well, Lauren, we're up before sunrise, we eat a good breakfast, then it's nothing but sex till noon. After lunch, we sleep till two, then have sex till five. After dinner, we go at it again till we fall asleep around 11."

"Joel, is that what heaven is really like?"

"Heaven? I'm not in heaven. I'm a jack rabbit in Arizona."

1327 Three married couples — one Jewish, one Irish, one American — all died on the same day and arrived in heaven. St Peter was waiting at the gates to take down their names. After telling St Peter about all the good works he had done, the Jew told him that his wife's name was Penny.

"I'm sorry," said St Peter, "but I can't admit anyone with a name connected to money."

Next up was the Irishman. He too told St Peter of his many charitable works and said that his wife's name was Brandy.

"I'm sorry," said St Peter, "but I can't admit anyone with a name linked to alcohol."

Hearing all this, the American guy turned to his wife and said: "Fanny, I think we may have a problem."

1328 A nun, Sister Margaret, went to heaven, only to be told by St Peter that there was a waiting list.

"Go home and relax," suggested St Peter. "Give me a call in a week and I'll let you know whether your accommodation is ready."

The following week she phoned up and said: "Peter, this is Margaret. I have a confession to make: I had my first-ever cigarette yesterday. Will it affect my chances of getting into heaven?"

"I'm sure it won't," said St Peter. "But your room still isn't ready yet. Call me in a week."

A week later, she calls again. "Peter, this is Margaret. I have a confession to make: I had my first-ever alcoholic drink yesterday. Will it affect my chances of getting into heaven?"

"I'm sure it won't," said St Peter. "But your room still isn't ready. Call me in three days."

Three days later, she rings again. "Peter, this is Margaret. I have a confession to make: last night I kissed a man for the first time. Do you think it will wreck my chances of getting into heaven?"

"I shouldn't think so," said St Peter. "But give me a ring tomorrow. By then I'll have checked it out with the boss man and I'll know about your accommodation."

The next day, she phones again. "Pete, this is Meg, forget about the room."

1329 Hugh Hefner and Madonna died and went to heaven, but St Peter was wary about admitting them. He told Hefner: "You have corrupted people with your pornography and so you must pass a test if you wish to remain in heaven. You must walk along a 100-foot tunnel without thinking any unclean thoughts. If you should have an unclean thought while in the tunnel, a trap door will open and you will fall down to hell."

Hefner thought the test was fair and was confident of negotiating 100 feet without an impure thought. But halfway along, St Peter leaned towards him and said: "Tits". The trap door opened and Hefner plunged down to hell.

Then St Peter turned to Madonna. He said: "You have corrupted people with your provocative clothes and videos and so you must pass the same test if you wish to remain in heaven. You must walk along a 100-foot tunnel without thinking any unclean thoughts. If you should have an unclean thought while in the tunnel, a trap door will open and you will fall down to hell."

Madonna agreed to take the test and was also confident of success. Halfway along the tunnel, St Peter leaned towards her, the trap door opened and St Peter plunged down to hell.

1330 Everybody on earth died and went to heaven. On their arrival, God announced that he wanted the men to form two lines – one for all the men who had dominated their women on earth, the other for all the men who had been dominated by their women. Then he told all the women to go with St Peter. When God turned around, he saw that the men had indeed formed two lines. The line of men who had been dominated by their woman stretched back 80 miles whereas the line of men who had dominated their women consisted of just one person.

God was furious. "You men should be ashamed of yourselves for having been so weak," he boomed. "Only one of my sons has been strong. He is the only one of whom I am truly proud." God addressed the man standing alone. "Tell me, my son, how did you manage to be the only one in this line?"

"I'm not sure," replied the man meekly. "My wife told me to stand here!"

Hollywood

1331 A place where they shoot too many pictures and not enough actors. (WALTER WINCHELL)

1332 A Hollywood director was shooting a big budget movie on location in the desert. One day an old Indian came up to him and said: "Tomorrow rain." And sure enough the next day it rained. A few days later, the old Indian appeared on set again, sidled up to the director and said: "Tomorrow storm." And sure enough, the following day there was a fearful storm which brought a temporary halt to filming.

The director was hugely impressed by the old Indian's weather predictions and told his secretary to put the tribesman on the payroll. However, after a number of other successful forecasts, the Indian didn't show for three weeks. Then the director sent for him. The director said: "I have to shoot a big scene tomorrow and I'm relying on you. What is the weather going to be like?"

The old Indian shrugged his shoulders. "Don't know. Radio broken."

1333 In Hollywood, brides keep the bouquets and throw away the groom. (GROUCHO MARX)

1334 The owner of a cinema chain died. The newspaper obituary read: "The funeral will be on Thursday at 2.10, 4.20, 6.30, 8.40 and 10.50."

1335 Mickey Rooney was getting married for the eighth time. The registrar asked: "Have you been married before, sir, and if so, to whom?"
"What is this?" said Rooney. "A memory test?"

1336 Living in Hollywood is like fibreglass underwear – interesting but painful. (ROBIN WILLIAMS)

1337 Two goats were behind a Hollywood studio eating an old movie film. One goat said to the other: "Pretty good, huh?"
The second goat said: "Yeah, but not as good as the book."

1338 How did Darth Vader know what Luke was getting for Christmas? – He felt his presents.

1339 Why does E.T. have such big eyes? – Because he saw the phone bill.

1340 What is E.T. short for? – Because he's got little legs.

Things we would never know without the movies:
1341 During all police investigations, it is necessary to visit a strip club at least once.
1342 When they are alone, all foreigners prefer to speak English to one another.
1343 All beds have special L-shaped sheets which reach up to armpit level on a woman but only to waist level on the man lying beside her.

1344 The ventilation system of any building is the perfect hiding place.

1345 It's easy for anyone to land a plane providing there is someone to talk you down.

1346 Police departments give their officers personality tests to ensure that they are assigned to a partner who is their polar opposite.

1347 You are likely to survive any battle in any war unless you make the mistake of showing someone a picture of your sweetheart back home.

1348 The Eiffel Tower can be seen from any window in Paris.

1349 All bombs are fitted with electronic timing devices that have large red readouts so you know exactly when they're going to go off.

1350 You never have to wait more than ten seconds when hailing a London taxi.

1351 Any lock can be picked by a credit card or a paper clip within seconds – unless it's the door to a burning building with a child trapped inside.

1352 Should you wish to pass yourself off as a German officer, it is not necessary to speak the language – a German accent will do.

1353 You can always find a chainsaw when you need one.

1354 A man shows no pain while taking the most ferocious beating but winces when a woman tries to clean his wounds.

1355 When paying for a taxi, don't look at your wallet as you take out a bill – just grab one at random and hand it over. It will always be the exact fare.

1356 Cars that crash nearly always burst into flames.

1357 A single match is sufficient to light up a room the size of the Millennium Stadium.

1358 Medieval peasants had perfect teeth.

1359 It's always possible to park directly outside the building you are visiting.

1360 A detective can only solve a case once he's been suspended from duty.

Honeymoon

1361 Two newlyweds walked up to the hotel clerk and asked for a suite.

"Bridal?" asked the clerk.

The new bride blushed and said: "No thanks, I'll hold on to his shoulders until I get the hang of it."

1362 An 88-year-old man married a 17-year-old girl. Returning from their honeymoon, he told a friend: "We made love almost every night."

"How did you manage that at 88?" asked the friend.

"Well," said the new groom, "we almost made love Monday, we almost made love Tuesday . . ."

1363 Two newlyweds spent their honeymoon at a remote log cabin. After booking in on the Saturday, they weren't seen again for another five days. The elderly couple who ran the resort were becoming concerned and so the husband went and knocked on the door of the cabin.

A young man answered the door, bleary-eyed.

"Are you two OK?" asked the old man. "Only nobody's seen you around since Saturday."

"Yes, we're fine. We're living on the fruits of love."

"I thought so. Would you mind not throwing the peelings out the window? They're choking my ducks!"

1364 On their first day home after honeymoon, the husband said: "If you make the toast and pour the juice, breakfast will be ready."

"How thoughtful," said the wife. "What are we having?"

"Toast and juice."

1365 A honeymoon couple returned home barely on speaking terms. The best man asked the groom what the problem was.

The groom explained: "After making love on the first night, I got up to go to the bathroom and I put a 50 dollar bill on the pillow without thinking."

"Don't worry," said the groom reassuringly. "She'll get over it. She surely didn't think you've been saving yourself all these years?"

"Maybe," said the groom, "but I don't know if I'll get over it – she gave me 20 dollars change!"

1366 A bride stepped out of the shower on her wedding night wrapped in a robe. Her husband said: "You don't have to be shy now – we're married." So she took off her robe to reveal her naked body.

"Wow," said the husband. "Let me take your picture."

"Why?" said the wife coyly.

"So I can carry your beauty next to my heart for ever."

He took his photo and then went to have a shower himself. A few minutes later he emerged wrapped in a robe.

"Why are you wearing a robe, honey?" she asked. "Remember, you don't have to be shy now – we're married." So he took off his robe to reveal his naked body.

"Let me take your picture," she said.

"Why?" he asked, grinning.

"So I can get it enlarged."

1367 Embarrassed that everyone at the hotel would know she was on honeymoon, the bride asked her husband if there was a way they could make it look as if they had been married a long time. "Sure," he said. "You carry the cases."

1368 Two newlyweds were so strapped for cash that they spent their wedding night at the bride's parents' house. They didn't show for breakfast the next morning and still hadn't put in an appearance by midday at which point the bride's mother asked: "Has anybody seen Tony and Marion?"

The bride's eight-year-old brother revealed: "I saw Tony at about 10.30 last night. He popped his head round the door. He said something about wanting to get stuck in and asked for some Vaseline. Since I didn't know where it was, I gave him my model airplane glue instead."

1369 On their wedding night, a husband and wife slowly undressed and sat nervously at opposite ends of the bed. He was terrified of her discovering that he had appallingly smelly feet while she was dreading him finding out that she suffered from awful halitosis.

After a while, she finally plucked up the courage to move closer and leaned over him. But before she could speak, he said: "I have a confession to make."

"Me too," she said.

"You don't have to tell me," he replied. "I know. You've eaten my socks."

Horses

1370 The Lone Ranger and Tonto were sitting drinking in a bar when a cowboy came in and asked: "Whose white horse is that outside?"

The Lone Ranger replied: "That's my horse – Silver."

"Well," said the cowboy, "he doesn't look too good left out there in the blazing midday sun."

So the Lone Ranger and Tonto went outside to take a look at Silver who was indeed suffering in the heat. The Lone Ranger gave him a bowl of water to drink and splashed some water over his back. But the problem was there was no breeze, so the Lone Ranger asked Tonto to run around Silver to get some air flowing and to cool the horse down. While Tonto was doing this, the Lone Ranger went back into the bar to finish his drink.

A few moments later, another cowboy walked in and asked: "Whose white horse is that outside?" he Lone Ranger turned to face him: "That's my horse," he said. "What's wrong with him now?"

"Nothing," replied the cowboy. "I just wanted to let you know that you left your Injun running."

1371 A man drove his car into a ditch on a quiet country lane. Fortunately a farmer passed by with a horse.

"Could your horse pull my car out of the ditch?" asked the driver.

"Buddy's a big strong horse," said the farmer. "We'll see what we can do."

The farmer hitched Buddy up to the car and said: "Pull, Blackie, pull." Buddy didn't move an inch. Then the farmer said: "Pull, Samson, pull." Buddy didn't move an inch. Then the farmer said: "Pull, Troy, pull." Buddy didn't move an inch. Then the farmer said: "Pull, Buddy, pull." And Buddy effortlessly pulled the car out of the ditch.

The driver was grateful but mystified: "Tell me, why did you keep calling your horse by the wrong name?"

"Ah, well," said the farmer, "you see, Buddy is blind. And if he thought he was the only one pulling, he wouldn't even try!"

1372 A cowboy rode into town and went into the saloon for a few drinks. When he came out again, his horse was gone. He stormed back into the saloon and shouted: "Who stole my horse?"

There was no reply.

He was getting angry. "Right, if no one owns up to stealing my horse, I'm going to do what I did in Arizona."

Still there was silence.

The cowboy was fuming. "This is your last chance. If no one owns up to stealing my horse, I'm going to do what I did in Arizona."

Just then, a lone voice piped up: "What did you do in Arizona?"

The cowboy said quietly: "I walked home."

1373 Another cowboy rode into town, got off his horse, lifted its tail and kissed it where the sun don't shine.

"What d'you do that for?" asked an old timer sitting outside the saloon.

"Got chapped lips," replied the cowboy.

"And does that help?"

"Nope, but it keeps me from lickin' 'em."

1374 Horses are what glue is made from, which is a bit odd because if you touch a horse, they're not sticky, are they? (HARRY HILL)

1375 A guy was driving along a country road when his car broke down. He got out and had just started to check the engine when an old horse trotted up the road. The horse peered into the engine, said, "You'd better check the fuel pump," and trotted on.

The motorist was so shaken that he ran straight to the nearest farmhouse and told the farmer what had happened.

"Was it an old white horse with a black patch on his hind quarters?" asked the farmer.

"Yes, yes, it was!" said the motorist.

"Well, don't pay any attention to him," continued the farmer. "He doesn't know the first thing about cars."

1376 A cowboy strolled out of a saloon, ready to ride out of town. But he saw that someone had painted his horse green from head to hoof. The cowboy stormed back into the saloon. "Which one of you painted my horse green?" he demanded.

"I did," said a huge, mean-looking guy rising to his feet.

"Right," said the cowboy. "Just letting you know that the first coat's dry."

Hospital

1377 Two eminent surgeons – one Indian, the other African – were arguing bitterly during an international convention.

"No," said the Indian, "I tell you it is woomba."

The African was equally adamant. "And I'm telling you it is whoooommm."

After ten minutes of this, an English surgeon interrupted. "Excuse me, chaps, but I think the word you're trying to say is womb."

When the Englishman had gone, the African turned to the Indian and said: "I bet he has never even seen a hippopotamus, never mind heard one fart under water!"

1378 Doctor: "Nurse, how is that little boy doing – the one who swallowed all those quarters?"

Nurse: "No change yet."

1379 No sooner had the elderly patient come round after an operation than the surgeon told her: "I'm sorry – we're going to have to open you up again. I've accidentally left my surgical gloves inside you."

"Oh, if that's all it is," said the patient, "I'd rather you left me alone and I'll buy you a new pair."

1380 A doctor was doing his rounds when he saw to his horror that one of his patients was half dead.

"Nurse, did you give this man two tablets every eight hours, as prescribed?"

The nurse consulted her notes. "No, I gave him eight tablets every two hours. Sorry."

The doctor moved swiftly on to the next bed. Here too the patient appeared near death.

"Nurse, did you give this man one spoonful of medicine every six hours, as prescribed?"

The nurse consulted her notes. "No, I gave him six spoonfuls of medicine every hour. My mistake."

The doctor moved on to the next bed where the patient was completely and utterly dead.

"Nurse," barked the doctor, "did you prick his boil?"

The nurse consulted her notes. "Oops."

1381 My girlfriend has to have a kidney transplant but I'm not worried. She hasn't rejected an organ for over 15 years. (TOM COTTER)

1382 An old man woke up in the recovery room after an operation and said: "Thank God that's over!"

"You're lucky," said the guy in the next bed. "They left a scalpel inside me and had to cut me open again."

"How terrible!" said the old man.

"They had to open me up again too," said the guy on the other side. "To find their sponge."

"That's dreadful," said the old man.

Just then, the surgeon who had operated on the old man stuck his head round the door and asked: "Has anybody seen my hat?"

The old man fainted.

You know you've been a nurse too long when:

1383 Discussing dismemberment over a meal seems perfectly normal.

1384 You believe that "shallow gene pool" should be a diagnosis.

1385 You believe that unspeakable evil will befall you if someone should say, "Boy, it sure is quiet around here!"

1386 You believe that chocolate is a food group.

1387 You admire a stranger's veins.

1388 You have referred to someone's death as a transfer to the "Eternal Care Unit".

1389 You believe in aerosol spraying of Prozac.

1390 You have had to leave a patient's room before breaking into uncontrollable laughter.

1391 You can work out the "tooth to tattoo" ratio without a calculator.

1392 You aren't sure who your boss is.

1393 You know how to say bedpan in five languages.

1394 You have ever bet on someone's blood alcohol level.

1395 You've called in sick on a full moon.

1396 You've got voodoo dolls labelled with doctors' names.

1397 You have restrained someone, and it was not a sexual experience.

1398 Four surgeons were on a coffee break. The first said: "I like operating on librarians best because you open them up and everything is in alphabetical order."

The second said: "I think accountants are the easiest to operate on because everything inside is numbered."

The third said: "I prefer electricians because everything is colour-coded."

And the fourth said: "I reckon lawyers are the easiest to operate on because they're heartless, spineless, gutless and their head and their ass are interchangeable."

1399 How is a hospital gown like insurance? — You're never covered as much as you think you are.

1400 The doctor pulled the sheet up over the patient's face and turned solemnly to the wife. "Well, the good news is that he's stable."

1401 An old man went into hospital for the first time in his life. Toying with the bell cord which had been fastened to his bed, he asked his son: "What's this thing?"

"It's a bell."

The old man pulled it several times. "I can't hear it ringing," he said.

"No," explained the son, "it doesn't ring. It turns on a light in the hall for the nurse."

The old man was indignant. "If the nurse wants a light on in the hall, she can damn well turn it on herself!"

1402 I took my husband to the hospital yesterday to have 17 stitches out — that'll teach him to buy me a sewing kit for my birthday. (JO BRAND)

1403 A surgeon was about to perform a haemorrhoidectomy. He summoned the nurse and gave her a list of the instruments he required for the operation. A few minutes later, she brought in a rubber glove, a large jar of Vaseline, a knife and a bottle of beer. The surgeon began the operation. First he picked up the rubber glove and put it on his hand, ensuring that all the wrinkles were smoothed out. The surgeon held out his hand and the nurse gave him the Vaseline which he proceeded to smooth over the glove. Then he held out his free hand and the nurse handed him the beer.

"Dammit, nurse!" he said in exasperation. "I wanted a butt-light!"

Genuine patients' charts

1404 She stated that she had been constipated for most of her life until 1989 when she got a divorce.

1405 The baby was delivered, the cord clamped and cut and handed to the pediatrician, who breathed and cried immediately.

1406 The patient was in his usual state of good health until his aircraft ran out of fuel and crashed.

1407 On the second day the knee was better, and on the third day it disappeared.

1408 Bleeding started in the rectal area and continued all the way to Los Angeles.

1409 She is numb from her toes down.

1410 The patient refused autopsy.

1411 Examination of genitalia reveals that he is circus sized.

1412 When she fainted, her eyes rolled around the room.

1413 The patient lives at home with his mother, father, and pet turtle, who is presently enrolled in day care three times a week.

1414 Patient has left his white blood cells at another hospital.

1415 Occasional, constant, infrequent headaches.

1416 The patient is a 79-year-old widow who no longer lives with her husband.

1417 Patient was to have a bowel resection. However he took a job as a stockbroker instead.

1418 She slipped on the ice and apparently her legs went in separate directions in early December.

1419 Between you and me, we ought to be able to get this lady pregnant.

1420 She has no rigours or shaking chills, but her husband states she was very hot in bed last night.

1421 The patient has no previous history of suicides.

1422 Discharge status: Alive but without permission.

1423 A God-fearing man was close to death in hospital, so his family called in the priest. As the priest stood by the bed, the man's condition seemed to deteriorate and he motioned frantically for something to write on. The priest handed him a pen and paper and he quickly scribbled a note. No sooner had he finished writing than he died. The priest left the note unread for three quarters of an hour while the family came to terms with their grief. But as he prepared to leave the hospital, he said: "I think now would be an appropriate time to read Bill's last note. It was obviously something which meant a lot to him, something he felt the need to say." The priest opened the piece of paper and read aloud: "Hey, you, you're standing on my oxygen tube."

1424 Did you hear about the gynaecologist who papered the hall through the letterbox?

1425 What do puppies and near-sighted gynaecologists have in common? – Wet noses.

1426 What does a gynaecologist do when he gets nostalgic? – He looks up an old friend.

1427 A man woke up in hospital after having a gangrenous leg amputated. The doctor told him: "There's good news and bad news."

"OK, doc, give me the bad news first."

"The bad news," said the doctor, "is that I'm afraid we've amputated the wrong leg."

"The wrong leg! My God! How could you do that to me? What's the good news?"

The doctor breathed in and said: "I think we're going to be able to save the other leg."

1428 What's the definition of macho? – Jogging home from your own vasectomy.

1429 There was a terrible mix-up at the hospital. A man who had been scheduled for a vasectomy was instead given a sex-change operation. When told of the mistake, he was understandably distraught.

"I'll never be able to experience an erection again," he wailed.

The surgeon tried to console him. "Of course you'll be able to experience an erection – it's just that it will have to be someone else's."

Hotels

1430 A couple who had been married for 35 years were lying in a hotel bed about to go to sleep. Then through the walls, they heard a girl's voice say: "Oh, honey, you're so strong."

The husband turned to his wife: "Why don't you ever say that to me?"

"Because," she replied, "you're not strong any more."

A few minutes later, they heard the girl's voice again: "Oh, honey, you're so romantic."

The husband turned to his wife: "Why don't you ever say that to me?"

"Because," she said, "you're not romantic any more."

Five minutes later, they heard the girl's voice groan: "Oh, honey, that was a wonderful climax. Thank you."

The husband turned to his wife. "Why don't you ever tell me when you have a wonderful climax?"

"Because," she said, "you're never around when I have them!"

1431 An American tourist came to London to stay at a top hotel. He picked up the phone one morning and asked for room service. He said: "I want three overdone fried eggs that are hard as a rock, toast that is burnt to a cinder and a cup of black coffee that tastes like mud."

"I'm sorry, sir," replied room service, "we don't serve a breakfast like that."

"Well, you did yesterday!"

1432 "Will there be anything else, sir?" asked room service after setting out dinner for two.

"No, thank you. That will be all."

As he turned to leave, he noticed a beautiful satin negligee on the bed. "Anything for your wife, sir?"

"Yes. Good idea. Bring up a postcard."

1433 A man checked in to a run-down hotel. "The room is 18 dollars a night," said the manager. "It's eight dollars if you make your own bed."

"OK, I'll make my own bed."

"Right, I'll get you some nails and wood."

1434 A hotel is a place that keeps the manufacturers of 25-watt bulbs in business. (SHELLEY BERMAN)

1435 A porter was whistling as he walked through the foyer of an exclusive hotel. The manager reprimanded him. "Do you not know that it is forbidden for hotel employees to whistle while on duty?"

"I wasn't whistling," said the porter. "I was paging a dog."

1436 A honeymoon couple stayed at the Watergate Hotel in Washington. The bride was worried in case the place was still bugged, so she asked her new husband to search the room thoroughly. He looked behind the curtains, under the bed, in the wardrobes, and finally under the rug. And there, beneath the rug, he found a mysterious disc with four screws. Using his Swiss army knife, he undid the screws and threw the disc out of the window.

The following morning as they checked out, the hotel manager asked: "How was your room? How was the service? How was your stay at the Watergate Hotel?"

"Why so many questions?" said the groom.

"Well," said the manager, "the room under you complained that the chandelier fell on them."

1437 An old woman from the country was visiting the big city for the first time in her life. She checked in at a smart hotel and let the bellboy take her bags. She followed him but as the door closed, her face fell.

"Young man," she said angrily. "I may be old and straight from the hills, but I ain't stupid. I paid good money and this room won't do at all. It's way short of what I expected. It's too small and there's no proper ventilation. Why, there's not even a bed!"

"Ma'am," replied the bellboy, "this isn't your room. It's the elevator!"

1438 Hotel guest: "Does the water always come through the roof like that?"
Proprietor: "No, sir, only when it rains."

1439 I'm not very wild. I tried to trash hotel rooms when I was younger, but I just ended up making the bed and leaving a small chocolate on the pillow for the maid. (ARDAL O'HANLON)

Hunting

1440 A city guy bought all the hunting gear from a department store and went for his first day's shooting in the country. However, he didn't bag a thing all day. Then just as he was on his way back to his car, he spotted a duck flying overhead. He took aim and, to his delight, scored a direct hit, the duck falling to earth in a farmyard. The city guy went to claim his prize but was challenged by the farmer.

"That's my duck," insisted the city guy. "I shot him out of the sky."

"But he fell on my land," insisted the farmer. "So he's mine. But I tell you what we'll do, we'll settle this dispute country-style."

"What's that?" asked the city guy.

"I kick you in the balls as hard as I can, then you kick me in the balls as hard as you can. And the last man standing keeps the duck."

"That sounds fair enough," said the city guy and he braced himself for the full force of the farmer's boot. Sure enough, the farmer wound himself up and landed a hefty blow to his opponent's genital area. It nearly doubled him up.

Now it was the city guy's turn. But before he could do anything, the farmer said: "It's OK, you can have the duck."

1441 A husband took his wife deer hunting for the first time. He explained that the most important thing was to claim your kill immediately, before anyone else could. They went off to their hunting boxes and waited for deer. Soon the husband heard his wife's gun go off. Keen to make sure she staked her claim to the kill, he rushed outside and found her involved in a bitter argument with a man.

"This is my kill," insisted the wife. "I can prove I shot this animal."

"OK, lady," said the man, realizing she wasn't going to back down. "But do you mind if I take my saddle off your deer before you take it away?"

1442 What's the American Indian word for "lousy hunter"? – Vegetarian.

1443 Two guys were out hunting when they accidentally dropped their guns over a cliff. They turned round and saw a bear making towards them. They climbed a tree, but the bear started to follow them up. Perched on a branch, the first guy swapped his hiking boots for trainers.

"What are you doing?" asked his friend.

"When the bear gets close to us, we'll jump down and make a run for it."

"Are you crazy? You can't outrun a bear."

"I don't have to. I only have to outrun you!"

1444 Two hunters went moose hunting every winter without success. So one year they hit upon a cunning plan. They decided to hire an authentic cow moose costume and learn the mating call. They would then hide in the costume, lure the bull moose, slip out of the costume and shoot the animal.

The pair set off for the woods, climbed into the costume and found a nice spot on the edge of a clearing. There they gave the moose love call. After a few minutes, a huge bull moose appeared. When it was close enough, the guy at the front said: "Let's get out and shoot him."

But the guy at the back said: "I can't! The zipper's stuck. What are we going to do?"

The guy at the front said: "Well, I'm going to start nibbling grass, but you'd better brace yourself."

1445 Hearing how a man had killed a dinosaur, a scientist went deep into the jungle to investigate. There he found a weedy little guy standing next to a 300ft-long dead dinosaur.

"That's amazing," said the scientist. "It's so big and you're so small. How on earth did you kill it?"

"With my club," replied the man.

"How big is your club?" asked the scientist.

"Well, there are about a hundred of us . . ."

1446 A woman went into a hunting store to buy a rifle. "It's for my husband," she explained.

"Did he tell you what gauge to get?" asked the store assistant.

"Are you kidding?" said the woman. "He doesn't even know I'm going to shoot him!"

1447 Two guys went duck hunting. One drank a bottle and a half of whisky while the other kept watch. After two hours, a solitary duck flew up. The sober man took aim but missed. "Quick," he said to his drunken friend, "try and hit that duck."

The drunk waved his shotgun in the vague direction of the sky, pulled the trigger and hit the duck.

"That's amazing," said the sober one.

"Not really," replied the drunk. "When there's a whole flock you can hardly miss!"

1448 Three men hired a plane to hunt moose in Canada but were warned by the pilot: "This is a very small plane, so you can only bring back one moose."

But they ended up killing three moose and tried to load their trophies on to the plane. The pilot repeated his warning: "I told you, only one moose!"

"That's what you said last year," protested one of the hunters, "but for an extra $150 you then let us take the three moose on the plane. So, here, take the money now."

The pilot relented and allowed the three moose on board, but shortly after take-off the plane crashed. Extricating himself from the wreckage, one hunter asked shakily: "Where are we?"

One of his companions muttered: "About a hundred yards from where we crashed last year."

Insanity

1449 In the course of his rounds at a mental hospital, a doctor entered a patient's room. One patient was sitting on the floor, sawing an imaginary piece of wood in half, while another patient was dangling from the ceiling by his feet.

"What are you doing?" the doctor asked the first patient.

"Can't you see? I'm sawing this piece of wood in half."

"And what's he doing?" said the doctor, indicating the other patient.

"Oh, he's my friend. He's a little crazy. He thinks he's a light bulb."

The doctor could see that the man's face was going red as he hung from the ceiling. "If he's your friend, you should get him down before he hurts himself."

"What, and work in the dark?"

1450 A patient had spent 12 years in an asylum but doctors were hopeful that he was beginning to respond to treatment. One day, they decided to test their beliefs by taking him to the movies. As they entered the cinema, there was a sign on the seats saying "wet paint". The doctors disregarded the sign but were delighted when the patient placed a newspaper on the seat before sitting down. They were certain his actions proved that he was finally in touch with reality, so they asked him why he had put the newspaper on the seat.

He replied: "So I'd be higher up and have a better view."

1451 The statistics on sanity are that one out of every four Americans is suffering from some form of mental illness. Think of your three best friends. If they're OK, then it's you. (RITA MAE BROWN)

1452 A man was convinced that he was a chicken. Every day he'd go around clucking noisily and pecking the ground. A neighbour asked the man's wife: "Why don't you take him to a doctor to get him cured?"

She said: "Because I need the eggs."

1453 An inmate in an asylum proclaimed loudly: "I am Napoleon!"

"How do you know?" asked a fellow inmate.

"God told me."

A voice from another room shouted: "I did not!"

1454 Three lunatics were trying to escape from an asylum. As the first one crept past the guard, he made the sound of a cat and continued on his way. The second lunatic also made a cat sound as he passed the guard. He too continued on his way. As the third lunatic reached the guard, he called out: "I'm a cat too!"

1455 After hearing that a patient in a mental hospital had saved another from a suicide attempt by pulling him out of a bathtub, the hospital director summoned the rescuer to his office.

"Looking through your file and taking into account your heroic behaviour, I am confident that you are ready to be allowed home. I am only sorry that the man you saved later killed himself with a rope around the neck."

"Oh no," said the rescuer. "He didn't kill himself. I hung him up to dry."

1456 Some mornings, it's just not worth chewing through the leather straps. (EMO PHILIPS)

1457 A man called the secretary at the mental hospital and asked who was in room 18.

"Nobody," said the secretary.

"Great," cried the man. "I must have escaped!"

Things that can drive a sane person crazy:

1458 There are always one or two ice cubes that won't pop out of the tray.

1459 You have to try on a pair of sunglasses with that stupid little plastic tag in the middle.

1460 The elevator stops at every floor but nobody gets in.

1461 You can never put anything back in the box the way it came.

1462 Three meetings after lunch you look in the mirror and discover a piece of parsley stuck to your front teeth.

1463 Your tyre gauge lets out half the air while you're trying to get a reading.

1464 You open a can of soup and the lid falls in.

1465 You set the alarm on your digital clock for 7pm instead of 7am.

1466 You have to inform six different salespeople in the same store that you're just browsing.

1467 You rub on hand cream and can't turn the bathroom doorknob to get out.

Insects

1468 A man went to answer a knock at the door of his house and saw a six-foot cockroach standing there. Without warning, the cockroach slapped him around the face and ran off.

The following night, the man answered another knock at the door. Again the huge cockroach was there. This time it bit him and ran off.

On the third night, the same thing happened again, but this time the cockroach kicked him hard before running off.

The man was so worried by this that he went to see the doctor. The doctor said: "Yes, there's a nasty bug going round."

1469 Time's fun when you're having flies. (KERMIT THE FROG)

1470 Two caterpillars were sunning themselves in the garden when they spotted a butterfly overhead. It fluttered, swooped, rose again and floated on the air currents.

One caterpillar turned to the other and said: "There's no way you'll ever get me up in one of those contraptions."

1471 Why couldn't the butterfly go to the dance? — It was a moth-ball.

1472 What's the difference between a sick horse and a dead bee? — One is a seedy beast, the other is a bee deceased.

1473 A guy was sitting in a bar one Monday lunchtime, fascinated by the movements of a spider. He watched intently as the spider came out of the kitchen, climbed up the wall, walked across the ceiling, round the chandelier and back down the opposite wall, coming to rest on the radiator pipe.

It was the same story on the Tuesday. The spider came out of the kitchen, climbed up the wall, walked across the ceiling, round the chandelier and back down the opposite wall, coming to rest on the radiator pipe.

By the Wednesday the guy was so intrigued that he shared his enthusiasm with a fellow customer. "You watch," he said, "any minute now a spider will come out of the kitchen, climb up the wall, walk across the ceiling, round the chandelier and back down the opposite wall, coming to rest on the radiator pipe."

Sure enough, within minutes, the spider came out of the kitchen, climbed up the wall, walked across the ceiling, round the chandelier and back down the opposite wall, coming to rest on the radiator pipe.

"That's amazing," said the other guy.

On Thursday lunchtime the first guy was in position ready for his entertainment, but this time the spider came from the toilets and did the whole trip in reverse order. It climbed over the radiator pipe, up the wall, walked across the ceiling, round the chandelier and back down the opposite wall.

The guy was mystified by this change in routine and waited to see what would happen on Friday. At exactly the same time as usual, the spider came out of the kitchen, climbed up the wall, walked across the ceiling, round the chandelier and back down the opposite wall, coming to rest on the radiator pipe.

The guy scratched his head. "Tell me, bartender," he said, "on Monday, Tuesday, Wednesday and today, I have watched a spider come out of the kitchen, climb up the wall, walk across the ceiling, round the chandelier and back down the opposite wall, coming to rest on the radiator pipe. But yesterday, it came from the toilets and made the trip in reverse. Why was that?"

"The kitchen window was closed."

1474 It's only when you look at an ant through a magnifying glass on a sunny day that you realize how often they burst into flames. (HARRY HILL)

1475 What do you get when you cross a centipede with a parrot? – A walkietalkie.

1476 What's worse than a giraffe with a sore neck? – A millipede with athlete's foot.

1477 What do you call a fly with no wings? – A walk.

1478 What do you call a greenfly with no legs? – A bogey.

1479 "This is an ideal spot for a picnic," said the husband.
"Yes, it must be," replied his wife. "A million insects can't be wrong!"

1480 What did the worm say to the caterpillar? – Who did you have to sleep with to get that fur coat?

1481 How did the firefly burn to death? – It tried to mate with a lit cigarette.

1482 One tick said to another: "Whatever happened to the two bedbugs who fell in love?"
"Didn't you know? They got married in the spring."

1483 I got stung by a bee this morning – £3 for a jar of honey! (JIMMY CARR)

1484 Two cockroaches were crawling around in a drain. One said to the other: "Did you hear about the new restaurant that's opened over the street? It's got a brand new, stainless steel refrigerator, the kitchen floor is sparkling clean and all the shelves are spotless."

The other cockroach grimaced and said: "Do you mind? Not while I'm eating!"

1485 Two fleas left a cinema. When they got outside, one turned to the other and said: "Shall we walk or take a dog?"

Irish jokes

1486 An Englishman, a Scotsman and an Irishman were working together on the same building site. Each took packed lunches which they ate at the same time every day. One day the Englishman opened his Tupperware container and cried out in anguish: "Oh no, not egg sandwiches again. If I have egg sandwiches one more time, I swear I'll kill myself."

Next the Scotsman opened his lunch box and screamed: "Och no, not beef sandwiches again. If I have beef sandwiches one more time, I swear I'll kill myself."

Then the Irishman opened his lunch container and yelled in horror: "Oh no, not cheese sandwiches again. If I have cheese sandwiches one more time, I swear I'll kill myself."

The following day, lunchtime came round again. The Englishman opened his food to find egg sandwiches again. With a despairing cry of "Egg sandwiches, I can't face them any more," he ran along the girder and threw himself off, plunging six floors to his death.

Moments later, the Scotsman opened his lunch and found beef sandwiches – again. Wailing "Beef sandwiches, I cannae face them any more," he ran along the girder and jumped to his death.

Finally the Irishman opened his lunch and saw cheese sandwiches. Yelling "Cheese sandwiches, I can't face them any more," he too ran along the girder and jumped to his death.

At the funeral for the three men, their widows were inconsolable. "I don't understand," sobbed the Englishman's wife, "I thought he liked egg."

The Scotsman's widow was equally puzzled. "I don't understand it either," she groaned, "I thought my husband loved beef."

Finally the Irishman's wife spluttered: "I just don't understand Paddy's behaviour at all – he always made his own sandwiches."

1487 What's Irish and stays out all night? – Paddy O'Furniture.

1488 How do you sink an Irish submarine? – Knock on the hatch.

1489 Why did the Irishman fall out of the window? – He was ironing the curtain.

1490 What do you call an Irishman with an IQ of 12? – A village.

1491 Why don't Irish women use vibrators? – They chip their teeth.

1492 An Irishman called a Dublin number at three o'clock in the morning. "Is that O'Malley's Bar?" he asked.
"No, it's not. This is a private residence."
"I must have the wrong number. Sorry to trouble you at this time of night."
"Ah, it's no trouble. I had to get up anyway to answer the phone."

1493 Mick and Paddy went into a diner and ordered two drinks. They then took their sandwiches from their lunch boxes and started to eat. Seeing this, the waiter told them: "Sorry, but you can't eat your own sandwiches in here!"
Mick and Paddy looked at each other, shrugged their shoulders, and exchanged sandwiches.

1494 Why do Irishmen wear two condoms? – To be sure, to be sure.

1495 An Irishman went into a pizza parlour in Dublin. The waiter said: "Would you like your pizza cut in six or eight slices, sir?"
"Make it six, I don't think I can eat eight."

1496 Paddy: "Seamus, did you hear that joke about the Egyptian guide who showed some tourists two skulls of Cleopatra – one as a girl and one as a woman?"
Seamus: "No, let's hear it."

1497 What's the definition of an Irish cocktail? – A pint of Guinness with a potato in it.

1498 Where is Cleanliness next to Godliness? – In the Irish dictionary.

1499 An Irishman went to a psychic for the first time. He knocked on the door and the psychic called out: "Who's there?" So he left.

1500 Brendan, Sean and Paddy entered a pub's weekly raffle. To their delight, each won a prize. Brendan won first prize – a case of Guinness. Sean won second prize – a joint of beef. And Paddy won third prize – a toilet brush. When they met up again in the pub the following week, Paddy asked the others how they were enjoying their prizes.

"The Guinness is beautiful," said Brendan.

"So was the beef," echoed Sean. "And how's your toilet brush, Paddy?"

"Not so good," frowned Paddy. "I think I'll go back to paper."

1501 What's black and fuzzy and hangs from the ceiling? – An Irish electrician.

1502 An Irishman came home unexpectedly and found his wife in bed with his best friend. He was so distressed that he rushed to the drawer, took out a revolver and pointed it to his head.

"I can't take this," he cried. "My wife and my best friend in bed together. I'm going to shoot myself."

At this, the wife began to laugh.

"I don't know what you're laughing it," said the Irishman. "You're next."

1503 What's the difference between an Irish wedding and an Irish funeral? – One less drunk.

1504 How do you tell which is the bride at an Irish wedding? – She's the one wearing white gumboots.

1505 Seamus Murphy phoned Pan-Am. "How long does it take to fly from Boston to Dublin?"

"Just a minute, sir."

"Ah, that is quick." And he hung up.

1506 An Irishman's wife gave birth to twins. Her husband demanded to know who the other man was.

1507 The doctor was explaining to Paddy how nature adjusted certain physical disabilities. "For example, if a man is blind, he develops a keen sense of hearing and touch. If he's stone deaf, he develops other senses."

"I know what you mean," said Paddy. "I've noticed that if a bloke has one short leg, then the other one is always a bit longer."

1508 An Irishman went to a carpenter and said: "Can you build me a box that is two inches high, two inches wide and fifty feet long?"

"I suppose so," said the carpenter, "but why do you want a box like that?"

"Well," replied the Irishman, "my neighbour moved away and forgot some things, so he asked me to send him his garden hose."

1509 An Irish couple were on holiday in Florida when they saw a sign saying "Helicopter tours 200 dollars." The husband turned to his wife and said: "Sure, isn't that a lot of money just to look around a helicopter?"

1510 What did St Patrick say to the snakes when he was driving them out of Ireland? – "Are ye all right in the back there, lads?"

1511 O'Flaherty was walking along the road when he saw a sign outside Murphy's house. It read, "Boat for sale".
"What's this sign all about, Murphy?" asked O'Flaherty. "You haven't got a boat. All you've got is a tractor and a trailer."
"That's right," said Murphy, "and they're boat for sale."

1512 Did you hear about the Irishman who wouldn't use Inter Flora for his wife's birthday because he didn't think she would want margarine as a present?

1513 Paddy and his two English friends were talking at a bar. The first friend said: "I think my wife is having an affair with an electrician. The other day I came home and found wire cutters under the bed, and they weren't mine."
The second friend said: "I think my wife is having an affair with a plumber. The other day I came home and found a wrench under the bed, and it wasn't mine."
Paddy said: "I think my wife is having an affair with a horse." His two friends looked at him in amazement. "No, I'm serious," continued Paddy. "The other day I came home and found a jockey under our bed."

1514 Did you hear about the Irish helicopter crash? – The pilot got cold, so he turned off the fan.

1515 Did you hear about the Irish attempt on Mount Everest? – They ran out of scaffolding.

1516 Did you hear about the Irish abortion clinic? – There's a 12-month waiting list.

1517 Did you hear what happened to the Irish Sea Scouts? – Their tent sank.

1518 Did you hear about the Irishman who tried sniffing Coke? – The ice cubes got stuck in his nose.

1519 Paddy was put in a line-up at the police station on an assault charge. When the female victim was led in, he shouted: "That's her!"

Jewish jokes

1520 Isaac Goldblum was sitting in a bar looking thoroughly miserable. After a while the customer at the next table said: "Excuse me, but you look really depressed. What's the problem?"

"You may well ask," sighed Isaac. "I'll tell you what the problem is. My mother died in June and left me 10,000 dollars."

"Gee, that's tough," said the customer sympathetically.

"Then in July," continued Isaac, "my father died, leaving me 50,000 dollars."

"I'm real sorry to hear that," said the customer. "Losing two parents in two months – no wonder you're depressed."

"And last month," added Isaac, "my aunt died and left me 15,000 dollars."

The customer shook his head in pity: "How terrible! Three close family members lost in three months!"

"Then this month," said Isaac. "Nothing."

1521 A Jewish gangster was dining at a kosher restaurant on New York's Lower East Side when members of the mob burst in and pumped him full of lead. He managed to stagger out of the restaurant and stumbled up the street to the tenement block where his mother lived. Clutching his bleeding stomach, he then crawled up the flight of stairs and banged on the door of his mother's apartment, screaming, "Mama, Mama! Help me, Mama!"

His mother opened the door, eyed him up and down and said: "Bubeleh, come in. First you eat, then you talk!"

1522 I landed at Orly Airport and discovered my luggage wasn't on the same plane. My bags were finally traced to Israel where they were opened and all my trousers were altered. (WOODY ALLEN)

1523 A Jewish businessman put in an insurance claim after one of his shops burned down. The insurance agent who came to settle the claim tried to sell him more insurance.

"You're covered by fire insurance," said the agent, "but why don't you take out insurance against storm damage?"

"Storm?" queried the Jew. "How do you start a storm?"

1524 What's a Jew's idea of Christmas? – A parking meter on the roof.

1525 Ruth took her boyfriend Bernie home to meet her parents, Mr and Mrs Bloom.
"What do you do for a living?" asked Mr Bloom.
"I own some property," replied Bernie.
"Some property!" exclaimed Ruth. "He owns a chain of fast-rising retail stores."
"And where do you live?" asked Mrs Bloom.
"I've got an apartment in town."
"An apartment!" cried Ruth. "He has a luxury apartment in the most sought-after block in Manhattan."
"And what are your prospects?" inquired Mr Bloom.
"I'm hoping to expand," said Bernie.
"Expand!" interrupted Ruth. "He's planning to buy Bloomingdale's!"
Just then Bernie sneezed.
"Have you got a cold?" asked Mrs Bloom.
"A cold?" shrieked Ruth. "Bernie's got pneumonia!"

1526 My parents worshipped old-world values: God and carpeting. (MEL BROOKS)

1527 "Hymie, wake up!" shouted his wife.
"What's the matter?" said Hymie.
"You're talking in your sleep again. Why don't you control yourself?"
"All right," said Hymie, "we'll make a bargain. You let me talk when I'm awake and I'll try to control myself when I'm asleep!"

1528 An elderly Jewish lady was leaving the garment district to go home from work one evening when suddenly a flasher appeared before her and opened his raincoat. She looked and said: "You call this a lining?"

1529 Back in the days of the Samurai warriors, there was a mighty emperor who needed a new head Samurai. There were three applicants for this prestigious post – one Japanese, one Chinese, and one Jewish.
"Show me what you can do," the emperor said to the Japanese warrior. With that, the Japanese swordsman released a fly from a matchbox and with a lightning swish from his sword, sliced the fly clean in half. "Very good," said the emperor.
Next it was the Chinaman's turn. He too released a fly from a matchbox and, with two instant flourishes of his sword, reduced the fly to four pieces. "Excellent," said the emperor.

Realizing he was out of his league, the Jew thought he would try the same trick and released a fly from a matchbox. He waved his sword about as if he knew what he was doing, but the fly continued to buzz around the room.

"But the fly is not dead," said the emperor.

"Maybe not," said the Jew, "but if you look closely, you will see that it has been circumcised."

1530 One summer's day, Mrs Rose took her son Reuben to the beach. As soon as she settled under her beach umbrella, she called out to him: "Reuben, Reuben, come here! Don't run into the water – you'll drown! Reuben, don't play with the sand – you'll get it in your eyes and you could end up blinded! Reuben, Reuben, don't stand in the sun – you'll get sunstroke! Oy Vey! Such a nervous child."

1531 Why did the Jews wander in the desert for 40 years? – Someone dropped a quarter.

1532 A Jewish landlord had just finished collecting the rents from the tenants in his apartment block. But when he got home he realized that his wallet was missing and burst into tears.

"What's the matter?" asked his wife.

"I've lost my wallet containing 500 dollars," he wailed. "I think I put it in my inside coat pocket, but it's not there now."

"Did you look in the pockets of your pants?"

"Yes, but the money isn't there either."

"What about the side pocket of your jacket? Did you look there?"

"Of course not!" he snapped. "Do you want me to lose the last bit of hope I have left?"

1533 Why don't Jews drink? – It interferes with their suffering.

1534 For her birthday, Naomi's mother gave her two silk scarves – one pink, one blue. On the Sabbath she went round to her parents, wearing her smartest dress and the pink scarf. Her mother took one look at her and said: "So you don't like the blue scarf?"

1535 How do you know when a Jewish woman has had an orgasm? – She drops her nail file.

1536 A Jewish tailor came to America from a small town in Russia. Although he was illiterate, his business prospered to the point where he decided to open a bank account. Unable to write, he always signed the bank documents with two crosses.

As the years went by, he expanded his business and bought larger premises. He returned to the bank to open a new account but instead of making his signature with two crosses, he now wrote it with three.

"Why three crosses instead of two?" inquired the bank president.

"You know what women are like," said the tailor. "Now we're moving up in the world, she wants me to take a middle name."

1537 A down and out walked up to a Jewish mother on the street and said: "Lady, I haven't eaten in three days."

"Force yourself," she said.

1538 A Jewish woman was on a plane travelling from New York to Miami. After a few minutes, she said to the businessman in the next seat: "You're Jewish, aren't you?"

"No, madam, I'm not Jewish," he replied politely.

"You are Jewish," she insisted.

"No, I'm not."

"Yes, you are. You're Jewish."

"Madam, I'm not."

"I'm sure you are . . ."

Just to shut her up, he said: "OK. I give up. Yes I am Jewish."

"Funny," she said. "You don't look Jewish!"

1539 Why is money green? – Because the Jews picked it before it was ripe.

1540 A man walked into a bar and spotted a beautiful woman sitting alone in the corner. He said to the bartender: "I want to buy that gorgeous-looking woman a drink. Have you got any Spanish Fly?"

"I'm sorry, we're fresh out of Spanish Fly. But I have got Jewish Fly and it's guaranteed to get her over here within 20 minutes of drinking it."

So the man forked out ten dollars and asked the bartender to mix the Jewish Fly into a champagne cocktail and to deliver it to the beautiful woman with his compliments. She drank it and, sure enough, 20 minutes later, she sauntered over to the bar, flung her arms around the man and whispered sensuously in his ear: "Hey, big boy, want to go shopping?"

1541 I saw my first porno film the other day. It was a Jewish porno film – one minute of sex, nine minutes of guilt. (JOAN RIVERS)

1542 Why do Jewish men like to watch porno movies backwards? — They like the part where the hooker gives the money back.

1543 Mrs Goldblum shocked her solicitor by telling him that she wanted to be cremated.

"But it's against your religion," protested the solicitor. "Your family will be devastated."

"I don't care," insisted Mrs Goldblum. "My mind's made up. And furthermore I want my ashes to be scattered in the entrance to the big clothing store in the shopping mall."

"Why on earth do you want to do that?" asked the solicitor.

"Because that way at least I'll be sure my daughter visits me twice a week!"

1544 What did the waiter ask the group of dining Jewish mothers? — Is anything all right?

1545 Three men — an Italian, a Spaniard and a Jew — were about to be executed. Each was asked what he would like as a last meal.

The Italian requested a pizza. He was served it and executed. The Spaniard requested paella. He was served it and executed. The Jew requested fresh strawberries.

"But they're out of season!" said the head of the firing squad.

"Then I'll wait," said the Jew.

1546 Two Jewish businessmen were discussing a mutual acquaintance.

"I put him on his feet," boasted the first.

"You did?" exclaimed the other. "Why, you have a reputation as the most hardhearted man in town! How come you put him on his feet?"

"Because he couldn't keep up with the payments. I repossessed his car!"

1547 A recently widowed Jewish lady was sitting on a Florida beach when a Jewish man of similar age placed his blanket nearby and began reading a book. Attempting to strike up conversation, she asked him how he was.

"Fine," he replied, and returned to his book.

"I love the beach," she persisted. "Do you come here often?"

"First time since my wife passed away last year," he answered, before going back to his book.

"Do you live around here?" she asked.

"Yes, I live over in Suntree," he said, and then resumed reading.

Trying to find a topic of common interest, she asked: "Do you like pussycats?" With that, the man threw down his book, tore off both their swimsuits and gave her the most passionate sex of her life.

Afterwards she gasped: "How did you know that was what I wanted?"

The man replied: "How did you know my name was Katz?"

1548 Mrs Rosenberg was so proud. "Did you hear about my son Isaac?" she asked Mrs Bernstein. "He's going to a psychiatrist, twice a week."

"Is that good?" queried Mrs Bernstein.

"Good?" exclaimed Mrs Rosenberg. "Of course it's good. Not only does he pay 35 dollars an hour but all he talks about is me!"

1549 Why do Jewish women go for circumcised men? – They can't resist anything with 10 per cent off.

1550 Manny was desperate to settle down with a nice girl, but every time he took a girl home to meet his parents, his mother said she didn't like her. Then one day a friend came up with a possible solution. "Why don't you find a girl who is just like your mother? That way she is sure to like her."

Manny thought it was a great idea and found a girl who was the spitting image of his mother. She looked like her, dressed like her and talked like her.

The following week he bumped into his friend again. "So, did you find a girl who was just like your mother?"

"I did," said Manny. "They could have been mistaken for sisters."

"And did you take her home to meet your parents?"

"I did."

"And was it a success?"

"No. My father couldn't stand her."

1551 A Jewish man was knocked down by a car. The paramedic loaded him on to a stretcher and asked: "Are you comfortable?"

"I make a good living," said the Jew.

1552 Old Mr Finkelstein's health was failing, so his family decided to send him to Palm Beach for two weeks. But as the short vacation drew to a close, the old man died and his body was shipped back to New York. As his family gathered around the open casket to pay their last respects, a nephew remarked: "Doesn't he look wonderful?"

"He sure does," said a cousin. "Those two weeks in Palm Beach did him the world of good."

1553 What's the difference between a Catholic wife and a Jewish wife? – A Catholic wife has real orgasms and fake jewellery.

1554 A grandmother was playing in the park with her two small grandchildren when an old friend appeared. After exchanging greetings, the friend asked: "And these must be your grandchildren. How old are they?"

"Well," said the proud grandmother, "the doctor is four and the lawyer is two."

1555 Isaac's wife could tell that her husband was obviously very worried about something. He wasn't sleeping at night, he had lost his appetite and looked permanently anxious. Eventually she asked him what was wrong.

"It's terrible," said Isaac. "I owe Manny Cohen £1,000, but I can't pay it back. I daren't tell him. What shall I do?"

"Why don't you ring Manny straight away," said the wife, "and tell him that you can't pay him back the £1,000. Then he'll do the worrying, not you."

1556 Morris called his son in New York and announced: "Benny, I'm divorcing your mother."

"But you can't," said Benny. "You've been married 52 years."

"I'm sorry," said Morris, "but I don't want to discuss it. My mind's made up. I just thought I should let you know."

"Can I talk to Mama?" asked Benny.

"No, you can't talk to your mother because I haven't told her yet. But I'm seeing a lawyer the day after tomorrow."

Benny couldn't believe what he was hearing. "Listen, Dad, don't do anything rash. I'm catching the first flight down to Florida. I'll be with you as soon as I can. So can we at least talk about this as a family before you start petitioning for a divorce?"

"All right," said Morris. "I'll postpone the lawyer for a day or so. Will you call your sister in New Jersey and break the news to her? I can't bear to talk about it any more."

Half an hour later, Morris received a call from his daughter in New Jersey who said that she and her brother had got tickets and that they and the children would be arriving in Florida the day after tomorrow. She made him promise not to do anything hasty. He promised, and put down the phone. Then he turned to his wife and said: "Well, it worked this time, but what are we going to do to get them to come down next year?"

1557 What's the definition of a Jewish nymphomaniac? – A woman who will have sex on the same day she has her hair done.

1558 To save on the expense of lessons, Manny offered to teach his wife Ruth to drive. On their first outing, she was going along nicely until she reached the top of one of the steepest hills in New York. Suddenly the car veered out of control down the incline.

"The brakes aren't working," screamed Ruth as the foot pedal went down to the floorboard. She grabbed the handbrake but it came away in her hand. "What shall I do?" she yelled as she careered downhill at 80 mph towards a row of parked cars.

"For God's sake, Ruth!" wailed Manny. "Hit something cheap!"

1559 What's the difference between an Italian mother and a Jewish mother? An Italian mother tells her child: "If you don't eat your dinner, I'll kill you." A Jewish mother tells her child: "If you don't eat your dinner, I'll kill myself."

1560 An Englishman, a Scotsman and a Jew had a five-course meal at a top London restaurant. At the end, the waiter presented them with a bill for £120.

"I'll pay that," said the Scotsman.

The front page of the following day's paper carried the headline: JEWISH VENTRILOQUIST FOUND DEAD IN ALLEY.

1561 Three Jews were sentenced to death and put in front of a firing squad. The officer turned to the first condemned man. "Do you want a blindfold?"

"Yes, sir."

The officer turned to the second condemned man. "Do you want a blindfold?"

"Yes, sir."

The officer turned to the third man. "Do you want a blindfold?"

"No, I don't want anything from you."

The second man turned to the third, and said to him in a worried voice: "Isaac, don't make trouble now."

1562 A Jewish husband returned from a business trip overseas. "Honey," he called out, "I'm home. Where are you?"

"I'm hiding."

"Honey," he continued, "I've got a surprise for you. Where are you?"

"I'm hiding."

"I bought you that diamond necklace you wanted. Where are you?"

"I'm hiding . . . behind the sofa in the living room."

1563 Miriam was woken by a strange noise in the middle of the night. She nudged her snoring husband. "Max, wake up! There's a burglar in the house!"

"All right," said Max unconcerned, "so there's a burglar in the house. Go back to sleep."

"Max," persisted Miriam, "don't you understand? Somebody has broken in?"

"Keep quiet!" hissed Max. "You know very well we have nothing worth stealing. You want me to go downstairs and admit it to a total stranger? Have you no shame?"

1564 A daughter phoned her mother to tell her that she was marrying a gentile. The mother seemed surprisingly unconcerned, even when the daughter added that her husband-to-be was unemployed and that they would have to live in the family home. The mother even offered her own bed.

"But where will you sleep?" asked the daughter.

"Don't worry about me," replied the mother. "The minute you hang up I'm going to kill myself anyway."

1565 When I was a kid, I had no watch. I used to tell the time by my violin. I used to practise in the middle of the night and the neighbours would yell, "Fine time to practise the violin, three o'clock in the morning!" (HENNY YOUNGMAN)

1566 An Oriental man was sitting in a restaurant in Chinatown when a Jew suddenly came up and tipped a bowl of fried rice over his head.

"That's for Pearl Harbour," said the Jew.

"But I'm Chinese," cried the man.

The Jew was unrepentant. "Chinese, Siamese, Japanese, you're all the same!"

At this, the Chinaman picked up his plate of sweet and sour chicken and threw it over the Jew.

"That's for sinking the *Titanic*," shouted the Chinaman.

"But the *Titanic* was sunk by an iceberg . . ."

"Goldberg, Greenberg, iceberg . . ."

1567 For their twentieth wedding anniversary, Bernstein bought his wife a family plot at a memorial park. As their twenty-first anniversary approached, Mrs Bernstein asked him what he was buying her this time.

"Nothing," he replied. "You still haven't used what I gave you last year.

1568 A wealthy Jewish businessman was travelling down a steep hill in a taxi when suddenly the driver announced: "The brakes have gone!"

At which, the Jew shouted: "Stop the meter!"

Lawyers

1569 A truck driver hated lawyers so much that if ever he saw any walking along the side of the road he would deliberately swerve his truck into them and run them down. The resounding THUD as truck hit lawyer made it all worthwhile.

One day the truck driver saw a priest hitchhiking by the side of the road. Always ready to offer a helping hand to a man of the cloth, the driver said: "Where are you going to, Father?"

"To St Matthew's Church eight miles along the road," replied the priest.

"Hop in," said the truck driver and he proceeded to set off in the direction of St Matthew's.

Half a mile on, the truck driver saw a lawyer walking along the side of the road and instinctively swerved to hit him. Then he remembered that he was carrying a priest in his truck, so at the last minute he swerved back into the centre of the road, narrowly missing the lawyer. But he still heard the THUD. Puzzled, he glanced in his mirrors and when he didn't see anything he turned to the priest and said, "I'm sorry, Father, I almost hit that lawyer."

"That's OK," replied the priest. "I got him with the door!"

1570 What do you call 1,000 lawyers at the bottom of the sea? – A start.

1571 A man was walking along the street when he noticed a bottle lying in the gutter. He picked up the bottle and decided to rub it for good luck. To his amazement, a genie appeared.

"I will grant you three wishes," said the genie, "but I must warn you, there is a catch. For each wish I grant, every lawyer in the world will receive double what you ask for. Do you understand?"

"Yes, I think so," said the man.

"Right," said the genie. "What is your first wish?"

"My first wish," replied the man, "is for a Ferrari. I've always wanted a Ferrari."

"Then you shall have a Ferrari," answered the genie, "and all the lawyers in the world will be given two Ferraris. Now what is your second wish?"

"I could do with a million dollars," said the man.

"Very well," said the genie, "and you do realize that means that every lawyer in the world will become 2 million dollars richer? Now what is your third wish?''

The man thought for a moment. "Well, I've always wanted to donate a kidney.''

1572 What is black and white and looks great wrapped around a lawyer's neck? – A pit bull terrier.

1573 What is the difference between a lawyer and a vampire? – A vampire only sucks blood at night.

1574 What's the ideal weight of a lawyer? – About 3 lbs, including the urn.

1575 A rabbi, a Hindu and a lawyer were driving late at night in the country when their car broke down. Desperate to find somewhere to sleep, they walked to an isolated farmhouse and asked the farmer whether they could stay the night. The farmer said they could, but pointed out that he had only two beds so that one of the three would have to sleep in the barn with the animals.

The rabbi said he didn't mind sleeping in the barn and went off to join the animals, leaving the Hindu and the lawyer to settle down in the bedroom. But five minutes later there was a knock on the bedroom door. It was the rabbi. "I can't sleep in the barn,'' he said. "There's a pig in there and it's against my religion to sleep in the same room as a pig.''

"Very well,'' said the Hindu, "I'll go and sleep in the barn.'' And he set off to spend the night with the animals. But five minutes later there was another knock on the bedroom door. It was the Hindu. "I can't sleep in the barn,'' he said. "There's a cow in there and it's against my religion to sleep in the same room as a cow.''

The lawyer now realized he had no alternative but to volunteer to sleep in the barn. So he went off to get some much-needed rest. But five minutes later, the bedroom door burst open. The pig and the cow were standing there.

1576 What does a lawyer use for birth control? – His personality.

1577 What do you call a lawyer with an IQ of 50? – Your honour.

1578 What do you call a lawyer gone bad? – Senator.

1579 Two lawyers arranged to meet for lunch. The first lawyer was on time but the second was over an hour late. When he eventually showed up, his friend asked. "What kept you?''

"I ran over a milk bottle and got a flat tyre."
"Didn't you see the milk bottle in the road?"
"No, the kid had it under his coat."

1580 How many lawyers does it take to roof a house? — Depends on how thin you slice them.

1581 An American tourist was being shown round London's Westminster Abbey. The guide pointed to a splendid monument and declared: "There lies a great and honest man and a most distinguished lawyer."

"That's interesting," said the American. "I never knew that in England you buried two men in the same grave."

1582 A lawyer was approached by the devil with a proposition. The devil said he'd arrange for the lawyer to win every case, make twice as much money, work half as hard, be appointed to the Supreme Court Bench at 49 and live to be 95. In return, the lawyer had to promise the devil the souls of his parents, his wife and his three young children.

The lawyer thought for a moment: "So what's the catch?"

1583 If it weren't for my lawyer, I'd still be in prison. It went a lot faster with two people digging. (MISTER BOFFO)

1584 What's the difference between a lawyer and a sperm? — A sperm has a one in a million chance of turning into a human being.

1585 What's the difference between a lawyer and a haddock? — One's cold and slimy, the other's a fish.

1586 What's the difference between a lawyer and a trampoline? — You take off your boots to jump on a trampoline.

1587 What's the difference between a lawyer and a leech? — A leech will let go when its victim dies.

1588 A man was sitting quietly in a bar when someone shouted: "All lawyers are assholes!"

The man jumped to his feet and said: "I resent that."

"Are you a lawyer?"

"No, I'm an asshole."

1589 What do you call parachuting lawyers? – Skeet.

1590 A long New Orleans-style funeral procession passed by but instead of a jazz band, it was led by a man walking a lion. Behind the coffin was a line of around 200 people.

A bystander asked the man: "What's going on?"

"My lion ate my lawyer," replied the man, "and this is his funeral."

"Hey," said the bystander, "could I borrow your lion? I've got a lawyer I'd like to have eaten."

"Sorry," said the man, indicating the 200 people following the coffin, "you'll have to get to the end of the queue."

1591 The celebrated American lawyer Clarence Darrow told a story about how easy it is for a lawyer in court to make the fatal mistake of asking one question too many.

The defendant was accused of biting off another man's ear. His lawyer cross-examined the witness: "Did you see my client biting off the victim's ear?"

"No, sir."

Instead of stopping there, the lawyer pressed on triumphantly: "So how can you testify that my client bit off the victim's ear?"

"Because I saw him spit it out."

1592 How do you get a lawyer out of a tree? – Cut the rope.

1593 A lawyer charged a client 800 dollars for legal services. The client paid him with crisp, new 100-dollar bills. After the client left, the lawyer discovered that two of the bills were stuck together with the result that the client had overpaid him by 100 dollars. This left the lawyer with an ethical dilemma: should he tell his partner?

1594 Aiming for a bank, a three-man gang of robbers broke into a lawyers' club by mistake. The old lawyers put up such a fierce struggle that the gang were just relieved to escape. In their getaway car, they tried to make the best of a bad job. "At least we got out with 25 dollars between us," said one.

The gang leader growled: "I warned you to stay clear of lawyers. We had over 100 dollars when we broke in!"

1595 Ninety-nine per cent of lawyers give the rest a bad name.

1596 A lawyer and a blonde were sitting at a bar. All the blonde wanted to do was sleep, but the lawyer saw the chance to make money.

"Why don't we play a game?" he suggested. "I ask you a question. If you don't know the answer, you pay me five dollars, and vice versa."

"No, I just wanna go to sleep," said the blonde.

The lawyer wasn't giving up that easily. He figured taking money from a blonde would be like taking candy from a baby so he gave her a greater incentive, feeling confident that she wouldn't prove his intellectual equal. "I'll tell you what I'll do," he persisted. "If you don't know the answer, you pay me five dollars, but if I don't know the answer, I have to pay you 50 dollars."

"OK," sighed the blonde. "Anything for a quiet life."

The lawyer asked the first question: "What is the circumference of the world?"

The blonde didn't even try to think, but just handed over her five dollars. The lawyer pocketed it with glee.

Then it was the blonde's turn. "What," she asked, "goes up a hill with three legs and comes down with four?"

The lawyer was stumped. He couldn't believe that the blonde could come up with a question he didn't know the answer to. While the blonde dozed, he consulted half a dozen encyclopaedias, e-mailed his lawyer friends, went on his laptop but still couldn't find the answer. After an hour, he finally had to admit defeat and handed over the 50 dollars.

"Right," he said tetchily. "What is the answer?"

The blonde silently reached into her purse, handed him five dollars and went back to sleep.

1597 A man with an alligator went into a bar and asked the bartender: "Do you serve lawyers here?"

"Yes."

"Good. I'll have a beer and my 'gator will have a lawyer."

1598 What's the difference between a good lawyer and a great lawyer? – A good lawyer knows the law, a great lawyer knows the judge.

1599 A Mexican bandit specialized in sneaking over the border to rob banks in Texas. Eventually a resourceful Texas Ranger tracked the bandit down to a bar near the Rio Grande and held a gun to his head. "Tell me where you hid the loot or I'll blow your brains out."

The bandit didn't speak English and the Texas Ranger didn't speak Spanish but in the saloon that day there happened to be a bilingual lawyer who agreed to act as translator. With a gun at his head, the terrified bandit blurted out in Spanish that the loot was buried under an oak tree at the back of the saloon.

"What did he say?" asked the Texas Ranger.

The lawyer replied: "He said, 'Get lost, Gringo. You wouldn't dare shoot me.'"

1600 When lawyers die, why are they buried in holes 20 feet deep? – Because deep down, they're all nice guys.

1601 How can you tell when a lawyer is lying? – His lips are moving.

1602 A lawyer died and arrived at the pearly gates. St Peter was waiting and, to the lawyer's delight and surprise, made a great fuss of him.

"What's the big deal?" asked the lawyer. "I know I was pretty good at my job, won a few major cases, but I didn't expect such a special welcome. Why me?"

"Well," said St Peter, "I've added up all the hours for which you billed your clients and, by my calculations, you must be about 179 years old."

1603 A lawyer's dog, running unleashed, stole a piece of meat from a butcher's shop. The butcher was furious and marched straight round to the lawyer's office. He asked the lawyer: "If a dog running unleashed steals a piece of meat from my store, do I have the right to demand payment for the meat from the dog's owner?"

"Definitely," said the lawyer.

"Then you owe me 8 dollars 50," said the butcher. "Your dog was loose and stole some meat from me today."

To the butcher's surprise, the lawyer promptly wrote out a cheque for 8 dollars 50 without making a fuss.

Two days later, the butcher opened his mail to find a bill from the lawyer – 100 dollars for legal consultation.

1604 Two boys were talking on their first day in school. "My daddy's an accountant," said one.

"What does your daddy do?"

"My daddy's a lawyer."

"Honest?"

"No, just the regular kind."

1605 After decades of conducting research experiments using rats, a team of eminent biological scientists announced that in future they would be using lawyers instead. Two reasons were given for changing to lawyers – the lab assistants don't get so attached to them, and also there are some things that even a rat won't do.

1606 A priest, a doctor and a lawyer were playing golf together one morning, but were stuck behind a particularly slow group. All three were complaining about how long the group were taking on each hole. Finally they spotted the greenkeeper, so they decided to have a word with him.

"That's a group of blind firefighters," explained the greenkeeper. "They lost their sight while saving our clubhouse last year. So we let them play here any time free of charge."

The priest said: "That's so sad. I think I'll say a special prayer for them tonight."

The doctor said: "That's a good idea. And I'm going to consult all my textbooks to see if there isn't anything that can be done for them."

The lawyer said: "Why can't these guys play at night?"

1607 A man went into a pet shop to buy a parrot. The shop owner pointed to three identical birds lined up on the perch.

"How much is the one on the left?" asked the customer.

"Five hundred dollars," said the shop owner.

"Why is it so expensive?"

"Because it knows how to do legal research."

"What about the one in the middle? How much is that?"

"One thousand dollars because it can do everything the other parrot can do, plus it knows how to write a brief that will win any case."

"And how much is the third parrot?"

"Five thousand dollars."

"What can it do that is so special?"

"To be honest, I've never seen him do a damn thing, but the other two call him Senior Partner."

1608 A lawyer's son wanted to follow in his father's footsteps. He went to law school, graduated with honours and joined his father's law firm. At the end of his first day there, he ran in excitedly to tell his father: "Guess what. On my first day, I've cracked that accident case you've been working on for the past four years."

"You idiot!" said the father. "What do you think put you through law school!"

1609 If you were stranded on a desert island with Hitler, Saddam Hussein and a lawyer and you had a gun with only two bullets, what would you do?
– Shoot the lawyer twice.

1610 A group of terrorists hijacked a plane full of lawyers. The terrorists called down to ground control with their list of demands and threatened that if the demands weren't met, they'd release one lawyer every hour.

1611 A defending attorney was cross-examining a coroner. "Before you signed the death certificate, had you taken the man's pulse?"
"No," said the coroner.
"Did you listen for a heart beat?"
"No."
"Did you check for breathing?"
"No."
"So when you signed the death certificate, you hadn't taken any steps to check that the man was dead, had you?"
The coroner was tired of this browbeating. "Let me put it this way," he said. "The man's brain was sitting in a jar on my desk, but for all I know he could be out there practising law somewhere!"

1612 Two tigers were prowling through the jungle. The male tiger kept licking the female's ass.
"I wish you'd stop that," she growled.
"Sorry," replied the male, "but I just ate a lawyer and I'm trying to get the taste out of my mouth."

1613 How can you tell if a lawyer is well hung? – You can't get a finger between the rope and his neck.

1614 St Peter had gone on vacation, leaving God in charge of the heavenly gates. One day an engineer arrived at the gates but God, who wasn't used to the procedure, took one look at him and said: "You're in the wrong place."
Dejected, the engineer caught the escalator down to hell where he received a warm welcome from the devil. But after a week, the engineer decided that hell was too hot and uncomfortable so he arranged with the devil for a few improvements to be made. The engineer said: "How about if I fix it for water to

be piped in, air conditioning to be installed and a few swimming pools to be built?"

"Sounds great," said the devil and within three weeks hell was transformed into a tropical paradise.

Not long after, God called the devil for one of their regular chats. "How's things down there," chortled God. "Pretty hot, huh?"

"As a matter of fact, no," said the devil. "It's fantastic. We've got an engineer down here who has worked wonders. We've got air conditioning, swimming pools, the lot."

"What!" boomed God. "That's a mistake, the engineer was supposed to be up here."

"Too bad," said the devil, "we're keeping him."

"That's what you think," stormed God. "I want that engineer. I'm going to sue."

The devil gave a supremely confident smile and replied: "Yeah? Where are you going to get a lawyer?"

1615 If a lawyer and a taxman were both drowning and you could save only one, would you go to lunch or read the paper?

1616 What do you call a lawyer who doesn't chase ambulances? — Retired.

1617 A Grade school teacher was asking the children what their parents did for a living. "What does your daddy do for a living, Mary?" she asked.

"My daddy is a doctor," replied Mary.

"And what does your daddy do for a living, Mark?"

"My daddy is a journalist," replied Mark.

"And what about you, James? What does your daddy do for a living?"

"My dad plays the piano in a whorehouse," replied James.

The teacher was horrified but thought there must be some logical explanation for the boy's reply. So the next time she saw James's father, she mentioned the incident.

"Well actually," said the father, "I'm a lawyer, but how can I explain a thing like that to a seven year old?"

1618 A man went to a lawyer for help. "What are your fees?" he asked.

"Fifty dollars for three questions," answered the lawyer.

"That's pretty expensive, isn't it?"

"Maybe," said the lawyer. "So, what's your third question?"

1619 What do you have if three lawyers are buried up to their necks in sand? – Not enough sand.

1620 The good news is a bus full of lawyers went over a cliff. The bad news is one of the seats was empty.

1621 A cardiac patient was told that he needed an urgent heart transplant. The surgeon said: "You can have a doctor's heart for 10,000 dollars, a rabbi's heart for 20,000 or a lawyer's heart for 100,000."

"Why are lawyers' hearts so expensive?" asked the patient.

"Well," said the surgeon, "we have to go through a lot of lawyers to find a heart."

1622 What's the definition of a lawyer? – The larval stage of a politician.

1623 A man's car was a total write-off and was covered with leaves, twigs, grass, mud and blood.

"What happened to your car?" asked a friend.

"I hit a lawyer."

"That explains the blood, but what about the leaves, twigs, grass and mud?"

"I had to chase him all through the park."

1624 A man phoned up a law firm and asked to speak to Mr Hanson, his ex-wife's lawyer.

"I'm sorry," said the secretary, "but Mr Hanson died last night."

Ten minutes later the phone rang again. The same voice asked: "Can I speak to Mr Hanson, my ex-wife's lawyer?"

"I'm afraid that's not possible," said the secretary. "As I told you a few minutes ago, Mr Hanson died last night."

Ten minutes later the phone rang again. The same voice said: "I'd like to speak to Mr Hanson, my ex-wife's lawyer."

"Look," said the secretary. "I've told you twice. Mr Hanson is dead. Why do you keep phoning? Don't you understand?"

"Sure I understand," said the caller. "I just enjoy hearing you say it over and over."

1625 The Post Office had to recall its series of stamps depicting famous lawyers. People were confused about which side to spit on.

1626 How do you keep a lawyer from drowning? – Take your foot off his head.

1627 A teacher, a garbage collector and a lawyer all died and went to heaven on the same day. St Peter was in a bad mood because so many people had been dying recently that heaven was getting overcrowded. So he told the three that they would each have to pass an entrance examination in the form of a single question. If they got it right, they would be allowed in; if not, hard luck.

St Peter addressed the teacher first: "Here is your question. What was the name of the ship which crashed into an iceberg in the Atlantic in 1912, resulting in a huge loss of life?"

"Was it the *Titanic*?" asked the teacher.

"Yes," said St Peter and allowed the teacher through the heavenly gates. St Peter didn't really want a garbage collector stinking out heaven so he decided to make his question a little more difficult. "How many people died on the *Titanic*?"

"Fifteen hundred and twenty-three," said the garbage man.

"That's right," said St Peter.

Then St Peter turned to the lawyer. "What were their names?"

1628 Why did New Jersey get all the toxic waste and California all the lawyers? – New Jersey got to pick first.

1629 What's the difference between a lawyer and an onion? – You cry when you cut up an onion.

1630 Shortly before her fourth marriage, a middle-aged woman went to see her doctor to ask for advice on sex, more particularly on how to do it. The doctor was amazed. He said: "You've been married three times before, surely you know what you have to do by now?"

"No, that's the point," said the woman, "I don't. My first husband was a gynaecologist and all he wanted to do was look at it; my second husband was a psychiatrist and all he wanted to do was talk about it; my third husband worked for the Post Office and he couldn't find it. Now I'm getting married to a lawyer so I'm bound to get screwed sometime!"

1631 Two lawyers were waiting in a bank queue when a gang of ten armed robbers burst in. While half of the gang jumped the counter, the others made the customers line up before snatching their money and jewellery. Just before the gang reached the lawyers, one lawyer pressed a wad of notes into the other's hand.

"Here's that 50 dollars I owe you."

1632 A young lawyer was involved in a dreadful car smash. The entire side of his BMW was ripped away, along with his arm. When a patrolman arrived on the scene, the lawyer was in a state of shock. "My car! My car!" he groaned.

The patrolman weighed up the extent of the injuries and said: "Sir, I think you ought to be more concerned about your arm than your car."

The lawyer looked down in horror at where his arm used to be and screamed: "My Rolex! My Rolex!"

Laziness

1633 A guy told the doctor that he could no longer do as much around the house as he used to. He didn't seem to have the energy for any chores. The doctor gave him a thorough examination and at the end the guy said: "OK, doc, I can take it. Tell me in plain English, what's wrong with me?"

"Well," said the doctor, "in plain English, you're just lazy."

"OK," said the guy, "now give me the medical term so I can tell my wife."

1634 It was a balmy summer's afternoon and an old timer and his wife were sitting rocking on the porch at the side of their house when they heard a funeral procession pass by the front door.

"That'll be old Jerry's funeral," said the husband. "They reckon it's the biggest there's been round here for years."

"I'd like to have seen it," said the wife.

"Me too. After all, he was best man at our wedding."

"That's right. Shame we ain't facin' that way!"

1635 It is better to have loafed and lost than never to have loafed at all. (JAMES THURBER)

1636 A city guy was touring the country when he came across an old farmer sitting on a tree stump and idly chewing a blade of grass.

"How's things?" asked the tourist.

"Can't complain," said the farmer. "I had some trees to cut down, but a cyclone came along and spared me the trouble."

"Well, they say it's an ill wind."

"Then a lightning storm set fire to the brush pile and saved me the trouble of burnin' it."

"Another stroke of luck. What are you going to do next?"

"Oh, nothin' much. Just waitin' for an earthquake to come along and shake them potatoes out of the ground."

1637 The laziest guy in America was sitting with his friend in a bar one day. Both were too idle to find a job. Suddenly the friend turned to him and said: "I'm thinking of going to Australia. On the news it says that someone's discovered a diamond mine in the Outback where the precious stones sit all over the ground. All you have to do is bend down and pick them up."

The other guy looked at him and said: "Bend down?"

1638 A farmer had ten employees on his farm, and all were notoriously lazy. One morning, he decided to try and cure them of their idleness once and for all.

"Men," he said, "I have a nice, easy job for the laziest man on the farm. Will the laziest man step forward?"

Immediately nine of them stepped forward. The farmer looked at the one man left behind and said: "Why didn't you step forward along with the others?"

"Too much trouble."

Lies

The world's biggest lies:

1639 I'll respect you in the morning.

1640 The cheque is in the mail.

1641 Officer, I only had two beers.

1642 The new ownership won't affect you: the company will remain the same.

1643 I won't come in your mouth.

1644 The river never gets high enough to flood this property.

1645 This won't hurt.

1646 I gave at the office.

1647 The puppy won't be any trouble, Mum – I promise I'll look after it myself.

1648 Come on, tell me. I promise I won't get angry.

1649 Eat this, you'll like it.

1650 Its only previous owner was a little old lady who used it for driving to the shops.

1651 My wife doesn't understand me.

1652 You don't look a day over 40.

1653 Don't worry, madam, we'll be with you first thing in the morning.

1654 We've had a lot of interest in this property.

1655 Of course I love you.

1656 You don't need it in writing – you have my word.

1657 I'll call you later.

1658 It's only a cold sore.

1659 It's an absolute bargain.

1660 The villa is less than 100 yards from the beach.

1661 We only had three days' rain here last summer.

1662 I am getting a divorce.

1663 It was delicious, but I couldn't eat another bite.

1664 I've never had a dissatisfied customer.

1665 Having a great time. Wish you were here.

1666 I'll only put the tip in.

1667 But we can still be friends.

1668 You made it yourself? I would never have guessed.

1669 I never inhaled.

1670 If it will make you happy, it will make me happy.

1671 It's supposed to make that noise.

1672 Your hair looks just fine.

1673 One size fits all.

1674 I'm only having a quick half.

1675 Your insurance policy covers you for full replacement value.

1676 You're lucky – this is the last one in stock.

1677 It's not the money, it's the principle of the thing.

1678 Sure, I've had an Aids test.

1679 The government will not raise taxes.

1680 It won't shrink in the wash.

1681 Our children never caused us a moment's worry.

1682 It's a very small spot – nobody will notice.

1683 I never received your fax.

1684 I don't work here for the money – I believe in what I do.

1685 It'll be as good as new.

1686 Size doesn't matter.

1687 The colour really suits you.

1688 Don't worry, he's never bitten anyone.

1689 She means nothing to me.

1690 Trust me.

1691 You won't find anyone cheaper.

1692 Don't worry, it's OK – I'm sterile.

1693 I never watch soaps.

1694 All our work is guaranteed.

1695 The sleeves will ride up with wear.

1696 The sleeves will ride down with wear.

1697 Now, I'm going to tell you the truth.

1698 I never argue with a lady.

1699 I'm on your side.

1700 Don't worry, I can go another 20 miles when the gauge is on empty.

1701 You must both come again.

Light bulb jokes

1702 How many psychiatrists does it take to change a light bulb? Only one, but the bulb has really got to want to change.

1703 How many lawyers does it take to change a light bulb? How many can you afford?

1704 How many Irishmen does it take to change a light bulb? Two. One to hold the bulb and another to drink whisky until the room spins.

1705 How many Marxists does it take to change a light bulb? None. The light bulb contains the seeds of its own revolution.

1706 How many Roman Catholics does it take to change a light bulb? Two. One to do the screwing, one to hear the confession.

1707 How many Californians does it take to change a light bulb? Seven. One to turn the bulb and six to share the experience.

1708 How many Los Angeles cops does it take to change a light bulb? Eight. One to change the bulb and seven to smash the old one to pieces.

1709 How many Virginia politicians does it take to change a light bulb? Three. One to change the bulb and two more to reminisce about how great the old light bulb was.

1710 How many New Yorkers does it take to change a light bulb? Five. One to change the bulb and four to protect him from muggers.

1711 How many straight San Franciscans does it take to change a light bulb? Both of them.

1712 How many Harvard grads does it take to change a light bulb? One. He grabs the bulb and waits for the world to revolve around him.

1713 How many Jewish mothers does it take to change a light bulb? None. "Don't worry about me, I'll sit here all alone in the dark."

1714 How many actors does it take to change a light bulb? Only one. They don't like to share the spotlight.

1715 How many mystery writers does it take to change a light bulb? Two. One to screw it almost all the way in and one to give it a surprising twist at the end.

1716 How many pessimists does it take to change a light bulb? None. The old one is probably screwed in too tight.

1717 How many economists does it take to change a light bulb? Eight – one to screw it in and seven to hold everything else constant.

1718 How many movie directors does it take to change a light bulb? One, but he wants to do it 19 times.

1719 How many California therapists does it take to change a light bulb? Just one, but it takes 25 visits.

1720 How many advertising executives does it take to change a light bulb? None – "because it's getting brighter! It's definitely getting brighter!"

1721 How many fishermen does it take to change a light bulb? One, but you should have seen the bulb. It was this big.

1722 How many Russians does it take to change a light bulb? That's a military secret.

1723 How many divorced men does it take to change a light bulb? Who knows – they never get to keep the house!

1724 How many divorced women does it take to change a light bulb? Four – one to change the bulb, three to form a support group.

1725 How many existentialists does it take to change a light bulb? Two. One to screw it in and one to observe how the light bulb itself symbolises a single incandescent beacon of subjective reality in a netherworld of endless absurdity reaching towards a maudlin cosmos of nothingness.

1726 How many doctors does it take to change a light bulb? Depends on whether it has health insurance.

1727 How many car mechanics does it take to change a light bulb? Six. One to scratch his head, one to say "We can't look at it till Thursday', and four to add up the bill.

1728 How many MPs does it take to change a light bulb? Twenty-one. One to change it and twenty to form a fact-finding committee to learn more about how it's done.

1729 How many Conservative MPs does it take to change a light bulb? Two. One to screw it in and the other to hang himself accidentally from the flex while performing a perverted sexual act involving woman's underwear.

1730 How many surrealists does it take to change a light bulb? Fish.

1731 How many real men does it take to change a light bulb? None. Real men aren't afraid of the dark.

1732 How many feminists does it take to screw in a light bulb? That's not funny!

1733 Why does it take three women with PMS to change a light bulb? It just does! All right?

1734 How does a spoiled rich girl change a light bulb? She says: "Daddy, I want a new apartment."

Love and marriage

1735 A wife told her husband that the cleaner was broken and ordered her husband to fix it.

"Do I look like the Hoover repairman?" he asked indignantly and carried on reading the newspaper.

The next day she told him that the washing machine had broken and ordered him to fix it.

"Do I look like the Zanussi repairman?" he snapped and carried on reading the paper.

The day after, she told him that the computer was broken and ordered him to fix it.

"Do I look like the IBM repairman?" he moaned and carried on reading the paper.

A few weeks later the husband said: "I see you got everything fixed. How did you get it all done so cheap?"

"Well," said the wife, "you know Pete next door? He agreed to do the repairs for free if I'd sleep with him or sing him a song."

"What song did you sing?" asked the husband.

The wife replied: "Do I look like Tina Turner?"

1736 Marriage is a wonderful institution, but who wants to live in an institution. (GROUCHO MARX)

1737 A wife woke up in the middle of the night to hear her husband sobbing uncontrollably downstairs. She put on her gown and went to investigate.

"Honey, whatever's the matter?" she asked.

"Remember 20 years ago I got you pregnant, and your father threatened to have me thrown in jail if I didn't marry you?"

"Of course I do," she said.

"Well, I'd have been released tonight."

1738 I was cleaning out the attic the other day with the wife. Filthy, dirty and covered with cobwebs . . . but she's good with the kids. (TOMMY COOPER)

1739 In the first year of marriage, the man speaks and the woman listens. In the second year, the woman speaks and the man listens. In the third year, they both speak and the neighbours listen.

1740 What's the only way to have your husband remember your anniversary? – Get married on his birthday.

1741 A man's description of marriage: a very expensive way to get your laundry done for free.

1742 A wealthy man met a beautiful woman and knew straight away that he wanted to marry her. He proposed on their second date.

"But we don't know anything about each other," she said.

"No matter. We'll learn about each other as we go along. That'll be part of the fun."

So she agreed and they got married. After the ceremony, they went on an expensive honeymoon to the finest hotel in Mauritius. On their first morning, they went to the hotel pool. He climbed to the top of the diving board and, with an elaborate double somersault, plunged into the water. As he surfaced, he said to his new bride: "Impressive, huh? You see, I used to be an Olympic diving champion. I told you we'd learn things about each other as we went along."

Then she jumped into the water and proceeded to complete 25 lengths of the pool without breaking sweat. As she climbed out, he said: "Wow! That was fantastic. Were you an Olympic endurance swimmer?"

"No," she said. "I was a hooker in Venice, and I worked both sides of the canal."

1743 The romance is dead if he drinks champagne from your slipper and chokes on a Dr Scholl's foot pad. (PHYLLIS DILLER)

1744 A guy knows he's in love when he loses interest in his car for a couple of days. (TIM ALLEN)

1745 A neighbour said to the newlywed bride: "I can't help noticing that you and your husband don't seem to have much in common. Why did you get married?"

The young woman sighed: "I guess it was the old story of opposites attract – he wasn't pregnant and I was."

1746 Two men were talking in a bar. One asked: "What are you going to get your wife for your twentieth wedding anniversary?"

"I was thinking about a trip to Australia," said the other. "She'd love that."

"A trip to Australia! That's mighty impressive. But how will you be able to top that for your twenty-fifth anniversary?"

"I'm not sure. Maybe I'll pay for her fare back."

1747 When you're in love, it's the most glorious two and a half days of your life. (RICHARD LEWIS)

1748 I'm a member of Bridegrooms Anonymous. Whenever I feel like getting married, they send over a lady in a housecoat and hair curlers to burn my toast for me. (DICK MARTIN)

1749 My wife made me join a bridge club. I jump off next Tuesday. (RODNEY DANGERFIELD)

1750 I take my wife everywhere, but she keeps finding her way back. (HENNY YOUNGMAN)

1751 I had my credit card stolen, but I didn't report it because the thief was spending less than my wife did. (HENNY YOUNGMAN)

1752 I married Miss Right. I just didn't know her first name was Always. (HENNY YOUNGMAN)

1753 When their marriage went through a rocky patch, a young couple went to see a marriage counsellor. The male counsellor listened while the wife outlined her grievances, the principal one being that her husband neglected her.

"We've only been married two years," she said, "but he never seems to take any interest in me. He never shows any affection. It seems as if he's bored with me already."

The husband simply shrugged his shoulders, so the counsellor decided to take drastic action. He went over to the wife and kissed her passionately. As the wife slumped back into her seat in shock, the counsellor turned to the husband and said: "Your wife needs that at least twice a week."

The husband replied: "Well, I can get her here Tuesdays and Thursdays."

1754 A woman yelled at her husband: "You're gonna be really sorry. I'm going to leave you!"

He said: "Make up your mind. Which is it gonna be?"

1755 A husband said to his wife: "Darling, let's go out and have some fun tonight."

"I suppose so," she said, "but if you get home before I do, leave the hallway light on."

1756 Getting married for sex is like buying a 747 for the free peanuts. (JEFF FOXWORTHY)

1757 "I am" is said to be the shortest sentence in the English language. "I do" is the longest.

1758 Marriage is an institution in which the man loses his Bachelor's Degree and the woman gets her Masters.

1759 An irate wife was waiting for her husband at the door. There was alcohol on his breath and lipstick on his collar.

"I assume," she snarled, "that there's a very good reason for you to come waltzing in here at eight o'clock in the morning!"

"There is," he said. "Breakfast."

1760 Boy: "Dad, how much does it cost to get married?"

Father: "Don't know, son. I'm still paying for it."

1761 My wife had a sex change. Now it's Wednesdays and Saturdays instead of Tuesdays and Fridays. (HENNY YOUNGMAN)

1762 Three men were sitting at a bar. Two of them were boasting about how they controlled their wives. The third man was conspicuously quiet. Eventually they turned to him and said: "So what about you?"

"As a matter of fact," he said, "only the other night my wife came to me on her hands and knees."

"Really?" they said, surprised. "And what did she want?"

"She said: 'Get out from under the bed and fight like a man!'"

1763 Why did the polygamist cross the aisle? – To get to the other bride.

1764 Husband: "Put your coat on, love, I'm going to the bar."

Wife: "Are you taking me out for a drink?"

Husband: "Don't be silly, woman. I'm turning the heating off!"

1765 Boy: "Is it true, Dad, that in some parts of Africa a man doesn't know his wife until he marries her?"

Father: "That happens in every country, son."

1766 A motorist was pulled over by a traffic cop. "Excuse me, sir," said the cop. "Do you realize your wife fell out of the car two miles back?"

"Thank God," he said. "I thought I'd gone deaf."

1767 Why get married and make one man miserable when I can stay single and make thousands miserable? (CARRIE SNOW)

Mixed marriages:

1768 If Yoko Ono married Bono, she'd be Yoko Ono Bono.

1769 If Dolly Parton married Salvador Dali, she'd be Dolly Dali.

1770 If Ella Fitzgerald married Darth Vader, she'd be Ella Vader.

1771 If Bea Arthur married Sting, she'd be Bea Sting.

1772 If Bo Derek married Don Ho, she'd be Bo Ho.

1773 If Irene Handl married David Broome, she could be Irene Broome-Handl.

1774 If Oprah Winfrey married Deepak Chopra, she'd be Oprah Chopra.

1775 If Olivia Newton-John married Wayne Newton, then divorced him to marry Elton John, she'd be Olivia Newton-John Newton John.

1776 If Snoop Doggy Dogg married Winnie the Pooh, he'd be Snoop Doggy Dogg Pooh.

1777 If G. Gordon Liddy married Boutros-Boutros Ghali, then divorced him to marry Kenny G, he'd be G. Ghali G.

1778 If Sondra Locke married Eliot Ness, then divorced him to marry Herman Munster, she'd become Sondra Locke Ness Munster.

1779 If Woody Allen married Natalie Wood, divorced her and married Gregory Peck, divorced him and married Ben Hur, he'd be Woody Wood Peck Hur.

1780 For a man, how is marriage like a tornado? – They both begin with a lot of blowing and sucking, and end with you losing your house.

1781 First man: "My wife's an angel."
Second man: "You're lucky – mine's still alive!"

1782 A husband never referred to his wife by her real name, but instead always called her pet names like Sugar Lump, Kitten, and Honey Bunch. His friend thought it was sweet. "I really like the way you call her those endearing names. It shows how much you care about her."
   "To tell the truth," said the husband, "I forgot her real name three years ago!"

1783 My wife and I have the secret to making a marriage last. Two times a week, we go to a nice restaurant, a little wine, good food. She goes Tuesdays, I go Fridays. (HENNY YOUNGMAN)

1784 "What would you like for your anniversary, darling?" asked the husband as the couple prepared to celebrate their thirtieth wedding anniversary. "How about a new wardrobe full of designer labels?"

"No, I don't think so," said the wife.

"Then what about a new Mercedes?"

"No, I don't think so."

"What about a holiday in Bali?"

"No, I don't think so. You see, what I really want is a divorce."

"A divorce?" said the husband. "Sorry, darling, I wasn't planning to spend that much!"

1785 The Invisible Man married an invisible woman. The kids were nothing to look at.

1786 Any husband who says, "My wife and I are completely equal partners" is talking about either a law firm or a hand of bridge. (BILL COSBY)

1787 A man was drowning his sorrows in a bar with a fellow drinker. "I had it all," he groaned, "money, a beautiful house, fast car and the love of a beautiful woman. Then suddenly it was all gone."

"What happened?" asked his companion.

"My wife found out."

1788 Bigamy is the only crime on the books where two rites make a wrong. (BOB HOPE)

1789 A woman I know has been married so many times she has rice marks on her face. She has a wash and wear bridal gown. (HENNY YOUNGMAN)

1790 Do you know what it means when you come home to a little affection, a little tenderness, and a little sympathy? – It means you're in the wrong house.

1791 A wife became increasingly annoyed by the fact that her shopkeeper husband was repeatedly home late from work. Every night he promised faithfully that he would be home in time for dinner but something always arose to keep him at the shop later than planned. Consequently, night after night she ended up throwing his dinner away. Eventually she got so mad that she Issued him with an ultimatum. "Tonight you get home at six o'clock sharp or it's the last meal I ever cook for you."

The husband was worried. He loved his wife dearly and couldn't help working late. After all, times were hard and business was business. But he decided to make a real effort to get home on time for once. So he closed the shop an hour early and set off to catch the bus. But as he crossed the street, he was struck down by a car. He was rushed to hospital but his injuries turned out to be minor and he was discharged shortly afterwards. Nevertheless the delay meant that it was eight o'clock before he arrived home.

His wife was raging. "What time do you call this?" she boomed. "You promised me you'd be home by six!"

"Darling, I can explain. I know I'm two hours late, but I was run over by a car."

"So what?" she said. "It takes two hours to get run over?"

1792 Marriage is a wonderful invention; but then again, so is a bicycle puncture repair kit. (BILLY CONNOLLY)

1793 Men who have pierced ears are better prepared for marriage. They've experienced pain and bought jewellery. (RITA RUDNER)

1794 A woman ran excitedly into her house one morning and yelled to her husband: "John, pack up your stuff. I just won the lottery!"

"Shall I pack for warm weather or cold?" he said.

"Whatever. Just so long as you're out of the house by noon."

1795 Courtship is like looking at the beautiful photos in a seed catalogue. Marriage is what actually comes up in your garden.

1796 Marriage is like the witness protection programme: you get all new clothes, you live in the suburbs and you're not allowed to see your friends anymore. (JEREMY HARDY)

1797 Why do most men die before their wives? – They want to.

1798 Why did Adam and Eve have the perfect marriage? – He didn't have to listen to her talk about all the other men she could have married, and she didn't have to put up with his mother.

1799 The honeymoon period is over when the husband calls home to say he'll be late for dinner, and the answering machine says it's in the microwave.

1800 Two married men, Norm and Dick, were having a beer after work. Norm said: "Have you ever said one thing when you meant to say something else?"

"How do you mean?" said Dick.

"Well, the other day instead of two tickets to Pittsburgh, I asked for two pickets to Titsberg."

"Yeah, I know what you mean," said Dick. "Last week I was having breakfast with my wife. I meant to say, "Pass the sugar." But what came out was, "You bitch, you ruined my life!'"

1801 I love being married. It's so great to find the one special person you want to annoy for the rest of your life. (RITA RUDNER)

1802 A marriage counsellor was asking a woman questions about her state of mind.

"Did you wake up grumpy this morning?"

"No, I let him sleep."

1803 An x-ray specialist married one of his patients. Everybody wondered what he saw in her.

1804 A woman went to the police to report her husband missing. "He's 35, six foot two inches tall, dark eyes, dark wavy hair, athletic build, weighs 185 lbs, softspoken, and he's good with the children."

Her neighbour protested: "He's five foot 2 inches, chubby, bald, has a big mouth and is mean to your children!"

"I know," said the wife, "but who wants him back?"

1805 A guy was drinking heavily in a bar. "I think you've had enough," said the bartender.

The drunk was indignant. "I just lost my wife."

The bartender sympathized. "Well, it must be hard losing a wife."

"Hard? It was almost impossible!"

1806 A guy told his pal: "My wife and I are inseparable. In fact, last week it took four State Troopers and a dog!"

1807 After 35 years of miserable marriage, a millionaire suddenly changed his will so that his wife would inherit everything, so long as she remarried within three months of his death.

"Why do you want to do that?" asked his lawyer.

"Because I want someone to be sorry I died."

1808 I recently read that love is entirely a matter of chemistry. That must be why my wife treats me like toxic waste. (DAVID BISONETTE)

1809 A couple had a furious row on their twenty-fifth wedding anniversary. He was so bitter that he presented her with a gift of a tombstone bearing the inscription: "Here lies my wife – cold as ever."

In retaliation she went out the next day and bought him a tombstone with the inscription: "Here lies my husband – stiff at last."

1810 You may marry the man of your dreams, but 14 years later you're married to a couch that burps. (ROSEANNE BARR)

1811 Husband: "Honey, why are you wearing your wedding ring on the wrong finger?"

Wife: "Because I married the wrong man."

1812 A guy went into a bar and ordered a double shot of bourbon. He downed it, reached into his pocket and pulled out a photo. After staring at the picture for a few moments, he put it away and ordered another double. When he had finished that drink, he pulled out the photo again, looked at it for a moment, put it back and ordered another double. He repeated this procedure for the next hour. Finally the bartender's curiosity got the better of him. "Excuse me," he said, "but after each drink, why do you keep taking out that picture and staring at it?"

"It's a picture of my wife," explained the customer, "and when she starts to look good, I'm going home."

1813 Why are married women heavier than single women? – Single women come home, see what's in the refrigerator and go to bed; married women come home, see what's in bed and go to the refrigerator.

1814 My ex-boyfriend came round last night, which was a bit weird because I didn't even know he was in a coma. (JO BRAND)

1815 Tony: "I hear you got married again, Mike."

Mike: "Yes, for the fourth time."

Tony: "What happened to your first three wives?"

Mike: "They all died."

Tony: "I'm sorry, I didn't know. That's terrible. How did they die?"

Mike: "The first ate poisonous mushrooms."

Tony: "How awful! What about the second?"

Mike: "She ate poison mushrooms."

Tony: "Oh no. What about the third? Did she die from poisonous mushrooms too?"

Mike: "No, she died of a broken neck."

Tony: "I see, an accident."

Mike: "Not exactly – she wouldn't eat her mushrooms."

Men

Men are like . . .

1816 Men are like mascara – they usually run at the first sign of emotion.

1817 Men are like parking spots – the good ones are already taken and the ones that are left are handicapped.

1818 Men are like blenders – you need one, but you're not quite sure why.

1819 Men are like bananas – the older they get, the less firm they are.

1820 Men are like mini skirts – if you're not careful, they'll creep up your legs.

1821 Men are like cement – after getting laid, they take ages to get hard.

1822 Men are like computers – hard to figure out and they never have enough memory.

1823 Men are like lava lamps – fun to look at, but not all that bright.

1824 Men are like bank accounts – without a lot of money, they don't generate much interest.

1825 Men are like coolers – load them with beer and you can take them anywhere.

1826 Men are like fragments of soap – they get together in bars.

1827 Men are like vacations – they never seem to last long enough.

1828 Men are like chocolate bars – sweet, smooth, and they usually go straight to your hips.

1829 Men are like place mats – they only show up when there's food on the table.

1830 Men are like commercials – you can't believe a word they say.

1831 Men are like curling irons – they're always hot and always in your hair.

1832 Men are like popcorn – they satisfy you, but only for a short while.

1833 Men are like horoscopes – they always tell you what to do and are usually wrong.

1834 Men are like noodles – they're always in hot water and they lack taste.

1835 Men are like lawn mowers – if you're not pushing one around, then you're riding it.

1836 Men are like copiers – you need them for reproduction, but that's about it.

1837 Men are like snowstorms – you never know when they're coming, how many inches you'll get, or how long they'll last.

1838 What is the difference between going to a singles bar and going to a circus? – At a circus the clowns don't talk.

1839 What's the difference between a Savings Bond and the typical male? At some point the Savings Bond will mature.

1840 What's the difference between a new husband and a new dog? – After a year, the dog is still excited to see you.

1841 What's the difference between a man and ET? – ET phoned home.

1842 What is the difference between a man and childbirth? – One is a constant pain and is almost unbearable, the other is simply having a baby.

1843 How do you scare a man? – Sneak up behind him and start throwing rice.

1844 How does a man show that he's planning for the future? – He buys two cases of beer instead of one.

1845 What's the one thing worse than a male chauvinist pig? – A woman who won't do what she's told.

1846 How can you tell if a man is a male chauvinist pig? – He thinks "harass" is two words.

1847 Why is a launderette a really bad place to pick up a woman? – Because a woman who can't even afford a washing machine will never be able to support you.

1848 Why do black widow spiders kill their males after mating? – To stop the snoring before it starts.

1849 I don't hate men. I think men are absolutely fantastic . . . as a concept. (JO BRAND)

1850 How to impress a woman: compliment her, cuddle her, kiss her, caress her, love her, tease her, comfort her, protect her, hug her, hold her, spend money on her, wine and dine her, listen to her, care for her, stand by her, support her, go to the ends of the earth for her.
   How to impress a man: turn up naked with beer.

1851 The quickest way to a man's heart is through his chest. (ROSEANNE BARR)

1852 Why do most men like smart women? – Because opposites attract.

1853 Why is it difficult to find men who are sensitive, caring and good looking? – Because they already have boyfriends.

1854 How do you get a man to exercise? – Tie the TV remote control to his shoelaces.

1855 How do men exercise on the beach? – By sucking in their stomach every time they see a bikini.

1856 What should you give a man who has everything? – A woman to show him how to work it.

1857 All men are afraid of eyelash curlers. I sleep with one under my pillow, instead of a gun. (RITA RUDNER)

1858 A girl and a boy had been in a relationship for four months. One Friday night they met in a bar after work, stayed for a few drinks, then went to get some food at a local restaurant. They ate, went back to his house and she stayed over.

Her story: He was in an odd mood when I got to the bar. I thought that it might have been because I was a bit late, but he didn't say much about it. The conversation was quite slow going, so I thought we should go off somewhere more intimate to talk. We went to this restaurant and he was still a bit strange. I tried to cheer him up, but it didn't seem to make any difference. I asked him if the problem was me, but he said that it wasn't. In the cab back to his house, I told him that I loved him, but he just put his arm around me. I didn't know what the hell that meant because he didn't say he loved me in return. By the time we got back to his place, I actually wondered if he was going to dump me. I tried to ask him about it, but he just switched on the TV. Reluctantly, I told him that I was going to bed. After ten minutes he joined me and we made love. But he still seemed really distracted, and afterwards I just wanted to leave. I don't really know what he thinks any more. I wonder if he's met someone else.

His story: Bad day at work, but at least I got laid.

1859 Did you hear about the new "morning after" pill for men? – It changes their blood type.

1860 Jesus was a typical man. They always say they'll come back but you never see them again.

1861 Actually there were four wise men on their way to Bethlehem. One of them said he knew a short cut.

1862 Why did God create woman? – Because after creating man, he was sure he could do better.

1863 What's the difference between a golf ball and a g-spot? A man will spend two hours searching for a golf ball.

1864 The problem is that God gives men a brain and a penis, and only enough blood to run one at a time. (ROBIN WILLIAMS)

1865 No man is an island, but some of us are pretty long peninsulas. (ASHLEIGH BRILLIANT)

1866 On the one hand, we'll never experience childbirth. On the other hand, we can open all our own jars. (JEFF GREEN)

What men say and what they really mean:

1867 "Take a break, honey, you're working too hard" MEANS "I can't hear the game over the vacuum cleaner."

1868 "I'm going fishing" MEANS "I'm going to drink myself into a stupor, stand by a stream with a stick in my hand while the fish swim by in total safety."

1869 "Can I help with dinner?" MEANS "Why isn't it on the table yet?"

1870 "I missed you" MEANS "My socks need washing and we're out of toilet paper."

1871 "It's a really good movie" MEANS "It's got guns, knives, fast cars and Heather Locklear."

1872 "I'm not lost, I know exactly where we are" MEANS "No one will ever see us alive again."

1873 "I don't believe in material possessions" MEANS "I'm poor."

1874 "I was listening to you – it's just that I have things on my mind" MEANS "I was wondering if that blonde over there is wearing a bra."

1875 "That's women's work" MEANS "I don't understand how to do it."

1876 "You cook just like my mother used to" MEANS "She used the smoke detector as a meal timer too."

1877 "What's wrong?" MEANS "What meaningless, self-inflicted psychological trauma are you going through now?"

1878 "I was just thinking about you, and got you these roses" MEANS "I fancy the flower-seller."

1879 "You look terrific" MEANS "Please don't try on any more outfits – I'm starving."

1880 "I've been thinking a lot" MEANS "You're not as attractive as when I was drunk."

1881 "I think we should just be friends" MEANS "You're downright ugly."

1882 "I can't find it" MEANS "It didn't fall into my outstretched hands."

1883 "You're the only girl I've ever cared about" MEANS "You're the only girl who hasn't dumped me."

1884 "I'm hungry" MEANS "Make me something to eat."

1885 "I do help around the house" MEANS "I once put a dirty towel in the laundry basket."

1886 "She's one of those rabid feminists" MEANS "She won't wait on me hand and foot."

1887 "Do you love me?" MEANS "I've done something stupid and you might find out."

1888 "Do you really love me?" MEANS "I've done something stupid and you're going to find out sooner or later."

1889 "How much do you love me?" MEANS "I've done something really stupid and someone's on their way to tell you now."

1890 "I have something to tell you" MEANS "Get tested."

1891 "Do you want to go to a movie?" MEANS "I really want to have sex with you."

1892 "Can I take you out to dinner?" MEANS "I really want to have sex with you."

1893 "May I have this dance?" MEANS "I really want to have sex with you."

1894 "Nice dress" MEANS "Nice cleavage."

1895 "You look tense, let me give you a massage" MEANS "I want to grope you."

1896 "I'm bored" MEANS "Do you want to have sex?"

1897 Man to God: "God, why did you make woman so beautiful?"
    God: "So that you would love her."
    Man: "But why did you make her so dumb?"
    God: "So that she would love you."

1898 A man is designed to walk three miles in the rain to phone for help when the car breaks down, and a woman is designed to say, "You took your time" when he comes back dripping wet. (VICTORIA WOOD)

1899 Men do not like to admit even momentary imperfection. My husband forgot the code to turn off the house alarm. When the police came, he wouldn't admit he'd forgotten the code. He turned himself in. (RITA RUDNER)

1900 If men can run the world, why can't they stop wearing neckties? How intelligent is it to start the day by tying a little noose around your neck? (LINDA ELLERBEE)

1901 A man walked into a florist's and said: "I'd like some flowers please."
"Certainly, sir. What did you have in mind?"
"I'm not sure."
"Perhaps I could help," suggested the florist. "What exactly have you done?"

1902 A woman needs a man like a fish needs a bicycle. (GLORIA STEINEM)

1903 What are the three words guaranteed to humiliate men everywhere? – "Hold my purse". (FRANCOIS MORENCY)

1904 Two women were talking about the new hunk in the neighbourhood.
"But he acts so stupid," said one. "I think he must have his brains between his legs."
"Yeah," smiled the other, "but I'd sure love to blow his mind."

1905 When women are depressed, they either eat or go shopping. Men invade another country. (ELAYNE BOOSLER)

1906 Only one man in 1,000 is a leader of men. The other 999 follow women. (GROUCHO MARX)

1907 When is the only time a man thinks about a candlelit dinner? – When there's a power cut.

1908 What does a man consider to be a seven-course meal? – A hot dog and a six-pack.

1909 What's the definition of a man with manners? – One who gets out of the bath to pee.

1910 What's a man's idea of doing housework? – Lifting his legs so you can hoover.

1911 How do men define a 50/50 relationship? – You cook, we eat.

1912 What is a man's idea of foreplay? – Half an hour of begging.

1913 What do you call a man who expects to have sex on the second date? – Slow.

1914 How can you tell if a man is sexually excited? – He's breathing.

1915 A woman's work that is never done is the stuff she asked her husband to do.

1916 If one man can wash one pile of dishes in one hour, how many piles of dishes can four men wash in four hours? – None – they'll all sit down together and watch football on TV.

1917 There are only two four-letter words that are offensive to men: "Don't" and "Stop" (unless they're used together).

1918 Husbands are like children – they're fine if they're someone else's.

1919 Diamonds are a girl's best friend. Dogs are man's best friend. So which is the dumber sex?

1920 Scientists have just discovered something that can do the work of five men – a woman.

1921 Women will never be equal to men until they can walk down the street bald and with a beer gut and still think they're beautiful.

What do you call a man . . . ?

1922 What do you call a man with a spade on his head? – Doug.
1923 What do you call a man without a spade on his head? – Douglas.
1924 What do you call a man with a seagull on his head? – Cliff.
1925 What do you call a man in debt? – Owen.
1926 What do you call a man with a car on his head? – Jack.
1927 What do you call a man with a government subsidy? – Grant.
1928 What do you call a man with 50 rabbits up his ass? – Warren.
1929 What do you call a man with three eyes? – Seymour.
1930 What do you call a man with sports equipment on his head? – Jim.
1931 What do you call a man who has lost 90 per cent of his brain? – A widower.
1932 What do you call a Brazilian with a rubber toe? – Roberto.

Why a cucumber is better than a man:

1933 A cucumber doesn't make you sleep on the wet spot it has made.

1934 You can enjoy a cucumber all night long.

1935 Cucumbers only get pickled if you want them too.

1936 Cucumber stains wash out.

1937 A cucumber won't get upset if you come home with another cucumber on your breath.

1938 Your cucumber will always wait patiently in the car while you go shopping.

1939 Cucumbers don't demand equality.

1940 A cucumber is nearly always hard.

1941 When your cucumber goes soft, you toss it.

1942 Cucumbers can't tell the time, so they don't know when you're late.

1943 Indigestion goes away in the morning.

1944 Cucumbers don't play around.

1945 Cucumber skins come off without a fight.

1946 It's easy to pick up a cucumber in a grocery store.

1947 You don't have to watch where a cucumber puts its hands.

1948 The older a cucumber, the larger it gets.

1949 You can have more than one cucumber a night and not feel guilty.

1950 You always know when you're the first one to eat a cucumber.

1951 You can keep a cucumber in your apartment without upsetting your mother.

1952 Women might be able to fake orgasms, but men can fake whole relationships. (JIMMY SHUBERT)

1953 A wealthy playboy was going out with three different girls at the same time. He wanted to settle down but couldn't decide which of the three to ask to be his bride. So he decided upon a test. He would give each girl 5,000 dollars to spend and would monitor what each did with the money.

The first girl spent the cash on a complete makeover – new clothes, new hairdo, the lot. She told him: "I wanted to look my best for you because I love you so much." He was impressed.

The second girl bought new golf clubs, a CD player, an expensive leather jacket and a wide screen TV, and gave them all to him as gifts. "These are a token of my love for you," she declared. He was impressed.

The third girl invested the 5,000 dollars in the stock market, tripled her initial investment and gave him his 5,000 dollars back . . . plus interest. She then reinvested the remainder "for our future, because I love you so." He was impressed.

Clearly it was a tough decision to choose between the three. He spent several days in deliberation before coming to the only rational conclusion – he chose the one with the biggest tits.

1954 Men hate to lose. I once beat my husband at tennis. I asked him, "Are we going to have sex again?" He said, "Yes, but not with each other." (RITA RUDNER)

1955 How many men does it take to open a beer? – None. It should be opened by the time she brings it to the couch.

1956 How many men does it take to change a roll of toilet paper? – Nobody knows, it's never happened.

Reasons why it's great to be a man:

1957 People never glance at your chest while you're talking to them.

1958 You can wear the same pair of underpants for a week.

1959 Phone calls are over in 30 seconds flat.

1960 Facial hair can be attractive.

1961 If another guy shows up at a party in the same outfit, you might become lifelong friends.

1962 Women almost expect you to belch.

1963 When your work is criticized, you don't have to panic that everyone secretly hates you.

1964 Not liking someone does not eliminate having great sex with them.

1965 You can buy condoms without the shopkeeper imagining you naked.

1966 A week's vacation requires only one suitcase.

1967 You can go to the bathroom without a support group.

1968 You can leave the bed in a hotel room unmade.

1969 You don't have to worry about your weight.

1970 Spiders don't reduce you to a quivering wreck.

1971 Your ass is never a factor in a job interview.

1972 All your orgasms are real.

1973 You can kill your own food.

1974 You don't have to lug a bag of useful stuff around wherever you go.

1975 You never have to clean the toilet.

1976 You can be showered and ready in ten minutes.

1977 Wedding plans take care of themselves.

1978 You can sleep around without any stain on your character.

1979 If someone forgets to invite you to something, they can still be your friend.

1980 You don't have to shave below your neck.

1981 You can write your name in the snow.

1982 Flowers fix everything.

1983 You don't get wolf whistles from workmen.

1984 You get to think about sex 90 per cent of your waking hours.

1985 You can wear a white shirt to a water park.

1986 Hot wax never comes near your pubic area.

1987 You don't have to learn how the washing machine works.

1988 Three pairs of shoes are more than enough.

1989 You can admire Leonardo DiCaprio without starving yourself to look like him.

1990 Nobody stops telling a dirty joke when you walk in the room.

1991 You can take your shirt off on a hot day.

1992 You don't care whether anyone notices your new haircut.

1993 You can sit with your knees apart.

1994 You can eat a banana in public.

1995 The world is your urinal.

1996 You have one mood all the time.

But it's not always easy being a man:

1997 If you put a woman on a pedestal and try to protect her from the rat race, you're a male chauvinist; if you stay home and do the housework, you're a sissy.

1998 If you work too hard, there's never any time for her; if you don't work enough, you're a good-for-nothing bum.

1999 If she has a boring repetitive job with low pay, it's exploitation; if you have a boring repetitive job with low pay, you should get off your butt and find something better.

2000 If you get a promotion ahead of her, it's favouritism; if she gets a job ahead of you, it's equal opportunity.

2001 If you mention how nice she looks, it's sexual harassment; if you don't, you're rude and arrogant.

2002 If you cry, you're a wimp; if you don't, you're an insensitive jerk.

2003 If you make a decision without consulting her, you're a chauvinist; if she makes a decision without consulting you, she's a liberated woman.

2004 If you ask her to do something she doesn't enjoy, it's domination; if she asks you, it's a favour.

2005 If she has a headache, she's tired; if you have a headache, you don't love her anymore.

2006 If you want it too often, you're oversexed; if you don't, there must be someone else.

Money

2007 It was the worst winter in living memory. Thousands of homes were cut off by deep snowdrifts, including a family in a remote mountain cabin in Canada. After three months with no contact with the outside world, the family became the target of a Red Cross rescue mission. But for weeks even the Red Cross team couldn't manage to force their way through to the cabin which by now was almost completely submerged in snow. Finally the brave rescuers succeeded in hacking out a path to the front door of the cabin. Not knowing what they would find, they knocked on the front door. The father answered the door.

"Red Cross," said the leader of the team.

"Sorry," said the father. "It's been such a tough winter that I don't think we can give anything this year."

2008 Misers are no fun to live with, but they make great ancestors. (TOM SNYDER)

2009 A father gave his three-year-old son his first pocket money. "I'll give you two pence a week, son, so you save them up and put them in this yellow box. Then when you've got five, I'll swap them for a ten pence coin and you can put that in this blue box. Then when you've got five of those, I'll swap them for a 50 pence coin and you can put that in this red box."

It was only 12 years later that the boy discovered that the red box was the gas meter.

2010 I have enough money to last me the rest of my life, unless I buy something. (JACKIE MASON)

2011 A couple had been spending money at such an alarming rate that they didn't think they would be afford a holiday next year. So the husband came up with a bright savings plan: whenever they had sex, he would put 20 dollars into a piggy bank.

A year later, he emptied the piggy bank to see how much they had collected. He was puzzled. "Every time we've had sex, I've put in a 20 dollar bill, but there are 50 and 100 dollar bills in here."

His wife said: "That's your trouble – you think everyone's as stingy as you."

2012 A little old lady was walking down the street, dragging two plastic garbage bags with her, one in each hand. There was a hole in one of the bags, leaving a trail of $20 bills on the sidewalk. Spotting this, a police officer stopped her: "Ma'am, there are $20 bills falling out of that bag."

"Damn!" said the little old lady. "I'd better go back and collect them. Thanks for the warning."

"Well now, not so fast," said the cop. "How did you get all that money? Did you steal it?"

"Oh no," said the little old lady. "You see, my garden backs on to the car park of the football stadium. Each time there's a game, a lot of fans come and pee in the bushes, right onto my flower beds. So I go and stand behind the bushes with a big pair of shears and each time someone sticks his thingie through the bushes, I say: '$20, or off it comes!'"

"Hey, not a bad idea!" laughed the cop. "OK, good luck! By the way, what's in the other bag?"

"Well," said the little old lady, "not all of them pay up . . ."

2013 There's always one of my uncles who watches a boxing match with me and says, "Sure. Ten million dollars. For that kind of money, I'd fight him." As if someone is going to pay $200 a ticket to see a 57-year-old carpet salesman get hit in the face once and cry. (LARRY MILLER)

2014 Wife: "Do you love me just because my father left me a fortune?"

Husband: "Not at all, darling. I would love you no matter who left you the money."

2015 A man was walking through a rough part of town when a bum in tattered clothes walked up to him and asked him for two dollars.

"What do you want the money for?" asked the man. "Will you use it to buy booze?"

"No."

"Will you gamble it away?"

"No."

"Then will you come home with me so my wife can see what happens to a guy who doesn't drink or gamble?"

2016 Money can't buy you friends, but you get a better class of enemy. (SPIKE MILLIGAN)

2017 An archaeologist working in the Israeli desert discovered a casket containing a mummy. He proudly announced: "I have just found a 3,000-year-old mummy of a man who died of heart failure."

Tests on the mummy confirmed the archaeologist's findings. "How did you know he had died of heart failure?" asked a journalist.

"It was simple," said the archaeologist. "There was a piece of paper in his hand that said '10,000 shekels on Goliath'."

2018 After the family barn burned down, the wife rang the insurance company. "We had that barn insured for 60,000 dollars. I want my money."

The insurance agent explained: "I'm sorry, madam, but insurance doesn't quite work like that. We will ascertain the value of what was insured and provide you with a replacement of comparable worth."

"Then I'd like to cancel the policy on my husband!"

2019 I was walking down Fifth Avenue today and I found a wallet, and I was gonna keep it, rather than return it. But I thought: if I lost $150, how would I feel? And I realized I would want to be taught a lesson. (EMO PHILIPS)

2020 A father came home from a long business trip to find his son riding a fancy new bike. "Where did you get the money for that?" he asked. "It must have cost 300 dollars."

"I earned it hiking," replied the boy.

"Come on, son, tell me the truth. Nobody gets that sort of money hiking. Where did you really get the cash?"

"It's like I say, Dad. Every night you were gone, Mr Gillespie from the bank would come over to see Mum. He'd give me a 20 dollar bill and tell me to take a hike."

2021 My parents were so poor, they got married for the rice. (BOB HOPE)

2022 Joe was broke. His business had gone bust and in desperation he prayed to God to make him win the lottery. But he was out of luck and had to sell his car. The next week he again prayed to God to make him win the lottery, but once more he was out of luck and had to sell his house. With his wife about to leave him, Joe made one last plea to God to make him win the lottery. God came back to him and said: "Listen, Joe, meet me halfway on this – buy a ticket."

2023 Mark went round to his friend's house one evening and rang the doorbell. "Is Tony in?" he asked.

"No," said Tony's wife, Vicky, dressed in a bathrobe, "but he should be in soon if you'd like to wait."

Mark sat down in the lounge with Vicky and waited. After a few minutes he said: "Vicky, I've always thought you had the most fantastic breasts. I'd pay you 100 bucks just to see one."

Vicky was taken aback, but thought that for that sort of money, it was worth it. So she opened her robe and allowed Mark to see one of her breasts. Mark gave her the 100 dollars and then said: "I'd give you another 100 bucks if I could see the other one."

So Vicky undid her robe a little more and this time let him have a really long look for his money. Then he gave her the 100 dollars and said: "I'm sorry, I can't wait for Tony any longer. I've got to go. Tell him I called."

When Tony arrived home, Vicky said: "Your friend Mark came round earlier."

"Oh yeah?" said Tony. "Did he drop off the 200 bucks he owes me?"

Mother-in-law jokes

2024 A big game hunter went on safari with his wife and mother-in-law. One evening, the husband and wife were sitting around the camp fire having supper when she realized that her mother was missing. The hunter picked up his rifle and, with his wife close behind, set off into the jungle to look for the missing woman. After searching for over an hour, they finally spotted her backed up against a cliff with a huge lion facing her.

"What are we going to do?" shrieked the wife.

"Nothing," said the husband. "The lion got himself into this mess . . ."

2025 A man took his dog to the vet and asked the vet to cut off its tail. The vet wanted to know why.

"Because," said the man, "my mother-in-law is arriving tomorrow, and I don't want anything to make her think she's welcome."

2026 What is the definition of mixed emotions? – When you see your mother-in-law backing off a cliff in your new car.

2027 I just got back from a pleasure trip. I took my mother-in-law to the airport. (HENNY YOUNGMAN)

2028 A lawyer cabled his client overseas: "Your mother-in-law passed away in her sleep. Shall we order burial, embalming or cremation?"

The reply came back: "Take no chances – order all three."

2029 What is the penalty for bigamy? – Two mothers-in-law.

2030 My mother-in-law broke up my marriage. One day my wife came home early and found us in bed together. (LENNY BRUCE)

2031 A husband was late home from work one evening. "I'm sure he's having an affair," said his wife to her mother.

"Why do you always think the worst?" said the mother. "Maybe he's just been in an accident."

2032 I said to my mother-in-law, "My house is your house." She said, "Get the hell off my property." (JOAN RIVERS)

2033 The wife's mother said: "When you're dead, I'll dance on your grave." I said: "Good, I'm being buried at sea." (LES DAWSON)

2034 The wife's mother said: "How would you like to have a chat with me?" I said: "Through a medium." (LES DAWSON)

2035 Two friends met in the street. "Where are you coming from?" asked Ted.

"The cemetery," answered Jim. "I just buried my mother-in-law."

"Oh, I'm sorry. But what are those scratches on your face?"

"She put up a heck of a fight."

2036 The front doorbell rang and a man opened the door to find his mother-in-law on the step with a suitcase. "Can I stay here for a few days?" she asked.

He said, "Sure you can," and shut the door in her face.

2037 The police chief addressed a new recruit. "As a recruit, you'll be faced with some difficult issues. For example, what would you do if you had to arrest your wife's mother?"

"Call for back-up."

2038 It took time but eventually I developed a special attachment to my mother-in-law. It fitted over her mouth. (LES DAWSON)

2039 I saw six men kicking and punching the mother-in-law.

My neighbour said, "Are you going to help?"

I said, "No, six should be enough." (LES DAWSON)

2040 A man came into work one Monday morning with his neck heavily bandaged.

"What happened to you?" asked his colleagues.

"I was playing golf yesterday with my mother-in-law and on the second hole she sliced her ball into a field full of cows. She wasn't going to give the ball up for lost and so she insisted that we search. We looked for a quarter of an hour, but there was no sign of the ball, just one old cow. Still my mother-in-law insisted that she wouldn't leave until we had found her ball. We searched for another 25 minutes, but still couldn't find it. I was just on the point of giving up when I thought I'd better check to make sure the ball hadn't somehow got lodged in the cow. So I lifted up the cow's tail and, sure enough, a ball was stuck there. I called my mother-in-law over and said: 'Does this look like yours?' And she hit me in the throat with a five iron."

Music

2041 I hate music, especially when it's played. (JIMMY DURANTE)

2042 The wife was upset: "Why do you go out on the balcony whenever I sing? Don't you like to hear me?"
"It's not that," said the husband. "I just want the neighbours to see that I'm not beating my wife."

2043 When Jack Benny plays the violin, it sounds as if the strings are still back in the cat. (FRED ALLEN)

2044 Jack Benny arrived at the gates of the White House carrying his violin case.
"What you got in there, Jack?" asked the security guard. Benny handed over the case. The guard opened it and found a sub-machine gun inside. "That's OK," said the guard. "I was worried you'd brought your violin."

2045 Why do bagpipers walk when they play? – To try to get away from the noise.

2046 What's the definition of a gentleman? – Someone who knows how to play the bagpipes, but doesn't.

2047 What's the difference between a banjo and a Harley-Davidson? – You can tune a Harley.

2048 What's the difference between a soprano and the PLO? – You can negotiate with the PLO.

2049 What's the difference between a soprano and a Porsche? – Most musicians have never been in a Porsche.

2050 What's the definition of an optimist? – An accordion player with a pager.

2051 What's the difference between an Uzi and an accordion? – An Uzi stops after 20 rounds.

2052 What is an accordion good for? – Learning how to fold a map.

2053 Why are accordionists' fingers like lightning? – They rarely strike the same spot twice.

2054 Following a late-night gig, an accordion player woke up in the morning and realized he had left his accordion on the back seat of his car which was parked out in the street. Convinced that the instrument would have been stolen overnight, he dashed out in his pyjamas and, sure enough, saw that the side rear window of the car had been smashed. But when he looked into the back seat, he saw not only his accordion but two more accordions.

2055 What do you call an oboist who is deaf? – Principal.

2056 Why did the chicken cross the road? – To get away from the cello recital.

2057 What's the difference between a cello and a chainsaw? – The grip.

2058 What do you call someone who hangs around with musicians? – A drummer.

2059 What do you call a drummer without a girlfriend? – Homeless.

2060 What's the difference between a drum kit and a lawnmower? – The neighbours are upset if you borrow a lawnmower and don't return it.

2061 How is a drum solo like a sneeze? – You can tell it's coming, but you can't do a thing about it.

2062 What's the last thing a drummer says in a band? – "Hey, guys, why don't we try one of my songs?"

2063 Man: "My doctor advised me to give up playing the drums?"
Friend: "Why?"
Man: "He lives in the apartment below."

2064 How do you get a drummer off your porch? – Pay for the pizza.

2065 What's the difference between a drummer and Dr Scholl's footpads? – Dr Scholl's bucks up the feet.

2066 An Amazon explorer went in search of a remote tribe thought to be hostile to strangers. He employed a local guide to act as translator. At dusk on the first day the pair were sitting around a campfire when they heard the sound of tribal drums in the distance. The drums got louder. The guide confessed: "I don't like the sound of those drums."
As darkness began to fall, the drums became even louder. The guide said: "I really don't like the sound of those drums."
Come nightfall and still the drums got louder. They were obviously very close. The guide repeated: "I really do not like the sound of those drums."
Suddenly the drums stopped and a voice from the darkness cried out: "Hey, man, he's not our regular drummer!"

2067 I play all my country and western music backwards – your lover returns, your dog comes back and you cease to be an alcoholic. (LINDA SMITH)

2068 A society hostess was talking to one of her guests as the two sat on the lawn listening to a cello recital.
"Beautiful, isn't it?" said the hostess.
"Pardon?" said the guest.
"I said it's beautiful, isn't it?"
"I'm sorry," yelled the guest. "I can't hear a thing for that damn cello!"

2069 An 11-year-old boy was doing his violin practice at home and the torturous noise was making the dog howl. Upstairs, the boy's father was trying to work on the computer. After putting up with the combined racket of violin and dog for 20 minutes, the father eventually called out: "Jason. Can't you play something the dog doesn't know?"

2070 What's the difference between a violinist and a dog? – A dog knows when to stop scratching.

2071 What's green and sings? – Elvis Parsley.

2072 What has 300 legs and seven teeth? – The front row at a Willie Nelson concert.

2073 What do a viola and a lawsuit have in common? – Everyone is happy when the case is closed.

2074 How do you get two viola players to play in perfect unison? – Shoot one of them.

2075 What's the difference between a viola and a coffin? – The coffin has the corpse *inside*.

2076 What's the difference between a vacuum cleaner and a viola? – A vacuum cleaner has to be plugged in before it sucks.

2077 What's the latest crime wave in New York? – Drive-by viola recitals.

2078 How can you tell if a viola is out of tune? – The bow is moving.

2079 Why do viola players stand for long periods outside people's houses? – They can't find the key and they don't know when to come in.

2080 Why shouldn't you drive off a cliff in a Mini with three violas in it? – You could fit in at least one more.

2081 What's the difference between a viola and fingernails scraping on a black-board? – Vibrato.

2082 Why shouldn't viola players take up mountain climbing? – If they got lost, no one would look for them.

2083 Why do viola players leave their cases on the dashboard of their car? – So they can park in handicapped zones.

2084 What's the difference between a cello and a viola? – A cello burns longer.

2085 What's the difference between viola players and terrorists? – Terrorists have sympathizers.

2086 What's the range of a viola? — Thirty yards if you've got a good arm.

2087 During a concert, a fight broke out between the oboe player and the viola player. At the interval, the orchestra leader went to investigate.
"He broke my reed," said the oboe player.
"He undid two of my strings," countered the viola player, "but he won't tell me which ones!"

2088 Why are so many viola players dating drummers? — It makes them feel superior.

2089 If you drop an accordion, a set of bagpipes and a viola off a fifteen-storey building, which one crashes to the ground first? — Who cares?

2090 A viola player came home late at night to find police cars and fire trucks outside his house. The chief of police intercepted him. "I'm afraid I have some terrible news for you," said the chief. "While you were out, the conductor came to your house, killed your family and burned your house down."
The viola player was stunned. "You're kidding! The conductor came to my house?"

2091 Man: "Was your uncle who died a band or orchestra conductor?"
Woman: "No, lightning."

2092 How can you tell a trumpeter's kids at a playground? — They're the ones who don't know how to swing.

2093 How can you tell a trombonist's kids at a playground? — They're the ones who don't know how to use the slide.

2094 What kind of calendar does a trombonist use for his gigs? — Year-at-a-glance.

2095 Now there's a boy band in Iraq: New Kids On What Used To Be The Block. (DENNIS MILLER)

2096 What do you get when you cross a French horn player with an ant? — An ant that can't march.

2097 Why did God give French horn players one more brain cell than horses? — So they wouldn't shit during a parade.

2098 I wrote a song, but I can't read music. Every time I hear a new song on the radio, I think: "Hey, maybe I wrote that." (STEVEN WRIGHT)

2099 I worry that the person who thought up Muzak may be thinking up something else. (LILY TOMLIN)

2100 How does Bob Marley like his donuts? – Wi' jammin'.

Mysteries of life

The imponderables . . .

2101 If one synchronized swimmer drowns, do the rest have to drown too?

2102 If you choke a Smurf, what colour does it turn?

2103 How do you tell when you've run out of invisible ink?

2104 If practice makes perfect and nobody's perfect, then why practise?

2105 Whose cruel idea was it to put an "s" in the word "lisp"?

2106 If diarrhoea runs down only one leg, is it monorrhoea?

2107 If swimming is so good for your figure, how come whales are so fat?

2108 If you are born again, do you have two belly buttons?

2109 If you ate pasta and antipasta, would you still be hungry?

2110 What happens if you get scared half to death twice?

2111 What if there were no hypothetical questions?

2112 If a man with no arms has a gun, is he armed?

2113 If Barbie is so popular, how come you have to buy her friends?

2114 Why did kamikaze pilots wear helmets?

2115 If all the world's a stage, where is the audience sitting?

2116 If a tree falls in the forest, do the other trees laugh at it?

2117 Occasional tables – what are they the rest of the time?

2118 Why is it that every time you lose weight, it finds you again?

2119 When cheese gets its picture taken, what does it say?

2120 Why isn't there mouse-flavoured cat food?

2121 If it's true that we're here to help others, then what exactly are the others here for?

2122 What is a free gift? Aren't all gifts free?

2123 Can atheists get insurance for acts of God?

2124 If space is a vacuum, who changes the bags?

2125 Why do they rarely sell car boots at car boot sales?

2126 What does God say when an angel sneezes?

2127 How come you never hear about gruntled employees?

2128 If a word in the dictionary was spelt wrongly, how would we know?

2129 When a paraplegic gets drunk, do you still call him legless?

2130 Why do they sterilize the needles for lethal injections?

2131 Why is it called lipstick if you can still move your lips?

2132 When sign workers go on strike, is anything written on their picket signs?

2133 God is love. Love is blind. Stevie Wonder is blind. Does that mean Stevie Wonder is God?

2134 Do people with psychic powers get nostalgic about next week?

2135 What should you do if you see an endangered animal eating an endangered plant?

2136 Do cemetery workers prefer the graveyard shift?

2137 If you are a complete pessimist, does it mean you are positively negative?

2138 Why is Ronnie Biggs called a Great Train Robber? He robbed one train, got caught, and lost all the money. He's a crap train robber.

2139 Why do people say, "You just want to have your cake and eat it too?" What use is a cake you can't eat?

2140 Why is lemon juice made with artificial flavour, and dishwashing liquid made with real lemons?

2141 If your yoga teacher doesn't like you, would it put you in a difficult position?

2142 Why do women wear evening gowns to nightclubs? Shouldn't they be wearing nightgowns?

2143 If you steal a clean slate, does it go on your criminal record?

2144 If a stealth bomber crashed in a forest, would it make a noise?

2145 Why do people with closed minds always open their mouths?

2146 What do you plant to grow a seedless watermelon?

2147 Why do you never see topless women on topless buses?

2148 Is there such a thing as a closet claustrophobic?

2149 Does a man who works in a bean factory always have his finger on the pulse?

2150 Do they have reserved car parking spaces for non-disabled people at the Paralympics?

2151 If a tin whistle is made of tin, what is a fog horn made of?

2152 Before they invented drawing boards, what did they go back to?

2153 Why do your nose run and your feet smell?

2154 Why did God give men nipples?

2155 Do people in Australia call the rest of the world "Up Over"?

2156 If blind people wear sunglasses, why don't deaf people wear earmuffs?

2157 Why are a wise man and a wise guy opposites?

2158 Do cats have to pay nine times more for their life insurance?

2159 Why, when a child is running, does a mother say, "Don't come running to me if you break your leg"?

2160 Do chickens think rubber humans are funny?

2161 How can there be self-help groups?
2162 If homosexuality is a disease, can you call in to work "gay"?
2163 If you jogged backwards, would you gain weight?
2164 If quitters never win and winners never quit, who came up with the phrase "Quit while you're ahead"?
2165 Do coffins have lifetime guarantees?
2166 Why do the signs that say "Slow Children" have a picture of a running child?
2167 If love is blind, why is lingerie so popular?
2168 Can mute people burp?
2169 If, instead of talking to your plants, you yelled at them, would they still grow but be troubled and insecure?
2170 Why is the time of day with the slowest traffic called rush hour?
2171 How come super glue doesn't stick to the tube?
2172 Does distressed leather come from very tense cows?
2173 In a world without walls and fences, who needs Windows and Gates?
2174 If the opposite of pro is con, does that make congress the opposite of progress?
2175 If dolphins are so clever, how come they're always getting caught in tuna nets?
2176 When French people swear, do they say pardon my English?
2177 Does killing time damage eternity?
2178 Under the sea, how come it's always the starfish that gets to be the sheriff?
2179 Have you ever seen a toad on a toadstool?
2180 Why do "fat chance" and "slim chance" mean the same thing?
2181 Should crematoriums give discounts for burns victims?
2182 Why is there an expiration date on sour cream?
2183 When shops have a sign on the door "Guide dogs only", who is supposed to read it? The dog?
2184 Are hungry crows ravenous?
2185 Aren't the "good things that come to those who wait" just the leftovers from the people that got there first?
2186 Since Americans throw rice at weddings, do Orientals throw burgers?
2187 If Spiderman became arachnophobic, would he be scared of himself?
2188 Why do people say, "It's always in the last place you look?" Of course it is. Why would you keep looking after you've found it? Do people do this? Who and where are they?
2189 Why does a cowboy wear two spurs? If one side of the horse goes, surely the other side does too?
2190 If a rabbit's foot is so lucky, what happened to the rabbit?
2191 Where can a man buy a cap for his knee?

2192 Do paediatricians play miniature golf on Wednesdays?

2193 If a book about failures doesn't sell, is it a success?

2194 If someone with multiple personality disorder threatens to kill himself, is it considered a hostage situation?

2195 If heat rises, shouldn't hell be cold?

2196 Why is it so hard to remember how to spell "mnemonic"?

2197 Despite the cost of living, have you noticed how it remains so popular?

2198 Why do joggers never smile?

2199 After eating, do amphibians have to wait an hour before getting out of the water?

2200 Why do they lock gas station bathrooms? Are they afraid someone will clean them?

2201 If time heals all wounds, how come the belly button always stays the same?

2202 Why do overlook and oversee mean opposite things?

2203 If man evolved from apes, why do we still have apes?

2204 If a guy is picked up for stealing human hearts from a morgue, is it a cardiac arrest?

2205 Just before you get nervous, do you experience cocoons in your stomach?

2206 If you're in the Los Angeles Dodgers and you get hit by a pitch, do they throw you off the team?

2207 When travelling at the speed of sound, can you still hear the radio?

2208 Why is it that if someone tells you there are one billion stars in the universe, you believe them, but if they tell you a wall has wet paint, you touch it to be sure?

2209 Why is it called a "building" when it is already built?

2210 When your pet canary sees you reading the newspaper, does he think you're just sitting there, staring at carpeting?

2211 If people dream in colour, is it a pigment of their imagination?

2212 How deep would the ocean be without the sponges?

2213 If you were under house arrest and lived in a mobile home, would you be able to go anywhere you wanted?

2214 Ever wonder what the speed of lightning would be if it didn't zig-zag?

2215 Since light travels faster than sound, is that why some people appear bright until you hear them speak?

2216 So what's the speed of dark?

2217 If you don't pay your exorcist, do you get repossessed?

2218 If we weren't meant to eat animals, why are they made of meat?

2219 What's another word for synonym?

2220 Why isn't phonetic spelt the way it sounds?

2221 Is a harp a piano with no clothes on?

2222 How does the guy who drives the snowplough get to work?

2223 If people from Poland are called Poles, why aren't people from Holland called Holes?

2224 Mustn't counting the pollen for the pollen count be really boring?

2225 If a man overdoses on Viagra, how do they get the coffin lid shut?

2226 Why can't they make an airplane out of the same material as the indestructible black box?

2227 Why do dogs sniff other dogs' bottoms to say hello? Why don't they just bark in their face?

2228 How do sheep know if you are pulling the wool over their eyes?

2229 Why don't we have cultured oil anywhere, instead of just crude oil?

2230 Why do mothers take their kids to the supermarket to smack them?

2231 Why do we wait until a pig is dead to cure it?

2232 How do "Do Not Walk On The Grass" signs get there?

2233 Why is it called the tourist season if we can't shoot them?

2234 Why don't sheep shrink when it rains?

2235 Why is abbreviation such a long word?

2236 What was the best thing before sliced bread?

2237 Is Jerry Garcia grateful to be dead?

2238 If nothing sticks to Teflon, how does Teflon stick to the pan?

2239 If the cops arrest a mime artist, do they tell him he has the right to remain silent?

2240 Why is there only one Monopolies Commission?

Navy

2241 The admiral was resting in his quarters when suddenly the lookout burst in. "Two enemy ships spotted on the horizon, sir."

"Right," said the admiral, "Fetch me my red shirt."

The danger passed but later in the day the lookout burst in once more. "Three enemy ships spotted on the horizon, sir."

"Right," said the admiral leaping to his feet. "Fetch me my red shirt."

Again the danger passed but the lookout felt compelled to ask the admiral why he always ordered his red shirt when battle was imminent.

"Well," explained the admiral. "It's a question of morale. If I'm wounded while wearing a red shirt, the men won't see the blood and will continue to fight."

When this answer was relayed to the men, all were agreed that their admiral was a remarkably courageous man.

The next morning, the admiral was resting in his quarters as usual when suddenly the lookout burst in. "Twelve enemy ships spotted on the horizon, sir."

"Right," said the admiral. "Fetch me my brown underpants."

2242 How do you knock out a marine? – Throw sand against a brick wall and say "Hit the beach".

2243 How do you separate the men from the boys in the navy? – With a crowbar.

2244 Through the pitch black of night, a navy captain saw a light dead ahead on collision course with his ship. He immediately sent a signal. "Change your course ten degrees east."

The light signalled back: "Change yours ten degrees west."

The captain was angry and sent another signal: "I'm a navy captain. Change your course, sir!"

The signal came back: "I'm a seaman, second class. Change your course, sir!"

The captain was furious at such insubordination and sent another signal: "I'm a battleship – I'm not changing course."

The reply came back: "And I'm a lighthouse."

2245 Why does the New Italian Navy have glass-bottomed boats? – To see the Old Italian Navy.

2246 An American tourist went to Portsmouth to see Nelson's flagship HMS *Victory*. On the tour of the ship, the guide pointed out a raised brass plaque on the deck.

"That's where Nelson fell," said the guide.

The tourist was unimpressed. "I nearly tripped on the damn thing myself."

2247 Did you hear about the incompetent navy captain? – He grounds the warship he walks on.

2248 A naval officer met a pirate at an inn and couldn't help but noticing that the pirate had a wooden leg, a hook and an eye patch.

"How did you get the wooden leg?" asked the officer.

"Well," said the pirate, "we were in a storm at sea and I was swept overboard into shark-infested waters. And one of the sharks bit off my leg."

"That's terrible," said the officer. "What about the hook? How did you come by that?"

"Well," said the pirate, "we were boarding an enemy ship and in the heat of battle, my right hand was sliced off by an enemy swordsman."

"How terrible," said the officer. "And the eye patch?"

"A seagull dropping fell into my eye."

"You lost your eye to a seagull dropping?"

"Well, it was my first day with the hook."

Neighbours

2249 A man collared his neighbour on the front drive. "Hey, Wayne, do you like a woman with a big, big stomach?"

"No, I don't."

"Do you like a woman whose breasts are so sagging they almost hang down to her feet?"

"No, I don't."

"Do you like a woman who has hips as wide as a truck?"

"No, no, I don't."

"Well then, keep your filthy hands off my wife!"

2250 Three Boy Scouts told their scoutmaster that they had done their good deed for the day.

"What did you do, boys?" asked the scoutmaster.

"We helped an elderly neighbour across the street," they chimed in unison.

The scoutmaster looked mystified. "Did it take all three of you to do that?"

"Yes, it did," said the boys. "She didn't want to go."

2251 A man called over the garden fence to his neighbour: "Tony, will you be using your lawn mower this afternoon?"

"Yes, I'm afraid I will."

"Good. Then can I borrow your tennis racket? The strings are broken on mine."

2252 A farmer owned a mule which was really docile until it was put in its stable. For whenever it was loaded into the stable, its ears brushed against the top of the doorway and the sensation made it buck and kick. The farmer decided to solve the problem by sawing away part of the doorway, allowing the mule greater clearance. For six hours, he and his farmhand toiled in the blazing heat, hacking away at the wooden frame. A passing neighbour remarked that they could save a lot of time and effort simply by taking a shovel and digging a shallow pit in the entrance to the stable. That, said the neighbour, would take them less than half an hour.

The farmer thanked the neighbour for the suggestion but when he had gone, the farmer turned to his assistant and said: "Stupid man! Anyone can see it's not the mule's feet that are too long, it's his ears!"

2253 My next-door neighbour is always bragging about the sex he and his wife have had. As if I hadn't been watching. (BRIAN KILEY)

2254 The wife was livid when her husband refused to go shopping with her. "For goodness sake," she cried, "the neighbours will soon be talking about us just like they did with poor Mr and Mrs Dawkins along the road. The only time they went out together was when their gas stove exploded!"

2255 A boy taunted his neighbour in the street. "I was looking in your bedroom window last night and I saw your wife giving you a blow job."

"Actually the joke's on you, sonny," replied the neighbour. "I wasn't even home last night."

2256 A wife was keeping a close watch on her new neighbours. "They seem perfectly devoted to each other," she told her husband. "He kisses her every time he goes out, and even blows kisses to her from the window. Why don't you do that?"

"I hardly know the woman."

Newspapers and magazines

2257 A newspaper photographer was assigned to take pictures of a huge forest fire. Owing to the density of the smoke at ground level, his editor had hired a light aircraft for aerial shots and the photographer was told that the plane would be waiting for him at a small rural airfield. The photographer drove at top speed to the airfield and saw a small plane warming up on the runway. He raced over to the plane, jumped in and yelled to the pilot: "Let's go! Let's go!"

As the aircraft soared into the sky, the photographer issued his instructions. "I want you to fly over the north side of the fire and make three or four low-level passes."

"Why?" asked the pilot.

"What do you mean, why?" said the photographer. "So I can take pictures. I'm a photographer and photographers take pictures."

The pilot thought for a moment. "So you mean you're not the instructor?"

2258 A reporter covering a Sunday morning soccer match was amazed to see that one of the teams included a wrinkled man clearly of advanced years. Sensing that he might be in the presence of the oldest player in the country, he thought it would make a good story. So he grabbed a word with the old timer just before kickoff.

"Tell me," said the reporter, "do you have a special diet?"

The man replied: "Every day I drink eight pints of beer and a bottle of Scotch, and I smoke 40 cigarettes. And all I ever eat are chips."

"That's incredible," said the reporter. "How old did you say you were?"

"Twenty-eight."

2259 The pen is mightier than the sword, and considerably easier to write with. (MARTY FELDMAN)

2260 A young reporter was covering a story about an escapee from a mental asylum. To accompany the story, he sent in the headline: WOMAN RAPED, MENTAL PATIENT ESCAPES. But the editor asked for something snappier. So the reporter suggested: NUT SCREWS AND BOLTS.

2261 Two years before the Gulf War, a female journalist had done a story on gender roles in Kuwait and had noted that it was the custom for women to walk several yards behind their husbands. But when she returned recently she observed that the roles had been reversed, and that the men now walked several yards behind their wives.

"This is wonderful news," the journalist enthused to an Arab woman. "Tell me, what enabled women here to achieve this reversal of roles?"

"Land mines."

2262 There's very little advice in men's magazines because men don't think there's a lot they don't know. Women do. Women want to learn. Men think: "I know what I'm doing, just show me somebody naked." (JERRY SEINFELD)

2263 A truck carrying hundreds of copies of Roget's Thesaurus overturned. The local newspaper reported that onlookers were "stunned, overwhelmed, astonished, gobsmacked, amazed, bewildered and dumbfounded."

2264 A reporter saw a crowd gathered around a road accident. Anxious to get a scoop, he told the bystanders: "Let me through, let me through! I'm the son of the victim."

The crowd made way for him. Lying in front of the car was a donkey.

2265 A woman phoned up the sports desk of her local newspaper to settle a family argument. "Tell me," she said, "who won Super Bowl XVI? Was it San Francisco or Cincinnati?"

The reporter, a keen 49ers' fan, replied: "It was San Francisco."

"Thank you," said the woman, before calling to her husband, "See, I told you it was Cincinnati!"

2266 Foreign newspapers: if they've got nothing to hide, how come they don't print them in English? (STEPHEN COLBERT)

2267 A visitor to a small town in Georgia was walking along the main street when a wild dog suddenly leaped out and attacked a small boy. Without thought for his own safety, the passer-by instinctively dragged the dog off the boy before throttling it with his bare hands.

The incident was witnessed by a reporter on the local newspaper who went up and shook the hero by the hand. The reporter told him that the headline in that week's paper would be: BRAVE LOCAL MAN SAVES CHILD BY KILLING VICIOUS BEAST.

"But I'm not from this town," said the man.

"No problem," replied the reporter. "The headline will be: GEORGIA MAN SAVES CHILD BY KILLING DOG."

"As a matter of fact," revealed the man, "I'm not from Georgia at all. I'm from Connecticut."

The reporter glared at him. "In which case the headline will be: YANKEE SLAYS FAMILY PET."

2268 A reporter was assigned to cover a rural area in Ireland. He asked a local: "Who is the oldest inhabitant of this village?"

"Well now, we haven't got one. We did have, but he died three weeks ago."

New York

2269 St Peter was manning the pearly gates when 40 New Yorkers showed up. Never having seen anyone from the Big Apple at heaven's door before, St Peter thought he had better consult God. So he left the group at the gates and went off to find God.

"I've got 40 people from New York," said St Peter. "Is it safe to let them in?"

"New York, huh?" mused God. "We certainly don't want heaven overrun with New Yorkers. Why don't you just admit the ten most virtuous?"

St Peter went back to relay the news but a few minutes later returned to God in a state of anxiety.

"What's happened?" asked God.

"They've gone," gasped St Peter.

"What, all of the New Yorkers?"

"No, the pearly gates!"

2270 When it's Chinese New Year in New York there are fireworks going off at all hours. New York mothers calm their frightened children by telling them it's only gunfire. (DAVID LETTERMAN)

2271 On extended vacation in Canada, a New Yorker went into a hardware store and asked for a chainsaw that would cut down six trees in an hour. The sales assistant showed him a top-of-the- range model and the New Yorker was so impressed that he bought it.

The following day he returned to the shop and complained that it had taken him all day to cut down just one tree. To find out what the problem was, the sales assistant took the chainsaw and started it up.

The New Yorker said: "What's that noise?"

Telltale signs that you're from New York:

2272 Your door has more than three locks.

2273 The most frequently used part of your car is the horn.

2274 You go to a hockey game for the fighting.

2275 You believe that being able to swear at people in their own language makes you multilingual.

2276 You get arthritis in your middle finger from over-use.

2277 You consider eye contact to be an overt act of aggression.

2278 You've never been to the Statue of Liberty or the Empire State Building.

2279 You envy cabbies for their driving skill.

2280 The subway makes sense.

2281 Only time four New Yorkers get into a cab together without arguing, a bank robbery has just taken place. (JOHNNY CARSON)

2282 A pollster was taking opinions outside the United Nations building in New York. He approached four men – a Saudi, a Russian, a North Korean and a resident New Yorker. To each one he said: "Excuse me, I would like to ask you your opinion on the current meat shortage."

The Saudi replied: "Excuse me, what is a shortage?

The Russian replied: "Excuse me, what is meat?"
The North Korean replied: "Excuse me, what is an opinion?"
The New Yorker replied: "Excuse me, what is 'excuse me'?"

2283 You don't see too many tourists in Brooklyn, and when you do see them, they are always pointing out the wrong stuff: "Look, honey, they're barbecuing!" No, they're burning evidence. (STEVEN ROBINS)

2284 A meek little man appeared before a judge. "In your own words," said the judge, "I want you to tell me exactly what happened."

The little man said: "I am a mathematician dealing in the nature of proof, and on 12 August last I was in the city library conducting some research. There were two books I wanted to take out, so I got in line. But when I reached the desk, I was told that my library card had expired. So I filled out the forms for another card, got in another line and waited patiently. Then when I got to the desk, the guy asked me whether I could prove I was from New York City. So I stabbed him."

Indications that it's cold in New York:
2285 Pickpockets put their hands in strangers' pockets to keep warm.
2286 Flashers are reduced to describing themselves.
2287 You can walk across the frozen East River, and see dozens of mob informants beneath you.
2288 The hookers wear long johns.
2289 Whenever a motorcycle messenger gets hit by a cab, he shatters into a thousand tiny pieces.
2290 Taxi drivers wear turbans with ear flaps.
2291 You can see people's breath when they yell: "Screw you!"
2292 A headline in the *New York Post* reads: MAN STABBED FOR EAR MUFFS.

Other countries

2293 It's a small world, but I wouldn't want to have to paint it. (STEVEN WRIGHT)

2294 I would love to speak a foreign language, but I can't. So I grew hair under my arms instead. (SUE KOLINSKY)

2295 I always enjoy appearing before a British audience. Even if they don't feel like laughing, they nod their heads to show they've understood. (BOB HOPE)

Australia

2296 An elderly couple were on a visit to Australia and were driving along in the Outback when they saw a man copulating with a kangaroo. A few miles on, they saw another man copulating with a kangaroo.

"That's disgusting," said the husband. "I'm going to report this to the hotel when we get back."

They arrived back at their hotel, only to see a man with a wooden leg masturbating on the front step of the hotel. The husband stormed in to see the hotel manager. "My wife and I are appalled. This is a five-star hotel and we've seen two men having sex with kangaroos and just now we saw a wretched man with a wooden leg masturbating on the steps of your hotel. What have you got to say?"

The manager replied: "Struth, mate, you expect a guy with a wooden leg to catch his own kangaroo?"

2297 What do you call a boomerang that doesn't come back? – A stick.

2298 Three Australians – Bruce, Bill and Herbie – were sitting in a bar in the Outback. Bruce and Bill were easy-going guys, but Herbie had a speech impediment which made him bad-tempered. As they were drinking, who should walk in but Red Adair, the famous oil-well firefighter!

Bruce recognized him immediately. "Look," he said. "It's Red Adair."

"Yeah, that's right," agreed Bill.

"No way," barked Herbie. "That's not Red Adair."

"Trust me," insisted Bruce. "It is."

"Sorry, Herbie," said Bill. "But I'm with Bruce on this one. It is Red Adair."

"No it's not," said Herbie, becoming more aggressive by the minute.

"It is Red Adair," said Bruce.

"Yeah, it is," echoed Bill.

Herbie slammed his fist down on the table. "No, it's not. I'm telling you, I know what Red Adair looks like. I've seen every picture he made with Ginger Rogers."

2299 An Australian asked a woman whether she would have sex with him. She refused. "In that case," he said, "do you mind lying down while I have some?"

Canada

2300 On the sixth day, God turned to the angel Gabriel and announced: "Today I shall create a land called Canada. It will be a land of outstanding natural beauty, with snow-capped mountains, shimmering blue lakes, forests of elk and moose and rivers of salmon. And the air will be clear and pure. I shall make the land rich in oil so that the inhabitants shall prosper. I shall call these inhabitants Canadians and they shall be known as the friendliest people on Earth."

"Don't you think you're being rather too generous to these Canadians?" asked Gabriel.

"Wait," said God. "You haven't seen the neighbours I'm going to give them!"

2301 An Ontarian wanted to become a Newfie (someone from Newfoundland). So he went to a neurosurgeon and said: "Is there anything you can do to make me a Newfie?"

"Sure," said the surgeon. "All I have to do is cut out one-third of your brain."

The man agreed to this, but during the operation the surgeon's knife slipped and instead of cutting out one-third of the brain, he accidentally removed two-thirds. The surgeon was deeply embarrassed and waited anxiously for the patient to regain consciousness. When the man finally came round, the surgeon said: "I'm very sorry, but instead of cutting out one-third of your brain, I accidentally cut out two-thirds."

The patient replied: "Qu'est-ce que vous avez dit, monsieur?"

2302 Canada: a country so square that even the female impersonators are women. (RICHARD BRENNER)

2303 An Albertan visited the Eiffel Tower. The first question he asked the tour guide was: "How many barrels a day do you get out of her?"

2304 A severe storm rumbled through the Canadian town of Guelph last week and destroyed everything in its path. The entire town was reduced to rubble. Ten dollars worth of damage was reported.

France

2305 A French guest, staying in a hotel in Washington, phoned room service for some pepper.

"Black pepper or white pepper?" asked the voice on the other end.

"No. Toilet pepper!"

2306 Did you hear about the new French tank? It has 14 gears – 13 reverse and one forward, in case the enemy attacks from behind.

Germany

2307 Have you heard about the new German-Chinese restaurant? – The food is great, but an hour later you're hungry for power.

2308 How does a German eat mussels? – Knock! Knock! Knock! Aufmachen!

2309 If you go to Germany and get drunk, at some point you're going to look up Hitler in the phone book. (DAVE ATTELL)

2310 I married a German. Every night I dress up as Poland and he invades me. (BETTE MIDLER)

2311 My sister married a German. He complained he couldn't get a good bagel back home. I said, "Well, whose fault is that?" (EMO PHILIPS)

Greece

2312 A Greek and an Italian were arguing over who had the superior culture. The Greek said: "We have the Parthenon."
The Italian replied: "And we have the Colosseum."
The Greek said: "We Greeks gave birth to advanced mathematics, to which the Italian retorted: "But we built the Roman Empire."
On and on they argued until the Greek played what he thought was his trump card. With a flourish of finality he announced: "We invented sex!"
The Italian smiled: "That is true, but it was the Italians who introduced it to women."

Italy

2313 A British woman, an American woman and an Italian woman were having lunch. The British woman said: "A while back, I told my husband that I wasn't going to clean the house any more. If he wanted it clean, he would have to do it himself. After the first day, I didn't see anything. On the second day, I didn't see anything. Then on the third day, magic – my husband had cleaned the entire house!"
The American woman added: "I told my husband that I wasn't going to do the laundry any more. If he wanted it done, he would have to do it himself. After the first day, I didn't see anything. On the second day, I didn't see anything. Then on the third day, magic – my husband had done both his and my laundry!"
The Italian woman said: "I told my husband that I wasn't going to cook any more. If he wanted home cooking, he would either have to go to his mother's or cook for himself. After the first day, I didn't see anything. On the second day,

I didn't see anything. Then on the third day, I began to see a little out of my left eye."

You know you're Italian when:

2314 You're 5ft 4in, can bench press 325lb, shave twice a day, but you still cry when your mother yells at you.

2315 Your mechanic, plumber, electrician, accountant and travel agent are all blood relatives.

2316 Your two best friends are your cousin and your brother-in-law.

2317 You are a card-carrying VIP at more than three strip clubs.

2318 A high school diploma and one year at the local community college has earned you the title of "professor" among your aunts.

2319 If someone in your family grows beyond 5ft 6in, it is presumed his mother had an affair.

2320 At least five of your cousins live on your street.

2321 All five of those cousins are named after your grandfather.

2322 It's impossible for you to talk with your hands in your pockets.

2323 You have ever been in a fight defending Sylvester Stallone's acting ability.

2324 There were more than thirty-one people in your bridal party.

2325 You have at least one sister who went to beauty school.

2326 You have been to a funeral where talk of the deceased is: "He shoulda kept his big mouth shut."

Mexico

2327 What do Mexicans and sperm have in common? – There are millions of them but few work.

2328 There's a Mexican and a Puerto Rican in a car. Who's driving? – The police.

2329 Why are there so few Mexican athletes in the Olympics? Because most of them who can run, jump or swim are already in the United States.

2330 Did you hear about the guy who was half Polish, half Mexican? – He made a run for the border and forgot where he was going.

2331 What were the names of the two Mexican firefighting brothers? – Hose A and Hose B.

2332 A man on a bicycle approached the US border from Mexico. He was carrying a heavy sack.

"What's in the sack?" asked the border guard.

"Sand," came the reply.

The guard checked, and sure enough it was sand. So he let the man through. A week later, the man on the bicycle appeared again, carrying a heavy sack.

"What's in the sack?" asked the border guard.

"Sand."

The guard checked, verified that it was sand and let the cyclist through.

This continued on a weekly basis for six months until one day the cyclist with the sack full of sand failed to show up. A few days later the guard chanced upon him in a downtown bar.

"Hey," said the guard. "You've been driving us crazy for the past six months. We're damn sure you were smuggling something through. In strictest confidence, tell me what it was."

"Bicycles," replied the man.

Poland

2333 How do you stop a Polish army on horseback? — Turn off the carousel.

2334 Three guys — a Jew, an Italian and a Pole — signed up for police academy. The Jew went in first and the captain said: "Before we admit you to the academy, we have to ask you one question: Who killed Jesus?"

"The Romans," answered the Jew.

"That's correct. You can enter the academy."

Next it was the Italian's turn. "Who killed Jesus?" asked the captain.

"The Romans," replied the Italian.

"That's correct. You can enter the academy."

Finally it was the Pole's turn. "Who killed Jesus?" asked the captain.

"I'm not sure," said the Pole.

"Well," said the captain, "why don't you go home and think about it?"

The Pole went home and said to his wife: "You won't believe this! My first day in the job and they give me a murder case to solve!"

2335 I'm half Italian and half Polish. So I'm always putting a hit out on myself. (JUDY TENUTA)

2336 Poland just bought 10,000 septic tanks. As soon as they learn how to drive them, they're going to invade Russia.

2337 Did you hear about the latest Polish invention? — It's a solar-powered flashlight.

2338 A Polish guy wanted to join an amateur baseball team. The coach looked him over and decided to give him a chance. "I'll give you three questions," said the coach. "If you come back in a week and answer all three correctly, you're on the team. The first question is, how many days of the week start with the letter T? The second question is, how many seconds are there in a year? And the third question is, how many Ds are there in 'Rudolph the Red Nosed Reindeer'?"

Next week, the Polish guy returned, confident that he had got the right answers. "OK," said the coach, "how many days of the week start with T?"

"Two," replied the Pole.

"Very good," said the coach. "What are they?"

"Today and tomorrow."

"Hmmm . . . OK, I'll let you have that. So how many seconds are there in a year?"

"Twelve."

"Twelve? How did you come up with twelve?"

"Well," said the Pole, "there's the second of January, the second of February, the second of . . ."

"OK, OK. How many Ds in 'Rudolph the Red Nosed Reindeer'?"

"Oh that's easy!" laughed the Pole. "240."

"What!" exclaimed the coach. How did you get that figure?"

To which the Pole started singing, "Dee-dee-dee-dee-dee-dee-dee . . ."

Romania

2339 Three men were sitting in a Romanian café. One man looked at the newspaper headlines, shook his head and sighed. Then the second man looked at his newspaper, shook his head and sighed. The third man reached for his hat and said: "If you two are going to discuss politics, I'm off."

Russia

2340 Two Russians were standing in a queue for bread. Eventually one said: "I've had enough of all these queues. I'm going to shoot Yeltsin."

Three hours later he returned and silently went back to his place in the queue.

"Well?" asked his friend. "Did you kill Yeltsin?"

"Not a chance. The queue was twice as long as this one!"

2341 We don't have American Express in Russia, we have Russian Express. Their slogan is "Don't Leave Home." (YAKOV SMIRNOFF)

2342 Why do Russians go around in threes? – So that there is one who can read, one who can write, and one who can keep an eye on the two intellectuals.

2343 A Muscovite saved hard for 15 years so that he could afford Russia's finest car, a Lada. When he finally accumulated sufficient cash, he dashed to the nearest showroom.

"Congratulations, comrade," said the salesman, "your car will be here in ten years' time."

"Great," replied the customer. "Will that be morning or afternoon?"

2344 Russian comedians must be careful about what jokes they tell. If you say, "Take my wife, please", when you get home, she's gone. (YAKOV SMIRNOFF)

2345 A Russian peasant woman bought a cow for her family's milk supply. The cow provided gallons of milk and was so profitable that the woman decided to try and breed from it. So she sought out a suitable bull, but the bull was simply not interested. He just stomped around the paddock all day but never showed the slightest interest in mating with the cow. In despair, the woman sought the advice of a lady vet. "I have tried everything," said the woman, "but the bull just doesn't seem interested."

"Did the bull come from Minsk?" asked the vet.

"As a matter of fact it did. Why do you ask?"

"My husband is from Minsk."

2346 I like American women. They do things sexually that Russian girls never dream of doing – like showering. (YAKOV SMIRNOFF)

2347 Boris Yeltsin died and went to hell. He pleaded with the devil to be allowed to stay in touch with political leaders on earth. Satan told him he could use the phone.

"How much are calls?" asked Yeltsin.

The devil replied: "To the United States 20 dollars; to South America 18 dollars; to Britain 15 dollars; to China 15 dollars; and to Russia, one dollar."

"Why is it so cheap to Russia?" asked Yeltsin.

"Because," said Satan, "it's a local call."

Scotland

2348 A Scotsman got on a bus in London, put his suitcase under the stairs and said "Tower of London, please."

The driver said, "That's 60p plus 10p for the suitcase."

"What!" exclaimed the Scotsman. "I'm not paying for the suitcase."

The driver said: "If you don't pay up, I'm throwing the suitcase off the bus."

Still the Scotsman refused to pay so the driver picked up the case and threw it off the bus – straight into the River Thames.

The Scotsman was furious. He screamed: "You're not satisfied with trying to rob me, you English crook, but you're also trying to drown my wee boy as well."

2349 A small boy fell into Glasgow's River Clyde but was saved from drowning by the intervention of a passer-by. When the hero had dried out a little, the boy's father came over to him.

"Are you the man that saved my laddie?"

"Aye."

"Where's his bonnet?"

2350 A Scotsman had just lost his wife and went round to the local newspaper to put a notice in the deaths column.

"What would you like to say?" asked the clerk.

"Moira's dead," replied the Scotsman.

"But you can put in a few more words than that," said the clerk, "and at no extra cost."

"Well," said the Scotsman, mulling over the proposition, "how about 'And second-hand Ford for sale . . .'?"

South Africa

2351 George W. Bush, Tony Blair and Nelson Mandela were flying around the world on a special goodwill mission. At one point Bush remarked: "Hey, we just flew over America because I touched the Empire State Building."

A few hours later, Blair said: "We just flew over Britain because I touched Big Ben."

Several hours later, Mandela said: "We just flew over South Africa."

"How do you know?" asked the others. "Did you touch Table Mountain?"

"No," said Mandela, "my watch got stolen."

Wales

2352 A Russian spy was sent to seek out a contact in a small Welsh village. The password he was given was "The Geese Are Landing". So he knocked on the door of a house and when a woman answered, he announced: "The Geese Are Landing."

Straight away she said: "Oh, you've come to the wrong house, dear. You want number 9, two doors along. That's where Jones the Spy lives."

2353 A young man moved to a village in Wales and got talking to an old man from the village. After a while the old man started to vent his frustration. "See that row of houses over there?", he said. "I built them, but do they call me Jones the builder? Do they hell! See that railway line? I laid it, but do they call me Jones the engineer? Do they hell! And see those two bridges over the river? I built those, but do they call me Jones the bridge builder? Do they hell! Years ago, I shagged one sheep . . ."

2354 What do you call a Welshman with lots of girlfriends? – A shepherd.

2355 On a visit to Wales, an Australian saw a Welshman cuddling a sheep. "Hey, mate," said the Australian, "where I come from, we shear our sheep."
The Welshman frowned: "Well, I'm not shearin' my sheep with anyone!"

2356 The day after his wedding, Dai Evans returned home.
"What's happened?" asked his mother.
"It's Gwyneth," he said. "I found out she is a virgin. So I've left her."
"Quite right," said his mother. "If she's not good enough for the rest of the boys in the village, she's not good enough for you."

2357 How does a Welshman find a sheep in tall grass? – Very satisfying.

2358 What's the definition of safe sex in Wales? – Branding the sheep which kick.

2359 What do you call a Welshman with a sheep under each arm? – A pimp.

2360 What do you call four sheep tied to a post in Wales? – A leisure centre.

Parents

2361 Four guys were sitting in a bar when one got up to go to the toilet. In his absence, the other three started to talk about their sons. The first said: "Mine was a big worry to me. I really didn't think he was ever going to make anything of himself. But I'm happy to say he's doing OK now. He owns a car dealership and just bought his best mate a new car."
The second said: "Mine was hopeless at school. He had failure written all over him. But he's pulled through. I'm real proud of him. He owns a bank and just gave his best friend a 1 million dollar savings bond."
The third said: "My son was bad at school too, but I'm glad to say he's doing fine now. He owns a pet shop and just gave his best pal a puppy."

Just then the fourth guy returned from the toilet. "We were talking about our sons," said the others.

"Mine was a real headache," said the fourth guy. "He's gay, but he's turned out OK. And he sure is popular. Just recently one of his boyfriends gave him a new car, another gave him a 1 million dollar savings bond and another gave him a puppy."

2362 My parents are from Glasgow which means they're incredibly hard, but I was never smacked as a child . . . well maybe one or two grams to get me to sleep at night. (SUSAN MURRAY)

2363 A teenage girl was forced to stay at a friend's house overnight and called her mother first thing in the morning to let her know she was safe. The words came out in a breathless torrent. "Mum, it's Caroline. I'm fine. I knew you'd be worried, but I didn't get a chance to call you last night. My car broke down and I had to stay at Moira's house, and by the time I got there it was gone midnight, so I knew you'd be asleep. Please don't be mad with me."

By now, the woman on the other end of the phone realized that the caller had got the wrong number. "I'm sorry," she said, "I don't have a daughter named Caroline."

"Gee, Mum, I didn't think you'd be this mad!"

2364 I could tell that my parents hated me. My bath toys were a toaster and a radio. (RODNEY DANGERFIELD)

2365 My mother had morning sickness after I was born. (RODNEY DANGERFIELD)

2366 Once I was lost. I saw a policeman and asked him to help me find my parents. I said to him: "Do you think we'll ever find them?" He said: "I don't know, kid — there are so many places they can hide." (RODNEY DANGERFIELD)

2367 My father carries around the picture of the kid who came with his wallet. (RODNEY DANGERFIELD)

2368 I remember the time I was kidnapped and they sent a piece of my finger to my father. He said he wanted more proof. (RODNEY DANGERFIELD)

2369 My mother never saw the irony of calling me a son-of-a -bitch. (RICH JENI)

2370 A girl invited her boyfriend to come to her parents' house for dinner. She realized it was a daunting prospect but as an inducement, she said that after the dinner she wanted to go out with him and lose her virginity. To prepare for this, the boy, who was also a virgin, went to a pharmacist to buy a packet of condoms. The pharmacist was extremely helpful and told him everything he wanted to know about sex. Finally he asked the boy whether he wanted a three-pack, a six-pack or a family pack.

"I think I'd better take a family pack," said the boy, "because I think I'm going to be busy over the next few nights."

The boy showed up on time for dinner and was greeted at the front door by his girlfriend. She then showed him into the dining room where her parents were already seated at the table. Sitting down, the boy quickly offered to say grace and bowed his head. After ten minutes, his head was still down. When after 20 minutes the boy's head was still bowed, his girlfriend leaned over and whispered: "I had no idea you were so religious."

The boy whispered back: "And I had no idea your father was a pharmacist."

2371 A husband, wife and their two young sons were watching TV until, after exchanging meaningful glances, the wife took the husband by the hand and said: "Excuse us for a few minutes, boys, we're going up to our room."

Soon one of the boys became curious and, seeing the door to his parents' bedroom was ajar, peeked inside. He then fetched his little brother but warned: "Before you look in there, remember this is the same woman who used to tell us off for sucking our thumbs."

2372 If your parents never had children, chances are you won't either. (DICK CAVETT)

2373 A man answered the phone. "Yes, Mother," he sighed. "I've had a hard day. Mildred has been in one of her difficult moods . . . I know I ought to be firmer with her, but it's not easy. You know what she's like . . . Yes, I remember you warned me . . . Yes, I remember you told me she was a vile creature who would make my life a misery . . . Yes, I remember you begged me not to marry her. You were right . . . You want to speak to her? OK." He put down the phone and called to his wife in the next room: "Mildred, your mother wants to talk to you!"

2374 My mother was like a sister to me, only we didn't have sex quite so often. (EMO PHILIPS)

Parties

2375 A preacher decided to call on a member of his church one Friday night, but arrived to find a party in full swing. On entering the house, he saw a circle of naked men with blindfolded women moving from man to man, fondling their genitals in an attempt to guess their identity.

The embarrassed preacher turned to the host and said: "I'm sorry, I don't think I'd fit in here right now."

"Nonsense," said the host. "Your name's been called three times already!"

2376 What's with the people who put carpeting on the lid of their toilet seat? What are they thinking: "Gosh, if we have a party, there may not be enough standing room; I'd better carpet the toilet too." (JERRY SEINFELD)

2377 Why did the guy bring toilet paper to a party? – Because he was a party pooper.

2378 A man tried to gatecrash a fancy dress party at a city centre bar. He was dressed as a pair of jump leads. After a bit of an argument, the bouncer on the door said: "All right, you can go in, so long as you don't start anything."

2379 You moon the wrong person at an office party, and suddenly you're not "professional" any more. (JEFF FOXWORTHY)

2380 A man went to a friend's fancy dress party with nothing but a girl on his back.

"What have you come as?" asked his friend.

"A snail."

"How can you be a snail when all you've got is that girl on your back?"

"That's not a girl – that's Michelle."

People not to invite to your party:

2381 Your parents.

2382 The local chapter of Hell's Angels.

2383 A delegation of Russian fishermen.

2384 Bill Clinton.

2385 Members of the temperance society.

2386 Members of a manic depressives' support group.

2387 Members of the local noise abatement society.

2388 The National Farting Champion.

2389 Jehovah's Witnesses.

2390 Karl Marx (because corpses make a terrible smell).
2391 The SAS.
2392 An avid trainspotter.
2393 Ted Bundy (see Karl Marx).

The following historical figures were invited to a party:
2394 Nelson said he'd give his right arm for a good party.
2395 Wilbur Wright accepted, provided he and Orville could get a flight.
2396 Einstein said that it would be relatively easy to attend.
2397 Pierre and Marie Curie radiated enthusiasm.
2398 Schubert said he'd come, but there was something he had to finish first.
2399 Archimedes was buoyant.
2400 King Alfred asked whether he should bring some cakes.
2401 Ohm resisted the idea at first.
2402 Boyle said he was under too much pressure.
2403 Edison said it would be an illuminating experience.
2404 Chairman Mao said he'd write the date in his little red book.
2405 Watt reckoned it would be a great way to let off steam.
2406 Dr Jekyll was in two minds.
2407 Darwin said he would have to see what evolved.
2408 Morse's reply was, "I'll be there on the dot. Can't stop now, must dash."

Philosophy

Think on the following maxims:
2409 The Internet isn't better than sex, but sliced bread is in serious trouble.
2410 You don't need a parachute to skydive: you only need a parachute to skydive twice.
2411 Animal testing is a terrible idea – they get all nervous and give the wrong answers.
2412 Avoid clichés like the plague.
2413 Never hit a man with glasses – use your fist.
2414 Eagles may soar but weasels don't get sucked into jet engines.
2415 The only substitute for good manners is fast reflexes.
2416 The nurse who can smile when things go wrong is probably going off duty.
2417 Never raise your hand to your kids – it leaves your groin unprotected.
2418 Nonconformists are all alike.
2419 Exaggeration is a billion times worse than understatement.
2420 Never try to out-stubborn a cat.
2421 It's far easier to forgive an enemy after you've got even with him.

2422 If guys had periods, they'd brag about the size of their tampons.

2423 It's bad luck to be superstitious.

2424 Be nice to your kids — they'll choose your nursing home.

2425 A chip on the shoulder is an indication of wood higher up.

2426 All generalizations are false.

2427 First impressions are often lasting — especially if they're made by a car bumper.

2428 Co-operation can only be reached if we work together.

2429 If everything's going your way, you're driving in the wrong lane.

2430 The best way to change someone's mind is with a machete.

2431 An oral contract isn't worth the paper it's written on.

2432 Prepositions are not words to end sentences with.

2433 Don't sweat the petty things and don't pet the sweaty things.

2434 The best way to serve cabbage is to someone else.

2435 Never tell a lie unless it is absolutely convenient.

2436 People would give their right arm to be ambidextrous.

2437 A clear conscience is usually the sign of a bad memory.

2438 If you want your wife to pay undivided attention to every word you say, talk in your sleep.

2439 When two egotists meet, it's an I for an I.

2440 An escalator can never break, it can only become stairs.

2441 Don't hate yourself in the morning — sleep till noon.

2442 You're never alone with schizophrenia.

2443 The worst thing about accidents in the kitchen is eating them.

2444 Practise safe eating: use condiments.

2445 Rehab is for quitters.

2446 Never test the depth of water with both feet.

2447 A day without sunshine is like . . . night.

2448 Do not argue with a spouse who is packing your parachute.

2449 Never take life seriously. Nobody gets out alive anyway.

2450 Sometimes the best helping hand you can give is a good, firm push.

2451 Bigamy is having one wife too many. Some say monogamy is the same.

2452 The world's full of apathy, but so what?

2453 The best way to keep your kids at home is to make the home a pleasant atmosphere . . . and let the air out of their tyres.

2454 Beat the five o'clock rush — leave work at noon.

2455 Always use tasteful words — you may have to eat them.

2456 Never stand between a dog and a hydrant.

2457 Never buy a portable TV in the street from a man who is out of breath.

2458 I have this nagging fear that everyone is out to make me paranoid.

2459 A good woman is like a good bar – liquor in the front and poker in the rear.

2460 The sooner you fall behind, the more time you'll have to catch up.

2461 The best way to forget all your troubles is to wear tight shoes.

2462 The only time the world beats a path to your door is if you're in the bathroom.

2463 Teamwork is essential – it allows you to blame someone else.

2464 Always talk to your wife while making love – if there's a phone handy.

2465 Don't be afraid of pressure. Remember that pressure is what turns a lump of coal into a diamond.

2466 Whatever hits the fan will not be evenly distributed.

2467 A tidy desk is a sign of an untidy desk drawer.

2468 If you can't beat them, arrange to have them beaten.

2469 If you can smile when things go wrong, you have someone in mind to blame.

2470 Clones are people two.

2471 A successful diet is the triumph of mind over platter.

2472 The more you complain, the longer God lets you live.

2473 Always be on the lookout for conspicuity.

2474 Blessed are those who have nothing to say and who cannot be persuaded to say it.

2475 Talk is cheap – until lawyers get involved.

2476 A weekend wasted isn't a wasted weekend.

2477 If tomorrow never comes, then you're dead.

2478 Laughter is the best medicine. Unless you're really sick. Then you should ring 999.

2479 An auctioneer has no friends, only nodding acquaintances.

2480 A good pun is its own reword.

2481 Don't judge a book by its movie.

2482 Alcohol is not the answer – it just makes you forget the question.

2483 Borrow money from pessimists – they don't expect it back.

2484 The easiest way to find something lost around the house is to buy a replacement.

2485 Smile – it makes people wonder what you're thinking.

2486 The human body is an interesting phenomenon – a pat on the back can result in a swollen head.

2487 If you can't be kind, at least have the decency to be vague.

2488 Sex is nobody's business but the three people involved.

2489 A face can say so many things. Especially the mouth part.

2490 Money is the root of all wealth.

2491 Sea captains don't like crew cuts.

2492 It's sad how whole people get torn apart by simple things, like wild dogs.

2493 When you're run down, the best thing to take is the licence number.

2494 A bird in the hand makes blowing your nose difficult.

2495 Early to rise and early to bed makes a man healthy but socially dead.

2496 Death is nature's way of saying "slow down".

2497 Cowboy philosophy: always drink upstream from the herd.

2498 A bartender is just a pharmacist with a limited inventory.

2499 Condoms are easier to change than nappies.

2500 Everybody is somebody else's weirdo.

2501 Money can't buy everything — that's what credit cards are for.

2502 The best way to keep the wolf from the door is to leave a sheep in the garden.

2503 Every snowflake in an avalanche pleads not guilty.

2504 Carpenter's rule: cut to fit, beat into place.

2505 God made pot. Man made beer. Who do you trust?

2506 Eat a live toad first thing in the morning. That way, nothing worse can happen to you for the rest of the day.

2507 If you can remain calm, you don't have all the facts.

2508 Drilling for oil is boring.

2509 Never play strip poker with a nudist: they have nothing to lose.

2510 All that glitters has a high refractive index.

2511 If you want to know more about paranoids, follow them around.

2512 If God had meant us to touch our toes, he would have put them further up our body.

2513 The road to success is always under construction.

2514 There is no such thing as absolute truth. This is absolutely true.

2515 One good turn gets most of the blankets.

2516 If the early bird catches the worm, the worm should sleep in.

2517 If you're not living life on the edge, you're taking up too much space.

2518 Time may be a great healer, but it's a lousy beautician.

2519 If you feel the world is moving too fast, take comfort from the queue for the supermarket checkout.

2520 If at first you don't succeed, destroy all evidence that you tried.

2521 Cloning is the sincerest form of flattery.

2522 Sure, you can't take it with you — but you can hide it where no other bastard can find it.

2523 Everyone is beautiful if you squint a bit.

2524 The trouble with half-truths is you never know which half you've got.

2525 The bigger they are, the harder they hit.

2526 If the Lord had wanted us to use the metric system, there would have been ten apostles.

2527 Be careful — the toes you step on today may be connected to the ass you have to kiss tomorrow.

2528 Some people say I'm superficial, but that's just on the surface.

2529 A student who changes the course of history is probably taking an exam.

2530 Prejudiced people are all alike.

2531 A bird in the hand is safer than one overhead.

2532 Nobody's ugly after 2 a.m.

2533 Never buy a car you can't push.

2534 Friendly fire isn't.

2535 Accept that some days you're the pigeon, and some days you're the statue.

2536 There are two sides to every story: the book and the movie.

2537 If there's one thing I can't stand, it's intolerance.

2538 Drink until she's cute, but stop before the wedding.

2539 Perspective is in the eye of the beholder.

2540 Golf scores are directly proportional to the number of witnesses.

2541 Getting married is like buying a dishwasher. You'll never need to do it by hand again.

2542 How long a minute is depends what side of the bathroom door you're on.

2543 If at first you don't succeed, then skydiving probably isn't for you.

2544 The severity of the itch is directly proportional to the reach.

2545 Suicide is a way of telling God, "You can't fire me – I quit!"

2546 There's no such thing as non-existent.

2547 Given a conflict, Murphy's law supersedes Newton's.

2548 It's not hard to meet expenses – they're everywhere!

2549 Children are like farts: your own are just about tolerable but everyone else's are horrendous.

2550 When a man talks dirty to a woman, it's sexual harassment. When a woman talks dirty to a man, it's 3 dollars 95 a minute.

2551 If you think nobody cares about you, try missing a couple of mortgage payments.

2552 If you aren't part of the solution, you're a precipitate.

2553 Where there's a will, make sure you're in it.

2554 A single fact can ruin a good argument.

2555 Never eat yellow snow.

2556 Before criticizing people, walk a mile in their shoes. Then when you do criticize them, you'll be a mile away and you'll have their shoes.

2557 A penny for some people's thoughts is still a fair price.

2558 On the other hand, the early worm gets eaten.

2559 Procrastination means never having to say you're sorry.

2560 Sex is like air – it's not important unless you aren't getting any.

2561 Success always occurs in private, and failure in full view.

2562 A beer in the hand is worth two in the fridge.

2563 It's only kinky the first time.

2564 Never moon a werewolf.

2565 A friend in need is a pest indeed.

2566 Eat, drink and be merry, for tomorrow they may cancel your VISA.

2567 Those who live by the sword get shot by those who don't.

2568 If money could talk, it would say goodbye.

2569 Marriage is a three ring-circus: engagement ring, wedding ring, and suffering

2570 If love is a dream, then marriage is an alarm clock.

2571 Never agree to plastic surgery if the doctor's office is full of portraits by Picasso.

2572 Marriage is one of the chief causes of divorce.

2573 A fool and his money are soon partying.

2574 Your temper is one of the few things that improves the longer you keep it.

2575 Sex is not the answer. Sex is the question. The answer is "yes".

2576 Work is for people who don't know how to fish.

2577 Work is a fine thing if it doesn't take up too much of your spare time.

2578 Never argue with an idiot. They drag you down to their level, then beat you with experience.

2579 Change is inevitable, except from a vending machine.

2580 The man who gives in when he is wrong is wise. The man who gives in when he is right is married.

2581 Nothing in the known universe travels faster than a bad cheque.

2582 It's not an optical illusion, it just looks that way.

2583 Honesty is the best policy, but insanity is a better defence.

2584 He who laughs last, thinks slowest.

2585 It's not whether you win or lose, but where you place the blame.

2586 Love thy neighbour, but make sure her husband is away first.

2587 Constipated people don't give a shit!

2588 Hard work has a future payoff, but laziness pays off now.

2589 If you can't laugh at yourself, make fun of other people.

2590 Friends help you move. Real friends help you move bodies.

2591 Twenty-four hours in a day, 24 beers in a case. Coincidence?

2592 "You'll never know until you try it" works pretty well for most unknowns, but "I wonder if it hurts to saw off the tip of my tongue" is probably not one of them. (DOUG RENDALL)

Police

2593 A traffic cop stopped a drunken driver just after midnight in Dublin. "Excuse me, sir," said the officer peering into the car window. "Have you been drinking?"

"I certainly have," replied the driver. "I had five pints of Guinness with my pals at lunchtime and then I spent the afternoon in O'Malley's Bar, drinking Guinness with whisky chasers. During Happy Hour I sank six double brandies and then I had a couple of drinks with old friends, just to be sociable like. And then I drove one of my friends home and had a few cans of beer at his house, because it would have been rude to refuse."

"I see," said the officer. "I'm afraid I'm going to have to ask you to step out of the car and take a breathalyzer test."

"Why?" said the drunk. "Don't you believe me?"

2594 How many police officers does it take to break an egg? – None, it "fell down the stairs".

2595 A man went to the police station demanding to speak with the burglar who had broken into his house the previous night.

"You'll get your chance in court," said the desk sergeant.

"No, you don't understand," said the man. "I want to know how he got into the house in the middle of the night without waking my wife. I've been trying to do that for years!"

2596 An ice cream seller was found lying on the floor of his van covered in hundreds and thousands. Police say he topped himself.

2597 A rookie New York cop was on his first day in a patrol car. The sergeant had teamed him up with a more experienced partner. After a quiet hour, a call came through asking them to disperse a group of people who were loitering on the corner of 43rd Street.

"I'll handle this," said the rookie excitedly. So when they got to 43rd Street and saw a small crowd on a corner, he leapt out of the car and yelled: "OK, move along now. Haven't you got homes to go to?" The crowd were reluctant to disperse, so he repeated the command: "Come on now, move on."

Puzzled, they slowly drifted off in different directions.

The rookie climbed back into the patrol car. "Not bad, huh?" he said proudly to his partner.

"Yeah, you did OK. Pity it was a bus stop . . ."

2598 As a police dog handler parked his van at the station, the dog started barking. A small boy asked: "Is that a dog you've got in the back of the van?"

"Sure is," replied the cop.

"Gee!" said the boy. "What did he do?"

2599 A cop spotted a woman driving and knitting at the same time. "Pull over!" he called.

"No, officer, it's a scarf."

2600 A five-year-old boy got lost in a shopping mall. Remembering what his mother had told him, he went up to a police officer and said: "Officer, did you happen to see a lady without a boy like me?"

2601 Police arrested two kids yesterday. One was drinking battery acid, the other was eating fireworks. They charged one and let the other one off. (TOMMY COOPER)

2602 Ed was driving along the highway when a cop pulled him over and informed that he'd won a 1,000-dollar safe driving award.

"So what are you gonna spend the money on?" asked the cop.

"I guess I'll use it to get that drivers' licence," smiled Ed.

"Take no notice, officer," said Jenny in the passenger seat. "He's a real smartass when he's drunk and stoned."

Just then Ray in the back seat hissed: "I told you guys we wouldn't get far in a stolen car!"

As the cop took all this in, there was a knock from the trunk and a muffled voice said: "Are we over the border yet?"

2603 Yesterday a basketball player and a jockey robbed a store. Police are looking high and low.

2604 After checking the licence of the driver he'd stopped, the police officer commented: "It says here you're supposed to be wearing glasses."

"But officer," said the motorist, "I have contacts."

"I don't care who you know," snapped the officer. "You're breaking the law."

Things not to say when stopped by a traffic cop:

2605 "I can't reach my licence unless you hold my beer."

2606 "Aren't you the guy from the Village People?"

2607 "Want to buy a cheap camcorder, no questions asked? I've got 50 in the trunk."

2608 "Is that your baton or are you just pleased to see me?"

2609 "You must have been doing 120 to keep up with me."

2610 "Here's ten dollars to forget all about it."

2611 "Want to race to the station?"

2612 "Sorry, officer, my guide dog usually barks if I'm driving too fast."

2613 "This is a typical case of harassment by a fascist police force."

2614 "Is it true that people become cops because they're too dumb to work at McDonalds?"

2615 "I pay your salary, you know!"

2616 "Thanks, officer. The officer yesterday let me off with a warning too."

2617 "Officer . . . I think I love you."

2618 A California traffic cop pulled a driver over for not stopping at a stop sign.
"Do you know why I pulled you over?" he asked.
"I slowed down, didn't I?" said the driver.
"But you must come to a complete stop at the sign."
"Stop. Slow down. What's the difference?"
The cop was so annoyed by the driver's attitude that he whipped out his baton and began pummelling him about the head, shouting: "Well, do you want me to stop or slow down!"

2619 We live in an age when pizza gets to your home before the police. (JEFF MARDER)

2620 A shipment of Viagra was hijacked last week. Police are on the lookout for two hardened criminals.

2621 A large hole was found in a fence surrounding a nudist colony. Police are looking into it.

2622 Following the theft of 100 wigs, police officers were reported to be combing the area.

2623 Thieves broke into a police station and stole all the toilets. Police say they have nothing to go on.

2624 A tourist asked a man in uniform: "Are you a policeman?"
"No, I'm an undercover detective."
"Then why are you in uniform?"
"It's my day off."

Political correctness

These are only a few examples:

2625 A man doesn't have a beer gut – he has developed a liquid grain storage facility.

2626 A man does not eat like a pig – he suffers from reverse bulimia.

2627 A man is not stupid – he suffers from minimal cranial development.

2628 A man doesn't get lost – he discovers alternative destinations.

2629 A man is not dishonest – he is ethically disoriented.

2630 A man is not short – he is anatomically compact.

2631 A man is not lazy – he is energetically declined.

2632 A man is not a psychopath – he is socially misaligned.

2633 A man is not going bald – he is in follicle regression.

2634 A man is not a cradle snatcher – he prefers generationally differential relationships.

2635 A man is not unsophisticated – he is socially malformed.

2636 A man is not impotent – he is procreationally disabled.

2637 A man does not fart and belch – he is gastronomically expressive.

2638 A man is not quiet – he is a conversational minimalist.

2639 A man is not a male chauvinist pig – he has swine empathy.

2640 A man does not get falling-down drunk – he becomes accidentally horizontal.

2641 A man does not behave like a total ass – he develops a case of rectalcranial inversion.

2642 A man does not have a dirty mind – he has introspective pornographic moments.

2643 A man is not sleeping around – he is monogamously challenged.

2644 A man is not weird – he is behaviourally different.

2645 A man does not snore – he is nasally repetitive.

2646 A man is not ignorant – he is factually unencumbered.

2647 A man does not hog the blankets – he is thermally unappreciative.

2648 A woman is not old – she is chronologically gifted.

2649 A woman is not overweight – she is gravity enhanced.

2650 A woman is not a bad cook – she is microwave compatible.

2651 A woman is not easy – she is horizontally accessible.

2652 A woman does not have a rich daddy – she is a recipient of parental asset infusion.

2653 A woman is not a bleached blonde – she is peroxide dependent.

2654 A woman does not get drunk – she becomes verbally dyslexic.

2655 A woman is not a bad driver – she is automotively challenged.

2656 A woman does not put on weight – she is a metabolic underachiever.

2657 A woman is not frigid – she is thermally incompatible.

2658 A woman is not dumb – she is a detour off the information superhighway.

2659 A woman does not get PMS – she becomes hormonally homicidal.

2660 A woman does not have a killer body – she is terminally attractive.

2661 A woman does not have a moustache – she's in touch with her masculine side.

2662 A woman does not wear too much make-up – she is cosmetically over-saturated.

2663 A woman is not too skinny – she is skeletally prominent.

2664 A woman does not have sexy lips – she is collagen dependent.

2665 A woman is not having a bad hair day – she is suffering from rebellious follicle syndrome.

2666 A woman is not hooked on soap operas – she is melodramatically fixated.

2667 A woman does not sunbathe – she experiences solar enhancement.

2668 A woman does not hate sport on TV – she is athletically biased.

2669 A woman is not a gossip – she specializes in the speedy transmission of near-factual information.

2670 A woman is not a shopaholic – she is overly susceptible to marketing ploys.

2671 A woman is not late – she has a rescheduled arrival time.

2672 A woman is not a hooker – she is a human relations specialist.

2673 A woman is not a housewife – she is a domestic engineer.

2674 A woman has not been around – she is a previously enjoyed companion.

2675 A teenager's bedroom is not cluttered – it is passage restrictive.

2676 A teenager's homework isn't missing – it's having an out-of-notebook experience.

2677 A teenager does not have smelly gym socks – he has odour retentive athletic footwear.

2678 A teenager is not in trouble – he's merely hit social speed bumps.

2679 A teenager is not sleeping in class – he is rationing consciousness.

2680 A teenager has not been sent to the principal's office – he was going on a mandatory field trip to the administrative building.

2681 A teenager has not got a detention at school – he's merely one of the "exit delayed".

Politics

2682 Laura Bush was out walking near the White House one day when she saw a young boy trying to sell a litter of tiny puppies. "My, they're so cute," said the First Lady.

"And they're all Republicans," replied the boy.

"Is that so?" said Laura. "I tell you, I'm so taken with these puppies that if you've got one left at the weekend, I'm going to buy one."

The following weekend, Laura passed the same spot and saw the boy with just two puppies left. "I'd like to buy one," she said. "How much?"

"Fifty dollars each," said the boy. "They're both Democrats."

"Wait a minute," snapped Laura. "The other day you said they were Republicans."

"Well, yes, ma'am," answered the boy. "But since then they've opened their eyes."

2683 Too bad all the people who know how to run the country are busy driving cabs and cutting hair. (GEORGE BURNS)

2684 If Presidents don't do it to their wives, they do it to the country. (MEL BROOKS)

2685 A bus load of politicians was speeding along a country road when it ploughed into a tree and overturned. There was blood and glass everywhere. An old farmer saw the crash and was first on the scene. Within two hours, he had dug a huge hole and buried all the politicians.

A few days later, the local sheriff was passing through when he saw the wreckage of the bus. The farmer explained what had happened.

"Were they all dead?" inquired the sheriff.

"Well," said the farmer. "Some of them said they weren't, but you know how them politicians lie."

2686 Now I know what a statesman is; he's a dead politician. We need more statesmen. (BOB EDWARDS)

2687 Americans have different ways of saying things. They say "elevator", we say "lift"; they say "President", we say "stupid psychopathic git". (ALEXEI SAYLE)

2688 Show me where Stalin is buried and I'll show you a Communist plot. (EDGAR BERGEN)

2689 A priest walked into a barber shop in Washington, DC. After getting his hair cut, he asked how much it would be. The barber said: "No charge. I consider it a service to the Lord."

The next morning the barber arrived for work to find 12 prayer books and a thank you note from the priest at the front door. Later that day, a police officer walked into the same barber shop. After getting his hair cut, he asked how much it would be. The barber said: "No charge. I consider it a service to the community."

The next morning the barber arrived for work to find 12 doughnuts and a thank you note from the police officer at the front door. Then a senator walked into the barber shop. After getting his hair cut, he asked how much it would be. The barber said: "No charge. I consider it a service to the nation."

The next morning the barber arrived for work to find 12 senators at the front door.

2690 I belong to no organized party – I'm a Democrat. (WILL ROGERS)

2691 Why don't politicians like golf? – Because it's too much like their work: trapped in one bad lie after another.

2692 How long does a US Congressman serve? – Until he gets caught.

2693 When a little boy desperately needed 100 dollars to buy a present, his mother suggested that he pray for it. So he wrote to God asking for the money. The Post Office intercepted the letter and forwarded it to the President who was so touched by the request that he instructed his secretary to send the boy 5 dollars.

On receiving the money, the boy wrote back: "Dear God, Thank you very much for sending me the money. I noticed that you had to send it through Washington. As usual, those thieving bastards deducted 95 dollars."

2694 Based on what you know about him in history books, what do you think Abraham Lincoln would be doing if he were alive today?
1. Writing his memoirs of the Civil War.
2. Advising the President.
3. Desperately clawing at the inside of his coffin. (DAVID LETTERMAN)

Prison

2695 Two prisoners were waiting to be executed. "Any last requests?" asked the jailer.

"Yes," replied one of the prisoners. "I love music, so before I die could you play me 'Everything I Do' by Bryan Adams."

And the second prisoner said: "Kill me first."

2696 After serving 18 months of a 25-year sentence, a man escaped from prison. His escape was the lead story on the early evening TV news and, knowing that there would be a huge search party out looking for him, he took care to make his way home via a long, cross-country route of fields and woodland. When he finally made it to his house, he looked around to make sure the coast was clear and knocked on the door. His wife answered. "You dirty stinkin' rat!" she screamed. "Where have you been? You escaped over five hours ago!"

2697 What do prisoners use to call each other? – Cell phones.

2698 A new prisoner was introduced to his cellmate. "I'll take you through the week," said the cellmate. "Sundays we go to church. Do you like church?"
"No, not much."
"Mondays we play cards. Do you like cards?"
"No, not much."
"Tuesdays we play football. Do you like football?"
"No, not much."
"Wednesdays we play snooker. Do you like snooker?"
"No, not much."
"You're hard to please, aren't you? Do you like sex?"
"Yeah."
"With men or women?"
"Women."
"So you don't like sex with men?"
"No way."
"Then you're not gonna like Thursdays either."

2699 Nelson Mandela, he's been out of prison for 16 years and hasn't reoffended. I think he's going straight. Which shows you, prison works. (RICKY GERVAIS)

2700 Two new prisoners were taken to their cell. "How long are you in for?" asked one.
"Fifteen years. What about you?"
"Twenty-two years. So as you're getting out first, you'd better have the bed by the door."

2701 Three men were sentenced to 25 years' solitary confinement. As a concession, the prison governor allowed each to take one item into his cell. The first asked for a pile of books; the second asked for his wife; and the third asked for 200 cartons of cigarettes.
At the end of the 25 years, the first prisoner was released and said: "Those books proved invaluable. I've studied so hard now I can train to be a lawyer. I'm really happy."

The second man stepped out of his cell with his wife and five new children. He enthused: "My wife and I have never been so close. I have a beautiful new family. I'm so happy."

And the third guy said: "Anybody got a match?"

2702 During his spell in prison, Michael learnt carpentry and became highly accomplished. He was also a model prisoner so when the governor wanted some work doing on his kitchen at home, he asked Michael whether he would help out.

"I've done the cupboards," said the governor, "but I promised my wife a nice counter top and, to be honest, I don't think I'm up to the job. So could you do it for me?"

"I'd like to," said Michael, "but you have to remember, it was counter fitting that got me into prison in the first place."

Psychiatrists

2703 A man walked into a psychiatrist's office with a pancake on his head, a fried egg on each shoulder and a piece of bacon over each ear.

"What seems to be the problem?" asked the psychiatrist, puzzled.

The man said: "I'm worried about my brother."

2704 A woman sat down in a psychiatrist's office. "I think I might be a nymphomaniac," she said.

"I see. Well, I can help you but I ought to tell you in advance that my fee is 75 dollars an hour."

"Hmmm," she said. "How much for all night?"

2705 A man thought he was a dog, so he went to see a psychiatrist. "It's terrible," said the man, "I walk around on all fours, I keep barking in the middle of the night and I can't go past a lamp-post any more."

"OK," said the psychiatrist. "Get on the couch."

The man replied: "I'm not allowed on the couch."

2706 Right now I'm having amnesia and déjà vu at the same time. I think I've forgotten this before. (STEVEN WRIGHT)

2707 A man went to a psychiatrist and said he was worried that he was becoming obsessed with sex. The psychiatrist showed him a photograph of a cow and asked him what it reminded him of.

"A man and a woman making love," replied the man.

Then the psychiatrist showed him a photo of a cardboard box. "Now what does this remind you of?"

"A man and a woman making love."

Next the psychiatrist showed him a photo of the Empire State Building. "What does this remind you of?"

"A man and a woman making love."

Finally the psychiatrist produced a photo of a pot of yoghurt. "What does this remind you of?" he asked.

"A man and a woman making love."

"Well," sighed the psychiatrist, "I have to say you do seem to be obsessed with sex."

"Me?" said the patient. "You're the one who keeps showing me dirty pictures."

2708 One behaviourist to another after lovemaking: "Darling, that was wonderful for you. How was it for me?"

2709 The psychiatrist told the patient that he was conducting a simple test to monitor normal human responses. "So," began the psychiatrist, "what would happen if I cut off your left ear?"

"I wouldn't be able to hear," replied the patient.

"And what would happen if I cut off your right ear?"

"I wouldn't be able to see?"

"Why do you say that?" asked the psychiatrist.

"Because my hat would fall over my eyes."

2710 Never get into an argument with a schizophrenic person and say, "Who do you think you are?" (RAY COMBS)

2711 A wife went to a psychiatrist in an attempt to sort out her sex life. For over half an hour, she talked about how unrewarding sex was with her husband, but the psychiatrist was struggling to reach the root of the problem. Then he asked: "Do you ever watch your husband's face while you're making love?"

"I did once," she replied.

"And how did he look?"

"Very angry."

"That's interesting. You say you have only once seen your husband's face during sex? That in itself is unusual. Tell me, what were the circumstances that led you to see his face on the occasion he appeared so angry?"

"He was looking through the window at me."

2712 A woman went to a psychiatrist and said: "You've got to help me – my husband thinks he's a greyhound. He eats dog food, sleeps in a kennel and even chases hares."

"Well," said the psychiatrist, "I can cure him but it's going to be costly."

"Oh, money isn't an issue," said the wife. "He's already won four races."

2713 A psychotherapist started up in business and, in order to attract patients, he asked a young artist to write a name sign above the front door. But three weeks later, in spite of the advertising, he was still awaiting his first patient. What seemed particularly strange was that a number of women had approached the building, but had then turned away suddenly. So he decided to take a look at the sign which the artist had written in case that was somehow to blame. Due to shortage of space, it read:

PSYCHO

THE

RAPIST

2714 A man was convinced he was dead, and nothing, it seemed, could persuade him otherwise. When words failed, his psychiatrist resorted to text books and, after three hours of careful argument, backed up by expert testimony, he got the man to agree that dead men don't bleed.

"So now," said the psychiatrist, "I will prick your finger with a needle." He jabbed a needle into the tip of the man's finger, and it started to bleed.

"What does that tell you?" asked the psychiatrist triumphantly.

"That dead men do bleed."

2715 I told my therapist I was having nightmares about nuclear explosions. He said: "Don't worry, it's not the end of the world." (JAY LONDON)

2716 Patient; "My wife thinks I'm crazy because I like sausages."

Psychiatrist: "Nonsense, I like sausages too."

Patient: "Great – you should come and see my collection. I've got hundreds of them."

2717 Four psychiatrists were attending an out-of-town convention. Sitting in the hotel lounge one night, they each agreed that it could get pretty tiresome listening to other people's hang-ups all the time. Wouldn't it be nice if someone listened to their complexes and problems for a change?

"OK," said one, "why don't we reveal our innermost feelings now, just between the four of us? I'll go first if you like. My big hang-up is sex. I can't get enough of it, and I have to confess that I frequently seduce my female patients."

The second said: "My problem is money. I lead an extravagant lifestyle way beyond my means, and to finance this, I regularly overcharge my patients."

The third said: "My trouble is drugs. I'm a pusher, and I often get my patients to sell drugs for me."

The fourth said: "My problem is that, no matter hard I try, I just can't keep a secret."

2718 A man went to see a psychiatrist and confessed that he had suicidal tendencies. "I suddenly get the urge to kill myself," he said. "I never know when these feelings are going to occur."

"Hmmm," said the psychiatrist. "In the circumstances, perhaps you had better pay in advance."

2719 I told my psychiatrist that everyone hates me. He said I was being ridiculous – everyone hasn't met me yet. (RODNEY DANGERFIELD)

2720 A man had been seeing a psychiatrist for three years in an attempt to cure his fear that there were monsters lurking under his bed. But all the psychiatrist's efforts were in vain and the man was no nearer to being cured. Eventually the man decided that further sessions were a waste of time and money. A few weeks later, the psychiatrist bumped into the man in a bar. The man was looking much happier.

"You look well," remarked the psychiatrist.

"Yes," beamed the man. "That's because I'm cured. After all this time, I can finally go to sleep at night and not worry that there are monsters lurking under my bed."

The psychiatrist was puzzled. "How have you managed to get cured? Nothing I tried with you seemed to work."

"I went to see a different doctor," explained the man. "He is a behaviourist and he cured me in one session."

"In one session!" exclaimed the psychiatrist. "How?"

"It was simple," said the man. "He told me to saw the legs off my bed."

2721 Psychiatrist hotline voice messaging system: If you are obsessive-compulsive, please press 1 repeatedly.

If you are co-dependent, please ask someone to press 2.

If you have multiple personality disorder, please press 3, 4, 5 and 6.

If you are schizophrenic, please listen carefully and a little voice will tell you which number to press.

If you are paranoid-delusional, we know who you are and what you want. Just stay on the line till we can trace the call.

If you are manic depressive, it doesn't matter which number you press – no one will answer.

Q&A jokes

2722 Why do seagulls live near the sea? – Because if they lived near the bay, they'd be called bagels.

2723 What's got a trunk, four legs, and lots of keys? – A piano up a tree.

2724 What do you get if you cross a chicken with a cement mixer? – A brick layer.

2725 What do you call a Telly Tubby that's just been burgled? – Tubby.

2726 What did the plate say to the other plate? – "Lunch is on me."

2727 How do we know the Indians were the first people in North America? – They had reservations.

2728 What did one toilet say to the other? – "You look flushed."

2729 What is small, red and whispers? – A hoarse radish.

2730 How do you make a hot dog stand? – Steal its chair.

2731 What do you get when you cross a stream and a brook? – Wet feet.

2732 Why did Henry VIII put skittles on his lawn? – So he could take Anne Boleyn.

2733 If Martians live on Mars and Venusians live on Venus, what lives on Pluto? – Fleas.

2734 Why was Queen Elizabeth II disappointed? – When she discovered that Philip's 24-inch was a television.

2735 What has fifty legs but still can't manage to walk? – Half a centipede.

2736 What has one horn and gives milk? – A milk truck.

2737 Why didn't the skeleton go to the party? – It had no body to go with.

2738 What is 150 yards long and eats potatoes? – A Moscow queue waiting to buy meat.

2739 What did one elevator say to the other? – "I think I'm coming down with something."

2740 Why couldn't the bicycle stand on its own? – Because it was two tyred.

2741 What did the necktie say to the hat? – "You go on ahead, I'll hang around a while."

2742 What do you get when you cross poison ivy with a four-leaf clover? – A rash of good luck.

2743 What did one eye say to the other? – Between you and me there's something that smells.

2744 Why was the electrician disqualified from the race? – Because he made a short circuit.

2745 What's red and invisible? – No tomatoes.

2746 What has six eyes but can't see? – Three blind mice.

2747 What did the rug say to the floor? – "Don't move, I've got you covered."

2748 What do you call a guy who's born in Columbus, grows up in Cleveland, and then dies in Cincinnati? – Dead.

2749 What's the biggest drawback in the jungle? – An elephant's foreskin.

2750 What cheese is made backwards? – Edam.

2751 Why does a squirrel swim on its back? – To keep its nuts dry.

2752 What lies on its back 100 feet in the air? – A centipede.

2753 What do you get when you cross a blue cat and a red parrot? – A purple carrot.

2754 What did one magnet say to the other? – "I find you very attractive."

2755 What do you get when you cross an octopus with a cow? – A farm animal that can milk itself.

2756 What do you get when you cross an elephant and a rhino? – El-if-i-no.

Rail travel

2757 A young man went for an interview for a signalman's job on the railways. The inspector asked: "What would you do if you realized that two trains were heading towards each other on the same track?"

"I'd switch the points for one of the trains," answered the young man confidently.

"But what would you do if the lever was broken?" said the inspector.

"I'd rush down from the signal box and use the manual lever."

"What if the manual lever had been struck by lightning?"

"I'd phone the next signal box."

"What if the phone was engaged?"

"I'd use the emergency phone at the level crossing."

"What if the emergency phone was vandalized?"

"In that case, I'd run to the village and fetch my uncle Joshua."

"Why would you do that?" asked the inspector.

"Because he's never seen a train crash."

2758 A man travelling on a train from London to Edinburgh asked the ticket collector what time the train stopped at Newark.

"This train doesn't stop at Newark," said the ticket collector.

The man was distraught. "But you don't understand. I have to get off at

Newark. My wife is waiting for me, and she's taking me straight to see our first grandson in hospital. There must be something you can do."

The ticket collector was sympathetic to the passenger's plight. "Well I suppose I could ask the driver to slow down as we approach Newark and then I could dangle you out the door and lower you on to the platform."

The plan was agreed, and the express approached the station at a modest 50 mph. The ticket collector opened the door and held the man out. He started running like crazy in mid-air and the ticket collector lowered him until first one foot and then both feet touched the platform. Sparks flew from his shoes and there was a terrible smell of burning rubber. The man was doing 30 mph, and running for his life. Finally the ticket collector let go and the man realized he'd made it. Safely on the platform, he started to reduce speed to 20 mph. But just as the last carriage drew alongside him, a hand suddenly grabbed the man by the collar and lifted him back on to the train. "Lucky I was here to help," said the buffet manager. "This train doesn't even stop at Newark."

2759 A slow-thinking country boy got off the train with a face as white as a sheet. A friend asked him what was wrong.

"Railroad sickness," said the country boy. "Whenever I travel by railroad, I always feel sick when I sit with my back to the engine."

"Why didn't you ask the person sitting opposite you to change places?" said the friend.

"I thought of that," replied the country boy, "but there wasn't anybody there."

2760 Last time I went Intercity there were a couple across the aisle having sex. Of course, this being a British train, nobody said anything. When they'd finished, they both lit up a cigarette and this woman stood up and said, "Excuse me, I think you'll find this is a non-smoking compartment." (VICTORIA WOOD)

2761 After travelling slowly for several minutes, an express train finally stopped in the middle of nowhere. Seeing the guard walking alongside the track, a passenger leaned out of the window and asked: "What's going on?"

"There's a cow on the track," replied the guard.

Eventually the train moved off and resumed its slow crawl, only to stop again 15 minutes later. The passenger saw the same guard walking past and inquired: "What happened? Did we catch up with the cow again?"

2762 It was a crowded train at the height of rush hour and the passengers were crushed together in the gangways. Suddenly a middle-aged woman turned to the man next to her and said firmly: "Sir, if you don't stop poking me with your thing, I'm going to the police."

"I don't know what you're talking about," protested the man. "It's just my wages packet in my pocket."

"Oh yes? Well that's some job you must have, because that's the fifth rise you've had in the last half-hour!"

2763 An English visitor to the United States was talking to a fellow passenger on the train. She told him that last year she came over to stay in San José.

"You pronounce that wrong," said the man. "It is San Hosay. In California, you should pronounce all Js as Hs."

"Oh, I see," said the woman. "Thank you for pointing that out."

"When were you there?"

"Hune and Huly."

2764 On a train, why do I always end up sitting next to the woman who's eating the individual fruit pie by sucking the filling out through the hole in the middle? (VICTORIA WOOD)

2765 A man was on a train from Milan to Rome. "I must get off at Prato," he told the ticket collector. "So if I fall asleep, you must wake me at Prato. Here's 10,000 lire for your trouble. Now don't forget!"

The man did indeed fall asleep and woke up to find himself in Rome. He raged at the ticket collector: "You are an imbecile. I told you I had to get off at Prato. I paid you money to wake me at Prato. Yet here I am in Rome!"

Two passengers witnessed this outburst. One said: "He's angry, isn't he?" The other said: "But not as angry as the guy who was thrown off the train at Prato."

2766 Two sardines were big tennis fans. "Let's go to Wimbledon this year," said one.

"How would we get there?" asked the other.

"On the London Underground, of course."

"What, and get packed in like commuters?"

Real estate

2767 The real estate agent was intent on selling an expensive summer house to the wealthy businessman.

"What a perfect location," enthused the agent. "Right on the bank of the river. Two steps from the back door and you're in the water, ready for a nice relaxing swim. Or you can go fishing – without leaving your porch. And if you like boating, see, there's a little pier, right on your doorstep. Believe me, sir, this house is ideal for you."

"I must say it's very nice," said the businessman, "but one thing troubles me. Suppose the river overflows its banks?"

"So what?" answered the agent smoothly. "How could that possibly affect your house? It's set back a long way from the river!"

2768 What was the worst selling-point about Robin Hood's house? – It had a little John.

2769 For once in his life, the estate agent decided to be honest with a prospective lady house-buyer. "This property is bordered on the north by gasworks, on the south by a rubber factory, on the east by a brewery, and on the west by a glue factory."

"My goodness!" said the woman. "It sounds absolutely appalling. Doesn't it have any redeeming features?"

"There is one," said the agent. "You can always tell which way the wind is blowing."

Genuine letters sent to landlords:

2770 The toilet is blocked and we cannot bathe the children until it is cleared.

2771 This is to let you know that there is a smell coming from the man next door.

2772 I want some repairs done to my stove as it has backfired and burnt my knob off.

2773 The toilet seat is cracked: where do I stand?

2774 I am writing on behalf of my sink, which is running away from the wall.

2775 Our kitchen floor is very damp, we have two children and would like a third, so will you please send someone to do something about it.

2776 I request your permission to remove my drawers in the kitchen.

2777 Our lavatory seat is broken in half and is now in three pieces.

2778 The person next door has a large erection in his back garden, which is unsightly and dangerous.

2779 Will you please send someone to mend our cracked sidewalk. Yesterday my wife tripped on it and is now pregnant.

2780 Will you please send a man to look at my water. It is a funny colour and not fit to drink.

2781 When the workmen were here they put their tools in my wife's new drawers and made a mess. Please send men with clean tools to finish the job and keep my wife happy.

2782 Will you please send a man to repair my down spout. I am an old age pensioner and need it straight away.

2783 Could you please send someone to fix our bath tap. My wife got her toe stuck in it and it is very uncomfortable for us.

2784 I want to complain about the farmer across the road. Every morning at five thirty his cock wakes me up, and it is getting too much.

Rednecks

You know you're a redneck if . . .

2785 Your dad walks you to school because you're both in the same grade.

2786 Your Christmas stocking is full of ammo.

2787 You go to church to pick up women.

2788 Your dog passes wind and you claim it.

2789 You think the stock market has a fence around it.

2790 You can tell your age by the number of rings in the bathtub.

2791 You think paprika is a third world country.

2792 The UFO hotline limits you to one call a day.

2793 You vacuum the sheets instead of washing them.

2794 You've ever used lard in bed.

2795 You own all the components of soap on a rope except the soap.

2796 You were taught to put your underwear on: yellow in front, brown behind.

2797 Birds are attracted to your beard.

2798 Your house has wheels and your car doesn't.

2799 Your pocket-knife has ever been referred to as Exhibit A.

2800 When a sign that reads "Say No To Crack!" reminds you to pull up your jeans.

2801 Your bathroom deodorizer is a box of matches.

2802 You own a homemade fur coat.

2803 The same pair of boots have been in your family for five generations and they're only 30 years old.

2804 There's a wasps' nest in your living room.

2805 Your vehicle has a two-tone paint job — primer red and primer grey.

2806 Bikers back down from your momma.

2807 There has ever been a scene-of-crime tape on your front door.

2808 The fifth grade is referred to as "your senior year".

2809 Your wedding was held in the delivery room.

2810 Your wife can climb a tree faster than your cat.

2811 Your toilet paper has page numbers on it.

2812 You think the mountain men in *Deliverance* were just misunderstood.

2813 You've ever bathed with flea and tick soap.

2814 Your e-mail address ends in "over.yonder.com".

2815 You go Christmas shopping for your mom, sister and girlfriend and only need to buy one gift.

2816 You've ever used scissors on your food.

2817 You've ever stood in line to have your picture taken with a freak of nature.

2818 Your good deed for the month was hiding your brother for a few days.

2819 There's a gun rack on your bicycle.

2820 You can recite every line from *The Dukes of Hazzard*.

2821 Your daddy has ever said, "You kids run down to the dump and see what they left."

2822 Your wife weighs more than your fridge.

2823 More than one living relative is named after a Southern Civil War general.

2824 You've ever stolen clothes from a scarecrow.

2825 Your momma keeps a spit cup on the ironing board.

2826 Your family tree does not fork.

2827 Your bathroom is a nearby creek.

2828 Your wife has a beer belly and you find it attractive.

2829 The Salvation Army rejects your mattress.

2830 There is a stuffed possum anywhere in your house.

2831 You think Dom Perignon is a mafia leader.

2832 You mow your lawn and find a car.

2833 Your wife's best shoes have steel toes.

2834 You clean your fingernails with a stick.

2835 Your idea of a neighbourhood watch programme is tuning in to America's Most Wanted.

2836 You have a special baseball cap for formal occasions.

2837 You've never paid for a haircut.

2838 Your dog acts as a dishwasher.

2839 You had to remove a toothpick for wedding pictures.

2840 You consider your licence plate to be personalized because your dad made it in prison.

2841 Your favourite T-shirt is offensive in 19 states.

2842 You think a computer hacker carries an axe.

2843 You've ever been involved in a custody battle over a hunting dog.

2844 A pretty girl was driving down a country road in Arkansas one night when her car broke down. Unable to fix the problem, she walked to a nearby farmhouse for help. The farmer said he would look at her car in the morning and in the meantime agreed to let her stay the night, but on one condition: "I don't want you messin' with my sons Jethro and Luke."

The girl promised, but in the middle of the night the temptation of sleeping in the next room to two strapping lads proved too great to resist. So she crept into their room and said: "Boys, how would you like me to show you the ways of the world?"

"Huh?" they chorused.

She explained to them exactly what she wanted to do, adding: "I don't want to get pregnant, so you have to wear these rubbers." She put the condoms on the boys and for the next four hours, the three of them enjoyed sex.

Thirty-five years later, Jethro and Luke were sitting on their front porch, watching the world go by. Jethro turned to his brother and said: "Luke, you remember that pretty gal who came by here 35 years or so ago, the one who showed us the ways of the world?"

"Yeah, I remember," said Luke.

"Well," continued Jethro, "do you care if she gets pregnant?"

"No," said Luke.

"Me neither. Let's take these things off."

2845 How can you tell which is the groom at an Arkansas wedding? – He's the one in the clean bowling shirt.

2846 Two good ol' boys bought a couple of horses and decided to put them out to pasture for the winter.

"How will we tell which horse belongs to who?" asked the first redneck.

The second had a bright idea. "We'll cut the mane off mine and the tail off yours, and that way we'll be able to tell them apart."

But when they came to collect the horses in the spring, the mane and tail had grown back to their normal lengths.

"Now what?" asked the first.

The second scratched his head for a moment. "Why don't you just take the black one and I'll take the white one?"

2847 What's the difference between a good ol' boy and a redneck? – The good ol' boy raises livestock, the redneck gets emotionally involved.

2848 What's redneck foreplay? – "Hey, sis, get in the back of the truck!"

2849 Why did O.J. Simpson want to move to Arkansas? – Everyone has the same DNA.

2850 What is the best redneck pick-up line? – Nice tooth.

2851 How does a guy from Arkansas spell the word "farm"? – E I E I O.

2852 Bubba died in a fire and was so badly burned that someone needed to identify the body. So the mortician called in Bubba's friends Jim-Bob and Billy-Joe. Jim-Bob looked at the body and said: "He sure is burnt to a cinder. Roll him over."

The mortician rolled the body over but Jim-Bob said: "That ain't Bubba."

Next, it was Billy-Joe's turn to study the body. "He sure is burnt. Roll him over."

The mortician rolled the body over again but Billy-Joe said: "That ain't Bubba."

The mortician asked: "How can you tell by rolling him over?"

"Because," they said, "Bubba had two assholes."

"What!" exclaimed the mortician.

"Yep, everyone round here knew. Every time the three of us went into town, people would say, 'Here comes Bubba with them two assholes.'"

2853 Two rednecks staggered out of a zoo, their clothes ripped and their faces covered in cuts and bruises. One turned to the other and said: "That lion dancing sure ain't as restful as they made out."

2854 A young man watched an old American Indian at a state fair. The Indian was charging 5 dollars a time for a special challenge – if he couldn't tell where you were from just by looking at you, he'd pay you 50 dollars.

The young man saw a cowboy try his luck first. The Indian looked him up and down, noticed some cow dung on his boots and declared: "You're from Wyoming."

"Gee, that's right," said the cowboy.

The young man then looked on as another cowboy took a turn. The Indian looked him up and down, spotted straw and cow dung on his boots and said: "You're from Montana."

"Gee, that's right," said the second cowboy.

The young man decided that he wanted to have a go, but thought of a way of confusing the Indian. Having observed that the Indian placed great store on boots, the young man polished his own boots until they were spotless and therefore offered no clues. He went into the Indian's booth, the Indian looked him up and down and said: "You're from Arkansas."

"Gee, that's amazing. How could you tell?"

"Your jeans are on back to front."

2855 The sheriff was alarmed to see Joe-Bob walking around town wearing nothing but his gun belt and boots.

"What in God's name do you think you're doing?" demanded the sheriff.

"Well, it's kind of a long story, Sheriff," drawled Joe-Bob.

"I'm listening."

"Well, you see, Mary-Jo and me were on the farm this morning, having a kiss and cuddle like. Then Mary-Jo said we should go into the barn, and we did. After a bit, Mary-Jo said we should go up on the hill, and we did. Then Mary-Jo took off all her clothes and said I should do the same, so I did. I took off all my clothes except my gun belt and my boots. Then Mary-Jo lay on the ground, opened her legs and said, 'Joe-Bob, go to town . . .'"

2856 What's the last thing you usually hear before a redneck dies? – "Hey, y'all, watch this!"

2857 A pair of Arkansas newlyweds were driving from Little Rock to a motel in Memphis for their honeymoon.

On their way, he put his hand on her knee. She smiled, blushed and said: "Oh, Elmer, we're married now – you can go farther than that."

So they drove to Nashville.

2858 A stranger walked into a run-down bar in Alabama and ordered a dry martini. All heads turned. The bartender looked at him and said: "You ain't from round these parts, are you?"

"No," said the stranger, "I'm from Pennsylvania."

"Yeah?" said the bartender suspiciously. "What d'you do up in Pennsylvania?"

"I'm a taxidermist," replied the stranger.

"A taxidermist, huh?" said the bartender. "What's one of those?"

"I mount dead animals," explained the stranger.

Hearing this, the bartender called to the other customers. "It's OK, boys, he's one of us."

2859 How do you know when you're at a redneck wedding? – Everyone is sitting on the same side of the church.

2860 Having moved from Arkansas, Joe-Bob was in his first day of grade three at a new school in Pennsylvania. The teacher asked the class to count to 50, which is about the standard for grade three. Most were able to count up to 20, a few managed 30, but Joe-Bob counted all the way up to 100 without any mistakes.

After school, he ran home to tell his dad how well he had done. His dad said: "That's because you come from Arkansas, son."

The next day, the teacher asked the class to recite the alphabet. Most got halfway, but Joe-Bob did it all without any mistakes. After school, he ran home to tell his dad how well he had done. His dad said: "That's because you come from Arkansas, son."

The next day after PE, the boys were taking showers. Joe-Bob couldn't help noticing he was much better endowed than all the other boys in his grade. After school, he ran home to tell his dad.

"Is that because I'm from Arkansas, Dad?"

"No, son, it's because you're 18."

Religion

2861 A man entered a Trappist monastery and was told that once every five years he would be allowed to utter two words. After the first five years, he was approached by the monsignor and asked what he wished to say. The monk said simply, "Bed hard." The monsignor promised to look into the problem.

Five years later, the monk was brought before the monsignor again. This time he said, "Food cold." The monsignor said that he would look into the matter.

Another five years later and the monk told the monsignor, "I quit."

The monsignor said: "I'm hardly surprised you're quitting. All you have done over the past 15 years is complain!"

2862 Priest: "Tell me, Rabbi, did you ever cheat and try eating ham?"

Rabbi: "Well, to tell you the truth, I did break down once, just out of curiosity. Since I've confessed my experiment to you, let me ask, have you ever had a woman?"

Priest: "Yes, though I hate to admit it, earlier in my career I just had to find out what it was like."

Rabbi: "A lot better than ham, no?"

2863 They say that God has existed from the beginning and will exist beyond the end of time. Can you imagine trying to sit through his home movies? (SCOTT ROEBEN)

2864 Mick went into confessional and told the priest: "Bless me, father, for I have sinned. I've been with a loose woman."

The priest said: "Oh dear. Who was it? Was it Mary O'Malley?"

"No, Father," said Mick.

"Was it Bernadette Casey?"

"No, Father."

"Was it Niamh O'Farrell?"

"No, Father."

"Was it Sheila Byrne?"

"No, Father."

"Was it Angela O'Flaherty?"

"No, Father."

"Then was it Siobhan McKenna?"

"No, Father."

A few moments later, Mick emerged from the confessional box and met his friend Seamus.

"What did you get?" asked Seamus.

"Four Our Fathers, five Hail Marys, and six good leads."

2865 A guy ran through a crowded train, looking very agitated and calling out: "Is there a Catholic priest on board?"

When he got no reply, he ran through the train again, shouting: "Is there an Anglican vicar on board?" Still no reply.

Becoming increasingly desperate, he then ran down the train shouting: "Is there a Rabbi on board?"

Eventually a gentleman stood up and said: "Can I be of any assistance, my friend? I'm a Methodist minister."

The guy said: "No, you're no good. I need a corkscrew!"

2866 A priest and a rabbi took confession together. The priest treated three women who confessed to committing adultery on three occasions by demanding ten "Hail Marys" and ten dollars for the collection plate. When the priest had to go to the bathroom, the rabbi took over. Another woman came in and confessed to committing adultery on two occasions. The rabbi invited her to take advantage of the special — three for ten dollars.

2867 What is the biggest problem for an atheist? — No one to talk to during orgasm.

2868 The Pope was in the middle of an audience when his principal adviser whispered in his ear: "Your holiness, the Messiah is on the phone and he wants to talk to you."

The Pope thought he had better not keep the Messiah waiting so he interrupted the audience to go and talk on the phone. He returned a few minutes later.

"I have good news and bad news," announced the Pope. "The good news is that the call was the Messiah and the time of the second coming is at hand. The bad news is he was calling from Salt Lake City."

2869 Sacred cows make the best hamburger. (MARK TWAIN)

2870 Christ was up high on the cross while Peter and the disciples watched in anguish from below. Suddenly Jesus called out: "Peter . . . Peter . . . Peter."

Peter rushed forward and attempted to climb the hill to reach Christ, but a centurion sliced off Peter's left arm and he fell back down the hill.

A few minutes later, Jesus again called out: "Peter . . . Peter . . . Peter."

Peter tried to break through once more but a centurion sliced off his other arm and he stumbled back down the hill.

Shortly afterwards, Jesus again shouted: "Peter . . . Peter . . . Peter."

Peter made another desperate attempt to reach Christ, but a centurion sliced off Peter's left leg and he collapsed down the hill in a heap.

A few minutes after, Jesus yelled plaintively: "Peter . . . Peter . . . Peter."

Peter hopped defiantly towards Christ, but a centurion sliced off Peter's other leg and he rolled back down the hill.

Moments later, Jesus screamed: "Peter . . . Peter . . . Peter."

Even though he had no arms or legs, Peter managed to propel himself forward. Touched by such devotion, the head centurion finally allowed him through to talk to Christ. Peter lay on the ground writhing in agony at the foot of the cross and, looking up at Jesus, gasped weakly: "Yes, Lord. What is it?"

Jesus said: "Peter . . . Peter . . . Peter, I can see your house from up here."

2871 Why is it that when we talk to God we're said to be praying, but when God talks to us we're schizophrenic? (LILY TOMLIN)

2872 Three men of God were asked the same question: "When does life begin?"

The Catholic priest answered: "At the moment of conception."

The Anglican vicar replied: "When the child is born."

And the rabbi said: "When the children are married and the mortgage has been paid off."

2873 What do you get when you cross a Jehovah's Witness with an atheist? – Someone who knocks on your door for no apparent reason.

2874 What do you get if you cross a Jehovah's Witness with a Hell's Angel? – Someone who knocks on your door on a Sunday morning and tells you to push off.

2875 An atheist was fishing in Scotland one day when his boat was suddenly attacked by the Loch Ness Monster. The boat capsized and the man was tossed skywards. As he flew through the air towards the monster's open mouth, he screamed: "Oh God, help me!"

Immediately everything was frozen in place. The ferocious attack stopped and the atheist was left suspended in mid-air. A booming voice came down from the clouds: "I thought you didn't believe in Me!"

"Come on God, give me a break," said the man. "Two minutes ago I didn't believe in the Loch Ness Monster either!"

2876 I admire the Pope. I have a lot of respect for anyone who can tour without an album. (RITA RUDNER)

2877 Two Irish Catholics were digging a ditch opposite a brothel. One morning they saw a rabbi slip into the brothel. "What's the world coming to," they said, "when a religious man goes into a house of ill-repute?"

Ten minutes later, they saw a Protestant minister sneak into the brothel. "It's no wonder the world's in such a terrible state," they said, "with this sort of thing going on."

Ten minutes later, they saw a priest creep into the brothel. "One of the poor lasses must be ill," they said.

2878 A Sunday school teacher asked her young class: "Why is it necessary to be quiet in church?"

One boy answered: "Because people are sleeping."

2879 A young Protestant couple wanted to convert to Catholicism but the priest told them that, in order to prove their sincerity, they would first have to perform an act of penance. He told them they had to abstain from making love for 30 days.

Thirty days later the husband called on the priest. "How did it go?" asked the priest.

"Well, Father, for 29 days it was fine. But then on the 30th day I saw her standing over the freezer and I just couldn't help myself."

"Then I'm sorry," said the priest, "but I can't allow you into the Catholic Church."

"That's OK," said the husband. "They won't allow me into the supermarket any more either."

2880 A deeply religious man lived in a house by the river, but one day the banks burst and the house was flooded. As the water level rose alarmingly, the man climbed on to the roof of the house. A boat came by. "Climb aboard," called the captain.

"No, I shall stay here," said the man. "God will take care of me."

Twenty minutes later, with the waters still rising, the man climbed on to the chimney. Another boat came past. "Jump aboard," said the captain.

"No, I shall stay here," said the man. "God will take care of me."

With the water now up to the man's waist, a helicopter suddenly swooped down. "Quick!" shouted the pilot. "Climb aboard!"

"No, I shall stay here," insisted the man. "God will take care of me."

The water level continued to rise and soon the man was swept from the chimney and drowned. Up in heaven, he sought out God. "I thought you said you would take care of me," he complained.

God said: "I sent you two boats and a helicopter. What more do you want?"

2881 What do priests and Christmas trees have in common? – The balls are just for decoration.

2882 A man went to confession and admitted to the priest that he had stolen some wood to build a kennel for his dog. The priest told him to say one Hail Mary for forgiveness. But the man wished to unburden himself further. He said that after building the kennel, he still had some stolen wood left and so he had constructed some decking for his garden.

"Very well," said the priest. "You'd better say three Hail Marys."

But the man wasn't finished yet. He said that after building the kennel and the decking, he still had some stolen wood left and so he had built a garage.

"I see," said the priest wearily. "In that case, you'd better say five Hail Marys."

But there was more. After building the kennel, the decking and the garage, the man said he still had some stolen wood left and so he had built an extension to his house.

By now, the priest had heard enough. Searching for a suitable punishment, he said: "Do you know what a novena is?"

The man replied: "I'm not certain, Father, but if you show me some blueprints, I'm sure I could build one for you."

2883 I would never want to be a member of a group whose symbol was a guy nailed to two pieces of wood. (GEORGE CARLIN)

2884 Three pastors were discussing the problems they had been experiencing with bats in their church lofts.

The first said: "I introduced half a dozen cats, but nothing seems to work. The bats are still there."

The second said: "I had the place fumigated, but even that didn't work. It's still infested with bats."

The third said: "I baptized all mine and made them members of the church. I haven't seen one of them back since!"

2885 A priest was strolling down the street when a woman in a tight skirt suddenly popped out of an alleyway. "Fancy a quickie for ten bucks?"

The priest said: "I have no idea what you mean. Leave me alone, please." And he continued on his way.

A little further down the street, he was accosted by another woman in a shop doorway.

"Fancy a quickie for ten bucks?"

"I do not know what you mean," said the priest, and continued on his way.

Shortly afterwards, he came face to face with another woman outside the bank. "Fancy a quickie for ten bucks?"

"I'm sorry," said the priest, "but I have absolutely no idea what you mean."

Puzzled by the terminology, he decided to drive to the convent and call on the Mother Superior. "Tell me," said the priest. "What's a quickie?"

The Mother Superior said: "Ten bucks. The same as in town."

2886 I was raised half Jewish and half Catholic. When I'd go to confession, I'd say, "Bless me, Father, for I have sinned – and you know my attorney, Mr Cohen." (BILL MAHER)

2887 How do you make holy water? – Boil the hell out of it.

2888 A minister sold a mule to a priest and told him that the animal was trained to obey two commands: "Praise the Lord" to go and "Amen" to stop. The priest climbed on board the mule, said "Praise the Lord" and the mule set off. The mule began to go faster and faster and the priest began to get worried. He wanted the animal to stop but he couldn't remember the key word. He kept saying "Whoa" but it had no effect. Finally he remembered and said "Amen". The mule stopped immediately. The priest looked down and saw that the mule had come to a halt right on the edge of a huge cliff with a 500-foot drop. Wiping his brow in relief, the priest sighed: "Praise the Lord."

2889 One Sunday morning a priest announced to his congregation: "I have here in my hands three sermons – a 500 dollars sermon that lasts five minutes, a 200 dollars sermon that lasts 15 minutes, and a 10 dollars sermon that lasts a full hour. Now we'll take the collection and see which one I'll deliver . . ."

2890 As a priest walked down the street, a drunk noticed his collar and said: "Excuse me, but why are you wearing your shirt backwards?"

The priest laughed: "Because, my son, I am a Father."

The drunk said: "But I'm a father too, and I don't wear my shirt backwards."

"But," continued the priest, "I am a Father of thousands."

To which the drunk replied: "Well maybe you should wear your shorts backwards!"

2891 A boy began dating a pretty Christian Fundamentalist and was keen to find out more about her religion. So he went to see the church elder. "Tell me," said the boy, "does your religion allow me to drink coffee?"

"No," replied the elder. "Coffee beans are treated to enhance their flavour, so we do not consider coffee to be completely natural. We will not permit anything that is not natural."

"What about tea?"

"Tea is fine."

The boy had more questions. "What is the view on dancing?"

"We do not permit dancing," replied the elder. "It is unnatural."

"What about sex?"

"Yes, sex is permissible as long as it is between two people who are married."

"What about kinky sex?"

"It depends what you mean by kinky sex."

"Well," said the boy, "I was thinking of different positions, like standing up."

"No – it could lead to dancing."

2892 Not only is there no God, but try getting a plumber at weekends. (WOODY ALLEN)

2893 A wealthy American had just one remaining wish in life – to meet the Pope in person – and was willing to stay in Rome for as long as it took to achieve his ambition. Week after week, he joined the crowds in St Peter's Square but never got any closer than the occasional glimpse of the Pope on the balcony. He was bemoaning his lack of success to an English tourist who offered to sell him his ticket for a garden party which the Pope was giving in the Vatican the next day. The American willingly paid £100 for the ticket but noticed that the invitation stipulated full morning dress. So he hurried off to an exclusive Italian tailor and hired some morning clothes.

The next day the American went to the Vatican dressed in his morning suit and top hat, and stood in a line of guests waiting for the Pope to appear. The guests were drawn up in two lines facing each other so that the Pope could walk down one line, turn and then go back along the other line. When the Pope finally appeared, there was polite applause. The American waited expectantly as the Pope proceeded down the first line but, to general dismay, he spoke to nobody. Instead he merely waved vaguely as he passed the American and made his way to the end of the line.

The last position in the line was occupied by a tramp, looking hopelessly out of place in his tattered clothes. But, to everyone's surprise, the Pope stopped when he reached the tramp, put his hands on the poor man's shoulders and whispered something in his ear. The American thought quickly. It was clear that the Pope would only talk to some hobo, someone who was in need of words of comfort, so the American grabbed hold of the tramp and persuaded him to swap clothes. Dressed in tatty rags and a battered hat, the American rushed to the end of the second line, along which the Pope was now making his way.

Once again, the Pope spoke to nobody until he reached the tramp-like figure at the end of the line. The American could hardly conceal his excitement as the Pope stopped and looked at him. Then the Pope put his hands on his shoulders and whispered in his ear: "I thought I told you a moment ago to bugger off!"

2894 A man came home from church sporting two black eyes. "What on earth happened to you?" asked his wife.

"Well, I was sitting there in church and I noticed the woman in front of me had her dress sticking in her crack. So I reached over the pew and pulled it out. And she turned round and hit me in the eye."

"OK. That explains one black eye, but what about the other one?"

"Well, I figured that must have been how she wanted her dress, so I put it back."

2895 An elderly priest invited a young priest over for dinner. The younger man couldn't help but notice that his colleague employed an extremely attractive housekeeper and was highly suspicious as to whether the relationship was purely platonic. When the subject was raised, the elderly priest insisted that it was all quite innocent.

A week later, the housekeeper said that she couldn't find a silver gravy ladle and hadn't seen it since the young priest had come to the house. "You don't think he could have taken it?" she said. The elderly priest said he would write to him.

His letter began: "Dear Father, I'm not saying you 'did' take my silver gravy ladle and I'm not saying you 'did not' take my silver gravy ladle, but it has been missing since you came to my house."

Two days later, the younger priest wrote back: "Dear Father, I'm not saying you 'do' sleep with your housekeeper and I'm not saying you 'do not' sleep with your housekeeper, but if you were sleeping in your own bed, you'd have found your silver gravy ladle by now."

2896 If there really is a God who created the entire universe with all of its glories, and He decides to deliver a message to humanity, He will not use, as His messenger, a person on cable TV with a bad hairstyle. (DAVE BARRY)

2897 What kind of fun does a priest have? – Nun.

2898 A priest had his bicycle stolen and thought a member of his flock was to blame. In need of advice, he consulted his bishop who suggested that he root out the thief by preaching a sermon on the Ten Commandments. The idea was that when the priest got to "Thou shalt not steal', he should pause and look around the church for anyone behaving in a guilty manner. In this way it was hoped that the culprit would give himself away.

A couple of weeks later, the bishop bumped into the priest and asked him whether the plan had worked. "Well, yes," said the priest, "but not quite in the way you had envisaged. I was going through the Ten Commandments, one by one, and when I got to 'Thou shalt not commit adultery', I remembered where I had left my bike."

2899 I once wanted to become an atheist, but I gave it up – they have no holidays. (HENNY YOUNGMAN)

2900 The Mother Superior was discussing the rising crime rate with one of her nuns. "Sister," she said, "what would you do if you were walking along the street at night and were accosted by a man?"

"I would lift my habit," replied the nun.

The Mother Superior was shocked to hear this. "Then what would you do?"

"I would tell him to drop his pants."

The Mother Superior was even more shocked. "And then what would you do?"

"I would run off, because I could run faster with my habit up than he could with his pants down!"

2901 A man went to confession and told the priest: "I have a steady girlfriend but last week I went to her house and there was nobody at home except her sister. We were all alone and we ended up having sex."

"That's bad, my son," said the priest, "but at least you can see that you have made a mistake."

The man continued: "Then later that day I went to my girlfriend's office to look for her, but nobody was around except one of her colleagues. So I had sex with her too."

"That's very bad, my son."

The man went on. "Then yesterday I went to my girlfriend's uncle's house to look for her, but nobody was home except her aunt. So I had sex with her too."

The priest made no reply.

"Father? . . . Father?" Realizing that the priest wasn't there, the man searched for him and found him hiding behind a wall. "What are you doing, Father?"

"I suddenly realized you and I are the only ones around . . ."

2902 Three nuns told a priest that they had sinned. The first nun laughed and said: "I had sex with a man."

The priest said: "Drink holy water."

The second nun laughed and said: "I was involved in a fight."

The priest said: "Drink holy water."

The third nun laughed even more. "I pissed in the holy water."

2903 Moses was sent by the Israelites to the top of Mount Sinai to negotiate with God over the Commandments. After two weeks of intense discussion, an exhausted Moses came down with a list of 250 Commandments. The Israelites were not happy with this and sent him back to negotiate a better deal. Four days later, a haggard-looking Moses returned from his mission. "I have some good news and some bad news," he told the Israelites. "The good news is I've got the list down to ten. The bad news is that adultery is still in."

2904 I do not believe in God. I believe in cashmere. (FRAN LEBOWITZ)

2905 A married man went to confession and told the priest: "Father, I had an affair with a woman – well, almost."

"What do you mean, almost?" said the priest.

"Well, we got undressed and rubbed together, but then I stopped."

"Rubbing together is the same as putting it in," insisted the priest. "Five Hail Marys and put 50 dollars in the poor box on your way out."

The man came out and stood by the poor box for a few seconds, but didn't reach for his wallet. Instead he headed for the church door. The priest saw this and shouted: "You didn't put any money in!"

The man replied: "But I rubbed against it and you said that's the same as putting it in!"

2906 A new pastor visited a children's Sunday school. After standing quietly at the back for a few minutes, he asked the youngsters: "Who tore down the walls of Jericho?"

"It wasn't me," shouted young Tommy.

The pastor was unfazed, and repeated: "Come on now, who tore down the walls of Jericho?"

The teacher took the pastor to one side. "Look, Pastor, Tommy's a good boy. If he says he didn't do it, I believe him."

The pastor couldn't comprehend what he was hearing and later that day he related the story to the director of the Sunday school. The director frowned. "I know we've had problems with Tommy in the past. I'll have a word with him."

By now totally baffled, the pastor left and approached the deacon. Once again, he told him the whole story, including the response of the teacher and the director.

The deacon listened patiently and smiled: "Yes, Pastor, I can see your problem. But I suggest we take the money from the general fund to pay for the walls and leave it at that."

2907 A drunk staggered into a bar and sat himself down next to a priest. The drunk had lipstick on his collar, booze on his breath and a half bottle of gin sticking out of his pocket. His clothes were heavily stained. He started reading a newspaper and then turned to the priest and said: "What causes arthritis?"

The priest, who was clearly uncomfortable in his presence, responded testily: "It's caused by loose living, too much alcohol, seeking the company of cheap women, and having a general contempt for one's fellow man!"

"Well, I'll be damned," muttered the drunk.

The priest immediately began to feel guilty about his outburst. "I'm sorry I came on a bit strong just then. How long have you had arthritis?"

"I don't have it, Father," said the drunk. "I was just reading here that the Pope does."

2908 A builder was fixing a nail into the church roof when he accidentally hit his thumb with the hammer. "Damn it, I missed!" exclaimed the builder in agony.

"You shouldn't say that," said the priest from below.

"Why not?" sneered the builder. "Will I be struck by a bolt of lightning or something?"

"Yes, you might well be," replied the priest.

A moment later there was a terrific flash and a bolt of lightning shot down from the sky. It narrowly avoided the builder but struck the priest dead. And a voice from above boomed out: Damn it, I missed!"

2909 How do you get rid of a nun's hiccups? – Tell her she's pregnant.

2910 What's black, white and red and swings from the ceiling? – A nun on a meathook.

2911 What do you call a sleepwalking nun? – A roamin' Catholic.

2912 A wife insisted that her husband accompany her to church every Sunday. But for him it was an ordeal and he always had difficulty staying awake. She was aware of this and so one week she took along a hat pin with which to poke him every time he fell asleep.

Five minutes into the service, just as the husband was dozing off, the preacher asked: "Who created the Universe?"

The wife poked her husband with the hat pin and he yelled loudly: "My God!"

A few minutes later, the husband's eyes were shutting again just as the preacher asked the flock: "And who died on the cross for you?"

The wife gave a sharp poke with the hat pin and the husband shouted: "Jesus Christ!"

Shortly afterwards the husband was asleep once more. The wife poked him with the hat pin just as the preacher asked: "And what did Eve say to Adam the second time she was pregnant?"

The husband woke with a start, jumped to his feet and yelled: "By God, if you poke me with that thing one more time, I'm going to break it off!"

2913 A priest went into a shop and said: "I'd like to buy a dead bluebottle."
The shopkeeper said: "We don't sell dead bluebottles."
The priest said: "Well, you've got one in the window."

2914 Jesus was really tired after the resurrection. So when he came to an inn, he put three nails on the counter and said to the innkeeper: "Can you put me up for the night?"

2915 Did you hear about the guy who told religious jokes and was put on the Sects Offenders List?

Restaurants

2916 A pretty waitress came over to take a man's order. "I want a quickie," he said. Appalled, she immediately slapped him around the face.
When she had regained her composure, she asked him again. "Now what would you like?"
"I want a quickie," he said.
Once again, she slapped him hard around the face. She decided to give him one last chance. "For the last time, what would you like?"
"I want a quickie," he replied.
She slapped him around the face again and went to fetch the manager. A customer at the next table then leaned over and whispered to the man: "I think it's pronounced quiche."

2917 Can't we just get rid of wine lists? Do we really have to be reminded every time we go out to a nice restaurant that we have no idea what we are doing? Why don't they just give us a trigonometry quiz with the menu? (JERRY SEINFELD)

2918 The chef flew into a rage at his new assistant. "Didn't I tell you to notice when the soup boiled over?" he yelled.
"I did," said the assistant. "It was half past eleven."

2919 A man was sitting alone in a restaurant, finishing his coffee and free after dinner mints when he suddenly heard a voice say: "Wow! You look great tonight. I love that shirt."
The man looked round to see where the voice was coming from but the only other person in the room was a waiter, so he called him over.
"Excuse me," said the man. "Did you say something?"

"Not me, sir," replied the waiter.

A few minutes later the same thing happened again. This time the voice said: "And your hair really suits you in that style. It makes you look years younger."

Once more, the man summoned the waiter. "Did you say something just then?" he inquired.

"No, sir," replied the waiter. "Not a word."

"Well, that's twice I've heard a voice and you're the only other person in the room."

The waiter thought for a moment. "This voice, did it say nice things or rude things?"

"Nice things," said the man.

"Well, that's it then," said the waiter. "It must have been the complimentary mints."

2920 I went to a restaurant that serves "breakfast at any time". So I ordered French toast during the Renaissance. (STEVEN WRIGHT)

2921 The diner had been waiting a long time for his meal and was on the point of walking out when the waiter appeared.

"I must apologize for the delay, sir," said the waiter, "but your fish will be coming in a minute."

The diner replied coldly: "What bait are you using?"

2922 A man went to a restaurant in Madrid. He ordered the house special and was brought a plate with potatoes, corn and two large meaty objects.

"What are these?" he asked the waiter.

"Cojones, señor," said the waiter.

"What exactly are cojones?"

"They are the testicles of the bull who lost at the arena this afternoon."

Overcoming his initial reservations, the man decided to try this local delicacy and found it very tasty. Indeed he liked it so much that he returned the following night and ordered the same again. The waiter appeared with a plate of potatoes and corn, but this time the two meaty objects were much smaller. Nevertheless, the man ate them and thoroughly enjoyed them.

"What were they?" he asked the waiter afterwards.

"Cojones, señor."

"No. I had the cojones yesterday and they were much bigger."

"Ah yes, señor, but the bull does not lose every time."

2923 Two customers were sitting in a shabby restaurant.

"What can I get you to drink?" asked the waiter.

"A Coke, please," said one customer.

"And I'll have the same," said his friend. "And make sure I get a clean glass."

The waiter took the order and five minutes later returned with the drinks. "Right, now which one asked for the clean glass?"

2924 Waitress: "Tea or coffee?

Customer: "Coffee — without cream."

Waitress: "You'll have to take it without milk. We have no cream."

2925 A middle-aged man was sitting in a truck stop when three rough bikers strode in. The first walked over to the man and stubbed a cigarette into his lunch. Then the second biker spat in the man's milk. Finally the third biker picked up the man's plate of food and threw it on to the floor. Without saying a word, the man got up and left.

"He wasn't much of a man, was he?" sneered one of the bikers to the waitress.

"Not much of a truck driver either," she said. "He just backed his truck over three motorcycles."

2926 A man went for a meal at a chicken restaurant. He asked the manager: "How do you prepare the chickens?"

The manager said: "We just tell them straight out that they're going to die."

2927 "Are you sure this place is hygienic?" asked the grumpy diner.

"Oh yes, sir," replied the manager. "You could eat off the floor."

"That's the problem. It looks as if somebody just has!"

2928 A man went into a restaurant called The Moon. The food was good, but there was no atmosphere.

2929 A customer wanted to ask his pretty waitress for a date but couldn't get her attention. When he was able to catch her eye, she quickly looked away. Finally he followed her into the kitchen and blurted out his invitation. To his amazement she readily consented. He said: "Why have you been avoiding me all this time? You wouldn't even make eye contact."

"Sorry," she replied. "I thought you wanted more coffee."

2930 Have you ever noticed that the waiter who takes your order is not the one who brings your food any more? What is that about? And which waiter are you tipping anyway? I think next time I go to a restaurant I'll just say, "Oh sorry, I only eat the food. The guy who pays the bill will be along shortly." (JERRY SEINFELD)

2931 A guy sat down in a restaurant and ordered a hot chilli. But the waitress said: "I'm sorry, the customer next to you had the last bowl."

The guy looked across the table and saw that the other customer had left most of his chilli. "Could I have that?" he asked.

"Sure," said the other guy.

So he started eating his way through the chilli but then halfway down, he discovered a dead mouse.

"Ugh!" he exclaimed. "I've just found a dead mouse in the chilli."

"That's as far as I got too," said the other guy.

2932 "Waiter! There's a fly in my soup."
"Don't worry, sir. The spider in the bread roll will get it."

2933 "Waiter! There's a fly in my soup."
"OK, I'll bring you a fork."

2934 "Waiter! There's a fly in my soup."
"So what, there's soup on your fly."

2935 "Waiter! What's this fly doing in my soup?"
"Looks like the backstroke, sir."

2936 "Waiter! There's a fly in my soup!"
"Can't be, sir. The cook used them all in the raisin bread."

2937 "Waiter! There's a fly in my soup."
"Don't worry, it's not hot enough to burn him."

2938 "Waiter! What's the meaning of this fly in my soup!"
"I don't know, sir. I'm a waiter, not a fortune-teller."

2939 "Waiter! There's a fly in my soup."
"No, sir, that's the essential vitamin bee."

2940 "Waiter! There's a dead fly in my soup."
"It must have committed insecticide."

2941 "Waiter! There's a dead beetle in my soup."
"Yes, sir, they're not very good swimmers."

2942 "Waiter! What's that in my soup?"
"I'd better call the manager, sir – I can't tell one insect from another."

2943 "Waiter! What's this?"
"It's bean soup, sir."
"I don't care what it's been. What is it now?"

2944 "Waiter! Your thumb's in my soup."
"That's all right, sir. The soup's not hot."

2945 "Waiter! My plate's wet."
"It's not wet, sir – that's the soup."

2946 "Waiter! Is there soup on the menu?"
"No, sir, I wiped it all off."

2947 "Waiter! There's a button in my soup."
"Thank you, sir. I wondered what had happened to it."

2948 "Waiter! Come here and taste this soup."
"Where's the spoon?"
"Gotcha!"

2949 "Waiter! There's a dead fly in my wine."
"Well, sir, you did ask for something with a little body to it."

2950 "Waiter! What is that fly doing on my sorbet?"
"Learning to ski, sir."

2951 "Waiter! This lobster's only got one claw."
"He must have been in a fight, sir."
"Well, bring me the winner!"

2952 "Waiter! Do you have frogs' legs?"
"No, sir, it's rheumatism that makes me walk like this."

2953 "Waiter! This coffee tastes like mud."
"Yes, sir, it's fresh ground."

2954 "Waiter! You're not fit to serve a pig!"
"I'm doing my best, sir."

2955 An American in a Chinese restaurant complained: "This chicken is rubbery."
The waiter said: "Thank you, sir."

2956 A man and a woman were sitting in a restaurant when the waitress noticed the man sliding down his chair and under the table. The woman appeared remarkably unconcerned but the waitress felt she ought to mention something.
"Excuse me," she said, "I think your husband just slid under the table."
"No," replied the woman coldly. "He just walked in the door."

2957 A waiter brought a customer the steak he ordered with his thumb pressing down on the meat.
The customer was appalled. "What are you doing putting your hand on my steak?"
"Well," replied the waiter, "you wouldn't want it falling on the floor again."

Salesmen

2958 A sales assistant reported for his first day at work at a major department store. The sales manager showed him around and was passing through the gardening department when he heard a customer asking for a packet of grass seed.
"Will you be needing a hose to water your new lawn?" interrupted the sales manager helpfully.
"Yes, I probably will," said the customer. "Thank you. I'll take a hose as well."
"And what about fertilizer," suggested the sales manager, "to make the grass grow green and strong?"
"Good idea," said the customer.
"But of course there are always troublesome weeds," continued the sales

manager. "So you'll be wanting a bottle of weed-killer to keep them down. The large bottles work out the most economical."

"Right," said the customer, "I'll take some weed-killer too."

"And how about a nice new lawn mower to do your grass justice?" said the sales manager.

"Why not?" replied the customer. "Add a lawn mower to the bill."

As the customer paid for the goods, the sales manager took the young assistant to one side and said: "See, that's how it's done. That customer only came in for one item, but ended up leaving with five. That's good sales technique. That's what you must try to emulate."

The assistant's first posting was to the pharmaceutical department. A man came in and asked for a pack of tampons.

The assistant seized his chance. "Are you sure you wouldn't like to buy a lawn mower as well?"

"Why would I want to do that?" asked the man.

"Well," said the assistant, "your weekend's ruined, so you might as well mow the lawn."

2959 A man went to a hardware store and asked for some nails.

"How long do you want them?" asked the sales assistant.

"Oh," said the customer. "I was rather hoping to keep them."

2960 A salesman called at a house and found a small boy sitting on the front step. "Is your mother in?" asked the salesman.

"Yes," said the boy.

The salesman rang the doorbell, but there was no answer. He tried again; still no answer. He turned to the boy. "I thought you said your mother was home?"

"She is, but this isn't where I live."

2961 I used to impale the heads of door-to-door salespeople on pikes in the garden as a warning to others – until I learned that it's bad Feng Shui. (GREG GLYNN)

2962 A keen sportsman spent the weekend at a hunting lodge and bagged a record number of birds with the help of a dog named Salesman. The man was so impressed that when making his reservation for the following year, he specifically requested the services of the same dog.

"Too bad," said the lodge manager. "Six months ago, some jerk who was here kept calling the dog 'Sales Manager' by mistake. Now all he does is sit on his tail and bark."

2963 A door-to-door vacuum cleaner salesman went to the first house in his new territory. A woman answered the door, but before she could say a word, he had rushed inside and dumped a pile of horse manure on her lounge carpet. "Lady," he said in his best sales talk, "if this vacuum cleaner don't do wonders cleaning up that horse shit, I'll eat every chunk of it."

The woman replied coldly. "Do you want ketchup on that?"

The salesman was taken aback. "How do you mean?"

"Well, we just moved in, and we haven't yet got the electricity turned on."

2964 A salesman rang the bell at a suburban home and was greeted by an eight-year-old boy puffing on a long cigar. Stifling his surprise, the salesman asked: "Is your mother home?"

The kid nonchalantly flicked the ash from his cigar and said: "What do you think?"

2965 A man was interviewed for a sales post with a small family-run firm, but throughout the interview he kept winking. He couldn't complete a sentence without winking. Eventually the proprietor of the firm felt it necessary to say something.

"You're an intelligent, well-dressed young man, and, under normal circumstances, I'd be happy to offer you the job but I have to say I'm worried that your facial tic might put some customers off."

"I'm glad you mentioned that," said the man. "All I need to make it go are a couple of aspirin. I've got some in my pocket."

With that, he emptied his pockets and dozens of condoms fell out in all shapes and sizes.

The proprietor was horrified. "I'm really not sure that this conveys the proper image for a family-run concern."

"Oh no, I'm happily married," protested the man.

"So what's with all these condoms?"

"Have you ever tried to go into a drug store, winking like crazy, and ask for a packet of aspirins?"

School

2966 A young boy arrived late for school.

"Why are you late, Johnny?" asked the teacher.

"I'm sorry, miss, but I had to get my own breakfast today."

"All right, Johnny," said the teacher, "never mind. Now today we are doing geography and here is a map of the British Isles. Can anyone tell me where the Scottish border is?"

"Yes, miss," said Johnny, "in bed with mum. That's why I had to get my own breakfast."

2967 A teacher was struggling to teach arithmetic to a young boy. So she said: "If you reached in your right pocket and found a nickel, and you reached in your left pocket and found another nickel, what would you have?"

The boy thought for a moment and replied: "Someone else's pants."

2968 "Can you help me put my boots on, miss?" said the small boy to his kindergarten teacher. She pulled and he pushed, but the boots seemed really tight. By the time she had finally managed to get the second boot on she had worked up a real sweat and so she nearly burst into tears when the boy said: "Teacher, they're on the wrong feet."

She looked, and sure enough they were on the wrong feet. Together they struggled to get his boots off and then back on again, this time on the correct feet. He then announced: "These aren't my boots."

"Why didn't you say so?" said the increasingly exasperated teacher as she struggled to help him pull off the ill-fitting boots.

"They're my brother's boots," he said. "My mom made me wear them."

The teacher was now near breaking point but she somehow managed to wrestle the boots back onto his feet. The job completed, she asked wearily: "Now, where are your mittens?"

The boy said: "I stuffed them in the toes of my boots . . ."

2969 There are three kinds of people – those who can count and those who can't.

2970 A mother and father were worried that their son would refuse to learn maths at school, so they sent him to a Catholic school which had a good reputation in the subject. But after his first day at the new school, the boy came home, ran straight to his room and slammed the door. This behaviour went on every school night for the next two months, at the end of which the parents were asked along to meet the teachers. They feared the worst but, to their surprise, their son's maths teacher revealed that the boy was doing excellent work and was top of the class.

"So what changed your mind about learning maths?" they asked the boy when they returned home.

"Well," said the boy, "on the first day I walked into the classroom, I saw a guy nailed to a plus sign at the back of the room, and I knew they meant business."

2971 Did you hear about the cross-eyed schoolteacher? – She couldn't control her pupils.

2972 Teacher: "It's clear that you haven't studied your geography. What's your excuse?"
   Pupil: "Well, my dad says the world is changing every day, so I decided to wait until it settles down."

2973 A history teacher had been taking a lesson about the kings and queens of England. "Do you know who followed Edward VI?" she asked.
   "Mary," replied a boy at the back.
   "That's right," said the teacher. "And who followed Mary?"
   "Her little lamb," said the boy.

2974 In elementary school, in case of fire you have to line up quietly in single file from the smallest to the tallest. What is the logic? Do tall people burn slower? (WARREN HUTCHERSON)

2975 A schoolteacher asked her class what their parents did for a living. Little Johnny put up his hand and said: "My mum is a substitute."
   Knowing something of the family background, the teacher said: "I think you mean she's a prostitute."
   "No," said Johnny. "My big sister's the prostitute but when she doesn't feel well, Mum acts as a substitute."

2976 Teacher: "If you had one dollar and you asked your father for another, how many dollars would you have?"
   Boy: "One dollar."
   Teacher: "You don't know your arithmetic."
   Boy: "You don't know my father."

2977 A child told her mother: "My teacher thinks I'm going to be famous. She said all I have to do is mess up one more time and I'm history!"

2978 Voice on phone: "Johnny has a cold and can't come to school today."
   School secretary:"Who is this?"
   Voice: "This is my dad."

2979 Teacher: "Johnny, did your father help you with your homework last night?"
Johnny: "No, he did it all."

2980 You don't appreciate a lot of stuff in school until you get older: little things like being spanked every day by a middle-aged woman – stuff you pay good money for in later life. (EMO PHILIPS)

2981 A teacher broke up a fight between two boys in the school corridor and took them to the headmaster.
"Right," said the headmaster. "Who was doing the fighting?"
"I think it was six of one and half a dozen of the other," said the teacher.
"No," protested one of the boys, "there were the just the two of us."

2982 The schoolchildren were asked to talk about something exciting that had happened to them recently. One small boy put up his hand and announced: "Daddy fell down a mineshaft last week."
"Oh dear!" exclaimed the teacher. "Is he all right now?"
"He must be," replied the boy. "He stopped yelling for help yesterday."

2983 Ever wonder if illiterate people get the full effect of alphabet soup? (JOHN MENDOZA)

2984 The children in class were asked to write a story with a moral. The next day, they read out their efforts to the teacher.
First to go was young Claire. She said: "My daddy owns a farm and every Sunday we put the chicken eggs on the truck and drive to town to sell them at market. But one Sunday we hit a bump and all the eggs fell on to the road and smashed. And the moral of the story is: don't put all your eggs in one basket."
"That's very good, Claire," said the teacher. "Now you, Emma."
Emma read out her story. "My daddy also owns a farm. Every weekend we take the chicken eggs and put them in an incubator. Last weekend, only eight of the 12 eggs hatched. And the moral of the story is: don't count your chickens before they hatch."
"Very nice, Emma," said the teacher. "Now, let's hear from you, Johnny."
Johnny read out his story. "My uncle Jim fought in the Vietnam war, but one day his plane was shot down. He parachuted out before it crashed but he could only take with him a case of beer, a machine gun and a machete. He drank the case of beer on the way down and landed in the middle of thousands of enemy soldiers. He shot 80 Vietnamese with the gun and when he ran out of

bullets, he killed another 25 with his machete and throttled ten more with his bare hands."

"That's very colourful, Johnny," said the teacher, "but what is the moral of the story?"

"Don't mess with my uncle Jim when he's drunk."

2985 I was bullied at school, called all kinds of different names. But one day I turned to my bullies and said, "Sticks and stones may break my bones but names will never hurt me." And it worked. From then on it was sticks and stones all the way. (HARRY HILL)

Actual school excuse notes:

2986 Please excuse Gloria from Jim today. She is administrating.

2987 Please excuse Roland from P.E. for a few days. Yesterday he fell out of a tree and misplaced his hip.

2988 Please excuse Tommy for being absent yesterday. He had diarrhoea and his boots leak.

2989 Please excuse Joe from school today as constipation has made him uptight.

2990 Please excuse Ray Friday from school. He has very loose vowels.

2991 Molly will not be attending school today because her fish died and we're planning the flushing.

2992 Please excuse Mary from gym today. She was watching TV yesterday and strained her eyes, so now she can't focus well.

2993 Please excuse Jeff from school. He hurt his hair.

2994 I kept Billie home because she had to go Christmas shopping because I don't know what size she wears.

2995 My daughter was absent yesterday because she was tired. She spent a weekend with the Marines.

2996 Please excuse Jenna for being absent yesterday. She was in bed with gramps.

2997 Carlos was absent yesterday because he was playing football. He was hurt in the growing part.

2998 Mom ate my homework. She's heavily pregnant and having very odd cravings.

2999 I made my homework into a paper plane, and it was hijacked by some bullies.

3000 Please excuse John from being absent on Jan 28, 29, 30, 31, 32, and also 33.

3001 A boy came home from his first day at school. "So what did you learn?" asked his mother.

"Not enough. They want me to come back tomorrow."

3002 Teacher: "This essay you've written about your pet dog is word for word exactly the same essay as your brother has written."
Little Johnny: "Of course. It's the same dog!"

3003 Teacher: "Where's the English Channel?"
Little Johnny: "I don't know. My TV doesn't pick it up."

3004 Teacher: "What do you want to be when you grow up?"
Little Johnny: "I want to follow in my father's footsteps and be a policeman."
Teacher: "I didn't know your father was a policeman."
Little Johnny: "He isn't. He's a burglar!"

3005 Teacher: "I told you to stand at the end of the line."
Little Johnny: "I tried, but somebody was already there."

3006 "Let me see your school report," said Little Johnny's father.
"I don't have it," said Johnny. "My friend borrowed it. He wants to scare his parents."

3007 An ironworker was nonchalantly walking along the narrow beams way above the street on a new skyscraper. Even though the structure was fragile and there was a hurricane blowing, he was always foot perfect and showed no fear. When he came down, a man who had been watching him from ground level went over to him and said: "I was really impressed with you up there. You were so calm. How did you get a job like this?"
"As a matter of fact," replied the ironworker, "I used to drive a school bus, but my nerves gave out."

3008 I won't say ours was a tough school, but we had our own coroner. (LENNY BRUCE)

3009 A boy said to his father: "Dad, can you sign your name without looking?"
"Yes, I think so," replied the father.
"Good," said the boy. "Close your eyes and sign my school report card."

3010 The schoolteacher was taking the class in basic maths. She said to little Johnny, "If I give you two rabbits and two rabbits and another two rabbits, how many have you got?"
"Seven," replied Johnny.

"No, Johnny," explained the teacher. "That's not the right answer. Listen. If I give you two apples, then I add another two apples and another two apples after that, how many have you got?"

"Six," replied Johnny.

"That's right," said the teacher. "So, let's try again. If I give you two rabbits and two rabbits and another two rabbits, how many have you got?"

"Seven," replied Johnny.

"Seven!" wailed the teacher. "How do you get seven?"

"Because I've already got one rabbit at home!"

3011 "What's your father's occupation?" asked the school secretary, filling in the forms at the start of the academic year.

"He's a magician," said the small boy.

"How interesting! What's his favourite trick?"

"Sawing people in half."

"Really? Now, next question. Any brothers or sisters?"

"Yes. One half-brother and two half-sisters."

Sex

3012 I believe that sex is a beautiful thing between two people. Between five it's fantastic. (WOODY ALLEN)

3013 A man and a woman were seated at a bar, both drinking champagne. Neither had met before. After a while, the man turned to the woman and said: "I see you're drinking champagne too. Are you celebrating something?"

"I sure am," replied the woman. "This is a special day for me. For years I've been trying to have a child and today my gynaecologist told me I'm pregnant."

"Congratulations," said the man. "I'm celebrating too. I'm a chicken farmer and for years all my hens were infertile, but today they're finally fertile."

"How did it happen?" asked the woman.

"I switched cocks," he replied.

"What a coincidence . . ."

3014 I love the lines men use to get us into bed. "Please, I'll only put it in for a minute." What am I, a microwave? (BEVERLY MICKINS)

3015 You know the worst thing about oral sex? The view. (MAUREEN LIPMAN)

3016 Two elderly men were talking about Viagra. One had never heard of it and asked the other what it was for.

"It's the greatest invention ever," he said. "It makes you feel like a man of 30."

"Can you get it over the counter?"

"Probably — if you took two."

3017 I went out with a promiscuous impressionist — she did everybody. (JAY LONDON)

3018 Did you hear about the side-effects of the Viagra pill for men? If you swallow it slowly, you'll get a stiff neck.

3019 What do you get if you mix Viagra and Prozac? — A guy who is ready to go, but doesn't really care where.

3020 Why is Viagra like Disneyworld? — You have to wait an hour for a three-minute ride.

3021 I blame my mother for my poor sex life. All she told me was "the man goes on top and the woman underneath." For three years my husband and I slept in bunk beds. (JOAN RIVERS)

3022 A man was prescribed Viagra by his doctor who told him to take it one hour before sex. The man collected his prescription and went home to wait for his wife to get in from work. An hour before she was due home, he took the Viagra pill. But just as he was expecting her, she phoned to say that she wouldn't be in for another two and a half hours.

In a panic, he phoned the doctor. "What should I do?" he asked. "I've taken the pill, but the effects will have worn off by the time my wife gets home."

"I see," said the doctor. "It is a pity to waste it. Do you have a maid?"

"Yes."

"Well, could you not occupy yourself with her instead?"

"But I don't need Viagra with the maid."

If men got pregnant:

3023 Morning sickness would rank as the nation's number one health problem.

3024 Maternity leave would last for two years with full pay.

3025 Children would be kept in hospital until toilet trained.

3026 Natural childbirth would become obsolete.

3027 All methods of birth control would be 100 per cent effective.

3028 Men would be eager to talk about commitment.

3029 There would be a cure for stretch marks.

3030 They'd serve beer instead of coffee at antenatal classes.

3031 Men wouldn't think twins were so cute.

3032 Sons would have to be home from dates by 10 p.m.

3033 Women need a reason to have sex. Men just need a place. (BILLY CRYSTAL)

3034 A fireman and his wife were bored with their sex life so he tried to liven it up by incorporating the bell system that was used at work. At the firehouse when the first bell rings, everyone runs to the trucks; on the second bell, they gear up; and on the third bell they jump on the trucks and head for the fire.

So he went home and told his wife: "I've got this great idea to spice up our sex life. We're gonna use the bell system. When I shout 'bell one', you run into the bedroom; when I shout 'bell two', you take off your clothes; and when I call 'bell three', you jump on the bed and we make passionate love."

The next evening he got home from work and immediately shouted "bell one". His wife ran into the bedroom. Then he called out "bell two" and she took off her clothes. Then he yelled "bell three" and the pair leaped on the bed together and started making love. But no sooner had they started than she suddenly cried: "Bell four, bell four!"

"What the hell's bell four?" he gasped.

"More hose! More hose! You're nowhere near the fire!"

3035 If it weren't for pick-pockets, I'd have no sex life at all. (RODNEY DANGERFIELD)

3036 Wife: "Why don't you ever call out my name when we're making love?"
Husband: "Because I don't want to wake you."

3037 On the night before his wedding, the shy young man thought he ought to ask his father what was expected of him in the bedroom.

"What exactly do I have to do?" he asked tentatively.

"Well, son," said his father. "You remember what you used to play with as a teenager? All you do is stick that where your wife pees."

So the following night the young man threw G.I. Joe down the toilet.

3038 I'm a practising heterosexual, but bisexuality immediately doubles your chances for a date on Saturday night. (WOODY ALLEN)

3039 A couple went to an agricultural show one weekend and watched the auction of some prize bulls. The auctioneer announced that the first bull had reproduced 72 times last year.

"Hey," said the wife, nudging her husband. "That's six times a month. A pity you can't match that."

The next bull for auction was revealed to have reproduced 144 times last year.

The wife prodded her husband again. "Did you hear that? Twelve times a month! He's way out of your league."

Then a third bull was led around. The auctioneer proudly stated that the animal had reproduced 365 times last year.

The wife elbowed her husband hard in the ribs. "Three hundred and sixty-five times!" she exclaimed. "That's every day of the year. That really puts you to shame."

By now, the husband was thoroughly irritated by the jibes. "Sure. Great," he said icily. "But I bet it wasn't all with the same cow."

3040 After making love, I said to my girl: "Was it good for you too?" She said: "I don't think this was good for anybody!" (GARRY SHANDLING)

Things a man shouldn't say to a woman during sex:
3041 "Oops! It seems to have come off."
3042 "If you come quick, I can catch the game on TV."
3043 "You look just like your mother."
3044 "You're better than your mother."
3045 "Did you remember to lock the back door?"
3046 "And to think, I was really trying to pick up your friend!"
3047 "You carry on, but do you mind if I finish this book?"
3048 "What's for dinner tomorrow?"
3049 "I thought you had the keys to the handcuffs."
3050 "It's my mobile! I must answer it."
3051 "I can see right up your nose."
3052 "Oh, by the way, the cat got run over this afternoon."
3053 "That boil on your chin looks nasty."
3054 "Did I tell you my aunt Agatha died in this bed?"
3055 "Linda used to do that."
3056 "Do you accept Visa?"
3057 "It's nice being in bed with a woman I don't have to inflate."
3058 "I keep having fantasies about Barbara Bush."
3059 "Did I mention the video camera?"

3060 "Hurry up – this room rents by the hour."

3061 "Sorry about that – must be the baked beans."

3062 "This would be fun with a few more people."

3063 "Try not to leave any stains, OK?"

3064 "I've just thought of the answer to 3 down. I won't be a second."

3065 "Shall I do my impression of Officer Dibble?"

3066 "Do you know the definition of statutory rape?"

3067 "Keep it down. My mother is a light sleeper."

3068 "I see that mad axeman's still on the loose."

3069 "Is that it? Can I go now?"

Things a girl shouldn't say to a man during sex:

3070 "And yet your feet are so big!"

3071 "Don't worry, we'll work around it."

3072 "I guess this makes me the early bird."

3073 "Try not to smear my make-up."

3074 "At least this won't take long."

3075 "I want a baby."

3076 "Do you know the ceiling needs painting?"

3077 "Maybe we should call Dr Ruth."

3078 "Is that blood on the headboard?"

3079 "It's just a rash."

3080 "Sorry about the name tags, but I'm not very good with names."

3081 "Does it come with an air pump?"

3082 "But it still works, right?"

3083 "Why don't we skip right to the cigarettes?"

3084 "But everybody looks funny naked."

3085 "Do you smell something burning?"

3086 "On second thoughts, let's turn off the lights."

3087 "You must be cold."

3088 "Don't mind me. I always file my nails in bed."

3089 "Maybe if we water it, it'll grow."

3090 "Maybe it looks better in natural light."

3091 "Maybe you're just out of practice."

3092 "When is this supposed to feel good?"

3093 "It's a good thing you're rich."

3094 A man living on the second storey of an apartment block was leaning out of the window one morning to check whether it was raining when a glass eye suddenly fell into his hand. Looking up, he saw a girl peering down from four storeys above.

"Is this yours?" he called out.

"Yes," she replied.

"Hold on," he said. "I'll bring it up to you."

So he took the glass eye up to the girl's apartment. She invited him in and they started chatting. Not only was she extremely grateful to him but she also found him incredibly attractive and so she asked him out to dinner that evening. He readily accepted. The meal was a great success and afterwards she suggested they go back to his place and go to bed.

She stayed the night and when she left the following morning, he said: "I'm sorry but I have to ask. Do you act like this with every man you meet?"

"No," she replied, "only those who catch my eye."

3095 We were having sex doggie style. I didn't plan on it, it's just how she passed out. (DAVE ATTELL)

3096 Why are condoms like cameras? – they both capture the moment.

3097 A young couple on their first date had sex which was over in a matter of seconds. Feeling rather proud of himself, the boy said: "If I'd known you were a virgin, I'd have taken more time."

The girl replied: "If I'd known you were going to take more time, I'd have taken off my panty hose."

3098 There's a new medical crisis. Doctors are reporting that many men are having allergic reactions to latex condoms. They say they cause severe swelling. So what's the problem? (JAY LENO)

3099 What is the definition of making love? – Something a woman does while a guy is shagging her.

3100 We got new advice as to what motivated men to walk upright: to free his hands for masturbation. (JANE WAGNER)

3101 The headmistress of a girls' school asked a male friend who was an author to give a talk to the pupils about sex. After much persuasion, the man agreed but was too embarrassed to tell his wife. So he told her that he was addressing the school on sailing and wrote an appropriate entry in his diary for that day.

The day after the talk, the headmistress met the wife in the street. "Your husband was wonderful yesterday, so illuminating. I know my girls learned a lot from him."

"I can't think how," said the wife. "He's only tried it twice. The first time he was sick and the second time he lost his hat."

3102 I'm not homophobic — I'm not scared of my house. (PETER KAY)

3103 A man said to his wife: "Honey, what do you say that tonight we change positions?"

"OK," she said. "You stand by the ironing board and I'll lie on the sofa and watch TV."

3104 When a man and woman are trying to have sex, he will often climax before she is ready. Sometimes he will climax before she is, technically, in the room. (DAVE BARRY)

3105 One day, God and Adam were walking in the Garden of Eden. God told Adam that it was time to populate the Earth. "Adam," he said, "you can start by kissing Eve."

"What's a kiss?" asked Adam.

God explained, and then Adam took Eve behind a bush and kissed her.

Adam returned with a big smile and said: "That was great. What's next?"

"Now you must caress Eve," said God.

"What's caress?" asked Adam.

God explained, and then Adam took Eve behind a bush and lovingly caressed her.

Adam returned with a big smile and said: "That was even better than a kiss. What's next?"

"I want you to make love to Eve," said God.

"What is make love?" asked Adam.

God explained, and then Adam took Eve behind the bush.

A few seconds later, Adam returned and asked God: "What is a headache?"

3106 I'm a double bagger. Not only does my husband put a bag over my head when we're making love, but he also puts a bag over his own head in case mine falls off. (JOAN RIVERS)

3107 Why don't women blink during foreplay? — There isn't time.

3108 Husband: "Want a quickie?"

Wife: "As opposed to what?"

3109 A middle-aged man was told at the hospital that he had only 24 hours to live. He went home in a state of shock and fell into his wife's arms.

"I've been told I've only got 24 hours to live," he said. "Can we have sex one last time?"

"Of course, honey," she said, and they went to bed.

Four hours later, he turned to her and said: "Could we have sex again? I've only got 20 hours to live. It will probably be our last chance."

"Sure, honey," replied his wife and they had sex.

Eight hours later, he asked her. "Do you think we could have sex one more time? After all, I've only got 12 hours to live."

"OK," said the wife and they had sex.

Four hours later, he nudged her in bed. "I just realized I've only got eight hours to live. Could we have sex one last time?"

"Very well," she sighed. "It's the least I can do in the circumstances."

Four hours later, he woke her again. "I've only got four hours to live. Would you mind if we had sex just one more time, our final act of love?"

This was too much for the wife. "Listen," she snapped, "you may not have to get up in the morning, but I do!"

3110 Why is sex like a game of bridge? – You don't need a partner if you have a good hand.

3111 Sex between a man and a woman can be wonderful, provided you get between the right man and the right woman. (WOODY ALLEN)

3112 A husband was feeling randy one night, but the wife pushed him away.

"Sorry, honey," she said, "I have a gynaecologist's appointment in the morning and I want to stay fresh."

He nuzzled up to her again. "Do you have a dental appointment?"

3113 I'm a bad lover. I once caught a peeping tom booing me. (RODNEY DANGERFIELD)

3114 I was making love to this girl and she started crying. I said, "Are you going to hate yourself in the morning?" She said, "No, I hate myself now." (RODNEY DANGERFIELD)

3115 A woman phoned the doctor in the middle of the night. "Doctor, please come over quick. My son has swallowed a condom."

The doctor quickly got dressed but just as he was about to leave, the phone rang again. It was the same woman.

"Don't worry," she said. "There's no need to come over after all. My husband just found another one."

3116 Hey, don't knock masturbation! It's sex with someone I love. (WOODY ALLEN, *Annie Hall*)

3117 I always thought music was more important than sex. Then I thought if I don't hear a concert for a year and a half it doesn't bother me. (JACKIE MASON)

3118 A couple decided that the only way to have a quickie while their ten-year-old son was in the apartment was to send him out on the balcony and let him give a running report on what was going on in the neighbourhood. So the boy stood on the balcony and reported on everything that was happening.

"A police car has just called at the Hamiltons' house, the Chandlers are taking delivery of a new wardrobe, and the Mitchells are having sex."

Hearing this, the boy's parents shot bolt upright. "How do you know the Mitchells are having sex?"

"Because their kid is standing on the balcony too."

3119 Superman was bored because Batman and Spiderman were on vacation and there was nothing much to do. Flying around New York one day, he spotted Wonder Woman lying on her back with her legs apart on the roof of a tall building. He had always lusted after Wonder Woman so he thought he would swoop down and have his wicked way with her.

"What was that?" said Wonder Woman afterwards.

The Invisible Man climbed off her and said: "I dunno, but it hurt."

3120 Whoever named it necking was a poor judge of anatomy. (GROUCHO MARX)

3121 A guy and his date were parked on a back road way out of town. Things started to heat up and he began to undo her dress.

"I probably should have mentioned this before," she said, "but I'm a prostitute and if you want to have sex with me, it will cost you 20 dollars."

The guy wasn't happy, but he paid up. Afterwards, he got dressed but just sat in the driver's seat without starting the engine.

"Why aren't we going anywhere?" asked the woman.

"I probably should have mentioned this before," he replied, "but I'm a taxi driver and if you want to get back to town, it will cost you 30 dollars!"

3122 What do hookers do on their night off: type? (ELAYNE BOOSLER)

3123 A male market researcher was calling on homes on behalf of Vaseline. A woman answered the door.

"Do you use Vaseline?" asked the researcher.

"Certainly," she said. "It's very good for cuts, grazes and burns."

"And what about anything else?" he asked.

"Like what?"

He became embarrassed. "Well, sex, maybe."

"Oh, of course," she said. "I smear it on the bedroom doorknob to keep my husband out."

3124 A hard man is good to find. (MAE WEST)

3125 My classmates would copulate with anything that moved, but I never saw any reason to limit myself. (EMO PHILIPS)

3126 With his wife away on an overseas trip, a guy decided to take his secretary back to his house for an evening of passion. They were rolling around on the bed when he suddenly remembered he didn't have any condoms.

"What are we gonna do?" he said.

"I don't know," answered the secretary. "I don't have any either."

Just then he hit upon an idea. "Hey!" he yelled exultantly. "No problem. I know where my wife keeps her diaphragm. You can use that."

So he searched the top drawer of the dressing table where the wife always kept her contraceptive device but it was nowhere to be found.

After 20 minutes, he gave up. "Goddam bitch!" he snarled. "She's taken it with her. I always knew she didn't trust me!"

3127 I once had a large gay following, but I ducked into an alleyway and lost him. (EMO PHILIPS)

3128 A guy was told he had just 24 hours to live, so he decided to go home and make passionate love to his wife. He crept into the bedroom, slid into bed and for the next three hours enjoyed the wildest sex he'd ever experienced. Finally exhausted, he crawled into the bathroom where he was surprised to find his wife lying in the bath with a mudpack on her face.

"How did you get in here?" he asked.

"Sssh!" she said. "You'll wake my mother."

3129 A man went into a store to buy some condoms. "That's 1 dollar 15 plus tax," said the store assistant.

"I don't need tacks," said the man. "It'll stay up all by itself."

Imaginary new condom brands:
3130 Nike condoms — Just do it.
3131 Toyota condoms — Oh what a feeling.
3132 Pringles condoms — Once you pop, you can't stop.
3133 KFC condoms — Finger-lickin' good.
3134 Ford condoms — The best never rest.
3135 Bounty condoms — The quicker picker-upper.
3136 Energizer condoms — It keeps going and going and going.
3137 M & Ms condoms — It melts in your mouth, not in your hands.
3138 Star Trek condoms — To boldly go where no man has gone before.

3139 I once made love for an hour and 15 minutes, but it was the night the clocks are set ahead. (GARRY SHANDLING)

3140 A truck driver was going down a steep incline when, at the foot of the hill, he was able to make out a couple having sex in the middle of the road. Five times on his descent he sounded his horn, but they didn't move. He finally brought the truck to a halt inches from them.

The truck driver got out and stormed: "What the hell's the matter with you two? Didn't you hear me? You could have been killed!"

The man replied nonchalantly: "Listen, I was coming, she was coming, and you were coming. You were the only one with brakes."

3141 He says, "Come on, honey. I can't remember the last time we made love." She says, "Well I can — and that's why we're not." (RODNEY DANGERFIELD)

3142 A woman went to the doctor and complained that she was suffering from knee pains.

"Do you indulge in any activity that puts a lot of pressure on your knees?" asked the doctor.

"Every night, my husband and I have sex on the floor doggy style."

"I see," said the doctor. "You know, there are plenty of other sexual positions?"

"Not if you want to watch TV there ain't!"

3143 You know why God is a man? Because if God was a woman she would have made sperm taste like chocolate. (CARRIE SNOW)

3144 Pinnochio had been getting complaints from his girlfriend. "Every time we make love," she said, "I get splinters."

So Pinocchio went back to his maker, Gipetto the carpenter, for advice.

"Sandpaper," said the carpenter. "That's what you need."

So Pinocchio took some sheets of sandpaper and went home. A few weeks later, the carpenter bumped into Pinocchio again. "How are you getting on with the girls now?" he asked.

"Who needs girls?" said Pinocchio.

Shopping

3145 Looking for something different one lunchtime, a man wandered into a newly opened magic shop. "I want a fun present for myself," he said.

The shop owner produced a special pair of glasses. "They're 1,000 dollars," he said, "but, believe me, they're worth it. When you wear them, you can see people naked."

The man tried them on and, sure enough, the shop owner appeared naked. And when his pretty female assistant walked through, she was naked too. When he took the glasses off, everyone was fully clothed.

"They're incredible," he said. "I'll buy them."

He left the shop, wearing the glasses, and headed back towards his office.

Everyone he passed was naked – pretty girls, old women, men with beer bellies, traffic wardens, the lot. He was delighted with his purchase. He thought he'd surprise his wife so before going back to work, he called in at home. He was still wearing them when he walked into the living room. There were his wife and his best friend sitting on the sofa completely naked.

"Hi, surprise!" he said, removing the glasses, but they were still naked.

"Look at that," he moaned, "A thousand dollars for a pair of magic glasses and after half an hour they're broken!"

3146 I was in the supermarket and I saw this man and woman wrapped in a barcode. I said, "Are you two an item?" (TIM VINE)

3147 A woman stormed into a soft furnishings shop. "I have come to return this rug which I bought from you last week. You promised me that it was in mint condition."

"So it is, madam," said the shop manager. "Look at that hole in the middle."

3148 I went down the street to the 24-hour grocery. When I got there, the guy was locking the front door. I said: "Hey, the sign says you're open 24 hours." He said, "Yes, but not in a row." (STEVEN WRIGHT)

3149 A teenager had just started work as an assistant in an Oklahoma grocery store. One day a man came in and asked for half a lettuce. "I'm not sure whether you can buy half a lettuce," said the young assistant.

"Why not?" asked the man. "I don't need a whole lettuce."

"But I don't think I am allowed to sell you half a lettuce."

"Right," said the man firmly. "Fetch me the manager."

So the assistant went to speak to the manager. "There's some jerk out there who only wants to buy half a lettuce." Just then he was aware of the man standing next to him. Without missing a beat, the young assistant added: "And this gentleman wants to buy the other half."

When the matter had been resolved, the manager told his assistant: "I was impressed with the way you handled things back there. You got yourself out of a tricky situation. Where are you from?"

"Minnesota."

"Why did you leave?"

"They're all just whores and hockey players up there."

The manager frowned. "My wife's from Minnesota."

"You don't say! Which team did she play for?"

3150 I went to a general store. They wouldn't let me buy anything specifically. (STEVEN WRIGHT)

3151 A man went into a bookstore and asked the saleswoman where the Self-Help section was.

She said: "If I told you, it would defeat the purpose."

3152 A guy in a supermarket noticed an old lady following him around. Whenever he stopped, she stopped. What's more, she kept staring at him. She finally overtook him just before the checkout where she turned to him and said: "I hope I haven't made you uncomfortable — it's just that you look so much like my late son."

"That's OK," he said.

"I know it's silly," she continued, "but if you'd call out 'Goodbye, Mother' as I leave, it would make me so happy."

The old lady went through the cash desk and as she left the supermarket, the man called out "Goodbye, Mother." The old lady waved back and smiled warmly.

Pleased that he had brought a little sunshine into someone's day, the man went to pay for his groceries.

"That comes to 117 dollars 95," said the clerk.

"How come?" said the man. "I've only bought a few things!"

"Yeah, but your mother said you'd pay for her."

3153 What is it that makes a shoe repairer think that he can also cut keys? (HARRY HILL)

3154 A man approached a pretty girl in a supermarket. "I've lost my wife. Can I talk to you?"

"Why?"

"Because every time I talk to a pretty girl, my wife appears out of nowhere!"

3155 My wife will buy anything marked down. Last year she bought an escalator. (HENNY YOUNGMAN)

3156 A native American Indian girl walked into a general store and asked for some toilet paper.

"We have two brands," said the shop assistant, "Toilet Paper Deluxe and the cheap brand which doesn't have a name."

She took a pack of the unnamed cheap brand but returned the following day to complain. "I have found a name for your toilet paper," she said. "John Wayne, because it's rough and it's tough, and it don't take no crap from Indians."

3157 A duck walked into a store and bought some lipstick.

"That'll be $3.99," said the cashier.

The duck said: "Put it on my bill."

Sleep

3158 A businessman booked a room in a hotel but was warned by the receptionist that the guest in the adjoining room was extremely nervous and had trouble getting to sleep at night. On reaching his room, the businessman was so exhausted after a long day that he thoughtlessly threw his shoe down very hard. He immediately remembered the nervous guest in the next room, so he laid the other shoe down very gently.

He went to bed but two hours later was woken by a knock at the door. He asked who it was, and a voice replied: "I'm the guest in the next room. For heaven's sake throw that other shoe down, will you?"

3159 Whenever you tell anyone you're an insomniac, you can guarantee what they'll say: "That's funny, because I'm asleep the moment my head hits the pillow."

But when I meet a blind man, I don't say: "That's funny, because I can see perfectly." (DAVID BADDIEL)

3160 A farmer slept peacefully night after night, week after week, even though at exactly seven minutes past three every morning a train passed by his house and blew its whistle long and loud. Then one night, the train was cancelled. At seven minutes past three the farmer sat bolt upright in bed and said: "What was that?"

3161 James Bond once slept through an earthquake. He was shaken, not stirred.

3162 A husband and wife were fast asleep in bed in the early hours of the morning when there was a knock at their front door. The husband tried to ignore it, but moments later the knocking was repeated, louder than before.

"Go and see who it is, dear," said the wife. "It must be important at this hour."

So the husband put on his dressing-gown and went downstairs to answer the door. He was greeted by a drunk who said in a slurred voice: "Will you give me a push?"

The husband was furious. "No, I will not," he raged. "It's half past three in the morning, and I was fast asleep in bed. Get lost!" And he slammed the door and went back up to bed.

When he told his wife what had happened, she was annoyed with him. "That wasn't a very nice thing to do, Peter," she said. "Remember the time when our car broke down late at night in the pouring rain on our way to pick the kids up from the baby-sitter, and you had to knock on that man's door to get us started again? What would we have done if he'd told us to get lost?"

"But this guy was drunk," protested the husband.

"It doesn't matter – he needs our help."

The husband could see that he wouldn't be allowed to get back to sleep, so he got dressed, went downstairs and opened the door. He couldn't see the drunk anywhere so he called out: "Do you still want a push?"

A voice came back out of the darkness: "Yeah, please."

"Where are you?" asked the husband, still unable to see him.

"I'm over here – on your swing."

3163 A couple woke up in the morning. "Did you hear the storm last night?" asked the husband.

"No," said his wife. "Was there thunder?"

"Yes, it was terrible. It sounded like the end of the world."

"Why didn't you wake me? You know I can never sleep when it thunders."

3164 I had a nightmare last night. I dreamed Dolly Parton was my mother and I was a bottle baby. (HENNY YOUNGMAN)

3165 A businessman arrived at a hotel so late one night that the only room available was one sharing with a stranger. The businessman was grateful for anything, but the manager did warn him that his fellow occupant snored so loudly that people in adjoining rooms had complained in the past.

The next morning, the businessman came down for breakfast and the manager asked him how he had slept.

"I had a really good night's sleep," he said.

"What about the snoring?"

"No problem. He was snoring away when I entered the room, but I simply went over, kissed him on the cheek, said 'Goodnight, darling', and he sat bolt upright for the rest of the night watching me like a hawk!"

3166 A librarian was fast asleep at three o'clock in the morning when the phone rang. The voice on the other end of the line said: "What time does the library open?"

"Nine o'clock," replied the librarian bleary-eyed. "And what's the idea of calling me at home in the middle of the night to ask a question like that?"

"Not until nine o'clock?" said the caller, disappointed.

"No, not until nine o'clock," repeated the librarian angrily. "Why do you want to get in before nine o'clock?"

"I don't want to get in," said the caller. "I want to get out."

3167 A woman had a dog which snored loudly in its sleep. Seeking a remedy, she consulted a vet who suggested tying a ribbon to the dog's testicles. So that evening, she tied a red ribbon to the dog's balls, and it worked. The dog didn't snore at all. An hour later, her husband rolled in drunk and started snoring loudly. Interested to discover whether the cure worked for humans, she tied a blue ribbon to his testicles while he was asleep. He immediately stopped snoring.

The husband woke up in the morning, feeling decidedly hung over. He lurched into the bathroom and saw his reflection in the mirror, ribbon and all.

Then he noticed that the dog was also sporting a ribbon. He turned to the dog and said: "I don't remember what happened last night, boy, but wherever you and I were, we won first and second prize."

3168 I slept like a log last night. I woke up in the fireplace. (TOMMY COOPER)

Soccer

3169 A soccor goalkeeper was walking along the street one day when he heard screams from a nearby building. He looked up to see smoke billowing from a fourth-floor window and a woman leaning out holding a baby.

"Help! Help!" screamed the woman. "I need someone to catch my baby!"

A crowd of onlookers had gathered, but none was confident about catching a baby dropped from such a great height. Then the goalkeeper stepped forward. "I'm a professional goalkeeper," he called to the woman. "I'm renowned for my safe hands. Drop the baby and I will catch it. For me, it will be just like catching a ball."

The woman agreed: "OK, then. When I drop my baby, treat it as if you were catching a ball."

On a count of three, the woman dropped the baby. Everyone held their breath as the goalkeeper lined himself up to catch it. There was a huge sigh of relief, followed by wild cheering as the goalkeeper caught the baby safely in his arms. Then he bounced it twice on the ground and kicked it 50 yards down the street.

3170 Embarrassed by revelations that she was to send her own daughters to a Swiss school, rather than one in Britain, the Duchess of York decided to offer to help out at her local comprehensive school. The delighted headmaster asked her to referee a soccer match.

Ten minutes into the game, the Duchess noticed that one of the boys was left all on his own, well away from the other players and the action. She asked him if he was OK, but he just nodded. Ten minutes later, she asked him again, but he insisted there was no problem.

She decided a pep talk was in order. "Why are you all on your own?" she asked. "Why don't you join in?"

The boy snapped: "Because I'm the goalkeeper!"

3171 The Seven Dwarfs got trapped in a mineshaft. Snow White ran to the entrance and yelled down to them. In the dark distance a voice called back: "Scotland will win the 2010 World Cup."

Snow White sighed: "Thank God – at least Dopey's still alive!"

3172 Two factory workers were talking about going to the United match. One said: "It's pointless even thinking about it – my wife will never let me go."

"It's easy," said his workmate. "All you have to do is pick her up, carry her to the bedroom, fling her on the bed, rip off her clothes, screw her and say, 'I'm going to the game.'"

The two men met up again on the Monday morning. "Did you do what I said?"

"Yeah. An hour before the game, I picked up my wife, carried her to the bedroom and flung her on the bed. Then just as I was pulling off her knickers and unzipping my fly, I thought: 'What the hell, United haven't been playing that well lately . . .'"

3173 Ronaldo went into the Brazil changing room to find his team-mates looking glum. "What's up?" he asked.

They replied: "We're having trouble getting motivated for this game – it's only Scotland."

Ronaldo said: "I reckon I can beat them by myself – you go to the pub."

So Ronaldo went and played Scotland by himself. After a few pints the rest of the team wondered how the score was going, so they asked the landlord to put teletext on. It said "Brazil 1 Scotland 0 (Ronaldo 10 min)". After several more drinks, they checked the final score on the TV. It said "Brazil 1 Scotland 1 (McFadden 89 min)". They couldn't believe that Ronaldo had single-handedly got a draw against Scotland, so they rushed to the stadium to congratulate him. Instead he was sitting with his head in his hands and wailing: "I've let you down."

"Don't be silly," they said. "You got a draw against Scotland – and they only scored at the very end."

"No, no," he cried, "I have, I've let you down – I got sent off after 12 minutes."

Stockbrokers

3174 Two women were walking in the woods one day when they came across a frog. "Please help me," cried the frog. "I'm a stockbroker, but because an evil witch put a curse on me, I've been turned into a frog. If one of you will kiss me, I'll be returned to my former state."

Hearing this, one of the women quickly stuffed the frog into her handbag.

"What are you doing?" asked her companion. "Didn't you hear what he said? If you kiss him, he'll turn into a stockbroker."

"Sure," said the other woman, "but these days a talking frog is worth more than a stockbroker."

3175 Who was the greatest financier that ever lived? – Noah, because he was able to float a company when the whole world was in liquidation.

3176 A stockbroker was in hospital. The nurse was taking his temperature.
"What is it now, nurse?" he asked.
"102."
"When it gets to 103, sell!"

3177 A stockbroker's secretary answered the phone. "Sorry, Mr Palmer is on another line."
The caller said: "This is Mr Rogers. I want to know if he's bullish or bearish right now."
"He's talking to his wife," said the secretary. "Right now I'd say he was sheepish!"

3178 On the stock market today: Helium was up, feathers were down, paper was stationary, fluorescent tubes were down in light trading, knives were up sharply, pencils were down a few points, elevators were up and down, escalators experienced a slight decline, mining equipment hit rock bottom, sun peaked at midday, the market for raisins dried up, there was no move for artists' models, vacuum cleaners picked up, caravans were trailing, socks were unchanged, balloon prices were inflated, and the bottom fell out of disposable nappies.

Stupidity

3179 Sherlock Holmes and Dr Watson went camping. After a good meal and an excellent bottle of wine, they lay down and went to sleep. A couple of hours later, Holmes woke up and nudged his faithful friend. "Watson, Watson," he said. "Look up at the sky and tell me what you see?"
"I see millions and millions of stars," replied Watson.
"And what does that tell you?" inquired the master detective.
Watson thought for a moment. "Well, Holmes, astronomically, it tells me that there are millions of galaxies and potentially billions of planets. Astrologically, I observe that Saturn is in Leo. Horologically, I deduce that the time is approximately two twenty-five. Theologically, I can see that God is all powerful and that we are small and insignificant. Meteorologically, I

believe we will have a glorious day tomorrow. What does it tell you, Holmes?"

"Watson, you imbecile! Some thief has stolen our tent!"

3180 Two British army captains, Carruthers and Fanshawe, decided to have a bet as to which of their batmen was the more stupid. Carruthers called for his batman and said: "Take this £1 coin and buy me a colour TV set in the village."

"Certainly, sir," replied the batman.

Fanshawe then rang for his batman. "Go to the orderly room at once," he commanded, "and see if I am there."

"Yes, sir," said the batman.

Outside the two batmen compared notes. "Fancy asking me to buy a colour TV set on an early closing day," said Carruthers' servant. And Fanshawe's replied: "Imagine making me walk half a mile when he could have used the telephone to see if he's in the orderly room!"

3181 Two truck drivers came to a low bridge. The clearance said 10 foot 8 inches, but when they got out and measured the truck, they realized the vehicle was 11 foot. The first man looked at the other and said: "I can't see any cops around. Let's go for it."

3182 A girl persuaded her boyfriend to take her to a restaurant. But he wasn't used to eating out and didn't know what to order from the menu.

"Why don't you have what I choose?" she suggested.

"What, and leave you hungry? No, I couldn't do that."

3183 A guy in a spelling bee was asked to spell Mississippi. "Which," he said, "the river or the state?"

3184 A supermodel was driving home in a flashy sports car when she got caught in a terrible hailstorm. The car became covered in tiny dents, so she stopped at a garage for help. The mechanic decided to have some fun at her expense. He told her that when she got home, all she had to do was blow into the exhaust pipe as hard as she could and all the dents would pop out again.

Back home, she followed the mechanic's instructions, huffing and puffing, but to no effect. Alerted by the strange noise, her yuppie boyfriend came to see what all the fuss was about. She repeated what the mechanic had told her to do.

The boyfriend rolled his eyes to heaven. He could not believe her stupidity. "Duh!" he exclaimed. "You have to wind up the windows first!"

3185 Two men were building a wooden house. One man picked up a nail, hammered it in, picked up another nail, threw it away. After that, he picked up a nail, hammered it in, picked up another nail, threw it away. After this had been going on for some time, his workmate finally came over and asked him why he was throwing half of the nails away.

"It's obvious," he said. "Those ones were pointed at the wrong end."

"How could you be so stupid?" said his friend. "They were for the other side of the house!"

3186 A man drained all the water from his swimming pool.

"Why did you do that?" asked his wife.

The man said: "I want to practise diving but I can't swim."

Taxation

3187 When old Barney died, he was initially refused admission to heaven because he had cheated on his income tax to the tune of 50,000 dollars. He was told that the only way he could get into heaven was to do penance for his tax evasion by sleeping with a really ugly woman. He didn't look forward to the prospect but realized there was no alternative.

A week later, his friend Joe also died and he too was initially refused admission to heaven because he had cheated on his income tax to the tune of 100,000 dollars. He was told that the only way he could get into heaven was to do penance for his tax evasion by sleeping with an even uglier woman, a hideous creature rarely allowed out in daylight. Reluctantly he too agreed.

A few weeks later, Barney and Joe were commiserating with each other about their fate and how they wished they had paid their taxes when they spotted their friend Wilbur walking on ahead. On his arm was the most gorgeous-looking blonde. The pair were insanely jealous and tackled Wilbur later that evening.

"How come you've got such a beautiful woman?" they demanded.

"I dunno," said Wilbur, "and I'm certainly not complaining. The thing I don't understand is that every time we have sex, she rolls over and mutters to herself, 'Damn income taxes!'"

3188 Why won't sharks attack tax inspectors? – Professional courtesy.

3189 A small boy was playing in the street in Los Angeles when he accidentally swallowed a coin which then became stuck in his throat. With the boy choking, his mother ran along the street screaming for help. Luckily, a passer-by intervened and hit the boy hard on the back so that he coughed up the coin.

"Thank you so much, doctor," said the mother.

"I'm not a doctor," said the passer-by. "I work for the Internal Revenue Service."

3190 The wages of sin are death, but by the time taxes are taken out, it's just sort of a tired feeling. (PAULA POUNDSTONE)

3191 Two junior doctors were involved in a fight in the hospital. The senior surgeon had to pull them apart.

"What's this all about?" said the surgeon angrily.

"It's the Internal Revenue inspector in G ward," said one. "He's only got two days to live."

"He had to be told," said the second doctor.

"I know," said the first, "but I wanted to be the one to tell him!"

Television

3192 I find television very educating. Every time someone turns on the set I go into the other room and read a book. (GROUCHO MARX)

3193 Two men were watching a Western on television. As the hero rode on horseback towards a cliff edge, one of the men said: "I bet you 50 dollars he goes over the cliff."

"You're on," said the other man.

The hero rode straight over the cliff.

As the second man handed over the money, the first man looked at it and said: "You know, I feel a bit guilty about winning this because I've seen the film before."

"So have I," said the second man. "But I didn't think he'd be stupid enough to make the same mistake twice."

3194 Did you hear about the Jewish game show? – The Price Is Too Much.

3195 If it weren't for electricity, we'd all be watching television by candlelight. (GEORGE GOBEL)

3196 A woman appeared as a contestant on a TV game show and did so well that she was in line to win the 100,000 dollars jackpot if she could answer tomorrow night's question correctly. While she tried to calm her nerves, her husband sneaked into the TV studio and found the question. then he rushed home to tell his wife.

"Guess what," he said. "I've found the question you'll have to answer tomorrow night. It is: 'What are the three main parts of the male anatomy?' And the answer is: 'The head, the heart and the penis.' All you have to do is say that and we've won 100,000 dollars! So remember: head, heart, ponis."

The wife eventually dozed off but kept waking up in the night, unable to remember the answer. Her husband reminded her: head, heart, penis. But when she woke up in the morning, she had forgotten it again. So he reminded her: head, heart, penis.

Come the evening and she appeared on the show. The tension built up as the quiz-master asked her: "For 100,000 dollars, what are the three main parts of the male anatomy? You have ten seconds in which to answer."

"Er, the head."

"Very good. Six seconds."

"Um, the heart."

"Excellent. Four seconds."

"Oh, er, oh, darn. My husband drilled it into me last night and I had it on the tip of my tongue this morning . . ."

"That's close enough! You've won 100,000 dollars!"

Answers given by contestants on Family Feud:

3197 Name a dangerous race – The Arabs.
3198 Name something associated with the police – Pigs.
3199 Name a non-living object with legs – A plant.
3200 Name something a blind person might use – A sword.
3201 Name a bird with a long neck – Naomi Campbell.
3202 Name an occupation where you need a torch – Burglar.
3203 Name something that floats in the bath – Water.
3204 Name something you wear on the beach – A deckchair.
3205 Name something red – My cardigan.
3206 Name something slippery – A conman.
3207 Name something with a hole in it – A window.
3208 Name a part of the body beginning with 'N' – Knee.
3209 Name a domestic animal – A leopard.
3210 Name something you open other than a door – Your bowels.

3211 Two television aerials met on a rooftop, fell in love and got married. The ceremony was awful, but the reception was excellent.

3212 A new study reveals that guests on daytime talk shows are predominantly female. Of course, most of them weren't born that way. (CONAN O'BRIEN)

3213 A man was a contestant on a TV game show and, for 500,000 dollars, was asked to name two of Santa's reindeer. "Rudolph and Olive," he answered confidently.

There was a stunned silence among the audience. They didn't know whether to laugh or cry. The host shuffled uneasily. "Er, we can accept Rudolph, but I'm not sure about Olive. How did you come by that?"

The man began to sing: "Rudolph the red-nosed reindeer had a very shiny nose, and if you ever saw it, you would even say it glows. Olive, the other reindeer . . ."

Texas

3214 A Texan guy bought a round of drinks after announcing that his wife had just produced "a typical Texas baby boy weighing twenty pounds." Gasps of admiration echoed around the bar.

Two weeks later he returned and the bartender said: "Hey, you're the father of the typical Texas baby that weighed twenty pounds at birth, aren't you?"

The father answered: "Fifteen pounds now."

"How come?" said the bartender. "He weighed twenty pounds at birth."

The Texan took a slow sip from his beer, wiped his lips on his shirt sleeves, leaned over to the bartender and said proudly: "Had him circumcised."

3215 A Texan on a steamer trip along the Alaskan coast was boasting to locals about how the Lone Star State had the biggest and best of everything. Just then a huge iceberg came into view. The Texan was rendered speechless for a second. "Hell," he said, "I have to admit you've got bigger ice cubes."

3216 A Texan oil baron went to the dentist for a check-up. "I'm pleased to say your teeth are just fine," said the dentist.

"I know," replied the oilman, "but drill anyway. I feel lucky."

3217 A Texan was standing admiring the beauty of Niagara Falls when a New Yorker standing next to him said sarcastically: "I bet you don't have anything like this in Texas."

"No," said the Texan, "but we've got plumbers who could fix it!"

3218 If God had meant for Texans to ski, he would have made bullshit white.

3219 A Texan tourist looked in awe at the London Eye millennium wheel. "Wow," he said, "we have nothing so enormous back home."

His London host replied: "If you think that's big, wait till you see the size of the hamster!"

3220 A visitor to Texas inquired: "Does it ever rain here?"

The rancher replied: "Yes. Remember that part in the Bible where it rained for 40 days and 40 nights?"

"You mean Noah's flood?"

"Yep. Well, we got about two and a half inches during that spell."

3221 An Englishman, a Frenchman, a Mexican and a Texan were traveling together on a small plane when the pilot suddenly announced: "We are in trouble. The only way we can make it to an airfield is for three of you to jump out. At least that way one of you will be saved."

The four opened the door and looked out at the 20,000-foot drop. With the stiffest of upper lips, the Englishman shouted, "God Save the Queen" and jumped out of the plane.

Inspired by this heroism, the Frenchman shouted, "Vive La France" and jumped out of the plane.

The Texan was really pumped up now. He hollered, "Remember the Alamo", grabbed the Mexican and threw him out of the plane.

3222 If a man's from Texas, he'll tell you. If he's not, why embarrass him by asking? (JOHN GUNTHER)

3223 A Texan farmer went on vacation to Australia. He met up with an Australian farmer who proudly showed off his wheat field.

"That's nothing," said the Texan. "Back home, we have wheat fields that are twice as large as this."

Next the Australian pointed out his cattle.

"They're nothing," said the Texan. "Back home, we have longhorns that are twice as big as your cows."

Just then, half a dozen kangaroos bounded across the road.

"What are those?" said the Texan.

The Australian replied: "Don't you have grasshoppers in Texas?"

Texas computer definitions:

3224 Hard drive: Trying to climb a steep, muddy hill with three flat tyres, pulling a flatbed trailer loaded with alfalfa hay.

3225 Mouse: Fuzzy, soft thing you stuff in your beer bottle to get a free case.

3226 Cursor: What you do when you find your wife drank the last beer.

3227 Website: Place in the kitchen where spiders live.

3228 Window: Place in the truck to hang your gun.

3229 Reboot: What you do when your old pair gets encrusted with barn droppings.

3230 Modem: How you got rid of weeds in the pasture.

3231 ROM: Delicious when you mix it with Coke.

3232 Byte: The next thing that happens after you hear that rattling sound down in the grass.

3233 Browser: What you do when a pretty gal walks past the general store.

3234 A Texas boy rushed home from kindergarten and told his mother: "I need a set of pistols, a gun belt and a holster."

"Whatever for?" asked the mother. "Surely you don't need them for school?"

"I do," he insisted. "Teacher said tomorrow she's going to teach us to draw."

3235 What is the definition of a Texan virgin? – A girl who can run faster than her brother.

3236 A blind man travelled by airplane to Texas. On board the plane, he felt the plush seats and remarked how big they were. The passenger next to him said: "Everything is big in Texas."

When he landed in Texas, he went straight to a hotel bar in Dallas and ordered a beer. The bartender served it in a mug. The blind man felt the mug and commented on its size. The bartender said: "Everything is big in Texas."

After three beers, the blind man needed the toilet, so he asked the bartender for directions. But he accidentally went to the swimming pool instead and fell in. As he flapped around terrified in the water, he screamed: "Don't flush! Don't flush!"

Theatre

3237 Why should I pay ten dollars for something I can see in the bathroom for nothing? (GROUCHO MARX on *Hair*)

3238 "I beg your pardon," said the man returning to his theatre seat at the end of the interval, "but did I step on your foot when I left?"

"Yes, you did."

"Oh, good, that means I'm in the right row."

3239 A couple were sent two theatre tickets as an anniversary present with the cryptic message: "Guess who sent them?"

They rang round all of their friends and family but nobody admitted sending the tickets. However, they weren't prepared to look an anonymous gift horse in the mouth and went to the theatre and had a wonderful time. But when they got home, they discovered that their house had been burgled. On the kitchen worktop was a note saying: "Now you know."

3240 A strained voice called out through the darkened theatre: "Please, is there a doctor in the house?"

As the lights came on, several men stood up. An older lady also rose to her feet and pulled her twenty-something daughter close to her. "Good," shouted the older woman. "Now are any of you doctors single and interested in a date with a nice Jewish girl?"

3241 The opening night of a new play was so bad that the audience started leaving the theatre at the end of the second act. As he got up from his aisle seat, a noted critic raised a restraining hand. "Wait!" he commanded loudly. "Women and children first!"

3242 During a performance of a school nativity play at the local theatre, a large crack suddenly appeared in the middle of the stage. As the performance progressed, the crack became bigger and bigger until it finally developed into a hole. Everyone else managed to avoid it but when young Johnny stepped forward as one of the Wise Men, he plunged straight through the hole.

The audience gasped. Johnny's father whispered to his mother: "Don't worry, dear. It's just a stage he's going through."

3243 A man walked into a grocery store and announced: "I want all the rotten eggs you have."

"What do you want with rotten eggs?" asked the shop assistant. "Unless you're going to see that terrible new comedian who's on at the theatre this week?"

The man replied icily: "I am the new comedian."

3244 At the interval of a play, the theatre manager spotted a man sprawled across three seats in the stalls and groaning loudly. Assuming him to be a drunk, he decided to monitor his behaviour for the next few minutes. When the man continued to moan and groan, the manager felt he had no option but to eject him. The manager marched over to him and said: "Where have you come from?"

The man replied weakly: "The balcony."

3245   A farmer went to town and bought a live chicken. With time to kill afterwards, he decided to catch a show at the local theatre, but the woman at the cash desk refused him entry.

"Sorry, sir," she said, "we don't allow live animals in the theatre."

The man was determined to get in, so he sneaked around the corner, stuffed the chicken down his trousers and tried again. This time, he was allowed in.

Soon two women came and sat down, one either side of him. He felt increasingly uncomfortable with the chicken which was becoming restless in the heat of the theatre, so he unzipped his fly to enable the chicken to extend its neck.

One woman said to the other: "Do you see what I see?"

"I do, Gloria, but I'm trying to ignore it. If you've seen one, you've seen them all."

"I'm not sure about that," said Gloria. "This is the first one I've seen that eats popcorn!"

3246   Two chorus girls were discussing what to buy as a birthday present for one of the other girls in the line.

"Why not get her a book?"

"No, she's already got a book."

3247   Audience with me all the way. Managed to shake them off at the station. (HARRY SECOMBE)

Time

3248   A tourist visiting an archaeological site in South America was intrigued by the display of dinosaur bones. She asked a local Indian, who was acting as tour guide, how old the bones were.

"Exactly 100 million and three years old," replied the Indian.

"That's amazing," said the tourist. "How can you be so precise?"

"Simple," said the Indian. "A geologist told me they were 100 million years old, and that was exactly three years ago."

3249   Whenever I think about the past, it brings back such memories. (STEVEN WRIGHT)

3250 What did the Leaning Tower of Pisa say to Big Ben? – If you've got the time, I've got the inclination.

3251 A man arrived at a small country station ready to catch the eight-thirty train. Spotting that the clock outside the station said eight twenty-five, he thought he had enough time to buy a newspaper. But after hurriedly purchasing his paper, he stepped on to the platform just as his train was disappearing into the distance. He looked up at the platform clock and saw that it said eight thirty-five. When he protested to the stationmaster about the discrepancy between the two clocks, the stationmaster replied: "Well, why would we need two clocks if they both told the same time?"

3252 Time flies like an arrow, but fruit flies like a banana. (GROUCHO MARX)

3253 After driving all night, a company rep was still a long way from home as dawn broke. He decided to pull over and catch up on his sleep for a couple of hours. Unbeknown to him, he had chosen to park his car on the city's main jogging route. Barely had he dozed off than he was startled by a knock on the car window. It was a jogger.

"What's the time?" asked the jogger.

"Seven-fifteen," said the man drowsily. He tried to doze but soon another jogger knocked on his window.

"What's the time?" yelled the jogger.

"Seven-thirty," said the man, irritated. Again, he tried to get to sleep, but was quickly woken by another jogger hammering on the window.

"What's the time?" he screamed.

"Seven forty-five." snapped the man. That was the last straw. Taking a pen and paper, he put a sign in his car window saying, "I DO NOT KNOW THE TIME!". No sooner had he fallen asleep again than another jogger was pounding on the window, shouting: "Hey, buddy. It's seven fifty-five."

3254 We spend our lives on the run. We get up by the clock, eat and sleep by the clock, get up again, go to work. And then we retire. And what do they give us? A bloody clock! (DAVE ALLEN)

3255 A smooth-talking guy at a bar kept looking at his watch. An attractive woman couldn't help noticing this and asked: "Is your date late?"

"No," he said. "I just bought this state-of-the-art watch and I was testing it. It uses alpha waves to talk to me."

"What's it telling you?"

"That you're not wearing any panties."

"Well, sorry," she said, "but I am."

"Damn, it must be an hour fast."

Vacations

3256 A man on vacation in North Africa ended up lost in the desert. The temperature was over 100 degrees and he was desperate for water. Through the heat haze he was just able to make out a tent in the distance. Somehow summoning up extra strength, he staggered to the tent where he was greeted by a Bedouin.

"Water," gasped the traveller. "I must have water."

"I'm sorry, sir," replied the Bedouin, "I have no water, but would you like to buy a tie?"

"A tie!" exclaimed the traveller as the Bedouin produced an array of brightly coloured silk ties. "You idiot! I don't need a bloody tie. I need water."

"Well," said the Bedouin, "if you really need water, there is another tent three kilometres to the east. I do know that they have water."

The weary traveller set off on his lonely crawl across the desert. The journey took him eight hours. Finally he arrived at the second tent. A Bedouin in a smart tuxedo was waiting at the entrance.

"Can I help?" he asked.

"Water," gasped the traveller with one last breath. "I must have water."

"Sorry, sir," replied the Bedouin. "You can't come in without a tie."

3257 Parents took their young son on vacation to a nudist beach. After spending some time happily digging in the sand, the boy ran back to his mother and said: "Mum, I saw ladies with bigger boobies than yours!"

His mother replied: "The bigger they are, the dumber they are."

The boy went off to play again but a few minutes later ran back to his mother. "Mum, I saw men with dingers a lot bigger than Daddy's."

His mother said: "The bigger they are, the dumber they are."

The boy scampered off again but came back a short while later. "Mum, I just saw Dad talking to the dumbest lady I've ever seen, and the more he talked, the dumber and dumber he got!"

3258 A couple from Seattle were talking about their holiday to a friend. "Sounds as if you had a great time in California," said the friend, "but I didn't know you were planning to take in Florida as well."

"We weren't," said the wife, "but Ted simply will not ask for directions."

3259 A man saw a cheap cruise advertised in a travel agent's. He handed over fifty dollars, the travel agent hit him over the head with a baseball bat and threw him in the river. A few minutes later, the same thing happened to a second man. As they floated down the river together, the first man said: "Do you think they'll serve any food on this cruise?"

"I doubt it," said the second. "They didn't last year."

3260 A man planning his holidays consulted a travel agent. "Last year you suggested the Maldives, and when I returned my wife was pregnant. The year before you suggested the Bahamas, and when I returned my wife was pregnant. And the year before that I went to Bali, and when I got back, my wife was pregnant. Could you suggest somewhere cheaper this year so I can take her with me?"

3261 A girl on vacation in Spain headed for the hotel roof for some sun. On her first day up there she wore a bathing suit but since there was nobody around, on the second day she removed it in order to acquire an all-over tan. She was lying on her stomach when she heard someone running up the stairs. She quickly pulled a towel over her and was confronted by the assistant hotel manager.

"Excuse me," he said. "The hotel doesn't mind you sunning yourself on the roof, but we would appreciate it if you wore a bathing suit as you did yesterday."

"What's the problem?" she asked. "No one can see me up here."

"That's not quite true," he replied. "You're lying on the dining-room skylight."

War

3262 During the Second World War, German soldiers were looting French villages of food, wine and women. In one village, everyone fled in advance except for a young man and his 90-year-old grandmother who refused to be driven out by the Germans. When the German tanks rumbled into the near-deserted village, the soldiers cornered the young man.

"Bring us food," they demanded.

"All I have left is half a loaf of bread," said the young man.

"War is war," said the soldiers and they forced him to hand over the last crumbs.

Then they shouted: "Bring us wine."

"All I have left is half a bottle," said the young man.

"War is war," insisted the soldiers, and they forced him to hand over the last half bottle of wine.

Then the soldiers shouted: "Bring us a woman."

"But there is only one left in the village," protested the young man.

"War is war," boomed the soldiers.

So he fetched his 90-year-old grandmother. The German soldiers took one look at her and said: "Er, maybe we'll let you off this time."

"No way," said Granny. "War is war."

3263 Sometimes I think war is God's way of teaching us geography. (PAUL RODRIGUEZ)

3264 A British soldier serving abroad was upset to receive a letter from his girlfriend breaking off their engagement and asking for her photo back. So he collected a stack of unwanted photos from the rest of the regiment and sent them back to Britain with a note saying: "Sorry, can't remember which one is you – please keep your photo and return the others."

3265 Three Vietnam war veterans were out fishing on a lake one day when Jesus walked across the water and joined them in their boat. Not surprisingly, the three men were amazed.

The first said humbly: "Jesus, I've suffered from back pain ever since I was hit by shrapnel in the Vietnam War. Can you help me?"

"Of course, my son," said Jesus and when he touched the man's back, the man felt relief for the first time in 30 years.

The second man, who wore thick glasses, said to Jesus: "I've never been able to see properly since a mine blew up in front of me in Vietnam. Is there anything you can do to help?"

Jesus smiled, removed the man's glasses and lobbed them into the lake. As soon as the glasses hit the water, the man's eyes cleared and he was able to see perfectly for the first time in 30 years.

Then Jesus turned to the third man who put up his arms defensively and cried: "Don't touch me – I'm on a disability pension!"

3266 The right to bear arms is slightly less ludicrous than the right to arm bears. (CHRIS ADDISON)

3267 A medieval knight and his men returned to the castle after a hard day's fighting. The knight informed the king: "Your majesty, I have been robbing and pillaging on your behalf all day, burning the villages of your enemies in the north."

The king looked perplexed. "But I don't have any enemies in the north."
"Ah," replied the knight, realizing his blunder. "I fear you do now."

3268 I did sympathize with Bush and Blair trying to find WMDs. I'm like that with my scissors. I put them down, then I search all over the house, and I never find them. Of course, I do know that my scissors exist. (LINDA SMITH)

3269 An army platoon became detached in the desert during the Gulf War. For three days and nights they waited for help until all their food supplies were exhausted. Finally in desperation they sent out a soldier to explore the wilderness and to report back as to whether there was any hope of food. The next day the soldier returned. "There is bad news and good news," he told the starving troops.

"The bad news is, there is only camel dung to eat. The good news is, there is plenty of it."

3270 In a world without men, there would be no war, just intense negotiations every 28 days. (ROBIN WILLIAMS)

3271 Last year in Brussels, a Belgian went to his local priest and confessed: "Forgive me, Father, for I have sinned. During the Second World War, I hid a Jewish man in my attic."

"That's not a sin," said the priest. "It was an act of great kindness."

"But I made him agree to pay me 30 francs for every week he stayed."

"I admit that wasn't particularly charitable," said the priest, "but you did it for a good cause."

"Thank you, Father," said the man. "That's a great relief to me. I have just one more question."

"What's that?"

"Do I have to tell him the war is over?"

Weddings

3272 A young couple met with the vicar to set a date for their wedding. When the vicar asked whether they would prefer a modern service or a traditional service, they opted for the modern service. On the day of the wedding, a terrible storm broke, forcing the groom to abandon the car and complete the journey to church on foot. The streets were flooded, so he rolled up his trousers in an attempt to keep them dry. He arrived late at the church and was immediately hustled up the aisle just as the ceremony was starting.

The vicar looked at him and whispered: "Pull down your trousers."

The groom said nervously: "Er, actually, Reverend, I've changed my mind. I think I'll go for the traditional service."

3273 A minister recognized the young man standing at the back of the church one Sunday as someone whose wedding ceremony he had conducted a few months earlier. After the service, the young man was waiting to talk to the minister.

"Tell me, Reverend, do you believe that someone should profit from the mistakes of others?"

"Definitely not," said the minister.

"In which case can I have back the 50 dollars I paid you for the wedding?"

3274 A woman rushed up the stairs to the church, late for the wedding. An usher asked to see her invitation.

"I don't have one," she said.

"Well, are you a friend of the groom?" asked the usher.

"Certainly not!" she stormed. "I'm the bride's mother!"

3275 During the wedding rehearsal, the groom took the minister to one side and said: "I'll give you 100 dollars if you change my wedding vows. When you reach the part where I promise to love, honour and obey and 'forsaking all others, be faithful to her for ever', I want you to leave that bit out." The minister duly accepted the 100 dollars.

At the ceremony itself, the minister got to the groom's vows and said: "Will you promise to obey her every command and wish, serve her breakfast in bed every morning, and swear that you will never look at another woman?"

The groom was horrified. "I thought we had a deal," he hissed.

"Yes," whispered the minister pressing the 100 dollars into the groom's hand. "But the bride made me a better offer."

3276 Just before his wedding, a naïve young man asked his mother: "Why are wedding dresses always white?"

"Because," she replied, "white is a sign of purity."

He was satisfied with the answer, but thought he had better double-check with his father.

"Dad, why are wedding dresses always white?"

His father replied: "Because kitchen appliances always come in white."

3277 A traffic cop in a small town stopped a motorist for speeding. "But, Officer," said the driver, "I can explain . . ."

"Save your excuses," said the cop. "You can cool your heels in jail till the chief gets back."

"But, Officer . . ."

"Shut up," snapped the cop. "You're going to jail. The chief will deal with you when he gets back."

A few hours later the officer looked in on the prisoner. "Lucky for you that the chief's at his daughter's wedding. It means he'll be in a good mood when he gets back."

"Don't count on it," said the prisoner. "I'm the groom."

Women

3278 Women complain about pre-menstrual syndrome, but I think of it as the only time of the month that I can be myself. (ROSEANNE BARR)

3279 Why does a woman close her eyes during sex? – Because no woman ever wants to see a man enjoying himself.

3280 Why do women have smaller feet than men? – So that they can stand closer to the sink.

3281 A radical feminist was travelling on a bus when, just in front of her, a man got up from his seat. She thought to herself, "Here's another man patronizing the female sex by offering a poor, defenceless woman a seat." And she pushed him back down into his seat.

A few minutes later, he again tried to get up but again she pushed him back down. "Look, lady," he protested, "you've got to let me up. I'm a mile past my stop already."

Reasons why bicycles are better than women:
3282 Bicycles don't get pregnant.
3283 You can ride your bicycle any time of the month.
3284 Bicycles don't have parents.
3285 Bicycles don't whine unless something is really wrong.
3286 You can share your bicycle with friends.
3287 Bicycles don't care how many other bicycles you've ridden.
3288 When riding, you and your bicycle can arrive at the same time.
3289 Bicycles don't care if you look at other bicycles.

3290 If your bicycle is too loose you can tighten it.

3291 You can stop riding your bicycle as soon as you want and it won't get frustrated.

3292 Bicycles don't care if you buy bicycle magazines.

3293 A bicycle never wants a night out with other bicycles.

3294 If you say horrible things to your bicycle, you don't have to apologize before you can ride it again.

3295 You can ride your bicycle as long as you want to and it won't get sore.

3296 Your parents won't keep in touch with your old bicycle after you dump it.

3297 A man's only as old as the woman he feels. (GROUCHO MARX)

3298 Anyone who says he can see through women is missing a lot. (GROUCHO MARX)

3299 Women have a passion for mathematics. They divide their age in half, double the price of their clothes and always add at least five years to the age of their best friend. (MARCEL ACHARD)

3300 It was early evening in a casino and the two dealers at the craps table were waiting patiently for the first punters to arrive. Just then a woman came over and said that she wanted to bet 25,000 dollars on a single roll of the dice.

"Certainly, madam," they said, happy to relieve the boredom.

"There's just one thing though," she added. "I hope you don't mind, but going bottomless always brings me luck. So since there's hardly anyone about, is it all right with you two if I pull down my skirt and knickers?"

She then stripped off, threw the dice and yelled: "I've won! I've won!" Then she scooped up the money, picked up her clothes and left.

The two dealers were dumbfounded. "What did she roll anyway?" asked one.

"I don't know," said the other. "I thought you were watching the dice!"

Big busted women:

3301 Can get a taxi on the worst days.

3302 Have a neat place to carry spare change.

3303 Make jogging a spectator sport.

3304 Can keep a magazine dry while lying in the tub.

3305 Can usually find leftover popcorn after a movie.

3306 Always float better.

3307 Know where to look for lost earrings.

3308 Rarely have to look for a slow dance partner.

Small busted women:

3309 Don't cause a traffic accident every time they bend over in public.

3310 Find that dribbled food makes it to the napkin on their lap.

3311 Can always see their shoes.

3312 Can sleep on their stomachs.

3313 Have no trouble sliding behind the wheel of small cars.

3314 Know that people can read the entire message on their T-shirts.

3315 Can come late to the theatre and not disrupt an entire aisle.

3316 Can take aerobics class without running the risk of knocking themselves out.

3317 If your dog is barking at the back door and your wife is yelling at the front door, who do you let in first? – The dog. At least he'll shut up after you let him in.

3318 At various times in her life, a woman is like the continents of the world. From 13 to 18, she's like Africa – virgin territory; from 18 to 30, she's like Asia – hot and exotic; from 30 to 45, she's like America – fully explored and free with her resources; from 45 to 55, she's like Europe – exhausted, but not without places of interest; from 55 onwards, she's like Australia – everybody knows it's down there, but nobody cares.

3319 Women say they want a man who knows what a woman's worth. That's a pimp. (RICH HALL)

3320 What do cow pies and cowgirls have in common? – The older they get, the easier they are to pick up.

3321 A woman walked into a drug store and asked the pharmacist if he sold extra large condoms.
"Yes, we do. Would you like to buy some?"
"No, but do you mind if I wait here till someone does?"

3322 A study has revealed that the kind of face a woman finds attractive on a man can differ depending on where she is in her menstrual cycle. For example, if she is ovulating, she is attracted to men with rugged and masculine features. However if she is menstruating, or menopausal, she tends to be more attracted to a man with scissors lodged in his temple and tape over his mouth while he is on fire.

3323 What do you call a woman tied up at a jetty? – Maud.

3324 What do you call a woman with a toothpick in her head? – Olive.

3325 What do you call a Chinese woman with a food processor on her head? – Brenda.

3326 What do you call a woman balancing a pint glass on each arm and another pint glass on her head? – Beatrix.

3327 What do you call a woman with a roulette wheel on her head? – Bette.

3328 What do you call a woman who sets fire to her bills? – Bernadette.

3329 What do you call a woman with a screwdriver in one hand, a knife in the other, a pair of scissors between the toes on her left foot, and a corkscrew between the toes on her right foot? – A Swiss Army wife.

3330 What's six inches long, two inches wide and drives women wild? – Money.

3331 Why did the woman cross the road? More to the point, what was she doing out of the kitchen?

3332 What would have happened if there had been Three Wise Women? They would have asked for directions, arrived on time, helped deliver the baby, cleaned the stable, made a nice casserole and given practical gifts for the home.

3333 What does a woman make best for dinner? – Reservations.

3334 You know, men and women are a lot alike in certain situations. Like when they're both on fire, they're exactly alike. (DAVE ATTELL)

What a woman says and what she really means:
3335 "We need" MEANS "I want."
3336 "Do what you want" MEANS "You'll pay for this later."
3337 "I heard a noise" MEANS "I noticed you were nearly asleep."
3338 "Do you love me?" MEANS "I'm going to ask for something expensive."
3339 "How much do you love me?" MEANS "I did something today you're not going to like."
3340 "We need to talk" MEANS "I need to complain."
3341 "You're certainly attentive tonight" MEANS "Is sex all you ever think about?"

3342 "Be romantic, turn out the lights" MEANS "I think I'm putting on weight."

3343 "This kitchen floor is so hard to clean" MEANS "I want a new house."

3344 "Hang the picture here" MEANS "Hang the picture there."

3345 "I'm not yelling" MEANS "I am yelling because I think this is important."

3346 "Is my butt fat?" MEANS "Tell me I'm beautiful."

3347 "Do I really look fat in this dress?" MEANS "We haven't had a fight for a while."

3348 "No, pizza's fine" MEANS "You tight-fisted slob."

3349 "Can we just be friends?" MEANS "There's no way I'm going to let any part of your body ever touch me again."

3350 "I see you more as a brother" MEANS "You have the sexual allure of a sea slug."

3351 "I just don't want a boyfriend now" MEANS "I just don't want you as a boyfriend now."

3352 "It's not you, it's me" MEANS "It's you."

3353 "I don't know, what do you want to do?" MEANS "I can't believe you have nothing planned."

3354 "I just need some space" MEANS "without you in it."

3355 "We're moving too quickly" MEANS "I'm not going to sleep with you till I find out whether the guy at the gym has a girlfriend."

3356 "I'm sorry" MEANS "You'll be sorry."

3357 "I'll be ready in a minute" MEANS "I'll be ready in an hour."

3358 "Yes" MEANS "No."

3359 "No" MEANS "No."

3360 "Maybe" MEANS "No."

3361 With the plane about to plunge into a mountain, a female passenger stood up and shouted: "If I'm going to die, I want to die feeling like a woman."

Then she took off her top and cried: "Is there someone on this plane who is man enough to make me feel like a woman?"

Hearing this, a man stood up, took off his shirt and said: "Iron this."

3362 Why did God make man first? — He didn't want a woman looking over his shoulder.

3363 In the beginning, God created earth and rested. Then God created man and rested. Then God created woman. Since then, neither God nor man has rested.

3364 When does a woman enjoy a man's company? — When he owns it.

3365 A woman said to her friend: "I made my husband a millionaire."
"And what was he before you married him?"
"A billionaire."

Reasons why it's great to be a woman:

3366 You never have to buy your own drinks.

3367 You can get laid any time you want.

3368 You don't look like a frog in a blender when you're dancing.

3369 You can get out of speeding tickets by crying.

3370 You're not expected to know how cars work.

3371 You can sleep your way to the top.

3372 You can scare bosses with mysterious gynaecological excuses.

3373 You don't worry about losing your hair.

3374 You always get to choose the movie.

3375 You don't have to mow the lawn.

3376 PMS is a legal defence for murder.

3377 You don't have to understand the offside rule.

3378 You don't have to adjust your genitals constantly.

3379 Sweat is sexy on you.

3380 You can marry rich and then not have to work.

3381 You never have to use a power drill.

3382 You never run out of excuses.

3383 You get expensive jewellery as gifts that you never have to give back.

3384 You get gifts all the time because men mess up so often.

3385 You can give "the look" that makes any man cower in the corner.

3386 You can always get a taxi to stop for you.

3387 You look good in shorts.

3388 You don't have to worry about being able to get it up.

3389 You have mastered civilized eating.

3390 You are better gossips.

3391 You look better naked than men.

3392 You don't have to pass wind to amuse yourself.

3393 If you forget to shave, no one has to know.

3394 You can congratulate your teammate without ever touching her rear.

3395 Women do less time for violent crime.

3396 You can wear no underwear and be considered wild and sexy; a man who does the same thing is merely thought of as disgusting.

3397 Short women are petite; short men are just short.

3398 You can talk to people of the opposite sex without having to picture them naked.

3399 If you marry someone twenty years younger, you're aware that you look like an idiot.

3400 You don't need an excuse to be in a bad mood.

3401 A pointy-shaped vegetable is all you need for a good time.

3402 Chocolate can solve all your problems.

3403 You'll never regret piercing your ears.

3404 You can fully assess a person just by looking at their shoes.

3405 You can make comments about how stupid men are in their presence, because they aren't listening anyway.

3406 You piss sitting down, so it's easier to pass out on the toilet when drunk.

3407 You got off the *Titanic* first.

Work

3408 Near the end of a job interview, the human resources officer asked the confident young applicant: "What salary are you looking for?"

"Something in the region of 90,000 dollars, depending on the benefits package."

"Well, what would you say to a package of six weeks' vacation plus 12 paid holidays, full medical and dental, and a new company car every year?"

"Wow! Are you kidding?"

"Certainly, but you started it!"

3409 I used to work in a fire hydrant factory. You couldn't park anywhere near the place. (STEVEN WRIGHT)

3410 One by one the directors of a Chicago finance company were called in to the chairman's office until only the newest, most junior executive was left sitting nervously outside. Finally it was his turn to be summoned. He entered the office to find the chairman and the other eight directors seated solemnly around a table. Suddenly the chairman turned to the young man and asked: "Have you ever slept with Miss Foyt, my secretary?"

"No, certainly not."

"Are you absolutely sure?" persisted the chairman.

"Absolutely. I've never laid a finger on her."

"You'd swear to that on the Bible?"

"Yes, I swear I've never had a sexual relationship with your secretary."

"Good. Then you can fire her."

3411 Employer: "In this job, we need someone who is responsible."

Applicant: "That's me. In my last job, whenever anything went wrong, they said I was responsible."

3412 I hate housework. You make the beds, you do the dishes — and six months later you have to start all over again. (JOAN RIVERS)

Actual employee evaluation reports:

3413 His men would follow him anywhere, but only out of morbid curiosity.

3414 Works well when under constant supervision and cornered like a rat in a trap.

3415 When she opens her mouth, it seems that it is only to change feet.

3416 He doesn't have ulcers, but he's a carrier.

3417 He has a knack for making strangers immediately.

3418 When his IQ reaches 50, he should sell.

3419 A prime candidate for natural de-selection.

3420 The wheel is turning but the hamster is dead.

3421 It's hard to believe he beat a million other sperm.

3422 If you see two people talking and one looks bored, he's the other one.

3423 Four men — a Californian, a Texan, a Bostonian and a New Yorker — were being interviewed for a prestigious job with a multi-national company. There was nothing to choose between them so the company president told them over dinner at a luxurious hotel that he would be conducting the decisive test the following morning. Each candidate would be asked the same question and the one who came up with the best answer would get the job.

First in the following morning was the Californian. "Here is your question," said the president. "What is the fastest thing in the world?"

Scarcely hesitating, the Californian replied: "A thought, because it takes no time at all. It is in your mind in an instant, then gone again."

"That's a very good answer," said the president.

Next in was the Texan. "What is the fastest thing in the world?" asked the president.

"A blink," replied the Texan instantaneously, "because you don't even think about a blink. It's a reflex."

"That's a fine answer," said the president.

Next in was the Bostonian. "What is the fastest thing in the world?" asked the president.

The Bostonian thought for a second. "I'd say electricity, because you can flip a switch and immediately ten miles away a light will go on."

"That's an excellent answer," said the president.

Finally it was the turn of the New Yorker. "What is the fastest thing in the world?" asked the president.

The New Yorker scratched his head and replied: "Diarrhoea, because last night after dinner I was lying on the bed when I got these terrible stomach cramps and before I could think, blink or turn on the light . . ."

3424 Employer: "Young man, do you think you can handle a variety of work?"

Applicant: "I should be able to — I've had eight different jobs in the past three months!"

3425 Employee of the month is a good example of how somebody can be both a winner and a loser at the same time. (DEMETRI MARTIN)

3426 Why are robots never afraid? — Because they have nerves of steel.

3427 A guy had a problem getting up for work in the mornings and was frequently reprimanded for being late. It got so bad that he went to see a doctor who gave him a pill to take at bedtime. After taking the pill, the man slept soundly, woke up refreshed, had a leisurely breakfast and went into work.

"Hi, I feel great," he told the boss. "I think all my timekeeping problems are a thing of the past."

"Terrific," said the boss. "But where were you yesterday?"

What employee evaluation reports really mean:

3428 Character above reproach . . . Still one step ahead of the law.

3429 Exceptionally good judgment . . . Lucky.

3430 Great presentation skills . . . Bullshitter.

3431 Independent worker . . . Nobody knows what he/she does.

3432 Experienced problem solver . . . screws up often.

3433 Relaxed attitude . . . Sleeps at desk.

3434 Career minded . . . Back stabber.

3435 Quick thinking . . . Offers plausible excuses for mistakes.

3436 Zealous attitude . . . Opinionated.

3437 Meticulous attention to detail . . . Nit picker.

3438 Shows leadership qualities . . . Big mouth.

3439 They say you can tell a British workman by his hands — they're always in his pockets.

3440 What's the difference between a rottweiler and a social worker? – It's easier to get your kids back from a rottweiler.

3441 A social worker asked a colleague: "What time is it?"
"Sorry, I don't know," replied the other, "I'm not wearing a watch."
"Never mind," said the first. "At least we talked about it."

3442 A puny guy went for a job as a lumberjack, but the head lumberjack told him: "Sorry, pal, you're too weak."
"I may look weak," protested the guy, "but I'm not. At least give me a chance to show what I can do."
"OK then, see that giant redwood over there. Let's see you chop it down."
Half an hour later, to the amazement of the head lumberjack, the giant redwood was lying on its side.
"Where did you learn to cut down trees like that?"
"The Sahara Forest."
"You mean the Sahara Desert?"
"Sure, if that's what they call it now."

3443 Tarzan came home from a hard day's work and said: "Jane, it's a jungle out there."

3444 The United States were competing against Japan in a boat race and, to the Americans' dismay, the Japanese team won by a mile. Determined to ensure that there would be no repetition of the national humiliation the following year, the Americans hired a firm of consultants to discover the reason for the defeat and to recommend corrective action. The consultants found that whereas the Japanese crew had seven people rowing and one steering, the Americans had one rowing and seven steering. After a year of study and millions of dollars spent analyzing the problem, the firm of consultants cautiously concluded that on the US team too many people were steering and not enough were rowing.
So as race day approached the following year, the US team's management structure was completely reorganized. The new structure was four steering managers, three area steering managers and a new performance review system for the person rowing the boat to provide work incentive. This time the Japanese team won by two miles. The US corporate management promptly laid off the rower for poor performance but gave the managers a bonus for discovering where the problem lay.

3445 A union leader was reading his granddaughter a bedtime story: "Once upon a time and a half . . ."

3446 Several weeks after being hired, the young man was called into the personnel manager's office. "When you applied for this job, you said you had a degree in English Language from Cambridge plus five years' experience in this line of work. Now we discover that you have absolutely no qualifications and that this is your first job of any kind. What do you have to say for yourself?"

"Well, your ad said you wanted somebody with imagination!"

3447 One day as I came home early from work, I saw a guy jogging naked. I said to the guy, "Hey, buddy, why are you doing that?" He said, "Because you came home early." (RODNEY DANGERFIELD)

3448 Every morning a guy took the ferry to work, but one morning his watch stopped and he thought he was running late. He rushed to the dock and saw the boat ten feet away. Taking a run at it, he jumped and, with a superhuman effort, just managed to land in the boat. The captain looked at him quizzically and said: "If you had waited another minute, we'd have docked."

3449 Hard work never killed anybody, but why take a chance? (CHARLIE MCCARTHY/ EDGAR BERGEN)

3450 At a job interview, an office manager asked a female applicant whether she had any unusual talents. She said that she had won several prizes in crossword puzzle and slogan-writing competitions.

"That's very good," said the manager, "but we want somebody who can be smart during office hours."

"Oh," said the applicant, "that was during office hours."

3451 I used to sell furniture for a living. The trouble was, it was my own. (LES DAWSON)

3452 Boss: "Is there anything you can do that other people can't?"

Applicant: "Yes, I'm the only person that can read my handwriting."

3453 A businesswoman was explaining her delicate problem to a doctor. She told him she couldn't help passing wind, which was particularly embarrassing for her in board meetings.

"I just can't control myself," she said. "The only consolation is that they neither smell nor make a noise. In fact since I've been in your office talking to you, it's happened twice."

The doctor reached for his notebook, scribbled a prescription and handed it to her.

"What, nasal drops?" she said.

"Yes, we'll fix your nose, then we'll have a go at your hearing."

Comparisons between prison and work:

3454 In prison, you spend most of your time in an eight by ten cell.

At work, you spend most of your time in an eight by eight cubicle.

3455 In prison, you get three free meals a day.

At work, you get a break for one meal and you have to pay for it.

3456 In prison, you get time off for good behaviour.

At work, you get rewarded for good behaviour with more work.

3457 In prison, a guard locks and unlocks all the doors for you.

At work, you have to carry around a security card and unlock and open all the doors yourself.

3458 In prison, you can watch TV and play games.

At work, you get fired for watching TV and playing games.

3459 In prison, you get your own toilet.

At work, you have to share a toilet.

3460 In prison, they allow your family and friends to visit.

At work, you're not allowed to speak to your family and friends.

3461 In prison, all expenses are paid by the taxpayer with no work required.

At work, you get to pay all expenses to go to work and then taxes are deducted from your salary to pay for prisoners.

3462 In prison, you spend most of your life looking through bars from the inside wanting to get out.

At work, you spend most of your time wanting to get out and go inside bars.

3463 In prison, there are officers who are often sadistic.

At work, they're called managers.

3464 I was doing some decorating, so I got out my step-ladder; I don't get on with my real ladder. (HARRY HILL)

3465 The CIA were holding interviews for the post of assassin. They were looking for someone who was utterly ruthless and had narrowed the field down to three candidates – two men and a woman.

The first applicant was handed a gun and told: "In that room your wife is sitting in a chair. You must go in and shoot her."

The man said: "I'm sorry, I just can't do that, not to my own wife." He knew he had blown his chance of getting the job.

The second applicant was also handed a gun and told: "In that room your wife is sitting in a chair. You must go in and shoot her in cold blood."

The man looked horrified. "No way. I'm not gunning down my wife." And with that he walked out.

Finally it was the turn of the woman candidate. She too was handed a gun and told: "In that room your husband is sitting in a chair. You must go in and shoot him."

Without protest, the woman opened the door and went into the room. From outside, the CIA officials heard gunfire, followed by screams and a lot of banging. Eventually the woman reappeared. "You guys didn't tell me the gun was loaded with blanks," she complained. "I had to beat him to death with the chair!"

3466 I think Mr Smithers picked me for my motivational skills. Everyone always says they have to work twice as hard when I'm around. (HOMER SIMPSON)

3467 Four workers – an engineer, an accountant, a milkman and a civil servant – were discussing how smart their dogs were.

The engineer, said his dog – called Compass – could draw. The engineer told the dog to get some paper and draw a square, a circle and a triangle. The dog performed the task to perfection.

The accountant reckoned his dog, Balance, could do better. He told the dog to fetch a dozen cookies and divide them into piles of three. The dog did it without any problem.

The milkman was convinced that his dog, Bottle, could outsmart the other two. He told the dog to fetch a pint of milk and then pour exactly four ounces into a glass. The dog did it precisely.

All three men agreed that their dogs were equally smart and then they turned to the civil servant and asked him what his dog, Coffee Break, could do. The civil servant simply said: "Show 'em what you can do, boy." The dog strolled over, ate the cookies, drank the milk, crapped on the paper, screwed the other three dogs and claimed he injured his back in doing so. He then filed a grievance for unsafe conditions, applied for compensation and went home on sick leave.

3468 A young man went to the job centre and said: "I want a job where I can start at the top."

"I've got the very thing," said the clerk. "Grave digging."

3469 On a baking hot day, a nasty smell wafted around the office. Eventually one of the workforce said loudly: "Obviously someone's deodorant isn't working."

A guy in the corner shouted back: "Well, it can't be me because I'm not wearing any."

3470 Three guys went for a job interview. The personnel officer conducting the interviews had no ears. He told the first candidate: "This job calls for observations, so I want you to make an observation about me."

The first guy said: "You've got no ears."

The personnel officer was furious and threw him out.

The second guy entered and was also invited to make an observation.

"You've got no ears," he said.

The personnel officer went crazy and threw him out.

Then the third guy came in and he too was asked to make an observation.

"You wear contact lenses," he said.

"Wow!" said the personnel officer. "That's amazing. How did you know?"

"Because you've got no ears to hold up glasses."

3471 A man was given the job of painting white lines down the middle of the highway. On his first day, he painted six miles; on his second day, he did three miles; and on his third day, he painted less than a mile.

The foreman was not pleased. "How come you're doing less each day?" he demanded.

"Because each day I keep getting further away from the can of paint!"

Zoos

3472 Two middle-aged spinsters – Kay and Matilda – went to the zoo one afternoon. When they reached the gorilla enclosure, the gorilla suddenly pulled Matilda into his den and molested her.

A few weeks later, the two women met in the street. Kay asked Matilda how she was doing after the attack.

"Well, how do you think?" snapped Matilda. "He hasn't called, he hasn't written . . ."

3473 In the United States, what's the difference between a southern zoo and a northern zoo? – A southern zoo has a description of the animal on the front of the cage, along with a recipe.

3474 A husband and wife visited the zoo on a steaming hot day. When they stopped at the gorilla cage, the husband could see that the gorilla was getting aroused by the sight of the wife's nipples through her blouse.

"Look," said the husband, "he's really getting worked up. Why don't you take off your blouse and see what he does?"

The wife was reluctant at first but eventually agreed. As she took off her blouse, the gorilla went ape and started jumping up and down and throwing his food bowl around.

"Wow!" said the husband. "That was pretty impressive. He obviously fancies you. Now let's see what he does if you strip off completely."

Again the wife hesitated but, since there was nobody about, she eventually agreed to take off all her clothes. As she stood there stark naked, the gorilla began pounding his chest in a display of masculinity and then started banging on the bars of his cage. Suddenly the husband opened the door of the cage and pushed the wife inside.

"Right," he said, "now tell him you've got a headache!"

3475 A baby camel turned to its father and said: "Dad, why do we have humps on our back?"

"Well, son," replied the father, "our humps contain the fat necessary to sustain us through all the days when we're out in the desert."

"Oh," said the baby camel. "Dad, why do we have long eyelashes?"

"They're to protect our eyes from the sandstorms which rage in the desert."

"Fine. Dad, why do we have big padded feet?"

"Because the sand in the desert is very soft and we need big feet so that we can walk on the sand without sinking."

"Thanks, Dad. So what are we doing in London Zoo?"

3476 A police officer saw a truck being driven erratically. On closer inspection, he noticed that there were 140 penguins on the back seat of the truck and pulled the driver over for unlawful possession of animals. But when the driver explained that he was taking the penguins to the zoo, the officer relented.

"OK, I'll let you off this time, so long as you are definitely taking them to the zoo."

The following day, the officer saw the same truck weaving along the road, and once again there were 140 penguins on the back seat. He stopped the truck and said to the driver: "I thought you told me yesterday you were taking the penguins to the zoo."

"I was," said the driver. "And today I'm taking them to a theme park."

3477 Needing a star attraction for the summer, a cash-strapped zoo persuaded a visitor to dress up in a gorilla costume and pretend to be a great ape. The ruse worked well as the man threw himself into the role with great enthusiasm, devouring bucket loads of bananas, prowling his cage with menace and banging his chest dramatically. But then one day, he went too far and accidentally fell into the lion cage next door.

"Help! Help!" cried the fake gorilla.

The lion let out an almighty roar, then rushed at him, put his paw on the gorilla's chest and growled: "Shut up, or we'll both lose our jobs!"

Part 2
MISCELLANEOUS

BUMPER STICKERS

These have been seen on vehicles around the world:

3478 Be alert. The world needs more lerts.

3479 If you can read this, I've lost my caravan.

3480 Go ahead and honk, I'm reloading.

3481 If you don't like the way I drive, get off the sidewalk!

3482 So many pedestrians, so little time.

3483 Veni, Vidi, Visa: I came, I saw, I did a little shopping.

3484 Veni, Vidi, Video: I came, I saw, I got it on tape.

3485 Veni, Vidi, Velcro: I came, I saw, I stuck around.

3486 Veni, Vidi, VD: I came, I saw, I cankered.

3487 Veni, Vidi, Icky: I came, I saw, I felt sick.

3488 Veni, Vidi, Vicky: I came, I saw, I got a talk show.

3489 Kids in the back seat cause accidents; accidents in the back seat cause kids.

3490 This car will explode upon impact.

3491 Jesus is coming, look busy!

3492 I've found Jesus — he's in my trunk.

3493 Make love not war — see driver for details.

3494 I Killed Kenny!

3495 Traffic wardens eat their young.

3496 I love my wife — and for 25 dollars you can too.

3497 I love animals, especially in gravy.

3498 Born again pagan.

3499 Gone crazy: back soon.

3500 Money is the route to all evil — send 9.95 dollars for more info.

3501 Horn broken, watch for finger.

3502 Honk if the twins fall out.

3503 Support your local Search and Rescue unit. Get lost.

3504 Minimum wage for politicians.

3505 Madness takes its toll. Please have exact change.

3506 Today is the day for decisive action. Or is it?

3507 10,000 sperm and you were the fastest?

3508 Mafia staff car.

3509 A waist is a terrible thing to mind.

3510 Abandon the search for truth; settle for a good fantasy.

3511 Give blood . . . play hockey.

3512 Diarrhoea is hereditary — it runs in your genes.

3513 To all you virgins — thanks for nothing.

3514 OK, so God made heaven and earth. But what has he done recently?

3515 Atheism is a non-prophet organization.

3516 Eat a prune and start a movement.

3517 Welcome to Utah! Set your watch back 20 years.

3518 Pigs may fly – this one drives.

3519 I'm a dyslexic Satanist – I worship the drivel.

3520 Procrastinate now!

3521 I took an IQ test – it came back negative.

3522 My wife keeps complaining I never listen to her . . . or something like that.

3523 Now that you're on my ass, you wanna get married?

3524 It's not pretty being easy.

3525 Viagra – the gift that keeps on coming.

3526 OK, who's been messing with my anti-paranoia medication?

3527 Pretend to spank me – I'm a pseudo-masochist!

3528 That's not a haircut – it's a cry for help.

3529 Feel safe tonight – sleep with a cop.

3530 My other wife is beautiful.

3531 I wouldn't be caught dead with a necrophiliac.

3532 Adrenalin is my drug of choice.

3533 I suffer from a sexually transmitted disease – children.

3534 I'm not in heat so get off my tail.

3535 When the going gets tough, the tough go shopping.

3536 Madam: welcome to the palindrome.

3537 Take an interest in your husband's activities – hire a detective.

3538 Ssssh. The driver is sleeping.

3539 Spelling is a lossed art.

3540 Proofread carefully to see if you any words out.

3541 Practise safe sex – go screw yourself.

3542 Forget the Joneses, I can't keep up with the Simpsons!

3543 Want a taste of religion? Bite a minister.

3544 Adults are just kids with money.

3545 There's no future in time travel.

3546 Mind like a steel trap – rusty and illegal in 37 states.

3547 Déjà flu: the feeling that somehow, somewhere, you've been kicked in the head like this before.

3548 Half the people you know are below average.

3549 My kid got inmate of the month award at the county jail.

3550 I planned to live forever – so far so good.

3551 Trust in God – but lock your car.

3552 Marriage is not a word – it's a sentence.

3553 I'm pink, therefore I'm Spam.

3554 Avoid hangovers. Stay drunk.

3555 Corduroy pillows – they're making headlines!

3556 Photons have mass? I didn't know they were Catholic!

3557 Hypochondria is the one disease I haven't got.

3558 Air pollution is a mist-demeanour.

3559 51 per cent love goddess, 49 per cent bitch. Care to push your luck?

3560 People who think they know everything are a great annoyance to those of us who do.

3561 If you don't believe in oral sex, keep your mouth shut.

3562 Stupidity is not a crime so you're free to go.

3563 Preserve nature – pickle a squirrel.

3564 Say no to shampoo – demand real poo.

3565 Prevent interbreeding – ban country music.

3566 Please tell your pants it's not polite to point.

3567 To err is human, to forgive is against company policy.

3568 Save the whales – collect the whole set.

3569 Buckle up – it makes it harder for the aliens to suck you out of your car.

3570 I'd kill for a Nobel Peace Prize.

3571 Wear short sleeves – support your right to bare arms!

3572 Of all the things I've lost, I miss my mind the most.

3573 Heck was created for those who refuse to believe in Gosh.

3574 I want to die in my sleep like my grandfather . . . not screaming and yelling like the passengers in his car.

3575 Beer, helping people have sex since 1865.

3576 Too close for missiles, switching to guns.

3577 Skydiving – good till the last drop.

3578 We're not old people, we're recycled teenagers.

3579 If that phone was up your ass, maybe you could drive better.

3580 I still miss my ex . . . but my aim is getting better.

3581 To err is human, to moo bovine.

3582 I didn't believe in reincarnation in the last life, why should I in this?

3583 Gun control means using both hands.

3584 Cleverly disguised as a responsible adult.

3585 Good cowgirls keep their calves together.

3586 A man needs a mistress, just to break the monogamy.

3587 What rear-view mirror?

3588 If ignorance is bliss, you must be orgasmic.

3589 I love to give home-made gifts – which one of my kids do you want?

3590 The earth is full – go home.

3591 I bet you I could stop gambling.

3592 I used to have a handle on life, but it broke.

3593 Very funny, Scotty. Now beam down my clothes.

3594 Out of my mind – back in five minutes.

3595 Coincidence is when God chooses to remain anonymous.

3596 This car protected by Smith and Wesson.

3597 Caution! Driver applying make-up.

3598 If it's not one thing, it's your mother.

3599 I'm not a complete idiot – some parts are missing.

3600 Five out of four people have trouble with fractions.

3601 The face is familiar but I can't quite remember my name.

3602 He who hesitates is not only lost, but miles from the next exit.

3603 I don't suffer from insanity – I enjoy every minute of it.

3604 Ex-wife in trunk.

3605 Dr Kevorkian can fit you in next Monday.

3606 If you lived in a car, you'd be home by now.

3607 I wouldn't touch the metric system with a 3.048 metre pole.

3608 Ask not what you can do for me – just do it!

3609 Never mind the dog – Beware of owner!

3610 I refuse to have a battle of wits with an unarmed person.

3611 Go ahead and hit me. I need the money.

3612 This car is constipated: it hasn't passed a thing all day.

3613 My wife's other car is a broom.

3614 Drugs may lead to nowhere, but at least it's the scenic route.

3615 You! Out of the gene pool!

3616 I fought the lawn and the lawn won.

3617 Funny, I don't remember being absent-minded.

3618 My karma ran over your dogma.

3619 Minds are like parachutes – they only function when open.

3620 I tried to daydream but my mind kept wandering.

3621 Evacuate the road – student driving!

3622 Bush/Cheney '04: making the world a better place, one country at a time.

3623 Where are we going and why am I in this handbasket?

3624 Honk once if you're Jesus – twice if you're Elvis.

3625 Incontinence hotline. Can you hold, please?

3626 If it's too loud, you're too old.

3627 Smile and the world smiles with you, fart and you stand alone.

3628 It's been lovely, but I have to scream now.

3629 I haven't lost my mind – it's backed up on disk somewhere.

3630 I'm straight: don't rear end me.

3631 Grow your own dope: plant a man.

3632 Fight crime: shoot back.

3633 Inflation is when the buck doesn't stop anywhere.

3634 I get enough exercise just pushing my luck.

3635 If you think I'm a lousy driver, wait till you see me putt.

3636 Don't piss me off, I'm running out of places to hide the bodies.

3637 Wanted: meaningful overnight relationship.

3638 I is a college student

3639 Get even — live long enough to be a problem to your children.

3640 Necrophilia — that uncontrollable urge to crack open a cold one.

3641 Conserve trees — eat a beaver.

3642 Lead me not into temptation — I can find it myself.

3643 Boldly going nowhere.

3644 I'm not as dumb as you look.

3645 Cover me. I'm changing lanes.

3646 All men are animals — some just make better pets.

3647 Ambivalent? Well, yes and no.

3648 Born free . . . taxed to death.

3649 Don't be sexist — broads hate that.

3650 I just got lost in thought. It was unfamiliar territory.

3651 I brake for scholars, priests, and no apparent reason.

3652 Be naughty — save Santa the trip.

3653 Beauty is only skin deep. Ugly goes straight to the bone.

3654 Disney World — a people trap operated by a mouse.

3655 When you do a good deed, get a receipt in case heaven is like the IRS.

3656 All things being equal, fat people use more soap.

3657 A man with worms is never alone.

3658 If it weren't for people like you, nobody else would have an above average IQ.

3659 Sex on TV can't hurt unless you fall off.

3660 Heart attacks — God's revenge for eating his animal friends.

3661 Who lit the fuse on your tampon?

3662 Don't take my signals literally.

3663 If you can read this, the bitch fell off.

3664 Rainy days and automatic weapons always get me down.

3665 Spell-checkers are hear two stay.

3666 Take me drunk occifer, I'm home.

3667 How many roads must a man travel down before he admits he is lost?

3668 We are the people your parents warned you about.

3669 Stop repeat offenders — don't re-elect them!

3670 Biology grows on you.

3671 Be safety conscious: 85 per cent of people are caused by accidents.

3672 My mother was a travel agent for guilt trips.

3673 Rap is to music what Etch-a-Sketch is to art.

3674 So you're a feminist. Isn't that cute?

3675 I can only please one person per day. Today is not your day and tomorrow doesn't look good either.

3676 A balanced diet is a cookie in each hand.

3677 Husbands are proof that women have a sense of humour.

3678 If you can't dazzle them with brilliance, riddle them with bullets.

3679 I didn't work my way to the top of the food chain to eat vegetables.

3680 Always remember – you're unique, just like everyone else.

3681 I love cats – they taste just like chicken.

3682 A husband is someone who takes out the trash and gives the impression he just cleaned the whole house.

3683 I can go from zero to bitch in 2.2 seconds.

3684 My brain just hit a bad sector.

3685 Hug your kids at home and belt them in the car.

3686 I'm as confused as a baby in a topless bar.

3687 Money isn't everything, but it sure keeps the kids in touch.

3688 I have PMS and a handgun. Any questions?

3689 Forget about world peace – visualize using your turn signal.

3690 We're staying together for the sake of our web site.

3691 I brake for hallucinations.

3692 Alcohol and calculus don't mix: Don't Drink and Derive.

3693 I'm not a vegetarian because I love animals, but because I hate plants.

3694 Support your local undertaker – DROP DEAD.

3695 Earn cash in your spare time – blackmail friends.

3696 I phoned the bondage helpline but all the operators were tied up.

3697 Drive defensively – buy a tank.

3698 It's lonely at the top, but you eat better.

3699 Hogwarts Dropout.

3700 Spare the fenders, save the trees, give your sober friend the keys.

3701 Give a man an inch and he thinks he's a ruler.

3702 Niagara Falls and Viagra Rises.

3703 She was only a moonshiner but I loved her still.

3704 Join the army, meet interesting people, kill them.

3705 Use caution in passing – driver chewing tobacco.

3706 Never, never, never, never repeat.

3707 My mother-in-law's web site is http://www.realwitch.com.

3708 Lost your cat? Look under my tyres.

3709 Born again voodooist.

3710 My dog Minton swallowed a shuttlecock – Bad Minton.

3711 On the other hand, you have different fingers.

3712 Don't honk – I'm pedalling as fast as I can.

3713 Love may be blind, but marriage is a real eye-opener.

3714 Warning: I have an attitude and I know how to use it.

3715 Flies spread disease. Keep yours closed.

3716 If the voices in my head paid rent, I wouldn't be broke.

3717 Mean people suck – nice people swallow.

3718 Next mood swing: six minutes.

3719 The sex was so good that even the neighbours had a cigarette.

3720 Don't drink and drive – if you hit a bump you spill your beer.

3721 Due to budget cuts, the light at the end of the tunnel will be out.

3722 Monday is a hell of a way to spend one-seventh of your life.

3723 Do Not Wash – this vehicle is undergoing a scientific dirt test.

3724 Ever stop to think, and forget to start again?

3725 I hate everybody and you're next.

3726 I used to be schizophrenic, but we're OK now.

3727 We're staying together for the sake of the cats.

3728 This car is like my husband – if it ain't yours don't touch it!

3729 Money can't buy love. But it can rent a very close imitation.

3730 Dyslexics of the world . . . UNTIE!

3731 Don't come knocking if the car is rocking.

CELEBRITIES' FAVOURITE JOKES

Woody Allen

3732 A guy went to a ranch to buy a horse. The animal looked good, but before selling it the owner warned: "I have to tell you one thing. He's got a bad habit. He likes to sit on grapefruits."

"And that's the only thing wrong with him?" asked the guy.

The owner said it was, and the deal was done.

So the guy took the horse home and they were crossing a stream when suddenly the horse sat down and wouldn't get up. The guy didn't know what to do and ran back to the ranch where he'd bought it.

"I bought a horse from you – you told me there was one thing wrong, that he likes to sit on grapefruits. Now he's sitting in the middle of a stream and I can't get him to move."

The old owner said: "Oh, I forgot to tell you. He also likes to sit on fish."

Tony Blair

3733 A man walked into a bar with a piece of tarmac over his shoulder and said to the bartender: "I'll have a pint of beer please and one for the road."

David Bowie

3734 What do you call a beautiful girl on a trombonist's arm? – A tattoo.

Jo Brand

3735 An overweight guy went to the doctor who advised him to try a keep fit video. But the guy said he couldn't be bothered. "Well," suggested the doctor, "try something that leaves you a little short of breath." So the guy took up smoking.

Gyles Brandreth

3736 What is the difference between the erotic and the perverse? With the erotic, you take a feather and use it tenderly, delicately, teasingly, playfully. You trace designs with it, and use it to play with your lover. With the perverse, you use the whole chicken.

Sir Richard Branson

3737 A Virgin Atlantic flight attendant was stationed at the departure gate to check tickets. As a man approached, she extended her hand for the ticket and he opened his trench coat and flashed her. Without missing a beat she said: "Sir, I asked to see your ticket, not your stub."

Marcus Brigstocke

3738 An inflatable boy goes to his inflatable school one day with a pin. He sees the inflatable headmaster walking towards him and pokes him with the pin. Sick of school, he then pokes the inflatable school with the pin. Finally he pokes himself with the pin. The headmaster tells him gravely: "You've let me down, you've let the school down, but worst of all you've let yourself down."

Basil Brush

3739 Why did the one-armed man cross the road? – To get to the second-hand shop.

Sandra Bullock

3740 A magician worked on a cruise ship in the Caribbean. The audience was different each week, so he did the same tricks over and over again. But the captain's parrot soon worked out how the tricks were done and began heckling "the card's up his sleeve" or "look behind his back". The magician was furious because the bird was ruining his act. Then one day there was an accident and the ship sank. The magician found himself floating in the middle of the ocean on a piece of wood, along with the parrot. The two enemies sat in stony silence for three days until, on the fourth day, the parrot couldn't hold back any longer. "Ok, I give up," he squawked. "Where's the boat?"

George W. Bush

3741 When I play golf, the only time I ever hit two good balls is when I step on a rake.

George Clooney

3742 A guy in a bar was so drunk he threw up all over himself. He said to the bartender: "When I go home, my wife's going to kill me."

So the bartender put $20 in the guy's shirt pocket and said: "Go home and tell your wife that a drunk threw up all over you and gave you $20 to get your shirt cleaned."

When he got home, his wife yelled: "Look at the state of you! You threw up all over yourself!"

The guy explained: "Honey, this drunk threw up on me but he put $20 in my shirt pocket."

The wife reached in and pulled out $40. "What's the other $20 for?" she demanded.

"He shit in my pants, too!"

John Corbett

3743 A guy was driving down the road when he saw a sign that said: "Talking Dog For Sale: Two Miles Ahead." So he pulled up at this little farmhouse, the farmer came out and the guy said: "I saw your sign, Talking Dog For Sale."

The farmer said: "The dog's around the back."

The guy went around the back and there was a collie in a cage. The dog said: "How you doing?"

The guy said: "Not bad, you?"

The dog said: "Hey I'm doing pretty good. I saved a family of six from a house fire last week. Pulled them all out. Even a little baby."

The guy was amazed. "Hold on," he said. "I'll be right back." The guy went over to the farmer and said: "That's the most incredible thing I've ever seen in my life. Why are you selling him?"

The farmer replied: "Cos that dog's a goddamned liar!"

Senator Jon Corzine

3744 What did the number 0 say to the number 8? — "Nice belt!"

Courteney Cox

3745 Four Catholic ladies were having coffee. The first said: "My son's a priest. When he walks into a room, everyone calls him 'Father.'"

The second lady said: "My son's a bishop. When he walks into a room, they say, 'Your Grace.'"

The third lady said: "My son's a cardinal. When he walks into a room, they say, 'Your Eminence.'"

The fourth lady sipped her coffee in silence.

"Well?" asked the other three.

Finally she said: "My son is 6ft 2in tall, wealthy, and gorgeous. When he walks into a room, people say, 'Oh my God!'"

Barry Cryer

3746 A man was driving down a country lane and ran over a cockerel. He went to the farmhouse and a woman answered the door. He said: "I appear to have killed your cockerel — I would like to replace him."

"Please yourself," she said. "The hens are round the back."

David Duchovny

3747 A cop stopped a young woman for speeding and asked her if she'd show him her driving licence. Huffily she replied: "I wish you guys would make up your mind. Just yesterday you take away my licence, then today you expect me to show it to you!"

Nick Faldo

3748 Mary Poppins went into a restaurant and ordered cauliflower cheese. The owner was so pleased to have her as a guest that he asked: "Will you sign the visitors' book and will you also write what you thought of my food?"

She signed her name in the book and added: "Super cauliflower cheese but eggs were quite atrocious!"

Anna Friel

3749 What do you call a lesbian dinosaur? — A lickalotopus.

Melissa George

3750 A blonde went into a library and said: "Hi, can I have a vodka and tonic?"

The librarian said: "Sorry, but this is a library."

So the blonde whispered: "Can I have a vodka and tonic?"

Dave Gorman

3751 What's black and white and eats like a horse? – A zebra.

Stuart Hall

3752 700 US soldiers have entered Jordan. George W. Bush is furious; he wants to know what she was doing there.

Anne Hathaway

3753 A rough-looking woman was sitting at a bar. She had the hairiest armpits so that whenever she raised her arm to order a drink, a mass of hair was visible to all her fellow drinkers. At closing time, a drunk at the far end of the bar pointed to the woman and said to the bartender: "I'd like to buy the ballerina a drink."

"She's not a ballerina," said the bartender. "What makes you think she's a ballerina?"

The drunk replied: "Any girl that can lift her leg that high has to be a ballerina!"

Dustin Hoffman

3754 A little boy was playing with his train set. His mum was suddenly startled as she listened to him playing. "All aboard for San Francisco," he said. "Anyone who wants to get off the train, then get the fuck off! Anyone who wants to get on the train, then get the fuck on!" Moments later she heard him say: "All aboard for Los Angeles! Anyone who wants toget off the train, then get the fuck off! Anyone who wants to get on the train, then get the fuck on!"

The mother was very upset and sent him to his room. After an hour, the little boy was allowed to play again but was told that he must not use bad language. The mother listened closely as he started to play again. "All aboard for California! Anyone who wants to get off the train, then get off! Anyone who wants to get on the train, then get on! And if you want to know why the train is an hour late, then ask the c**t in the kitchen!"

Jude Law

3755 A guy had a huge boil on his ass. He went to his doctor who said there was nothing he could do about it and referred him to a specialist. The specialist couldn't help either but wrote down the name and address of someone who might be able to. The guy traced the address to a ramshackle old building in the docks. On the door it said: "Peter Pus-sucker". Inside was an old timer with only one tooth.

"Drop your pants," said Peter.

The guy dropped his pants to reveal the huge boil on his ass.

"OK," said Peter. "Bend over. What I'm going to do is bite into this boil and suck out the poison — it's the only thing we can do."

So the guy bent over, and Peter had just started sucking out the poison when the guy farted in his face. Peter stood up and yelled: "Jesus, man! Blokes like you make this job disgusting!"

Jon Lovitz

3756 A Polish couple were having dinner with their kids who were aged five and six. The husband said to the wife: "Hey, honey, maybe after dinner we could send the kids out to a M-O-V-I-E, so we can go upstairs and fuck."

Matthew McConaughey

3757 A farmer named Muldoon lived alone with his beloved dog. When the dog died, Muldoon went to the parish priest and said: "Father, my dog is dead. Could ya be saying a Mass for the creature?"

The priest replied: "I'm afraid not. We cannot have services for an animal in the church, but there's a new denomination down the road, and there's no telling what they believe. Maybe they'll do something for the creature."

Muldoon said: "I'll go right away. Do you think $5,000 is enough to donate for such a service?"

The priest exclaimed: "Glory be to God! Why didn't ya tell me the dog was Catholic?"

Mike Malinin, Goo Goo Dolls

3758 What do a bunch of grapes and an elephant have in common? —They both have trunks. Except for the grapes.

Bernard Manning

3759 I went to see Pavarotti sing last week. Terrible, miserable man. He doesn't like you joining in, does he?

Chris Moyles

3760 A guy was walking past a suit shop when he saw a suit he really liked. He went in to try it on but wasn't really sure. He went back the next day, taking a friend with him to see what she thought of the suit. As he stood outside and pointed at the suit, the guy said: "That's the one I'd get." And a cyclops, who was walking past, went over and hit him.

Suzi Perry

3761 Just got back from B & Q. Some bloke in an orange apron asked if I wanted decking. Luckily, I got the first punch in.

Raj Persaud

3762 How many psychoanalysts does it take to change a lightbulb? – Two, one to change the lightbulb and one to hold the penis, sorry ladder . . . don't know why I keep making that slip.

Mark Radcliffe

3763 A guy was stranded on a desert island with Michelle Pfeiffer. At first, she tried to keep her distance but, out of sheer loneliness, the relationship became physical and for the next four months they enjoyed fantastic sex.

Then one day the guy said to her: "Can I borrow your eyebrow pencil?" Michelle was surprised, all the more so when he then asked: "Can I use it to draw a moustache on you?"

"I suppose so," she said warily. So he drew a moustache on her.

Then he said: "Will you wear some of my clothes?" Michelle thought it a bit weird, but reluctantly agreed. So he got her to put on an old check shirt and trousers.

Then he said: "Would you mind if I called you Frank?" By now, Michelle was really fed up with this apparent change in their relationship, but she went along with it. "OK, I guess you can call me Frank," she said.

Then he grabbed her by the arm and said: "Hey, Frank, you'll never guess who I'm shagging!"

Gordon Ramsay

3764 Three middle-aged women died and went to heaven. As they reached the Pearly Gates, Angel Gabriel appeared and welcomed them. "You will have a great time here," he said. "Just ensure one thing. Never tread on any of the ducks." The three women entered and saw at once what Angel Gabriel meant because everywhere there were ducks.

The next day one of the middle-aged women trod on a duck and before she could say anything Angel Gabriel appeared with the ugliest man this unfortunate woman had ever seen. "I told you not to tread on a duck," said Angel Gabriel, "and your punishment is to be chained to this very ugly man forever."

A week later another of the middle-aged women accidentally trod on a duck. Immediately Angel Gabriel appeared at her side with another very ugly man and said: "I told you not to tread on a duck. Your punishment is to be chained to this very ugly man forever."

The third middle-aged woman was so traumatized by this that she took great care not to tread on any ducks. Then after three months the Angel Gabriel turned up with the most amazing looking guy. Big pecs, oiled body and a full head of hair. The woman asked Angel Gabriel hopefully: "Am I to be chained to this man forever?"

"Yes," replied Angel Gabriel. "You are. He trod on a duck."

Ellen Reid, Crash Test Dummies

3765 Two cows were standing in a field. One said to the other: "Are you scared about all of this Mad Cow business?"

"Nope."

"How come you're not scared?"

"Because I'm a chicken."

Joely Richardson

3766 A vicar, a priest and a rabbi walked into a bar. The bartender said: "What is this, a joke?"

Joan Rivers

3767 I wanted to do something special for my husband, so I got dressed up in nothing but saran wrap [clingfilm]. When I answered the door he took one look at me and said: "Leftovers again!"

Chris Rock

3768 A woman accosted me on the street and said that for $200 she would do anything I wanted, anything at all. I said: "Bitch, paint my house!"

David Schwimmer

3769 A traffic cop was waiting outside a popular bar at closing time hoping for a bust. As everyone came out, he spotted a potential quarry — a guy so drunk that he could barely walk. The officer watched the guy stumbling around the parking lot for a few minutes looking for his car. After trying his keys on five other cars, he finally found his own vehicle. He turned his lights on, then off; he started to pull forward, then stalled. When his was the last car in the lot, he carefully pulled on to the road and began to drive home. Seizing his opportunity, the cop pulled him over and told him to breathe into the breathalyzer bag but to his amazement, the test was negative.

"I don't understand it," said the cop. "The equipment must be broken."

"No it isn't," said the guy. "You see, I'm the designated decoy."

Chris Tarrant

3770 Mahatma Gandhi walked barefoot most of the time, which produced an impressive set of calluses on his feet. He also ate very little, which made him rather frail and, with his odd diet, he suffered from bad breath. This made him a super calloused fragile mystic hexed by halitosis.

Alan Titchmarsh

3771 A small child was asked by his teacher to compose a sentence which included the word 'diadem'. He offered: "Children who don't look before they cross the road diadem sight sooner than those who do."

Lars Ullrich, Metallica

3772 What has three legs and a prick on top of it? – A drum stool.

Jonathan Wilkes

3773 What's worse than a bull in a china shop? – A hedgehog in a condom factory.

COLLECTIVE NOUNS

Here are some suggestions for new collective nouns:

3774 An absence of waiters.

3775 An ambush of widows.

3776 An assemblage of jigsaw puzzlers.

3777 An attitude of teenagers.

3778 A bevy of alcoholics.

3779 A billow of smokers.

3780 A chapter of authors.

3781 A charm of politicians.

3782 A clamour of journalists.

3783 A click of computer mice.

3784 A clipping of geldings.

3785 A clutch of kleptomaniacs.

3786 A cupful of starlets.

3787 A density of meatheads.

3788 A disputation of lawyers.

3789 A dose of doctors.

3790 A drove of cabbies.

3791 An embarrassment of parents.

3792 A fidget of suspects.

3793 A flood of plumbers.

3794 A flunk of students.

3795 A fold of chairs.

3796 A formation of geologists.

3797 A freeze of Eskimos.

3798 A fright of ghosts.

3799 A galaxy of chocoholics.

3800 A geek of train-spotters.

3801 A giggle of schoolgirls.

3802 A gossip of relatives.

3803 A groan of puns.

3804 A gross of farts.

3805 A handful of palm readers.

3806 A heard of town criers.

3807 A hoard of misers.

3808 A hug of teddy bears.

3809 An imposition of in-laws.

3810 An incantation of witches.

3811 An incision of surgeons.

3812 An indecision of managers.

3813 A jam of tarts.

3814 A knuckle of gangsters.

3815 A magnum of hitmen.

3816 A mass of Catholics.

3817 A maul of bears.

3818 A murder of crime writers.

3819 A nag of women.

3820 A number of mathematicians.

3821 A pack of holidaymakers.

3822 A plump of weightwatchers.

3823 A ponder of philosophers.

3824 A pod of vegetarians.

3825 A prevarication of consultants.

3826 A pride of actors.

3827 A rhyme of poets.

3828 A screech of mothers-in-law.

3829 A shortage of dwarves.

3830 A skulk of foxes.

3831 A smarm of game show hosts.

3832 A snap of photographers.

3833 A snatch of muggers.

3834 A swarm of sycophants.

3835 A treachery of spies.

3836 A volume of scientists.

3837 A wave of surfers.

COMIC DICTIONARY

3838 Absentee – A missing golf peg.

3839 Accordion – A bagpipe with pleats.

3840 Accountant – A man hired to explain that you didn't make the money you did.

3841 Acquaintance – A person whom we know well enough to borrow from, but not well enough to lend to.

3842 Adamant – The very first insect.

3843 Admiration – Our polite recognition of another's resemblance to ourselves.

3844 Adolescence – The stage between puberty and adultery.

3845 Adorn – What comes after the darkest hour.

3846 Adult – Someone who has stopped growing at both ends and started growing in the middle.

3847 Advertising – Makes you think you've longed all your life for something you've never even heard of before.

3848 Afternoon – The part of the day spent working out how you wasted the morning.

3849 Airhead – What a woman intentionally becomes when pulled over by a traffic cop.

3850 Alarms – What an octopus is.

3851 Alcohol – A liquid good for preserving almost anything except secrets.

3852 Alimony – The cost of loving.

3853 Americans – People with more time-saving devices yet less time than anybody else in the world.

3854 Amnesia – Condition that enables a woman who has gone through labour to have sex again.

3855 Announce – One-sixteenth of a pound.

3856 Antique – An object that has made a round-trip to the attic and back.

3857 Appellate – Hamster food.

3858 Archaeologist – Someone whose career is in ruins.

3859 Architect – One who drafts a plan of your house, and plans a draft of your money.

3860 Archive – Where Noah kept his bees.

3861 Armour – Clothing worn by someone whose tailor is a blacksmith.

3862 Aromatic – Auto pilot for archers.

3863 Arraign – Stormy weather.

3864 Autobiography – A car's log book.

3865 Automobile – A mechanical device that runs up hills and down people.

3866 Autopsy – A dying practice.

3867 Baby – A loud noise at one end and no sense of responsibility at the other.

3868 Bachelor – A man who prefers to ball without the chain.

3869 Bacteria – Back door to the cafeteria.

3870 Balderdash – A rapidly receding hairline.

3871 Baldness – When you have less hair to comb but more face to wash.

3872 Baloney – Where some hemlines fall.

3873 Barbecue – A wait at the hairdresser's.

3874 Barium – What doctors do when the treatment fails.

3875 Baseball – Twelve minutes of excitement crammed into two and a half hours.

3876 Beauty – The power by which a woman charms a lover and terrifies a husband.

3877 Book – A utensil used to pass time while waiting for the computer repairman.

3878 Bookmaker – A pickpocket who lets you use your own hands.

3879 Bore – A man who, when asked how he is, tells you.

3880 Boy – A noise with dirt on it.

3881 Brain – The apparatus with which we think that we think.

3882 Bride – A woman with a fine prospect of happiness behind her.

3883 Broadband – Musical group of female gender.

3884 Budget – A family's attempt to live below its yearnings.

3885 Businessman – One who talks golf all morning at the office and business all afternoon on the links.

3886 Calendar – Something that goes in one year and out the other.

3887 Cannibal – Someone who is fed up with people: one who loves his fellow man . . . with gravy.

3888 Cantaloupe – Having to get married in church.

3889 Capitalism – Survival of the fattest.

3890 Carefully – Variety of cheese made to exacting standards.

3891 Catalyst – Several cows' names written in alphabetical order.

3892 Chef – A cook with a large hat and a head to fill it.

3893 Chicken – A creature you eat before its born and after its dead.

3894 Children – Creatures who disgrace you by exhibiting in public the example you set for them at home.

3895 Christmas – Holiday in which neither the past nor the future is of as much interest as the present.

3896 Circumspection – Inspection after the circumcision.

3897 Coach – One who is always willing to lay down your life for his job.

3898 Cocktail party – A gathering where you spear olives and stab friends.

3899 Coffee – A person who is coughed upon.

3900 Cognition – That which is used to start your brain in the morning.

3901 College dean – A man who doesn't know enough to be a professor, but who is too smart to be a president.

3902 College professor– Someone who talks in other people's sleep.

3903 Committee – A group of the unwilling, chosen from the unfit, to do the unnecessary.

3904 Commuter – A traveller who pays short visits to home and the office.

3905 Computer – A device designed to speed up and automate errors.

3906 Conclusion – The place where you get tired of thinking.

3907 Condescend – A prisoner escaping down the wall using a rope.

3908 Confidence – That quiet assured feeling you have before you fall flat on your face.

3909 Connoisseur – A specialist who knows everything about something and nothing about anything else.

3910 Conscience – What hurts when all your other parts feel great.

3911 Consciousness – That annoying time between naps.

3912 Constipation – To have and to hold.

3913 Consultant– Someone who takes the watch off your wrist and tells you the time.

3914 Cosmetics – A woman's means for keeping a man from reading between the lines.

3915 Court of law– A place where a suit is pressed and a man may be taken to the cleaners.

3916 Courtship – The period during which the girl decides whether or not she can do any better.

3917 Coward – One who in a perilous emergency thinks with his legs.

3918 Dancing – A perpendicular expression of a horizontal desire.

3919 Dentist – One who, while putting metal into your mouth, pulls coins out of your pocket.

3920 Depression – Anger without the enthusiasm.

3921 Dermatologist – One who makes rash judgments.

3922 Diagnosis – The physician's art of determining the condition of the patient's purse in order to find out how sick to make him.

3923 Dictionary – The only place where divorce comes before marriage.

3924 Diet – A short period of starvation followed by a gain of five pounds.

3925 Dilate – To live long.

3926 Diplomacy – Lying in state.

3927 Diplomat – An ex-politician who has mastered the art of holding his tongue.

3928 Disarmament – Agreement between nations to get rid of all weapons that are obsolete.

3929 Divorce – The screwing you get for the screwing you got: the transformation from a duet to a duel.

3930 Dockyard – A physician's garden.

3931 Dreadlocks – The fear of opening the dead-bolt.

3932 Dust – Mud with the juice squeezed out.

3933 Dynamite – Take a flea out to dinner.

3934 Easy – A term used to describe a woman who has the sexual morals of a man.

3935 Echo – The only thing that can cheat a woman out of the last word.

3936 Economist – Someone who works with numbers but doesn't have the personality to be an accountant.

3937 Efficiency expert – Someone smart enough to tell you how to run a business but too smart to start his own.

3938 Egotist – Someone who is usually me-deep in conversation.

3939 Epitaph – A belated advertisement for a line of goods that has been permanently discontinued.

3940 Executive – An ulcer with authority.

3941 Experience – The name men give to their mistakes.

3942 Extradition – More maths homework.

3943 Eyedropper – Clumsy ophthalmologist.

3944 Fad – Something that goes in one era and out the other.

3945 Faucet – What you do when the tap won't turn on.

3946 Feedback – The result when a baby doesn't appreciate the strained carrots.

3947 Fib – A lie that has not cut its teeth.

3948 Fisherman – A jerk on one end of the line waiting for a jerk on the other end.

3949 Flabbergasted – Amazed at how much weight you've gained.

3950 Flattery – An insult in gift wrapping.

3951 Flatulence – The effect of sitting on your glasses.

3952 Friend – A person who dislikes the same people you do.

3953 Friendship – A ship big enough to carry two in fair weather, but only one in foul.

3954 Funeral director – A guy who tries to look sad during a 10,000 dollars funeral.

3955 Gambling – The sure way of getting nothing for something.

3956 Genius – Someone who is a crackpot until he hits the jackpot.

3957 Gentleman – A man who, when his wife drops her knitting, kicks it over to her so that she can easily pick it up.

3958 Glutton – Someone who eats the slice of cake you wanted.

3959 Golf ball– A sphere made of rubber bands wound up about half as tensely as the man trying to hit it.

3960 Golf flag– Beacon to a rallying point where members of a foursome meet every 20 minutes or so to exchange alibis.

3961 Golf hazard – Man-made difficulties, consisting of equal parts of sand, water, profanity and ulcers.

3962 Gossip– Letting the chat out of the bag.

3963 Grandparents – The people who think your children are wonderful even though they're sure you're not raising them right.

3964 Gross ignorance – 144 times worse than ordinary ignorance.

3965 Hairdresser's – A place where some women go to dye.

3966 Handicap – Ready-to-use hat.

3967 Handkerchief – A small square of linen, useful at funerals to conceal a lack of tears. Also a form of cold storage.

3968 Hanging – A suspended sentence.

3969 Happiness – An agreeable sensation arising from contemplating the misery of another.

3970 Health – The slowest possible rate of dying.

3971 Heroes – What a guy in a boat does.

3972 Honesty – Fear of being caught.

3973 Honeymoon – Vacation a man takes before starting work under a new boss.

3974 Hormone – Complaint from a hooker.

3975 Horse sense– Something a horse has to prevent it from betting on men.

3976 Hotel – A place where a guest often gives up good dollars for poor quarters.

3977 Hunch – An idea you're afraid is wrong.

3978 Husband – A person who expects his wife to be perfect and to understand why he isn't.

3979 Hypochondriac – Someone who won't let well enough alone.

3980 Impolite – A burning elf.

3981 Impotence – Nature's way of saying, "No hard feelings".

3982 Independent – How we want our children to be, as long as they do everything we say.

3983 Inflation – What used to cost 20 dollars to buy now costs 40 dollars to repair.

3984 In-patient – Where the lost scalpel can be found.

3985 Intoxication – To feel sophisticated, but not be able to say it.

3986 Jazz – Five men on the same stage all playing a different tune.

3987 Job – A place where you work just hard enough to avoid getting fired while getting paid just enough to avoid quitting.

3988 Judge – A law student who marks his own paper.

3989 Justice – A decision in your favour.

3990 Kangaroo – Spiritual advisor for metal food containers.

3991 Knighthood – Honour bestowed by a monarch to change the subject.

3992 Lactose – Consequence of frostbite.

3993 Lawyer – One skilled in circumvention of the law: a person who writes a 10,000 word document and calls it a "brief".

3994 Lecture – Means of transferring information from the notes of the lecturer to the notes of the student without passing through the minds of either.

3995 Liability – A talent for fibbing.

3996 Liar – A lawyer with a roving commission.

3997 Lymph – Walks with a lisp.

3998 Marriage – A romance in which the hero dies in the first chapter.

3999 Martyr – One who sacrifices himself to the unavoidable.

4000 Matrimony – A knot tied by a preacher, untied by a lawyer.

4001 Maturity – That stage in your life when you are finally able to determine which bridges to cross and which to burn.

4002 Middle age – When you're willing to get up and give your seat to a lady, but can't.

4003 Miser – A person who lets the world go buy.

4004 Moonlighting – The sun's other job.

4005 Morbid – Higher offer.

4006 Mosquito – A small insect designed by God to make us think better of flies.

4007 Mother-in-law– A woman who destroys her son-in-law's peace of mind by giving him a piece of hers.

4008 Multitasking – Reading in the bathroom.

4009 Negligent – The condition in which you absent-mindedly answer the door in your nightie.

4010 Nitrate – Rate of pay lower than day rate.

4011 Node – Was aware of.

4012 Oblivion – Fame's eternal dumping-ground.

4013 Optimist – Someone who believes what's going to be will be postponed.

4014 Originality – Undetected plagiarism.

4015 Ostracized – The same size as an ostrich.

4016 Outpatient – A person who was fainted.

4017 Pacifist – Someone who fights everybody but the enemy.

4018 Paradox – Two physicians.

4019 Parasites – What you see from the top of the Eiffel Tower.

4020 Pasteurize – Too far to see.

4021 Patience – What you have when you don't know what to do next.

4022 Pessimist – Someone who looks both ways before crossing a one-way street.

4023 Pharmacist – A helper on a farm.

4024 Philanthropist – One who returns to the people publicly a small percentage of the wealth he steals from them privately.

4025 Philosopher – A person who confuses you sufficiently to make you believe he knows what he is talking about.

4026 Plagiarism – A wise crack that knows its own father.

4027 Poise – The ability to be ill at ease naturally.

4028 Polarize – What penguins see with.

4029 Politeness – Not speaking evil of people with whom you have just dined until you are at least 100 yards from their house.

4030 Politician – Someone who divides his time between running for office and running for cover.

4031 Praise – Letting off esteem.

4032 Procrastination – The art of keeping up with yesterday.

4033 Propaganda – A gentlemanly goose.

4034 Prosperity – A period when you spend money you don't have.

4035 Protein – In favour of young people.

4036 Psychiatrist – Someone who finds you cracked and leaves you broke.

4037 Psychologist – Someone to whom you pay a lot of money to ask you questions your wife asks free of charge.

4038 Psychopath – The road nut taken.

4039 Punctuality – The art of guessing how late the person you are meeting will be.

4040 Raisin – A worried-looking grape.

4041 Regret – Make the final payment on the engagement ring three months after the divorce becomes final.

4042 Reindeer – A horse with a hat rack.

4043 Relief – What trees do in spring.

4044 Repartee – What a person thinks of after he becomes a departee.

4045 Resolve – That admirable quality in ourselves that is detestable stubbornness in others.

4046 Rheumatic – Storage area at the top of the house.

4047 Rhubarb – Celery gone bloodshot.

4048 Sadist – A person who is kind to a masochist.

4049 Sardines – Little fish that crawl into a tin, lock themselves up, and leave the key outside.

4050 Secret – Something you tell to one person at a time.

4051 Selfish – What the owner of a seafood store does.

4052 Sesame – Seed useful for opening caves.

4053 Shin – A device for finding furniture in the dark.

4054 Show-off – A child who is more talented than yours.

4055 Silence – Conversation with an Englishman.

4056 Skeleton – A bunch of bones with the person scraped off.

4057 Skier – Person who jumps to contusions.

4058 Sleep — That fleeting moment that ends alarmingly.

4059 Stalemate — A husband who has lost his ardour.

4060 Streaker — Someone who is unsuited for work.

4061 Stress — When you wake up screaming and realize you haven't fallen asleep yet.

4062 Suburbia — Where they tear out the trees and then name streets after them.

4063 Sweater — Garment worn by a child when the mother feels chilly.

4064 Synonym — A word you use when you can't spell the other one.

4065 Syntax — A way by which you pay for your misdemeanours.

4066 Tabloid reporter — To whom the belles told.

4067 Tact — Changing the subject without changing your mind.

4068 Tea — Break fluid.

4069 Teenager — One whose hang-ups don't include clothes.

4070 Thesaurus — Dinosaur with an excellent vocabulary.

4071 Toad — What happens to an illegally parked frog.

4072 Tomcat — A ball bearing mouse trap.

4073 Tomorrow — The day you are going to clean out the garage.

4074 Toothache — The pain that drives you to extraction.

4075 Tough neighbourhood— One in which any cat with a tail is a tourist.

4076 Transvestite — A guy who likes to eat, drink and be Mary.

4077 Undertaker — The last guy to let you down.

4078 Upper crust— A lot of crumbs held together with dough.

4079 Vacuum cleaner — A broom with a stomach.

4080 Waiter — One who thinks money grows on trays.

4081 Walnut — One who is mad about climbing vertical barriers.

4082 Warehouse — What you ask when you are lost.

4083 Wedding — A funeral where you smell your own flowers.

4084 Wedding ring— The world's smallest handcuffs.

4085 Weed — A plant whose virtues have not yet been discovered.

4086 Wholesale — Where a gopher goes to buy a home.

4087 Willy-nilly — Impotent.

4088 Worry — Interest paid on trouble before it falls due.

4089 Wrinkles — Something other people have. You have character lines.

4090 Writ — Past tense of write.

4091 X-Files — Where you keep records on your former spouse.

4092 Yawn — An honest opinion openly expressed.

4093 Yearning — A Texan's current salary.

4094 Yelping — Shouting half the name of a table tennis game.

EPIGRAMS

4095 If with the literate, I am
Impelled to try an epigram,
I never seek to take the credit;
We all assume that Oscar said it. (DOROTHY PARKER)

Ability
4096 Ability is the art of getting credit for all the home runs somebody else hits. (CASEY STENGEL)

Abuse
4097 It seldom pays to be rude. It never pays to be only half-rude. (NORMAN DOUGLAS)

Acting
4098 An actor is a guy who, if you ain't talking about him, ain't listening. (MARLON BRANDO)

4099 A fan club is a group of people who tell an actor he's not alone in the way he feels about himself. (JACK CARSON)

Advertising
4100 Advertising may be described as the science of arresting the human intelligence long enough to get money from it. (STEPHEN LEACOCK)

4101 Advertising is the art of making whole lies out of half truths. (EDGAR A. SHOAFF)

4102 Doing business without advertising is like winking at a girl in the dark. You know what you are doing, but nobody else does. (STUART HENDERSON BRITT)

4103 Advertising is the rattling of a stick inside a swill bucket. (GEORGE ORWELL)

4104 Advertising is like learning. A little is a dangerous thing. (PHINEAS T. BARNUM)

Advice
4105 Advice is what we ask for when we already know the answer but wish we didn't. (ERICA JONG)

4106 The only thing one can do with good advice is to pass it on. It is never of any use to oneself. (OSCAR WILDE)

Age

4107 Time and tide wait for no man – but time always stands still for a woman of 30. (ROBERT FROST)

4108 The old believe everything; the middle-aged suspect everything; the young know everything. (OSCAR WILDE)

4109 Middle age: when you begin to exchange your emotions for symptoms. (IRVIN SHREWSBURY COBB)

4110 Boys will be boys, and so will a lot of middle-aged men. (KIN HUBBARD)

4111 Old men are fond of giving good advice, to console themselves for being no longer in a position to give bad examples. (FRANÇOIS DE LA ROCHEFOUCAULD)

4112 Old age isn't so bad when you consider the alternative. (MAURICE CHEVALIER)

4113 The years that a woman subtracts from her age are not lost. They are added to the ages of other women. (DIANE DE POITIERS)

Alimony

4114 Alimony is like buying oats for a dead horse. (ARTHUR BAER)

Ambition

4115 Ambition is but avarice on stilts and masked. (WALTER SAVAGE LANDOR)

Americans

4116 Nobody ever went broke underestimating the taste of the American public. (H.L. MENCKEN)

4117 The 100 per cent American is 99 per cent idiot. (GEORGE BERNARD SHAW)

Antiques

4118 An antique is something that's been useless so long it's still in pretty good condition. (FRANKLIN P. JONES)

Apologies

4119 To apologize is to lay the foundation for a future offence. (AMBROSE BIERCE)

Architecture

4120 Architecture is the art of how to waste space. (PHILIP JOHNSON)

4121 The physician can bury his mistakes, but the architect can only advise his client to plant vines. (FRANK LLOYD WRIGHT)

Army

4122 Being in the army is like being in the Boy Scouts, except that the Boy Scouts have adult supervision. (BLAKE CLARK)

4123 Soldiers in peace are like chimneys in summer. (LORD BURGHLEY)

Art

4124 Abstract art: A product of the untalented, sold by the unprincipled to the utterly bewildered. (AL CAPP)

4125 What garlic is to salad, insanity is to art. (AUGUSTUS SAINT-GAUDENS)

4126 The more minimal the art the more maximum the explanation. (HILTON KRAMER)

4127 An artist cannot speak about his art any more than a plant can discuss horticulture. (JEAN COCTEAU)

4128 Everyone wants an artist on the wall or on the shelf, but nobody wants him in the house. (JAMES BALDWIN)

4129 Bad artists always admire each other's work. (OSCAR WILDE)

Assassination

4130 Assassination is the extreme form of censorship. (GEORGE BERNARD SHAW)

Banking

4131 A bank is a thing that will always lend you money if you can prove you don't need it. (JOE E. LEWIS)

4132 A banker is a fellow who lends you his umbrella when the sun is shining and wants it back the minute it begins to rain. (MARK TWAIN)

Beauty

4133 Wrinkles are hereditary. Parents get them from their children. (DORIS DAY)

Bigamy

4134 The maximum penalty for bigamy is two mothers-in-law. (OLIVER STAINTON)

Blame

4135 The man who smiles when things go wrong has thought of someone he can blame it on. (ARTHUR BLOCH)

Britain

4136 The British tourist is always happy abroad as long as the natives are waiters. (ROBERT MORLEY)

Bureaucracy

4137 The longer the title, the less important the job. (GEORGE MCGOVERN)

Canada

4138 You have to know a man awfully well in Canada to know his surname. (JOHN BUCHAN)

4139 A Canadian is somebody who knows how to make love in a canoe. (PIERRE BERTON)

4140 Quebec does not have opinions — only sentiments. (SIR WILFRID LAURIER)

4141 Canada has never been a melting pot; more like a tossed salad. (ARNOLD EDINBOROUGH)

4142 In any world menu, Canada must be considered the vichyssoise of nations — it's cold, half-French, and difficult to stir. (STUART KEATE)

Cauliflower

4143 Cauliflower is nothing but cabbage with a college education. (MARK TWAIN).

Celebrity

4144 A celebrity is a person who works hard all his life to become well known, and then wears dark glasses to avoid being recognized. (FRED ALLEN)

Chastity

4145 The most unnatural of the sexual perversions. (ALDOUS HUXLEY)

Children

4146 There is nothing so aggravating as a fresh boy who is too old to ignore and too young to kick. (KIN HUBBARD)

4147 Only the young die good. (OLIVER HERFORD)

4148 Having one child makes you a parent; having two you are a referee. (DAVID FROST)

Christmas

4149 A woman may race to get a man a gift but it always ends in a tie. (EARL WILSON)

Commerce

4150 Businessmen must not break their word twice. (THOMAS FULLER)

Committees

4151 A committee is a cul de sac to which ideas are lured and then quietly strangled. (JOHN A. LINCOLN)

4152 A committee is a group that keeps the minutes and loses hours. (MILTON BERLE)

Compliments

4153 Nothing is so silly as the expression of a man who is being complimented. (ANDRÉ GIDE)

4154 Whenever a man's friends begin to compliment him about looking young, he may be sure that they think he is growing old. (WASHINGTON IRVING)

Computers

4155 To err is human, but to really foul things up requires a computer. (PAUL EHRLICH)

Conference

4156 A conference is a gathering of important people who singly can do nothing, but together can decide that nothing can be done. (FRED ALLEN)

Congress

4157 Every time they make a joke, it's a law, and every time they make a law, it's a joke. (WILL ROGERS)

Conscience

4158 The inner voice which warns us that someone may be looking. (H.L. MENCKEN)

Consistency

4159 The last refuge of the unimaginative. (OSCAR WILDE)

4160 The only completely consistent people are the dead. (ALDOUS HUXLEY)

Contraceptives

4161 Contraceptives should be used on every conceivable occasion. (SPIKE MILLIGAN)

Cookery

4162 There is one thing more exasperating than a wife who can cook and won't, and that is the wife who can't cook and will. (ROBERT FROST)

Courage

4163 Bravery is being the only person who knows you're afraid. (FRANKLIN P. JONES)

4164 A hero is no braver than an ordinary man, but he is braver five minutes longer. (RALPH WALDO EMERSON)

Crime

4165 A kleptomaniac can't help helping himself. (HENRY MORGAN)

Critics

4166 A good review from the critics is just another stay of execution. (DUSTIN HOFFMAN)

4167 A critic is a man who knows the way but can't drive the car. (KENNETH TYNAN)

4168 Those who can't, teach. And those who can't do either, review. (BURT REYNOLDS)

4169 Critics are like eunuchs in a harem: they know how it's done, they've seen it done every day, but they're unable to do it themselves. (BRENDAN BEHAN)

4170 Asking a working writer what he feels about critics is like asking a lamppost what he feels about dogs. (JOHN OSBORNE)

4171 A critic is one who goes along for deride. (L.L. LEVINSON)

4172 The strength of criticism lies only in the weakness of the thing criticized. (HENRY LONGFELLOW)

4173 A drama critic is a man who leaves no turn unstoned. (GEORGE BERNARD SHAW)

Crying
4174 Crying is the refuge of plain women, but the ruin of pretty ones. (OSCAR WILDE)

Curling
4175 Housework on ice. (LINDA SMITH)

Cynicism
4176 A cynic is a man who knows the price of everything and the value of nothing. (OSCAR WILDE)

4177 A cynic is a man who, when he smells flowers, looks around for a coffin. (H.L. MENCKEN)

4178 Cynicism is humour in ill-health. (H.G. WELLS)

Death
4179 Man weeps to think he will die so soon; woman, that she was born so long ago. (H.L. MENCKEN)

Democracy
4180 Democracy is a form of religion. It is the worship of jackals by jackasses. (H.L. MENCKEN)

4181 Democracy is the art of running the circus from the monkey cage. (H.L. MENCKEN)

4182 An institution in which the whole is equal to the scum of the parts. (KEITH PRESTON)

4183 Democracy means government by the uneducated, while aristocracy means government by the badly educated. (G.K. CHESTERTON)

4184 Democracy is being allowed to vote for the candidate you dislike least. (ROBERT BYREN)

4185 The ballot is stronger than the bullet. (ABRAHAM LINCOLN)

Dictatorship
4186 A place where public opinion can't even be expressed privately. (WALTER WINCHELL)

Dinner parties
4187 Conversation is the enemy of good wine and food. (ALFRED HITCHCOCK)

Diplomacy
4188 A diplomat is a man who always remembers a woman's birthday, but never remembers her age. (ROBERT FROST)

4189 Diplomacy is the art of jumping into troubled waters without making a splash. (ART LINKLETTER)

Discretion
4190 A wise man sees as much as he ought, not as much as he can. (MICHEL DE MONTAIGNE)

Divorce
4191 The happiest time of anyone's life is just after the first divorce. (J.K. GALBRAITH)

Doctors
4192 God heals, and the doctor takes the fee. (BENJAMIN FRANKLIN)

4193 Doctors are men who prescribe medicines of which they know little, to cure diseases of which they know less, in human beings of whom they know nothing. (VOLTAIRE)

4194 Never go to a doctor whose office plants have died. (ERMA BOMBECK)

Drink
4195 One of the disadvantages of wine is that it makes a man mistake words for thoughts. (DR SAMUEL JOHNSON)

Economics
4196 It's a recession when your neighbour loses his job; it's a depression when you lose your own. (HARRY S. TRUMAN)

4197 The one profession where you can gain great eminence without ever being right. (GEORGE MEANY)

Education

4198 He who can does. He who cannot, teaches. (GEORGE BERNARD SHAW)

Egotism

4199 Egotism Is the anaesthetic that the dulls the pains of stupidity. (FRANK LEAHY)

Enemies

4200 Always forgive your enemies — nothing annoys them so much. (OSCAR WILDE)

4201 It takes your enemy and your friend, working together, to hurt you to the heart; the one to slander you, and the other to get the news to you. (MARK TWAIN)

4202 One should forgive one's enemies, but not before they are hanged. (HEINRICH HEINE)

4203 Forgive your enemies, but don't forget their names. (JOHN F. KENNEDY)

Experience

4204 Experience is the worst teacher; it gives the test before presenting the lesson. (VERNON LAW)

Expert

4205 A man who has stopped thinking. (FRANK LLOYD WRIGHT)

4206 One who knows more and more about less and less. (NICHOLAS MURRAY BUTLER)

Fame

4207 You're not a star until they can spell your name in Karachi. (HUMPHREY BOGART)

4208 You can't get spoiled if you do your own ironing. (MERYL STREEP)

Familiarity

4209 Familiarity breeds contempt — and children. (MARK TWAIN)

Fashion

4210 Fashion is a form of ugliness so intolerable that we have to alter it every six months. (OSCAR WILDE)

4211 Brevity is the soul of lingerie. (DOROTHY PARKER)

Food
4212 Anything you have to acquire a taste for was not meant to be eaten. (EDDIE MURPHY)

Friends
4213 Friendship is like money, easier made than kept. (SAMUEL BUTLER)

Gambling
4214 The only man who makes money following the races is one who does it with a broom and shovel. (ELBERT HUBBARD)

Genius
4215 A genius is one who can do anything except make a living. (JOEY ADAMS)

4216 Every man of genius is considerably helped by being dead. (ROBERT LYND)

Gentlemen
4217 A gentleman is any man who wouldn't hit a woman with his hat on. (FRED ALLEN)

Golf
4218 Golf is a good walk spoiled. (MARK TWAIN)

Guests
4219 Some people can stay longer in an hour than others can in a week. (W.D. HOWELLS)

4220 Fish and visitors smell in three days. (BENJAMIN FRANKLIN)

Guilt
4221 The gift that keeps on giving. (ERMA BOMBECK)

Hair
4222 The only thing that can stop hair falling is the floor. (WILL ROGERS)

Happiness
4223 Happiness is good health and a bad memory. (INGRID BERGMAN)

Hippies

4224 A hippie is someone who looks like Tarzan, walks like Jane and smells like Cheeta. (RONALD REAGAN)

History

4225 History is a set of lies agreed upon. (NAPOLEON BONAPARTE)

Hollywood

4226 They've got great respect for the dead in Hollywood, but none for the living. (ERROL FLYNN)

4227 A world of dwarfs casting long shadows. (SHEILA GRAHAM)

4228 Hollywood is a place where they'll pay you 1,000 dollars for a kiss and 50 cents for your soul. (MARILYN MONROE)

4229 Hollywood is a place where people from Iowa mistake themselves for stars. (FRED ALLEN)

4230 Hollywood is a locality where people without reputation try to live up to it. (TOM JENK)

4231 Hollywood – a place where the inmates are in charge of the asylum. (LAURENCE STALLINGS)

4232 A place where you spend more than you make, on things you don't want, to impress people you don't like. (KEN MURRAY)

4233 Directors are people too short to be actors. (JOSH GREENFELD)

4234 Behind the phoney tinsel of Hollywood lies the real tinsel. (OSCAR LEVANT)

4235 In Hollywood, if you don't have happiness, you send out for it. (REX REED)

4236 Hollywood is a sewer with service from the Ritz Carlton. (WILSON MIZNER)

Hope

4237 Hope is merely disappointment deferred. (W. BURTON BALDRY)

Humour

4238 An epigram is only a wisecrack that's played Carnegie Hall. (OSCAR LEVANT)

4239 Tragedy is when I cut my finger. Comedy is when you fall down an open manhole cover and die. (MEL BROOKS)

Idealism

4240 An idealist is one who, on noticing that a rose smells better than a cabbage, concludes that it will also make better soup. (H.L. MENCKEN)

4241 Idealism increases in direct proportion to one's distance from the problem. (JOHN GALSWORTHY)

Ignorance

4242 It's innocence when it charms us, ignorance when it doesn't. (MIGNON MCLAUGHLIN)

4243 Everybody is ignorant, only on different subjects. (WILL ROGERS)

Intelligence

4244 The brain is a wonderful organ. It starts working the moment you get up in the morning, and does not stop until you get into the office. (ROBERT FROST)

4245 A highbrow is the kind of person who looks at a sausage and thinks of Picasso. (A.P. HERBERT)

4246 An intellectual is a man who takes more words than necessary to tell more than he knows. (DWIGHT D. EISENHOWER)

Lawyers

4247 A countryman between two lawyers is like a fish between two cats. (BENJAMIN FRANKLIN)

4248 A jury consists of twelve persons chosen to decide who has the better lawyer. (ROBERT FROST)

Life

4249 Life is rather like a tin of sardines: we're all of us looking for the key. (ALAN BENNETT)

4250 Life is like a sewer. What you get out of it depends on what you put in. (TOM LEHRER)

Literature

4251 A writer is somebody for whom writing is more difficult than it is for other people. (THOMAS MANN)

4252 Every great man nowadays has his disciples, and it is always Judas who writes his biography. (OSCAR WILDE)

4253 An autobiography usually reveals nothing bad about its writer except his memory. (FRANKLIN P. JONES)

4254 A classic is something that everybody wants to have read and nobody wants to read. (MARK TWAIN)

4255 To write a diary every day is like returning to one's own vomit. (ENOCH POWELL)

4256 An optimist is one who believes everything he reads on the jacket of a new book. (MILWAUKEE JOURNAL)

Love

4257 Love is not the dying moan of a distant violin – it is the triumphant twang of a bedspring. (S.J. PERELMAN)

4258 Love's like the measles – all the worse when it comes late in life. (DOUGLAS JERROLD)

4259 Never let a fool kiss you or a kiss fool you. (JOEY ADAMS)

4260 Scratch a lover and find a foe. (DOROTHY PARKER)

Marriage

4261 Keep your eyes wide open before marriage and half shut afterwards. (BENJAMIN FRANKLIN)

4262 I have always thought that every woman should marry, and no man. (BENJAMIN DISRAELI)

4263 Marriage is the deep, deep peace of the double bed after the hurly-burly of the chaise longue. (MRS PATRICK CAMPBELL)

4264 A bachelor is a man who never makes the same mistake once. (ED WYNN)

4265 Many a man in love with a dimple makes the mistake of marrying the whole girl. (STEPHEN LEACOCK)

4266 When a girl marries she exchanges the attentions of many men for the inattention of one. (HELEN ROWLAND)

4267 Before marriage, a man will lie awake thinking about something you said; after marriage, he'll fall asleep before you finish saying it. (HELEN ROWLAND)

Masturbation

4268 The good thing about masturbation is you don't have to dress up for it. (TRUMAN CAPOTE)

Mediocrity

4269 Only a mediocre person is always at his best. (SOMERSET MAUGHAM)

Men

4270 Man is the only animal that blushes. Or needs to. (MARK TWAIN)

4271 Men are those creatures with two legs and eight hands. (JAYNE MANSFIELD)

4272 A husband is what is left of the lover after the nerve has been extracted. (HELEN ROWLAND)

4273 Behind every successful man you'll find a woman who has nothing to wear. (JAMES STEWART)

4274 Behind every successful man stands a proud wife and a surprised mother-in-law. (BROOKS HAYS)

Military

4275 There are no bad regiments, only bad colonels. (NAPOLEON BONAPARTE)

Money

4276 Money is a terrible master but an excellent servant. (PHINEAS T. BARNUM)

4277 A rich man is nothing but a poor man with money. (W.C. FIELDS)

4278 All heiresses are beautiful. (JOHN DRYDEN)

4279 There are two times in a man's life when he should not speculate: when he can't afford it and when he can. (MARK TWAIN)

Morality
4280 Moral indignation is jealousy with a halo. (H.G. WELLS)

4281 An ethical man is a Christian holding four aces. (MARK TWAIN)

Music
4282 Classical music is the kind we keep thinking will turn into a tune. (KIN HUBBARD)

Newspapers
4283 The most truthful part of a newspaper is the advertisements. (THOMAS JEFFERSON)

4284 An editor is one who separates the wheat from the chaff and prints the chaff. (ADLAI STEVENSON)

4285 The press is like the peculiar uncle you keep in the attic — just one of those unfortunate things. (G. GORDON LIDDY)

Opera
4286 Opera is when a guy gets stabbed in the back and instead of bleeding he sings. (ED GARDNER)

4287 Sleep is an excellent way of listening to opera. (JAMES STEPHENS)

4288 Of all the noises known to man, opera is the most expensive. (MOLIÈRE)

Patriotism
4289 The last refuge of a scoundrel. (DR SAMUEL JOHNSON)

4290 A real patriot is the fellow who gets a parking ticket and rejoices that the system works. (BILL VAUGHAN)

Pessimism

4291 A pessimist is one who, when he has the choice of two evils, chooses both. (OSCAR WILDE)

Philosophy

4292 Philosophy is common sense in a dress suit. (OLIVER S. BRASTON)

Plagiarism

4293 If you steal from one person, it's plagiarism; if you steal from many, it's research. (WILSON MIZNER)

Politics

4294 A politician is a man who approaches every question with an open mouth. (ADLAI STEVENSON)

4295 Nothing is so admirable in politics as a short memory. (J.K. GALBRAITH)

4296 Politicians make strange bedfellows, but they all share the same bunk. (EDGAR A. SHOAFF)

4297 A political war is one in which everyone shoots from the lip. (RAYMOND MOLEY)

4298 A radical is a man with both feet planted firmly in the air. (FRANKLIN D. ROOSEVELT)

4299 A liberal is one who is too broadminded to take his own side in a quarrel. (ROBERT FROST)

4300 A conservative is a man who is too cowardly to fight and too fat to run. (ELBERT HUBBARD)

4301 A conservative is a man who thinks and sits, mostly sits. (WOODROW WILSON)

Prodigy

4302 A child who plays the piano when he ought to be in bed. (J.B. MORTON)

Psychiatrists

4303 Anyone who goes to a psychiatrist ought to have his head examined. (SAM GOLDWYN)

4304 A psychiatrist is a man who goes to the Folies-Bergère and looks at the audience. (MERVYN STOCKWOOD)

4305 Psychiatrist: a person who pulls habits out of rats. (DR DOUGLAS BUSH)

4306 A neurotic is a man who builds a castle in the air. A psychotic is the man who lives in it. A psychiatrist is the man who collects the rent. (JEROME LAWRENCE)

Religion

4307 A Christian is a man who feels repentance on a Sunday for what he did on a Saturday and is going to do on Monday. (THOMAS YBARRA)

4308 A Puritan is a person who pours righteous indignation into the wrong things. (G.K. CHESTERTON)

4309 Puritanism is the haunting fear that someone, somewhere, may be happy. (H.L. MENCKEN)

4310 An atheist is a man with no invisible means of support. (JOHN BUCHAN)

4311 The worst moment for an atheist is when he is really thankful and has nobody to thank. (DANTE GABRIEL ROSSETTI)

4312 The Eleventh Commandment: Thou shalt not be found out. (GEORGE WHYTE MELVILLE)

Russia

4313 A riddle wrapped in a mystery inside an enigma. (WINSTON CHURCHILL)

Science

4314 Science is a collection of successful recipes. (PAUL VALÉRY)

Sentimentality

4315 A sentimentalist is simply one who desires to have the luxury of an emotion without paying for it. (OSCAR WILDE)

Sex

4316 A mistress is what goes between a mister and a mattress. (JOE E. LEWIS)

4317 Older women are best because they always think they may be doing it for the last time. (IAN FLEMING)

4318 Sex is an emotion in motion. (MAE WEST)

4319 Never go to bed with anyone crazier than yourself. (KRIS KRISTOFFERSON)

Society

4320 There is only one thing in the world worse than being talked about, and that is not being talked about. (OSCAR WILDE)

Statistics

4321 There are three kinds of lies: lies, damned lies, and statistics. (BENJAMIN DISRAELI)

Success

4322 The one unpardonable sin against one's fellows. (AMBROSE BIERCE)

4323 Success is going from failure to failure without losing enthusiasm. (WINSTON CHURCHILL)

4324 Nothing recedes like success. (WALTER WINCHELL)

Tact

4325 Tongue in check. (SUE DYTRI)

4326 Tact is the ability to tell a man he's open-minded when he has a hole in his head. (F.G. KERNAN)

Technology

4327 Nothing you can't spell will ever work. (WILL ROGERS)

Telephone

4328 The telephone is a good way of talking to people without having to offer them a drink. (FRAN LEBOWITZ)

Television

4329 TV is an invention that permits you to be entertained in your living room by people you wouldn't have in your home. (SIR DAVID FROST)

4330 A device that permits people who haven't anything to do to watch people who can't do anything. (FRED ALLEN)

4331 TV is a medium, because it is neither rare nor well done. (ERNIE KOVACS)

4332 Television is chewing gum for the eyes. (FRANK LLOYD WRIGHT)

Theatre

4333 The theatre is the aspirin of the middle-classes. (WOLCOTT GIBBS)

4334 A play is like a cigar. If it is a failure no amount of puffing will make it draw. If it is a success everybody wants a box. (HENRY J. BRYAN)

4335 Opening night is the night before the play is ready to open. (GEORGE J. NATHAN)

4336 There are no dull subjects, only dull playwrights. (ROBERT ANDERSON)

Time

4337 Time wounds all heels. (JANE ACE)

Travel

4338 In America there are two classes of travel – first-class and with children. (ROBERT BENCHLEY)

4339 Travel is only glamorous in retrospect. (PAUL THEROUX)

Truth

4340 Truth is the most valuable thing we have. Let us economize it. (MARK TWAIN)

Vanity

4341 Most of the shadows of this life are caused by standing in one's own sunshine. (RALPH WALDO EMERSON)

4342 He that falls in love with himself will have no rivals. (BENJAMIN FRANKLIN)

4343 To love oneself is the beginning of a lifelong romance. (OSCAR WILDE)

Vulgarity

4344 Vulgarity is simply the conduct of other people. (OSCAR WILDE)

Wit

4345 Wit is cultured insolence. (ARISTOTLE)

Women

4346 A woman's place is in the wrong. (JAMES THURBER)

4347 It is God who makes woman beautiful; it is the devil who makes her pretty. (VICTOR HUGO)

4348 The only time a woman really succeeds in changing a man is when he's a baby. (NATALIE WOOD)

4349 The more underdeveloped the country, the more overdeveloped the women. (J.K. GALBRAITH)

4350 Woman begins by resisting a man's advances and ends by blocking his retreat. (OSCAR WILDE)

4351 A woman is like a teabag – only in hot water do you realize how strong she is. (NANCY REAGAN)

Work

4352 Work is the curse of the drinking classes. (OSCAR WILDE)

4353 Work is the province of cattle. (DOROTHY PARKER)

4354 All work and no play makes Jack a dull boy – and Jill a wealthy widow. (EVAN ESAR)

Youth

4355 Youth is a wonderful thing; what a crime to waste it on children. (GEORGE BERNARD SHAW)

EPITAPHS

4356 A glassblower lies here at rest
Who one day burst his noble chest
While trying, in a fit of malice,
To blow a second Crystal Palace. (J.B. MORTON from *The Best of Beachcomber*)

4357 Here lie I, Martin Elginbrod.
Have mercy on my soul, Lord God.
As I on you, were I Lord God
And you were Martin Elginbrod. (Aberdeen)

4358 Here lie the bones of Elizabeth Charlotte,
Born a virgin, died a harlot.
She was aye a virgin at seventeen
A remarkable thing in Aberdeen. (Aberdeen)

4359 Here I lie bereft of breath
Because a cough carried me off;
Then a coffin they carried me off in. (Boston, Massachusetts)

4360 Sacred to the memory of Anthony Drake,
Who died for peace and quietness sake;
His wife was constantly scolding and scoffin',
So he sought for repose in a twelve-dollar coffin. (Burlington, Massachusetts)

4361 Here lies the body of Marry Ann Lowder,
She burst while drinking a Seidlitz Powder.
Called from the world to her heavenly rest,
She should have waited till it effervesced. (Burlington, Massachusetts)

4362 Here lies Dr Keene, the good Bishop of Chester,
Who ate up a fat goose, but could not digest her. (Cheshire)

4363 Stephen and Time are now both even, Stephen beats Time, but now Time's
beaten Stephen. (Grave of a music teacher, Cornwall)

4364 The wedding day appointed was,
The wedding clothes provided.
But ere the day did come, alas,
He sickened, and he dieded. (Devon)

4365 Here Lies
Ezekial Aikle
Aged 102.
The Good
Die Young. (East Dalhousie, Nova Scotia)

4366 Stranger, tread this ground with gravity
Dentist Brown is filling his last cavity. (Edinburgh)

4367 Here snug in grave my wife doth lie,
Now she's at rest and so am I. (Edinburgh)

4368 He passed the bobby without any fuss,
And he passed the cart of hay,
He tried to pass a swerving bus.
And then he passed away. (England)

4369 Here lies the body of our Anna
Done to death by a banana.
It wasn't the fruit that laid her low
But the skin of the thing that made her go. (Enosburg, Vermont)

4370 Here lies Johnny Cole,
Who died, on my soul,
After eating a plentiful dinner,
While showing his crust
He was turned into dust,
With his crimes undigested, poor sinner. (Essex)

4371 Honey you don't know what you did for me,
Always playing the lottery.
The numbers you picked came in to play,
Two days after you passed away.
For this, a huge monument I do erect,
For now I get a yearly check.
How I wish you were alive,
For now we are worth 8.5.
(on the tombstone of the aptly named Elizabeth Rich, Eufaula, Alabama)

4372 Here lie I and my four daughters,
Killed by drinking Cheltenham waters.
Had we but stuck to Epsom salts,
We wouldn't have been in these here vaults. (Gloucestershire)

4373 Here lies a poor woman who always was tired,
For she lived in a place where help wasn't hired.
Her last words on earth were, Dear friends I am going
Where washing ain't done nor sweeping nor sewing,
And everything there is exact to my wishes,
For there they don't eat and there's no washing of dishes.
Don't mourn for me now, don't mourn for me never,
For I'm going to do nothing for ever and ever. (Hertfordshire)

4374 This good old woman of Ryde
Ate some apples and died.
The apples fermented inside the lamented
Made cider inside her inside. (Isle of Wight)

4375 Wherever you be
Let your wind go free.
For it was keeping it in
That was the death of me. (Ireland)

4376 Fear God, keep the Commandments and
Don't attempt to climb a tree,
For that's what caused the death of me. (Kent)

4377 A victim of fast women and slow horses. (Kirkland Lake, Ontario)

4378 Here lieth John Cruker, a maker of bellows,
His craft's master and king of good fellows;
Yet when he came to the hour of his death,
He that made bellows, could not make breath. (Lancashire)

4379 Open wide ye heavenly gates
That lead to the heavenly shore;
Our father suffered in passing through
And mother weighs much more. (Lee, Massachusetts)

4380 Poor John Scott lies buried here;
Although he was both hale and stout
Death stretched him on the bitter bier.
In another world he hops about. [Epitaph on a Liverpool brewer]

4381   Owen Moore
Gone away
Owing more
Than he could pay. (London)

4382   Whoever treadeth on this stone
I pray you tread most neatly
For underneath this stone do lie
Your honest friend
Will Wheatley. (London)

4383   Here lies one Foote, whose death may thousands save,
For death has now one foot within the grave.
(On the comedian Samuel Foote, in London's Westminster Abbey)

4384   Here lies the body of W.W.,
Who never more will trouble you, trouble you. (On the grave of William
Wilson, London)

4385   Curious enough, we all must say,
That what was Stone should now be clay.
More curious still, to own we must,
That what was Stone will soon be dust. (Grave of a Mr Stone, London)

4386   Here lies the clay of Mitchell Coots,
Whose feet yet occupy his boots.
His soul has gone – we know not where
It landed, neither do we care. (Lost Creek, Colorado)

4387   Here lies the body of Sarah Sexton,
She was a wife that never vexed one;
I can't say so much for the one at the next stone.
(The two wives of Tom Sexton, buried near Newmarket, Cambridgeshire)

4388   He's done a-catching cod
And gone to meet his God.
(Epitaph on Captain Thomas Coffin, New Shoreham, Rhode Island)

4389 Underneath this pile of stones
Lies all that's left of Sally Jones.
Her name was Briggs, it was not Jones,
But Jones was used to rhyme with stones. (New York State)

4390 Here lies my wife,
In carthy mould,
Who, when she lived,
Did naught but scold.
Good friends go softly
In your walking
Lest she should wake
And rise up talking. (Northumberland)

4391 John Adams lies here, of the parish of Southwell
A carrier who carried his can to his mouth well;
He carried so much, and he carried so fast,
He could carry no more — so was carried at last!
For the liquor he drunk, being too much for one,
He could not carry-off — so he's now carri-on. (Nottinghamshire)

4392 Here lies old twenty-five per cent,
The more he had, the more he lent.
The more he had, the more he craved,
Great God, can this poor soul be saved?
(On the grave of a money lender, Nova Scotia)

4393 I laid my wife
Beneath this stone,
For her repose
And for my own. (Ottawa)

4394 Here lies one
Blown out of breath
Who lived a merry life
And died a Merideth. (The gravestone of Mr Merideth, Oxford)

4395 Here lie two poor lovers, who had the mishap
Tho' very chaste people, to die of a clap. (Alexander Pope's epitaph on John
Hewet and Sarah Drew, killed by lightning, Oxfordshire)

4396 This blooming youth in health most fair
To his uncle's mill-pond did repair;
Undressed himself and so plunged in
But never did come out again. (Plainsfield, Vermont)

4397 Here lies as silent clay
Miss Arabella Young
Who on the 21st of May 1771
Began to hold her tongue. (Pownal, Vermont)

4398 Here lies the body of Bob Dent;
He kicked up his heels and to hell he went. (Port Gibson, Mississippi)

4399 Here lies Johnny Yeast
Pardon me for not rising. (Ruidoso, New Mexico)

4400 At rest beneath this slab of stone,
Lies stingy Jimmy Wyett.
He died one morning just at ten
And saved a dinner by it. (Scotland)

4401 Beneath this silent tomb is laid
A noisy antiquated maid;
Who from her cradle talked till death
And ne'er before was out of breath. (Scotland)

4402 This stone was raised to Sarah Ford
Not Sarah's virtues to record
For they're well known by all the town
No, Lord, it was raised to keep her down. (Scotland)

4403 Here lies my wife,
A sad slattern and shrew.
If I said I regretted it,
I should lie too. (Scotland)

4404 Here lies the body of Martha Dias,
Who was always uneasy and not over pious;
She lived to the age of threescore and ten,
And gave that to the worms she refused to the men. (Shropshire)

4405 On a Thursday she was born;
On a Thursday made a bride;
On a Thursday put to bed;
On a Thursday broke her leg; and
On a Thursday died. (Shropshire)

4406 Against his will
Here lies George Hill
Who from a cliff
Fell down quite stiff. (Surrey)

4407 Here lies an atheist:
All dressed up and no place to go. (Thurmont, Maryland)

4408 Here lies
Lester Moore
Four slugs from a 44
No Les
No More. (Tombstone, Arizona)

4409 Reader pass on and ne'er waste your time
On bad biography and bitter rhyme
For what I am this cumb'rous clay insures,
And what I was, is no affair of yours.
(An anonymous grave, Topsfield, Massachusetts]

4410 When I am dead and in my grave,
And all my bones are rotten.
While reading this you'll think of me
When I am long forgotten! (Toronto)

4411 Here lies the body
Of Jonathan Blake
Stepped on the gas pedal
Instead of the brake. (Uniontown, Pennsylvania)

4412 Underneath this stone lies Meredith Morgan,
Who blew the bellows of our church organ.
Tobacco he hated, to smoke most unwilling,
Yet never so pleased as when pipes he was filling.

No reflection on him for rude speech could be cast,
Though he gave our old organ many a blast!
No puffer was he, though a capital blower;
He could blow double G, and now lies a note lower. (Wales)

4413   Here I lie and no wonder I'm dead,
For the wheel of the wagon went over my head. (Wales)

4414   Here lies Mary the wife of John Ford,
We hope her soul is gone to the Lord;
But if for hell she has chang'd this life,
She had better be there than be John Ford's wife. (Wiltshire)

4415   Here sleeps in peace a Hampshire Grenadier
Who caught his death by drinking cold small beer.
Soldiers, be wise from his untimely fall,
And when you're hot, drink strong or none at all. (Winchester, Hampshire)

4416   Here lies one Wood
Enclosed in wood
One Wood
Within another.
The outer wood
Is very good:
We cannot praise
The other. (In memory of Beza Wood, Winslow, Maine)

4417   The children of Israel wanted bread
And the Lord sent them manna;
Old clerk Wallace wanted a wife,
And the devil sent him Anna.
(On the stone of Anna Wallace, Worcestershire)

4418   Here lies the body of John Trollope
Whose hands made these stones to roll up;
When God Almighty took his soul up
His body went to fill the hole up. (Yorkshire)

4419   Her tongue and her hands
Were not governable

But the rest of her members
She kept in subjection. (On the stone of Anna Harrison, Yorkshire)

4420   Sudden and unexpected was the end
       Of our esteemed and beloved friend:
       He gave to all his friends a sudden shock
       By one day falling into Sunderland Dock. (Yorkshire)

4421   Here lies the body of Edith Bone,
       All her life she lived alone,
       Until Death added the final S
       And put an end to her loneliness. (Epitaph on a woman imprisoned by the
       Hungarian Communist regime for seven years)

4422   At last she sleeps alone. (ROBERT BENCHLEY's epitaph for a promiscuous
       actress)

4423   That's All Folks. (MEL BLANC's epitaph in Hollywood)

4424   I'll be right back. (JOHNNY CARSON's proposed epitaph)

4425   Posterity will ne'er survey
       A nobler grave than this;
       Here lie the bones of Castlereagh:
       Stop, traveller, and piss. (LORD BYRON's epitaph to Viscount Castlereagh)

4426   Here lies our mutton-eating king,
       Whose word no man relies on;
       Who never said a foolish thing,
       Nor ever did a wise one. (THE EARL OF ROCHESTER's epitaph to King Charles II)

4427   Here lies Mr Chesterton,
       Who to heaven might have gone,
       But didn't when he heard the news
       That the place was run by Jews.
       (HUMBERT WOLFE's epitaph to G.K. Chesterton)

4428   On the whole, I'd rather be in Philadelphia. (W.C. FIELDS' suggested
       epitaph)

4429 The body of Benjamin Franklin, Printer,
(Like the cover of an old book, its contents worn out
And stript of its lettering and gilding)
Lies here, food for worms.
But the work itself shall not be lost,
For it will, as he believed,
Appear once more
In a new and more elegant edition,
Revised and corrected
By The Author. (BENJAMIN FRANKLIN's suggested epitaph for himself)

4430 Here lies Fred
Who was alive and is dead:
Had it been his father,
I had much rather;
Had it been his brother,
Still better than another;
Had it been his sister,
No one would have missed her;
Had it been the whole generation,
So much better for the nation.
But since 'tis only Fred,
Who was alive and is dead,
There's no more to be said. (on Frederick, Prince of Wales, a member of the
Hanoverian royal family)

4431 Back to the silents. (CLARK GABLE's planned epitaph)

4432 This is the grave of Edmund Gray
Who died maintaining his right of way.
He was right – dead right – as he drove along,
But he's just as dead as if he'd been wrong.

4433 Here lies the body of Sir John Guise,
Nobody laughs, and nobody cries;
Where his soul is, and how it fares,
Nobody knows, and nobody cares.

4434 Pardon me for not getting up. (ERNEST HEMINGWAY's suggestion for his own
epitaph)

4435 Here lies the body of William Jones
Who all his life collected bones,
Till Death, that grim and boney spectre,
That universal bone collector,
Boned old Jones, so neat and tidy,
And here he lies, all bona fide.

4436 Here lies Groucho Marx and Lies and Lies and Lies.
P.S. He never kissed an ugly girl.(GROUCHO MARX's suggested epitaph)

4437 Bust to dust.
Lashes to ashes. (Epitaph on Marilyn Monroe)

4438 Excuse my dust. (DOROTHY PARKER's suggested epitaph for herself)

4439 Here lies the body of Dame Margaret Pegg
Who never had issue except in her leg;
So great was her art, so deep was her cunning,
While one leg kept still the other kept running. (Epitaph for an old lady who
had an ulcerated leg)

4440 Beneath these poppies buried deep,
The bones of Bob the bard lie hid;
Peace to his manes; and may he sleep
As soundly as his readers did! (Epitaph on Robert Southey who became Poet
Laureate in 1813)

4441 Here lies an honest lawyer –
That is Strange. (On the eminent barrister, Sir John Strange)

4442 Neath this sod another lies,
An aristocrat of Scots assize,
Long dead but not forgotten.
When writhe and maggots eat his eyes,
They'll cause his lordship no surprise,
For while he lived, the man was rotten. (On the 14th Earl of Strathmore and
Kinghorne)

HUMOROUS QUOTATIONS

Acting

4443 To act with my clothes on is a performance; to act with my clothes off is a documentary. (JULIA ROBERTS)

4444 You spend all your life trying to do something they put people in asylums for. (JANE FONDA)

4445 I've made so many movies playing a hooker that they don't pay me in the regular way any more. They leave it on the dresser. (SHIRLEY MACLAINE)

4446 Left eyebrow raised, right eyebrow raised. (ROGER MOORE on his acting range)

4447 My acting is a bit like basketball. Most females in my films come off very well. I give great assist. And if I'm lucky, I even score. (BURT REYNOLDS)

4448 One tends to forget the pain of movie-making. I guess it's like pregnancy — something compels you to go through it again. (GENE HACKMAN)

4449 I wanted to win an Oscar so that I'd get more scripts without other actors' coffee-stains on them. (MICHAEL CAINE)

4450 My dear boy, forget about the motivation. Just say the lines and don't trip over the furniture. (NOEL COWARD)

4451 My problem is reconciling my gross habits with my net income. (ERROL FLYNN)

4452 I didn't even know my bra size until I made a movie. (ANGELINA JOLIE)

Advice

4453 Never try to teach a pig to sing; it wastes your time and it annoys the pig. (PAUL DICKSON)

4454 If you've got them by the balls, their hearts and minds will follow. (JOHN WAYNE)

4455 My mother gave me this advice: trust your husband, adore your husband and get as much as you can in your own name. (JOAN RIVERS)

Age

4456 The secret of staying young is to live honestly, eat slowly, and lie about your age. (LUCILLE BALL)

4457 There was no respect for youth when I was young, and now that I am old, there is no respect for age. I missed it coming and going. (J.B. PRIESTLEY)

4458 I refuse to admit I'm more than 52 even if that does make my sons illegitimate. (LADY ASTOR)

Agents

4459 My agent gets ten per cent of everything I get, except my blinding headaches. (FRED ALLEN)

America

4460 The trouble with America is that there are far too many wide open spaces surrounded by teeth. (CHARLES LUCKMAN)

4461 A country that has leapt from barbarism to decadence without touching civilization. (JOHN O'HARA)

4462 Thanks to the Interstate Highway System, it is now possible to travel from coast to coast without seeing anything. (CHARLES KURALT)

4463 America is a large, friendly dog in a very small room. Every time it wags its tail it knocks over a chair. (ARNOLD TOYNBEE)

4464 America is the country where you buy a lifetime supply of aspirin for one dollar, and use it up in two weeks. (JOHN BARRYMORE)

4465 I come from a part of the world where the Egg McMuffin would be a heritage object. (BILL BRYSON)

4466 America is a nation that conceives many odd inventions for getting somewhere but can think of nothing to do when it gets there. (WILL ROGERS)

4467 It is wonderful to find America, but it would have been more wonderful to miss it. (MARK TWAIN)

4468 Of course America had often been discovered before Columbus, but it had always been hushed up. (OSCAR WILDE)

4469 Never criticize Americans. They have the best taste that money can buy. (MILES KINGTON)

4470 Americans will put up with anything provided it doesn't block traffic. (DAN RATHER)

4471 You cannot gauge the intelligence of an American by talking with him. (ERIC HOFFER)

4472 The average American's day planner has fewer holes in it than Ray Charles's dartboard. (DENNIS MILLER)

Ancestors

4473 My folks didn't come over on the *Mayflower*, but they were there to meet the boat. (WILL ROGERS)

4474 My ancestors wandered lost in the wilderness for forty years because even in biblical times, men would not stop to ask for directions. (ELAYNE BOOSLER)

Animals

4475 We hope that, when the insects take over the world, they will remember with gratitude how we took them along on all our picnics. (BILL VAUGHAN)

4476 Scientists tell us that the fastest animal on earth, with a top speed of 120ft per second, is a cow that has been dropped out of a helicopter. (DAVE BARRY)

Architecture

4477 Most architects think by the inch, talk by the yard, and should be kicked by the foot. (PRINCE CHARLES)

4478 You have to give this much to the Luftwaffe — when it knocked down our buildings it did not replace them with anything more offensive than rubble. We did that. (PRINCE CHARLES)

4479 What has happened to Architecture since the Second World War that the only passers-by who can contemplate it without pain are those equipped with a white stick and a dog? (BERNARD LEVIN)

4480 I did not fully understand the dread term "terminal illness" until I saw Heathrow Airport for myself. (DENNIS POTTER)

4481 If you have to keep the lavatory door shut by extending your left leg, it's modern architecture. (NANCY BANKS-SMITH)

4482 We used to build civilizations. Now we build shopping malls. (BILL BRYSON)

Aristocracy
4483 The aristocracy is composed of asses — asses who talk about horses. (HEINRICH HEINE)

Art
4484 One reassuring thing about modern art is that things can't be as bad as they're painted. (M. WALTHALL JACKSON)

4485 Buy old masters. They fetch a better price than old mistresses. (LORD BEAVERBROOK)

Australia
4486 To live in Australia permanently is rather like going to a party and dancing all night with your mother. (BARRY HUMPHRIES)

4487 Australia may be the only country in the world in which the word "academic" is regularly used as a term of abuse. (LEONIE KRAMER)

Aviation
4488 I feel about airplanes the way I feel about diets. It seems to me that they are wonderful things for other people to go on. (JEAN KERR)

4489 The average airplane is 16 years old. And so is the average airplane meal. (JOAN RIVERS)

Baseball
4490 Baseball is the favourite American sport because it's so slow. Any idiot can follow it. And just about any idiot can play it. (GORE VIDAL)

4491 A great catch is like watching girls go by — the last one you see is always the prettiest. (BOB GIBSON)

4492 For the parents of a Little Leaguer, a baseball game is simply a nervous breakdown in innings. (EARL WILSON)

Beauty

4493 They used to photograph Shirley Temple through gauze. They should photograph me through linoleum. (TALLULAH BANKHEAD)

4494 I have no face — only two profiles clapped together. (MARGOT ASQUITH)

4495 I'm tired of all this nonsense about beauty being only skin-deep. That's deep enough. What do you want — an adorable pancreas? (JEAN KERR)

Birth

4496 There are two things in this life for which we are never fully prepared and that is twins. (JOSH BILLINGS)

Bores

4497 Bores can be divided into two classes; those who have their own particular subject, and those who do not need a subject. (A.A. MILNE)

Business

4498 Every crowd has a silver lining. (PHINEAS T. BARNUM)

California

4499 Los Angeles: 19 suburbs in search of a metropolis. (ANON)

4500 I have a theory about LA architecture. I think all the houses came to a costume party and they all came as other countries. (MICHAEL O'DONOGHUE)

Canada

4501 Canada has a climate nine months winter and three months late in the fall. (EVAN ESAR)

4502 I don't even know what street Canada is on. (AL CAPONE)

4503 Montreal is the only place where a good French accent isn't a social asset. (DAN BEHAN)

4504 Canada's national bird is the grouse. (STUART KEATE)

Cats

4505 Women and cats will do as they please, and men and dogs should relax and get used to the idea. (ROBERT A. HEINLEIN)

4506 When my cats aren't happy, I'm not happy. Not because I care about their mood but because I know they're just sitting there thinking up ways to get even. (PENNY WARD MOSER)

4507 To bathe a cat takes brute force, perseverance, courage of conviction, and a cat. The last ingredient is usually hardest to come by. (STEPHEN BAKER)

Chicago

4508 That's great advertising when you can turn Chicago into a city you'd want to spend more than three hours in. (JERRY DELLA FEMINA)

4509 Loving Chicago is like loving a woman with a broken nose. (NELSON ALGREN)

Children

4510 I love children, especially when they cry, for then someone takes them away. (NANCY MITFORD)

4511 In general my children refused to eat anything that hadn't danced on TV. (ERMA BOMBECK)

4512 If thine enemy offend thee, give his child a drum. (FRAN LEBOWITZ)

Christmas

4513 I stopped believing in Santa Claus when I was six. Mother took me to see him in a department store and he asked for my autograph. (SHIRLEY TEMPLE)

Cinema

4514 My interest in the cinema has lapsed since women began to talk. (GEORGE J. NATHAN)

Civilization

4515 You can't say that civilization doesn't advance, for in every war they kill you a new way. (WILL ROGERS)

Courage

4516 I'm a hero with coward's legs. (SPIKE MILLIGAN)

4517 If God wanted us to be brave, why did he give us legs? (MARVIN KITMAN)

4518 Courage is walking naked through a cannibal village. (L.L. LEVINSON)

4519 He was a bold man that first ate an oyster. (JONATHAN SWIFT)

4520 We can't all be heroes because someone has to sit on the kerb and clap as they go by. (WILL ROGERS)

Crime and punishment

4521 When I came back to Dublin I was court-martialled in my absence and sentenced to death in my absence, so I said they could shoot me in my absence. (BRENDAN BEHAN)

4522 If England treats her criminals the way she treated me, she doesn't deserve to have any. (OSCAR WILDE)

4523 I'm for bringing back the birch, but only for consenting adults. (GORE VIDAL)

Dating

4524 When a man goes on a date he wonders if he is going to get lucky. A woman already knows. (FREDERICK RYDER)

4525 As you get older, the pickings get slimmer, but the people don't. (CARRIE FISHER)

Death

4526 It's funny how most people love the dead. Once you're dead, you're made for life. (JIMI HENDRIX)

4527 They say such nice things about people at their funerals that it makes me sad that I'm going to miss mine by just a few days. (GARRISON KEILLOR)

4528 You can spend your whole life trying to be popular but, at the end of the day, the size of the crowd at your funeral will be largely dictated by the weather. (FRANK SKINNER)

4529 Die, my dear doctor, that's the last thing I shall do! (LORD PALMERSTON, on his deathbed)

4530 Those who welcome death have only tried it from the ears up. (WILSON MIZNER)

Divorce

4531 You never realize how short a month is until you pay alimony. (JOHN BARRYMORE)

4532 A lawyer is never entirely comfortable with a friendly divorce, any more than a good mortician wants to finish his job and then have the patient sit up on the table. (JOHN F. KENNEDY)

Dogs

4533 A dog teaches a boy fidelity, perseverance, and to turn around three times before lying down. (ROBERT BENCHLEY)

4534 I loathe people who keep dogs. They are cowards who haven't got the guts to bite people themselves. (AUGUST STRINDBERG)

4535 Don't accept your dog's admiration as conclusive evidence that you are wonderful. (ANN LANDERS)

Drink

4536 I saw a notice which said "Drink Canada Dry" and I've just started. (BRENDAN BEHAN)

4537 You can tell German wine from vinegar by the label. (MARK TWAIN)

4538 I always wake up at the crack of ice. (JOE E. LEWIS)

4539 Anybody who hates dogs and loves whisky can't be all bad. (W.C. FIELDS)

4540 Don't put ice in my drink: it takes up too much room. (GROUCHO MARX)

Drugs

4541 Cocaine isn't habit-forming. I should know — I've been using it for years. (TALLULAH BANKHEAD)

4542 Cocaine is God's way of saying you're making too much money. (ROBIN WILLIAMS)

Economists

4543 If all economists were laid end to end, they would not reach a conclusion. (GEORGE BERNARD SHAW)

Education

4544 Economists report that a college education adds many thousands of dollars to a man's lifetime income – which he then spends sending his son to college. (BILL VAUGHAN)

4545 If all the girls attending it were laid end to end, I wouldn't be at all surprised. (DOROTHY PARKER on the Yale Prom)

England

4546 The Englishman has all the qualities of a poker except its occasional warmth. (DANIEL O'CONNELL)

4547 Continental people have sex lives; the English have hot-water bottles. (GEORGE MIKES)

4548 Summer has set in with its usual severity. (SAMUEL TAYLOR COLERIDGE)

Evil

4549 When choosing between two evils, I always like to try the one I've never tried before. (MAE WEST)

Exercise

4550 Whenever I feel like exercise, I lie down until the feeling passes. (ROBERT HUTCHINS)

4551 I like long walks, especially when they are taken by people who annoy me. (NOEL COWARD)

4552 I get my exercise acting as a pallbearer to my friends who exercise. (CHAUNCEY DEPEW)

Fame

4553 I think that's just another word for washed-up has-been. (BOB DYLAN on being an "icon")

4554 You're not famous until my mother has heard of you. (JAY LENO)

Families

4555 The trouble with incest is that it gets you involved with relatives. (GEORGE S. KAUFMAN)

Folk dancing

4556 Try everything once except incest and folk dancing. (SIR THOMAS BEECHAM)

Food

4557 An Englishman teaching an American about food is like the blind leading the one-eyed. (A.J. LIEBLING)

4558 If the English can survive their food, they can survive anything. (GEORGE BERNARD SHAW)

4559 Jack Sprat could eat no fat, his wife could eat no lean. A real sweet pair of neurotics. (JACK SHARKEY)

Football (American)

4560 Football combines two of the worst things about American life. It is violence punctuated by committee meetings. (GEORGE WILL)

4561 Football is not a contact sport; it is a collision sport. Dancing is a contact sport. (VINCE LOMBARDI)

4562 Pro football is like nuclear warfare. There are no winners, only survivors. (FRANK GIFFORD)

France

4563 How can one conceive of a one-party system in a country that has over 200 varieties of cheeses? (CHARLES DE GAULLE)

4564 France is a country where the money falls apart in your hands and you can't tear the toilet paper. (BILLY WILDER)

4565 Mankind in general occupies the position between the angels and France. (MARK TWAIN)

Germany

4566 One thing I will say for the Germans, they are always perfectly willing to give somebody else's land to somebody else. (WILL ROGERS)

Golf

4567 The reason most people play golf is to wear clothes they would not be caught dead in otherwise. (ROGER SIMON)

4568 Alaska would be an ideal place for a golf course – mighty few trees and damn few ladies' foursomes. (REX LARDNER)

4569 If there's a thunderstorm on a golf course, walk down the middle of the fairway, holding a one-iron over your head. Even God can't hit a one-iron. (LEE TREVINO)

Greatness

4570 Some are born great, some achieve greatness, and some have PR officers. (DANIEL J. BOORSTIN)

Happiness

4571 Happiness? A good cigar, a good meal and a good woman . . . or a bad woman; it depends on how much happiness you can handle. (GEORGE BURNS)

Hate

4572 I never hated a man enough to give him his diamonds back. (ZSA ZSA GABOR)

Health

4573 Everything that used to be a sin is now a disease. (BILL MAHER)

4574 Gout is the only enemy which I don't wish to have at my feet. (SYDNEY SMITH)

4575 I have Bright's disease and he has mine. (S.J. PERELMAN)

Heaven and hell

4576 I don't want to express an opinion. You see, I have friends in both places. (MARK TWAIN)

4577 Heaven for climate, hell for society. (MARK TWAIN)

4578 I'd like to go to heaven. But if Jeffrey Archer is there I want to go to Lewisham. (SPIKE MILLIGAN)

Hollywood

4579 Hollywood is the only place in the world where an amicable divorce means each one gets 50 per cent of the publicity. (LAUREN BACALL)

4580 Ever since they found out that Lassie was a boy, the public has believed the worst of Hollywood. (GROUCHO MARX)

4581 "You will have the tallest, darkest leading man in Hollywood." Those were the first words I heard about King Kong. (FAY WRAY)

Home
4582 All I need is room enough to lay a hat and a few friends. (DOROTHY PARKER)

Ice hockey
4583 I went to a fight the other night and an ice hockey game broke out. (RODNEY DANGERFIELD)

Ireland
4584 The Irish are a fair people; they never speak well of one another. (DR SAMUEL JOHNSON)

4585 Put an Irishman on the spit, and you can always get another Irishman to turn him. (GEORGE BERNARD SHAW)

Journalists
4586 All day long, Hollywood reporters lie in the sun, and when the sun goes down, they lie some more. (FRANK SINATRA)

4587 Most rock journalism is people who can't write interviewing people who can't talk for people who can't read. (FRANK ZAPPA)

Leadership
4588 If you want to be a leader with a large following, just obey the speed limit on a winding, two-lane road. (CHARLES FARR)

Life
4589 Millions who long for immortality do not know what to do with themselves on a rainy Sunday afternoon. (SUSAN ERTZ)

4590 I like life. It's something to do. (RONNIE SHAKES)

Marriage
4591 My mother said it was simple to keep a man – you must be a maid in the living

room, a cook in the kitchen and a whore in the bedroom. I said I'd hire the other two and take care of the bedroom bit. (JERRY HALL)

4592 A girl must marry for love, and keep on marrying until she finds it. (ZSA ZSA GABOR)

4593 A man in love is incomplete until he has married. Then he's finished. (ZSA ZSA GABOR)

4594 I know nothing about sex because I was always married. (ZSA ZSA GABOR)

4595 Not all women give most of their waking thoughts to the problem of pleasing men. Some are married. (EMMA LEE)

4596 I'm the only man who has a marriage licence made out To Whom It May Concern. (MICKEY ROONEY)

4597 When a man opens the car door for his wife, it's either a new car or a new wife. (PRINCE PHILIP, DUKE OF EDINBURGH)

4598 When you see what some girls marry, you realize how much they must hate to work for a living. (HELEN ROWLAND)

Men
4599 God must love the common man. He made so many of them. (ABRAHAM LINCOLN)

4600 Men should be like Kleenex: soft, strong, and disposable. (CHER)

4601 One hell of an outlay for a very small return. (GLENDA JACKSON)

Miniskirts
4602 Never in the history of fashion has so little material been raised so high to reveal so much that needs to be covered so badly. (SIR CECIL BEATON)

Money
4603 Money is like manure. If you spread it around, it does a lot of good, but if you pile it up in one place, it stinks like hell. (CLINT W. MURCHISON)

4604 Money won't buy happiness, but it will pay the salaries of a large research staff to study the problem. (BILL VAUGHAN)

4605 A successful man is one who makes more money than his wife can spend. A successful woman is one who can find such a man. (LANA TURNER)

4606 I don't do the lottery, which means I'm marginally less likely to win than someone who does. (LINDA SMITH)

Morality
4607 All the things I really like to do are either immoral, illegal, or fattening. (ALEXANDER WOOLLCOTT)

4608 It's the good girls who keep diaries; the bad girls never have the time. (TALLULAH BANKHEAD)

4609 The only thing I regret about my past is the length of it. If I had to live my life again, I'd make the same mistakes, only sooner. (TALLULAH BANKHEAD)

4610 I'm as pure as the driven slush. (TALLULAH BANKHEAD)

4611 I used to be Snow White, but I drifted. (MAE WEST)

Music
4612 Karaoke is God's way of letting you know you've drunk too much. (DYLAN JONES)

4613 I know only two tunes: one of them is "Yankee Doodle", and the other isn't. (ULYSSES S. GRANT)

4614 An intellectual snob is someone who can listen to the William Tell Overture and not think of the Lone Ranger. (DAN RATHER)

4615 Jazz is not dead, it just smells funny. (FRANK ZAPPA)

Nudity
4616 It's not true that I had nothing on. I had the radio on. (MARILYN MONROE)

4617 The trouble with nude dancing is that not everything stops when the music does. (SIR ROBERT HELPMANN)

Orgasm
4618 I may not be a great actress but I've become the greatest at screen orgasms.

Ten seconds of heavy breathing, roll your head from side to side, simulate a slight asthma attack and die a little. (CANDICE BERGEN)

Patience

4619 I'm extraordinarily patient provided I get my own way in the end. (MARGARET THATCHER)

4620 Patience is what parents have when there are witnesses. (FRANKLIN P. JONES)

Photography

4621 If you look like your passport photo, in all probability you need the holiday. (EARL WILSON)

Police

4622 I have never seen a situation so dismal that a policeman couldn't make it worse. (BRENDAN BEHAN)

4623 Perhaps the crime situation would be improved if we could get more cops off television and onto the streets. (BILL VAUGHAN)

Politics

4624 Nobody believes a rumour here in Washington until it's officially denied. (EDWARD CHEYFITZ)

4625 You can always get the truth from an American statesman after he has turned 70 or given up all hope of the presidency. (WENDELL PHILLIPS)

4626 Being president is like being a jackass in a hailstorm. There's nothing to do but stand there and take it. (LYNDON B. JOHNSON)

4627 The constitution provides for every accidental contingency in the Executive — except a vacancy in the mind of the president. (JOHN SHERMAN)

4628 Office hours are twelve to one with an hour off for lunch. (GEORGE S. KAUFMAN on Congress)

4629 Fleas can be taught nearly anything that a congressman can. (MARK TWAIN)

4630 It could probably be shown by facts and figures that there is no distinctly native American criminal class except Congress. (MARK TWAIN)

4631 If the Republicans stop telling lies about us, we will stop telling the truth about them. (ADLAI STEVENSON)

4632 I have often wanted to drown my troubles, but I can't get my wife to go swimming. (JIMMY CARTER)

4633 I have orders to be awakened at any time in the case of a national emergency, even if I'm in a cabinet meeting. (RONALD REAGAN)

4634 Politics is supposed to be the second oldest profession. I have come to realize that it bears a very close resemblance to the first. (RONALD REAGAN)

4635 If I had stood unopposed at the last election, I would still have come second. (JOHN MAJOR)

Poverty
4636 I've known what it is to be hungry, but I always went right to a restaurant. (RING LARDNER)

4637 Poverty must have many satisfactions, else there would not be so many poor people. (DON HEROLD)

Prejudice
4638 I am free of all prejudices. I hate everyone equally. (W.C. FIELDS)

Presidency
4639 In America any boy may become president. I suppose it's just one of the risks he takes. (ADLAI STEVENSON)

4640 (On the virtues of being President) The pay is good and I can walk to work. (JOHN F. KENNEDY)

Punctuality
4641 I've been on a calendar, but never on time. (MARILYN MONROE)

Royalty
4642 There will soon be only five kings left: the kings of England, Diamonds, Hearts, Spades and Clubs. (KING FAROUK OF EGYPT on being deposed)

Scotland

4643 It requires a surgical operation to get a joke well into a Scotch understanding. (SYDNEY SMITH)

4644 Much may be made of a Scotchman, if he be caught young. (DR SAMUEL JOHNSON)

4645 There are few more impressive sights in the world than a Scotsman on the make. (J.M. BARRIE)

Sex appeal

4646 Sex appeal is 50 per cent what you've got and 50 per cent what people think you've got. (SOPHIA LOREN)

Shopping

4647 Shopping is better than sex. If you're not satisfied after shopping, you can make an exchange for something you really like. (ADRIENNE GUSOFF)

4648 Why would anyone steal a shopping cart? It's like stealing a two-year-old. (ERMA BOMBECK)

Sport

4649 The only thing on the level is mountain climbing. (EDDIE QUINN)

4650 In Russia, if a male athlete loses, he becomes a female athlete. (YAKOV SMIRNOFF)

4651 Swimming isn't a sport. It's just a way to keep from drowning. (GEORGE CARLIN)

Taxation

4652 It has made more liars out of the American people than golf. (WILL ROGERS)

4653 The art of taxation consists in so plucking the goose as to obtain the largest amount of feathers with the least amount of hissing. (JEAN BAPTISTE COLBERT)

Television

4654 Getting an award from TV is like getting kissed by someone with bad breath. (MASON WILLIAMS)

4655 Television has brought murder back into the home – where it belongs. (ALFRED HITCHCOCK)

4656 Today, watching television often means fighting, violence, and foul language – and that's just deciding who gets to hold the remote control. (DONNA GEPHART)

4657 I'm getting tired of cable. Day after day it's the same 97 channels. (JOE HICKMAN)

4658 The weirdest thing on the show was the guy that married his horse – and tho horse wasn't even that attractive. (JERRY SPRINGER)

Texas
4659 If I owned Texas and Hell, I would rent out Texas and live in Hell. (GENERAL PHILIP H. SHERIDAN)

Theatre
4660 Long experience has taught me that in England nobody goes to the theatre unless he or she has bronchitis. (JAMES AGATE)

4661 If Attila the Hun were alive today, he'd be a dramatic critic. (EDWARD ALBEE)

4662 Things are so bad on Broadway today an actor is lucky to be miscast. (GEORGE S. KAUFMAN)

4663 There are two kinds of directors in the theatre. Those who think they are God and those who are certain of it. (RHETTA HUGHES)

4664 Nudity on stage? I think it's disgusting. But if I were 22 with a great body, it would be artistic, tasteful, patriotic and a progressive religious experience. (SHELLEY WINTERS)

Vegetarians
4665 Most vegetarians I ever see look enough like their food to be classed as cannibals. (FINLEY PETER DUNNE)

Virtue
4666 Virtue has its own reward, but no sale at the box office. (MAE WEST)

4667 People with no vices usually have some pretty annoying virtues. (LIZ TAYLOR)

4668 Never practise two vices at once. (TALLULAH BANKHEAD)

4669 Some people say that I must be a horrible person, but that's not true. I have the heart of a young boy . . . in a jar on my desk. (STEPHEN KING)

Women

4670 To succeed with the opposite sex, tell her you're impotent. She can't wait to disprove it. (CARY GRANT)

4671 Being a woman is of special interest only to aspiring male transsexuals. To actual women it is merely a good excuse not to play football. (FRAN LEBOWITZ)

4672 You don't know a woman till you've met her in court. (NORMAN MAILER)

Work

4673 I always arrive late at the office, but I make up for it by leaving early. (CHARLES LAMB)

4674 I like work: it fascinates me. I can sit and look at it for hours. (JEROME K. JEROME)

LIMERICKS

4675 A fellow with passions quite gingery
Was exploring his young sister's lingerie
When with evident pleasure
He plundered her treasure,
Adding incest to insult and injury.

4676 There once was a pious young priest
Who lived almost wholly on yeast;
He said, "For it's plain
We must all rise again
And I wanted to get started, at least."

4677 A cat in despondency sighed
And resolved to commit suicide.
She passed under the wheels
Of eight automobiles
And after the ninth one she died.

4678 There was a young girl in the choir
Whose voice went up higher and higher,
Till one Sunday night
It vanished from sight
And turned up next day in the spire.

4679 A flea and a fly in a flue,
Were imprisoned, so what could they do?
Said the fly, "Let us flee!"
"Let us fly!" said the flea,
And they flew through a flaw in the flue.

4680 A widow whose singular vice
Was to keep her late husband on ice,
Said, "It's been hard since I lost him,
I'll never defrost him!
Cold comfort, but cheap at the price!"

4681 Said an ovum one night to a sperm,
"You're a very attractive young germ.
Come join me, my sweet,
Let our nuclei meet,
And in nine months we'll both come to term."

4682 It is the unfortunate habit
Of the rabbit to breed like a rabbit.
One can say without question
This leads to congestion
In the burrows that rabbits inhabit.

4683 Said the potentate gross and despotic,
"My tastes are more rich than exotic.
I've always adored
Making love in a Ford
Because I am auto-erotic."

4684 There once were two people of taste
Who were beautiful down to the waist.
So they limited love
To the regions above
And thus remained perfectly chaste.

4685 An accident really uncanny
Befell a respectable granny:
She sat down in a chair
While her false teeth were there
And bit herself right in the fanny.

4686 Said a woman with open delight,
"My pubic hair's perfectly white.
I admit there's a glare,
But the fellows don't care –
They locate it more quickly at night."

4687 Said an envious, erudite ermine,
"There's one thing I can't quite determine:
When a dame wears my coat,
She's a lady of note;
When I wear it, I'm called only vermin."

4688 A gentle old lady I knew
Was dozing one day in her pew.
When the preacher yelled "Sin!"
She exclaimed, "Count me in,
As soon as the service is through!"

4689 A golfer, who sought to survive
With grit, dedication and drive,
"Inflation," he'd claim,
"Is affecting my game,
I used to shout 'fore' – now it's 'five'."

4690 There once was a man not unique
In fancying himself quite a shique
But the girls didn't fall
For this fellow at all
For he only made sixty a wique.

4691 A young curate, just new to the cloth,
At sex was surely no sloth.
He preached masturbation
To his whole congregation,
And was washed down the aisle on the froth.

4692 There was an old lady who lay
With her legs wide apart in the hay;
Then, calling the ploughman,
She said, "Do it now, man!
Don't wait till your hair has turned grey."

4693 Ferrets live by a code tried and true,
From which humans can benefit too:
Teach your sons and daughters
To do unto otters,
As otters would do unto you.

4694 A lady with features cherubic
Was famed for her area pubic.
When they asked her its size
She replied in surprise,
"Are you speaking of square feet, or cubic?"

4695 A surgeon of some imprecision
Decided on self-circumcision.
A slip of the knife —
"Oh, dear," said his wife,
"Our sex life will need some revision."

4696 Consider the poor hippopotamus:
His life is unduly monotonous.
He lives half asleep
At the edge of the deep,
And his face is as big as his bottom is.

4697 A bather whose clothing was strewed
By breezes that left her quite nude
Saw a man come along
And, unless I'm quite wrong,
You expected this line to be lewd.

4698 There was a young girl of Aberystwyth
Who took grain to the mill to get grist with.
The miller's son, Jack,
Laid her flat on her back,
And united the organs they pissed with.

4699 In the garden of Eden lay Adam,
Massaging the bust of his madam,
And loud was his mirth
For he knew that on earth
There were only two boobs — and he had 'em.

4700 There once was a man from Algiers
Who tried growing corn in his ears.
When the temperature rose,
He leapt to his toes,
Now popping is all that he hears.

4701 A nymphomaniac named Alice
Used a dynamite stick for a phallus.
They found her vagina
In North Carolina
And her ass-hole in Buckingham Palace.

4702 A sleeper from the Amazon
Put nighties of his gra'mazon —
The reason: that
He was too fat
To get his own pajamazon.

4703 A lady there was in Antigua
Who said to her spouse, "What a pigua."
He answered, "My queen,
Is it manners you mean?
Or do you refer to my figua?"

4704 There was a young man from Australia,
Who painted his butt like a dahlia.
The drawing was fine,
The colour divine,
But the scent — ah! that was a failure.

4705 Another young man from Australia
Went on a wild bacchanalia.
He buggered a frog,
Two mice and a dog,
And a bishop in fullest regalia.

4706 There was a young girl of Baroda
Who built a new kind of pagoda.
The walls of its halls
Were hung with the balls
And the tools of the fools that bestrode her.

4707 A flatulent actor named Barton
Led a life exceedingly spartan,
Till a playwright one day
Wrote a well-received play
With a part for Barton to fart in.

4708 There was an old pirate named Bates
Who was learning to rumba on skates.
He fell on his cutlass,
Which rendered him nutless
And practically useless on dates.

4709 There once was a man from Bellaire
Who screwed his wife on the stair.
The banister broke,
He quickened his stroke
And finished her off in the air.

4710 There was a young girl from Berlin
Whose nose was exceedingly thin.
She could slice up the butter
With barely a mutter,
And flip it down onto her chin.

4711 I wooed a stewed nude in Bermuda,
I was lewd, but my God! she was lewder.
She said it was crude
To be wooed in the nude –
I pursued her, subdued her, and screwed her!

4712 There once was a student named Bessor
Whose knowledge grew lessor and lessor
It at last grew so small
He knew nothing at all,
And today he's a college professor!

4713 There was a young lady of Bicester
Who was nicer by far than her sister:
The sister would giggle
And wiggle and jiggle,
But this one would come if you kissed her.

4714 There once was a man of Blackheath
Who sat on his pair of false teeth.
He said with a start,
"Oh dear, bless my heart,
For I've bitten myself underneath!"

4715 Bill Bounce, being fat for a jockey,
Tried steaming to make him less stocky.
This heated him so
That he had to eat snow,
And change his profession to hockey.

4716 A young trapeze artist named Bract
Is faced by a very sad fact.
Imagine his pain
When, again and again,
He catches his wife in the act!

4717 A squeamish young fellow named Brand
Thought caressing his penis was grand.
But he viewed with distaste
The gelatinous paste
That it left in the palm of his hand.

4718 An indolent vicar of Bray
His roses allowed to decay;
His wife, more alert,
Bought a powerful squirt,
And said to her spouse, "Let us spray."

4719 A maiden at college, Miss Breeze,
Weighed down by BAs and LitDs
Collapsed from the strain.
Said her doctor, "It's plain —
You're killing yourself by degrees."

4720 There was a discreet Brigadier,
Very fond of four thousand a year;
Who, when he heard the guns rattle,
Fiercely cried: "Ha! The battle!" –
Then complacently slid to the rear.

4721 There was a young lady named Bright
Whose speed was far faster than light.
She set off one day
In a relative way
And came back the previous night.

4722 There once was a sailor from Brighton
Who said to a lass, "You're a tight one."
She replied "'Pon my soul,
You're in the wrong hole!
There's plenty of room in the right one."

4723 There was a young lady called Brigid
Whose sex life was apt to be frigid
So they used to begin
With a bottle of gin
Till the boy friend (not Brigid) was rigid.

4724 An Argentine gaucho named Bruno
Once said, "There is something I do know;
A woman is fine
And a sheep is divine
But a llama is Numero Uno!"

4725 There once was a Queen of Bulgaria
Whose bush had grown hairier and hairier,
Till a Prince from Peru
Who came up for a screw
Had to hunt for her hole with a terrier.

4726 There was a young cashier of Calais
Whose accounts when reviewed wouldn't talais.
But his chief smelled a rat
When he furnished a flat
And was seen every night at the balais.

4727 There was an old man of Calcutta
Who coated his tonsils with butta,
Thus converting his snore
From a thunderous roar
To a soft, oleaginous mutta.

4728 There was a young girl of Cape Cod
Who thought babies were fashioned by God.
But it wasn't the Almighty
Who lifted her nighty
But Roger the lodger, the sod!

4729 There once was a man from Cape Horn
Who wished that he'd never been born.
He wouldn't have been
If his father had seen
That the end of his condom was torn.

4730 There was a young fellow named Charteris
Put his hand where his young lady's garter is.
Said she, "I don't mind,
And up higher you'll find
The place where my fucker and farter is."

4731 There was a young lady from Cheam
Who tried out a breast-growing cream;
She woke in the night
With a terrible fright –
Another had grown in between.

4732 The robes of the Vicar of Cheltenham
Gave him pleasure whenever he knelt in 'em.
But they got rather hot
When he wore them a lot,
And the Vicar of Cheltenham smelt in 'em.

4733 There was a young lady of Chichester
Who made all the saints in their niches stir.
One morning at Matins
Her breasts in white satins
Made the Bishop of Chichester's britches stir.

4734 When they catch a chinchilla in Chile,
They cut off its beard, willy-nilly,
With a small razor blade,
Just to say that they've made
A Chilean chinchilla's chin chilly.

4735 There was a fat lady of China
Who had an enormous vagina,
And when she was dead,
They painted it red
And used it for docking a liner.

4736 There was a young lady named Clair
Who possessed a magnificent pair,
Or at least so I thought
Till I saw one get caught
On a thorn and begin losing air.

4737 There once was a man named Clegm
Who had a great deal of phlegm.
Ahegm, ahegm,
Ahegm, ahegm,
Ahegm, ahegm, ahegm.

4738 There once was a fellow named Clyde
Who went to a funeral and cried.
When asked who was dead,
He stammered and said,
"I don't know, I just came for the ride."

4739 There was a brave girl of Connecticut
Who signalled the train with her pecticut,
Which the papers defined
As presence of mind,
But deplorable absence of ecticut.

4740 A lady while dining at Crewe
Found an elephant's whang in her stew.
Said the waiter, "Don't shout,
And don't wave it about,
Or the others will all want one too."

4741 There once was a man name of Crocket
Who stuck his foot in a socket.
Then along came a witch
Who turned on the switch
And Crocket went up like a rocket!

4742 A huge-organed female in Dallas,
Named Alice, who yearned for a phallus,
Was virgo intacto,
Because, ipso facto,
No phallus in Dallas fit Alice.

4743 There was a young girl of Darjeeling
Who could dance with such exquisite feeling
There was never a sound
For miles around,
Save for fly-buttons hitting the ceiling.

4744 There was a faith healer of Deal
Who said: "Although pain is not real,
When I sit on a pin,
And puncture my skin,
I dislike what I fancy I feel."

4745 There was a young lady from Del.
Who was most undoubtedly wel.
That to dress for a masque   (Note abbreviation
Wasn't much of a tasque,   of American state:
But she cried, "What on earth will my fel.?"   Del. = Delaware)

4746 There was a young man from Devizes
Whose balls were of different sizes
The one that was small
Was no use at all,
But the other won several prizes.

4747 A mouse in her room woke Miss Dowd
Who was frightened and screamed very loud.
Then a happy thought hit her
To scare off the critter
She sat up in bed and miaowed.

4748 I sat next to the Duchess at tea,
Distressed as a person could be.
Her rumblings abdominal
Were simply phenomenal –
And everyone thought it was me!

4749 There was a young girl from Dumfries
Who said to her boy: "If you please
It would give me great bliss
If, while fondling this,
You would pay some attention to these."

4750 When twins came, their father, John Dunn,
Gave "Edward" as name to each son.
When folks said, "Absurd!"
He replied, "Haven't you heard
That two Eds are better than one?"

4751 There once was a lady, Eileen,
Who lived on distilled kerosene.
But she started absorbin'
A new hydrocarbon
And since then she's never benzene.

4752 There was a young lady in Eton
Whose figure had plenty of meat on.
She said, "Marry me, dear,
And you'll find that my rear
Is a nice place to warm your cold feet on."

4753 A gardener, living in Ewell,
Found his bonfire wanted more fuel;
So they threw Uncle James
To heighten the flames –
A measure effective though cruel.

4754 There once was a lady from Exeter
So pretty that men craned their necks at her.
One was even so brave
As to take out and wave
The distinguishing mark of his sex at her.

4755 There's an arthritic lady in Fakenham
Whose joints have a worsening ache in 'em;
Her pain level's rising,
Which isn't surprising:
She's got pills, but hasn't been takin' 'em.

4756 There was a young fellow named Feeney
Whose girl was a terrible meanie.
The hatch of her snatch
Had a catch that would latch –
She could only be screwed by Houdini.

4757 There once was a man name of Finnigin
Who broke out of jail just to sinnigin;
He broke laws by the dozen,
Even stole from his cousin
– Now the jail he broke out of, he's innigin.

4758 There was a young fellow named Fisher,
Who was fishing for fish in a fissure,
When a trout, with a grin,
Pulled the fisherman in;
Now they're fishing the fissure for Fisher.

4759 A newspaper man name of Fling
Could make "copy" from any old thing.
But the copy he wrote
Of a five dollar note
Was so good he is now in Sing Sing.

4760 A handsome young gent down in Fla.
Collapsed in a hospital ca.
A young nurse from Me.   (Note the abbreviation for
Sought to banish his pe.   American states: Fla. = Florida
And shot him. Now what could be ha.?   and Me. = Maine)

4761 A publisher went off to France
In search of a tale of romance.
A Parisian lady
Told a story so shady
That the publisher made an advance.

4762 There once was a baker named Fred
Whose success never went to his head.
Instead of just looking,
He ate all his cooking,
So it went to his waistline instead.

4763 There once was a young man named Gene
Who invented a screwing machine.
Concave and convex,
It could please either sex,
And it played with itself in between.

4764 There was an old maid of Genoa
I blush when I think what Iowa.
She's gone to her rest,
And it's all for the best;
Otherwise I would borrow Samoa.

4765 There was a young lady from Gloucester
Whose husband once thought that he'd loucester.
But he found her that night
In the icebox, locked tight.
We all had to help him defroucester.

4766 Another young lady of Gloucester
Had friends who thought they had lost her,
Till they found on the grass
The marks of her arse,
And the knees of the man who had crossed her.

4767 There once was a man from Great Britain
Who interrupted two girls at their knittin'.
Said he with a sigh,
"That park bench, well I
Just painted it right where you're sittin'."

4768 There was an old fellow named Green
Who grew so abnormally lean,
And flat, and compressed,
That his back touched his chest,
And sideways he couldn't be seen.

4769 There once was a lady from Guam
Who said, "Now the ocean's so calm
I will swim, for a lark."
She encountered a shark.
Let us now sing the 90th psalm.

4770 "Far dearer to me than my treasure,"
Miss Guggenheim said "Is my leisure.
For then I can screw
The whole Harvard crew –
They're slow, but it lengthens the pleasure."

4771 A mathematician named Hall
Had a hexahedronical ball.
And the cube of its weight
Times his pecker's, plus eight
Is his phone number – give him a call.

4772 There was a young lady named Hannah
Who slipped on a peel of banana.
More stars she espied
As she lay on her side
Than are found in the Star Spangled Banner.

4773 There once was a lady named Harris
That nothing seemed apt to embarrass
Till the bath salts she shook
In a tub that she took
Turned out to be plaster-of-Paris.

4774 There was a young fellow from Harrow
Whose cock was the size of a marrow.
He said to his tart,
"How's this for a start?
My balls are outside in a barrow."

4775 A lovely young girl named Anne Heuser
Declared that no man could surprise her;
But a fellow named Gibbons
Untied her Blue Ribbons,
And now she is sadder Budweiser.

4776 There was a young girl from Hong Kong
Who said, "You are utterly wrong
To say my vagina
's the largest in China,
Just because of your mean little dong."

4777 There was an old fellow from Hyde
Who fell down a closet and died.
He had a young brother
Who fell down another
And now they're interred side by side.

4778 There was an old barber from Hythe
Who shaved stubbly chins with a scythe.
He said: "It comes cheaper
Than using a reaper,
Though it does make the customers writhe."

4779 There once was a guy named Jake
Who had very bad stomach ache;
He sat in his chair
Saying, "Tis only fair,
For I ate the entire chocolate cake."

4780 There once was a woman named Jane
With a soft and pliable brain.
When she went to the pool
At her junior high school,
They used her to plug up the drain.

4781 There once was a couple named Kelly
Who lived their life belly to belly.
Because in their haste,
They used paper paste
Instead of petroleum jelly.

4782 There was a young fellow of Kent
Whose prick was so long that it bent.
So to save himself trouble,
He put it in double,
And instead of coming he went.

4783 There once was a Curate from Kew
Who preached with his vestments askew:
A lady called Morgan
Caught sight of the organ,
And promptly passed out in the pew.

4784 There was a young harlot from Kew
Who filled her inside up with glue.
She said with a grin,
"If they pay to get in
They'll pay to get out of it too."

4785 A faggot who lived in Khartoum
Took a lesbian up to his room
And they argued all night
As to who had the right
To do what, and with which, and to whom.

4786 There once was a man from Khartoum
Who was exceedingly fond of the womb.
He thought nothing finer
Than the human vagina,
So he kept three or four in his room.

4787 A lady who lived in Killean
Was notoriously stingy and mean.
"If a sandwich," she said,
"Had but one slice of bread,
There'd be no need for meat in between."

4788 There was a young lady of Lancashire,
Who once went to work as a bank cashier.
But she scarcely knew
One plus one equalled two
So they had to revert to a man cashier.

4789 There was a young fellow called Lancelot
Whom his neighbours all looked on askance a lot
Whenever he'd pass
A presentable lass
The front of his pants would advance a lot.

4790 There was a young girl of La Plata
Who was widely renowned as a farter.
Her deafening reports
At the Argentine Sports
Made her much in demand as a starter.

4791 There was a young salesman of Leeds
Rashly swallowed six packets of seeds.
In a month, silly ass,
He was covered with grass
And couldn't sit down for the weeds.

4792 There was a young plumber of Leigh
Who was plumbing a girl by the sea.
She said, "Stop your plumbing,
There's somebody coming!"
Said the plumber, still plumbing, "It's me."

4793 A precocious young lady named Lillian
Protruded her tongue at a Chilean;
Her mother said, pleading,
"Remember your breeding,
That trick is distinctly reptilian."

4794 There once was a walrus named Lou
Who lived in a place called the zoo.
He said to his friend,
"Do my teeth ever end?
I can't see past them, can you?"

4795 There was a young man from Lundu
Who was only just learning to screw,
But he hadn't the knack,
And he got too far back —
In the right church, but in the wrong pew.

4796 There once was an old man of Lyme
Who married three wives at a time:
When asked, "Why a third?"
He replied, "One's absurd,
And bigamy, sir, is a crime."

4797 There once was a lady named Lynn
Who was so uncommonly thin
That when she assayed
To drink lemonade,
She slipped through the straw and fell in.

4798 There once was a farm girl named Mabel
Who at milking was not very able.
To get over her fright,
She practised at night
With sausages under the table.

4799 There was a young girl from Madras
Who had the most beautiful ass.
But not as you'd think
Firm, round and pink,
It was grey, had long ears, and ate grass.

4800 There once was a man from Madras
Whose balls were constructed of brass.
In stormy weather
They clanged together
And sparks flew out of his ass.

4801 There was a young lady of Malta
Who strangled her aunt with a halter.
She said, "I won't bury her,
She'll do for my terrier;
She'll keep for a month if I salt her."

4802 There was a young girl named Mariah
Who succumbed to her lover's desire.
She said, "It's a sin,
But now that it's in,
Could you shove it a few inches higher?"

4803 A hungry young fellow named Marvin
Sat dreaming of turkeys and carvin'.
So a lady brought Spam,
But he said: "Thank you, ma'am;
I prefer the alternative: starvin'."

4804 Have you heard of knock-kneed Sam McGuzzum
Who wed Samantha, his bow-legged cousin?
Some people say
Love finds a way
But for Sam and Samantha it doesn'.

4805 She frowned and called him Mr
Because he boldly Kr
And so in spite
That very night
This Mr Kr Sr.

4806 A dentist named Archibald Moss
Fell in love with the dainty Miss Ross,
But he held in abhorrence
Her Christian name, Florence,
So he renamed her his Dental Floss.

4807 There was a young belle of old Natchez
Whose garments were always in patchez.
When comment arose
On the state of her clothes
She drawled, "When ah itchez, ah scratchez."

4808 There once was a man from New Haven
Whose daughter resembled a raven.
He daily would feed
Her only birdseed —
Just think of the money he's savin'.

4809 There once was a girl of New York
Whose body was lighter than cork;
She had to be fed
For six weeks upon lead
Before she went out for a walk.

4810 There was a young lady of Niger
Who smiled as she rode on a tiger.
They returned from the ride
With the lady inside
And the smile on the face of the tiger.

4811 There was a young lady of Norway
Swung on a trapeze in a doorway.
With her legs opened wide,
To her lover she cried,
"I think I've discovered one more way."

4812 An alluring young pig in Paree
Fills all of her suitors with glee,
For when they implore
Her to give a bit more
She invariably answers, "Wee, wee."

4813 An impetuous swordsman from Parma
Was lovingly fondling a charma.
Said the maiden demure,
"You'll excuse me, I'm sure,
But I think you're still wearing your arma."

4814 There was a young fellow named Paul
Who attended a fancy dress ball.
They say, just for fun,
He dressed up as a bun,
And a dog ate him up in the hall.

4815 A lecherous Bishop of Peoria,
In a state of constant euphoria,
Enjoyed having fun
With a whore or a nun
While chanting the Sanctus and Gloria.

4816 There was a young lady named Perkins
Who just simply doted on gherkins.
In spite of advice,
She ate so much spice
That she pickled her internal workin's.

4817 There once was a Jew from Peru
Who was vainly attempting to screw.
His wife said, "Oy-vey!
If you keep up this way,
The messiah will come before you."

4818 There once was a man from Peru
Who dreamed of eating his shoe.
He awoke with a fright
In the middle of the night
And found that his dream had come true.

4819 There once was a man from Peru
Whose limericks always end on line two.

4820 There once was a young man named Pete
Who was more than a shade indiscreet.
He pulled on his dong
Till it grew very long
And actually dragged in the street.

4821 There was a small dog of Pirbright
Who would play at the organ all night;
And in this shrewd way
It kept burglars at bay,
For its Bach was much worse than its bite.

4822 The President's loud protestation
On his fall to the intern's temptation:
"This affair is still moral,
As long as it's oral —
Straight screwing I save for the nation."

4823 There was a young student of Queen's
Who was fond of explosive machines.
He once blew up a door,
But he'll do it no more
For it chanced that the door was the Dean's.

4824 A young violinist from Rio
Was seducing a lady named Cleo.
As she took down her panties,
She said: "No andantes;
I want this allegro con brio!"

4825 There once was a man from St Paul
Who swore that he had but one ball.
Two dirty young bitches
Tore down his breeches
And found that he had none at all.

4826 Meanwhile a young girl from St Paul
Wore a newspaper dress to a ball.
But the dress caught on fire
And burned her entire,
Front page, sporting section and all.

4827 There was a young man from Seattle
Who bested a bull in a battle.
With fire and gumption,
He assumed the bull's function
And deflowered a whole herd of cattle.

4828 There was a hillbilly named Shaw
Who envied his maw and his paw.
To share in their life,
He adopted his wife
And became his own father-in-law.

4829 There was a young hunter named Shepherd
Who was eaten for lunch by a leopard.
Said the leopard, "Egad!
You'd be tastier, lad,
If you had only been salted and peppered."

4830 There once was a monk from Siberia
Whose manners were somewhat inferior.
He did to a nun
What he shouldn't have done
And now she's a Mother Superior.

4831 There was a young lady named Stella
Fell in love with a bowlegged fella.
The venturesome chap
Let her sit on his lap
And she plummeted down to the cellar.

4832 A man in a bus queue at Stoke
Unzipped his fly for a joke.
An old man gave a shout
And almost passed out
And a lady close by had a stroke.

4833 A young schizophrenic named Struther,
When told of the death of his mother,
Said, "Yes, it's too bad,
But I can't feel too sad.
After all, I still have each other."

4834 Undressing a maiden called Sue,
Her seducer exclaimed, "If it's true
That a nipple a day
Keeps the doctor away,
Think how healthy you must be with two!"

4835 There was a young lady from Sydney
Who could take it right up to her kidney.
But a man from Quebec
Shoved it up to her neck.
Now he had a long one, didn' he?

4836 A lady once triplets begat,
Named Nat and Pat and Tat.
Though it was fun breeding,
The trouble was feeding,
Because there was no tit for Tat.

4837 There was a young girl of Tonga
Used to diddle herself with a conger.
When asked how it feels
To be pleasured by eels,
She said, "Just like a man, only longer."

4838 There once was a woman called Toni
Who ate lots of steamed macaroni.
She grew quite fat
But she didn't mind that
Cos she bounced when she fell off her pony.

4839 There was a young lady of Tottenham,
Her manners — she'd wholly forgotten'em.
While at tea at the vicar's
She took off her knickers
Explaining she felt much too hot in 'em.

4840 There was a young dentist called Trevor
Whose technique was deplorably clever:
Since, out of depravity,
He filled the wrong cavity,
He's more women patients than ever.

4841 There was a young fellow from Tyne
Put his head on the South-Eastern line.
But he died of ennui
For the 5.53
Didn't come till a quarter past nine.

4842 An oldish maid, born in Vancouver,
Once captured a man by manoeuvre;
She jumped on his knee
With a chortle of glee,
And nothing on earth could remove her.

4843 There was a young lady called Valerie
Who started to count every calorie.
Said her boss in disgust,
"If you lose half your bust
Then you're worth only half of your salary."

4844 A golfer who hailed from Verdun
Was intent on not being outdone.
To avoid any glitches,
He carried spare britches
In case he got a hole in one.

4845 There was a young fellow named Vivian
Who had a dear friend, a Bolivian,
Who dropped his cigar
In a gunpowder jar —
His spirit is now in oblivion.

4846 Said a foolish young lady of Wales,
"A smell of escaped gas prevails."
Then she searched with a light
And later that night
Was collected — in seventeen pails!

4847 There once was a woodsman named Weaver
Whose wife had a face like a beaver.
But her sharp teeth with ease
Could cut down tall trees,
And so no way could Weaver leave 'er.

4848 The bottle of perfume that Willie sent
Was highly displeasing to Millicent.
Her thanks were so cold
That they quarrelled, I'm told,
Through that silly scent Willie sent Millicent.

4849 There was a young fellow called Willie
Whose behaviour was frequently silly.
At a big UNO ball,
Dressed in nothing at all,
He claimed that his costume was Chile.

4850 A progressive professor named Winners
Held classes each evening for sinners.
They were graded and spaced
So the very debased
Would not be held back by beginners.

4851 On the chest of a harlot from Yale
Were tattooed the prices of ale,
And on her behind,
For the sake of the blind,
Was the same information in Braille.

4852 A cheerful old bear at the Zoo
Could always find something to do.
When it bored him to go
On a walk to and fro,
He reversed it and walked fro and to.

MISPRINTS AND HOWLERS

News and Sport

4853 Cynthia Bertross, the celebrated soprano, was involved in a serious car accident last month. We are happy to report that she was able to appear this evening in four pieces. (*Worthing Gazette*)

4854 Belcoo police seized 20 cattle and 30 small pigs on suspicion of having been smuggled, assisted by Miss K. McDermott (violin) and Mrs P. O'Rourke (percussion and effects). (*Fermanagh Herald*)

4855 Winners in the home-made claret section were Mrs Davis (fruity, well rounded), Mrs Rayner (fine colour and full-bodied) and Miss Ogle-Smith (slightly acid, but should improve if laid down). (Leicestershire parish magazine)

4856 The Vicar, the Rev. C.O. Marston, reported an increased number of communicants during the year. He also stated that the death watch beetle had been confirmed in the church. (*Banbury Guardian*)

4857 Towards the end of the day souffles broke out in the crowd. (*Daily Star* report of a troublesome Notting Hill Carnival)

4858 He told police that one of the men menaced him with a wench while the other covered him with a revolver. (Ohio paper)

4859 Miss Mary Salter rendered three vocal solos and a return to orchestral music was greatly appreciated. (Surrey paper)

4860 The public will be allowed to inspect the Crematorium on Sundays. Other amusements will be found advertised in the local Press. (Canadian paper)

4861 In my opinion he will make a great king. He is a young man wise beyond his ears. (Armand Hammer's opinion of Prince Charles, as quoted by the *Sunday Times*)

4862 "In most associations half the committee does all the work, whilst the other half does nothing. I am pleased to put on record that in this society it is just the reverse." (*Liverpool Echo*)

4863 The district game warden filed four complaints, charging illegal fishing in Judge J.J. Padgett's court. (*Waco News-Tribune*)

4864 Before Miss Jenkinson concluded the concert by singing "I'll walk beside you" she was prevented with a bouquet of red roses. (Sussex paper)

4865 The Sunbeam Band of Central Baptist Church, meeting at ten o'clock at the church where transportation will be provided to a picnic which will be hell in the county. (Kentucky paper)

4866 Peanut-butter grilled corn. Let everyone grill his own ears, using long skewers to do so. (*American Weekly*)

4867 "This budget leakage is something that's got to stop," said the President, with what seemed to be more than a trace of irrigation in his voice. (*Jackson* [Missouri] *State Times*)

4868 Arthur Kitchener was seriously burned Saturday afternoon when he came into contact with a high voltage wife. (Surrey paper)

4869 The best plan is to hold the bottle firmly and remove the cook as gently as possible. (Women's magazine)

1070 Your food stamps will be stopped effective March 1992 because we received notice that you passed away. May God bless you. You may reapply if there is a change in your circumstances. (Department of Social Services, Greenville, South Carolina)

4871 There was a good number present at the Bible class on Monday and a keen discussion took place on the subject, 'Are there stages in Sin?' On Monday night a practical class was held. (Welsh paper)

4872 According to the complaint, Mrs O'Donnell says her husband started amusing her three days before the marriage. [Texas paper]

4873 The glamorous 17-year-old wants to be a policewoman some day, just like her father. (New Zealand paper)

4874 A heavy pall of lust covered the upper two-thirds of Texas last night and was expected to drift south-east over the state by morning. (*Yankton Press*)

4875 Chiu Mei Au Yeung, who works for VNU's Computer Business Week, was particularly thrilled as the holiday will give her an opportunity to sell her Hong Kong-based family, whom she has not seen for many years. (*Magazine Week*)

4876 The ladies of the Helping Hand Society enjoyed a swap social on Friday evening. Everybody brought something they didn't need. Many of the ladies were accompanied by their husbands. (Massachusetts paper)

4877 Some 40 per cent of female gas station employees in Metro Detroit are women. (Detroit paper)

4878 The region, developed as America's first national seashore park, was visited by 306,328 persons, three times the attendance for the previous year when no attendance figures were kept. (US magazine)

4879 Out of those 50 guests more than 30 had been married to the same man for more than 20 years. (*Los Angeles Times*)

4880 The ladies of the Cherry Street Church have discarded clothing of all kinds. Call at 44 North Cherry Street for inspection. (Louisiana paper)

4881 Let there be no misunderstanding. A mating of two champion sheepdogs is more likely to produce a super Border Collie than the mating of two champion cattle or horses. (*Scotsman*)

4882 She was married in Evansville, Indiana, to Walter Jackson, and to this onion was born three children. (Ohio paper)

4883 The driver involved in this incident asked that her gender not be revealed. (Sydney paper)

4884 What is more beautiful for a blonde to wear for formal dances than white tulle? My answer – and I'm sure you will agree with me – is "Nothing". (Massachusetts paper)

4885 At next Wednesday's children's party it is expected that in two hours 300 children will consume 1,800 sandwiches and 900 fancy cakes, gallons of milk and tea, pounds of butter and a fishfryer, a plumber, a schoolmaster and a railway inspector. (Yorkshire paper)

4886 As maintenance of this churchyard is becoming increasingly difficult and expensive, it will be appreciated if parishioners will cut the grass around their own graves. (Essex newspaper)

4887 Dr Gordon Nikiforuk of Toronto University told the Ontario Dental Association that a person can help prevent decay by vigorously rinsing his mother after each meal. (Toronto paper)

4888 Mr and Mrs Remington Taylor of Verona, formerly of Ithaca, were weakened guests of Mrs J. H. Barron of 145 Cascadilla Park. (*Ithaca Journal*)

4889 The strike leaders had called a meeting that was to have been held in a bra near the factory, but it was found to be too small to hold them all. (*South London Press*)

4890 Due to a typing error, Gov. Dukakis was incorrectly identified in the third paragraph as Mike Tyson. (Massachusetts paper)

4891 Mr Firestone argued that his client was a student, had not been found guilty, and should not be subhauled by tank steamer to the east coast and then pumped back into the middle-west and the Great Lakes area through pipelines. (*Cleveland Press*)

4892 The murder of the man and the finding of the body was followed by a series of tragedies, including the suicide of the murdered man. (*Idaho Falls Times-Register*)

4893 The season for grass fires seems to have arrived, so stamp out that cigarette end before you throw it down. (*Herne Bay Press*)

4894 A new swimming pool is rapidly taking shape since the contractors have thrown in the bulk of their workers. (East African paper)

4895 We are sorry to announce that Mr Albert Brown has been quite unwell, owing to his recent death, and is taking a short holiday to recover. (US parish magazine)

4896 The first essential in the treatment of burns is that the patient should be removed from the fire. (*First Aid Journal*)

4897 Three children died in a cloudburst near Memphis, Texas, as floods swept that section of the Southwest. Beneficial rains also fell in the San Angelo area. (California paper)

4898 At the fair they will be exhibiting a full range of shoes for girls with low-cut fancy uppers. (*Leicester Mercury*)

4899 A cup of good English tea, with a few biscuits, is frequently his only food at breakfast, and this after he has devoured all the morning newspapers at nine o'clock. (Buckinghamshire paper)

4900 The motorist approached the coroner at 90 mph. (US paper)

4901 The bride, who was given away by her father, wore a dress of white figured brocade with a trailing veil held in place by a coronet of pearls. She carried a bouquet of rose buds and goods vehicles, leaving free access to all private vehicles not built for more than seven passengers. (*Atherstone News and Herald*)

4902 Seven children of this community took advantage of the clinic in Rogers and were examined for tuberculosis and other diseases which the clinic offered free of charge. (Arkansas paper)

4903 The piano accompanist was Miss Margaret Mander, whose delightful talent for striking the right note is so much appreciated. (Scottish paper)

4904 After Governor Baldridge watched the lion perform, he was taken to Main Street and fed 25 pounds of raw meat in front of the Fox Theater. (*Idaho Statesman*)

4905 Miss Penneway is in hospital this morning after having been bitten by a spider in a bathing suit. (US paper)

4906 The spacious home of Judge and Mrs Woodbury was the scene of a beautiful wedding last evening when their youngest daughter, Dorothy, was joined in holy deadlock to Mr Wilkie. (Nebraska paper)

4907 Bedford firemen today received 28 letters thanking them for their efforts which destroyed three houses last Wednesday night. (Bedford paper)

4908 On July 11 he suffered a stroke but with the loving care of his family and his efficient nurse, he never fully recovered. (Wisconsin paper)

4909 Wrap poison bottles in sandpaper and fasten with scotch tape or a rubber band. If there are children in the house, lock them in a small metal box. (*Philadelphia Record*)

4910 Very Rev M. Canon Doherty, ugly and unsightly debris heap, was being transformed into a delightful miniature park. (*Limerick Chronicle*)

4911 Columbia, Tennessee, which calls itself the largest outdoor mule market in the world, recently held a mule parade, headed by the governor. (New York magazine)

4912 We wish to thank our many friends and neighbours for their kind assistance in the recent destruction of our home by fire. (US paper)

4913 Mr and Mrs Kenneth Walts of Vendocia are announcing the approaching marriage of their daughter, Carole, to Mr John H. Buchanan. The couple will exchange cows at 7.30 Saturday evening. (*Delphose Herald* [Ohio])

4914 A carpet was stolen last night from Ryde Council building. Measuring almost six feet square, the thief has baffled council officers. (Sydney, Australia, paper)

4915 Anyone can plant radishes; it takes courage to plant acorns and wait for the oats. (*Boy Scouts Association Weekly*)

4916 Much has been written on the subject of rose cultivation. Let us take soil preparation first. You will want a loam containing plenty of humans and good drainage. (*San Francisco Examiner*)

4917 We note with regret that Mrs Calhoun is recuperating from an automobile accident. (*Florida Baptist-Witness*)

4918 It is thought that he was beaten to death, possibly during a family fun day in the park. (*Wolverhampton Express & Star*)

4919 The local ladies, who were on duty in the church and elsewhere, were by no means ornamental additions to the gathering. (Hertfordshire paper)

4920 Mr Travis lost a finger when a poisoned dog to which he was administering an anecdote bit him. (El Paso paper)

4921 Mr and Mrs Charles Cooper announce the betrayal of their daughter Miss Margaret to Ensign Raymond McKee. (US paper)

4922 In America it is true that our general rules of evidence and principles of law are mainly followed, and there is very little danger of an innocent man being acquitted. (*The Globe*)

4923 If the motion were passed, no strike action would be taken by NALGO without a ballet of all its members. (*Bristol Evening Post*)

4924 A screaming crowd of 200 men and women to-night attempted to lynch Kinsey. Two policemen defended the prisoner until refreshments arrived. (Honolulu paper)

4925 Amazing luck in the Irish Sweep fell to a Kentish man who drew two tickets and a Sussex woman. (Yorkshire paper)

4926 The bride wore a gown of heavy Oldham Corporation Gasworks. (*Manchester Evening News*)

4927 George Burrell has had charge of the entertainment during the past year. His birth-provoking antics were always the life of the party and he will be greatly missed. (Ohio paper)

4928 "After finding no qualified candidates for the position of principal, the school department is extremely pleased to announce the appointment of Charles Stanton to the post," said Philip Stauffer, superintendent. (US paper)

4929 Fire broke out on the prairie near the CPR viaduct on Monday evening but the blaze was extinguished before damage could be done by the local fire brigade. (Canadian paper)

4930 Mr and Mrs Wyglass of New York have completed their holiday at Angus. They have been shooting tenants at Burg House. (Dundee paper)

4931 Dale Martin, an entertainer, has been ordered by a provincial court judge to avoid making anyone pregnant for the next three years. The order not to impregnate any girls came from Judge Leslie Bewley, who gave Martin a suspended sentence and three years probation for possession of an offensive weapon. (*Toronto Globe*)

4932 The club's celebration will also include a DJ and balloons falling from the ceiling at midnight. (US paper)

4933 If the baby does not thrive on fresh milk it should be boiled. (Women's magazine)

4934 March 18: Outdoor Adventure Series: Indoor Rock Climbing. (School newsletter)

4935 Our office policy is that we will do our utmost to see patients in discomfort as soon as possible. (California dental newsletter)

4936 Dr Smith is associated with societies for the prohibition of cruel sports, recorder playing and Welsh folk songs. (*Yorkshire Post*)

4937 She enjoyed talking with people, cooking her infamous lasagna meals, walking, reading, and bowling (US obituary)

4938 The next meeting of the Legion will take place on February 10. Every man who died for his country is cordially invited to attend. (North Dakota paper)

4939 Miss Hazel Foster's gladioli garden has been attracting considerable attention of late. She spends many hours among her large collection of pants. (Pennsylvania paper)

4940 The new lizard, 21 inches long, is said at the zoo to be settling down well. It is described by a keeper as being as lively as the cricketers that are part of its favourite diet. (*Lincolnshire Echo*)

4941 To serve, dip moulds in water to loosen the contents and serve with passion fruit and cream. British housewives can substitute pineapple, cherries or apricots for passion. (*Romford Recorder*)

4942 The license fee for altered dogs with a certificate will be $3 and for pets owned by senior citizens who have not been altered the fee will be $1.50. (US leaflet)

4943 Fog and smog rolled over Los Angeles today, closing two airports and slowing snails to a traffic pace. (Los Angeles paper)

4944 Miss Gorman, in a quiet part as a nice woman, makes it obvious that she is a very good actress indeed. (Canadian paper)

4945 Our paper carried the notice last week that Mr Shaw is a defective in the police force. This was a typographical error. Mr Shaw is really a detective in the police farce. (*Ely Standard*)

4946 Your thumb or fingerprint will be taken. (California Driver Handbook)

4947 In the handicrafts exhibition at Wordsley Community Centre, the contribution of the Misses Smith was "smocking and rugs" and not "smoking drugs" as stated in last week's report. (*County Express*, Stourbridge)

4948 Owing to a printer's error in the "Fairy-ring" cake recipe last week "two ounces castor oil" was given for "two ounces caster sugar". (*Reveille*)

4949 Sir Hugh and Lady Carlton received many congratulations after their horse's success. The latter wore a yellow frock trimmed with picot-edged frills and a close-fitting hat. (Berkshire paper)

4950 A lot of water has been passed under the bridge since this variation has been played. (Russian chess book)

4951 The goalkeeper was then troubled by a 20-yard shit from Macdonald. (*Sunday Post*)

4952 Willie Carson, riding his 180th winner of the season, spent the last two furlongs looking over one shoulder then another, even between his legs but there was nothing there to worry him. (*Sporting Life*)

4953 Men's and Ladies' Singles, Pairs and Triples as well as Mixed Pairs are invited to the Yarmouth Bowling Green to compete for £5,000 of prize money at the Great Yarmouth Open Bowels Festival. (*Where and When in East Anglia*)

4954 Correction: Hakin girl wins lap dancing certificate. The headline should have read: Hakin girl wins tap dancing certificate. (*Milford and West Wales Mercury*)

Advertisements

4955 Try our homemade pies – they are a real threat. (Restaurant ad.)

4956 Call Wieser's for Home Made Fruit Cake: Solid Mahogany. (*Fredericksburg Free Lance-Star*)

4957 A superb and inexpensive restaurant. Fine food expertly served by waitresses in appetizing forms.

4958 Mixing bowl designed to please a cook with round bottom for efficient beating.

4959 And now, the Superstore – unequalled in size, unmatched in variety, unrivalled inconvenience. (US paper)

4960 The hotel has bowling alleys, tennis courts, comfortable beds, and other athletic facilities.

4961 Top of the bill: Glen Campbell – "The Nine Stone Cowboy". (*Stoke Evening Sentinel*)

4962 This is the model home for your future. It was panned by *Better Homes and Gardens*.

4963 Washing done – in my home including bachelors. (*Allentown Chronicle*)

4964 One week sale of blankets: These bargain lots are rapidly shrinking.

4965 We do not tear your clothing with machinery. We do it carefully by hand. (Boston paper)

4966 We will oil your sewing machine and adjust tension in your home for one dollar.

4967 Sheer stockings. Designed for fancy dress, but so serviceable that lots of women wear nothing else.

4968 Tired of working for only $9.75 per hour? We offer profit sharing and flexible hours. Starting pay: $7-$9 per hour.

4969 Dogs called for, fleas removed and returned to you for one dollar. (Washington paper)

4970 Sexual abuse centre looking for volunteers. (Surrey paper, UK)

4971 With the advent of spring, the carpet beetle commences its ravenous inroads into your carpets. Have them treated now before irreparable damage is done by the Nelson firm with ten years guarantee. (Lancashire paper, UK)

4972 Get rid of aunts: Zap does the job in 24 hours. (Iowa paper)

4973 Our bikinis are exciting. They are simply the tops!

4974 15 Men's Wool Suits. Three dollars. They won't last an hour! (*Tacoma News Tribune*)

4975 Wasps nests destroyed £20. OAPs £15. (*Yours* magazine)

4976 Used cars: Why go elsewhere to be cheated? Come here first. (Oregon paper)

4977 Modular sofas. Only 299 dollars. For rest or fore play. (Chicago paper)

4978 Widows made to order: send us your specifications. (El Paso paper)

4979 Auto Repair Service. Free pickup and delivery. Try us once, you'll never go anywhere again.

4980 On 28th inst. To Mr and Mrs Arthur French, a bony daughter. (South African paper)

4981 Try our herbal remedies. You can't get better. (UK paper)

4982 PARKYNS – to the memory of Mr Parkyns, passed away September 10. Peace at last. From all the neighbours of Princes Avenue. (*Leicester Mercury*, UK)

4983 Retraction: The "Greek Special" is a huge 18-inch pizza and not a huge 18-inch penis, as described in an ad. Blondie's Pizza would like to apologize for any confusion Friday's ad may have caused. (*Daily Californian*)

Church bulletins

4984 We shall be meeting on Wednesday 11 April when the subject will be: "Heaven: How do we get there?" Transport is available at 7.55pm from the bus stop opposite the Harewood Arms.

4985 Wednesday: the ladies liturgy society will meet. Mr Johnson will sing "Put Me In My Little Bed" accompanied by the pastor.

4986 This being Easter Sunday we will ask Mrs Fisher to come forward and lay an egg at the altar.

4987 Miss Charlene Mason sang "I Will Not Pass This Way Again", giving obvious pleasure to the congregation.

4988 The third verse of Blessed Assurance will be sung without musical accomplishment.

4989 Please place your donation in the envelope along with the deceased person you want remembered.

4990 Thursday at 5 p.m. there will be a meeting of the little mothers club. All ladies wishing to be little mothers, please meet with the pastor in his study.

4991 There was a break-in at the Open Door Baptist Church last week. Burglars entered through a rear window.

4992 Thank you, Lord, for the many miracles we are too blond to see.

4993 The ladies of the church have cast off clothing of every kind and they may be seen in the church basement on Friday afternoon.

4994 The rosebud on the altar this morning is to announce the birth of David Alan Belzer, the sin of Rev. and Mrs Julius Belzer.

4995 Low Self-Esteem Support Group will meet Thursday 7 to 8.30pm. Please use the back door.

4996 The Ladies Bible Study will be held Thursday morning at 10. All ladies are invited to lunch in the Fellowship Hall after the B.S. is done.

4997 The pastor would appreciate it if the ladies of the congregation would lend him their electric girdles for the pancake breakfast next Sunday morning.

4998 The concert held in Fellowship Hall was a great success. Special thanks are due to the minister's daughter who labored the whole evening at the piano, which as usual fell upon her.

4999 There will be a procession next Sunday afternoon in the grounds of the monastery, but if it rains in the afternoon, the procession will take place in the morning.

5000 Pastor is on vacation. Massages can be given to church secretary.

5001 This afternoon there will be a meeting in the south and north ends of the church. Children will be baptized at both ends.

5002 Weight watchers will meet at the Presbyterian Church. Please use the large double doors.

5003 Barbara remains in the hospital and needs blood donors for more transfusions. She is also having trouble sleeping and requests tapes of Pastor Jack's sermons.

5004 Due to the rector's illness, Wednesday's healing services will be discontinued until further notice.

5005 (Announcing the visit of an African missionary speaker named Bertha Belch to the Calvary Memorial Church, Racine, Wisconsin.) Come tonight and hear Bertha Belch all the way from Africa.

5006 Thanks to two special people who picked my wife up after a fall from her bike and broke her pelvis and severely damaged her back.

5007 Tonight's sermon: What is hell? Come early and listen to our choir practice.

5008 Mrs Crutchfield and Mrs Rankin sang a duet, The Lord Knows Why.

5009 The Rev. Merriweather spoke briefly, much to the delight of the audience.

5010 Tuesday at 4 p.m. there will be an ice cream social. All ladies giving milk come early.

5011 Don't forget, Ash Wednesday is Monday, March 5th.

5012 The baby shower will be at 2pm Saturday. All ladies invited. No clothing needed.

5013 Sermon tonight: it will be gin at 8.

5014 Allison Perozzo is recovering from having her wisdom taken out last week.

5015 Scouts are saving aluminium cans, bottles and other items to be recycled. Proceeds will be used to cripple children.

5016 The church will host an evening of fine dining, superb entertainment, and gracious hostility.

5017 Today's sermon: "How Much Can a Man Drink?" with hymns from a full choir.

5018 The eighth graders will be presenting Shakespeare's *Hamlet* in the church basement on Friday at 7pm. The congregation is invited to attend this tragedy.

5019 The pastor will preach his farewell message, after which the choir will sing "Break Forth Into Joy".

5020 For those of you who have children and don't know it, we have a nursery downstairs.

5021 The Johnson family will attend the funeral of Susie's former husband, who died in Flint, Michigan tomorrow.

5022 Next Sunday a special collection will be taken to defray the cost of the new carpet. All those wishing to do something on the new carpet should come forward.

5023 The choir invited any member of the congregation who enjoys sinning to join the choir.

5024 Pot luck supper: prayer and medication to follow.

5025 Eight new choir robes are currently needed, due to the additions of several new members and to the deterioration of some older ones.

5026 The Lutheran men's group will meet at 6pm. Steak, mashed potatoes, green beans, bread and dessert will be served for a nominal feel.

5027 Don't let worry kill you off — let the church help.

5028 The sermon this morning: Jesus Walks On The Water. The sermon tonight: Searching For Jesus.

5029 Remember in prayer the many who are sick of our church and community.

Wanted ads

5030 Wanted: Chambermaid in rectory. Love in, 200 dollars a month. (US paper)

5031 Lost: Small apricot poodle – Reward. Neutered, like one of the family. (Florida paper)

5032 Dog for sale: Eats anything, fond of children. (Washington paper)

5033 Man wanted to work in dynamite factory. Must be willing to travel. (US paper)

5034 Snow blower for sale – only used on snowy days.

5035 Must sell: Plymouth 4-door Sedan, complete with actress. (*Philadelphia Enquirer*)

5036 For sale: An antique desk suitable for lady with thick legs and large drawers.

5037 For sale: Large crystal vase by lady slightly cracked. (Long Island paper)

5038 Gents three-speed bicycle, also two ladies for sale, in good running order. (Lancashire paper)

5039 Drop-leaf table. The leaves when opened will seat six people comfortably and there's an automatic hinge that holds them firmly in place. (Washington paper)

5040 For sale: Registered Jersey cow, giving three gallons of milk, two tons of hay, a number of chickens and a cook stove. (UK paper)

5041 Cook wanted. Comfortable room with radio. Two in family. Only one who can be well recommended. (Hereford paper)

5042 Motor-bike, complete, less engine, frame, tank, coil, saddle, handlebar, tyres, etc (*Motor Cycling*)

5043 For sale: Complete mahogany Chip & Dale dining-room set, in good condition. (Long Island paper)

5044 School. Wanted in January. Experienced man to take almost entire responsibility for the lowest form of boys. (Manchester paper)

5045 Wanted: Unmarried girls to pick fresh fruit and produce at night.

5046 Wanted: Wet fish or experienced man or woman to take charge of business. (*Bristol Evening Post*)

5047 Amana washer $100. Owned by bachelor who seldom washed.

5048 Shop assistant required: no objection to sex.

5049 A young woman wants washing and cleaning daily. (*Toronto Daily Star*)

5050 Free puppies: half cocker spaniel, half sneaky neighbour's dog. (US paper)

5051 Wanted: Man to take care of cow that does not smoke or drink.

5052 Antique card table for sale. No dealers. (UK paper)

5053 Precast concrete foremen required in Hampshire. (London paper)

5054 For sale – eight puppies from a German Shepherd and an Alaskan Hussy.

5055 1959 Austin A35, black, heater, new tyres, immaculate, elderly owner exchanged for bath chair. (*Cambridge Daily News*)

5056 Wanted: Mother's helper, peasant working conditions.

5057 For sale: '83 Toyota hunchback. $2000.

5058 Wanted: Widower with school-age children requires person to assume general housekeeping duties. Must be capable of contributing to growth of family.

5059 Ford Granada Hearse. Superb engine and gearbox. Body in good condition.

5060 Wanted: Girls to sew on men's pants. (*Baltimore Sun*)

5061 Tired of cleaning yourself? Let me do it.

5062 Complete home for sale: two double, one single bed, dining-room 3 piece suite, wireless, television, carpets, lion etc. (*Portsmouth News*)

5063 Illiterate? Write for free information.

5064 Ear piercing while you wait. (*Herts Advertiser*)

5065 Four-poster bed, 101 years old. Perfect for antique lover.

5066 Wanted: Preparer of food. Must be dependable, like the food business and be willing to get hands dirty.

5067 Woman wanted, to share fat with another (Berkshire newspaper)

5068 Our experienced Mom will care for your child. Fenced yard, meals and smacks included.

5069 Now is your chance to have your ears pierced and get an extra pair to take home too.

5070 Man, honest. Will take anything. (Jacksonville paper)

5071 E. Cramer Ltd require beamer, presser and girl for stripping. (*Long Eaton Advertiser*)

5072 Have several very old dresses from grandmother in beautiful condition.

Strange signs

5073 At a railroad station: Beware! To touch these wires is instant death. Anyone doing so will be prosecuted.

5074 In a greengrocer's: Please don't handle the fruit. Ask for Debbie.

5075 In a clothing store: Wonderful bargains for men with 16 and 17 necks.

5076 In an Austrian hotel: In case of fire, please do your utmost to alarm the hall porter.

5077 At a Texas diner: Mattie's Restaurant and Yoghurt Palace, An Alternative to Good Eating.

5078 In a Bombay tailor's shop: Customers giving orders will be promptly executed.

5079 In a Tokyo hotel: You are requested to take advantage of the chambermaid.

5080 In a New York restaurant: Customers who consider our waitresses uncivil ought to see the manager.

5081 In an Irish hotel: Please do not lock the door as we have lost the key.

5082 In a Bucharest hotel lobby: The lift is being fixed for the next day. During that time we regret that you will be unbearable.

5083 On an electrician's truck: Let us remove your shorts.

5084 On a farmer's gate: Please shut gate to stop sheep worrying.

5085 At a level crossing: Beware of trains going both ways at once.

5086 In a hotel: Ladies are requested not to have children in the Cocktail Room.

5087 Outside a radiator repair shop: The best place in town to take a leak.

5088 On an asphalt truck: Let us fill your crack.

5089 Over a gynaecologist's office: Dr Jones, at your cervix.

5090 In a department store: Bargain basement upstairs.

5091 On a taxidermist's window: We really know our stuff.

5092 In a veterinarian's waiting room: Be back in five minutes. Sit! Stay!

5093 In a hospital: Visitors – husbands only. One per patient.

5094 Outside a maternity clothes store: We are open on labour day.

5095 On the menu of a Baltimore restaurant: If you don't say Mrs Globus' chocolate pudding is the finest you ever tasted, tear up the cashier and walk out.

5096 In a butcher's shop: And remember you can make a wonderfully nourishing broth from the remains if you have an invalid in the house.

5097 On a testimonial dinner menu: We are honored to saute Megan Casey and Brian Cafferty.

5098 Outside a public toilet: The ladies bathroom is manned at all times.

5099 Inside a bowling alley: Please be quiet, we need to hear a pin drop.

5100 In a Paris hotel: Please leave your values at the front desk.

5101 In an Athens hotel: Visitors are expected to complain at the office between the hours of 9 and 11 a.m. daily.

5102 In a Brazilian resort brochure: We offer you peace and seclusion. The paths to our resort are only passable by asses. Therefore, you will certainly feel at home here.

5103 In an Austrian ski resort hotel: Not to perambulate the corridors in the hours of repose in the boots of ascension.

5104 At a Warsaw restaurant: As for the tripe served here, you will be singing its praises to your grandchildren on your deathbed.

5105 Outside a Hong Kong tailor's: Ladies may have a fit upstairs.

5106 At a convenience store: No Checks Excepted! No Acceptions!

5107 In a Rome laundry: Ladies, leave your clothes here and spend the afternoon having a good time.

5108 At Gatwick Airport: Your nearest alternative toilet is located on this level – towards the spectators' viewing facility.

5109 In a Swedish furrier: Fur coats made for ladies from their own skin.

5110 In a Finnish washroom: To stop the drip, turn cock to right.

5111 In a Moscow hotel lobby: You are welcome to visit the cemetery where famous Russian and Soviet composers, artists and writers are buried daily except Thursday.

5112 In a Copenhagen airline ticket office: We take your bags and send them in all directions.

5113 At a Hong Kong dentist: Teeth extracted by the latest methodists.

5114 In a Dublin barber's: Haircutting while you wait.

5115 In a Florida maternity ward: No children allowed.

5116 On a dock in Alaska: Safety ladder, climb at own risk.

5117 In a doctor's waiting room: Stroke patients: don't feel alone.

5118 On a tree: No Trespassing. Violators will be prosecuted to the fullest extent of the law – Sisters of Mercy.

5119 In a launderette: Automatic washing machines. Please remove all your clothes when the light goes out.

5120 On the door of a maternity ward: Push, push, push.

5121 Outside a restaurant: If you enjoy good food, eat at our other branches.

5122 In a shop window: We exchange everything – bicycles, washing machines etc, etc. Bring your wife and get the deal of your life.

5123 In an African hotel brochure: Mt Kilimanjaro, the breathtaking backdrop for the Serena Lodge. Swim in the lovely pool while you drink it all in.

5124 On an office photocopying machine: The typists' reproduction equipment is not to be interfered with without the prior permission of the manager.

5125 In a loan company office: Ask about our plans for owning your home.

5126 For donkey rides in Thailand: Would you like to ride on your own ass?

5127 On the door of a Maine shop: Our motto is to give our customers the lowest possible prices and workmanship.

5128 In a restaurant: Steaks and chops are grilled before our customers.

5129 In a churchyard: Due to increasing problems with litter louts and vandals, we must ask anyone with relatives buried in the graveyard to do their best to keep them in order.

5130 In a dry cleaner's: Anyone leaving their garments here for more than 30 days will be disposed of.

5131 In a health shop window: Closed due to illness.

5132 In a London office block: Toilet out of order. Please use floor below.

5133 On the menu of a Swiss restaurant: Our wines leave you nothing to hope for.

5134 In a Yugoslav hotel: The flattening of underwear with pleasure is the job of the chambermaid.

5135 In an Acapulco hotel: The manager has personally passed all the water served here.

5136 On a repair shop door: We can repair anything (Please knock hard on the door – the bell doesn't work).

5137 Outside a social club: Closed tonight for special opening.

5138 Outside a Bangkok cleaner's: Drop your trousers here for best results

5139 On the door of a Moscow hotel room: If this is your first visit to the USSR, you are welcome to it.

5140 In a Tokyo shop: Our nylons cost more than common, but you'll find they are best in the long run.

5141 In a hotel: All fire extinguishers must be examined at least ten days before any fire.

5142 In a club: Anyone breaking this rule will be dismembered.

5143 On a plumber's van: Don't sleep with a drip, call your plumber.

5144 Outside a hospital: Please help our nurses home.

5145 Outside a factory: Closing down, thanks to all our customers.

5146 Outside a dance hall: Saturday night dance – very exclusive. Everybody welcome.

5147 On the van of Patel Bros builders: You've had the cowboys, now try the Indians.

5148 At a Japanese hairdresser's: Artistic barber for cutting off of head.

5149 On a building site: Night-watchman patrols this area 24 hours a day.

5150 At a Santa Fe gas station: We will sell gasoline to anyone in a glass container.

5151 In a shop: Customers should note that any complaints of incivility on the part of any member of our staff will be severely dealt with.

5152 On an Italian hotel brochure: There is a French window in every bedroom, with balcony imminent to a romantic gorge, affording delightful prospects. We hope you want to drop in.

5153 In a hotel brochure: Enjoy our breath-taking view of the Atlantic Ocean that is eliminated by our special lighting at night.

5154 In a hospital: Dangerous drugs must be locked up with Matron.

5155 At an arts centre: Push button to open automatic doors.

5156 On a plumber's van: We repair what your husband fixed.

5157 At a Shanghai buffet: You will be able to eat all you wish until you are fed up.

5158 In an office: Staff should empty the tea-pot and then stand upside down on the tea tray.

5159 On a Milwaukee tyre shop: Invite us to your next blow-out.

5160 In the grounds of a public school: No trespassing without permission.

5161 Outside a restaurant: Open seven days a week and weekends.

5162 Inn sign: The Greyhound Inn – An old coaching inn dating from the fifteenth century. No coaches.

5163 Outside a Mexican disco: Members and non-members only.

5164 On a Chinese menu: Special cocktails for women with nuts.

5165 At a towing company: We don't charge an arm and a leg. We want tows.

5166 In an Italian doctor's: Specialist in women and other diseases.

5167 Outside a New Mexico dry cleaner's: 38 years on the same spot.

5168 Outside a Los Angeles dance hall: Good clean dancing every night but Sunday.

5169 In a barber's shop: Haircuts half price today. One only per customer.

5170 In a leisure centre café: Shoes are required to eat in the cafeteria.

5171 On a lift: Please do not use this lift when it is not working.

5172 At a cemetery: Persons are prohibited from picking flowers from any but their own graves.

5173 In a shop window: Model willing to pose for nude artist.

5174 On a Budapest menu: Special today: no ice cream.

5175 In a dress shop: Wedding gear for all occasions.

5176 In a jeweller's shop: Our gifts will not last long at these prices.

5177 In a church: This is the gate of heaven – enter ye all by this door. This door is kept locked because of the draught.

5178 In the front yard of a funeral home: Drive carefully. We'll wait.

Label instructions

5179 On Sears hair dryer: Do not use while sleeping.

5180 On a bag of Fritos: You could be a winner! No purchase necessary. Details inside.

5181 On a bar of Dial soap: Directions: Use like regular soap.

5182 On a pushchair: Remove child before folding

5183 On a string of Christmas lights: For indoor or outdoor use only.

5184 On a Tropicana Twisters drink bottle: Flavors Mother Nature never intended.

5185 On a bottle of Nytol (a sleep aid): Warning: may cause drowsiness.

5186 On a frozen dinner: Serving suggestion: Defrost.

5187 On a hotel shower cap box: Fits one head.

5188 On a restroom dryer: Do not activate with wet hands.

5189 On a dessert package: This packet of ready-made pastry will make enough for four persons or 12 tarts.

5190 On cat furniture: Real wooden furniture for cats with removable parts.

5191 On a self-build chair: Do not sit in chair without being fully assembled.

5192 On a bottle of children's cough medicine: Do not drive car or operate machinery.

5193 On Sainsbury's peanuts: Warning: contains nuts.

5194 On a microwave oven: Do not use for drying pets.

5195 On a bottle of dog shampoo: Caution – the contents of this bottle should not be fed to fish.

5196 On a wok: Do not use mental tools for prolonging the life of the pan.

5197 On packaging for a Rowenta iron: Do not iron clothes on body.

5198 On a push-up deodorant stick: Remove cap and push up bottom.

5199 On a bottle of rum: Open bottle before drinking.

5200 On a curling iron: Do not insert curling iron into any bodily orifice.

5201 On a carpet cleaner: Safe for carpets, too.

5202 On a bathroom heater: This product is not to be used in bathrooms.

5203 On a box for an illuminated screwdriver: Now you can see what you're screwing in the dark.

5204 On a shipment of hammers: May be harmful if swallowed.

5205 On instructions for an electric thermometer: Do not use orally after using rectally.

5206 On a Japanese medicine bottle: Adults – one tablet three times a day until passing away.

5207 On a Spanish oven: Do not use soup for cleaning oven.

5208 On a Swedish chainsaw: Do not attempt to stop chain with your hands.

5209 On a Korean kitchen knife: Warning – keep out of children.

5210 On a Taiwanese puzzle toy: Let's decompose and enjoy assembling.

Office memos

5211 Joe Harrigan's father passed away yesterday from a massive heart attack. He won't be back in the office until Tuesday.

5212 A son was born to Mr and Mrs Charles Mulkahey, Garrison St, during the past week. Congratulations, Pete!

5213 Due to repairs to the air-conditioning system, offices will be very humid for the next three days. Please bare with us.

5214 We need candid photos for the yearbook. Only decent pictures will be excepted. Sex should not be aloud.

5215 In an emergency situation, call security at extension 3069, and we will determine if the situation is emergent.

5216 Will the person who took the step ladder yesterday please bring it back, or further steps will be taken.

5217 Employees requesting safety shoe reimbursement, limited to one pair per year, must complete and submit an expense account form, attaching proof of purchase to their supervisor.

Headlines

5218 WOMAN KICKED BY HER HUSBAND SAID TO BE GREATLY IMPROVED (Illinois paper)

5219 POPE CITES DANGERS FACING THE WORLD: NAMES EIGHT CARDINALS (New York paper)

5220 PUBLIC HEALTH PROBLEM: SPECIAL COMMITTEE TO SIT ON BED BUG (*Liverpool Echo*)

5221 MACARTHUR FLIES BACK TO FRONT (US paper)

5222 NIGHT SCHOOL TO HEAR PEST TALK (*Oakland Tribune*)

5223 GORILLAS VOW TO KILL KHOMEINI (*Valley Independent*)

5224 MAGNATE USED TO REMOVE NAIL IN STOMACH (*Los Angeles Times*)

5225 STRIP CLUBS SHOCK: MAGISTRATES MAY ACT ON INDECENT SHOWS (*Daily Mirror*)

5226 NEW HOUSING FOR ELDERLY NOT YET DEAD (US paper)

5227 COMMUNITY BANDS TOGETHER TO HELP BURN VICTIM'S FAMILY (*Bay City Times*)

5228 LOCAL HIGH SCHOOL DROPOUTS CUT IN HALF (US paper)

5229 STARR AGHAST AT FIRST LADY SEX POSITION (*Washington Times*)

5230 PANDA MATING FAILS: VETERINARIAN TAKES OVER (US paper)

5231 STUDY FINDS SEX, PREGNANCY LINK (*Cornell Daily Sun*)

5232 SIX SENTENCED TO LIFE IN CLARKSVILLE (*Nashville Banner*)

5233 SANTA ROSA MAN DENIES HE COMMITTED SUICIDE IN SOUTH SAN FRANCISCO (California paper)

5234 QUEEN MARY HAVING BOTTOM SCRAPED (US paper)

5235 LONG ISLAND STIFFENS FOR LILI'S BLOW (*Newsday*)

5236 JUVENILE COURT TO TRY SHOOTING DEFENDANT (US paper)

5237 LEGISLATOR WANTS TOUGHER DEATH PENALTY (US paper)

5238 GOVERNOR CHILES OFFERS RARE OPPORTUNITY TO GOOSE HUNTERS (*Tallahassee Democrat*)

5239 TEXTON INC. MAKES OFFER TO SCREW COMPANY STOCKHOLDERS (*Miami Herald*)

5240 GATORS TO FACE SEMINOLES WITH PETERS OUT (*Tallahassee Bugle*)

5241 SQUAD HELPS DOG BITE VICTIM (US paper)

5242 MALF NATURIST MEMBERS RISE (*Big Issue*)

5243 MAN ATTACKED BY CANAL (UK paper)

5244 TWO HOLD UP DUNKIN' DONUTS, FLEA WITH $176 (*New Haven Register*)

5245 FOUR SHEEP FOR EVERY WELSHMAN (*Independent on Sunday*)

5246 TWELVE-YEAR WAIT FOR TOILETS (*Long Eaton Advertiser*)

5247 NEW STUDY OF OBESITY LOOKS FOR LARGER TEST GROUP (US paper)

5248 SHELL FOUND ON BEACH (UK paper)

5249 SEVEN ROAD DEATHS IN VERMONT, BUT GOOD TIMES ABOUND EVERYWHERE (*Rutland* [VT] *Herald*)

5250 AUDIENCE TRIED TO SPOIL PLAY – BUT ST CHAD'S PLAYERS SUCCEEDED (*Sunderland Echo*)

5251 LUNG CANCER IN WOMEN MUSHROOMS (US paper)

5252 PROSECUTOR RELEASES PROBE INTO UNDERSHERIFF (US paper)

5253 DIVORCES ARE FEWER AMONG SINGLE PEOPLE, CHICAGO FIGURES SHOW (*Chicago Tribune*)

5254 GRANDMOTHER OF EIGHT MAKES HOLE IN ONE (US paper)

5255 ANTIQUE STRIPPER TO DISPLAY WARES AT STORE (UK paper)

5256 STOLEN PAINTING FOUND BY TREE (US paper)

5257 FATHER SHOULD BE INCLUDED IN PLANNING FOR FIRST CHILD (*Richmond News-Leader*)

5258 STUD TIRES OUT (US paper)

5259 TIGER WOODS PLAYS WITH OWN BALLS, NIKE SAYS (US paper)

5260 DOG FOULING – IT'S IN YOUR HANDS (*Exeter Citizen*)

5261 MEDINA TO HAVE PARENT TEACHER ASSASSINATION (*Medina Sentinel*, Oregon)

5262 KICKING BABY CONSIDERED TO BE HEALTHY (US paper)

5263 BRITISH LEFT WAFFLES ON FALKLAND ISLANDS (*Guardian*)

5264 CHILD TEACHING EXPERT TO SPEAK (*Birmingham Post-Herald*)

5265 AIR HEAD FIRED (*Chicago Sun-Times*)

5266 CHEF THROWS HIS HEART INTO HELPING FEED NEEDY (US paper)

5267 PLANE TOO CLOSE TO GROUND, CRASH PROBE TOLD (US paper)

5268 TAXMAN CRUSHED IN ORANGE JUICE CASE (*London Evening Standard*)

5269 BELFAST MAN CHARGED FOR HARRODS BOMB (*Chicago Tribune*)

5270 NEW VACCINE MAY CONTAIN RABIES (US paper)

5271 ARSON SUSPECT HELD IN MASSACHUSETTS FIRE (US paper)

5272 MARCH PLANNED FOR NEXT AUGUST (US paper)

5273 FORMER PYTHON TO OPEN GIRAFFE HOUSE (*The News, Portsmouth*)

5274 BLOODHOUND IN CHILD HUNT FOUND, PICKING BLACKBERRIES (*Daily Express*)

5275 CLINTON PLACES DICKEY IN GORE'S HANDS (*Bangor* [Maine] *News*)

5276 SAFETY EXPERTS SAY SCHOOL BUS PASSENGERS SHOULD BE BELTED (US paper)

5277 FIRE OFFICIALS GRILLED OVER KEROSENE HEATERS (US paper)

5278 GOLFER CHARGED WITH DRUNKEN DRIVING (Associated Press)

5279 PASSENGERS HIT BY CANCELLED TRAINS (*Manchester Evening News*)

5280 PRINCE ANDREW TAKES KOO PEASANT HUNTING IN SCOTLAND (*Atlanta Journal-Constitution*)

5281 SOMETHING WENT WRONG IN JET CRASH, EXPERTS SAY (US paper)

5282 RALLY OFFERS TO HELP RAPE SURVIVORS (US paper)

5283 AIRLINE TRAVEL SAFER DESPITE MORE ACCIDENTS (Reuters)

5284 CROWDS RUSHING TO SEE POPE TRAMPLE SIX TO DEATH (US paper)

5285 TEENAGE GIRLS OFTEN HAVE BABIES FATHERED BY MEN (*Sunday Oregonian*)

5286 PAIR CHARGED WITH BATTERY (*Denver Post*)

5287 20-YEAR FRIENDSHIP ENDS AT ALTAR (US paper)

5288 HENMAN SEES BALLS AS KEY TO HIS SUCCESS (*Evening Standard*)

5289 CHILD'S DEATH RUINS COUPLE'S HOLIDAY (US paper)

5290 HOTEL BURNS. TWO HUNDRED GUESTS ESCAPE HALF GLAD (US paper)

5291 POLICE FOUND SAFE UNDER BLANKET (*Gloucestershire Echo*)

5292 JERK INJURES NECK, WINS AWARD (*Buffalo News*)

5293 IRAQI HEAD SEEKS ARMS (US paper)

5294 MAN HERE TO SEE WIFE ROBBED AND BEATEN (*Philadelphia Enquirer*)

5295 DEFENDANT'S SPEECH ENDS IN LONG SENTENCE (US paper)

5296 PROSTITUTES APPEAL TO POPE (US paper)

5297 MAN SHOOTS NEIGHBOR WITH MACHETE (*Miami Herald*)

5298 POLICE DISCOVER CRACK IN AUSTRALIA (US paper)

5299 FALSE CHARGE OF THEFT OF HENS: POLICE ON WILD GOOSE CHASE (Kent paper)

5300 GIVE THE PALESTINIANS A HOMELAND – OTTAWA (*Toronto Star*)

5301 THUGS EAT THEN ROB PROPRIETOR (Dallas paper)

5302 REAGAN WINS ON BUDGET, BUT MORE LIES AHEAD (US paper)

5303 ALBANY TURNS TO GARBAGE (*New York Daily News*)

5304 FISH LURK IN STREAMS (*Rochester Democrat & Chronicle*)

5305 FORD, REAGAN NECK IN PRESIDENTIAL PRIMARY (*Ethiopian Herald*)

5306 MINERS REFUSE TO WORK AFTER DEATH (US paper)

5307 THANKS TO PRESIDENT CLINTON, STAFF SGT FRUER NOW HAS A SON (*Arkansas Plainsman*)

5308 GOVERNOR'S PENIS BUSY – (*New Haven* [Connecticut] *Register*)

5309 DRIVER OF DEATH CAR HELD ON SUSPICION OF NEGLIGIBLE HOMICIDE (California paper)

5310 CHEF THROWS HIS HEART INTO HELPING FEED NEEDY (*Louisville Courier Journal*)

5311 MAN RUN OVER BY FREIGHT TRAIN DIES (*Los Angeles Times*)

5312 POLICE CAN'T STOP GAMBLING (*Detroit Free Press*)

5313 TWO SOVIET SHIPS COLLIDE, ONE DIES (US paper)

5314 POPE LAUNCHES TALKS TO END LONG DIVISION (US paper)

5315 ROBBER HOLDS UP ALBERT'S HOSIERY (US paper)

5316 ASTRONAUT TAKES BLAME FOR GAS IN SPACECRAFT (US paper)

5317 DOG BAN: MATRON TURNS DOWN POST (*Glasgow Evening Citizen*)

5318 BAR TRYING TO HELP ALCOHOLIC LAWYERS (*Seattle Times*)

5319 MAN IS FATALLY SLAIN (US paper)

5320 DOCTOR TESTIFIES IN HORSE SUIT (US paper)

5321 TENANT FAILED TO GIVE NOTICE BEFORE DYING (US paper)

5322 LACK OF BRAINS HINDERS RESEARCH (*Columbus Dispatch*)

5323 LAWMEN FROM MEXICO BARBECUE GUESTS (*San Benito News*)

5324 SAVE STREAMS, FISH HEAD WARNS (*Bainbridge* [Georgia] *Review*)

5325 A FARMER'S WIFE IS BEST SHOT (*Glasgow Evening Citizen*)

5326 BLIND WOMAN GETS KIDNEY FROM DAD SHE HASN'T SEEN IN YEARS (US paper)

5327 BRANCH AVENUE BRIDGE TO BE FIXED BEFORE FALL (*Providence Evening Bulletin*)

5328 MARIJUANA ISSUE SENT TO A JOINT COMMITTEE (*Toronto Star*)

5329 WOMAN SWIMS 12 MILES AFTER SINKING (*Irish Times*)

5330 COLD WAVE LINKED TO TEMPERATURES (US paper)

5331 BEATING WITNESS PROVIDES NAMES (US paper)

5332 NEVER WITHHOLD HERPES INFECTION FROM LOVED ONE (US paper)

5333 INFERTILITY UNLIKELY TO BE PASSED ON (*Montgomery Advertiser*)

5334 DRUNK GETS NINE MONTHS IN VIOLIN CASE (US paper)

5335 TRANSSEXUALS BENEFITS CUT OFF (*Highbury & Islington Express*)

5336 DEAD OFFICER ON S.F. FORCE FOR 18 YEARS (San Francisco paper)

5337 AFTER DETOUR TO CALIFORNIA SHUTTLE RETURNS TO EARTH (US paper)

5338 WILD WIFE LEAGUE WILL MEET TO-NIGHT (West Virginia paper)

5339 WAR DIMS HOPE FOR PEACE (US paper)

5340 COMPLAINTS ABOUT NBA REFEREES GROWING UGLY (*Chicago Sun-Times*)

5341 UNDERTAKER'S FAILURE: LET DOWN BY CUSTOMERS (Lancashire paper)

5342 'NAGGING' WIFE CRITICAL AFTER HAMMER ATTACK (US paper)

5343 HOSPITALS ARE SUED BY 7 FOOT DOCTORS (US paper)

5344 TUNA BITING OFF WASHINGTON COAST (US paper)

5345 ORGAN FESTIVAL ENDS IN SMASHING CLIMAX (*San Antonio Rose*)

5346 STUDY REVEALS THOSE WITHOUT INSURANCE DIE MORE OFTEN (US paper)

5347 CHANNEL SWIM ATTEMPT: BOSTON GIRL'S ARRIVAL IN LIVERPOOL (*Liverpool Echo*)

5348 RED TAPE HOLDS UP NEW BRIDGE (US paper)

5349 USE OF HEROIN SHOOTING UP (*Huntingdon Town Crier*)

5350 BRIDE REPLACED ON HIGHWAY 82 (Texas paper)

5351 NUDIST NABBED — UNCLOTHED MAN WHO ADMITS BRANDISHING PISTOL IS CHARGED WITH CARRYING CONCEALED WEAPON (*Providence Journal*)

5352 DR RUTH TO TALK ABOUT SEX WITH NEWSPAPER EDITORS (US paper)

5353 TYPHOON RIPS THROUGH CEMETERY: HUNDREDS DEAD (US paper)

5354 DEFENDER'S BROKEN LEG HITS HAVERHILL (*Cambridge Evening News*)

5355 POLICE DISCOVERED POT PLANTS WERE REALLY CANNABIS (US paper)

5356 HEADLESS BODY FOUND IN TOPLESS BAR (US paper)

5357 TRAFFIC DEAD RISE SLOWLY (US paper)

5358 2 CONVICTS EVADE NOOSE: JURY HUNG (*Oakland Tribune*)

5359 INFANT MORALITY SHOWS DROP HERE (Connecticut paper)

5360 FRIED CHICKEN COOKED IN MICROWAVE WINS TRIP (US paper)

5361 ALZHEIMER'S CENTER PREPARES FOR AN AFFAIR TO REMEMBER (US paper)

5362 LUCKY VICTIM WAS STABBED THREE TIMES (*Hackney Gazette*)

5363 MILK DRINKERS ARE TURNING TO POWDER (US paper)

5364 MAN MINUS EAR WAIVES HEARING (US paper)

5365 HUNTINGTON CEMETERY REPORTS GOOD YEAR: NO DEPRESSION (Long Island paper)

5366 PIPELINE RAPTURED (*Ghanaian Times*)

5367 DEALERS WILL HEAR CAR TALK AT NOON (US paper)

5368 TWO SISTERS REUNITED AFTER 18 YEARS AT CHECKOUT COUNTER (US paper)

5369 OFFICER CONVICTED OF ACCEPTING BRIDE (*Raleigh News and Observer*)

5370 INCLUDE YOUR CHILDREN WHEN BAKING COOKIES (US paper)

Bloomers

5371 If the terriers and bariffs are torn down, this economy will grow. (GEORGE W. BUSH)

5372 Rarely is the question asked: Is our children learning? – (GEORGE W. BUSH, self-styled education governor)

5373 The problem with the French is that they don't have a word for entrepreneur. (GEORGE W. BUSH)

5374 More and more of our imports come from overseas. (GEORGE W. BUSH)

5375 Our enemies are innovative and resourceful, and so are we. They never stop thinking about new ways to harm our country and our people, and neither do we. (GEORGE W. BUSH)

5376 A tax cut is really one of the anecdotes to coming out of an economic illness. (GEORGE W. BUSH)

5377 We cannot let terrorists and rogue nations hold this country hostile. (GEORGE W. BUSH)

5378 Families is where our nation takes hope, where our wings take dream. (GEORGE W. BUSH)

5379 We look forward to hearing your vision, so we can more better do our job. (GEORGE W. BUSH)

5380 I refuse to be sucked into your hypnotheoretical arguments. (GEORGE W. BUSH)

5381 The thing that's important for me is to remember what's the most important thing. (GEORGE W. BUSH)

5382 My trip to Asia begins here in Japan for an important reason. It begins here because for a century and a half now, America and Japan have formed one of the great and enduring alliances of modern times. (GEORGE W. BUSH)

5383 They misunderestimated me. (GEORGE W. BUSH)

5384 Osama Bin Laden is either alive and well, or alive and not too well, or not alive. (DONALD RUMSFELD)

5385 There are known knowns. These are things we know that we know. There are known unknowns. That is to say, there are things we know we don't know. But there are also unknown unknowns. These are things we don't know we don't know. (DONALD RUMSFELD)

5386 I believe that people would be alive today if there were a death penalty. (NANCY REAGAN)

5387 For seven and a half years I've worked alongside President Reagan. We've had triumphs. Made some mistakes. We've had some sex – er – setbacks. (GEORGE BUSH)

5388 I believe we are on an irreversible trend toward more freedom and democracy. But that could change (DAN QUAYLE)

5389 If we don't succeed, we run the risk of failure. (DAN QUAYLE)

5390 We don't want to go back to tomorrow, we want to go forward. (DAN QUAYLE)

5391 It isn't pollution that's harming the environment. It's the impurities in our air and water that are doing it. (DAN QUAYLE)

5392 The Holocaust was an obscene period in our nation's history . . . this century's history . . . We all lived in this century . . . I didn't live in this century. (DAN QUAYLE)

5393 I was recently on a tour of Latin America, and the only regret I have was that I didn't study Latin harder in school so I could converse with those people. (DAN QUAYLE)

5394 I love California. I practically grew up in Phoenix. (DAN QUAYLE)

5395 It is wonderful to be here in the great state of Chicago. (DAN QUAYLE)

5396 Republicans understand the importance of bondage between a mother and child. (DAN QUAYLE)

5397 We are ready for any unforeseen event that may or may not occur. (DAN QUAYLE)

5398 What a waste it is to lose one's mind. Or not to have a mind is being very wasteful. How true that is. (DAN QUAYLE)

5399 I desire the Poles carnally. (JIMMY CARTER whose innocuous comments about his hopes for the future of the Polish people lost something in the translation.)

5400 My vision is to make the most diverse state on earth, and we have people from every planet in the earth in this state. (GRAY DAVIS, Governor of California)

5401 Outside of the killings, Washington has one of the lowest crime rates in the country. (MAYOR MARION BARRY, Washington, DC)

5402 The streets are safe in Philadelphia. It's only the people who make them unsafe. (FRANK RIZZO, ex-police chief and mayor of Philadelphia)

5403 The police are not here to create disorder, they're here to preserve disorder. (RICHARD DALEY, Mayor of Chicago)

5404 We are not without accomplishment. We have managed to distribute poverty equally. (NGUYEN CO THATCH, Vietnamese foreign minister)

5405 Nixon has been sitting in the White House while George McGovern has been exposing himself to the people of the United States. (FRANK LIGHT, governor of Rhode Island, 1972)

5406 Four people and Congressman Ryan were killed. (US newscaster)

5407 I haven't committed a crime, what I did was fail to comply with the law. (New York City mayor DAVID DINKINS answering accusations that he failed to pay his taxes)

5408 Belgrade is now in darkness for as far as the eye can see. (TV newscaster)

5409 The mother killed herself and then the child. (TV newscaster)

5410 We all have ancestors, and in this series I will encourage you to dig up yours. (TV presenter)

5411 The tickets to the free concert have been sold out. (Radio announcer)

5412 And don't forget, on Sunday, you can hear the two-minute silence on Radio 1. (STEVE WRIGHT)

5413 I am honoured today to begin my first term as the governor of Baltimore – that is, Maryland. (WILLIAM DONALD SCHAEFER)

5414 It's no exaggeration to say that the undecideds could go one way or another. (GEORGE BUSH)

5415 I have opinions of my own – strong opinions – but I don't always agree with them. (GEORGE BUSH)

5416 Now we are going to get unemployment to go up and I think we're going to succeed. (RONALD REAGAN)

5417 You read what Disraeli had to say. I don't remember what he said. He said something. He's no longer with us. (BOB DOLE)

5418 If this thing starts to snowball, it will catch fire right across the country. (ROBERT THOMPSON)

5419 I think incest can be handled as a family matter within the family. (JAY DICKEY)

5420 Those who survived the San Francisco earthquake said, "Thank God, I'm still alive." But of course those who died, their lives will never be the same again. (Senator BARBARA BOXER)

5421 I think that gay marriage should be between a man and a woman. (ARNOLD SCHWARZENEGGER)

5422 Smoking kills. If you're killed, you've lost a very important part of your life. (BROOKE SHIELDS)

5423 This is the worst disaster in California since I was elected. (Governor PAT BROWN)

5424 You should hear her sing. She's a female Lena Horne. (JOE PASTERNAK)

5425 We are not prepared to stand idly by and be murdered in our beds. (REV. IAN PAISLEY)

5426 This is unparalyzed in the state's history. (GIB LEWIS)

5427 I can't believe that we are going to let a majority of the people decide what's best for this state. (JOHN TRAVIS, Louisiana state legislator)

5428 That lowdown scoundrel deserves to be kicked to death by a jackass, and I'm just the one to do it. (Texas congressional candidate)

5429 This year's hairstyle is called a shag and our resident stylist is here to give our model one. (LORRAINE KELLY)

5430 For those of you who haven't read the book, it's being published tomorrow. (DAVID FROST)

5431 And now, the moment you have been waiting for — the Chancellor of the Exchequer, Sir Stifford Crapps. (BBC broadcaster MCDONALD HOBLEY introducing a 1951 political broadcast from Chancellor Sir Stafford Cripps)

5432 Why do you think marriage is a bum deal, for you as a gay person? (ANN LESLIE)

5433 Our walking encyclopaedia on disablement problems, Ann Davies, is waiting in her wheelchair to hear from you. (ROBBIE VINCENT)

5434 I didn't even know Elvis was from Memphis, I thought he was from Tennessee. (DREW GOODEN)

5435 Born in Italy, most of his fights have been in his native New York. (DES LYNAM)

5436 It's about 90 per cent strength and 40 per cent technique. (World middleweight wrist-wrestling champion JOHNNY WALKER on the secret of his success)

5437 Arnie Palmer, usually a great putter, seems to be having trouble with his long putts. However he has no trouble dropping his shorts. (US golf commentator)

5438 And here's Moses Kiptanui, the 19-year-old Kenyan who turned 20 a few weeks ago. (DAVID COLEMAN)

5439 She's really tough; she's remorseful. (DAVID MOORCROFT)

5440 We didn't underestimate them. They were just better than we thought. (BOBBY ROBSON)

5441 Not only is he ambidextrous, but he can throw with either hand. (American Football coach (DUFFY DAUGHTERTY)

5442 And referee Richie Powers called the loose bowel foul on Johnson. (FRANK HERZOG)

5443 My parents have always been there for me, ever since I was about seven. (DAVID BECKHAM)

5444 I've never had major knee surgery on any other part of my body. (University of Kentucky basketball forward WINSTON BENNETT)

5445 Michelle Ford is Australia's first Olympic medal for four years. (NORMAN MAY)

5446 What will you do when you leave football, Jack — will you stay in football? (STUART HALL)

5447 The ball came back, literally cutting Graham Thorpe in half. (COLIN CROFT)

5448 Paul Gascoigne has pissed a fartness test. (BOB WILSON)

5449 A lot of horses get distracted. It's just human nature. (NICK ZITO)

5450 Girls shouldn't play with men's balls. Their hands are too small. (SENATOR WALLY HORN of Iowa, on basketball)

5451 Fred Davis, the doyen of snooker, now 67 years of age and too old to get his leg over, prefers to use his left hand. (TED LOWE)

5452 Ballesteros felt much better today after a 69. (STEVE RIDER)

5453 There's going to be a real ding-dong when the bell goes. (DAVID COLEMAN)

5454 I don't want to tell you any half-truths unless they're completely accurate. (Boxing manager DENNIS RAPPAPORT)

5455 Billie Jean has always been conscious of wind on the centre court. (DAN MASKELL)

5456 We haven't had any more rain since it stopped raining. (HARRY CARPENTER)

5457 Stephen Hendry jumps on Steve Davis's misses every chance he gets. (Snooker commentator MIKE HALLETT)

5458 As Phil De Glanville said, each game is unique, and this one is no different to any other. (JOHN SLEIGHTHOLME)

5459 He's in front of everyone in this race except for the two in front of him. (MURRAY WALKER)

5460 I imagine that the conditions in those cars today are totally unimaginable. (MURRAY WALKER)

5461 Knowing exactly where Nigel Mansell is because he can see him in his earphones. (MURRAY WALKER)

5462 You can see now that the gap between Mansell and Piquet is rather more than just visual. (MURRAY WALKER)

5463 I make no apologies for their absence; I'm sorry they're not here. (MURRAY WALKER)

5464 The doctors X-rayed my head and found nothing. (Baseball star DIZZY DEAN after being hit on the head during the World Series)

5465 Fans, don't fail to miss tomorrow's game. (DIZZY DEAN, still feeling the aftereffects of the blow when he turned to commentating)

5466 I can see the carrot at the end of the tunnel. (STUART PEARCE)

5467 Ah! Isn't that nice – the wife of the Cambridge President is kissing the cox of the Oxford crew? (HARRY CARPENTER)

5468 He treats us like men. He lets us wear ear-rings. (TORRIN POLK)

5469 The word "genius" isn't applicable in football. A genius is a guy like Norman Finstein. (NFL quarterback JOE THEISMAN)

5470 Sure there have been injuries and deaths in boxing, but none of them serious. (ALAN MINTER)

5471 The Port Elizabeth ground is more of a circle than an oval. It's long and square. (TREVOR BAILEY)

5472 A lot of people my age are dead at the present time. (CASEY STENGEL of the New York Yankees baseball team)

5473 We are going to turn this team around 360 degrees. (Dallas Mavericks' basketball player JASON KIDD)

5474 If history repeats itself, I should think we can expect the same thing again. (TERRY VENABLES)

5475 It's like learning to play golf. Just when you think you've cracked it, they move the goalposts. (ADRIAN LOVE)

5476 It seems like déjà vu all over again. (Baseball legend YOGI BERRA)

5477 The similarities between me and my father are different. (DALE BERRA, son of Yogi)

5478 A brain scan revealed that Andrew Caddick is not suffering from a stress fracture of the shin. (TV reporter)

5479 Once Tony Daley opens his legs, you've got a problem. (HOWARD WILKINSON on the speedy former Aston Villa soccer player)

5480 Bobby Gould thinks I'm trying to stab him in the back. In fact I'm right behind him. (STUART PEARSON)

5481 You weigh up the pros and cons and try to put them in chronological order. (DAVE BASSETT)

5482 I'd like to play for an Italian club, like Barcelona. (MARK DRAPER)

5483 He's a guy who gets up at six o'clock in the morning regardless of what time it is. (Boxing trainer LOU DUVA, on the strict training regime of heavyweight Andrew Golota)

5484 This is Gregoriava from Bulgaria . . . I saw her snatch this morning and it was amazing. (Weightlifting commentator PAT GLENN)

5485 One of the reasons Arnie Palmer is playing so well is that, before each tee-shot, his wife takes out his balls and kisses them. (US golf commentator)

5486 Even Napoleon had his Watergate. (DANNY OZARK, manager of the Philadelphia Phillies baseball team)

5487 I'll fight Lloyd Honeyghan for nothing, if the price is right. (MARLON STARLING)

5488 Julian Dicks is everywhere. It's like they've got eleven Dicks on the field. (Metro Radio)

5489 I'd like to think it was a case of crossing the i's and dotting the t's. (DAVE BASSETT, preparing to make a signing)

5490 The beauty of Cup football is that Jack always has a chance of beating Goliath. (TERRY BUTCHER)

5491 What I said to them at half-time would be unprintable on the radio. (GERRY FRANCIS)

5492 We only have one person to blame, and that's each other. (LARRY BRECK)

5493 I have other irons in the fire, but I'm keeping them close to my chest. (JOHN BOND)

5494 I can count on the fingers of one hand ten games when we've caused our own downfall. (JOE KINNEAR)

5495 Good night. And don't forget tonight to put your cocks back. (JIMMY HILL, signing off *Match of the Day* on the night before the end of British Summer Time)

5496 Here we are in the Holy Land of Israel — a Mecca for tourists. (DAVID VINE)

5497 I've got ten pairs of trainers — that's one for every day of the week. (SAM FOX)

5498 Agatha Christie is such a well-known name. Her books sell all over the world — and other places as well. (MICHAEL GRADE)

5499 I owe a lot to my parents, especially my mother and my father. (GREG NORMAN)

5500 We didn't have metaphors in our day. We didn't beat about the bush. (FRED TRUEMAN)

5501 Fiction writing is great. You can make up almost anything. (IVANA TRUMP, upon finishing her first novel)

5502 I don't think anyone should write his autobiography until after he's dead. (SAM GOLDWYN)

5503 That's the trouble with directors – always biting the hand that lays the golden egg. (SAM GOLDWYN)

5504 If I could drop dead right now, I'd be the happiest man alive. (SAM GOLDWYN)

5505 Thank heaven. A bachelor's life is no life for a single man. (SAM GOLDWYN, on hearing that his son was getting married)

5506 I don't want any yes-men around me. I want everyone to tell me the truth – even if it costs him his job. (SAM GOLDWYN)

5507 You don't get once-in-a-lifetime offers like this every day. (Radio advert)

5508 Ladies and gentlemen, now you can have a bikini for a ridiculous figure. (US radio station)

5509 We are unable to announce the weather. We depend on weather reports from the airport, which is closed, due to weather. Whether we will be able to give you a weather report tomorrow will depend on the weather. (Arab news report)

PICK-UP LINES AND REJECTIONS

Pick-up lines

5510 The word of the day is "legs". Let's go back to my place and spread the word.

5511 Do you believe in love at first sight, or should I walk by again?

5512 That outfit would look great in a crumpled heap on my bedroom floor tomorrow morning.

5513 Inheriting 70 million bucks doesn't mean much when you've got a weak heart.

5514 If you've lost your virginity, can I have the box it came in?

5515 Do your legs hurt from running through my dreams all night?

5516 Y'know – your hair and my pillow are perfectly colour co-ordinated.

5517 Do I know you from somewhere, or is it just that you have your clothes on?

5518 I like every muscle in your body, especially mine.

5519 Do you know why you should masturbate with these two fingers? Because they're mine.

5520 Hi, I'm conducting a feel test of how many women have pierced nipples.

5521 Anything drugs can do, I can do with my tongue.

5522 That's a really nice smile you've got; shame that's not all you're wearing.

5523 I want to melt in your mouth, not in your hands.

5524 Your face or mine?

5525 Really like your peaches, wanna shake your tree.

5526 All those curves, and me with no brakes.

5527 I suffer from amnesia. Do I come here often?

5528 There must be something wrong with my eyes – I can't take them off you.

5529 I can sense you're a terrific lover, and it intimidates me a little.

5530 Let's go back to my place and get something straight between us.

5531 I'm an organ donor, and I have an organ you might need.

5532 If I said you had a beautiful body, would you hold it against me?

5533 My friend and I have a bet that you won't take your top off in a public place.

5534 I miss my teddy bear. Would you sleep with me?

5535 You've got the whitest teeth I've ever come across.

5536 Gorgeous hair. But it'd be even better brushing against my thighs.

5537 (Pulling trouser pockets inside out): Have you ever kissed a rabbit between the ears?

5538 Let's do breakfast tomorrow. Shall I call you or nudge you?

5539 I've lost my phone number. Can I have yours?

5540 Smile. It's the second best thing you can do with your lips.

5541 I've got a pimple on my butt. Wanna see it?

5542 If it's true that we are what we eat, then I could be you by the morning.

5543 Do you know the essential difference between sex and conversation? No? Wanna go upstairs and talk?

5544 Would you be my love buffet so I can lay you out on the table and take what I want?

5545 I'd buy you a drink but I'd be jealous of the straw.

5546 I wanna floss with your pubic hair.

5547 Do you know how to use a whip?

5548 Are you religious, because I'm the answer to your prayers?

5549 You are truly absolutely beautiful. Can you cook and clean too?

5550 Stand back, I'm a doctor! You get an ambulance – I'll loosen her clothes.

5551 Is it that cold out or are you just smuggling tic-tacs?

5552 How about you sit on my lap and we'll talk about the first thing that comes up?

5553 Can I be your slave for the night?

5554 Are those space pants? Because your ass is out of this world.

5555 My love for you is like the Energizer bunny — it keeps going and going.

5556 Since we shouldn't waste this day and age, what say we use these condoms in my pocket before they expire?

5557 I've got the ship, you've got the harbour. How about I dock for the night?

5558 If I help you screw Uncle Sam, can I be next? (Accountants' pick-up line)

5559 Did it hurt — when you fell from heaven?

5560 Excuse me, but are those stretch marks around your mouth?

5561 Are you a screamer or a moaner?

5562 I'm no Fred Flintstone, but I can make your Bedrock.

5563 I'm choking — I need mouth to mouth.

5564 I'm new in town. Can you give me directions to your apartment?

5565 I must be lost. I thought paradise was further south.

5566 My face is leaving in five minutes. Be on it.

5567 Wanna go halves in a baby?

5568 Do you have a map? I just got lost in your eyes.

5569 Do you have 40 cents? No? I wanted to call my mother to tell her I just found the girl of my dreams.

5570 Hey, baby, wanna play lion? You go kneel right there and I'll throw you my meat.

5571 I'll cook you dinner if you cook me breakfast.

5572 Would you touch me so I can tell my friends I've been touched by an angel?

5573 What do you say we go behind that rock and get a little boulder?

5574 If you're going to regret this in the morning, we can sleep till the afternoon.

5575 Nice ass. May I wear it as a hat?

5576 Would you like to join me in some arithmetic? We'll add you and me, subtract our clothes, divide your legs, and multiply.

5577 Wow! Are those real?

5578 Would you like gin and platonic, or would you prefer Scotch and sofa?

5579 Was your father a thief? Because someone stole the stars from the sky and put them in your eyes.

5580 Hi, I'm Big Brother. And I've been watching you!

5581 Stand back, I'm a police officer! You call for backup while I frisk her.

5582 Can I see your tan lines?

5583 Do you know what would look good on you? Me.

5584 I'm Italian. Have you got some Italian in you? No? Want some?

5585 I'm gonna have sex with you tonight so you might as well be there.

5586 Is it hot in here or is it just you?

5587 Hi. Do you swallow?

5588 Can I tickle your belly-button from the inside?

5589 I'm writing a phone book. Can I have your number?

5590 I'm sorry, I'm an artist and it's my job to stare at beautiful women.

5591 You may not be the best looking girl here, but beauty is only a light switch away.

5592 Hi, I'm a love machine. Wanna strap yourself to my engine?

5593 I think I could fall madly in bed with you.

5594 Hey, can I use your thighs as earmuffs?

5595 You're good at maths, right? Is 69 a perfect square?

5596 Nice dress. Can I talk you out of it?

5597 I'd love to be a bar of soap in your shower.

5598 C'mon, baby, light my fire.

5599 Are you from Tennessee? Because you're the only ten I see.

5600 You know what I like about you? – My arms.

5601 We've got to keep meeting like this.

5602 Do you sleep on your stomach? No? Can I?

5603 Is there an airport nearby or is that just my heart taking off?

5604 Do you wanna see something really swell?

5605 If I could rearrange the alphabet, I'd put U and I together.

5606 My name's Paul. That's so you know what to scream in the night.

5607 I was sitting here holding my drink when I realized I'd rather be holding you.

5608 You know what I'd like to see you in? – Nothing.

5609 Fuck me if I'm wrong, but I think you want to kiss me.

5610 Man: "You look like my third wife."
Woman: "How many times have you been married?"
Man: "Twice."

Inadvisable pick-up lines

5611 Wanna see my collection of Jack the Ripper memorabilia?

5612 You look just like Joan Rivers.

5613 Let's make the most of this, because I'm only on day release.

5614 You'd be a real babe if you lost a couple of stone.

5615 Do you like children?

5616 That tape on your glasses really sets off your eyes.

5617 Excuse me while I use the phone. I have to ring my mother if I'm out after ten.

5618 I may not be the best looking guy here, but I am the only one talking to you.

5619 I'm from Arkansas.

5620 I'm undergoing treatment for clinical depression.

5621 Who wants safe sex anyway?

5622 It's late — you'll do.

5623 Did you see my picture on America's Most Wanted?

5624 There's ten dollars riding on you.

5625 Is that a glass eye you've got?

5626 I work in a slaughterhouse. How about you?

5627 What are your views on manacles?

5628 A Porsche is all very well, but for reliability you can't beat a Yugo.

5629 You're so much cuter than some of the other trash I've got off with this week.

5630 I share everything with my best friend.

5631 I'm a lawyer. Trust me.

Smart rejections

5632 Hey, beautiful, what are you doing tonight?
    Sorry, I don't date outside my species.

5633 Hi, gorgeous. Where have you been all my life?
    Well, for most of it I wasn't born.

5634 They say I'm a smooth talking guy. What do you think?
    If I wanted to hear from an ass, I'd fart.

5635 Is this seat empty?
    Yes, and this one will be too if you sit down.

5636 Your body is like a temple.
    Sorry, there are no services today.

5637 May I have the last dance?
    You've just had it.

5638 Hi, sexy, fancy a drink?
    I like your approach. Now let's see your departure.

5639 We could step outside and watch the sunrise.
    You're starting to sound OK. Time to up my medication.

5640 Wanna go back to my place?
    I don't know. Will two people fit under a stone?

5641 If I could see you naked, I'd die happy.
    If I could see you naked, I'd die laughing.

5642 Hey, baby, wanna come outside?
    I see you've set aside this special time to humiliate yourself in public.

5643 If you come home with me, I can show you a real good time.
    You know your problem? Your mouth is writing cheques that your body can't cash.

5644 When can I take you out?
    How about never. Is never good for you?

5645 Why won't you come out with me? Lower your standards a little.

I did, and the answer's still no.

5646 I'd really like to get into your pants.

No thanks, there's already one asshole in there.

5647 Hey, baby, what's your sign?

Do not enter.

5648 I reckon we'd be great together.

Any connection between your reality and mine is purely coincidental.

5649 So how about you and I go away somewhere?

I couldn't go away with you. I feel I'd be depriving your village of its idiot.

5650 I'd go through anything for you.

Let's start with your bank account.

5651 Y'know, I really like you.

I like you. You remind me of when I was young and stupid.

5652 I haven't been able to take my eyes off you.

I know, I just found your eyeballs in my cleavage.

5653 Y'know, heads turn when they see your face.

And stomachs turn when they see yours.

5654 I really think this could be the start of something beautiful.

Keep talking. I always yawn when I'm interested.

5655 I want to give myself to you.

Sorry, I don't accept cheap gifts.

5656 I'm as particular about my clothes as I am about my women.

Hmm, nice suit. Were you there for the fitting?

5657 D'you mind if I kiss the back of your neck?

Look, I don't know what your problem is, but I bet it's hard to pronounce.

5658 I would go to the end of the world for you.

Yes, but would you stay there?

5659 What's a nice girl like you doing in a place like this?

What's a nice guy like you doing with a face like that?

5660 Haven't we met before?

Yes, I'm a receptionist at a VD clinic.

5661 You knock me dead with your looks.

You knock me dead with your breath.

5662 Let me buy you a drink.

Sorry, I'd rather pass a kidney stone than another five minutes with you.

5663 Your place or mine?

Both. You go to your place, and I'll go to mine.

5664 So how about a date?

I'm busy now. Can I ignore you some other time?

5665 We could make sweet music together.
  I'm looking for a guy with a grand piano, not a penny whistle.
5666 I can tell that you want me.
  Yes, I want you to leave.
5667 Do you mind if I sit here?
  Sorry, I can't talk to you right now. Tell me, where will you be in ten years?
5668 What are your sexual preferences?
  My sexual preference is "no".
5669 Wow, what a body!
  Please don't talk to my breasts. You won't be meeting them.
5670 How about you and me get together some time?
  I'm busy. You're ugly. Have a nice day.
5671 What do you do for a living?
  I'm a female impersonator.
5672 I know how to please a woman.
  Then please leave me alone.
5673 Haven't I seen you some place before?
  Yes, that's why I don't go there any more.
5674 Fancy a quick one?
  What am I? Flypaper for freaks?
5675 I happen to think you're great.
  And I happen to think you grate.
5676 Listen, honey, you and I were meant for each other.
  Save your breath for your inflatable date.
5677 Hey, come on, we're both here at this bar for the same reason.
  Yeah, let's pick up some chicks!
5678 After picking up a girl in a club, a Romeo was desperate to get her to stay the night. She clearly wasn't interested but he wouldn't give up.
  "Say, honey," he asked her suggestively, "how do you like your eggs in the morning?"
  She looked at him and replied coldly: "Unfertilized."

Handy excuses for getting out of a date –
I'd love to go out with you but . . .
5679 I have to worm my dog.
5680 I want to spend more time with my blender.
5681 The man on TV told me to stay tuned.
5682 I'm staying home to work on my cottage cheese sculpture.
5683 I'm teaching my ferret to yodel.
5684 I have to check the sell-by dates on all my dairy products.

5685 I'm sandblasting my oven.

5686 My patent is pending.

5687 I'm trying to see how long I can go without saying the word "yes".

5688 I'm trying to be less popular.

5689 I'm being deported.

5690 My yucca plant is unwell.

5691 I'm attending the opening of my garage door.

5692 I'm not allowed out at night.

5693 I'm going to count the bristles in my toothbrush.

5694 The Pope might drop by.

5695 My gerbil is about to give birth.

5696 You know how we psychos are.

5697 Having fun gives me prickly heat.

5698 I promised to help a friend fold road maps.

5699 It's too close to the start of the century.

5700 I just picked up a book on the History of Superglue, and I can't put it down.

5701 There are important world issues that need worrying about.

5702 I have to jog my memory.

5703 I have to stay home and see if I snore.

5704 I'm busy cleaning the blood off my axe.

5705 My dad said I can't date till I'm married.

5706 None of my socks match.

5707 My bathroom tiles need grouting.

5708 My favourite commercial is on TV.

5709 I have to study for my blood test.

5710 I prefer to remain an enigma.

5711 My grandma is on fire.

5712 I have to put my CDs in alphabetical order.

5713 I swallowed my gold crown this morning, and I have to wait here till it comes out the other end.

5714 I need to trim my nose hairs.

5715 My plot to take over the world is gathering pace.

5716 I'm observing National Apathy Week.

5717 I'm going through strawberry cheesecake withdrawal.

5718 I never go out on days that end in a Y.

5719 My palm reader advised against it.

5720 I feel a song coming on.

5721 It would be a complete waste of make-up.

POLITICALLY INCORRECT JOKES

Blonde jokes

5722 I'm not offended by all the dumb blonde jokes because I know I'm not dumb . . . and I also know that I'm not blonde. (DOLLY PARTON)

5723 What do you call a blonde with two brain cells? – Pregnant.

5724 What is the difference between a blonde and a bowling ball? – You can only put three fingers in a bowling ball.

5725 How are a turtle and a blonde the same? – Once on their backs, they're both screwed.

5726 What is the difference between a blonde and the *Titanic*? – They know how many men went down on the *Titanic*.

5727 Why do blondes wear pony-tails? – To hide the air valve.

5728 Why did the blonde go out with her purse open? – Because she was expecting some change in the weather.

5729 How can you tell when a blonde is dating? – By the buckle print on her forehead.

5730 How can you tell when a fax has been sent by a blonde? – There's a stamp on it.

5731 Why did the blonde throw bread into the toilet? – She wanted to feed the toilet duck.

5732 How do you get a blonde to marry you? – Tell her she's pregnant.

5733 What do blondes wear behind their ears to attract men? – Their heels.

5734 What's the difference between a blonde and a supermarket trolley? – A supermarket trolley has a mind of its own.

5735 A brunette, a redhead and a blonde were all pregnant. One afternoon they were sitting at the doctor's discussing what sex they thought their babies would be. The brunette said: "I'm going to have a boy because I was on top during sex."

The redhead said: "I'm going to have a girl because I was underneath during sex."

And the blonde screamed: "Oh my God, I'm going to have puppies!"

5736 A blonde phoned her boyfriend in despair. "I'm doing a jigsaw puzzle and I can't fit any of the pieces together."

"What's the puzzle of?" he asked.

"It's of a big rooster, and I can't get any of it together. None of the edge pieces will fit. Please come and help."

When the boyfriend arrived, she directed him to the kitchen. "The pieces are all over the kitchen table," she wailed.

He took one look at the problem and said: "Honey, put the corn flakes back in the box."

5737 A blonde hailed a passing policeman to report that thieves had been in her car. "Officer," she cried, "they've stolen the dashboard, the steering wheel, the brake pedal, even the accelerator."

"Madam," he replied, "you're in the back seat . . ."

5738 What do you call two nuns and a blonde? – Two tight ends and a wide receiver.

5739 What do you call 20 blondes standing ear to ear? – A wind tunnel.

5740 What does a blonde call safe sex? – A padded dashboard.

5741 How do you know when a blonde has been at the computer? – There's white-out all over the screen.

5742 Why did the blonde climb the glass wall? – To see what was on the other side.

5743 Why did the blonde bury her driver's licence? – Because it had expired.

5744 What's the difference between a blonde and a brick? – When you lay a brick, it doesn't follow you around.

5745 An interior designer was talking with a woman about decorating her apartment. The woman said she would like the lounge in shades of lilac.

The designer wrote this down, went over to the window and shouted: "Green side up!"

Moving to the kitchen, the woman said she envisaged pale blue. The designer wrote this down, went over to the window and shouted: "Green side up!"

When they reached the bedroom, the woman said she wanted it pink. The designer wrote this down, went over to the window and shouted: "Green side up!"

The woman was puzzled. "Why do you keep going to the window and shouting "Green side up!"?

"I'm sorry," said the designer, "but across the street I've got a crew of blondes laying turf."

5746 Why can blondes only count to 68? – Because 69's a bit of a mouthful.

5747 Three blondes were walking through the forest when they came upon a set of tracks.
"These are deer tracks," said the first.
"I think they're elk," said the second.
"No, they're moose," said the third.
They were still arguing when the train hit them.

5748 What's the difference between a blonde and a mosquito? – When you slap a mosquito, it stops sucking.

5749 What did the blonde ask when told she was pregnant? – How do you know it's mine?

5750 What does a blonde say after having sex for the first time? – "So you guys are all on the same team?"

5751 What's the difference between an ironing board and a blonde? – It's hard to get an ironing board's legs open.

5752 What do you call a blonde with a balloon on her shoulder? – Siamese twins.

5753 What is the mating call of a blonde? – "I'm soooo drunk!"

5754 How do you get a blonde to burn her ear? – Phone her while she's ironing.

5755 How do you get a blonde to burn her ear twice? – Phone her again while she's ironing.

5756 What do blondes and beer bottles have in common? – Both are empty from the neck up.

5757 How can you tell which blonde is the waitress? – She's the one with the tampon behind her ear, wondering what she did with her pencil.

5758 Why do blondes have orgasms? – So they know when to stop having sex.

5759 A blonde went to the doctor. He examined her and said: "Stay out of bed for two days."

5760 What do you do when a blonde throws a pin at you? – Run like hell, she's got a grenade in her mouth.

5761 A tearful blonde ran to her father and wailed: "You gave me bad financial advice. You told me to put my money in that big bank and now that big bank is in trouble."

"What are you talking about?" said the father. "That's one of the biggest banks in the world. There must be some mistake."

"I don't think so. They just returned one of my cheques with a note saying 'No Funds'."

5762 What do you see when you look into a blonde's eyes? – The back of her head.

5763 What is the difference between a blonde and the Grand Old Duke of York? – The Grand Old Duke of York only had 10,000 men.

5764 Why can't a blonde waterski? – Because her legs spread the moment her crotch gets wet.

5765 A blonde waitress was in floods of tears. Her boss asked her what the problem was.

"I'm sorry," sobbed the blonde, "but this morning I got a phone call saying that my mother died."

"That's terrible," said the boss sympathetically. "Why don't you take the rest of the day off?"

"No, it's all right," she answered. "Being at work and being surrounded by people helps me to take my mind off it."

"Well, only if you're sure," he said. "Remember, if you need time off or someone to talk to, just come and see me."

"That's very kind of you," she said, "but I'm sure I'll be fine now that I've had a little cry."

Nevertheless he continued to keep an eye on her and was horrified to see her sobbing her heart out again a couple of hours later.

"What's happened?" he asked.

"It's too awful," said the blonde. "I've just had a phone call from my sister and her mum died too!"

5766 Why did the blonde tiptoe past the medicine cabinet? – She didn't want to wake the sleeping pills.

5767 Two blondes were on board an airplane. Fifteen minutes into the flight, the captain announced: "One of the engines has failed and I am afraid the flight will therefore be an hour longer. But don't worry, we have three engines left."

Fifteen minutes later, the captain announced: "Our second engine has failed, and so I am afraid the flight will be two hours longer."

Fifteen minutes after that, the captain came on over the intercom again. "I am afraid our third engine has failed. As a result, our flight will be three hours longer."

One blonde turned to the other and moaned: "I don't know. If we lose one more engine, we'll be up here all day!"

5768 A blonde went for a job interview.

"How old are you?" asked the interviewer.

The blonde started counting on her fingers. "Uh, let me see now, 22."

"And what is your height?"

The blonde got out a tape measure and measured herself from head to toe. "Uh, five foot two."

The interviewer could see this was going to be a struggle, so he slipped her an easier question. "What is your name?"

The blonde mouthed something to herself for a few moments before replying: "Mandy."

"What were you saying to yourself just then?"

"Oh, I was remembering that song: 'Happy birthday to you, happy birthday to you . . .'"

5769 A blonde had a terrifying experience riding a horse. For no apparent reason, the beast started to get out of control. It became wild and frisky. The blonde desperately tried to hang on to the reins but the horse was so unpredictable that she was eventually thrown off. As she fell, her foot caught in the stirrup and her head bounced repeatedly on the ground with the horse refusing to stop or even slow down. Finally she was saved when the manager of Woolworth's came out and unplugged the machine.

5770 The blonde came in from the kitchen with a look of bewilderment on her face. "I don't know what's happened," she told her boyfriend. "I was rinsing some ice cubes a few minutes ago and now I can't find them!"

5771 What do you call a blonde grabbing at air? – Collecting her thoughts.

5772 What do an intelligent blonde and a UFO have in common? – You often hear about them but you never see one.

5773 What's the first thing a blonde does after sex? – She opens the car door.

5774 Why do blondes drive cars with sunroofs? – There's more leg room.

5775 Why did the blonde only change her baby's disposable nappy once a month? – Because it said on the bag "good for up to 20 lb".

5776 What have blondes and computers got in common? – You never fully appreciate them till they go down on you.

5777 What did the blonde's right leg say to the left leg? – Nothing, they've never met.

5778 How do you change a blonde's mind? – Blow in her ear.

5779 What do you call a blonde golfer with an IQ of 125? – A foursome.

5780 Why don't blondes eat bananas? – They can't find the zippers.

5781 Why don't they hire blondes as pharmacists? – They keep breaking the prescription bottles in their typewriters.

5782 What did the blonde say when she saw the sign in front of the YMCA? – "Look, they spelled MACY's wrong!"

5783 Did you hear about the blonde who got AM radio? – It took her a month to realize she could play it in the afternoon.

5784 Have you heard about the blonde virgin? – She hangs out with the Easter Bunny and Santa Claus.

5785 What's the difference between a prostitute, a nymphomaniac and a blonde?
    The prostitute says: "Are you done yet?"
    The nymphomaniac says: "Are you done already?"
    The blonde says: "Magnolia . . . I think I'll paint the ceiling magnolia."

5786 A blonde was out with her boyfriend when his car broke down. He asked her to check that the hazard warning lights were working. So she got out and walked round the back to take a look.
    "Are they on?" he called.
    "Yes, no, yes, no, yes, no, yes . . ."

5787 Two blondes were in a parking lot trying in vain to unlock the door of their Mercedes with a coat hanger. When the girl with the hanger paused for breath, her friend said: "Hurry up! It's starting to rain and the top is down!"

5788 Two blondes went duck hunting for the first time, but after three hours hadn't bagged a thing. One said to the other: "Maybe we're not throwing the dog high enough."

5789 A guy wanted to get an all-over tan before going on a hot date with a gorgeous blonde. So he went sunbathing on the flat roof of his house, but unfortunately he fell asleep and ended up with terrible sunburn on his penis. Nevertheless he went to her apartment and they sat watching a video. But as the film went on, his sunburn started to cause him considerable pain. Eventually he could stand it no longer and excused himself to the kitchen. There he poured a glass of ice cold milk and dipped his burning penis into it. The relief was instant.
    Just then the blonde, wondering where he had gone, peered around the kitchen door. "Oh," she exclaimed. "So that's how you guys load those things!"

5790 A blonde was really proud of herself for finishing a jigsaw puzzle in three months. After all, the box said two to five years.

5791 Why did the blonde climb on the roof? – She heard drinks were on the house.

5792 What do you call a blonde with half a brain? – Gifted.

5793 Why did the blonde wash her hair in the kitchen sink? – Because that's where you're supposed to wash vegetables.

5794 How do you make a blonde laugh on Friday? – Tell her a joke on Monday.

5795 How do you know when a blonde reaches orgasm? – She says "next".

5796 Why do blondes have TGIF on their shoes? – Toes go in first.

5797 Two blondes were driving to Disneyland. On the way they saw a sign on the freeway which said, Disneyland Left. So they turned round and went home.

5798 Why do blondes wear their hair up? – To catch everything that goes over their heads.

5799 Why do blondes wear hoop ear-rings? – So they have somewhere to rest their ankles.

5800 How do you confuse a blonde? – Put her in a round room and tell her to sit in the corner.

5801 Why did the blonde stare at the carton of orange juice? – Because it said "concentrate".

5802 What's the difference between a blonde and a Porsche? – You don't lend the Porsche out to your friends.

5803 Why do employers give blondes only half an hour for lunch? – Any longer and they'd have to retrain them.

5804 A blonde went to the library and ordered a book called *How to Hug*. It turned out to be volume seven of an encyclopaedia.

5805 Blonde: "Excuse me, what time is it?"
Man: "Two-thirty."
Blonde: "Gee, that's weird. I've been asking that question all day and each time I get a different answer."

5806 A man arrived home from work to find his blonde girlfriend sliding down the banister.
"What are you doing?" he asked.
"I'm just heating up dinner."

5807 A blonde went to get her hair cut. The stylist noticed that all the time she was there she never removed her headphones and was puzzled as to what could be so important to listen to. So when the blonde dozed off, the stylist gently removed the headphones and listened to the tape. It said: "Breathe in, breathe out, breathe in . . ."

5808 A college tutor asked the group: "What's the capital of Nebraska?"
"That's easy," said the blonde student. "N."

5809 A man was impressed that his blonde girlfriend was able to paint her apartment without help. "You're doing a great job," he said, "but there's just one thing which puzzles me. Why are you wearing a ski jacket over your fur coat?"
"Because," she replied, "it says on the tin: 'For best results, put on two coats'."

5810 Why did the blonde move to LA? – It was easier to spell.

5811 Why did the blonde fail her driving test? – Every time the car stopped, she hopped in the back seat.

5812 How do you drown a blonde? – Put a mirror in the bottom of your swimming pool.

5813 What do you call a dead blonde in a closet? – The winner of last year's hide and seek contest.

5814 Why do blondes take the Pill? – So they know what day of the week it is.

5815 Why did the blonde stop taking the Pill? – Because it kept falling out.

5816 Why is it good to have a blonde passenger? – You can park in the handicap zone.

5817 A traffic cop stopped a blonde who was driving erratically.
"Can I see your driver's licence?" he asked.

The blonde looked blank. "What's a driver's licence?"

"A little card with your picture on it."

"Oh, that. Here it is." And she handed him the licence.

"And may I have your car insurance?"

"What's that?" asked the blonde.

"It's the document which says you're allowed to drive the car."

"Oh, that. Here it is." And she handed him the car insurance.

The cop then reached into his pants and whipped out his cock.

"Oh, no," groaned the blonde, "not another breathalyzer test!"

5818 A blonde decided to go ice-fishing so she read up on what to do, packed her stool, her rod, her ice-pick and a thermos flask and set off for a suitable spot. She settled down and made a large cut in the ice but no sooner had she done so than she heard a mysterious deep voice boom out: "Hey, you! There are no fish there."

Unsettled by the experience, she thought she'd try a little further along the ice. Again, she hacked out a hole, only to hear the voice boom: "Hey, you! There are no fish there."

This was too much for the blonde. She looked skywards and pleaded: "Who are you – God?"

The voice came back: "No, I own the goddamn ice rink!"

5819 A blonde was driving down the road when she spotted another blonde sitting in a boat in the middle of a cornfield, rowing away. The first blonde got out of her car and shouted: "It's blondes like you that give all us blondes a bad name. If I could swim, I'd come out there and kick your ass!"

5820 A brunette and a blonde prepared for a long trek across the desert. The brunette was carrying a flask of water, and the blonde was carrying a car door.

"Why are you carrying a car door?" asked the brunette.

The blonde said: "So I can wind down the window when I get hot."

5821 A blonde and a brunette were discussing their boyfriends.

Brunette: "Last night I had three orgasms in a row."

Blonde: "That's nothing. Last night I had over 30."

Brunette: "Wow! I had no idea he was that good."

Blonde: "Oh! You mean with one guy?!"

5822 A blonde was walking along the sidewalk when she saw a brunette apparently walking down the middle of the street saying "92" over and over again.

"What are you doing?" asked the blonde.

The brunette replied: "It's great fun. You should try it."

So the blonde stepped into the middle of the street and started saying "92, 92, 92." Then a truck hit her.

And the brunette said: "93, 93 . . ."

5823 What does a blonde do if she's not in bed by ten? – She picks up her purse and goes home.

5824 What do you call a brunette between two blondes? – An interpreter.

5825 What do you call a blonde between two brunettes? – A mental block.

5826 If a blonde and a brunette fall from a building, who hits the ground first? – The brunette: the blonde has to stop to ask for directions.

5827 A brunette went to the doctor's and as she touched every part of her body with her finger, she said: "Doctor, it hurts everywhere. My leg hurts, my arm hurts, my neck hurts, my head hurts."

The doctor said: "Were you ever a blonde?"

"Yes. Why?"

"Because your finger is broken."

5828 A blonde and a brunette were talking. The brunette said that her boyfriend had a slight dandruff problem but she gave him Head and Shoulders and it cleared up. The blonde looked at her in bewilderment and asked: "How do you give shoulders?"

5829 What happens when a blonde gets Alzheimer's? – Her IQ goes up.

5830 What's the difference between butter and a blonde? – Butter is difficult to spread.

5831 What do you call a smart blonde? – A golden retriever.

5832 What do bleached blondes and 747s have in common? – Black boxes.

5833 Why did the blonde have a sore navel? – Because her boyfriend was also blonde.

5834 Why are blonde jokes so short? – So that men can remember them.

And a blonde's revenge:
5835 What do brunettes miss most about a party? – The invitation.

5836 Why do brunettes have to pay an extra $2,000 for a breast job? – Because the plastic surgeon has to start from scratch.

5837 Why didn't Indians scalp brunettes? – The hair from a buffalo's butt was more manageable.

5838 What is the most frustrated animal in the world? – A brunette rabbit.

5839 What's the difference between a brunette and the garbage? – At least the garbage gets taken out once a week.

5840 What did the frustrated brunette say to her boyfriend? – What part of "yes" don't you understand?

5841 What do you call a redhead with an attitude? – Normal.

5842 How does a redhead change a light bulb? – She doesn't, she bitches until someone else does.

5843 How do you get a redhead's mood to change? – Wait ten seconds.

5844 How do you know when a redhead has been using a computer? – There's a hammer embedded in the monitor.

5845 Why do redheads burn easily? – It's nature's way of telling us they should be kept indoors.

5846 How do you know when you've satisfied a redhead? – She unties you.

Confucius jokes

Confucius, he say:

5847 Man who eat crackers in bed wake up feeling crummy.

5848 Man who fart in church sit in own pew.

5849 Seven-day honeymoon make hole weak.

5850 Woman who sleep with judge get honourable discharge.

5851 Man who go to bed with hard problem wake up with solution in hand.

5852 Woman who stay on bedspring too long get offspring.

5853 Woman's charms like spider's web — lead to flies undoing.

5854 Man who drive like hell bound to get there.

5855 He who sleep on bed of nails is holy.

5856 He who eat too many prunes, sit on toilet many moons.

5857 Man who put head on railroad track to listen for train likely to end up with splitting headache.

5858 Man who sink into woman's arms soon have arms in woman's sink.

5859 Man who sit on tack bound to get point.

5860 He who place head in sand will get kicked in the end.

5861 Man who keep feet firmly on ground have trouble putting on pants.

5862 Man with hand in pocket always on the ball.

5863 Man who stand on toilet high on pot.

5864 Man who live in glass house should change in basement.

5865 Man who leap off cliff jump to conclusion.

5866 Panties not best thing on earth, but next to it.

5867 Nail on head not as good as screw on bench.

5868 Man who put head in fruit drink get punch in nose.

5869 He who fish in other man's well often catch crabs.

5870 Man with one chopstick go hungry.

5871 Baby conceived in automatic car grow up to be shiftless bastard.

5872 Man who want pretty nurse must be patient.

5873 Man who snatch kisses when young, kiss snatches when old.

5874 Man who run in front of car get tired.

5875 Man who run behind car get exhausted.

5876 Better to be pissed off than pissed on.

5877 Man who fight with wife all day get no piece at night.

5878 Girl who sit on jockey's lap get hot tip.

5879 War does not determine who is right; war determines who is left.

5880 It take many nails to build crib, but one screw to fill it.

5881 Man who walk sideways through airport turnstile going to Bangkok.

5882 Man who paint toilet not necessarily shithouse painter.

5883 Man who handles privates all day not necessarily sergeant.
5884 Man who do pushups in tall grass not necessarily fitness fanatic.
5885 Man who put cream in tart not necessarily baker.

Do it jokes

5886 Accountants do it with double entry.
5887 Acupuncturists do it with a small prick.
5888 Australians do it down under.
5889 Bankers use the withdrawal method.
5890 Bartenders do it on the rocks.
5891 Booksellers do it over the counter.
5892 Broadcasters do it with frequency.
5893 Cheese makers do it Caerphilly.
5894 Chess players check their mates.
5895 Detectives do it under cover.
5896 Disc jockeys do it on request.
5897 Divers do it deeper.
5898 Elevator operators do it up and down.
5899 Engineers do it to specifications.
5900 English cricketers are in and out.
5901 Firemen do it with a big hose.
5902 Gardeners do it in the potting shed.
5903 Gas attendants pump all day.
5904 Glider pilots stay up longer.
5905 Kamikaze pilots do it once.
5906 Landlords do it on the first day of every month.
5907 Lawyers do it in their briefs.
5908 Librarians do it in silence.
5909 Linguists do it orally.
5910 Lumberjacks do it with their choppers.
5911 Marathon runners keep it up for hours.
5912 Miners do it with the light on.
5913 Missionaries have their own position.
5914 Mountain climbers like to be on top.
5915 Musicians use the rhythm method.
5916 Photographers do it in a flash.
5917 Pizza delivery men come in 30 minutes, or it's free.
5918 Politicians just talk about it.
5919 Psychiatrists do it on the couch.

5920 Santa Claus comes once a year.

5921 Scaffolders have a mighty erection.

5922 Shot-putters do it on one leg.

5923 Skiers go down faster.

5924 Snooker players do it bending over.

5925 Squash players do it against a wall.

5926 Swimmers do it with the breast stroke.

5927 Teachers do it with class.

5928 Trapeze artists do it in mid-air.

5929 Travel agents do it in lots of different places.

5930 Windsurfers do it standing up.

5931 Don't do it with bankers — most of them are tellers.

5932 And beware of tennis players — love means nothing to them.

Good, Bad, Worse

5933 Bad: You can't find your vibrator. Worse: Your daughter borrowed it.

5934 Bad: You find a porn movie in your son's room. Worse: You're in it.

5935 Bad: Your kids are sexually active. Worse: With each other.

5936 Bad: Your wife's pregnant. Worse: The father's Gerald the Afghan Hound.

5937 Bad: Your husband's a cross-dresser. Worse: He looks better than you.

5938 Bad: Your son's involved in Satanism. Worse: As a sacrifice.

5939 Bad: You're arrested for flashing. Worse: The victim decides it's not worth pressing charges.

5940 Bad: Your wife wants a divorce. Worse: She's a lawyer.

5941 Good: You came home for a quickie. Bad: So did the mailman.

5942 Good: You came home for a quickie. Bad: Your wife walks in.

5943 Good: Your mother-in-law's going home. Bad: To put her house up for sale.

5944 Good: Your daughter's boss raves about her work. Bad: He's a pimp.

5945 Good: You get tickets to the theatre. Bad: It's performance art.

5946 Good: Your wife buys a new black dress. Bad: For your funeral.

5947 Good: Your neighbour exercises in the nude. Bad: She weighs 18 stone.

5948 Good: Your girlfriend's got soft, long, dark hair. Bad: On her top lip.

5949 Good: Your husband says you look 23. Bad: In dog years.

5950 Good: Your wife meets you at the door naked. Bad: She's coming home.

5951 Good: Your wife's kinky. Bad: With the neighbours. Worse: And the city orchestra.

5952 Good: The mailman's early. Bad: He's wearing camouflage gear and carrying an AK-47 rifle. Worse: You put nothing in his Christmas box.

Medical

5953 Adam went to God and said: "Eve has a problem – she's bleeding."
"Where from?" asked God.
"Between her legs."
"No problem. She is supposed to do that. I made her that way."
"That's a relief," said Adam. "We were really worried."
"Where is she now?"
"Down at the stream, washing."
"Oh great!" said God. "Now I'll never get the smell out of those fish!"

5954 A woman picked up the phone. On the other end was her husband's doctor.
"We've made an awful mistake," admitted the doctor. "We mixed up your husband's test results. He's either got Alzheimer's Disease or Aids."
"What shall I do?" wailed the woman.
"I tell you what," said the doctor. "Send your husband out for a walk. If he comes back, don't sleep with him."

5955 A man went to the doctor's. "Doctor, I can't get aroused for my wife any more."
"Very well," said the doctor. "Bring her with you tomorrow and I'll see what I can do."
The next day the man returned with his wife. The doctor told the wife to take off all her clothes and to sit on the bed with her legs apart. After a moment or two, he asked her to get dressed again. While she was getting dressed, the doctor took the husband to one side. "Don't worry," he said. "You're in perfect health – your wife didn't give me an erection either."

5956 What do you get when an epileptic falls into a lettuce patch? – Seizure salad.

5957 While performing a vasectomy, the surgeon slipped and accidentally cut off one of the patient's testicles. With the patient still under anaesthetic, the surgeon decided to replace the missing testicle with an onion and hope that nobody would ever know.
A few weeks later, the patient returned for a check-up.
"How's things?" asked the surgeon.
"Not bad," replied the patient. "Apart from a few side effects."
"What sort of side effects?" asked the surgeon apprehensively.
"Well," said the patient. "Every time I urinate, my eyes water; whenever

my wife gives me a blow job, she gets heartburn; and every time I pass a hamburger stand I get an erection."

5958 Doctor to patient: "I've got some good news and some bad news. The bad news is that we've got to amputate both your legs. The good news is that the guy in the next bed wants to buy your slippers."

5959 Doctor to patient: "I've got some good news and some bad news."
"What's the bad news?" asked the patient.
"You've only got three weeks to live."
"Only three weeks to live?" shrieked the patient. "That's terrible. What's the good news?"
"My numbers came up on the lottery."

5960 "Doctor, doctor, I can't feel my legs."
"Of course you can't. We had to amputate both arms."

5961 What do you call the costume of a ballerina with one leg? — A one-one.

5962 Why don't blind people go skydiving? — It scares the hell out of their dogs.

5963 An old man went to the doctor's accompanied by his equally aged wife. Since he was deaf, he relied on his wife to act as a sort of interpreter.
"Right," said the doctor to the old man. "Take off your shirt, please."
"What did he say?" asked the old man.
"They want your shirt," replied the wife.
The man took off his shirt which was encrusted with food. Next the doctor said: "Would you mind removing your socks so that I can examine your feet?"
"What did he say?" boomed the old man. "I didn't hear a word."
"They want your socks," explained the wife.
As the old man was removing his smelly socks, the nurse said: "Excuse me, sir, we need a stool sample and a urine sample."
"What did she say?" asked the old man.
The wife said: "They want your underpants."

5964 Why was time out called at the leper hockey game? — There was a face-off in the corner.

5965 Why do women get PMS? — Because they deserve them.

5966 A woman went to see a psychiatrist because she was concerned about her looks. "Doctor," she said, "I'm so depressed because I feel so ugly. I can't get a man because my self-esteem is so low. I just think that nobody finds me attractive. Can you help me feel better about myself?"

"I'm sure I can," said the psychiatrist. "Just go over and lie face down on that couch."

5967 What's the difference between an oral and a rectal thermometer? – The taste.

5968 A woman went to the doctor complaining of feeling lethargic. After a thorough examination, he prescribed the male hormone testosterone for her.

Two months later, she returned to the doctor. "The hormones you've been giving me have really helped," she said. "But I'm worried that the dosage is too high because I've started growing hair in places where I've never grown hair before."

"That's nothing to worry about," said the doctor reassuringly. "A little hair growth is a perfectly normal side effect of testosterone. Now where exactly has the hair appeared?"

"On my balls."

5969 What is the best thing about Alzheimers? – You meet new people every day.

5970 A man complained to a friend about a pain in his elbow and the friend recommended a computer at the local drug store. "It's amazing," said the friend. "It can diagnose anything cheaper and much quicker than a doctor. All you have to do is pay ten dollars, feed in a urine sample and the computer will tell you what the problem is. Just like that."

The man liked the sound of it so he went to the drug store, paid his ten dollars and fed in his urine sample. Two minutes later, the computer issued a print-out. It read: "You have tennis elbow. Soak your arm in warm water. Avoid heavy labour. It will clear up in two weeks."

The man was intrigued and that evening decided to try and outsmart the computer. He mixed together some tap water, a stool sample from his dog and urine samples from both his wife and his daughter. And to complicate the sample even more, he masturbated into it. Then he went down to the drug store, paid his ten dollars, fed in the sample and waited for the computer's reply. Two minutes later came the print-out: "Your tap water is too hard – get a water softener. Your dog has ringworm – bathe him with anti-fungal shampoo. Your daughter is using cocaine – put her in rehab. Your wife is pregnant with two girls. They aren't yours – get a lawyer. And if you don't stop jerking off, your tennis elbow will never get better."

5971 Why do nurses give Viagra to elderly male patients in old folks' homes? – To stop them rolling out of bed.

5972 A man was driving along the road when a cop stopped him and asked: "Have you been drinking, sir?"
"Why?" snorted the man. "Is there a fat bird in my car?"

5973 A 98-year-old man and a 98-year-old woman were close friends in an old folks' home. The highlight of their week was every Friday evening when she would jerk him off in her room. This ritual went on for 18 months until one Friday evening, he didn't show for their rendezvous.
"Where were you?" she asked him the following morning.
"I was with another woman."
"Another woman! I suppose it was someone younger. Tell me, who was it?"
"Minnie Gray."
"But she's 98, the same age as me. I cater to all your needs. What's she got that I haven't?"
"Parkinson's."

5974 Why did Dr Kevorkian cross the road? – To help the patient find the other side.

5975 Stephen had felt guilty all day long. He knew what he had done was wrong, but every now and then, he would hear a soothing inner voice trying to reassure him: "Stephen. Don't worry about it. You aren't the first doctor to sleep with one of your patients and you won't be the last."
But invariably another inner voice would bring him back to reality: "Stephen, you're a veterinarian."

5976 Why can't women play ice hockey? – They have to change their pads after every period.

5977 How can you spot a macho woman? – She rolls her own tampons.

5978 An army major was visiting sick soldiers in hospital.
"What's your problem, soldier?" he asked.
"Chronic syphilis, sir."

"What treatment are they giving you?"

"Five minutes with a wire brush each day."

"And what's your ambition?"

"To get back to the front, sir."

The major moved on to the next bed. "And what's your problem, soldier?"

"Chronic diarrhoea, sir."

"What treatment are they giving you?"

"Five minutes with a wire brush each day."

"And what's your ambition?"

"To get back to the front, sir."

The major moved to the next bed. "And what's your problem, soldier?"

"Chronic gum disease, sir."

"What treatment are they giving you?"

"Five minutes with a wire brush each day."

"And what's your ambition?"

"To get the wire brush before the other two, sir."

5979 What do you do if your wife has a fit in the bath? – Put the dishes in.

5980 Towards closing time in a bar, a man fell off his stool and couldn't get back up. Watching him struggling to stand on his own two feet, a stranger took pity on the poor drunk and offered to drive him home. He was in such a bad way that he had to be dragged to the car. Reaching the drunk's house, the stranger realized that the drunk couldn't make it up his front drive so he carried him to the door. The wife answered the door.

"I've had to bring your husband home from the bar," explained the stranger, "because I'm afraid he's just not capable of standing up, let alone walking."

"I understand," said the wife. "But tell me, where's his wheelchair?"

5981 What do you call a tablet that is a combination of aphrodisiac and laxative? – Easy come, easy go.

5982 A blind man with a guide dog went into a store. Suddenly the man picked the dog up by the tail and started swinging the animal above his head. The store assistant was alarmed by this behaviour. "Can I help you?" he inquired.

"No, it's all right," said the blind man. "Just looking around."

5983 Why do farts smell? – So that deaf people can appreciate them too.

5984 A 93-year-old man lived in a rest home but had a weekend pass to visit town. One Saturday night he went into a bar and met a 70-year-old woman. They got chatting and ended up back at her apartment where they got it together.

Five days later, he noticed he was developing a drip so he went to see his doctor.

"Have you engaged in sex recently?" asked the doctor.

"As a matter of fact I have," said the old man.

"Can you remember the name of the woman and where she lives?"

"Yes, I can. Why?"

"Well, you'd better get over there – you're about to come!"

5985 Two old men were sitting in a bar. One said to the other: "My wife's a mess. She has gonorrhoea, diarrhoea and ascariasis."

"Why do you stay with her?" said the other.

"Because I love to fish and she has great worms."

5986 How do you get a one-armed man out of a tree? – Wave at him.

5987 What do you call a guy at your front door with no arms and no legs? – Matt.

5988 What do you call a guy on your wall with no arms and no legs? – Art.

5989 What do you call a guy buried up to the neck with no arms and no legs? – Spike.

5990 What do you call a guy waterskiing with no arms and no legs? – Skip.

5991 What do you call a guy in a pile of leaves with no arms and no legs? – Russell.

5992 What do you call a guy in a meat grinder with no arms and no legs? – Chuck.

5993 What do you call a guy stuffed in a mailbox with no arms and no legs? – Bill.

5994 What do you call a guy in a flower pot with no arms and no legs? – Pete.

5995 What do you call a guy in a pot of boiling water with no arms and no legs? – Stu.

5996 What do you call two guys on your wall with no arms and no legs? – Kurt and Rod.

5997 What do you call a guy who has no arms and no legs but is a good swimmer? – Bob.

5998 What do you call a guy with no arms and no legs swimming the English Channel? – Clever Dick.

5999 What do you call a guy whose legs are cut off at the knees? – Neil.

6000 What do you say to a Spanish footballer with no legs? – Grassiass.

6001 A lonely widow put an advertisement in the newspaper for a dream man. She wanted someone who (a) won't beat me up; (b) won't run away; (c) must be great in bed. For weeks, she didn't receive a single reply and had almost given up hope when there was a ring at her doorbell. She answered it to find a man with no arms and no legs lying on the doormat.
"Who are you?" she asked.
"I'm your dream man," he replied.
"What makes you think you fit the bill?" she asked frostily.
"I've got no arms so I can't beat you up, and I've got no legs so I can't run away."
"What makes you think you're great in bed?"
"Well I rang the doorbell, didn't I?"

6002 A pilot and co-pilot boarded an airplane. The pilot had a white stick and kept bumping into passengers while the co-pilot had a guide dog. Both men wore dark glasses. At first, the passengers thought it was a joke but they became slightly more apprehensive when the engines started up. As the plane gathered speed along the runway, they became distinctly worried. They looked to the stewardess for signs of comfort but when none was forthcoming, panic began to set in. The end of the runway moved closer and closer. The passengers became hysterical. Finally with the plane less than 20 feet from the end of the runway, everybody screamed. Just then the plane at last soared into the air.
Up in the cockpit, the co-pilot breathed a huge sigh of relief. He turned to the pilot and said: "One of these days the passengers aren't going to scream, and we're going to get killed!"

6003 A woman had just stepped out of the shower when the doorbell went.
"Who is it?" she called through the intercom.
"Blind man," came the reply.

She was stark naked but figured that it didn't really matter too much for a blind man, so she released the lock and called out: "Come on up."

Not bothering to cover herself with a towel, she greeted him at the top of the stairs. He said: "Now where do you want these blinds?"

6004 A young man went to see the doctor about his lisp. The doctor told the young man that the lisp was caused by the size of his member – it was so big that it was pulling his tongue off-centre.

"Can you do anything about it?" asked the young man.

"Well," said the doctor, "I could perform an operation to shorten the length of your penis. That should get rid of your lisp."

Two months after the operation, the patient returned to the doctor and complained that while his lisp had gone, his sex life had been ruined. "I want my penis back," he demanded.

"Thcrew you," said the doctor.

6005 Why did the Siamese twins leave England for the US? – So the other one could have a chance to drive.

6006 A guy had been suffering from blinding headaches, so he went to see his doctor. The doctor revealed that he used to suffer from them too until he found a miraculous cure.

"The headache is caused by tension in the scalp muscles," explained the doctor. "I cured it by giving my wife oral sex on a daily basis. When she came, she would squeeze her legs together with all her strength, and the pressure would relieve the tension in my head. Try that every day for two weeks and come back and let me know how it goes."

Two weeks later, the guy returned.

"So how do you feel?" asked the doctor.

"Wonderful. I feel great. I haven't had a headache since I started this treatment. It certainly works. And by the way, doctor, you have a lovely home."

6007 What was the centrepiece of the annual Anorexia and Bulimia Sufferers' Convention? – A cake jumping out of a girl.

6008 A man went to see a psychiatrist. "Doctor, I'm having that dream again."

"Which one?"

"The one where I'm into sadism, necrophilia and bestiality."

"I should forget it," advised the shrink. "You're flogging a dead horse."

6009 Thirty years after attending school together, two women met up at a class reunion. They were discussing their respective husbands when one suddenly blurted out: "John and I have never looked back since we got into S & M."

"You, the head girl into S & M? I can't believe it."

"Yeah. He snores while I masturbate."

6010 A blind man walked into a restaurant. "I can't read the menu," he told the owner, "but if you bring me a dirty fork from the previous customer, I'll sniff it and order from that."

The owner was baffled by such a request, but went along with it. He went into the kitchen, fetched a dirty fork and handed it to the blind man who smelled it and promptly ordered meatloaf with mashed potato.

A week later, the blind man came in again and repeated his request for a dirty fork. The owner obliged, the blind man sniffed it and ordered spaghetti bolognese.

The third time the blind man came into the restaurant, the owner decided to try and catch him out. So he went into the kitchen and said to his wife Angela: "Will you rub this fork around your vagina before I take it to the blind man?"

The wife did so and the owner took the fork out to the blind man who sniffed it and said: "Hey, I didn't know Angela worked here!"

6011 Three old men were talking about their health problems. The 70-year-old said: "My problem is I wake up every morning at seven and it takes me at least 20 minutes to pee."

The 80-year-old said: "My problem is I get up at eight and it takes me at least half an hour to have a bowel movement."

The 90-year-old said: "At seven I pee like a horse, and at eight I crap like a cow."

"So what's your problem?" asked the others.

"I don't wake up till nine!"

6012 What is six feet long and smells like urine? – A line dance at a nursing home.

6013 An old man, hunched and bowed, hobbled into an ice cream shop. The waitress looked on sympathetically as he made his way slowly to the counter and ordered a banana split.

"Crushed nuts?" she asked.

"No, arthritis."

6014　A man contracted a terrible disease of the penis in the Far East. Every European doctor he consulted told him that it would have to be amputated. As a desperate last resort, he went to see a doctor in Thailand which, after all, was the country where he had picked up the disease. The Thai doctor examined him closely and announced: "There is no need to amputate your penis."

"That's fantastic!" said the man.

"Any doctor worth his salt can see that it will drop off of its own accord in three weeks."

6015　A young man woke up one morning to find a strange rash on his penis so he went to the doctor. The doctor gave him some cream to rub in and also advised him that exposing that part of his body to sunlight would help cure the infection. Since it was a nice day, the young man decided to go to a deserted beach and, with no one about, he thought he would follow the doctor's advice by stripping off. He lay on his back for a few minutes, soaking up the sunlight, but was startled to hear voices in the distance. To cover his embarrassment, he quickly dug a hole in the sand, broke off a reed from a plant for breathing purposes, and buried himself. However because he wanted the infected organ to get as much sunlight as possible, he left it protruding through the sand.

The voices turned out to be those of two old women. As they wandered along the beach, they spotted the curious shape sticking up through the sand and began to snigger. One said to the other: "When I was young, I couldn't get enough of it. As I matured, I was even more desperate for it. When I aged, I even started to pay for it. Now, just my luck, it's growing wild and I'm too old to bend down!"

6016　What did the vet say to the dog who kept licking his balls? – Thanks.

6017　Solly agreed to find a bride for his friend Cohen's son, but when he brought along the prospective wife, the boy was horrified. "She's as ugly as sin," he said. "Her hair's falling out, she's hardly got any teeth, she's got a wooden leg and she's only got one eye."

"Why are you whispering?" said Solly. "She is deaf too."

6018　A man went to the doctor. "It's my penis, doctor," said the man. "But when you look at it, you must promise not to laugh."

"Of course I won't laugh," said the doctor. "Now remove your pants, please."

So the man took off his pants. The doctor took one look at his penis and burst out laughing. "In all my years as a doctor," he shrieked, "that is the smallest, tiniest penis I have ever seen. I didn't know it was possible to have one so minute. So tell me what the problem is."

"It's swollen."

6019 What did the leper say to the prostitute? – Keep the tip.

6020 A man needed a pacemaker, but the Health Service waiting list was so long that he chose to go private. He visited a distinguished surgeon who said that he was perfectly happy to fit a pacemaker, but that it would cost over £7,000.

"I'm afraid these gadgets are very expensive," said the surgeon.

"I've got an idea," said the man. "I know someone who is brilliant with gadgets and electronics. If I provide my own pacemaker with his help, will you do the implant for me?"

The surgeon agreed. The man produced the pacemaker and the surgeon planted it in his chest and wired him up.

Three months later, the man returned for a check-up.

"Any problems?" asked the surgeon.

"Only one," said the man. "Whenever I get an erection, the garage door opens!"

6021 What is the difference between a genealogist and a gynaecologist? – A genealogist looks up the family tree and a gynaecologist looks up the family bush.

6022 A beautiful woman went to see a gynaecologist. He was so captivated by her beauty that he started behaving in a highly unethical manner, but he just couldn't help himself. First he told her to undress and he started to caress her inner thighs. As he did so, he asked: "Do you know what I'm doing?"

"Yes," replied the woman. "You're checking for any abrasions or skin abnormalities."

"That's right," said the gynaecologist.

Next he started to fondle her breasts. "Do you know what I'm doing?" he asked.

"Yes," she replied,. "You're checking for lumps."

"That's right," he answered.

Then he started to have sex with her. "Do you know what I'm doing now?" he panted.

"Yes," she replied. "You're getting herpes."

6023 Doctor: "I've got some very bad news. You've got cancer and Alzheimer's."

Patient: "Well, at least I don't have cancer."

Mommy, Mommy jokes

6024 Mommy, Mommy, why is Daddy running away?
Shut up and help me reload.

6025 Mommy, Mommy, are you sure this is how to learn to swim?
Shut up, and get back in the sack.

6026 Mommy, Mommy, Daddy's been run over in the street.
Don't make me laugh — you know my lips are chapped.

6027 Mommy, Mommy, why is Daddy so pale?
Shut up and keep digging.

6028 Mommy, Mommy, why do other kids tell me I have a big head?
Pay no attention. Now take your cap and go get me 40 lbs of potatoes at the store.

6029 Mommy, Mommy, when is the garden pond going to be ready?
Shut up and keep spitting.

6030 Mommy, Mommy, why am I running around in circles?
Shut up or I'll nail your other foot to the floor.

6031 Mommy, Mommy, what's an orgasm?
I dunno. Ask your father.

6032 Mommy, Mommy, can I lick the bowl?
Shut up and flush.

6033 Mommy, Mommy, what's a vampire?
Shut up and eat your soup before it clots.

6034 Mommy, Mommy, Daddy's on fire.
Quick, fetch the sausages.

6035 Mommy, Mommy, what's a nymphomaniac?
Shut up and help me get Grandma off the doorknob.

6036 Mommy, Mommy, I don't want my hair braided.
Shut up and lift the other arm.

6037 Mommy, Mommy, are you sure this is the way to make gingerbread men?
Shut up and get back in the oven.

6038 Mommy, Mommy, I don't like shark fishing.
Shut up and stop squirming.

6039 Mommy, Mommy, what's a lesbian?
Go ask your father – she'll know.

6040 Mommy, Mommy, can I play in the sandbox?
Not till I find a better place to bury Daddy.

6041 Mommy, Mommy, what happened to all that dog food Fido wouldn't eat?
Shut up and eat your meat loaf.

6042 Mommy, Mommy, I don't want to go to Australia.
Shut up and keep swimming.

6043 Mommy, Mommy, Sally won't come skipping with me.
Don't be cruel dear, you know it makes her stumps bleed.

6044 Mommy, Mommy, Grandma's got a bruise.
Well eat around it.

6045 Mommy, Mommy, when are we going to have Aunt Mary for dinner?
Shut up – we haven't finished your grandma yet.

6046 Mommy, Mommy, why are we celebrating Christmas in July?
Shut up, you know you have cancer.

6047 Mommy, Mommy, Laura's been run over by a steamroller.
Get the maple syrup.

6048 Mommy, Mommy, I don't like tomato soup.
Shut up, we only have it once a month.

6049 Mommy, Mommy, what's a werewolf?
  Shut up and comb your face.

6050 Mommy, Mommy, Grandpa's going out.
  Well throw some more gasoline on him then.

6051 Mommy, Mommy, why are we pushing the car off the cliff?
  Sssh, you'll wake your father.

6052 Mommy, Mommy, why can't I play with the other kids?
  Shut up and deal.

6053 Mommy, Mommy, I want to play marbles.
  Shut up, you can't use Grandpa's glass eye today.

6054 Mommy, Mommy, what happened to all your scabs?
  Shut up and eat your cornflakes.

6055 Mommy, Mommy, Daddy puked.
  Shut up and get a fork before your sister gets all the big chunks.

6056 Mommy, Mommy, can I play with Grandma?
  Not today – we already dug her up three times this week.

6057 Mommy, Mommy, can I wear a bra now I'm 16?
  No, you can't, Eric.

6058 Mommy, Mommy, can I have a cookie?
  Yes, cookies are on the top shelf.
  But, mom, I haven't got any arms.
  No arms, no cookie . . .

Sexual

6059 A poodle and a Great Dane were waiting in separate cages at the vet's. To ease the tension, the poodle struck up conversation with the Great Dane.

"I did a really stupid thing yesterday," confided the poodle. "My owner is devoutly religious and he invited some church friends round for tea. I don't know what came over me but I saw this woman's leg and I started humping it furiously. Three of them had to drag me off and chuck a bucket of cold water over me. Now I'm here to be castrated."

"I sympathize with your predicament," said the Great Dane. "My owner is an aged spinster who never lets me out. Yesterday she was bent over the bathtub after taking a shower and the sight of her bare butt in the air was simply too much for me. I lost control, mounted her and rode her for all she was worth. I stayed on for half an hour."

The poodle said: "So I guess you're here to be castrated too?"

"No," replied the Great Dane, "I'm here to get my nails clipped."

6060 What's the definition of trust? – Two cannibals giving each other a blow job.

6061 An old man of 85 married an 18-year-old nymphomaniac. On their wedding night, they got into bed and he held up four fingers. Her eyes lit up. "Does that mean we're going to have sex four times?"

"No," said the old man, "it means you can take your pick."

6062 What's the difference between a girlfriend and a wife? – 45lbs.

6063 Why do women play with their hair at traffic lights? – Because they don't have any balls to scratch.

6064 A woman was frustrated with her sex life because her husband had a crush on Brigitte Bardot. He was so obsessed with the French actress that his wife resorted to drastic measures to win back his interest. She went to a tattooist and asked for a large letter B to be tattooed on each breast. However the tattooist pointed out that, as her breasts sagged with age, it might eventually lose its effect and so he recommended that she have a B tattooed on each buttock instead. The woman agreed to this and had a letter B tattooed on each buttock.

As soon as her husband arrived home that evening, she took off her knickers, bent over and showed off the artwork.

He took one look and said: "Who the hell is Bob?"

6065 What did the banana say to the vibrator? – "What are you shaking for? She's going to eat me."

6066 A woman woke up and told her husband about a dream she'd had last night. "I was at an auction for penises," she said. "The big ones sold for 1,000 dollars and the tiny ones for 10."

"What about one my size?" asked the husband.

"No bids."

The husband felt crushed and decided to seek revenge. So the next morning he told his wife that he'd had a dream too. "I was at an auction for vaginas," he said. "The really tight ones sold for 1,000 dollars and the loose ones for 10."

"What about one like mine?" asked the wife.

"That's where they held the auction."

6067 Why does a bride smile when she walks up the aisle? – She knows she's given her last blow job.

6068 A man walked into a bar with an octopus. He perched the octopus on a stool and announced that it was the smartest octopus in the world. "This octopus," he boasted, "is a musical genius. And I will give 50 dollars to anyone here who can find a musical instrument which my octopus can't play."

A man came forward with a guitar. The octopus picked it up and played better than Jimi Hendrix. Another man brought out a trumpet. The octopus played it better than Louis Armstrong. A third man handed the octopus a set of bagpipes. The octopus looked bemused.

"Ha!" said the challenger. "You can't play it."

"Play it?" said the octopus. "I'm going to fuck it as soon as I get its pyjamas off!"

6069 How do you know when your wife has died? – Sex is still the same, but the dishes start piling up.

6070 Shortly after teeing off, a woman golfer ran into the clubhouse screaming in pain.

"What happened?" asked the professional.

"I got stung by a bee," she replied.

"Where?"

"Between the first and second holes."

"Mmm," said the professional. "Sounds like your stance was a little too wide."

6071 What do a clitoris, an anniversary and a toilet have in common? – Men always miss them.

6072 Billy was 12 and wanted to know all about courting. His mother was too embarrassed to tell him so instead she suggested that he hide behind the living-room curtains one night and watch his older sister and her boyfriend. The following morning, he told his mother what he had seen.

"Sis and Wayne talked for a bit, then he turned off the lights. Then he started kissing her. I could tell Sis was feeling sick because her face looked funny. Wayne must have thought so too because he put his hand inside her blouse to feel her heart. But he seemed to have trouble finding it. I guess he was getting sick too because he started panting and getting out of breath. His other hand must have been cold because he put it under her skirt. That was when Sis started to moan. I guess she was feeling feverish because she told Wayne she felt really hot. Then I saw what was making them both sick – a big eel had somehow got into his pants. It just jumped out and stood there, about eight inches long. He had to grab it with one hand to stop it getting away. When Sis saw it, she was really scared: her eyes got big, her mouth was open and she screamed to God. She said it was the biggest one she'd seen. She got brave and tried to kill the eel by biting its head off. Then she grabbed it with both hands while Wayne took a muzzle out of his pocket and slipped it over the eel's head to stop it biting Sis. Next she lay back and spread her legs so she could get a scissor lock on it. The eel kept on fighting but after a couple of minutes I thought it was dead because it just hung there and some of its insides were hanging out. Sis and Wayne were so happy about this that they kissed and hugged each other but when, what do you know, the eel suddenly came back to life again. It wasn't dead after all and began to straighten up and fight again. This time Sis jumped up and tried to kill the eel by sitting on it. After about five minutes, they finally killed it. I knew it was dead for sure because Wayne peeled its skin off and flushed it down the toilet."

6073 What do you get when you cross a rooster with an owl? – A cock that stays up all night.

6074 A man was driving along the road when a prostitute suddenly stepped right out in front of him. The resulting collision left her lying dazed in the road. The man jumped out of the car and ran to her aid. All the time she was moaning: "I think I'm blind. I think I'm blind."

The man quickly held up three fingers in front of her face and said: "How many fingers do I have up?"

"Oh God, no," she cried. "Don't say I'm paralyzed too!"

6075 What's the height of conceit? – Calling out your own name during orgasm.

6076 Two old ladies were smoking cigarettes while waiting for a bus. When it started to rain, one of the women reached into her purse, took out a condom, cut off the tip, slipped it over the cigarette and continued to smoke. That's a good idea, thought her friend, and so the next day she went into a pharmacist's and asked for a condom.

"What size?" asked the pharmacist.

"One that will fit a Camel."

6077 How do you make a dishwasher into a snow blower? – Give the bitch a shovel.

6078 A man walked into a bar with his arm in a plaster cast. "What happened to you?" asked the bartender.

"I got in a fight with Kelly."

"Kelly? He's only a small guy – he must have had something in his hand."

"He did – a shovel."

"Didn't you have anything in your hand?"

"I did – Mrs Kelly's tit. And a beautiful thing it was too, but not much use in a fight!"

6079 Why don't they teach driver's education and sex education on the same day in Iraq? – They don't want to wear out the camel.

6080 A nun climbed into a taxi cab. As they drove along, the driver stared at her and finally admitted: "I've always wanted to have a nun perform oral sex on me."

The nun said: "Well, I could perhaps arrange that provided you are single and Catholic."

"As a matter of fact I am single and Catholic," said the driver.

"Very well," said the nun. "Pull into an alley."

The driver pulled into a dark alley, but suddenly burst into tears.

"What is it?" asked the nun.

"I lied to you," said the driver. "I'm married and Jewish."

"That's OK," said the nun. "My real name's Kevin and I'm on my way to a Hallowe'en party!"

6081 A lonely reporter, sent out to cover the gold rush, walked into a small town bar. He asked one of the prospectors what they did for female companionship and was told: "We shag sheep."

The reporter was disgusted but, after considering the local women, he eventually agreed that the sheep were prettier. Nevertheless he resisted temptation for several months until he could stand it no longer. Rounding up a nice sheep, he took it to the local hotel and bedded it. The next day he took his four-legged lover into the bar. As he and the sheep walked in, everyone put down their drinks and stared at him as if he was crazy.

"You goddam bunch of hypocrites!" he raged. "You've all been shagging sheep for years and now that I've finally stooped to your level, you all stare at me like I'm some kind of crazy pervert."

A lone cowboy spoke up from the back. "But tenderfoot, don't you know? That's the sheriff's gal!"

6082 What did the Seven Dwarfs say when the prince awakened Snow White? – "I guess it's back to jerking off."

6083 A middle-aged woman hosted a regular weekly game of bridge but frequently annoyed her fellow players with her crude comments. They were thinking about dropping her from their little clique, but decided to give her one last chance. However she had no intention of changing her ways and couldn't wait to relay a juicy item of gossip. "Hey, girls," she said, "there's a rumour that a busload of prostitutes are leaving town in the morning for a big gold find up in Alaska. I hear . . ."

This was too much for the blue-rinsed matrons and they got up to leave. "Hold on," said the host. "The bus doesn't leave till morning!"

6084 What's grey and comes in pints? – An elephant.

6085 A hard-up elderly couple, Doris and Bert, advertised for a lodger so that they could make ends meet. A model applied and after inspecting their modest terraced house, she thought it would suit her ideally.

"There's only one slight problem," she said. "In my line of work, cleanliness is essential. I need to take a bath every night, but I couldn't help noticing that you don't appear to have either a bath or a shower."

"We have," said Doris. "There's a tin bath out in the yard and we can bring that into the lounge for you. And there's no need to worry about Bert – he's off playing darts most nights."

So the model took the room and moved in straight away. That night Bert went off to darts and Doris brought the bath into the lounge. As the model stripped off to step into the piping hot bath, Doris remarked that the girl had no pubic hair. "You see," explained the model, "I have to shave it for swimwear and underwear shots."

That night in bed, Doris was telling Bert all about the model's shaved bush. Bert didn't believe her, but Doris said she'd prove it to him. The following night, she would leave the lounge curtains slightly open so that he could see for himself.

Bert went off to his darts as usual and Doris prepared the bath, taking care to leave the curtains open a little. As the model was about to step into the bath, Doris glanced towards the curtains, gestured towards the girl's shaven hair and at the same time lifted up her own skirt which, since she wasn't wearing any knickers, revealed her hairy mound in all its glory.

In bed that night, Doris said to Bert: "Now do you believe me?"

"Yes," said Bert, "but why did you show me yours?"

"To show you the difference," said Doris. "But anyway, what's the problem? You've seen my pussy thousands of times."

"I know," replied Bert, "but the rest of the darts team haven't!"

6086 What do a condom and a coffin have in common? – They're both filled with stiffs, except one's coming and one's going.

6087 A cucumber and a pickle were talking. The pickle said: "My life sucks. Whenever I get big, fat and juicy, they sprinkle seasoning all over me and stick me in a jar."

"You think that's bad!" said the cucumber. "Whenever I get big, fat and juicy, they slice me up and put me over salad."

A penis was passing and overheard the conversation. "Believe me, that's nothing!" said the penis. "Whenever I get big, fat and juicy, they put a plastic bag over my head, stick me in a dark, smelly room and make me do push-ups till I throw up!"

6088 "Mummy, I've got the biggest dick in our primary school!"

"Yes, son, but do remember – you are the headmaster!"

6089 A woman climbed stark naked into the back of a taxi cab and told the driver to take her to the station. As they went along, she noticed that he was staring at her through his rear-view mirror.

"What's your problem?" she snapped. "Why are you staring at me?"

"You're naked," he said, glancing again in the mirror. "How are you going to pay the fare?"

With that, she opened her legs, put her feet up on the front seat, grinned and said: "Does this answer your question?"

Still looking in his mirror, he said: "Got anything smaller?"

6090 What do you say to a man with two black eyes? – Nothing, he's already been told twice.

6091 A guy went to a fancy dress party wearing nothing but a jam jar on his dick. A woman asked: "What are you dressed as?"
He replied: "A fireman. You break the glass, pull the knob, and I'll come as fast as I can."

6092 An asylum nurse spotted a patient walking around his room as if he was driving a car. "What are you doing, Terry?" she asked.
"I'm driving to Chicago."
She wished him a good trip and continued with her rounds.
The next day she saw him again. He was still pretending to drive a car. "And how are you today, Terry?"
"I just arrived in Chicago."
"That's nice," she said and continued with her rounds. In the next room, she found Walter masturbating furiously. "Walter, what do you think you're doing?"
"I'm screwing Terry's wife while he's in Chicago!"

6093 Who is the most popular man at a nudist colony? – The one who can carry two cups of coffee and 12 ring doughnuts.

6094 Who is the most popular woman at a nudist colony? – The one who can eat the last two doughnuts.

6095 A golfer met a woman on the first tee and agreed to join her for the round. To his surprise and disappointment, she turned out to be a good player and beat him. Although he was angry at losing, he liked the woman and bought her a drink in the bar afterwards. He then offered to drive her home. She was so grateful for the lift that, half-way home, she told him to stop the car and proceeded to give him the best blow job he'd ever had in his life.
The following day he bumped into her again on the first tee. Again she beat him – much to his annoyance – and again she gave him a fantastic blow job on the way home. This went on for a week. By the Friday, he was experiencing mixed emotions. He was sick to death of being beaten by a woman day after day but he did enjoy the blow jobs on the way home. So he arranged to take things a step further and booked them into a hotel for a passionate weekend. But when he told her, she burst into tears.
"I can't," she sobbed. "I'm a transvestite."

He was furious. "You dirty stinking cheat!" he raged. "You've been playing off the ladies' tee all week!"

6096   What's the difference between a hooker and a drug dealer? – A hooker can wash her old, used crack and re-sell it.

6097   Three women in their sixties were hanging out their washing. Over the past couple of years, the other two had noticed that whenever it rained, Shirley never had her washing on the line. It was uncanny, as if she always knew what the weather was going to be. So they finally decided to ask her what was her secret.

"It's simple," said Shirley. "When I wake up in the morning, I look over at Ted. If his penis is hanging over his right leg, I know it will be sunny and I can hang out the washing. If his penis is hanging over his left leg, I know it's going to rain, so I don't hang out the wash."

"What if he has an erection?" asked one of the neighbours.

"Honey," said Shirley, "on a day like that, you don't do the washing!"

6098   What's hard and straight going in, soft and sticky coming out? – Chewing gum.

6099   After striking gold in Montana, a miner headed straight for the nearest bar and announced: "I'm lookin' for the meanest, roughest, toughest whore in town."

The bartender said: "I reckon we can help you there. She's upstairs, second room on the right."

The miner handed the bartender a gold nugget to pay for the whore and two beers, and marched upstairs. He flung open the door to the second room on the right and said: "I'm lookin' for the meanest, roughest, toughest whore in town."

"Well you found her," said the woman occupant. Then she stripped naked, bent over and grabbed her ankles.

The miner said: "How d'you know I want to do it in that position?"

"I don't, but I thought you might like to open those beers first."

6100   Why do men have a hole in their penis? – So that oxygen can get to their brains.

6101   One Christmas morning a cop on horseback was patrolling the streets when a young kid stopped next to him on his new bike. The cop said: "Nice bike you got there. Was it a present from Santa?"

"Yeah," replied the kid.

"Well next year," said the cop, "tell Santa to put a tail-light on that bike."
And with that he issued the kid with a 20-dollar bicycle safety violation ticket.

The kid took the ticket but before riding off he said to the cop: "By the way,
that's a nice horse you get there. Was it a present from Santa?"

The cop thought he'd humour the kid. "As a matter of fact it was."

"Well," said the kid, "next year tell Santa to put the dick underneath the
horse instead of on top."

6102 How did Pinocchio find out he was made of wood? – His hand caught fire.

6103 A couple were driving along the highway when they saw an injured skunk lying
by the side of the road. The wife said: "We must stop and take it to a vet."

So the husband stopped the car and they went over to look at the wounded
skunk. "Look," he said, "the poor thing is shivering. Why don't you wrap it in
your skirt?"

"But what about the smell?"

"Well, if it dies, it dies!"

6104 What do you call two skunks having a 69? – Odour eaters.

6105 Two eggs, one male and one female, were boiling in a pan. The female egg
said: "Look, I've got a crack."

"No good telling me," replied the male egg. "I'm not hard yet."

6106 An elderly couple arrived at their honeymoon suite. He put his glasses on
the bedside table and went into the bathroom to freshen up after the ordeal
of the wedding. While he was in the bathroom, she took off her clothes and
began limbering up on the bed in readiness for their night of passion. After
touching her toes and flexing her arms, she lay back and began to bicycle.
She then stretched her legs farther back, trying to touch the bed behind her
head, only to get her feet caught in the headboard. Just as she was
attempting to extricate herself, her husband returned. He squinted at her and
said: "For God's sake, comb your hair and put your teeth back in. You look
just like your mother!"

6107 What's the difference between light and hard? – You can sleep with a light on.

6108 Why don't guys like to perform oral sex on a woman the morning after sex? –
Have you ever tried pulling apart a grilled cheese sandwich?

6109 An Italian, a Frenchman and a Jew were boasting about how adept they were at bringing their respective wives to orgasm.

The Italian said: "My wife screams for 15 minutes after we have sex."

The Frenchman said: "My wife screams for 30 minutes after we have sex."

The Jew said: "The last time we had sex, I got out of bed, wiped my dick on the bedroom curtain, and my wife is still screaming!"

6110 How do you turn a fox into an elephant? – Marry it.

6111 Two guys were close friends. One told the other that his sex life had become so boring that he'd like to change spouses for the day. His friend thought it was a good idea. That night in bed, the first guy lay back contented and said to his new spouse: "What do you think our wives are doing now?"

6112 A mother and her young son were strolling through the park one Sunday afternoon when the boy spotted two birds mating. "What are they doing, Mummy?" he asked.

Embarrassed, his mother answered: "Oh, they're making sandwiches, dear."

A few minutes later, the boy saw two dogs mating.

"What are they doing, Mummy?"

"Er, they're making sandwiches too, dear."

That night the boy was in bed when he heard noises coming from his parents' room. He called for his mother. Thinking something was wrong, she rushed straight into his room.

"What is it?" she said.

The boy replied: "You were making sandwiches."

She blushed and said: "How can you tell?"

"Because you've got mayonnaise all over your face."

6113 What do you call a hooker with her hand up her skirt? – Self-employed.

6114 A captain in the Foreign Legion was transferred to a desert outpost. On his tour of inspection, he noticed a camel tethered at the rear of the enlisted men's barracks. He asked the sergeant for an explanation.

"Well," replied the sergeant, "it's a long way from civilization here and naturally the men have sexual urges. So when they do, we have the camel."

"I see," said the captain. "Well if it's good for morale, it's fine by me."

After six months at the posting, the captain was becoming desperate. One day he instructed the sergeant to bring in the camel. The sergeant was surprised but did as he was told. Then he watched as the captain climbed on to a foot stool and proceeded to have passionate sex with the camel. As he stepped down from the stool, satisfied, he asked the sergeant: "Is that how the enlisted men do it?"

The sergeant said: "Well, sir, usually they just use it to ride into town."

6115 What's 12 inches long and hangs in front of an ass? – George W. Bush's tie.

6116 Child: "Mum, where do babies come from?"

Mother: "Mummy and Daddy fall in love and get married and they have sex. That means Daddy puts his penis into Mummy's vagina. That's how you get a baby."

Child: "But the other night when I came into your room, you had daddy's penis in your mouth. What do you get when you do that?"

Mother: "Jewellery, dear."

6117 What have you got if you've got a green ball in your left hand and a green ball in your right hand? – Kermit's undivided attention.

6118 A worm living underneath a golf course decided to check out the weather early one morning. Meanwhile above ground, a lady golfer had been caught short and was forced to squat in the long grass for a pee. She urinated just as the worm stuck its head above ground. The worm got soaked and quickly dived back beneath the soil. It said to its friend: "Not only is it raining, but it's raining so hard the birds are building their nests upside down!"

6119 Girl: "Do you believe in puppy love?"

Boy: "I tried it once but their assholes are too small."

6120 A man was sitting next to the Pope on a plane. The Pope was doing a crossword puzzle and the man, being something of a crossword buff, was hoping that the Pontiff would ask him for help with some of the clues. Sure enough after a few minutes, the Pope turned to him and said: "Do you know a four-letter word ending in 'unt' that refers to a woman?"

The first word that came into the man's head was one that he knew he couldn't possibly repeat to the Pope, but luckily another word presented itself.

"I think the word you're looking for is 'aunt'," said the man.

"Oh, of course," said the Pope. "I don't suppose you happen to have an eraser?"

6121 Mums have Mother's Day, dads have Father's Day. What do single men have? – Palm Sunday.

6122 Two aliens landed in a quiet American town. The nearest building was the gas station. The aliens walked over to it and the alien chief addressed the gas pump: "Take me to your leader."

When the gas pump failed to comply, the alien chief became angry and shot the pump with a ray gun. There was a huge explosion. The second alien asked him why he had felt it necessary to fire the gun. The chief said: "I certainly wasn't going to mess with anyone who can stretch his penis to the ground, wrap it around his body twice and still stick it in his ear!"

6123 If your wife keeps coming out of the kitchen to nag you, what have you done wrong? – Made her chain too long.

6124 A Jew, a Catholic and a Mormon were drinking at the bar following an interfaith meeting. The Jew, boasting about his virility, said: "I have four sons. One more and I'll have a basketball team."

The Catholic said: "That's nothing. I have ten sons. One more and I'll have a soccer team."

The Mormon snorted: "Big deal! I have 17 wives. One more and I'll have a golf course."

6125 An old sailor went to a brothel and chose a girl. As they got down to it, he asked: "How am I doing?"

"Three knots," she replied.

"Three knots? What do you mean?"

"You're not hard, you're not in and you're not getting your money back."

6126 The members of a farming family were coming down to breakfast one morning. As the boy sat down at the table, his mother told him that he'd get nothing until he had been to the barn and fed the animals. The boy stormed off to the barn in a foul mood. He threw the chickens their corn, but as they fed, he kicked one in the leg. Next he fed the cows and as they bent down, he kicked one on the rump. Finally he fed the pigs and as they put their snouts in the trough, he deliberately kicked one in the side. Then he marched back into the kitchen. His mother was waiting for him. "I saw what you did!" she yelled. "Since you kicked a chicken, you'll get no eggs for breakfast. Since you kicked a cow, you'll get no milk. And since you kicked a pig, you'll get no bacon or sausage."

Just then the father came down the stairs and tripped over the family cat. Instinctively, he kicked the cat off the stairs. The boy looked at his mother and said: "Are you gonna tell him or shall I?"

6127 What happens when a Jew with an erection walks into a wall? – He breaks his nose.

6128 A young couple got married. Both were virgins and were embarrassed about discussing sex, so they coined a phrase to spare their blushes. Instead of referring openly to sex, they called it "doing the laundry".

On the first night of their honeymoon they "did the laundry". It was so great that half an hour later the husband asked: "Can we do the laundry again?"

"I'm sorry, honey," said his bride, "but I'm a little tired right now. Tomorrow, yeah?"

However, in the middle of the night she woke up feeling guilty about having rejected him. She put her arm around him and said: "I'm sorry I pushed you away earlier. We can do the laundry again if you want."

"That's OK," he said. "It was only a small load so I did it by hand."

6129 What did the penis say to the condom? – "Cover me, I'm going in."

6130 A chicken and an egg were lying in bed. The chicken was smiling and smoking a cigarette while the egg looked decidedly miserable. The egg muttered: "Well, I guess we answered that question."

6131 A Texan went to a New York clothes store to buy a new city outfit. He walked into the men's department where a sweet young girl was serving. "Excuse me, miss," he announced, "I'm up from Texas and I want a complete outfit of new clothes, right from the tip of my hat to the soles of my shoes."

"Certainly, sir," replied the girl. "We'll start from the top. What size hat are you?"

"Eight and five-eighths," he replied.

The girl looked astonished. "That's really big."

"I know," he said. "They grow them big in Texas."

The girl wrote down the measurements. "And what size shirt do you wear?"

"Extra extra large," replied the Texan, "with a 21-inch collar."

"That's certainly big," said the girl.

"Like I say, miss, they grow them big in Texas."

"What about your pants?" inquired the girl.

"A 52-inch waist, 40-inch outside leg. They grow them big in Texas."

"And finally your shoes?" asked the girl.

"Size 19," he answered. "Wide fitting. You see, they grow them big in Texas."

The girl began to redden. "I hope you don't mind," she said hesitantly, "but I really have to ask, how big is your . . ."

The Texan anticipated her question. "I know what you're going to say, and the answer is four inches."

The girl was shocked. "Four inches! My boyfriend's bigger than that!"

"That's from the ground, miss," added the Texan.

6132 A guy couldn't work out what to wear to a fancy dress party. Then suddenly he had a bright idea. When the host answered the door, she found the guy standing there with no shirt and socks.

"What on earth are you supposed to be?" she asked.

"A premature ejaculation," he replied. "I just came in my pants."

6133 What do a walrus and Tupperware have in common? – They're both looking for a tight seal.

6134 A couple celebrating their fiftieth wedding anniversary decided to recapture the magic of years ago by booking into the same hotel where they had spent their honeymoon. Over breakfast, the wife said excitedly: "Oh, Alfred, it's just like 50 years ago. My breasts feel all warm and tingly."

"So they should, Mavis, since one's hanging in your porridge and the other's in your coffee!"

6135 A young man went to a pharmacy and asked the little old lady behind the counter if he could speak to the pharmacist. "That's me," she replied. "My sister and I have been pharmacists for 45 years, and there's nothing we ain't heard. So what's your problem?"

The man explained sheepishly: "I have a problem with my erections. Once I get hard, it won't go soft for hours and hours, no matter how often I have intercourse. It's really embarrassing. Please can you give me something for it?"

The old lady said: "I'll have to go in the back and talk to my sister. Wait there."

Ten minutes later she returned. "Young man, I have consulted with my sister and the best we can give you is 3,000 dollars a month and a third interest in the pharmacy."

6136 A rich American woman of 50 was eager to get married, but she was very specific about her future husband. She wanted a man who had never before had sex with a woman. After years of searching, she took out personal ads in newspapers and magazines all over the world. She ended up corresponding with a man who had lived his entire life in the Australian outback and soon they got married.

On their wedding night, she went to the bathroom to freshen herself up and when she returned to the bedroom, she found her new husband standing naked in the middle of the room with all the furniture piled in a corner.

"Why have you moved all the furniture?" she asked.

"Well," he replied. "I've never been with a woman, but if it's anything like screwing a kangaroo, I'm gonna need all the room I can get!"

6137 A four-year-old boy returned home from Sunday school and wanted to talk about what he had learned. "Dad," he said, "have any of the men in our family had their penises criticized?"

The boy's mother laughed and told him that the word was "circumcised", but that the answer was still "yes".

6138 A hot chick walked up to a bartender and purred: "May I speak with your manager?"

The bartender was eager to be of service. "Can I help you?" he said.

"Well, it's kinda personal."

"I'm sure I can help," he said.

She smiled and slipped two of her fingers into his mouth. He was instantly turned on and began sucking them. She whispered seductively: "Tell your manager there's no toilet paper in the ladies' restroom."

6139 Husband and wife American sociologists were on vacation in Saudi Arabia. Anxious not to miss lunch at their hotel, they desperately wanted to know the time. They chanced upon an old camel herder who was sitting by the side of the street on a stool. His camel was standing beside him.

"Excuse me," they said. "Could you tell us the time?"

The old man calmly reached under the camel, raised its testicles, held them in his hands for a few moments and announced: "Twelve fifteen."

"Thank you," they said, and hurried on their way.

All through lunch they talked about the amazing camel herder who could tell the time just by feeling the camel's testicles. Was it some Arab tradition, they wondered?

Later that day, they saw the old man again, still perched on a stool beside his camel. "Could you tell us the time?" they asked.

The old man reached under the camel, raised its testicles, held them for a few moments and said: "Four twenty-five."

"That's incredible," said the woman. "Can you show us how you tell the time just from the touch of the camel's testicles?"

"Very well," said the old man. "Squat down next to me. Now grasp his balls gently and lift them up to his belly."

"Fine," she said. "What now?"

"Well if you look through the gap where his balls were, you can see the clock tower."

6140 A man conducting a sex survey was interviewing a farmer in a remote rural area. The interviewer began: "I hear it's so isolated in these parts that you folks screw cows, pigs, sheep and chickens?"

The farmer was horrified at the suggestion. "Chickens?!" he exclaimed.

6141 A man arrived home early from work to find his wife in bed with a midget. "This is the third time this week I've caught you," he raged. "First, it was with a lumberjack, then it was with the coalman, now it's with a midget."

She said: "At least I'm cutting back."

6142 Why are men like linoleum? – If you lay them right the first time, you can walk on them for the next 50 years.

6143 Why are women like condoms? – They spend 90 per cent of their time in your wallet and the other 10 per cent on your dick.

6144 Two men in a hotel were comparing notes after their respective wedding nights.

"How's your wife?" asked one.

"She's lying on the bed, smoking."

"Jesus! Mine only got a bit sore."

6145 Did you hear about the girl who went fishing for the day with her six male friends? – She came home with a red snapper.

6146 A nun and a priest were crossing the Sahara desert by camel. Three days into their journey, the camel suddenly dropped dead. With no means of transport and precious little water, death seemed inevitable. The priest sat on a sand dune and said: "Sister, since we're unlikely to make it out of here alive, will you do something for me? In all my years on this earth, I've never seen a woman's breasts. Will you show me yours?"

"In the circumstances," replied the nun, "I don't see why not."

So she opened her habit and let him touch her breasts.

"Thank you, Sister," he said.

"You're very welcome," she replied. "Father, would you now do something for me? In all my years on this earth, I've never seen a man's penis. Would you show me yours?"

"All things considered, I am sure the Lord would not object," said the priest.

He lifted his robe and allowed her to stroke it. By now he was sporting a huge erection. "Sister," he said, "you know that if I insert my penis in the right place, it can give life?"

"Is that true, Father?"

"Yes, it is."

"Then why don't you stick it in that camel so we can get the hell out of here?"

6147 A man was lying back relaxing in a garden chair while his wife mowed the lawn. A neighbour poked his head over the fence and told him in no uncertain terms: "That's terrible, letting your wife do the work. How lazy can you get! You should be damn well hung!"

"I am," replied the man. "That's why she mows the lawn."

6148 Two guys, Dennis and Carl, were just about to start their regular round of golf when they were approached by a third player whom they had never met before.

"Do you mind if I join you?" asked the stranger.

"Sure," said Dennis. "I'm Dennis and I'm an accountant. And this is Carl — he's a mechanic. What do you do for a living?"

"Actually," said the stranger, "you'll find this hard to believe, but I'm a hitman."

"A hitman?" said Dennis. "I don't believe you."

"Take a look in my golf bag," said the stranger.

So Dennis looked in the golf bag and found a powerful rifle with a huge scope attached.

"Jesus!" exclaimed Dennis to Carl. "It's true, this guy really is a hitman. This scope is really awesome. I bet I can see my house through it. Yeah, there's my wife naked . . . and there's our next door neighbour. And he's naked too! Oh my God!"

Dennis was livid and handed the gun back to the stranger. "How much do you charge for a hit?"

"It's 1,000 dollars for every time I pull the trigger."

"Right, I want two hits. I want you to shoot my wife in the mouth to pay her back for all her nagging. And I want you to shoot my neighbour in the penis for screwing around with my wife."

The hitman pointed the rifle at the house and lined up his aim through the scope. This went on for about five minutes, by which time Dennis was growing impatient.

"What are you waiting for?" he demanded.

"Hold on," said the hitman, squeezing the trigger, "I'm about to save you 1,000 dollars."

6149 Why did God put men on earth? — Because a vibrator can't mow the lawn.

6150 On the night before her wedding, an Italian bride-to-be talked with her mother.

"Mama," she said, "I want you to teach me how to make my new husband happy."

The mother replied gently: "When two people love, honour and respect each other, love can be a beautiful thing . . ."

The daughter interrupted. "I know how to fuck, Mama — I want you to teach me how to make great lasagne!"

6151 What do you get when you cross an apple and a nun? — A computer that won't go down.

6152 Two nuns were cycling along a cobbled street. One said: "I've never come this way before."

The other said: "It must be the cobbles."

6153 What's the difference between a nun, and a woman taking a shower? — The nun has hope in her soul.

6154 Three nuns died and went up to heaven, but before they were allowed to enter, St Peter told them they each had to answer a question. St Peter turned to the first nun and said: "What were the names of the two people in the Garden of Eden?"

"Adam and Eve," replied the first nun.

At that, the lights which surrounded the pearly gates began to flash. "You may enter," said St Peter.

Then he addressed the second nun. "What did Adam eat from the forbidden tree?"

"An apple," replied the second nun.

At that, the lights which surrounded the pearly gates flashed and the second nun was permitted to enter.

Finally St Peter turned to the third nun. "What was the first thing that Eve said to Adam?"

The third nun looked puzzled. "Gosh, that's a hard one."

And the lights around the pearly gates flashed.

6155 What do you call the useless bit of fatty tissue at the end of a penis? – A man.

6156 A man was walking through a hotel lobby when he accidentally bumped into a woman, his elbow hitting her in the right breast.

"Ma'am," he apologized, "if your heart is as soft as your breast, I know you'll forgive me."

"Sir," she replied, "if your penis is as hard as your elbow, I'm in room 219."

6157 A guy was sitting in a bar with his dog, a friendly labrador. Soon an attractive woman came in and began to make a fuss of the dog. The guy told her that the dog possessed a unique talent – it could perform oral sex on women. The woman's initial reaction was one of revulsion, but after a few drinks she started to warm to the prospect and suggested that the dog show her its special trick.

So they all went to her flat and she took off her clothes and lay on the bed. The guy stood next to the dog and gave the command: "OK, boy, go get it." The dog didn't move an inch.

The guy tried again. "OK, boy, go get it." The dog sat perfectly still. He tried a third time, but still the dog did nothing. Finally in exasperation, the guy said: "OK, boy, I guess I'll have to show you one last time . . ."

6158 Did you hear about the hooker who had her appendix out? – The doctor sewed up the wrong hole and now she's making money on the side.

6159 A young couple were about to get married. The girl explained that the reason she hadn't been keen on pre-marital sex was because she was flat-chested.

The boy was sympathetic. "It doesn't matter," he said. "Sex isn't the most important thing in a marriage."

After dwelling on what she had said, he made a confession of his own later that day. "Actually," he admitted, "below my waist, it's just like a baby."

"That doesn't matter," said the girl reassuringly. "Like you say, sex isn't the most important thing in a marriage."

Delighted that they could be so honest with each other, they duly got married. On their wedding night, she took off all her clothes and was indeed as flat as a pancake. Then he took all his clothes off and the girl fainted. When she came round, she said: "I thought you said it was just like a baby."

"It is," he said. "Eight lbs and 21 inches."

6160 What was black and slid down Nelson's column? — Winnie Mandela.

6161 One day in class, a schoolteacher brought in a bag full of fruit. She said: "I'm going to reach into the bag and describe a piece of fruit, and I want you to tell me what fruit I'm talking about. My first fruit is round and red. Now what do you think it might be?"

Johnny raised his hand at once but the teacher ignored him and chose Julie instead.

"An apple, ma'am," said Julie.

"No," said the teacher, "it's a tomato, but I like your thinking. My second fruit is small, green and hairy. What do you think it might be?"

Johnny raised his hand but again the teacher ignored him. This time she asked Wendy. "A gooseberry, ma'am," said Wendy.

"Actually, it's a kiwi fruit, Wendy," said the teacher, "but I like your thinking. My third fruit is small, black and round."

Johnny's hand went up in a flash. But once more the teacher ignored him and chose Ann. "A blackberry, ma'am," said Ann.

"No, it's a grape, but I like your thinking."

By now Johnny was fed up with being continually overlooked so he called out: "I've got one for you, teacher. Let me put my hand in my pocket. I've got it — it's round, hard, and it's got a head on it."

"Johnny, that's disgusting," shouted the teacher.

"No," said Johnny. "It's a quarter, but I like your thinking."

6162 A man went to see a doctor, complaining that he was feeling run-down.

The doctor examined him and said: "I can see the problem. Your penis is burned out. You've been overdoing it all these years. You can only make love another 30 times."

The man was devastated and when he got home he tearfully told his wife that he could only have sex another 30 times.

She was sympathetic and suggested: "We mustn't waste that – we should make a list."

He said: "I already made a list on my way home. Sorry, your name's not on it."

6163 What does a woman have in common with Kentucky Fried Chicken? – When you've had the thigh and the breast, you've got a greasy box to stick your bone in.

6164 What do pussy and a warm toilet seat have in common? – They're both nice, but you always wonder who was there before you.

6165 An impoverished farmer and his wife were lying in bed when he leaned over and started to rub her breasts. "If only these would give milk," he sighed, "we could get rid of the cows."

Then he began massaging her butt. "If only this would lay eggs," he sighed, "we could get rid of the chickens."

At this, she leaned across and started to rub his penis. "If only this would get hard more often," she sighed, "we could get rid of the farmhand!"

6166 Why do tampons have strings? – So you can floss after every meal.

6167 A young married couple enjoyed a full sex life and she became accustomed to rewarding him between the sheets for any act of kindness. But he wanted to prove to her that he wanted her for more than just sex so one day, on the spur of the moment, he bought her a huge bouquet of flowers.

"They're lovely," she said before adding suspiciously, "I suppose now you'll expect me to spend the weekend on my back with my legs apart?"

"Why?" said the husband, puzzled. "Haven't we got a vase?"

6168 What's the difference between a woman and a washing machine? – You don't have to hug a washing machine after you put your load in it.

6169 At five o'clock one morning, a sadistic drill sergeant with the US Marines announced that the men would have to undergo an immediate birthday suit inspection. He boomed: "I wanna see you all outside butt naked NOW!"

The men lined up in three rows and the drill sergeant, brandishing his swagger stick, began his tour of inspection. He came to a guy who wasn't standing straight so he hit him hard across the chest with the stick.

"Did that hurt?" barked the sergeant.

"No, sir."

"Why not?"

"Cos I'm a US Marine, sir."

Further along the first line, the sergeant saw a guy with a twitch in his toes. So he whacked him hard on the butt with the stick.

"Did that hurt?"

"No, sir."

"Why not?

"Cos I'm a US Marine, sir."

The sergeant made his way along the line until he spotted a guy with a huge erection. He immediately whacked it hard with the stick.

"Did that hurt?" he bellowed.

"No, sir."

"Why not?"

"Cos it belongs to the guy behind me, sir!"

6170 Why are men like trains? – They always stop before you get off.

6171 A guy had just started a new job but on the Monday he called in to say: "I can't come in today, I'm sick." And it was the same for the next four Mondays – each time the guy phoned in to say he was sick.

His boss rated him and didn't want to lose him. "You're a good worker," said the boss, "but you seem to have a problem getting to work on Mondays. Is there anything we can help you with? Do you have a problem, maybe with drugs or alcohol?"

"No, I don't do drugs and I don't drink. But my brother-in-law drinks heavily every weekend and then starts hitting my sister. So every Monday morning I go over to make sure she's OK. I comfort her and, well, one thing always leads to another, and we end up in bed."

The boss was horrified. "You screw your own sister?"

"Hey," said the guy, "I told you I was sick."

6172 Why should you never trust a woman? – How can you trust something that bleeds for a week and doesn't die?

6173 A girl went to the doctor's for a check-up. When she removed her top, he saw that she had a big Y on her chest.

"How did you get that Y?" inquired the doctor.

"Well," said the girl, "my boyfriend goes to Yale and he likes it so much he wears his sweater whenever we have sex."

The next day another girl went to the same doctor for a check-up. She had a big S on her chest.

"How did you get that large S?" asked the doctor.

"Because," said the girl, "my boyfriend likes Stanford College so much that he always wears his Stanford sweater when we have sex."

The day after, a third girl went to see the same doctor for a check-up. She had a big W imprinted on her chest.

"Let me guess," said the doctor, "your boyfriend goes to a Wisconsin college and wears his sweater every time you have sex?"

"No," she said. "My girlfriend goes to Michigan."

6174 What's the difference between a wife and your job? – After five years your job still sucks.

6175 A husband and wife were keen golfers but both were having problems with their swing. The husband consulted the club professional who told him: "Your grip is too tight. Loosen it so that you hold the club as you would hold your wife's breasts."

The husband took the advice and it worked. He walked straight on to the first tee and hit a colossal drive 300 yards down the centre of the fairway.

"That's great," said the professional.

Next the wife went in to see the professional. "You have the same problem," he said. "Your grip is too tight. Loosen it so that you hold the club as you would hold your husband's penis."

She followed the advice, went to the first tee but only hit the ball a few yards. "That's OK," said the professional, "but this time let's try holding the club in your hands rather than in your mouth."

6176 Three personal hygiene product salesmen were discussing business. All were jealous of a fourth guy, Hermann, who was making a fortune. He had won every award going in the region and they were desperate to know the secret of his success.

"It's simple," said Hermann. "I get a pile of dog shit, garnish it with some lettuce, parsley, onion, tomato and a few olives and serve it up on a wafer to shoppers in the street. As soon as people taste it, they go, "Yuk! This tastes like shit." And I say: "That's exactly what it is. Would you care to buy a toothbrush?"

6177 A deeply depressed young woman was contemplating suicide. She went down to the New York docks with the intention of throwing herself in. While she was standing there at the quayside, a sailor came over and engaged her in conversation. He talked her out of killing herself and persuaded her to come to Europe, stowing away on his ship. "I know I can make you happy," he said.

She agreed, and that night the sailor hid her in a lifeboat on his ship. Every night after that, he brought her food and drink and had sex with her till dawn. Finally after three weeks, she was discovered by the captain.

"What are you doing on board this vessel?" he demanded.

"You don't understand," she said. "I have an arrangement with one of the sailors. He's taking me to Europe, and he's screwing me."

"He sure is, lady. This is the Staten Island Ferry!"

6178 A city dweller bought a farm and decided to purchase his stock from an old farmer.

"I'd like to buy a rooster," he told the farmer.

"Sure," said the farmer, "but in these parts we call 'em cocks."

"Right, and I also want to buy a chicken."

"No problem," said the farmer, "but in these parts we call 'em pullets."

The city guy paid for the two birds and put each one in a cage. Worried about transportation, he said: "Maybe I ought to buy a donkey too."

"Good idea," said the farmer, "but in these parts we call 'em asses. I tell you what, I'll let you have old Jake. He's a good animal, but a bit stubborn. Sometimes you have to scratch him between the ears to get him to move."

"Right, I'll remember that," said the city guy.

So he set off with the donkey and the cages, but half a mile down the road, the donkey stopped and refused to move. Just then a lady passed by on her way back from church.

"Excuse me, ma'am," said the city guy, "would you hold my cock and pullet while I scratch my ass?"

6179 A woman walked into a tattoo parlour and asked for a tattoo of a turkey on her left inner thigh. Beneath it, she said she wanted the words "Happy Thanksgiving". And for her right inner thigh, she said she wanted a picture of Santa Claus accompanied by the words "Merry Christmas".

The tattooist was puzzled by such a strange request and asked her why she wanted it.

She replied: "Because I'm sick of my husband complaining that there's nothing to eat between Thanksgiving and Christmas."

6180 A couple were at their honeymoon hotel and the bride couldn't stop talking about her hero – golfer Tiger Woods. After the couple had made love, the husband picked up the phone to order room service. But the wife grabbed the phone off him and said: "Tiger wouldn't do that – he'd make love to me again."

The husband obliged and afterwards picked up the phone to order some food. Again she snatched it from him, saying: "Tiger wouldn't do that – he'd make love to me again."

Somehow the husband summoned up the energy to perform for a third time. By now, he was absolutely starving so he made another attempt to order some food from room service. Once more, she seized the phone and said: "Tiger wouldn't do that – he'd make love to me again."

So they had sex again and afterwards the exhausted husband reached wearily for the phone.

"Are you calling room service?" she asked accusingly.

"No, I'm calling Tiger Woods to find out what par is for this hole!"

6181 A redneck boy went up to his dad and said: "Hey, Dad, I know how old I am today – I'm 12."

"That's very good, son," said the father.

Then the boy went into the kitchen and said to his grandma. "Hey, Grandma, know how old I am today?"

"Come closer," said Grandma. Then she unzipped his jeans, slipped her wrinkled hand into his underpants, fondled his genitals for a few seconds and said: "You're 12."

"How could you tell?" asked the boy.

"I heard you tell your father."

6182 A retired priest was recalled to duty while the regular parish priest was off sick. During confession, he heard one of the parishioners confess to sodomy. Unable to remember the proper penance, he asked an altar boy: "What does Father McKendrick give for sodomy?"

The boy said: "He usually gives us a candy bar and a Coke."

6183 What's the difference between a bitch and a whore? A whore sleeps with everyone at the party, and the bitch sleeps with everyone at the party but you.

6184 An elderly woman came home one night to find her daughter in bed with a vibrator.

"What on earth are you doing?" shrieked the mother.

The daughter said: "Mom, I'm 42 years old, I'm not married and I don't have a date. It's the twenty-first century. Give me a break!"

The mother shook her head and left the room.

The next day the father walked in on the daughter and he too found her with the vibrator.

"What's going on?" he demanded.

"Dad," she sighed. "I'm 42 years old, I'm not married and I don't have a date. This is the twenty-first century. Give me a break, please!"

The father shook his head and left the room.

That night, the mother went into the kitchen and found the father sitting at the table, with a beer in one hand and the vibrator in the other.

"What are you doing with that?" she demanded.

"Leave me alone," he said. "Can't a guy have a beer with his son-in-law?"

6185 Did you hear about the flasher who was thinking of retiring? He decided to stick it out for one more year.

6186 A penguin was out driving in the wilderness when his car broke down. He pushed it for ten miles to the nearest town and took it to a garage. While the mechanic tried to fix the car, the penguin went to a supermarket to cool down after all the exertion. He positioned himself by the freezer and devoured box loads of vanilla ice cream. Suddenly remembering the time, he decided he ought to get back to the garage and arrived covered from head to toe in ice cream.

The mechanic walked slowly towards him, shaking his head. "Looks like you blew a seal."

"No," said the penguin, "it's just ice cream."

6187 What's the difference between a woman with PMS and a pit bull? – Lipstick.

6188 A guy at a bar was eyeing up a girl wearing the tightest pants he'd ever seen. Finally curiosity got the better of him and he asked her: "Tell me, how do you get into those pants?"

"Well," she replied, "you could start by buying me a drink?"

6189 Two men are on opposite sides of the world. One is walking a tight-rope between two skyscrapers; the other is getting oral sex from a 95-year-old woman. What are both men thinking? – Don't look down.

6190 Three guys – Phil, Don and Jerry – were in a bar one night when they decided to wage a bet as to which of them had the ugliest wife. Phil assured them that his wife was truly ugly, so they went round to his house and recoiled in horror when she answered the door. But Don was sure he could top that, so they called in at his house. When his wife answered the door, she was so repulsive that Phil and Jerry were sick on the spot.

But Jerry insisted, "You ain't seen nothin' yet" and took them round to his house. He opened the door, walked into the garage and stamped on a trap door leading to the cellar.

"Is that you, honey?" called a voice from below. "Do you want me to come out?"

"Yes," said Jerry.

"Should I put the bag on my head?"

"No," said Jerry, "I don't want to screw you, I just want to show you off."

6191 How can you tell if your girlfriend's frigid? – When you open her legs, the lights go on.

6192 A mother took her young daughter to the zoo one day. After seeing the lions and tigers, they reached the elephant enclosure. The bull elephant looked mad and, to the embarrassment of the mother, had a huge erection.

"Do you think he'll charge?" asked the little girl.

"I think he'd be entitled to," sighed her mother.

6193 What's the difference between a sumo wrestler and a feminist? – A sumo wrestler shaves his legs.

6194 Santa asked the little girl what she would like for Christmas.

"I want a Barbie and G.I. Joe," said the little girl.

"I thought Barbie comes with Ken," said Santa.

"No," said the girl, "Barbie comes with G.I. Joe. She fakes it with Ken."

6195 A woman went into a small town hardware store and told the owner that she needed a new door handle.

He fetched one and asked: "You wanna screw for that?"

She looked around the store and said: "No, but I'll blow ya for that toaster over there."

6196 A doctor, a lawyer and a biker were standing at a bar talking. The doctor finished his Martini and said: "Tomorrow is my anniversary. I got my wife a diamond ring and a Mercedes. I figure that if she doesn't like the diamond ring, at least she will like the Mercedes and will know that I love her."

The lawyer finished his Scotch and said: "On my last anniversary, I got my wife a string of pearls and a trip to the Bahamas. I figured that if she didn't like the pearls, she'd like the Bahamas and would know that I love her."

The biker swigged his beer and growled: "For my anniversary, I got my old lady a T-shirt and a vibrator. I figured if she didn't like the T-shirt, she could go fuck herself."

6197 What is the difference between a battery and a woman? — A battery has a positive side.

6198 What is the difference between a heterosexual man and a homosexual? — Three beers.

6199 A young woman appeared in court on a public disorder charge. The prosecutor turned to her and said: "Is it true that on 3 February you committed an act of gross indecency with a one-legged dwarf and a donkey on the roof of a car while travelling through the centre of New York at 100 mph in a blizzard?"

The woman turned to the prosecutor and said: "What was the date again?"

6200 What did the hurricane say to the coconut tree? — Hold on to your nuts, this is no ordinary blow job.

6201 A man found himself sitting next to a gorgeous woman on a plane. They exchanged smiles but he was looking for an excuse to talk to her. Then he glanced over and noticed that she was reading a book on sexual statistics.

"Is that interesting?" he asked.

"Yes," she replied. "there's a lot of fascinating information. For instance, did you know that American Indians have, on average, the longest penis and that Scotsmen have, on average, the biggest diameter penis. By the way, my name's Marie. What's yours?"

"Tonto McTavish. Pleased to meet you."

6202 What do elephants use as tampons? — Sheep.

6203 A single woman went shopping for groceries late one night. Taking a small basket, she filled it with soup for one, a frozen meal for one and a small bottle of milk. At the checkout, the male attendant said: "You're single, aren't you?"

"Yes, how did you know?"

"Because you're so goddam ugly."

6204 What has 100 balls and fucks rabbits? — A shotgun.

6205 Three honeymoon couples were staying in adjoining rooms at a hotel. As he and his wife were getting undressed, the first man exclaimed: "Wow! what huge buttocks!" His wife was furious and threw him out into the corridor.

A few minutes later the second couple were getting undressed. The second man looked at his wife and remarked: "What huge tits!" She was outraged and threw him out into the corridor.

Five minutes later the two men were joined in the corridor by the third new husband. They said: "Did you put your foot in it?"

"No," he said, "but I could have done!"

6206 Why did God give men penises? – So there'd be at least one way to shut a woman up.

6207 Why do women have breasts? – So that men will talk to them.

6208 Memo to male office managers: if you keep the sexual harassment complaint forms in your bottom drawer, when your secretary gets one out, you'll get a great view of her butt.

6209 When is a pixie not a pixie? – When she's got her head down an elf's pants: then she's a goblin.

6210 A young man walked into a bar. "What can I get you?" asked the bartender. "I want six shots of Jagermeister."

"Six shots?" queried the bartender. "Are you celebrating something?"

"Yeah," replied the young man. "My first blow job."

"Well, in that case," said the bartender, "let me give you a seventh – on the house."

"No offence, sir," said the young man, "but if six shots won't get rid of the taste, nothing will."

6211 How do you get four gays on a barstool? – Turn it upside down.

6212 Stuck in the wilds of Canada, a lumberjack became restless, frustrated and bored. "Are there any women around?" he asked the foreman.

"No," said the foreman, "but if it's excitement you're looking for, there's an old guy named Charlie lives in a cabin a mile down the track. If you don't mind spending a little money, Charlie will show you the time of your life."

The lumberjack was appalled at the prospect. "No way," he said. "I don't go for that kinda stuff!"

Six months on, and the lumberjack was more bored and frustrated than ever. He was desperate for sex. So he decided to ask the foreman about Charlie. "This guy Charlie – how much will it cost?"

"Five hundred dollars," said the foreman.

"That's a hell of a lot of money. Why so much?"

"Well," said the foreman, "there's 200 dollars for Charlie, and 100 dollars apiece for the three guys who have to hold Charlie down. You see, old Charlie don't go for that kinda stuff either . . ."

6213 Why is a man so clever when he's having sex? – Because he's plugged into a woman.

6214 A man arrived home and found his wife in bed with his best friend. He shouted at his wife: "You whore, you've betrayed me. Pack your things and go. I never want to see you again!"

Then he turned to his best friend and said: "And as for you . . . bad dog!"

6215 A man walked into a bar and ordered a stiff drink. "You look a bit down," said the bartender. "What's the matter?"

"I've just found out that my eldest son is homosexual," moaned the man.

A few months later, the man returned to the bar and ordered another stiff drink.

"More problems?" inquired the bartender.

"I've just found out that my second son is homosexual," wailed the man.

Eight weeks later, he was back in the bar again, still looking thoroughly miserable. "I've just found out that my youngest son is homosexual," he told the bartender.

"Jesus Christ," said the bartender, "isn't there anybody in your family that likes women?"

"Yeah," groaned the man. "My wife does."

6216 What do you call a lesbian with fat fingers? – Well hung.

6217 What did one lesbian vampire say to the other? – See you next month.

6218 Driving across America, an Englishman chanced upon a small town in the wilds of Wyoming which proclaimed that it was a town with no women. He went for a drink in the local bar and asked the bartender: "How can you live in this town without any women?"

"Well, sir," said the bartender. "It's not that bad really. When we get lonely, we go out back where there's a barrel with a knothole in it. It doesn't sound very appealing at first, but, believe me, after one try you're hooked."

After a few beers, the Englishman started to feel lonely so he took the bartender's advice and sought out the barrel. When he found it, he inserted his penis into the knothole. Five minutes later, he returned to the bar and said to the bartender: "You were right. That was great. What do I owe you?"

"Nothing," said the bartender, "but it's your turn to get in the barrel."

6219 What's the difference between a gay rodeo and a straight rodeo? – At a straight rodeo they yell, "Ride that sucker!"

6220 What's the latest chat-up line in a gay bar? – Can I push your stool in?

6221 A general was incredibly proud of his son when he joined the Marines. He told everyone how well his boy was doing, and what a man he was, and he looked forward to hearing about further tales of heroism when the boy came home on a week's vacation.

But the boy appeared troubled. "Dad, there's something I have to tell you, and I don't think you're going to like it. I had to do my first jump out of a plane and I was absolutely terrified. I was the last one to jump and when I got to the door, I just froze. I couldn't do it. My drill sergeant glared at me and yelled: "Soldier, if you don't jump out of this plane this damn instant, I'm going to stick my big, hairy cock right up your little ass!"

The father's eyes widened. "Did you jump?"

"Only at first."

6222 How do you make a fruit cordial? – Pat him on the behind.

6223 A guy joined a nudist club. On his first day there, he strolled in the picturesque gardens where he saw a large sign: "Beware of Gays". A hundred yards further along, he spotted another sign: "Beware of Gays". He turned a corner into a pretty glade and noticed a bronze plaque set in the ground. He bent over to read it. It said: "Sorry, but you've had two warnings!"

6224 What do you say to a lesbian with no arms and no legs? – Nice tits, bitch.

6225 A cowboy was sitting in a bar when a young woman came and sat next to him. After a while they got talking.

"Are you a real cowboy?" she asked.

"Well, ma'am, I've spent all my life herding cows and breaking horses so I guess I must be."

A few minutes later, he said: "And what are you?"

"I'm a lesbian," she said. "I spend my whole day and all night thinking about women. Whether I'm eating, in the shower or watching TV, I think about women."

Soon she left and was replaced by a young couple. The woman got chatting to the cowboy and said: "Are you a real cowboy?"

"Well," he drawled, "I always thought I was, but I just found out I'm a lesbian."

6226 A lesbian went to see a gynaecologist. The gynaecologist enthused: "I must say, this is the cleanest pussy I've seen in months."

"Thanks, I have a woman in three times a week."

6227 Three young priests were about to take their final vows. The last test they had to take was a celibacy test. For this, all three had to strip naked and tie a little bell around their penis. A belly-dancer entered the room and began slinking around the first priest.

Ting-a-ling.

"Oh, Patrick," said the head priest, "I am disappointed in you. You have failed. Go and take a shower."

Then the belly-dancer went over to the second priest and began rubbing herself up against him.

Ting-a-ling.

"Oh, Michael," said the head priest. "I'm afraid you too have failed. Go and take a shower."

Finally the belly-dancer went over to the third priest. She pressed herself against him, whispered in his ear, licked his body, but got absolutely no reaction.

"Well done, Joseph!" said the head priest. "You have passed the test. You have shown that you can resist the temptation of women. Now go and relax and take a shower with Patrick and Michael."

Ting-a-ling.

6228 A husband took his wife and young daughter to the zoo. While he went off to fetch the ice creams, wife and daughter went to see the rhinoceros. The animal had a massive erection.

"What's that, Mummy?" asked the little girl.

"Oh, that's nothing," said the wife embarrassed. And she quickly changed the subject.

A few minutes later the husband returned. The little girl ran up to him and pointed to the rhinoceros's huge member.

"What's that, Daddy?" she asked.

The husband was flustered. "Er, well, darling, er, um, what did your mother say?"

"She said it was nothing," replied the little girl.

"Well, your mother's been spoilt."

6229 One morning a little girl was distressed to find her pet cat lying on the floor with its legs in the air.

"I'm afraid Sooty is dead," said her father.

The girl wiped away her tears and asked: "But Daddy, why is Sooty lying with his legs in the air?"

The father thought quickly. "Because that way it's easier for Jesus to come down, take hold of Sooty's legs and carry him off to heaven."

The little girl was satisfied with the explanation and the father went off to work. But when he came home in the evening, she ran sobbing to the door. "Daddy! Daddy!" she shouted, "Mummy nearly died this morning."

"Why? What happened?" asked the father anxiously.

"Well," said the little girl, "soon after you left for work, I saw her lying on the floor with her legs in the air. She was shouting 'Jesus, I'm coming, I'm coming' and if it hadn't been for the milkman holding her down, she would definitely have gone, Daddy."

6230 One day an elephant was lumbering through the jungle when he fell into a deep pit. Knowing that he would die if he wasn't rescued quickly, he cried out for help. Luckily his calls were heard by a passing chicken who immediately contacted the King of the Jungle. Ten minutes later the King of the Jungle arrived in a gleaming red Porsche, tied a strong rope to the rear bumper of the car and pulled the elephant to safety. The elephant was so grateful to the chicken for summoning help that he promised to help if the chicken ever found itself in trouble.

A few days later, the chicken fell into the same pit. The elephant heard its cries and raced to the rescue. He tried to pull the chicken out with his tail, but it was too short for the chicken to reach. Then he offered his trunk, but that wasn't long enough either. Finally he thrust his enormous member into the pit and told the chicken to grab hold of it. The chicken did so and was duly pulled to safety.

And the moral of the story is: if you've got a big dick, you don't need a red Porsche to pull a chick.

Yo mama jokes

6231 Yo mama is so fat her high school graduation picture was an aerial photo.

6232 Yo mama is so fat she had to go to Sea World to get baptized.

6233 Yo mama is so fat I had to ride a bus and two trains to get on her good side.

6234 Yo mama is so fat that when she was diagnosed with a flesh-eating disease, the doctors gave her 14 years to live.

6235 Yo mama is so fat she shows up on radar.

6236 Yo mama is so fat that when she goes to the zoo, elephants throw her peanuts.

6237 Yo mama is so fat the back of her neck looks like a pack of hot dogs.

6238 Yo mama is so fat her blood type is Ragu.

6239 Yo mama is so fat she's got smaller women orbiting around her.

6240 Yo mama is so fat that when she goes to a restaurant, she doesn't get a menu, she gets an estimate.

6241 Yo mama is so fat she has to fly cargo class.

6242 Yo mama is so fat the National Weather Agency assigns names to her farts.

6243 Yo mama is so fat she wakes up in sections.

6244 Yo mama is so fat people jog around her for exercise.

6245 Yo mama is so fat if she got her shoes shined, she'd have to take his word for it.

6246 Yo mama is so fat she can't even jump to a conclusion.

6247 Yo mama is so fat she has to wear a sock on each toe.

6248 Yo mama is so fat that when she goes to an all-you-can-eat buffet, they have to install speed bumps.

6249 Yo mama is so fat she has been declared a natural habitat for condors.

6250 Yo mama is so fat her belly button's got an echo.

6251 Yo mama is so fat that when she sits in front of the Hollywood sign, you can only see the H and the D.

6252 Yo mama is so fat that when you get on top of her, your ears pop.

6253 Yo mama is so fat she has to iron her pants on the drive.

6254 Yo mama is so fat she qualifies for group insurance.

6255 Yo mama is so fat the only thing attracted to her is gravity.

6256 Yo mama is so fat that when she has sex, she has to give directions.

6257 Yo mama is so fat that when she wears a yellow raincoat, people shout, "Taxi!"

6258 Yo mama is so fat she had to have her ears pierced with a harpoon.

6259 Yo mama is so fat her driver's license says "Picture continued on other side".

6260 Yo mama is so fat she's got shock absorbers on her toilet seat.

6261 Yo mama is so fat that when she went to the movies, she sat next to everyone.

6262 Yo mama is so fat she's on both sides of the family.

6263 Yo mama is so fat every time she walks in high heels, she strikes oil.

6264 Yo mama is so fat that when she bungee jumps, she goes straight to hell.

6265 Yo mama is so fat she could be the eighth continent.

6266 Yo mama is so fat her cereal bowl comes with a lifeguard.

6267 Yo mama is so fat that when she bends over, we lose an hour of daylight.

6268 Yo mama is so fat that when she cut her leg, gravy poured out.

6269 Yo mama is so fat she jumped in the air and got stuck.

6270 Yo mama is so fat she uses a mattress for a tampon.

6271 Yo mama is so fat that when she gets in an elevator, it has to go down.

6272 Yo mama is so fat she puts lipstick on with a paint-roller.

6273 Yo mama is so fat that when she lies on the beach, she's the only one to get the sun.

6274 Yo mama is so fat that when she bungee jumps, she brings down the bridge.

6275 Yo mama is so fat that when she steps on a scale, it reads, "one at a time, please."

6276 Yo mama is so fat she influences the tides.

6277 Yo mama is so fat even her clothes have stretch marks.

6278 Yo mama is so fat that when she sits on your face, you can't hear the stereo.

6279 Yo mama is so fat she's got her own area code.

6280 Yo mama is so hairy Big Foot took a picture of her.

6281 Yo mama is so old her social security number is 1.

6282 Yo mama is so old that when she reads the Bible she reminisces.

6283 Yo mama is so old that when she was in school there was no history class.

6284 Yo mama is so old that when God said "Let there be light", she flipped the switch.

6285 Yo mama is so old she was a waitress at The Last Supper.

6286 Yo mama is so old her birth certificate is in Roman numerals.

6287 Yo mama is so old she's got a picture of Moses in her school yearbook.

6288 Yo mama is so old she remembers the Grand Canyon when it was a ditch.

6289 Yo mama is so old that when she ran track in high school, they timed her with a sundial.

6290 Yo mama is so old she used to babysit Cain and Abel.

6291 Yo mama is so poor she waves an ice lolly and calls it air conditioning.

6292 Yo mama is so poor she hangs the toilet paper to dry.

6293 Yo mama is so poor that when you ring her doorbell, she has to say "Ding".

6294 Yo mama is so poor she wrestles squirrels for peanuts.

6295 Yo mama is so poor she can't even afford to pay attention.

6296 Yo mama is so poor she goes to KFC to lick other people's fingers.

6297 Yo mama is so poor, her TV has two channels — on and off.

6298 Yo mama is so poor your family ate cereal with a fork to save milk.

6299 Yo mama is so stupid she put lipstick on her forehead to make up her mind.

6300 Yo mama is so stupid that when she saw the "under 18 not admitted" sign, she went home and got 17 friends.

6301 Yo mama is so stupid she thought a quarterback was a refund.

6302 Yo mama is so stupid that when she hears it's chilly outside, she gets a bowl.

6303 Yo mama is so stupid that when she got locked in a grocery store, she starved.

6304 Yo mama is so stupid she sold her car for gas money.

6305 Yo mama is so stupid she could trip over a cordless phone.

6306 Yo mama is so stupid it took her a week to get rid of a 24-hour virus.

6307 Yo mama is so stupid that at the bottom of the application where it says "Sign here", she put Aquarius.

6308 Yo mama is so stupid she got fired from the M & M factory for throwing away the Ws.

6309 Yo mama is so stupid she is thicker than whale phlegm.

6310 Yo mama is so stupid that instead of taking the 44 bus, she took the 22 twice.

6311 Yo mama is so stupid she cooks with Old Spice.

6312 Yo mama is so stupid that when she asked "what's that letter after 'x' " and I said, " 'y' ", she said, "'cause I want to know."

6313 Yo mama is so stupid she took the Pepsi challenge and chose Jif.

6314 Yo mama is so stupid if she spoke her mind, she'd be speechless.

6315 Yo mama is so stupid that when you stand next to her, you hear the ocean.

6316 Yo mama is so stupid she said "What's the number for 911?"

6317 Yo mama is so stupid she thought a hot meal was stolen food.

6318 Yo mama is so stupid she thought Boyz II Men was a daycare centre.

6319 Yo mama is so ugly the last time she heard a whistle was when she got hit by a train.

6320 Yo mama is so ugly that when she gets up, the sun goes down.

6321 Yo mama is so ugly she made an onion cry.

6322 Yo mama is so ugly that on Hallowe'en people go as her.

6323 Yo mama is so ugly she put her head out of the window and was arrested for mooning.

6324 Yo mama is so ugly that when they took her to the beautician, it took 12 hours – for a quote.

6325 Yo mama is so ugly she tried to take a bath and the water jumped out.

6326 Yo mama is so ugly even Rice Krispies won't talk to her.

6327 Yo mama is so ugly that in strip joints, they pay her to put her clothes on.

6328 Yo mama is so ugly that your father takes her to work with him so that he doesn't have to kiss her goodbye.

6329 Yo mama is so ugly that when she was born, the doctor smacked the wrong end.

6330 Yo mama is so ugly that her parents had to feed her with a slingshot.

6331 Yo mama is so ugly that when she was born, she was put in an incubator with tinted windows.

6332 Yo mama is so ugly they know what time she was born because her face stopped the clock.

6333 Yo mama is so ugly they have to tie a steak around her neck to get the dog to play with her.

6334 Yo mama is so ugly that when she entered an ugly contest, they said, "Sorry, no professionals."

6335 Yo mama is so ugly that for Hallowe'en she tricks or treats over the phone.

6336 Yo mama is so ugly that when she walks into a bank, they turn off the surveillance cameras.

6337 Yo mama's teeth are so yellow traffic slows down when she smiles.

6338 Yo mama's teeth are so yellow I can't believe it's not butter.

6339 Yo mama's got so many teeth missing it looks like her tongue is in jail.

6340 Yo mama's breath is so bad, when she exhales her teeth have to duck.

6341 Yo mama's so dirty you can tell her age by the rings under her armpits.

6342 Yo mama's so dirty her Sure deodorant is now Confused.

6343 Yo mama's house is so dirty she has to wipe her feet before she goes outside.

6344 Yo mama's house is so dusty the roaches ride around on dune buggies.

6345 Yo mama's house is so small she has to go outside to eat a large pizza.

6346 Yo mama's house is so small you have to go outside to change your mind.

General

6347 A man went to confession and confessed to having used the F word. The priest said: "That's four Hail Marys and watch your language."

But the man said: "I want to explain why I used the F word."

"Very well, then," sighed the priest, looking at his watch.

"You see," said the man, "I played golf on Sunday instead of going to church."

"Was that why you swore?" interrupted the priest.

"No. I was on the first tee and I hooked my drive."

"Was that when you swore?"

"No, because when I got to my ball, I saw I had a clear shot to the green. But before I could play my second shot, a squirrel grabbed my ball and ran up a tree with it."

"Was that when you swore?"

"No, because an eagle flew by, caught the squirrel in its talons and flew off with it."

"Was that when you swore?"

"No, because the eagle flew over the green and the dying squirrel let go of my ball and it landed four inches from the hole."

"Don't tell me you missed the fucking putt!"

6348 What do you get if you cross an insomniac, an agnostic and a dyslexic? – Someone who's up all night wondering if there is a dog.

6349 What do you get when you cross the Atlantic Ocean with the *Titanic*? – Halfway.

6350 A man adored baked beans but when he got married, he agreed to give them up because they gave him such terrible gas. However on his way home from work one evening, he caught the smell of baked beans wafting from a café and gave in to temptation. He ate three platefuls but was confident that he could get rid of all the gas on the 20-minute walk home.

He arrived home, buttocks clenched, to find his wife waiting for him. "Darling, I've got a surprise for you tonight," she said. And with that, she put a blindfold on him, led him to his chair at the head of the dinner table and made him promise not to look. Just then the phone rang, and she went into the hallway to answer it.

Sat on the chair, he couldn't hold his gas in any longer. He could hear his wife's voice in the hallway, so he figured it was safe to let a few rip. He leaned one way and then the other and released them like machine-gun fire. They were loud and they stank. Then he lifted his right cheek up and released a veritable torpedo. The smell was so bad even he felt faint. He tried to wave the stench away with his hands and prayed that it would be gone by the time his wife returned. Finally she came back into the room, removed his blindfold and said, "Surprise!"

He opened his eyes to see 12 dinner guests seated around the table.

6351 Waiting by the side of the road, a fat woman said to a schoolboy: "Sonny, could you see me across the road?"

"Of course I can," he said. "I could see you a mile away!"

6352 The curator of a leading American art gallery commissioned an artist to do a painting depicting General Custer's last thoughts. For nine months, the artist kept his work a closely guarded secret and so its unveiling was eagerly anticipated. But when the great day came, the curator was horrified to see the result. Instead of a fine battle, the painting showed a large lake with fish leaping from the water with halos around their heads. And on the shore of the lake were hundreds of Indians fornicating.

The curator was furious. "What on earth is this supposed to be?" he raged.

The artist said: "You asked for a painting of Custer's last thoughts. This is it.

Custer was thinking: 'Holy mackerel, where did all those fucking Indians come from?' "

6353 Why don't they have toilet paper in KFC? – 'Cos it's finger lickin' good.

6354 A bear had to go for a crap in the woods. As he squatted down behind a bush, he found a rabbit doing the same.

"Say," said the bear, "do you have trouble with shit sticking to your fur?"

"No," said the rabbit.

So the bear picked up the rabbit and wiped his ass with it.

6355 Why did Hitler commit suicide? – He got the gas bill.

6356 In the heart of the Big Forest, the three bears woke up one morning. Baby bear went downstairs, sat in the small chair at the table, looked in his bowl and saw it was empty. "Who's been eating my porridge?" he squeaked.

Daddy bear arrived at the table, sat in the big chair, looked in his bowl and saw it was empty. "Who's been eating my porridge?" he roared.

Mummy bear put her head through the serving hatch and yelled: "For God's sake, how many times do we have to go through this? I haven't made the fucking porridge yet!"

6357 What do the letters DNA stand for? – National Dyslexics Association.

6358 Did you hear about the dyslexic Satanist? – He sold his soul to Santa.

6359 Did you hear about the paranoid with low self-esteem? He thought that nobody important was out to get him.

6360 What did the cannibal do after he dumped his girlfriend? – Wiped his ass.

6361 A guy walked into a bar with a pet monkey. The monkey immediately snatched handfuls of olives, limes and peanuts and started eating them. Then it grabbed the cue ball from the pool table, stuck it in its mouth and swallowed it whole.

The bartender complained about the monkey's behaviour, but the owner said: "There's nothing much I can do about him. He'll eat anything in sight."

Two weeks later, the man and the monkey were back in the same bar. The monkey immediately snatched a maraschino cherry from the bar, stuck it up its ass, pulled it out and ate it.

"Did you see what your monkey did?" said the bartender. "It put a cherry up its ass, pulled it out and then ate it. That's disgusting."

"I know," said the owner. "You see, he still eats anything in sight but ever since he ate that cue ball, he measures everything first."

6362 What do you call 123 white guys chasing after one black guy? — The PGA tour.

6363 At the end of the school year a kindergarten teacher received gifts from her pupils. First, the florist's son handed her a beautifully wrapped gift. The teacher held the gift above her head, shook it and said: "I think it's flowers. Am I right?"

"Yes," said the boy.

Her second gift was from the daughter of a sweet shop owner. The teacher held the beautifully wrapped gift above her head, shook it and said: "I think it's a box of sweets. Am I right?"

"Yes," said the girl.

The teacher's third gift was from a boy whose father ran the local liquor store. Once again, it was beautifully wrapped. The teacher held it above her head and shook it, but as she did so, it started to leak. She touched a drop of the leakage with her finger and put it on her tongue. "I think it's wine. Am I right?"

"No," said the boy.

So the teacher tasted another drop of the leakage. "Is it champagne?"

"No," said the boy.

The teacher tasted another drop, but, unable to recognize it, conceded defeat. "OK,

I give up. What is it?"

The boy said: "It's a puppy."

6364 A dyslexic man walked into a bra . . .

6365 A boy was apprehensive about being invited round to dinner to meet his girlfriend's parents for the first time. In fact, he was so worried he couldn't help passing wind throughout the meal. The first time he did it, the girl's father turned pointedly to the family dog which was sitting next to the table and said: "Rover, move away will you." The boy was relieved and extremely grateful to the father for getting him out of an awkward situation.

A minute or so later, the boy dropped another one. Again the considerate father turned to the dog and said: "Rover, move away will you."

Two minutes later, the poor boy struck again. Once more the father bailed him out, saying firmly: "Rover, move away will you."

A couple of minutes later, the boy let out a real snorter — louder and smellier than before. The father turned to the dog and said: "For Christ's sake, Rover. You'd better hurry up and move before he craps all over you!"

6366 Two airplane mechanics from Denver were regular drinking buddies. However because of thick fog one night, they were stranded in the hangar, unable to get into town. The only liquid available was jet fuel. Neither relished the thought of drinking jet fuel, but there seemed little alternative. They each drank four pints of jet fuel and slept it off. In the morning, one guy woke, expecting a massive hangover. But he felt fine. However there was no sign of his buddy. Just then the phone rang. It was his buddy.

"How are you feeling?" said the voice on the other end of the phone.

"Fine."

"Well, whatever you do, don't fart."

"Why not?"

"Because I'm in Phoenix!"

6367 A kindergarten teacher was trying to explain the meaning of the word "definitely" and asked the children to use it in a sentence.

One boy raised his hand and said: "The sky is definitely blue."

"That's not entirely correct," said the teacher, "because sometimes it's grey and cloudy."

Another child raised his hand and suggested: "Grass is definitely green."

"But," said the teacher, "if grass doesn't get enough water it turns brown, so that isn't really correct either."

Then a third boy raised his hand and asked: "Do farts have lumps?"

The teacher was horrified. "That isn't a question you want to ask in a class discussion. But the answer is no."

"Oh, then I've definitely crapped in my pants."

6368 What did Quasimodo's wife get him for his birthday? — A wok. She thought it would help her iron his shirts.

6369 Two lumps of vomit were walking down the street when suddenly one began to cry.

"What's wrong?" asked the other.

The first lump of vomit sobbed: "This is where I was brought up."

6370 A teacher asked her class to use the word "contagious". Roland, the class geek, stood up and said: "Last year I got measles and my mother said it was contagious."

"Well done, Roland," said the teacher. "Can anyone else try?"

Then Katie, a sweet child, announced: "My grandma says there's a bug going round, and it's contagious."

"Well done, Katie," said the teacher. "Anyone else?"

Little Shaun O'Malley jumped up and said: "Our next door neighbour is painting his house with a two-inch brush and my Dad says it will take the contagious."

PUNS

6371 Two pieces of tarmac were having a drinking contest to see which was the hardest. After 12 shots of vodka, both were still stone cold sober when suddenly the door opened and a piece of red tarmac walked in. Immediately, one piece of tarmac abandoned his drink and ran out of the bar.

The other piece of tarmac caught up with him the following day. "Why did you suddenly run off like that when that piece of red tarmac came into the bar?"

"Haven't you heard about him? He's a cycle-path!"

6372 A group of chess enthusiasts were waiting to check into a hotel and were discussing their recent tournament victories in the lobby. After an hour, the manager came out of his office and asked them to leave.

"But why?" they protested.

"Because," he said, "I can't stand chess nuts boasting in an open foyer."

6373 A man who specialized in puns thought he had an outstanding chance of winning a pun contest run by his local newspaper. He sent the paper no fewer than ten different entries in the hope that one of them might win. Unfortunately, no pun in ten did.

6374 Swedish explorer Leif Erikkson returned from his voyage to the New World only to discover that his name had been removed from his home town register. He was appalled and complained bitterly to the leader of the town council. After investigating the oversight, the council leader apologized, saying he must have taken Leif off his census.

6375 What do you call a one-eyed dinosaur? – D'yathinkesaurus?

6376 What do you call a one-eyed dinosaur's dog? – D'yathinkesaurus Rex.

6377 What do you do if you see a spaceman? – Park your car in it man.

6378 A mushroom walked into a bar and announced: "The drinks are on me."
The bartender said: "Why are you buying everybody drinks?"
"Because I'm a fungi."

6379 A wealthy lawyer had a summer house in the backwoods of Maine. One weekend he invited a Czech friend to stay with him. The pair were out picking berries for breakfast when they were approached by two huge bears – one male, one female. The lawyer managed to escape but his friend was swallowed whole by the male bear.
The lawyer drove to the sheriff's office and begged him to come and help his friend before it was too late. The sheriff grabbed his shotgun and the two men drove back to the place of the attack. The bears were still there.
"He's in that one," cried the lawyer, pointing to the male bear, but the sheriff shot the female instead.
"What did you do that for?" screamed the lawyer. "I said he was in the other one."
"Exactly," said the sheriff. "Would you believe a lawyer who told you the Czech was in the male?"

6380 What's white, light and sugary and swings from trees? – A meringue-utan.

6381 Roy Rogers put his cowboy boots out on the porch one night but when he went to collect them in the morning, he found that the heels had been ripped off. Thinking that a mountain lion was probably to blame, he rode into town to buy a new pair. That night, he left the new boots out on the porch as usual, but once again in the morning he found that they had been torn to shreds.
"It can only have been a mountain lion," growled Roy and he set off to seek revenge.
Two hours later, he returned with the carcass of a mountain lion strapped to his saddle. As Roy dismounted, his hired hand walked over to him and said: "Pardon me, Roy, is that the cat who chewed your new shoes?"

6382 What do Eskimos get from sitting on the ice too long? – Polaroids.

6383 What do you get when you drop a piano down a mine shaft? – A flat minor.

6384 What do you shout when you drop a piano down a mine shaft? – C sharp. Or B flat minor.

6385 What happened to the survivors of a collision between a red ship and a blue ship? – They were marooned.

6386 Fred Astaire and Ginger Rogers were having dinner at an expensive New York restaurant. It was the place to be seen and both had dressed for the occasion. Ginger was resplendent in a ball gown and diamond tiara while Fred wore his smartest morning suit. But the evening was marred when the waiter bringing their desserts tripped and covered Fred from head to toe in treacle sponge.

"I'm terribly sorry," said the waiter.

"So you should be," replied Fred. "Thanks to you I've got pudding on my top hat, pudding on my white tie, pudding on my tails."

6387 What do you get when you cross a snowman with a vampire? – Frostbite.

6388 Did you hear about the Buddhist who refused his dentist's Novocain during root canal work? – He wanted to transcend dental medication.

6389 What do you get if you divide the circumference of a pumpkin by its diameter? – Pumpkin pi.

6390 A man suffered for months with chronic back pain and was eventually persuaded by his doctor to go and see a chiropractor. But he didn't have much faith in such people and was convinced they wouldn't be able to help him. Yet after a few minutes' treatment, his back felt like new.

"How do you feel about chiropractors now?" asked the doctor.

The man said: "I stand corrected."

6391 A group of journalists formed a clothing optional track club. Their motto was: "All The Nudes That's Fit To Sprint."

6392 Why is a pig's tail like getting up at three o'clock in the morning? – It's twirly.

6393 Why was the theatre crying? – The seats were all in tiers.

6394 Doctor: "Have your eyes been checked?"
Patient: "No, they've always been blue."

6395 What do you call a chicken crossing the road? – Poultry in motion.

6396 A woman went into a bar with a newt perched on her shoulder. She ordered a drink for herself and one for the newt.
"What's its name?" asked the bartender.
"Tiny," replied the woman.
"Why Tiny?"
"Because he's my newt."

6397 Why do ghouls and demons hang out together? – Because demons are a ghoul's best friend.

6398 If you are American when you go into a toilet and you are American when you come out of the toilet, what are you while you are in the toilet? – European, of course.

6399 What soldiers smell of salt and pepper? – Seasoned troopers.

6400 What's made of plastic and hangs around French cathedrals? – The lunchpack of Notre Dame.

6401 Sherlock Holmes turned to Dr Watson and announced: "The murderer lives in the house with the yellow door."
"Good grief, Holmes," said Watson. "How on earth did you deduce that?"
"It's a lemon entry, my dear Watson."

6402 What do you get if you buy crayons for your children? – A gift to make your kin scrawl.

6403 What happens if you eat Christmas decorations? – You get tinselitis.

6404 How do you kill a circus? – Go for the juggler.

6405 What did the egg in the monastery say? – Ah, well, out of the frying pan and into the friar.

6406 An Englishman travelling in the desert saw a mirage on the distant horizon. It was of a huge market with bowls of jelly and custard, cream, sponge and hundreds and thousands.

He turned to his companion and said: "It's a trifle bazaar."

6407 An Irish band were doing a gig at a Dublin discotheque owned by their manager, Sam Frank. The gig was a great success and afterwards they all went out to dinner to celebrate. They didn't want to leave their instruments in the van for fear of theft so they decided to take them into the restaurant. The guitarist collected his guitar from the back of the van, the flautist picked up his flute, but the harpist couldn't find her instrument anywhere. She was beside herself with worry.

"What's the matter?" asked one of the band.

And the poor girl burst into song: "I left my harp in Sam Frank's disco."

6408 What do you call an unemployed jester? – Nobody's fool.

6409 What's a Hindu? – Lays eggs.

6410 Two herrings, Cain and Abel, were regular visitors to a bar. One day, Cain showed up alone and the bartender asked: "Where's your brother?"

"How should I know?" said Cain. "Am I my brother's kipper?"

6411 A royal castle was under siege from an infidel army. The only hope was to send one of the knights to get help, but the problem was that all of the horses had been killed in the battle.

"We must get help," said the king.

"I know," replied the leader of his army, "but we have no horses. If a knight goes on foot, he will be slain at once."

"Is there not another animal he can ride?" demanded the king. "What about that mighty wolfhound? It could surely bear the weight of a man."

"No, no," pleaded the army leader. "The wolfhound is too dangerous. Look at its snarling teeth. I wouldn't send a knight out on a dog like this."

6412 Two peanuts were walking down a sidewalk. One was assaulted . . .

6413 A man forgot to buy his wife her favourite anemones on her birthday. By the time he got to the florist's, all the shop had left were bits of greenery. Nevertheless he decided to buy the foliage and was pleasantly surprised when his wife expressed her delight at the gift. "With fronds like these," she exclaimed, "who needs anemones?"

6414 Two female rhinoceroses at the zoo were eagerly awaiting the arrival of a new male. When he was led into the paddock, they wasted no time in introducing themselves.

"Hi, I'm Julie, and this is Sandra."

"Hi," said the male. "My name's Neil."

"Ooooh!" they trilled. "Not the rhino Neil?"

6415 A three-legged dog walked into a bar and said: "I'm looking for the man who shot my paw."

6416 How did the butcher introduce his wife? – Meat Patty.

6417 A man was driving along a country road when he saw a farmer standing in the middle of a huge field. The farmer wasn't doing anything and appeared to be staring blankly at nothing in particular.

"What are you doing?" called the driver.

"I'm trying to win a Nobel Prize," said the farmer.

"How's that?"

"Well, I heard they give the Nobel Prize to people who are out standing in their field."

6418 A man went to a seance and flew into a temper because the psychic was laughing her head off at fooling the gullible public. So he hit her. He was subsequently arrested for striking a happy medium.

6419 During a great Australian tea famine, the small Queensland town of Mercy developed a tea made from koala bears. The tea became famous throughout Australia.

One day a visitor from Sydney tried a cup, but was disgusted to find bits of fur and flesh floating in it. He asked the waiter if it could be filtered.

The waiter replied firmly: "The koala tea of Mercy is not strained."

6420 What is a bigamist? – An Italian fog.

6421 A clown moved into an apartment block reserved solely for circus performers. He liked everything about the apartment. The kitchen was modern, the bedroom was comfortable and the lounge was spacious. And there were plenty of facilities – cooker, hoover, refrigerator, washing machine. The only thing that was missing was an ironing board, something on which he could press his circus uniform after washing it.

"Why is there no ironing board?" he asked the agent. "The lion tamer and the juggler have both got one."

"You use the window ledge, like the other clowns," explained the agent. "It's in your contract. Every clown has a sill for ironing."

6422 In Beijing there is a wooden sculpture of the Emperor Chung. It's titled Chung in Teak.

6423 A boy got a Saturday job bagging groceries at a supermarket. One day, the store put in a machine for squeezing oranges. The boy asked if he could work on the machine.

"Sorry," said his boss, "but baggers can't be juicers."

6424 A magazine photographer was sent on an assignment to a haunted house to take some shots of an apparition said to be residing there. To the photographer's amazement, as soon as the clock struck midnight, the apparition appeared on the landing at the top of the stairs and stood there for several minutes, posing. Unfortunately the light was very bad and the photographer had forgotten to charge his batteries. He kept snapping away but, because of the low batteries, none of the pictures came out. He explained to his editor: "The spirit was willing, but the flash was weak."

6425 Did you hear about the Old Testament hooker who was arrested for trying to make a Prophet?

6426 What is a cobra? – A bra for Siamese twins.

6427 Two boll weevils grew up in South Carolina. One went to Hollywood and became an international film star but the other stayed behind in the cotton fields and never really amounted to much. Naturally enough this second one was known as the lesser of two weevils.

6428 An Indian chief was feeling sick and summoned the medicine man to his tepee. After a brief examination, the medicine man cut off a thong of elk hide from his belt and handed it to the chief, instructing him to eat one inch of leather a day. A month later, the medicine man returned to check on the chief's progress. The chief complained: "The thong is ended, but the malady lingers on."

6429 What is a quark? – The noise a well-bred duck makes.

6430 A businesswoman led such a hectic life that she decided to ease the load by making a clone of herself. The clone was a perfect replica except for the fact that it swore a lot. No matter what the woman did, she could not stop it swearing. In the end, she was losing so much business because of her clone's foul mouth that she decided to end the experiment by pushing the clone off a tall building. She was subsequently charged with making an obscene clone fall.

6431 What do sad owls sing in a rainstorm? – Too wet to woo.

6432 What do you get if you feed lemon to a cat? – A sour puss.

6433 Cole's Law – Thinly sliced cabbage.

6434 A frog wanted to buy a new lily pond but had run out of money so he went to the bank for a loan. He sat down at a desk and introduced himself as Kermit Jagger, son of Mick Jagger. He was interviewed by a bank official named Patty Whack who asked the frog what he could offer as collateral. The frog reached into his briefcase and produced a vase but Patty was unimpressed. "I'm afraid we'll need something more than that," she told the frog. "It's just a cheap knick-knack."

But just to be sure, she decided to show the vase to the bank manager who knew a lot about antiques. "I've got this frog named Kermit Jagger and he's brought in this vase as collateral. What do you think?"

The manager registered the name, took one look at the vase and said: " It's a knick-knack, Patty Whack, but give the frog a loan. His old man's a Rolling Stone."

6435 Did you hear about the man at the flower shop who was robbed at gunpoint? – He was a petrified florist.

6436 A man joined a ballroom dancing club and claimed to be an expert dancer. However it quickly emerged that he couldn't dance at all. He was accused of bearing waltz fitness.

6437 A police officer made the mistake of arresting a judge who went to a party dressed as a convict. The episode taught the cop a valuable lesson – that you should never book a judge by his cover.

6438 What have you got when your parrot escapes? – Nil parity.

6439 Two cowboys in the kitchen – which one is the real cowboy? – The one on the range.

6440 Why do anarchists drink horrible tea? – Because all proper tea is theft.

6441 A doctor was in the habit of stopping off at a bar for a hazelnut daiquiri on his way home. The bartender knew of his habit but one day was dismayed to find that he was clean out of hazelnut extract. Thinking quickly, he threw together a daiquiri made of hickory nuts and placed it on the bar in readiness for the doctor's arrival. When the doctor turned up, he took one sip of the drink and exclaimed: "This isn't a hazelnut daiquiri!"
    "No, I'm sorry," replied the bartender, "it's a hickory daiquiri, doc."

6442 Did you hear about the cat that swallowed a ball of wool? – She had mittens.

6443 Johnny's mother told him that he had been a very naughty boy and, as punishment, she decided to omit his favourite vegetable from his dinner. That evening he sat down at the table and moaned: "I've only got beans, carrots and potatoes. Where are . . . ?"
    His mother interrupted him. "You know what they say, Johnny: no peas for the wicked."

6444 Why are there no aspirins in the jungle? – Because the parrots eat 'em all.

6445 If your partner is giving birth, and the midwife doesn't turn up on time, is it a midwife crisis?

6446 Did you hear about the cannibal who had a wife and ate kids?

6447 An Indian chief had three wives, each of whom was pregnant. The first wife gave birth to a boy and the chief was so pleased that he built her a tepee made of deer hide. A few days later, the second wife also gave birth to a boy and, to express his gratitude, the chief built her a tepee made of cow hide. The third wife gave birth a week later, but the chief decided to keep the details a secret. However he built this wife a two-storey tepee made of hippopotamus hide. Then he challenged the tribe to work out what had happened. Some warriors guessed a daughter or triplets but nobody came up with the right answer until one young brave declared confidently: "She has had twins."
    "That is correct," said the chief. "How did you know?"

"It is elementary," explained the brave. "The value of the squaw of the hippopotamus is equal to the sons of the squaws of the other two hides."

6448 Why was the man arrested for waiting in the marquee? – He was loitering within tent.

6449 Every day at six p.m. on a game reserve in Kenya, a pride of lions gathered at a watering hole. They didn't drink from it, and they made no attempt to attack passing impala or zebra. Instead, they just sat and watched. After a week of this, an elephant came over and asked them what they were doing.

The leader of the pride said: "We're waiting for the early evening gnus."

6450 An American couple, Hank and Kitty, and a Russian, Rudolph, were travelling by train to an international conference in Warsaw. As the weather closed in, Kitty asked: "Is it rain or sleet out there?"

"It looks like rain," said Hank.

"I agree," added Rudolph.

"Well, it looks like sleet to me," insisted Kitty.

"I can assure you that it's rain," said Rudolph firmly.

"Well, I say you're wrong," snapped Kitty.

"Please," said Hank, trying to calm his wife, "surely you realize that Rudolph the Red knows rain, dear?"

6451 What do you have if you have 20 rabbits all in a row and they all back up one step? – A receding hare-line.

6452 A shy boy met a girl at a nightclub and wanted to invite her back to his house. He asked her whether she would like to see his collection of stamps.

"Huh!" she snorted. "Philately will get you nowhere."

6453 Two Eskimos were paddling their kayak along the Alaskan coast. The temperatures were so freezing that even beneath their layers of clothing, the Eskimos started to feel the cold. In a desperate attempt to keep warm, they lit a fire but the wooden kayak went up in flames and the pair drowned. The moral of the story is that you can't have your kayak and heat it too.

6454 What do you get when you cross a humming-bird with a doorbell? – A humdinger.

6455 A remote monastery was home to an order of monks who communicated with each other solely by chanting. Every morning, they would assemble in the chapel and the abbot would chant: "Good morning, assembled brethren." And the monks would dutifully reply: "Good morning, Father Abbot."

But one morning a maverick monk instead chanted: "Good evening, Father Abbot."

The abbot glared at the monks and proclaimed: "Someone chanted evening!"

6456 Did you hear about the man who fell into an upholstery machine? – He's fully recovered.

6457 What did the chick say when its mother produced an orange instead of an egg? – Look at the orange mama laid.

6458 Did you hear about the mathematician who turned off his heating so he could be cold and calculating?

6459 The human cannonball decided to quit the circus. The owner was furious. "You can't quit!" he raged. "Where will I find another man of your calibre?"

6460 What happened to the man who used to pick fluff out of his belly button? – He gave it up for lint.

6461 What is the fear of meeting a fat man in a red suit in a confined space? – Santaclaustrophobia.

6462 What phobia is the fear of being asked "Who goes there"? – Friendorphobia.

6463 A farmer was milking a cow when a fly appeared in the barn. After circling around the cow's head, it flew into the cow's ear. Then a few minutes later, as the farmer continued milking, the fly squirted out into his bucket. Recounting the story to his son, the farmer explained: "It went in one ear and out the udder."

6464 What did the farmer say to the goat who wouldn't reproduce? – You must be kidding.

6465 What do you get if you cross a strong onion with a goat? – Garlic butter.

6466 While searching for Esmerelda, Quasimodo became so frustrated that he attacked a young woman in the streets of Paris. In an attempt to identify her assailant, the woman was taken to the police station and shown photographs of Paris's Most Wanted. When she reached the mugshot of Quasimodo, she hesitated.

"Was that the man?" asked the gendarme. "Do you know him?"

"I'm not sure of his name," said the woman, "but his face rings a bell."

6467 What do you call a witch who verifies her incantations? – A spell checker.

6468 A man and his five-year-old son were walking in South America when a baby aardvark ran towards them. The boy was scared: "Daddy, Daddy, will it bite?"

"No, Son. A little aardvark never hurt anyone."

6469 What do you call Santa's helpers? – Subordinate Clauses.

6470 The young lassie asked the ageing Scotsman: "What exactly is under your kilt?"

"Why don't you take a look?" said the Scotsman.

"Och," she shrieked lifting up his kilt, "it's gruesome!"

"Aye," replied the Scotsman, "and if you stay a few moments it'll have grue some more!"

6471 A bear marched into a bar and demanded a beer. "I'm sorry," said the bartender, "but we don't serve beers to bears."

The bear was annoyed by this and threw the contents of the ice bucket over the bartender. "Now can I have a drink?" he growled.

"I wish you hadn't done that," replied the bartender patiently. "And anyway, like I say, we don't serve beers to bears."

The bear was furious so he picked up a chair and smashed it over the bar. "NOW can I have a drink?" he growled menacingly.

"I do wish you hadn't done that," said the bartender, "because it has done you no good. We just don't serve beers to bears."

The bear was beside himself with rage. He looked along the bar and saw a rough-looking biker chick perched on a stool. "See her?" said the bear to the bartender. "I'm going to rip her to shreds, and then you'll have to give me a drink."

"I really don't think you should," said the bartender. "She's one mean woman."

But the bear didn't care. He stalked over to the biker chick, tore her leather jacket to shreds with his claws, ripped off her arms and head and ate her.

"Now do I get that beer?" he snarled at the bartender.

"I'm sorry," said the bartender. "But we don't serve beers to people who do drugs either."

"What do you mean, drugs?" said the bear. "I don't do drugs."

"Oh yeah?" said the bartender. "What about that barbitchyouate?"

6472 A camping store was holding a Christmas sale and the manager put the young English Literature student, who had a holiday job there, in charge of thinking up a suitable slogan. He came up with: "Now is the winter offer – discount tents."

6473 Two atoms ran into each other. One atom said: "I think I've lost an electron."
The second atom said: "Are you sure?"
The first atom said: "I'm positive."

6474 If you have a bee in your hand, what do you have in your eye? – Beauty, because beauty is in the eye of the bee-holder.

6475 What's the difference between unlawful and illegal? – Unlawful is against the law, illegal is a sick bird.

6476 Did you hear about the bumper car operator who got fired? He's suing his boss for funfair dismissal.

6477 A piece of string walked into a bar and asked for a Budweiser.
"I'm afraid we don't serve pieces of string," said the bartender.
Dejected, the piece of string went outside, back-combed his hair and went back in to the bar.
The bartender eyed him suspiciously. "Are you that same piece of string that was in a few moments ago?"
"No, I'm a frayed knot."

How different professions lose their jobs:
6478 Baseball players get debased.
6479 Bed-makers get debunked.
6480 Butchers get disjointed.
6481 Cashiers get distilled.
6482 Clothes designers get defrocked.
6483 Cowboys get deranged.
6484 Dry cleaners get depressed.

6485 Electricians get delighted.

6486 Fishermen get debated.

6487 Gamblers get discarded.

6488 Gardeners get deflowered.

6489 Hookers get delayed.

6490 Judges get dishonoured.

6491 Laboratory technicians get detested.

6492 Laundry workers get decreased.

6493 Locomotive engineers get derailed.

6494 Male dancers get decamped.

6495 Models get deposed.

6496 Musicians get decomposed.

6497 Organ donors get delivered.

6498 Pig farmers get disgruntled.

6499 Politicians get devoted.

6500 Publicans get disbarred.

6501 Secretaries get defiled.

6502 Ski resort managers get dislodged.

6503 Students get degraded.

6504 Traffic wardens get defined.

6505 Underwear salesmen get debriefed.

The teacher asked little Johnny to put the following words into a sentence to show their meaning. Here are his answers:

6506 Aftermath: Tuesday is the worst day at school because aftermath we have science.

6507 Ammonia: Billy's mum offered me a lift after school, but I said ammonia short way from home.

6508 Antidotes: My uncle likes me very much and my antidotes on me.

6509 Aperitif: If he has to eat anything crunchy, my grandad takes aperitif from a glass in the bathroom.

6510 Attitude: When I saw our dog with Billy's cap in his mouth, I was just glad it wasn't my attitude.

6511 Avalanche: In our house, we have a breakfast at eight and we always avalanche at 12.30.

6512 Avenue: Thanks to Mum and Dad, I avenue baby brother.

6513 Avoidable: When you walk into a field of cattle, you should always take care to avoidable.

6514 Bellicose: You shouldn't hit someone in the bellicose it hurts.

6515 Benign: Last year I was eight, so this year I'll benign.

6516 Bulletin: The cowboy limped because he'd got a bulletin his leg.

6517 Centimetre: Aunt Daisy arrived last night and I was centimetre at the station.

6518 Climate: The tree in our back garden is really tall, but one day I'll climate.

6519 Contrite: Jimmy writes great stories, but I contrite a thing.

6520 Crustacean: When Mr Patel at no. 17 was run over by a steamroller, Mum said he was a crustacean.

6521 Deceit: In our garden there's always a rush to see who can be first to sit on deceit.

6522 Diarrhoea: When we went on holiday last summer, my dad took one look at the run-down campsite and said: "It's pretty diarrhoea."

6523 Eclipse: Every month my dad gets the garden shears and eclipse the hedge.

6524 Efficient: On my way home from school, I stopped for a bag of yum efficient chips.

6525 Falsify: When I balance a book on my head, it falsify move.

6526 Fascinate: I have nine buttons on my shirt, but I can only fascinate.

6527 Festival: I have geography homework to do tonight, but festival I'm going to watch TV.

6528 Gladiator: That vicious old hen always used to peck me, so I'm gladiator.

6529 Judicious: On TV adverts, they say that hands that judicious can be soft as your face.

6530 Nuisance: Mum was complaining that she hadn't had anything nuisance she was married.

6531 Offence: Dad's get four wooden panels and four posts lying in the garden, but he doesn't want to put them up because he thinks they'll cause offence.

6532 Propagate: Dad knocked down the old wooden fence, so now we've got a propagate.

6533 Reverend: Teacher says if I don't study I'll be in this grade for reverend ever.

6534 Ruminate: When we got to the hotel, the receptionist said that our family wouldn't all fit in room 9 but that there was plenty of ruminate.

6535 Tenderize: I heard my sister's boyfriend tell her she'd got tenderize.

6536 Urinate: You're great looking, Ma'am — in fact urinate, and if you had bigger boobs, you'd definitely be a ten.

6537 Winsome: As the football coach said after the game: "You win some, you lose some."

What happens to old professionals?

6538 Old accountants never die, they just lose their balance.

6539 Old actors never die, they just drop apart.

6540 Old anthropologists never die, they just become history.

6541 Old archers never die, they just bow and quiver.

6542 Old astronauts never die, they just go to another world.

6543 Old auditors never die, they just lose their figures.

6544 Old bakers never die, they just stop making dough.

6545 Old bankers never die, they just lose interest.

6546 Old beekeepers never die, they just buzz off.

6547 Old burglars never die, they just steal away.

6548 Old canners never die, they're preserved.

6549 Old cartographers never die, they just lose their way.

6550 Old cartoonists never die, they just go into suspended animation.

6551 Old cashiers never die, they just check out.

6552 Old chauffeurs never die, they just lose their drive.

6553 Old chemists never die, they just don't react any more.

6554 Old college deans never die, they just lose their faculties.

6555 Old dentists never die, they just lose their pull.

6556 Old dieticians never die, they just waist away.

6557 Old doctors never die, they just lose their patience.

6558 Old farmers never die, they just go to seed.

6559 Old florists never die, they make alternative arrangements.

6560 Old gardeners never die, they just go to pot.

6561 Old hippies never die, they just take a trip.

6562 Old hookers never die, they just down tools.

6563 Old informers never die, they just get put out to grass.

6564 Old insurance agents never die, it's against their policy.

6565 Old investors never die, they just roll over.

6566 Old judges never die, they just cease to try.

6567 Old lawyers never die, they just lose their appeal.

6568 Old limbo dancers never die, they just go under.

6569 Old milkmaids never die, they just lose their whey.

6570 Old Monkees never die, they go to Davy Jones's locker.

6571 Old musicians never die, they just get played out.

6572 Old number theorists never die, they just get past their prime.

6573 Old owl-keepers never die, they just don't give a hoot.

6574 Old pacifists never die, they just go to peaces.

6575 Old photographers never die, they just stop developing.

6576 Old pilots never die, they just go to a higher plane.

6577 Old plumbers never die, they just pipe down.

6578 Old policemen never die, they just cop out.

6579 Old professors never die, they just lose their class.

6580 Old sailors never die, they just get a little dingy.

6581 Old sculptors never die, they just lose their marbles.

6582 Old sewage workers never die, they just waste away.

6583 Old shoemakers never die, they just pop their clogs.

6584 Old skiers never die, they just go downhill.

6585 Old soccer players never die, they just go on dribbling.

6586 Old statisticians never die, they just average out.

6587 Old steelmakers never die, they just lose their temper.

6588 Old tanners never die, they just go into hiding.

6589 Old truckers never die, they just retire.

6590 Old typists never die, they just lose their justification.

6591 Old window-cleaners never die, they just kick the bucket.

6592 Old wrestlers never die, they just lose their grip.

6593 Old fishermen never die, they just smell that way.

PUT-DOWNS

6594 If you haven't got anything good to say about anyone, come and sit by me.
(ALICE ROOSEVELT LONGWORTH)

Art

Sandro Botticelli
6595 If Botticelli were alive today, he'd be working for Vogue. (PETER USTINOV)

Paul Gauguin
6596 A decorator tainted with insanity. (art critic KENYON COX)

Edouard Manet
6597 You are the first in the decadence of your art. (CHARLES BAUDELAIRE)

Claude Monet
6598 It is only too easy to catch people's attention by doing something worse than anyone else has dared to do it before. (ANON)

Pablo Picasso
6599 Many painters and writers have made beautiful works out of repulsive subjects; Picasso enjoys making repulsive works out of beautiful objects.
(RAYMOND MORTIMORE)

Dante Rossetti
6600 Rossetti is not a painter, Rossetti is a ladies' maid. (JAMES WHISTLER)

Walter Sickert

6601 I give you this cigar because I so much admire your writings. If I liked your paintings, I'd give you a bigger one. (PERCY W. LEWIS)

Tintoretto

6602 He will never be anything but a dauber. (TITIAN)

J.W.M. Turner

6603 It resembles a tortoiseshell cat having a fit in a plate of tomatoes. (MARK TWAIN's appraisal of Turner's painting *The Slave Ship*)

Leonardo da Vinci

6604 He bores me. He ought to have stuck to his flying machines. (AUGUSTE RENOIR)

6605 Leonardo da Vinci did everything, and did nothing very well. (MARIE BASH-KIRTSEFF)

Andy Warhol

6606 The only genius with an IQ of 60. (GORE VIDAL)

6607 Warhol's art belongs less to the history of painting than the history of publicity. (HILTON KRAMER)

James Whistler

6608 With our James vulgarity begins at home, and should be allowed to stay there. (OSCAR WILDE)

Cinema

Woody Allen

6609 His mouth is a no-go area. It's like kissing the Berlin Wall. (HELENA BONHAM CARTER)

Pamela Anderson

6610 Hollywood is full of pale imitations of Pamela Anderson and, worse still, Pamela Anderson herself. (LISA MARCHANT)

Julie Andrews

6611 Working with her is like being hit over the head with a Valentine card. (CHRISTOPHER PLUMMER after starring with Julie Andrews in *The Sound of Music*)

Fred Astaire

6612 Can't act. Slightly bald. Can dance a little. (ANON. screen test)

Alec Baldwin

6613 He has eyes like a weasel. He makes Clint Eastwood look like a flirt. (SANDY DENNIS)

Tallulah Bankhead

6614 A day away from Tallulah Bankhead is like a month in the country. (HOWARD DIETZ)

6615 Watching Tallulah on stage is like watching someone skating on thin ice – everyone wants to be there when it breaks. (MRS PATRICK CAMPBELL)

Drew Barrymore

6616 Drew Barrymore sings so badly, deaf people refuse to watch her lips move. (WOODY ALLEN)

Kim Basinger

6617 A blow-up doll come to life: leggy legs, stick-on breasts, pumped-up lips – like a custom-built woman who's been ordered à la carte. (MARK STEYN)

Warren Beatty

6618 He's the type of man who will end up dying in his own arms. (MAMIE VAN DOREN)

Candice Bergen

6619 As an actress her only flair is her nostrils. (PAULINE KAEL)

Ingrid Bergman

6620 Dear Ingrid – speaks five languages and can't act in any of them. (JOHN GIELGUD)

Humphrey Bogart

6621 Bogey's a helluva nice guy until 11.30 p.m. After that he thinks he's Bogart. (DAVE CHASEN)

Ernest Borgnine

6622 You look at him and you think to yourself: was there anybody else hurt in the accident? (DON RICKLES)

Marlon Brando

6623 Most of the time he sounds like he has a mouth full of wet toilet paper. (REX REED)

Michael Caine

6624 A master of inconsequence masquerading as a guru, passing off his vast limitations as pious virtues. (RICHARD HARRIS)

6625 Can out-act any, well nearly any, telephone kiosk you care to mention. (HUGH LEONARD)

Capucine

6626 Kissing you is like kissing the side of a beer bottle. (LAURENCE HARVEY)

Richard Chamberlain

6627 A man with the sex appeal of a sheep and the comic timing of a manatee. (ANON)

Charlie Chaplin

6628 If people don't sit at Chaplin's feet, he goes out and stands where they are sitting. (HERMAN J. MANKIEWICZ)

Cher

6629 Working with Cher was like being in a blender with an alligator. (PETER BOGDANOVICH)

Maurice Chevalier

6630 A great artiste, but a small human being. (JOSEPHINE BAKER)

Harry Cohn

6631 It proves what they always say: give the public what they want, and they'll come out for it. (RED SKELTON, noting the large crowd attending the funeral of Harry Cohn, unpopular head of Columbia Pictures)

6632 You had to stand in line just to hate him. (HEDDA HOPPER)

Claudette Colbert

6633 I'd wring your neck, if you had one. (NOEL COWARD)

Joan Collins

6634 She looks like she combs her hair with an egg-beater. (LOUELLA PARSONS)

6635 Joan Collins told a reporter that she hasn't had plastic surgery. Come on! She's had more tucks than a motel bedsheet. (JOAN RIVERS)

Gary Cooper
6636 When he puts his arms around me, I feel like a horse. (CLARA BOW)

Kevin Costner
6637 Kevin Costner has personality minus. (MADONNA)

Joan Crawford
6638 She's slept with every male star at MGM except Lassie. (BETTE DAVIS)

6639 The best time I ever had with Joan Crawford was when I pushed her down the stairs in *Whatever Happened to Baby Jane?* (BETTE DAVIS)

6640 There is not enough money in Hollywood to lure me into making another film with Joan Crawford. (STERLING HAYDEN)

Tom Cruise
6641 Little Nicole Kidman has always needed a shoulder to cry on, and she couldn't with Tom. He'd have had to stand on a box. (DAME EDNA EVERAGE)

Marion Davies
6642 She has two expressions — joy and indigestion. (DOROTHY PARKER)

Bette Davis
6643 Surely no one but a mother could have loved Bette Davis at the height of her career. (BRIAN AHERNE)

Doris Day
6644 I knew Doris Day before she was a virgin. (OSCAR LEVANT)

6645 She is as wholesome as a bowl of cornflakes and at least as sexy. (DWIGHT MACDONALD)

James Dean
6646 What I disliked was the Dean legend. He was a hero to the people who saw him only as a little waif, when actually he was a pudding of hatred. (ELIA KAZAN)

6647 Another dirty shirt-tail actor from New York. (HEDDA HOPPER)

Sandy Dennis
6648 She has made an acting style out of a postnasal drip. (PAULINE KAEL)

Bo Derek
6649 She is so stupid she returns bowling balls because they've got holes in them. (JOAN RIVERS)

Kirk Douglas
6650 Boastful, egotistical, resentful of criticism — if anyone dare give it. (SHEILA GRAHAM)

6651 Kirk would be the first to tell you that he's a difficult man. I would be the second. (BURT LANCASTER)

6652 I'm here to speak about his wit, his charm, his warmth, his talent . . . At last, a real acting job! (BURT LANCASTER, at a tribute to Douglas)

Frances Farmer
6653 The nicest thing I can say about Frances Farmer is that she is unbearable. (WILLIAM WYLER)

Farrah Fawcett
6654 She is uniquely suited to play a woman of limited intelligence. (HARRY and MICHAEL MEDVED)

Clark Gable
6655 His ears make him look like a taxi-cab with both doors open. (HOWARD HUGHES)

6656 He's the kind of guy who, if you say, "Hiya, Clark, how are you?", is stuck for an answer. (AVA GARDNER)

Zsa Zsa Gabor
6657 She has discovered the secret of perpetual middle age. (OSCAR LEVANT)

6658 Zsa Zsa Gabor is an expert house-keeper. Every time she gets divorced, she keeps the house. (HENNY YOUNGMAN)

Greta Garbo

6659 Making a film with Greta Garbo does not constitute an introduction. (ROBERT MONTGOMERY)

6660 Boiled down to essentials, she is a plain mortal girl with large feet. (HERBERT KRETZMER)

6661 Dry and draughty, like an abandoned temple. (TRUMAN CAPOTE)

Judy Garland

6662 Mother was the real-life Wicked Witch of the West. (LIZA MINNELLI)

Mel Gibson

6663 He seems to think he's Lee Marvin – except he's two feet shorter and about one third the talent (JOHN BOORMAN)

Sam Goldwyn

6664 The only man who could throw a seven with one dice. (HARPO MARX) .

Hugh Grant

6665 A self-important, boring, flash-in-the-pan Brit. (ROBERT DOWNEY JR.)

Melanie Griffith

6666 Very sweet but dumb – the lights are on but the dogs aren't barking. (JOAN RIVERS)

Jean Harlow

6667 The "t" is silent, as in Harlow. (MARGOT ASQUITH, irritated when Jean Harlow repeatedly pronounced the "t" in Margot)

Katharine Hepburn

6668 She ran the whole gamut of emotions from A to B. (DOROTHY PARKER, on Katharine Hepburn's performance in *The Lake*)

6669 A cross between Donald Duck and a Stradivarius. (ANON)

Charlton Heston

6670 Charlton Heston throws all his punches in the first ten minutes (three grimaces and two intonations] so that he has nothing left long before he stumbles to the end, four hours later, and has to react to the crucifixion. (He does make it clear,

I must admit, that he disapproves of it.) (DWIGHT MACDONALD's review of *Ben Hur*)

Dustin Hoffman

6671 My experience with him was an unhappy one. There seemed to be a malevolence in him, a determination to make other human beings unhappy. (DAVID PUTTNAM)

6672 Never argue with a man who is shorter than his Oscar. (LARRY GELBART)

Bob Hoskins

6673 Just a testicle with legs. (PAULINE KAEL)

Glenda Jackson

6674 In almost every play or film she inflicts her naked body on us which, considering its quality, is the supreme insult. (JOHN SIMON)

Val Kilmer

6675 There are two things I would never do — climb Mount Everest and work with Val Kilmer again. (JOHN FRANKENHEIMER)

Alan Ladd

6676 A small boy's idea of a tough guy. (RAYMOND CHANDLER)

Jerry Lewis

6677 This arrogant, sour, ceremonial, pious, chauvinistic egomaniac. (ELLIOTT GOULD)

Gina Lollobrigida

6678 Her personality is limited. She is good as a peasant but incapable of playing a lady. (SOPHIA LOREN)

Sophia Loren

6679 I do not talk about Sophia. I do not wish to make for her publicity. She has a talent, but it is not such a big talent. (GINA LOLLOBRIGIDA)

George Lucas

6680 He reminded me a little bit of Walt Disney's version of a mad scientist. (STEVEN SPIELBERG)

Steve McQueen

6681 A Steve McQueen performance just naturally lends itself to monotony. Steve doesn't bring much to the party. (ROBERT MITCHUM)

6682 His features resemble a fossilized wash rag. (ALAN BRIEN)

Madonna

6683 She's jumped right into the movie game . . . but I think people should learn to act first, you know what I mean? (ROSANNA ARQUETTE)

6684 *Who's That Girl* is a vehicle for material womanhood, but Madonna, harshly photographed, armed with a wiggle and a Minnie Mouse squawk, is coarse and charmless: a performer to be kept tightly reined. (SHEILA JOHNSTON)

6685 Who's that girl? Who cares? (ALAN FRANK)

Jayne Mansfield

6686 Dramatic art, in her opinion, is knowing how to fill a sweater. (BETTE DAVIS)

Dean Martin

6687 Martin's acting is so inept that even his impersonation of a lush seems unconvincing. (HARRY MEDVED)

Walter Matthau

6688 He looked like a half-melted rubber bulldog. (JOHN SIMON)

Victor Mature

6689 I never go to movies where the hero's tits are bigger than the heroine's. (GROUCHO MARX)

Louis B. Mayer

6690 The only reason so many people showed up was to make sure he was dead. (SAM GOLDWYN, after Mayer's funeral)

Marilyn Monroe

6691 It's like kissing Hitler. (TONY CURTIS)

6692 Next to her, Lucrezia Borgia was a pussy-cat. (DAVID HALL)

6693 She was good at playing abstract confusion in the same way that a midget Is good at being short. (CLIVE JAMES)

6694 She has no charm, delicacy, or taste. She's just an arrogant little tailtwitcher who's learned to throw sex in your face. (NUNNALLY JOHNSON)

6695 A vacuum with nipples. (OTTO PREMINGER)

6696 Directing her was like directing Lassie. You need 14 takes to get each one of them right. (OTTO PREMINGER)

6697 Breasts like granite and a brain like Swiss cheese. (BILLY WILDER)

Paul Newman
6698 He delivered his lines with the emotional fervour of a conductor announcing local stops. (*The New Yorker* review of *The Silver Chalice*)

Jack Nicholson
6699 A legend in his own lifetime and in his own mind. (JENNIFER LOPEZ)

Margaret O'Brien
6700 If this child had been born in the Middle Ages, she'd have been burned as a witch. (LIONEL BARRYMORE)

Maureen O'Hara
6701 She looks as though butter wouldn't melt in her mouth – or anywhere else for that matter. (ELSA LANCHESTER)

Gwyneth Paltrow
6702 She lives in rarefied air that's a little thin. It's like she's not getting quite enough oxygen. (SHARON STONE)

Otto Preminger
6703 I don't think he could direct his nephew to the bathroom. (DYAN CANNON)

6704 Martin Bormann in elevator shoes. (BILLY WILDER)

6705 I hear Otto Preminger's on holiday. In Auschwitz. (BILLY WILDER)

Robert Redford

6706 Nowadays, his skin looks like a child's sandpit after heavy rain. (LYNN BARBER)

Debbie Reynolds

6707 Debbie Reynolds was indeed the girl next door. But only if you lived next door to a self-centred, totally driven, insecure, untruthful phony. (EDDIE FISHER)

Ken Russell

6708 An arrogant, self-centred, petulant individual. I don't say this in any demeaning way. (BOB GUCCIONE)

Norma Shearer

6709 A face unclouded by thought. (LILLIAN HELLMAN)

Maggie Smith

6710 She's better on stage, from a distance. On a screen, close up, she makes you want to dive for cover. (ELSA LANCHESTER)

Steven Spielberg

6711 Spielberg isn't a film-maker, he's a confectioner. (ALEX COX)

Sylvester Stallone

6712 He is to acting what Liberace was to pumping iron. (REX REED)

6713 His big asset: a face that would look well upon a three-toed sloth. (RUSSELL DAVIES)

Oliver Stone

6714 Oliver Stone, I don't like. But then nobody likes Oliver. He's just an aggressive man like me. But he hasn't my sense of humour. (ALAN PARKER)

Sharon Stone

6715 It's a new low for actresses when you have to wonder what's between her ears instead of her legs. (KATHARINE HEPBURN)

Barbra Streisand

6716 I have more talent in my smallest fart than you have in your entire body. (WALTER MATTHAU to Streisand, on the set of *Hello Dolly*)

6717 I had no disagreement with Barbra Streisand. I was merely exasperated at her tendency to be a complete megalomaniac. (WALTER MATTHAU)

6718 I'd love to work with Barbra Streisand again. In something appropriate. Perhaps *Macbeth*. (WALTER MATTHAU)

6719 Filming with Streisand is an experience which may have cured me of movies. (KRIS KRISTOFFERSON)

6720 She looks like the masculine Bride of Frankenstein. (MR BLACKWELL)

Elizabeth Taylor
6721 I knew Elizabeth Taylor when she didn't know where her next husband was coming from. (ANNE BAXTER)

6722 She had the face of an angel and the morals of a truck driver. (EDDIE FISHER)

6723 Elizabeth Taylor's so fat, she puts mayonnaise on an aspirin. (JOAN RIVERS)

Shirley Temple
6724 Shirley Temple had charisma as a child. But it cleared up as an adult. (TOTIE FIELDS)

Uma Thurman
6725 She looks like a giraffe that has wandered off the Nature Reserve and panicked. (ANON)

Lana Turner
6726 She's a nice girl, but it's like sitting in a room with a beautiful vase. (JUDY GARLAND)

6727 She is not even an actress . . . only a trollop. (GLORIA SWANSON)

Jack L. Warner
6728 He never bore a grudge against anyone he wronged. (SIMONE SIGNORET)

Raquel Welch
6729 One of the few actresses in Hollywood history who looks more animated in still photographs than she does on the screen. (MICHAEL MEDVED)

Mae West

6730 She did her own thing to the detriment of everyone around her. (CARY GRANT)

6731 A plumber's idea of Cleopatra. (W.C. FIELDS)

Esther Williams

6732 Wet she's a star, dry she ain't. (FANNY BRICE)

Michael Winner

6733 To say that Michael Winner is his own worst enemy is to provoke a ragged chorus from odd corners of the film industry of "Not while I'm alive!" (BARRY NORMAN)

Comedy

Desi Arnaz

6734 The Cuban heel. (WILLIAM FRAWLEY)

Roseanne Barr

6735 She went on *Saturday Night Live* and said I had a three-inch penis. Well, even a 747 looks small if it's landing in the Grand Canyon. (TOM ARNOLD)

Jack Benny

6736 He couldn't ad-lib a belch after a goulash. (FRED ALLEN)

Milton Berle

6737 The Thief of Bad Gags. (WALTER WINCHELL)

6738 He's been on TV for years and I finally figured out the reason for his success — he never improved. (STEVE ALLEN)

Cheech and Chong

6739 If dope smoking doesn't damage your brain, how come so many teenyboppers think Cheech and Chong are funny? (TONY HENDRA)

John Cleese

6740 He emits an air of overwhelming vanity combined with some unspecified nastiness, like a black widow spider in heat. But nobody seems to notice. (ROGER GELLERT)

Phyllis Diller

6741 She's so ancient she's just a carcass with a mouth. (RUBY WAX)

Bob Hope

6742 Bob Hope is still about as funny as he ever was. I just never thought he was that funny in the first place. (CHEVY CHASE)

6743 Hope is not a comedian. He just translates what others write for him. (GROUCHO MARX)

Groucho Marx

6744 He had the compassion of an icicle and the generosity of a pawnbroker. (S.J. PERELMAN)

6745 A male chauvinist piglet. (BETTY FRIEDAN)

Frank Skinner

6746 The amount of money he's earned for not making me laugh is staggering. (WILL SELF)

Jimmy Tarbuck

6747 Jimmy Tarbuck doesn't tell gags – he just refreshes your memory. (BERNARD MANNING)

Robin Williams

6748 A fellow with the inventiveness of Albert Einstein but with the attention span of Daffy Duck. (TOM SHALES)

Henny Youngman

6749 He's beautiful. He'll tell 30 jokes and only get laughs with four of them. That kind of heroism is exquisite to me. (JACKIE GLEASON)

Literature

Steve Allen

6750 When I can't sleep, I read a book by Steve Allen. (OSCAR LEVANT)

Jeffrey Archer

6751 Is there no beginning to your talents? (TV chat show host CLIVE ANDERSON)

6752 Archer has issued a strenuous denial — as good as a signed confession, really. (DES LYNAM)

Margot Asquith
6753 The affair between Margot Asquith and Margot Asquith will live as one of the prettiest love stories in all literature. (DOROTHY PARKER reviewing Asquith's four-volume autobiography)

Jane Austen
6754 It seems a great pity they allowed Jane Austen to die a natural death. (MARK TWAIN)

Robert Benchley
6755 Has a style that is weak and lies down frequently to rest. (MAX EASTMAN)

Truman Capote
6756 Truman Capote has made lying an art. A minor art. (GORE VIDAL)

Thomas Carlyle
6757 It was very good of God to let Carlyle and Mrs Carlyle marry one another and so make only two people miserable instead of four. (SAMUEL BUTLER)

Agatha Christie
6758 To say Agatha's characters are cardboard cut-outs is an insult to cardboard. (RUTH RENDELL)

Joseph Conrad
6759 What is Conrad but the wreck of Stevenson floating about in the slip-slop of Henry James? (GEORGE MOORE)

Charles Dickens
6760 One must have a heart of stone to read the death of Little Nell without laughing. (OSCAR WILDE)

John Dryden
6761 His imagination resembles the wings of an ostrich. (THOMAS BABINGTON MACAULAY)

Ralph Waldo Emerson
6762 Waldo is one of those people who would be enormously improved by death. (SAKI (H.H. MUNRO))

William Faulkner

6763 Poor Faulkner. Does he really think big emotions come from big words? (ERNEST HEMINGWAY)

Edward Gibbon

6764 Gibbon's style is detestable; but it is not the worst thing about him. (SAMUEL TAYLOR COLERIDGE)

Andrew Greeley

6765 Enough to give trash a bad name. (*The Chicago Sun-Times*, 1982 review of Andrew Greeley's *The Cardinal Sins*)

Thomas Hardy

6766 An abortion of George Sand. (GEORGE MOORE)

Frank Harris

6767 Frank Harris is invited to all of the great houses in England – once. (OSCAR WILDE)

Ernest Hemingway

6768 Always willing to lend a helping hand to the one above him. (F. SCOTT FITZGERALD)

6769 He has never been known to use a word that might send the reader to a dictionary. (WILLIAM FAULKNER)

6770 Remarks are not literature. (GERTRUDE STEIN)

Henry James

6771 Henry James had a mind so fine that no idea could violate it. (T.S. ELIOT)

6772 Mr Henry James writes fiction as if it were a painful duty. (OSCAR WILDE)

6773 Once you've put one of his books down, you simply can't pick it up again. (MARK TWAIN)

Ben Jonson

6774 Reading him is like wading through glue. (ALFRED, LORD TENNYSON)

James Joyce

6775 The work of a queasy undergraduate scratching his pimples. (VIRGINIA WOOLF's view of *Ulysses*)

Jack Kerouac

6776 That's not writing, that's typing. (TRUMAN CAPOTE's review of Jack Kerouac's *On the Road*)

Katherine Mansfield

6777 She stinks like a civet cat that has taken to street walking. (VIRGINIA WOOLF)

George Meredith

6778 As a writer, he has mastered everything except language. (OSCAR WILDE)

S. J. Perelman

6779 From the moment I picked up your book until I laid it down I was convulsed with laughter. Some day I intend reading it. (GROUCHO MARX on Perelman's first book, *Dawn Ginsbergh's Revenge*)

6780 He is just as unassuming, as comfortable to be with as an old glove — and just about as interesting. (GROUCHO MARX)

Alexander Pope

6781 There are two ways of disliking poetry: one way is to dislike it, the other is to read Pope. (OSCAR WILDE)

Ezra Pound

6782 To me Pound remains the exquisite showman minus the show. (BEN HECHT)

George Bernard Shaw

6783 It is his life work to announce the obvious in terms of the scandalous. (H.L. MENCKEN)

Dame Edith Sitwell

6784 She is genuinely bogus. (CHRISTOPHER HASSALL)

6785 In full regalia, she looked like Lyndon B. Johnson dressed up like Elizabeth I. (*Time* magazine)

Gertrude Stein

6786 Miss Stein was a past master in making nothing happen very slowly. (CLIFTON FADIMAN)

6787 I found nothing really wrong with this autobiography except poor choice of subject. (CLIFTON FADIMAN)

Jacqueline Susann

6788 She looks like a truck driver in drag. (TRUMAN CAPOTE)

Evelyn Waugh

6789 His style has the desperate jauntiness of an orchestra fiddling away for dear life on a sinking ship. (EDMUND WILSON)

William Wordsworth

6790 A bell with a wooden tongue. (RALPH WALDO EMERSON)

Military

General Alexander Haig

6791 One thing I don't want around me is an intellectual military. I don't have to worry about you on that score. (HENRY KISSINGER)

Earl Douglas Haig

6792 Haig was devoid of the gift of intelligible and coherent expression. (DAVID LLOYD GEORGE)

Saddam Hussein

6793 He's not a tactician. He's not a general. He's not a soldier. Other than that, he's a great military man. (GENERAL H. NORMAN SCHWARTZKOPF)

Marshal Jean-Jacques Joffre

6794 The only time he ever put up a fight in his life was when we asked him for his resignation. (GEORGES CLEMENCEAU)

General Douglas MacArthur

6795 MacArthur is the type of man who thinks that when he gets to heaven, God will step down from the great white throne and bow him into His vacated seat. (HAROLD ICKES)

6796 I fired him because he wouldn't respect the authority of the President. I didn't fire him because he was a dumb son-of-a-bitch, although he was, but that's not against the law for generals. If it was, half to three-quarters of them would be in jail. (HARRY S. TRUMAN)

General George B. McClellan
6797 My Dear McClellan: If you don't want to use the army I should like to borrow it for a while. (ABRAHAM LINCOLN in a letter to his inactive Civil War General)

Viscount Montgomery
6798 In defeat unbeatable; in victory unbearable. (WINSTON CHURCHILL)

General George S. Patton Jr
6799 Patton was an acolyte to Mars. (COLONEL J. FARLEY)

General Philip H. Sheridan
6800 The general is a stumpy, quadrangular little man, with a forehead of no promise and hair so short that it looks like a coat of black paint. (GEORGE STRONG)

Duke of Wellington
6801 Waterloo was a battle of the first rank won by a captain of the second. (VICTOR HUGO)

Music
AC/DC
6802 Some hints on how to enjoy this LP. Give your brain the evening off. (Smash Hits review of *Blow Up Your Video*)

Aerosmith
6803 Aerosmith were inducted into the Rock and Roll Hall of Fame for their uncanny ability to do the same song seven times with no one noticing. (CRAIG KILBORN)

Christina Aguilera
6804 I've seen drag queens who look better. (KELLY OSBOURNE)

Johann Sebastian Bach
6805 All Bach's last movements are like the running of a sewing machine. (ARNOLD BAX)

Ludwig van Beethoven

6806 Beethoven's last quartets were written by a deaf man and should only be listened to by a deaf man. (SIR THOMAS BEECHAM)

Hector Berlioz

6807 Berlioz composes by splashing his pen over the manuscript and leaving the issue to chance. (FREDERIC CHOPIN)

Chuck Berry

6808 I think for the lifespan he's lasted, Chuck Berry's productivity has been nil, more or less. (ELTON JOHN)

6809 I love his work but I couldn't warm to him even if I was cremated next to him. (KEITH RICHARDS)

Cilla Black

6810 Her voice is like labour pains set to music. (BOB MONKHOUSE)

Jovi Jon Bon

6811 Bon Jovi sounds like bad fourth-generation metal, a smudgy Xerox of Quiet Riot. (JIMMY GUTERMAN)

Boy George

6812 Boy George is all England needs – another queen who can't dress. (JOAN RIVERS)

Johannes Brahms

6813 It annoys me that this self-inflated mediocrity is hailed as a genius. What a giftless bastard! (PYOTR TCHAIKOVSKY)

Kate Bush

6814 Sounds like the consequences of mating Patti Smith with a Hoover. (ANON)

Maria Callas

6815 When Callas carried a grudge, she planted it, nursed it, fostered it, watered it, and watched it grow to sequoia size. (HAROLD C. SCHONBERG)

Frederic Chopin

6816 A composer for the right hand. (RICHARD WAGNER)

Eric Clapton

6817 If I go round to someone's house and there's an Eric Clapton record, I just walk out. (JOHN MOSS)

Leonard Cohen

6818 He gives you the feeling that your dog just died. (*Q* magazine)

Claude Debussy

6819 Debussy played the piano with the lid down. (ROBERT BRESSON)

Frederick Delius

6820 The musical equivalent of blancmange. (BERNARD LEVIN)

Celine Dion

6821 Celine Dion's in a 4,000-seat auditorium built specially to handle her voice. But it doesn't work. I could still hear her. (LEWIS BLACK)

Bob Dylan

6822 I always thought he sounded just like Yogi Bear. (MICK RONSON)

Art Garfunkel

6823 He makes Paul Simon look like LL Cool J. (IAN GITTINS)

Macy Gray

6824 Four of the fittest women in the world, and Macy Gray. (satirist ALI G introducing the contenders for Best International Female (Britney Spears, Whitney Houston, Jennifer Lopez, Mary J. Blige and Macy Gray) at the Brit Awards 2000)

Geri Halliwell

6825 She can't sing, she can't dance, and by the looks of things she can't hold down a meal. (GINA YASHERE)

Buddy Holly

6826 The biggest no-talent I ever worked with. (PAUL COHEN)

Billy Idol

6827 The Perry Como of Punk. (JOHNNY ROTTEN)

Michael Jackson

6828 His album was only called 'Bad' because there wasn't enough room on the sleeve for "Pathetic". (PRINCE)

6829 With his womanly voice, stark white skin and Medusa hair, his gash of red lipstick, heavy eyeliner, almost non-existent nose and lopsided face, Michael Jackson was making this appearance in order to scotch all rumours that he is not quite normal. (CRAIG BROWN)

Mick Jagger

6830 I think Mick Jagger would be astounded and amazed if he realized to how many people he is not a sex symbol. (ANGIE BOWIE)

6831 He moves like a parody between a majorette girl and Fred Astaire. (TRUMAN CAPOTE)

6832 This man has got childbearing lips. (JOAN RIVERS)

Elton John

6833 His writing is limited to songs for dead blondes. (KEITH RICHARDS)

Janis Joplin

6834 I couldn't stand Janis Joplin's voice. She was just a screaming little loudmouthed chick. (ARTHUR LEE)

Frankie Laine

6835 His approach to the microphone is that of an accused man pleading with a hostile jury. (KENNETH TYNAN)

Jennifer Lopez

6836 I'd rather be on stage with a pig. (MARIAH CAREY)

Madonna

6837 She is so hairy. When she lifted up her arm, I thought it was Tina Turner in her arm-pit. (JOAN RIVERS)

6838 She is closer to organized prostitution than anything else. (MORRISSEY)

6839 She sings like Mickey Mouse on helium. (ANON)

Yoko Ono

6840 Her voice sounded like an eagle being goosed. (RALPH NOVAK)

6841 If I found her floating in my pool, I'd punish my dog. (JOAN RIVERS)

Cliff Osmond

6842 He has Van Gogh's ear for music. (BILLY WILDER, after heavyweight American comedy actor Cliff Osmond had auditioned for a singing role)

Marie Osmond

6843 She is so pure even Moses couldn't part her knees. (JOAN RIVERS)

Cole Porter

6844 He sang like a hinge. (ETHEL MERMAN)

Elvis Presley

6845 Elvis was pretty far gone by the first time I saw him. It made sense when women threw their bras at him. Obviously he needed them. (TOM KENNY)

Prince

6846 Bambi with testosterone. (*ENTERTAINMENT WEEKLY*)

Helen Reddy

6847 She ought to be arrested for loitering in front of an orchestra. (BETTE MIDLER)

Keith Richards

6848 Like a monkey with arthritis, trying to go on stage and look young. (ELTON JOHN)

Lionel Richie

6849 He's got a chin like an ironing board. (PETE BURNS)

Diana Ross

6850 She is a piece of liquorice in shoes. She walks into a pool hall and they chalk her head. (JOAN RIVERS)

Arnold Schoenberg

6851 He would be better to shovel snow instead of scribbling on music paper. (RICHARD STRAUSS)

Frank Sinatra

6852 He's the kind of guy that, when he dies, he's going to heaven and give God a bad time for making him bald. (MARLON BRANDO)

Grace Slick

6853 She's like somebody's mum who'd a few too many drinks at a cocktail party. (NICK LOWE)

Ringo Starr

6854 Ringo wasn't even the best drummer in the Beatles. (JOHN LENNON)

Rod Stewart

6855 He was so mean, it hurt him to go to the bathroom. (BRITT EKLAND)

6856 Rod Stewart has an attractive voice and a highly unattractive bottom. He now spends more time wagging the latter than exercising the former. (CLIVE JAMES)

Sting

6857 Somebody should clip Sting around the head and tell him to stop singing in that ridiculous Jamaican accent. (ELVIS COSTELLO)

Richard Strauss

6858 Such an astounding lack of talent was never before united to such pretentiousness. (PYOTR TCHAIKOVSKY)

6859 Whatever I may once have learned from him, I am thankful to say I misunderstood. (ARNOLD SCHOENBERG)

Igor Stravinsky

6860 Bach on the wrong notes. (SERGEY PROKOFIEV)

Shirley Temple

6861 I can't hear "On The Good Ship Lollipop" without tasting vomit at the back of my throat. (PAUL MERTON)

Arturo Toscanini

6862 A glorified bandmaster! (SIR THOMAS BEECHAM)

Tina Turner

6863 You mean you can actually spend 70,000 dollars at Woolworth's? (BOB KRASNOW, after seeing inside Tina Turner's house)

Richard Wagner

6864 Wagner's music is better than it sounds. (MARK TWAIN)

6865 A composer who had some wonderful moments but awful quarter hours. (GIOACCHINO ROSSINI)

6866 One can't judge Wagner's opera *Lohengrin* after a first hearing, and I certainly don't intend hearing it a second time. (GIOACCHINO ROSSINI)

6867 I like Wagner's music better than anybody's. It is so loud that one can talk the whole time without people hearing what one says. (OSCAR WILDE)

6868 I love Wagner, but the music I prefer is that of a cat hung up by its tail outside a window and trying to stick to the panes of glass with its claws. (CHARLES BAUDELAIRE)

Robbie Williams

6869 A fat dancer from Take That. (NOEL GALLAGHER)

Frank Zappa

6870 Frank Zappa couldn't write a decent song if you gave him a million and a year on an island in Greece. (LOU REED)

Politics

Spiro T. Agnew

6871 Agnew reminds me of the kind of guy who would make a crank call to the Russians on the hot line. (DICK GREGORY)

Chester A. Allen

6872 A nonentity in side whiskers. (WOODROW WILSON)

Lady Astor

6873 Lady Astor to Winston Churchill: "Winston, if I were married to you, I'd put poison in your coffee."
Churchill: "Nancy, if you were my wife, I'd drink it."

Clement Attlee

6874 He is a sheep in sheep's clothing. (WINSTON CHURCHILL's view of the mild-mannered English prime minister)

6875 A modest little man with much to be modest about. (WINSTON CHURCHILL)

6876 He reminds me of nothing so much as a dead fish before it has time to stiffen. (GEORGE ORWELL)

Stanley Baldwin

6877 Baldwin occasionally stumbles over the truth, but he always hastily picks himself up and hurries on as if nothing had happened. (WINSTON CHURCHILL)

James G. Blaine

6878 No man in our annals has filled so large a space and left it so empty. (CHARLES E. RUSSELL)

6879 Wallowing in corruption like a rhinoceros in an African pool. (E.L. GODKIN)

Tony Blair

6880 The great prime ministers, those who leave a mark on history, are those who make the political weather and not those who skilfully avoid its storms and shelter from its downpours. (LORD JENKINS)

6881 He's done more U-turns than a dodgy plumber. (IAIN DUNCAN SMITH)

6882 They call him Teflon Tony because nothing sticks to him. (WILL SELF)

6883 Tony Blair is the ultimate air guitarist of modern political rhetoric. (WILL SELF)

Bessie Braddock

6884 The Rt Hon Bessie Braddock MP, to Winston Churchill: "Winston, you're drunk."
    Churchill: "And madam, you're ugly. Tomorrow morning, however, I shall be sober."

Gordon Brown

6885 When he leaves a room the lights go on. (ANON)

William F. Buckley Jr.

6886 Looks and sounds not unlike Hitler, but without the charm. (GORE VIDAL)

George Bush

6887 George Bush doesn't have the manhood to apologize. (WALTER MONDALE)
Bush's reply: On the manhood thing, I'll put mine up against his any time.

6888 If ignorance ever gets to $40 a barrel, I want drilling rights on that man's head. (JIM HIGHTOWER)

George W. Bush

6889 Bush is like if Reagan and Quayle had a kid. (WILL DURST)

6890 This is a guy who could not find oil in Texas. (AL FRANKEN)

6891 Peace, prosperity and a president smarter than his dog – already the Clinton years seem a golden age by comparison. (*ARKANSAS TIMES*)

6892 Bush is like McDonald's: pre-packaged, filled with empty calories and controlled by corporate interests. (PAUL BEGALA)

6893 Sometimes when you look in his eyes you get the feeling that someone else is driving. (DAVID LETTERMAN)

6894 George W. Bush is like a bad comic working the crowd. (MARTIN SHEEN)

6895 Bush has surrounded himself with smart people the way a hole surrounds itself with a doughnut. (DENNIS MILLER)

6896 Apparently Bush likes working out every day because it "clears his mind". Sometimes it works a little too well. (JAY LENO)

6897 He's as purposeful as a wind-up toy boat with a bent rudder doing circular putt-putts in the bathtub. (NICHOLAS VON HOFFMAN)

6898 What's his accomplishment? That he's no longer an obnoxious drunk? (RON REAGAN)

Alastair Campbell

6899 Being out of power is a shock. Temporarily at least, he's grown too small for his boots. (ANDREW MARR)

Jimmy Carter

6900 Sometimes when I look at all my children, I say to myself, "Lillian, you should have stayed a virgin." (LILLIAN CARTER)

6901 Jimmy Carter needs Billy like Van Gogh needs stereo. (JOHNNY CARSON, on the President's brother Billy)

6902 He would cut the cards if he was playing poker with his mother. (ANON)

6903 He smiles like a Christian with four aces. (BILL MOYERS)

6904 If you're in the peanut business, you learn to think small. (EUGENE MCCARTHY)

Neville Chamberlain

6905 Listening to a speech by Chamberlain is like paying a visit to Woolworth's: everything in its place and nothing above sixpence. (WINSTON CHURCHILL)

Dick Cheney

6906 He adds one thing to the Republican ticket: adult supervision. (BILL MAHER)

Randolph Churchill

6907 A typical triumph of modern science to find the only part of Randolph that was not malignant and remove it. (EVELYN WAUGH, after Churchill had a lung removed and it proved to be benign]

Sir Winston Churchill

6908 He would kill his own mother just so that he could use her skin to make a drum to beat his own praises. (DAVID LLOYD GEORGE)

6909 The mediocrity of his thinking is concealed by the majesty of his language. (ANEURIN BEVAN)

Bill Clinton

6910 The prince of sleaze. (JERRY BROWN)

6911 I have never seen . . . so slippery, so disgusting a candidate. (NAT HENTOFF)

6912 A hard dog to keep on the porch. (HILLARY CLINTON)

6913 Bill Clinton is the Willy Loman of Generation X, a travelling salesman who has the loyalty of a lizard with his tail broken off and the midnight tastes of a man who'd double date with the Rev. Jimmy Swaggart. (HUNTER S. THOMPSON)

Hillary Clinton
6914 A raisin-eyed, carrot-nosed, twig-armed, straw-stuffed mannequin trundled on a go-kart by the mentally bereft powerbrokers of the Democratic Party. (CAMILLE PAGLIA)

Calvin Coolidge
6915 I do wish he did not look as if he had been weaned on a pickle. (ALICE ROOSEVELT LONGWORTH)

6916 Calvin Coolidge's perpetual expression was of smelling something burning on the stove. (SHERWIN L. COOK)

6917 Calvin Coolidge didn't say much, and when he did he didn't say much. (WILL ROGERS)

6918 The greatest man who ever came out of Plymouth Corner, Vermont. (CLARENCE DARROW)

6919 How can they tell? (DOROTHY PARKER, learning that the ineffective President Coolidge had died)

Sir Stafford Cripps
6920 Sir Stafford has a brilliant mind until it is made up. (MARGOT ASQUITH)

Edwina Currie
6921 When she goes to the dentist, he's the one who needs the anaesthetic. (FRANK DOBSON)

Thomas E. Dewey
6922 You really have to get to know Dewey to dislike him. (ROBERT A. TAFT)

Benjamin Disraeli
6923 A self-made man who worships his creator. (JOHN BRIGHT)

Bob Dole
6924 When he does smile, he looks as if he's just evicted a widow. (MIKE ROYKO)

Michael Dukakis

6925 He's the stealth candidate . . . His campaign jets from place to place, but no issues show up on the radar screen. (GEORGE BUSH)

John Foster Dulles

6926 Foster Dulles is the only case I know of a bull who carries a china shop with him. (WINSTON CHURCHILL)

Iain Duncan Smith

6927 He looks like a Kinder egg with no toy inside. (SEAN LOCK)

Anthony Eden

6928 He is not only a bore, but he bores for England. (MALCOLM MUGGERIDGE)

Dwight D. Eisenhower

6929 As an intellectual, he bestowed upon the games of golf and bridge all the enthusiasm and perseverance that he withheld from his books and ideas. (EMMET JOHN HUGHES)

6930 The General has dedicated himself so many times, he must feel like the cornerstone of a public building. (ADLAI STEVENSON)

6931 Why, this fellow don't know any more about politics than a pig knows about Sunday. (HARRY S. TRUMAN)

6932 The only living unknown soldier. (ROBERT S. KERR)

Millard Fillmore

6933 At a time when we needed a strong man, what we got was a man who swayed with the slightest breeze. (HARRY S. TRUMAN)

Michael Foot

6934 A kind of walking obituary for the Labour Party. (CHRIS PATTEN)

Gerald Ford

6935 Richard Nixon impeached himself. He gave us Gerald Ford as his revenge. (BELLA ABZUG)

6936 He looks and talks like he just fell off Edgar Bergen's lap. (DAVID STEINBERG)

6937 He looks like the guy in the science fiction movie who is first to see "the Creature". (DAVID FRYE)

6938 Gerald Ford was unknown throughout America. Now he's unknown throughout the world. (ANON)

6939 Gerry Ford is so dumb that he can't fart and chew gum at the same time. (LYNDON B. JOHNSON)

6940 Gerry Ford is a nice guy, but he played too much football with his helmet off. (LYNDON B. JOHNSON)

6941 In the Bob Hope Golf Classic the participation of President Gerald Ford was more than enough to remind you that the nuclear button was at one stage at the disposal of a man who might have either pressed it by mistake or else pressed it deliberately to obtain room service. (CLIVE JAMES)

Charles de Gaulle
6942 He is like a female llama surprised in her bath. (WINSTON CHURCHILL)

William Ewart Gladstone
6943 A misfortune is if Gladstone fell into the Thames; a calamity would be if someone pulled him out. (BENJAMIN DISRAELI)

Al Gore
6944 Al Gore turned down a chance to be on *The Simpsons*. He explained, "I've never been animated and I'm not going to start now." (CONAN O'BRIEN)

Horace Greeley
6945 A self-made man who worships his creator. (HENRY CLAPP)

Thomas Jefferson Green
6946 He has all the characteristics of a dog except loyalty. (SAM HOUSTON)

William Hague
6947 They have elected a foetus as Conservative leader. I bet there's a lot of Tory MPs who wish they hadn't voted against abortion now. (TONY BANKS)

Warren G. Harding
6948 He has a bungalow mind. (WOODROW WILSON)

Gary Hart
6949 Hart is Kennedy typed on the eighth carbon. (LANCE MORROW)

Edward Heath
6950 A shiver looking for a spine to run up. (HAROLD WILSON)

Adolf Hitler
6951 He is inconsequent and voluble, ill-poised, insecure. He is the very prototype of the Little Man. (DOROTHY THOMPSON)

J. Edgar Hoover
6952 You should trust him as much as you would a rattlesnake with a silencer on its rattle. (DEAN ACHESON)

John Howard
6953 He is the greatest job and investment destroyer since the bubonic plague. (PAUL KEATING)

Michael Howard
6954 He has something of the night in him. (ANN WIDDECOMBE)

Sir Geoffrey Howe
6955 Being attacked in the House by him is like being savaged by a dead sheep. (DENIS HEALEY)

Hubert Humphrey
6956 He talks so fast that listening to him is like trying to read *Playboy* magazine with your wife turning the pages. (BARRY GOLDWATER)

Andrew Jackson
6957 A barbarian who could not write a sentence of grammar and could hardly spell his own name. (JOHN QUINCY ADAMS)

Thomas Jefferson
6958 A slur upon the moral government of the world. (JOHN QUINCY ADAMS)

Lyndon B. Johnson
6959 A man of his most recent word. (WILLIAM F. BUCKLEY JR)

John F. Kennedy

6960 The enviably attractive nephew who sings an Irish ballad for the company and then winsomely disappears before the table-clearing and dishwashing begin. (LYNDON B. JOHNSON)

Henry Kissinger

6961 When Kissinger can get the Nobel Peace Prize, what is there left for satire? (TOM LEHRER)

Fiorello La Guardia

6962 Anyone who extends to him the right hand of fellowship is in danger of losing a couple of fingers. (ALVA JOHNSON)

Jean Lesage

6963 The only person I know who can strut sitting down. (JOHN DIEFENBAKER)

Abraham Lincoln

6964 A first-rate second-rate man. (WENDELL PHILLIPS)

6965 Nothing more than a well-meaning baboon. (GENERAL GEORGE MCCLELLAN)

6966 The Illinois Baboon. (ANON)

Edward Livingstone

6967 He was a man of splendid abilities but utterly corrupt. Like rotten mackerel by moonlight, he shines and stinks. (JOHN RANDOLPH)

Ken Livingstone

6968 Ken Livingstone suffers from the politician's most debilitating disease: the need to see his picture in the papers every day. (LORD HATTERSLEY)

Joseph McCarthy

6969 Joseph McCarthy is the only major politician in the country who can be labelled "liar" without fear of libel. (JOSEPH ALSOP)

John Major

6970 He makes George Bush seem like a personality. (JACKIE MASON)

David Mellor

6971 The last woman to run her fingers through his hair was the nit nurse. (LINDA SMITH)

Walter Mondale

6972 He has all the charisma of a speed bump. (WILL DURST)

Richard Nixon

6973 Richard Nixon means never having to say you're sorry. (WILFRID SHEED)

6974 Would you buy a second-hand car from this man? (MORT SAHL)

6975 Nixon's motto was, "If two wrongs don't make a right, try three." (NORMAN COUSINS)

6976 Avoid all needle drugs. The only dope worth shooting is Richard Nixon. (ABBIE HOFFMAN)

6977 If he had an affair while in office, I misjudged him. I thought he was just doing that to the rest of the country. (JOHN GAVIN)

6978 He told us he was going to take crime off the streets. He did. He took it into the White House. (RALPH ABERNATHY)

6979 History buffs probably noted the reunion at a Washington party a few weeks ago of three ex-presidents: Carter, Ford and Nixon – See No Evil, Hear No Evil, and Evil. (SENATOR BOB DOLE)

6980 Nixon is the kind of politician who would cut down a redwood tree, then mount its stump for a speech on conservation. (ADLAI STEVENSON)

6981 Where is Lee Harvey Oswald now that his country needs him? (ANON)

Sir Robert Peel

6982 The Right Honourable Gentleman's smile is like the silver fittings on a coffin. (BENJAMIN DISRAELI)

Ross Perot

6983 All hawk and no spit. (MOLLY IVINS)

John Prescott

6984 He looks like a terrifying mixture of Hannibal Lecter and Terry Scott. (GYLES BRANDRETH)

Nancy Reagan

6985 She has agreed to be the world's first artificial heart donor. (ANDREA C. MICHAELS)

Ronald Reagan

6986 A triumph of the embalmer's art. (GORE VIDAL)

6987 Reagan is proof that there is life after death. (MORT SAHL)

6988 The battle for the mind of Ronald Reagan was like trench warfare in World War One: never have so many fought so hard for such barren terrain. (PEGGY NOONAN)

6989 We've got the kind of President who thinks arms control means some kind of deodorant. (PAT SCHROEDER)

6990 You could walk through Ronald Reagan's deepest thoughts and not get your ankles wet. (ANON)

6991 I believe that Ronald Reagan can make this country what it once was – an Arctic region covered with ice. (STEVE MARTIN)

6992 Ronald Reagan has two books on economics, but he hasn't finished colouring the first one yet. (ANON)

6993 You've got to be careful quoting Ronald Reagan because when you quote him accurately it's called mud-slinging. (WALTER MONDALE)

6994 Satire is alive and well and living in the White House. (ROBIN WILLIAMS)

Cecil Rhodes

6995 I admire him, I frankly confess it; and when his time comes I shall buy a piece of the rope for a keepsake. (MARK TWAIN)

Franklin D. Roosevelt

6996 He had every quality that morons esteem in their heroes. He was the first American to reach the real depths of vulgar stupidity. (H.L. MENCKEN)

6997 If he became convinced tomorrow that coming out for cannibalism would get him the votes he so sorely needs, he would begin fattening a missionary in the White House backyard come Wednesday. (H.L. MENCKEN)

6998 Thomas Jefferson founded the Democratic Party; Franklin Roosevelt dumb-founded it. (DEWEY SHORT)

Theodore Roosevelt

6999 His idea of getting hold of the right end of the stick is to snatch it from the hands of somebody who is using it effectively, and to hit him over the head with it. (GEORGE BERNARD SHAW)

7000 An old maid with testosterone poisoning. (PATRICIA O'TOOLE)

Donald Rumsfeld

7001 The most hated man in the Bush Administration against some pretty hot competition. (MAX HASTINGS)

Lord John Russell

7002 If a traveller were informed that such a man was leader of the House of Commons, he may well begin to comprehend how the Egyptians worshipped an insect. (BENJAMIN DISRAELI)

Earl of Sandwich

7003 Earl of Sandwich: "I do not know whether you will die on the gallows or of the pox."

John Wilkes: "My Lord, that will depend on whether I embrace your principles or your mistress."

Arnold Schwarzenegger

7004 In his bodybuilding days, he was known as the Austrian Oak. Then he started acting and was known as . . . the Austrian Oak. (JACK DEE)

7005 He has acted in plenty of movies but spoken less dialogue than any actor except maybe Lassie. (ROBIN WILLIAMS)

7006 (on his election as Governor of California) It's a triumph of grope over experience. (BORIS JOHNSON)

Margaret Thatcher

7007 She is democratic enough to talk down to anyone. (AUSTIN MITCHELL)

7008 She cannot see an institution without hitting it with her handbag. (JULIAN CRITCHLEY)

7009 I wouldn't say she is open-minded on the Middle East, so much as empty headed. She probably thinks Sinai is the plural of sinus. (JONATHAN AITKEN)

7010 Attila the Hen. (ANON)

Pierre Trudeau
7011 In Pierre Elliott Trudeau, Canada has at last produced a political leader worthy of assassination. (IRVING LAYTON)

Harry S. Truman
7012 Harry Truman proves that old adage that any man can become President of the United States. (NORMAN THOMAS)

Harold Wilson
7013 He is going round the country stirring up apathy. (WILLIAM WHITELAW)

Woodrow Wilson
7014 I feel certain that he would not recognize a generous impulse if he met it on the street. (WILLIAM HOWARD TAFT)

7015 Mr Wilson's mind will be closed all day Sunday. (GEORGE S. KAUFMAN)

Royalty

Anne The Princess Royal
7016 Such an active lass. So outdoorsy. She loves nature in spite of what it did to her. (BETTE MIDLER)

Queen Anne
7017 Anne when in good humour was meekly stupid, and when in bad humour was sulkily stupid. (THOMAS MACAULEY)

Camilla Parker Bowles, Duchess of Cornwall
7018 Camilla Parker Bowles is so ugly she has to frisk herself at airports. (JOAN RIVERS)

Prince Charles
7019 The idea of Prince Charles conversing with vegetables is not quite so amusing when you remember that he's had plenty of practice chatting to members of his own family. (JACI STEPHEN)

King Edward VII
7020 Bertie seemed to display a deep-seated repugnance to every form of mental exertion. (LYTTON STRACHEY)

King Edward VIII
7021 He had hidden shallows. (CLIVE JAMES)

Queen Elizabeth I
7022 She was bald and had wooden teeth and yet somehow managed to remain a virgin. (JACK DEE)

7023 Oh dearest Queen, I've never seen, a face more like a soup-tureen. (ANON)

Queen Elizabeth II
7024 She's head of a dysfunctional family. If she lived on a council estate in Sheffield, she'd probably be in council care. (MICHAEL PARKINSON)

King George III
7025 George the Third
  Ought never to have occurred.
One can only wonder
  At so grotesque a blunder. (E. CLERIHEW BENTLEY)

King George IV
7026 A more contemptible, cowardly, selfish, unfeeling dog does not exist than this King. (CHARLES GREVILLE)

King Henry VIII
7027 A pig, an ass, a dunghill, the spawn of an adder, a basilisk, a lying buffoon, a mad fool with a frothy mouth. (MARTIN LUTHER)

Napoleon III of France
7028 His mind is like an extinct sulphur-pit giving out the smell of rotten eggs. (THOMAS CARLYLE)

Prince Philip, Duke of Edinburgh
7029 I'm prepared to take advice on leisure from Prince Philip. He's a world expert on leisure. He's been practising for most of his adult life. (NEIL KINNOCK)

7030 He has perfected the art of saying hello and goodbye in the same handshake. (JENNIE BOND)

King Philip II of Spain
7031 I cannot find it in me to fear a man who took ten years a-learning his alphabet. (QUEEN ELIZABETH I)

Queen Victoria
7032 Nowadays, a parlour maid as ignorant as Queen Victoria was when she came to the throne, would be classed as mentally defective. (GEORGE BERNARD SHAW)

King William IV
7033 The King blew his nose twice, and wiped the royal perspiration repeatedly from a face which is probably the largest uncivilized spot in England. (OLIVER WENDELL HOLMES)

Duchess of Windsor
7034 The people are used to looking up to their King's representatives – the Duchess of Windsor is looked upon as the lowest of the low. (THE QUEEN MOTHER)

Sport

Peter Beardsley
7035 He's the only player who, when he appears on TV, Daleks hide behind the sofa. (NICK HANCOCK)

David Beckham
7036 He can't kick with his left foot, he doesn't score many goals, he can't head a ball and he can't tackle. Apart from that he's all right. (GEORGE BEST)

7037 He's had his eyebrows plucked, so now he's got nothing in front of his eyes either. (JACK DEE)

Larry Bird
7038 As long as Larry's around, I'll only be the second-worst defensive player in basketball. (CHARLES BARKLEY)

Bjorn Borg
7039 Like a Volvo, Bjorn Borg is rugged, has good after-sales service, and is very dull. (CLIVE JAMES)

Trevor Brooking
7040 Floats like a butterfly, and stings like one. (BRIAN CLOUGH)

Chris Evert
7041 The champion of monotony. (PAUL WEST)

Rio Ferdinand
7042 What can one say about a man who once damaged a tendon while watching TV with his feet on a coffee table? (ANON)

Joe Frazier
7043 He's so ugly they ought to donate his face to the World Wildlife Fund. (MUHAMMAD ALI)

Tim Henman
7044 He's the human equivalent of beige. (LINDA SMITH)

Merv Hughes
7045 His mincing run-up resembled someone in high heels and a panty-girdle running after a bus. (MARTIN JOHNSON)

Don King
7046 Don King doesn't care about black or white. He just cares about green. (LARRY HOLMES)

John McEnroe
7047 As charming as a dead mouse in a loaf of bread. (CLIVE JAMES)

7048 Hair like badly turned broccoli. (CLIVE JAMES)

Colin Montgomerie
7049 Looks like a bulldog chewing a wasp. (ANON)

Martina Navratilova
7050 Martina was so far in the closet she was in danger of being a garment bag. (RITA MAE BROWN)

Dennis Rodman
7051 He has so many fish hooks in his nose, he looks like a piece of bait. (BOB COSTAS)

Ronaldo

7052 He must be the only man alive who can eat an apple through a tennis racket. (GARY LINEKER)

Hugo Sanchez

7053 He is as welcome in Spanish football as a piranha in a bidet. (JESUS GIL)

Robbie Savage

7054 There's more meat on a toothpick. (ALAN BIRCHENALL)

Monica Seles

7055 I'd hate to be next door to her on her wedding night. (PETER USTINOV)

Alan Shearer

7056 A man so dull he once made the papers for having a one-in-the-bed romp. (NICK HANCOCK)

Jeremy Tree

7057 English racehorse trainer Jeremy Tree to legendary jockey Lester Piggott: "I've got to speak to my old school, Lester, and tell them all I know about horse racing. What should I tell them?"

Lester Piggott: "Tell 'em you have got the flu."

Jacques Villeneuve

7058 The man is a millionaire but always looks like an unmade bed. (Melbourne's *Herald Sun* newspaper)

Ray Wilkins

7059 The only time he goes forward is to toss the coin. (TOMMY DOCHERTY)

Serena Williams

7060 Her breasts alone must weigh more than Justine Henin-Hardenne. (MATTHEW NORMAN)

Dennis Wise

7061 He could start a row in an empty house. (SIR ALEX FERGUSON)

Television

7062 Acting on television is like being asked by the captain to entertain the passengers while the ship goes down. (PETER USTINOV)

Johnny Carson

7063 It has always been my personal conviction that Carson is the most overrated amateur since Evelyn and her magic violin. (REX REED)

7064 He's an anaesthetist – Prince Valium. (MORT SAHL)

Willie Carson

7065 Top hats look 100 per cent ridiculous on anybody, but on, for example, Willie Carson, it's like attaching a factory chimney to a bungalow. (GILES SMITH)

Terry Christian

7066 I can't stand people from Manchester like Terry Christian. Makes you wish Myra Hindley had been given a few more years of freedom. (ROB NEWMAN)

Angus Deayton

7067 You must have some talent locked up in that body of yours. It can't be reading out loud and that's it, surely! (PAUL MERTON)

Sir David Frost

7068 He rose without a trace. (KITTY MUGGERIDGE)

Kelsey Grammer

7069 He has launched his own website to refute stories about him in the tabloids. Check it out at likeyoureallycare.com. (ANDY WAITS)

Anne Robinson

7070 Quite attractive – in a Mr Burns from *The Simpsons* kind of way. (MATT BLAIZE)

Andy Rooney

7071 I don't know how Andy can make 60 seconds on *60 Minutes* seem like 60 hours. (WALTER CRONKITE)

Dinah Shore

7072 I never watch the Dinah Shore Show – I'm a diabetic. (OSCAR LEVANT)

Ed Sullivan

7073 Ed Sullivan will be around as long as someone else has talent. (FRED ALLEN)

Barbara Walters

7074 A hyena in syrup. (YEVGENY YEVTUSHENKO)

Bruce Willis

7075 His idea of a romantic kiss was to go "blaaah" and gag me with his tongue. (Moonlighting co-star CYBILL SHEPHERD)

Theatre

7076 With the collapse of Vaudeville new talent has no place to stink. (GEORGE BURNS)

7077 For those of you who missed it the first time, this is your golden opportunity: you can miss it again. (MICHAEL BILLINGTON on the revival of *Godspell*)

7078 It contains a number of tunes one goes into the theatre humming. (KENNETH TYNAN on a musical)

7079 I saw this show under adverse circumstances — my seat was facing the stage. (JOHN DAVID KLEIN on the 1985 production *Three Guys Naked From The Waist Down*)

7080 I have seen stronger plots in a cemetery. (STEWARD KLEIN'S review of a 1979 play *Break a Leg*)

7081 *Starlight Express* is the perfect gift for the kid who has everything except parents. (FRANK RICH)

7082 *Perfectly Scandalous* was one of those plays in which all of the actors, unfortunately, enunciated very clearly. (ROBERT BENCHLEY)

7083 Most of the heroes are in the audience. (WALTER WINCHELL'S review of *The Hero in Man*)

7084 *Hook and Ladder* is the sort of play that gives failures a bad name. (WALTER KERR)

7085 Oh, for an hour of Herod! (ANTHONY HOPE reviewing J.M. Barrie's *Peter Pan*)

Tallulah Bankhead
7086 Tallulah Bankhead barged down the Nile last night as Cleopatra and sank. (JAMES MASON BROWN)

Sarah Bernhardt
7087 A great actress, from the waist down. (DAME MARGARET KENDAL)

Bertolt Brecht
7088 A theatrical whore of the first quality. (PETER HALL)

Sarah Brightman
7089 She still simulates fear and affliction alike by screwing up her face into bug-eyed, chipmunk-cheeked poses more appropriate to the Lon Chaney film version. (FRANK RICH on Sarah Brightman's performance in *Phantom of the Opera*)

7090 Sarah Brightman couldn't act scared on the New York subway at four o'clock in the morning. (JOEL SEGAL)

Simon Callow
7091 Mozart, played by Simon Callow as a goonish cross between a chimp and a donkey. (BENEDICT NIGHTINGALE's review of Simon Callow's role in *Amadeus*)

Mrs Patrick Campbell
7092 It is greatly to Mrs Patrick Campbell's credit that, bad as the play was, her acting was worse. It was a masterpiece of failure. (GEORGE BERNARD SHAW's review of *Fedora*)

Dame Edith Evans
7093 To me, Edith looks like something that would eat its young. (DOROTHY PARKER)

Lillian Gish
7094 Lillian Gish may be a charming person, but she is not Ophelia. She comes on stage as if she had been sent for to sew rings on the new curtains. (MRS PATRICK CAMPBELL)

Farley Granger

7095 Farley Granger played Mr Darcy with all the flexibility of a telegraph pole. (BROOKS ATKINSON's review of a musical version of *Pride and Prejudice* on Broadway)

Cedric Hardwicke

7096 He conducted the soul-selling transaction with the thoughtful dignity of a grocer selling a pound of cheese. (A 1948 review of *Dr Faustus* by Christopher Marlowe)

Sir Anthony Hopkins

7097 Hopkins was dressed like a cross between a fisherman and an SS man, evoking doggedly a Welsh rugby captain at odds with his supporters' club. (A 1971 review of *Coriolanus*)

Sir Michael Hordern

7098 Michael Hordern's Cassius has an anxious air. This Cassius watches John Phillips' alarmingly tall Brutus like an insurance agent estimating how much life cover he can offer without insisting on a medical examination. (*Sunday Times* review of a 1958 production of *Julius Caesar*)

Henry Arthur Jones

7099 The first rule for a playwright is not to write like Henry Arthur Jones. The second and third rules are the same. (OSCAR WILDE)

Andrew Lloyd Webber

7100 Andrew Lloyd Webber was born with a face like a melted Wellington boot. (JEREMY CLARKSON)

Martine McCutcheon

7101 The only way she could crack America is by sitting on it. (ANON)

Diana Rigg

7102 Diana Rigg is built like a brick mausoleum with insufficient flying buttresses. (JOHN SIMON's review of the nude scene in *Abelard and Heloise* from *New York Magazine*)

George Bernard Shaw

7103 Shaw writes his plays for the ages, the ages between five and twelve. (GEORGE J. NATHAN)

7104 Shaw inviting Winston Churchill to the opening night of *Pygmalion*: "Am reserving two tickets for you for my premiere. Come and bring a friend – if you have one."

Churchill: "Impossible to be present for the first performance. Will attend the second – if there is one."

Tennessee Williams

7105 If a swamp alligator could talk, it would sound like Tennessee Williams. (REX REED)

Edward Woodward

7106 As swashbuckling Cyrano, Mr Woodward's performance buckles more often than it swashes. (KENNETH HURREN in the *Spectator*)

To whom it may concern

Put-downs aimed at unnamed victims:

7107 Tell me the story of that frock. It's obviously an old favourite. You were wise to remove the curtain rings. (DAME EDNA EVERAGE)

7108 She tells enough white lies to ice a cake. (MARGOT ASQUITH on a gossip columnist)

7109 Her singing reminds me of a cart coming downhill with the brake on. (SIR THOMAS BEECHAM on a soprano)

7110 I liked your opera. I think I will set it to music. (LUDWIG VAN BEETHOVEN to a fellow composer)

7111 The covers of this book are too far apart. (AMBROSE BIERCE)

7112 It opened at 8.40 sharp and closed at 10.40 dull. (HEYWOOD C. BROUN'S review of an unnamed play]

7113 Fine, if you like acting with two and a half tons of condemned veal. (CORAL BROWNE on her leading man)

7114 Her Victoria made me feel that Albert had married beneath his station. (NOEL COWARD on an actress playing Queen Victoria)

7115 Two things should be cut: the second act and the child's throat. (NOEL COWARD's review of a play featuring a child actor)

7116 She's the original good time that was had by all. (BETTE DAVIS on an unnamed actress)

7117 He played the King as though somebody else might be about to play the Ace. (EUGENE FIELD on an unnamed actor's understated performance as King Lear)

7118 Your manuscript is both good and original; but the part that is good is not original, and the part that is original is not good. (DR JOHNSON to an aspiring author)

7119 There was laughter at the back of the theatre, leading to the belief that someone was telling jokes back there. (GEORGE S. KAUFMAN's review of a Broadway comedy)

7120 He has delusions of adequacy. (WALTER KERR on an unnamed actor)

7121 I've had a wonderful evening, but this wasn't it. (GROUCHO MARX to a dinner party hostess)

7122 She was a large woman who seemed not so much dressed as upholstered. (J.M. BARRIE)

7123 This is not a novel to be tossed aside lightly. It should be thrown with great force. (DOROTHY PARKER)

7124 That girl speaks 18 languages and she can't say "no" in any of them. (DOROTHY PARKER)

7125 She's as tough as an ox. When she dies she'll be turned into Bovril. (DOROTHY PARKER)

7126 I did not attend his funeral, but I wrote a nice letter saying I approved of it. (MARK TWAIN on a recently deceased politician)

7127 One of those characteristic British faces that, once seen, are never remembered. (OSCAR WILDE)

7128 I've seen more excitement at the opening of an umbrella. (EARL WILSON reviewing an opening night)

7129 I thought I saw your name on a bag of bread, but when I reread it, it said "Thick Cut". (JACK DEE to a heckler)

Insults for all occasions

7130 He's a few sandwiches short of a picnic.

7131 He's a few trees short of a forest.

7132 He's a few beers short of a six-pack.

7133 He's a few bricks short of a wall.

7134 He's a few planes short of an Air Force.

7135 He's a few fries short of a happy meal.

7136 He's a few pickles short of a jar.

7137 He's a few pages short of a book.

7138 He's a flower short of an arrangement.

7139 He's a flying buttress short of a cathedral.

7140 He's a pane short of a window.

7141 He's a button short of a shirt.

7142 He's a six-iron short of a full bag.

7143 He's a span short of a bridge.

7144 He's one sock short of a pair.

7145 He's one tree short of a hammock.

7146 He's not playing with a full deck.

7147 He's knitting with only one needle.

7148 His clock doesn't have all its numbers.

7149 He's missing a few buttons on his remote control.

7150 He's not the sharpest knife in the drawer.

7151 He's not the brightest bulb on the Christmas tree.

7152 His brain waves fall a little short of the beach.

7153 He's got a photographic memory, but the lens cap is on.

7154 He has a mind like a steel trap — always closed.

7155 The receiver is off the hook.

7156 The cursor's flashing, but there's no response.

7157 The wheel is still spinning but the hamster is dead.

7158 The mouth is in gear, but the brain's in neutral.

7159 He's all mouth, no trousers.

7160 He's all missile, no warhead.

7161 He's all crown, no filling.

7162 He's all hammer, no nail.

7163 He's all foam, no beer.

7164 He's all hat, no cattle.

7165 He's all wax, no wick.

7166 He's full throttle, dry tank.

7167 He's half a bubble off plumb.

7168 He's swimming in the shallow end of the gene pool.

7169 He has reached rock bottom and has started to dig.

7170 Some drink from the fountain of knowledge – he only gargled.

7171 He's as much use as an ashtray on a motorcycle.

7172 He's as much use as a chocolate teapot.

7173 He's as much use as a lead parachute.

7174 He's as useful as dinosaur repellent.

7175 He's as quick as a corpse.

7176 He's as sharp as a beachball.

7177 He's as smart as bait.

7178 He's as popular as a French kiss at a family reunion.

7179 He has all the sex appeal of a wet paper bag.

7180 The twinkle in his eyes is actually the sun shining between his ears.

7181 He's got bubbles in his think tank.

7182 He's been short on oxygen one time too many.

7183 He's taken one too many punches to the head.

7184 He's so dense, light bends around him.

7185 His elevator doesn't go all the way to the top floor.

7186 If brains were bird droppings, he'd have a clean cage.

7187 If brains were dynamite, he wouldn't have enough to blow his nose.

7188 If brains were lard, he'd be hard pressed to grease a small pan.

7189 If brains were taxed, he'd get a rebate.

7190 If brains were water, his wouldn't be sufficient to baptize a flea.

7191 If brains were chocolate, he wouldn't have enough to fill an M&M.

7192 If intelligence were rain, he'd be holding an umbrella.

7193 If his IQ was two points higher, he'd be a rock.

7194 If he were any more stupid, he'd have to be watered twice a week.

7195 If what you don't know can't hurt you, he's invulnerable.

7196 If you gave him a penny for his thoughts, you'd get change.

7197 Anyone who told you to be yourself couldn't have given you worse advice.

7198 Are your parents siblings?

7199 Do you ever wonder what life would be like if you'd had enough oxygen at birth?

7200 As an outsider, what do you think of the human race?

7201 So a thought crossed your mind? It must have been a long and lonely journey.

7202 He's better at sex than anyone; now all he needs is a partner.

7203 His head is so far up his own ass, he can chew his food twice.

7204 The closest he'll ever get to a brainstorm is a slight drizzle.

7205 His own father looks on him as the son he never had.

7206 I used to think you were a pain in the neck. Now I have a much lower opinion of you.

7207 Did your parents ever ask you to run away from home?

7208 I hear you were born on a farm. Any more in the litter?

7209 I've seen people like you before, but I had to pay admission.

7210 You'd be out of your depth in a puddle.

7211 Don't you have a terribly empty feeling – in your head?

7212 Don't you need a licence to be that ugly?

7213 If I throw a stick, will you leave?

7214 Don't let your mind wander – it's too little to be let out alone.

7215 If you ever had a bright idea, it would be beginner's luck.

7216 Are you the first in your family to be born without a tail?

7217 Have you considered suing your brain for non-support?

7218 Make a mental note – oh, I see you're out of paper.

7219 Every girl has the right to be ugly, but you abused the privilege.

7220 Did someone leave your cage open?

7221 I don't think you're an idiot. But then what's my opinion against thousands of others?

7222 I hear the only place you're ever invited is outside.

7223 I'd like to see things from your point of view but I can't get my head that far up my ass.

7224 I bet your mother has a loud bark.

THE WISDOM OF CHILDREN

Exam howlers

English

7225 When a man is married to one woman it is called monotony.

7226 Spaghetti is thrown on people at weddings.

7227 A senator is half horse, half man.

7228 An optimist is a doctor who treats your eyes.

7229 Philatelists were a race of people who lived in biblical times.

7230 An epistle is the wife of an apostle.

7231 When letters are in sloping type, they are in hysterics.

7232 The feminine of bachelor is lady-in-waiting.

7233 Baboons live in an apiary.

7234 The future of "I give" is "I take".

7235 A myth is a female moth.

7236 A troubador is a Spanish bullfighter.

7237 Inflation is the material you put in your attic and in the walls. It helps keep your house warm in winter.

7238 Trigonometry is having three wives at one time.

7239 Vacuum: a large, empty space where the Pope lives.

7240 The pleasures of childhood are great but not compared with the pleasures of adultery.

7241 The parts of speech are lungs and air.

7242 An executive is the man who puts murderers to death.

7243 An antidote is a funny story.

7244 A census taker is a man who goes from house to house increasing the population.

7245 A tambourine is a curved club which can be hurled so that it will come back near the place from which it was thrown.

7246 An aviary is the place where aviators sleep.

7247 Germinate: to become a naturalized German.

7248 A magnet is something you find crawling over a dead cat.

7249 A Pomegranate is a lap dog.

7250 A monastery is where monsters live.

7251 A diva is a swimming champion.

7252 A tantrum is a bicycle for a man and his wife.

7253 Shakespeare was born in the year 1564, on his birthday.

7254 Shakespeare lived in Windsor with his merry wives.

7255 Romeo and Juliet are an example of a heroic couplet.

7256 Romeo's last wish was to be laid by Juliet.

7257 Writing at the same time as Shakespeare was Miguel Cervantes. He wrote Donkey Hote.

7258 John Milton wrote Paradise Lost. Then his wife died and he wrote Paradise Regained.

Geography

7259 A fjord is a Scandinavian car.

7260 The people of Japan ride about in jigsaws.

7261 The eastern part of Asia is called Euthanasia.

7262 People go about Venice in gorgonzolas.

7263 The inhabitants of Moscow are called Mosquitos.

7264 Most of the houses in France are made of plaster of Paris.

7265 Climate lasts a long time, but the weather is only a few days.

7266 A virgin forest is a forest where the hand of man has never set foot.

7267 The Tropic of Cancer is a rare and dangerous disease.

7268 The Matterhorn was a horn blown by the ancients when anything was the matter.

7269 The Pyramids are a range of mountains between France and Spain.

7270 Equinox is a country near the Panama Canal.

7271 The climate is hottest next to the Creator.

7272 Floods from the Mississippi may be prevented by putting big dames in the river.

7273 One by-product of raising cattle is calves.

7274 The four seasons are salt, pepper, mustard and vinegar.

History

7275 Ancient Egypt was inhabited by mummies and they all wrote in hydraulics.

7276 And Sir Francis Drake said: "Let the Armada wait. My bowels can't."

7277 The sun never set on the British Empire because the British Empire is in the east and the sun sets in the west.

7278 Julius Caesar extinguished himself on the battlefields of Gaul.

7279 The Natchez Indians rose up and massaged all the French at Fort Rosalie.

7280 William Tell invented the telephone.

7281 Moses went up on Mount Cyanide to get the Ten Commandments.

7282 Homer wrote the Oddity.

7283 Martin Luther lived on a diet of worms.

7284 The people who followed the Lord were called the 12 opossums.

7285 Noah's wife was called Joan of Ark.

7286 The Jews were a proud people and throughout history they had trouble with the unsympathetic Genitals.

7287 The Romans were so-called because they never stayed long in one place.

7288 David was a Hebrew king skilled at playing the liar.

7289 Solomon, one of David's sons, had 500 wives and 500 porcupines.

7290 A gladiator is something that keeps a room warm.

7291 Socrates died from an overdose of wedlock.

7292 Joan of Arc was burnt to a steak.

7293 King Arthur lived in the age of Shivery.

7294 Sir Francis Drake defeated the Spanish Armadillo.

7295 Edward VI could not rule alone because he was a miner.

7296 Abraham Lincoln's mother died in infancy, and he was born in a log cabin which he built with his own hands.

7297 Lincoln went to the theatre and got shot in his seat.

7298 Louis XVI was gelatined.

7299 The Pope was inflammable.

7300 William Tell shot an arrow through an apple while standing on his son's head.

7301 Queen Victoria's death was the final event which ended her reign.

7302 Queen Victoria sat on a thorn for 63 years. She was the longest queen.

7303 The Magna Carta proved that no free man should be hanged twice for the same offence.

7304 Suffragettes were things the Germans shot under water to kill the British in the First World War.

7305 The winter of 1620 was a hard one for the settlers. Many people died and many babies were born. Captain John Smith was responsible for all this.

7306 One of the causes of the Revolutionary War was that the English put tacks in their tea.

7307 Benjamin Franklin died in 1790 and is still dead.

7308 Christopher Columbus circumcised the world with forty-foot clippers.

7309 Christopher Columbus was a great navigator who discovered America while cursing about the Atlantic.

7310 The Edict of Nantes was a law passed by Louis XIV forbidding all births, marriages and deaths in France for a period of one year.

7311 Henry VIII found walking difficult because he had an abbess on his knee.

7312 After his divorce from Catherine of Aragon, Henry VIII married Anne Boleyn, and Archbishop Cranmer consummated the marriage.

7313 Queen Elizabeth I never had any peace of mind because Mary Queen of Scots was always hoovering in the background.

7314 When Queen Elizabeth I exposed herself before her troops, they all shouted "hurrah".

7315 Queen Elizabeth knitted Sir Walter Raleigh on the deck.

7316 Karl Marx was one of the Marx brothers.

7317 Christianity was introduced in to Britain by the Romans in 55 BC.

7318 Rome was overthrown by invasions of the Huns, Visigoths and Osteopaths.

7319 The French Revolution was caused by overcharging taxis.

Music

7320 Johann Bach wrote a great many musical compositions and had a large number of children. In between, he practised on an old spinster, which he kept in his attic.

7321 Refrain means don't do it.

7322 A virtuoso is a musician with high morals.

7323 Sherbet composed the Unfinished Symphony.

7324 Music sung by two people at the same time is called a duel.

7325 Just about any animal skin can be stretched over a frame to make a pleasant sound once the animal is removed.

7326 If people sing without music, it is called Acapulco.

7327 Handel was half German, half Italian, and half English.

7328 The principal singer of nineteenth century opera was called pre-Madonna.

7329 Beethoven was so deaf he wrote loud music.

7330 Beethoven expired in 1827 and later died from this.

7331 Most composers do not live until they are dead.

Science

7332 Three kinds of blood vessels are arteries, vanes and caterpillars.

7333 A molecule is so small that it cannot be seen by the naked observer.

7334 A kangaroo keeps its baby in the porch.

7335 The Earth makes one resolution every 24 hours.

7336 The pistol of a flower is its only protection against insects.

7337 The cuckoo does not lay his own eggs.

7338 In spring, the salmon swim upstream to spoon.

7339 Mushrooms always grow in damp places and that is why they look like umbrellas.

7340 When you smell an odourless gas, it is probably carbon monoxide.

7341 Hydrogin is made up of gin and water.

7342 When people run around and around in circles, we say they are crazy, when planets do it, we say they are orbiting.

7343 The wind is like the air, only pushier.

7344 Madame Curie discovered radio.

7345 Marie Curie did her research at the Sore Buns Institute in France.

7346 To prevent conception when having intercourse, the male wears a condominium.

7347 For asphyxiation, apply artificial respiration until the patient is dead.

7348 Nitrogen is not found in Ireland because it is not found in a free state.

7349 A vibration is a motion that cannot make up its mind which way it wants to go.

7350 Blood flows down one leg and up the other.

7351 A city purifies its water supply by filtering the water, then forcing it through an aviator.

7352 Electric volts are named after Voltaire, who invented electricity.

7353 Water freezes at 32 degrees and boils at 212 degrees. There are 180 degrees between freezing and boiling because there are 180 degrees between north and south.

7354 One of the main causes of dust is janitors.

7355 Clouds are high-flying fogs.

7356 Rain is saved up in cloud banks.

7357 I am not sure how clouds get formed. But the clouds know how to do it, and that is the important thing.

7358 Thunder is a rich source of loudness.

7359 Gravity was invented by Isaac Walton. It is chiefly noticeable in the autumn when the apples are falling off the trees.

7360 Charles Darwin was a naturalist who wrote the organ of the species.

7361 Some people can tell what time it is by looking at the sun. But I have never been able to make out the numbers.

7362 Benjamin Franklin discovered electricity by rubbing cats backwards.

7363 A triangle which has an angle of 135 degrees is called an obscene triangle.

7364 Louis Pasteur found a cure for rabbis.

7365 The process of turning steam back into water again is called conversation.

7366 A monsoon is a French gentleman.

7367 There are 26 vitamins in all, but some of the letters are yet to be discovered.

7368 Genetics explains why you look like your father, and if you don't, why you should.

7369 When you breathe, you inspire. When you do not breathe, you expire.

7370 The alimentary canal is located in the northern part of Indiana.

7371 To collect fumes of sulphur, hold a deacon over a flame in a test tube.

7372 H_2O is hot water and CO_2 is cold water.

7373 A fossil is an extinct animal. The older it is, the more extinct it is.

7374 Many dead animals in the past changed to fossils while others preferred to be oil.

7375 In some rocks, you can find the fossil footprints of fish.

7376 Reproduction is the life process by which an orgasm produces others of its kind.

Proverbs

A junior school teacher gave her class the first halves of well-known proverbs and asked the children to finish them.
These are their genuine answers:

7377 If you can't stand the heat . . . get a pool.

7378 Don't count your chickens . . . eat them.

7379 A watched pot never . . . disappears.

7380 Better to be safe than . . . punch a fifth former.

7381 Don't bite the hand that . . . looks dirty.

7382 You can't teach an old dog new . . . maths.

7383 The pen is mightier than the . . . pigs.

7384 Too many cooks . . . so few meals.

7385 Two's company. Three's . . . the Musketeers.

7386 Laugh and the world laughs with you, cry and . . . you have to blow your nose.

7387 Children should be seen and not . . . spanked.

7388 Strike while the . . . bug is close.

7389 A miss is as good as a . . . mister.

7390 Look before you . . . run into a pole.

7391 It's always darkest before . . . Daylight Savings Time.

7392 Happy the bride who . . . gets all the presents.

7393 Never underestimate the power of . . . termites.

7394 When the blind leadeth the blind . . . get out of the way.

7395 If you lie down with dogs you'll . . . stink in the morning.

7396 An idle mind is . . . the best way to relax.

7397 Where there's smoke, there's . . . pollution.

7398 A penny saved is . . . not much.

7399 There's no fool like . . . Aunt Edie.

Part 3
TOASTS

To absent friends

7400 Here's to our faraway friends. May their spirits be with us as soon as these spirits are in us.

7401 Here's to absent friends – especially prosperity.

To accountants

7402 Here's to my accountant. May he make many brilliant deductions.

To ambition

7403 Here's to a man who is a true inspiration to the rest of us. If he can make it, we've all got a chance!

To bankers

7404 To our friend the banker – may he never lose interest.

Birthdays

7405 Another candle on your cake –
Well, that's no need to pout.
Be glad that you have strength enough
To blow the damn thing out!

7406 Many happy returns of the day of your birth;
Many blessings to brighten your pathway on earth;
Many friendships to cheer and provoke you to mirth;
Many feastings and frolics to add to your girth.

7407 To the nation's best kept secret – your true age.

To bosses

7408 To the boss – the person who's early when you're late, and late when you're early.

7409 Here's to our boss – may he never hear what we say about him.

To children

7410 To babies. They will make love stronger, days shorter, nights longer, bank accounts smaller, homes happier, clothes shabbier, the past forgotten and the future worth living for.

7411 As they say in the disposable nappy business, bottoms up!

At Christmas

7412 Here's wishing you the kind of troubles that will last as long as your New Year's resolutions.

7413 May you have a Christmas you won't forget . . . and a New Year's Eve you'll never remember!

7414 I wish you a Merry Christmas
And a Happy New Year,
A stocking full of presents
And a fridge full of beer.

Drinking

7415 Here's to a temperance supper
With water in glasses tall,
And coffee and tea to end with –
And me not there at all.

7416 To champagne – a drink that makes you see double and feel single.

7417 Here's to champagne, a drink divine
That makes us forget all our troubles.
It's made of a dollar's worth of wine,
And twenty bucks worth of bubbles.

7418 To wine. It improves with age – the older I get, the more I like it.

7419 To a man who doesn't just drown his sorrows, he irrigates them.

7420 Here's to a long life and a merry one.
A quick death and an easy one.
A pretty girl and an honest one.
A cold beer and another one!

7421 To the hangover – something to occupy the head that wasn't used the night before.

7422 Here's to the good time I must have had.

7423 Here's to abstinence – as long as it's practised in moderation.

Food

7424 Eat, drink and be merry – for tomorrow we diet.

7425 Here's to us, my good, fat friends,
To bless the things we eat;
For it has been full many a year
Since we have seen our feet.

7426 To soup – may it be seen and not heard.

7427 To bread – for without bread, there could be no toast.

To friends

7428 May your joys be as deep as the ocean and your sorrows as light as its foam.

7429 May we never have friends who, like shadows, keep close to us in the sunshine, but desert us on a cloudy day.

7430 Here's champagne to our real friends, and real pain to our sham friends. To the lamp of true friendship. May it burn brightest in our darkest hours and never flicker in the winds of trial.

7431 To a friend who remembers all the details of our childhood but is discreet enough not to mention them.

7432 To our best friends, who know the worst about us but refuse to believe it.

7433 May Dame Fortune ever smile on you, but never her daughter – Miss Fortune.

7434 May our house always be too small to hold all our friends.

At funerals

7435 To our dear departed, that the devil might not hear of his death till he's safe inside the walls of heaven.

To grandchildren

7436 To our grandchildren – our revenge on our children!

To grandparents

7437 Here's to grandparents – the cheapest (and best) babysitters on earth.

To health

7438 I drink to your health when I'm with you
I drink to your health when alone;
I drink to your health so often
I've just about wrecked my own!

7439 May you live to be a hundred – and then decide if you want to go on.

7440 May you die in bed aged 97, shot by the jealous husband of a teenage wife.

7441 May you live to be as old as your jokes.

To love

7442 Here's to the prettiest, here's to the wittiest,
Here's to the truest of all who are true,
Here's to the neatest one, here's to the sweetest one,
Here's to them all wrapped in one – here's to you.

7443 Here's to the wings of love –
May they never moult a feather,

Till my big boots and your little shoes
Are under the bed together.

7444 Let's drink to love, which is nothing – unless it's divided by two.

7445 Here's to this water,
Wishing it were wine,
Here's to you, my darling,
Wishing you were mine.

7446 Here's to love: A little sighing, a little crying, a little dying – and a touch of white lying.

7447 Here's to the man who's decided to take a wife – but hasn't yet decided whose.

To men

7448 To men – who divide our time, double our cares, and triple our troubles.

7449 To men – creatures who buy play-off tickets months in advance but wait until Christmas Eve to buy presents.

7450 Women's faults are many,
Men have only two –
Everything they say
And everything they do.

7451 To the two things that delight a young girl's heart – fresh flowers and fresh men.

To parents

7452 To my parents who have spoiled me all my life. Don't stop!

Patriotic

7453 The American Eagle and the Thanksgiving Turkey.
May one give us peace in all our States,
And the other a piece for all our plates.

To prosperity

7454 Here's to beefsteak when you're hungry,
Whisky when you're dry;
All the girls you ever want,
And heaven when you die.

7455 May the most you wish for be the least you get.

7456 May bad fortune follow you all of your days – and never catch up with you!

7457 May you be hung, drawn and quartered –
Hung in the hall of fame,
Drawn by a golden chariot,
And quartered in the arms of the one you love.

To space

7458 When God made Man,
He made him out of string;
He had a little left over,
So he made a little thing.
When God made Woman,
He made her out of lace;
He didn't have enough,
So he left a little space.
Here's to space . . .

Weddings

7459 To marriage – the last decision a man is allowed to make.

7460 May your love be modern enough to survive the times
And old-fashioned enough to last forever.

7461 Here's to me and here's to you
And here's to love and laughter.
I'll be true as long as you,
But not a minute after.

7462 May our marriages never interfere with our love lives!

7463 Here's to you and here's to me,
I hope we never disagree.
But if, perchance, we ever do,
Then here's to me, to hell with you.

7464 May you grow old on one pillow.

7465 Congratulations on the termination of your isolation and may I express an
appreciation of your determination to end the desperation and frustration
which has caused you so much consternation in giving you the inspiration to
make a combination to bring an accumulation to the population.

7466 To keep a marriage brimming
With love in the loving cup,
When you are wrong, admit it
And when you're right, shut up!

7467 I hope the only ups and downs you two have are between the sheets.

7468 Here's to the man who is wisest and best,
Here's to the man who with judgment is blest.
Here's to the man who's as smart as can be –
I mean the man who agrees with me.

7469 Here's to your new bride who has everything a girl could want in her life,
except for good taste in men.

7470 John, you are a lucky man – you've got Linda. She's beautiful, intelligent,
funny, warm and loving. Linda, you've got John . . .

To women

7471 To wine and women. May we always have a taste for both.

7472 Here's to our wives,
They keep our hives
In little bees and honey.
They darn our socks,

They soothe life's shocks,
And don't they spend the money!

7473 Here's to the ladies — first in our hearts and first in our wallets.

7474 To our sweethearts and wives. May they never meet . . .

INDEX

NB: subjects are indexed by joke number